RISE UP AND CALL THEM BLESSED

~~ THE LOCHLAINN SEABROOK COLLECTION ~~

AMERICAN CIVIL WAR
Abraham Lincoln Was a Liberal, Jefferson Davis Was a Conservative: The Missing Key to Understanding the American Civil War
Confederacy 101: Amazing Facts You Never Knew About America's Oldest Political Tradition
Confederate Blood and Treasure: An Interview With Lochlainn Seabrook
Everything You Were Taught About African-Americans and the Civil War is Wrong, Ask a Southerner!
Everything You Were Taught About the Civil War is Wrong, Ask a Southerner!
Give This Book to a Yankee! A Southern Guide to the Civil War For Northerners
Lincoln's War: The Real Cause, the Real Winner, the Real Loser
The Great Yankee Coverup: What the North Doesn't Want You to Know About Lincoln's War!
The Ultimate Civil War Quiz Book: How Much Do You Really Know About America's Most Misunderstood Conflict?

CONFEDERATE FLAG
Confederate Flag Facts: What Every American Should Know About Dixie's Southern Cross

SECESSION
All We Ask Is To Be Let Alone: The Southern Secession Fact Book

SLAVERY
Everything You Were Taught About American Slavery is Wrong, Ask a Southerner!
Slavery 101: Amazing Facts You Never Knew About America's "Peculiar Institution"

CHILDREN
Honest Jeff and Dishonest Abe: A Southern Children's Guide to the Civil War
Saddle, Sword, and Gun: A Biography of Nathan Bedford Forrest For Teens

NATHAN BEDFORD FORREST
A Rebel Born: A Defense of Nathan Bedford Forrest - Confederate General, American Legend (winner of the 2011 Jefferson Davis Historical Gold Medal)
A Rebel Born: The Screenplay
Forrest! 99 Reasons to Love Nathan Bedford Forrest
Give 'Em Hell Boys! The Complete Military Correspondence of Nathan Bedford Forrest
Nathan Bedford Forrest and African-Americans: Yankee Myth, Confederate Fact
Nathan Bedford Forrest and the Battle of Fort Pillow: Yankee Myth, Confederate Fact
Nathan Bedford Forrest and the Ku Klux Klan: Yankee Myth, Confederate Fact
Nathan Bedford Forrest: Southern Hero, American Patriot - Honoring a Confederate Icon and the Old South
The Quotable Nathan Bedford Forrest: Selections From the Writings and Speeches of the Confederacy's Most Brilliant Cavalryman

QUOTABLE SERIES
The Alexander H. Stephens Reader: Excerpts From the Works of a Confederate Founding Father
The Quotable Alexander H. Stephens: Selections From the Writings and Speeches of the Confederacy's First Vice President
The Quotable Jefferson Davis: Selections From the Writings and Speeches of the Confederacy's First President
The Quotable Robert E. Lee: Selections From the Writings and Speeches of the South's Most Beloved Civil War General
The Quotable Stonewall Jackson: Selections From the Writings and Speeches of the South's Most Famous General

CONSTITUTIONAL HISTORY
The Articles of Confederation Explained: A Clause-by-Clause Study of America's First Constitution
The Constitution of the Confederate States of America Explained: A Clause-by-Clause Study of the South's Magna Carta

VICTORIAN CONFEDERATE LITERATURE
Rise Up and Call Them Blessed: Victorian Tributes to the Confederate Soldier, 1861-1901
The Old Rebel: Robert E. Lee As He Was Seen By His Contemporaries
Victorian Confederate Poetry: The Southern Cause in Verse, 1861-1901

ABRAHAM LINCOLN
Abraham Lincoln: The Southern View - Demythologizing America's Sixteenth President
Lincolnology: The Real Abraham Lincoln Revealed in His Own Words - A Study of Lincoln's Suppressed, Misinterpreted, and Forgotten Writings and Speeches
The Great Impersonator! 99 Reasons to Dislike Abraham Lincoln
The Unholy Crusade: Lincoln's Legacy of Destruction in the American South
The Unquotable Abraham Lincoln: The President's Quotes They Don't Want You To Know!

CIVIL WAR BATTLES
Encyclopedia of the Battle of Franklin - A Comprehensive Guide to the Conflict that Changed the Civil War

PARANORMAL
Carnton Plantation Ghost Stories: True Tales of the Unexplained from Tennessee's Most Haunted Civil War House!
UFOs and Aliens: The Complete Guidebook

FAMILY HISTORIES
The Blakeneys: An Etymological, Ethnological, and Genealogical Study - Uncovering the Mysterious Origins of the Blakeney Family and Name
The Caudills: An Etymological, Ethnological, and Genealogical Study - Exploring the Name and National Origins of a European-American Family
The McGavocks of Carnton Plantation: A Southern History - Celebrating One of Dixie's Most Noble Confederate Families and Their Tennessee Home

MIND, BODY, SPIRIT
Autobiography of a Non-Yogi: A Scientist's Journey From Hinduism to Christianity (Dr. Amitava Dasgupta, with Lochlainn Seabrook)
Britannia Rules: Goddess-Worship in Ancient Anglo-Celtic Society - An Academic Look at the United Kingdom's Matricentric Spiritual Past
Christ Is All and In All: Rediscovering Your Divine Nature and the Kingdom Within
Christmas Before Christianity: How the Birthday of the "Sun" Became the Birthday of the "Son"
Jesus and the Gospel of Q: Christ's Pre-Christian Teachings As Recorded in the New Testament
Jesus and the Law of Attraction: The Bible-Based Guide to Creating Perfect Health, Wealth, and Happiness Following Christ's Simple Formula
Seabrook's Bible Dictionary of Traditional and Mystical Christian Doctrines
The Bible and the Law of Attraction: 99 Teachings of Jesus, the Apostles, and the Prophets
The Book of Kelle: An Introduction to Goddess-Worship and the Great Celtic Mother-Goddess Kelle, Original Blessed Lady of Ireland
The Goddess Dictionary of Words and Phrases: Introducing a New Core Vocabulary for the Women's Spirituality Movement
The Way of Holiness: The Story of Religion and Myth From the Cave Bear Cult to Christianity

WOMEN
Aphrodite's Trade: The Hidden History of Prostitution Unveiled
Princess Diana: Modern Day Moon-Goddess - A Psychoanalytical and Mythological Look at Diana Spencer's Life, Marriage, and Death (with Dr. Jane Goldberg)
Women in Gray: A Tribute to the Ladies Who Supported the Southern Confederacy

Five-Star Books & Gifts From the Heart of the American South
SeaRavenPress.com

RISE UP
AND CALL THEM BLESSED

Victorian Tributes to the Confederate Soldier, 1861-1901

COLLECTED & EDITED, WITH AN INTRODUCTION & NOTES, BY THE AUTHOR,
"THE VOICE OF THE TRADITIONAL SOUTH," COLONEL

LOCHLAINN SEABROOK

JEFFERSON DAVIS HISTORICAL GOLD MEDAL WINNER

Generously Illustrated and Diligently
Researched for the Elucidation of the Reader

2017
Sea Raven Press, Nashville, Tennessee, USA

RISE UP AND CALL THEM BLESSED

Published by
Sea Raven Press, Cassidy Ravensdale, President
PO Box 1484, Spring Hill, Tennessee 37174-1484 USA
SeaRavenPress.com • searavenpress@gmail.com

Copyright © 2017 Lochlainn Seabrook
in accordance with U.S. and international copyright laws and regulations, as stated and protected under the Berne Union for the Protection of Literary and Artistic Property (Berne Convention), and the Universal Copyright Convention (the UCC). All rights reserved under the Pan-American and International Copyright Conventions.

1st SRP paperback edition, 1st printing: November 2017, ISBN: 978-1-943737-57-4
1st SRP hardcover edition, 1st printing: November 2017, ISBN: 978-1-943737-58-1

ISBN: 978-1-943737-57-4 (paperback)
Library of Congress Control Number: 2017958432

This work is the copyrighted intellectual property of Lochlainn Seabrook and has been registered with the Copyright Office at the Library of Congress in Washington, D.C., USA. No part of this work (including text, covers, drawings, photos, illustrations, maps, images, diagrams, etc.), in whole or in part, may be used, reproduced, stored in a retrieval system, or transmitted, in any form or by any means now known or hereafter invented, without written permission from the publisher. The sale, duplication, hire, lending, copying, digitalization, or reproduction of this material, in any manner or form whatsoever, is also prohibited, and is a violation of federal, civil, and digital copyright law, which provides severe civil and criminal penalties for any violations.

Rise Up and Call Them Blessed: Victorian Tributes to the Confederate Soldier, 1861-1901, by Lochlainn Seabrook. Includes an index, endnotes, and bibliographical references.

Front and back cover design and art, book design, layout, and interior art by Lochlainn Seabrook.
All images, graphic design, graphic art, and illustrations copyright © Lochlainn Seabrook.
All images selected, placed, manipulated, and/or created by Lochlainn Seabrook.
Cover images & design copyright © Lochlainn Seabrook.

The views on the American "Civil War" documented in this book are those of the publisher.

The paper used in this book is acid-free and lignin-free. It has been certified by the Sustainable Forestry Initiative and the Forest Stewardship Council and meets all ANSI standards for archival quality paper.

PRINTED & MANUFACTURED IN OCCUPIED TENNESSEE, FORMER CONFEDERATE STATES OF AMERICA

DEDICATION

To he who fought to preserve the government of the Founding Fathers: the Confederate soldier.

EPIGRAPH

That I did rebel against such authority as Mr. Lincoln assumed, and defy his armies on the field without reference to cost, I not only do not regret, but consider that occasion was thus furnished me for great personal gratification. I regard, indeed, this act of mine as not only altogether justifiable in every sense, but as constituting the most momentous and loftiest movement of my life or that is possible to any man. To have been a Confederate soldier in the true sense is to have done the sublimest thing that could have been done. The children of Confederate soldiers rise up and call them blessed, as will also the generations which are, in succession, to follow.

Albert Theodore Goodloe
FIRST LIEUTENANT COMPANY D
35TH REGIMENT ALABAMA VOLUNTEER INFANTRY, C.S.A.

Historical Outline of The Southern Confederacy
1861-1865

National Title:
CONFEDERATE STATES IN AMERICA

Capital
RICHMOND, VIRGINIA

Government Instituted:
FEBRUARY 18, 1861

Administration:
DAVIS (Pres't), STEPHENS (V. Pres't),
HUNTER (Sec.), MEMMINGER (Treas.)

Ambassadors:
MASON, SLIDELL

Army:
CONFEDERATE STATES ARMY

Navy:
CONFEDERATE STATES NAVY

Ensigns:
THE STARS AND BARS, THE STARRY CROSS

Cause of the War Combined:
NATIONAL INTERFERENCE IN STATES' RIGHTS

When the War Commenced:
APRIL 12, 1861

Where the War Commenced:
FORT SUMTER, SOUTH CAROLINA

Three Leading Generals:
LEE, BEAUREGARD, A. P. HILL

Three Great Battles of the War:
MANASSAS, GETTYSBURG, SHILOH

Three Leading Naval Officers:
SEMMES, BUCHANAN, MITCHELL

Three Best Naval Vessels:
MERRIMAC, ALABAMA, ARKANSAS

Three Distinguished Naval Actions:
HAMPTON ROADS, CHERBOURG, GALVESTON

Three Noted Sieges:
VICKSBURG, PORT HUDSON, LEXINGTON

Three Destructive Bombardments:
CHARLESTON, MOBILE, SAINT PHILLIP

Three Distinguished Private Soldiers:
CHESTNUT, PELHAM, MUMFORD

Three State Capitals not Captured during the War:
TALLAHASSEE, FLA.; AUSTIN, TEXAS; MONTGOMERY, ALA.

Three of the oldest Southern Newspapers not Suppressed during the War:
MERCURY (Charleston), *EXAMINER* (Richmond), *REGISTER* (Mobile)

When the War Closed:
APRIL 9, 1865

Where the War Closed:
APPOMATTOX, VIRGINIA[1]

CONTENTS

Historical Outline of the Southern Confederacy - 9
Notes to the Reader - 13
Introduction, by Lochlainn Seabrook - 19

CHAPTER 1: 1861 - 27
CHAPTER 2: 1862 - 31
CHAPTER 3: 1863 - 35
CHAPTER 4: 1864 - 38
CHAPTER 5: 1865 - 40
CHAPTER 6: 1866 - 44
CHAPTER 7: 1879 - 46
CHAPTER 8: 1886 - 47
CHAPTER 9: 1887 - 48
CHAPTER 10: 1891 - 49
CHAPTER 11: 1892 - 57
CHAPTER 12: 1893 - 60
CHAPTER 13: 1894 - 179
CHAPTER 14: 1895 - 291
CHAPTER 15: 1896 - 342
CHAPTER 16: 1897 - 383
CHAPTER 17: 1898 - 426
CHAPTER 18: 1899 - 446
CHAPTER 19: 1900 - 488
CHAPTER 20: 1901 - 535

Appendix A: - 557
Notes - 560
Bibliography - 567
Index - 573
Meet the Author - 590

NOTES TO THE READER

"NOTHING IN THE PAST IS DEAD TO THE MAN WHO WOULD
LEARN HOW THE PRESENT CAME TO BE WHAT IT IS."

WILLIAM STUBBS, VICTORIAN ENGLISH HISTORIAN

THE TWO MAIN POLITICAL PARTIES IN 1860

☛ In any study of America's antebellum, bellum, and postbellum periods, it is vitally important to understand that in 1860 the two major political parties—the Democrats and the newly formed Republicans—were the opposite of what they are today. In other words, the Democrats of the mid 19th Century were Conservatives, akin to the Republican Party of today, while the Republicans of the mid 19th Century were Liberals, akin to the Democratic Party of today.[2]

Thus the Confederacy's Democratic president, Jefferson Davis, was a Conservative (with libertarian leanings); the Union's Republican president, Abraham Lincoln, was a Liberal (with socialistic leanings).[3] This is why, in the mid 1800s, the conservative wing of the Democratic Party was known as "the States' Rights Party."[4]

Hence, the Democrats of the Civil War period referred to themselves as "conservatives," "confederates," "anti-centralists," or "constitutionalists" (the latter because they favored strict adherence to the original Constitution—which tacitly guaranteed states' rights—as created by the Founding Fathers), while the Republicans called themselves "liberals," "nationalists," "centralists," or "consolidationists" (the latter three because they wanted to nationalize the central government and consolidate political power in Washington, D.C.).[5]

The author's cousin, Confederate Vice President and Democrat Alexander H. Stephens: a Southern Conservative.

Since this idea is new to most of my readers, let us further demystify it by viewing it from the perspective of the American Revolutionary War. If Davis and his conservative Southern constituents (the Democrats of 1861) had been alive in 1775, they would have sided with George Washington and the American colonists, who sought to secede from the tyrannical government of Great Britain; if Lincoln and his Liberal Northern constituents (the Republicans of 1861) had been alive at that time, they would have sided with King George III and the English monarchy, who sought to maintain the American colonies as possessions of the British Empire. It is due to this very comparison that Southerners often refer to their secession as the Second Declaration of Independence and the "Civil War" as the Second American Revolutionary War.

Without a basic understanding of these facts, the American "Civil War" will forever remain incomprehensible. For a full discussion of this topic see my book, *Abraham Lincoln Was a Liberal, Jefferson Davis Was a Conservative: The Missing Key to Understanding the American Civil War.*

THE TERM "CIVIL WAR"

☛ As I heartily dislike the phrase "Civil War," its use throughout this book (as well as in my other works) is worthy of explanation.

Today America's entire literary system refers to the conflict of 1861 using the Northern term the "Civil War," whether we in the South like it or not. Thus, as all book searches by readers, libraries, and retail outlets are

The American "Civil War" was not a true civil war as Webster defines it: "A conflict between opposing groups of citizens of the *same* country." It was a fight between two individual countries; or to be more specific, two separate and constitutionally formed confederacies: the U.S.A. and the C.S.A.

now performed online, and as all bookstores categorize works from this period under the heading "Civil War," book publishers and authors who deal with this particular topic have little choice but to use this term themselves. If I were to refuse to use it, as some of my Southern colleagues have suggested, few people would ever find or read my books.

Add to this the fact that scarcely any non-Southerners have ever heard of the names we in the South use for the conflict, such as the "War for Southern Independence"—or my personal preference, "Lincoln's War." It only makes sense then to use the term "Civil War" in most commercial situations, distasteful though it is.

We should also bear in mind that while today educated persons, particularly educated Southerners, all share an abhorrence for the phrase

"Civil War," it was not always so. Confederates who lived through and even fought in the conflict regularly used the term throughout the 1860s, and even long after. Among them were Confederate generals such as Nathan Bedford Forrest, Richard Taylor, and Joseph E. Johnston, not to mention the Confederacy's vice president, Alexander H. Stephens.

Confederate General James Longstreet was just one of many Southern officials who referred to the conflict of 1861 as the "Civil War."

In 1895 Confederate General James Longstreet wrote about his military experiences in a work subtitled, *Memoirs of the Civil War in America*. Even the Confederacy's highest leader, President Jefferson Davis, used the term "Civil War,"[6] and in one case at least, as late as 1881—the year he wrote his brilliant exposition, *The Rise and Fall of the Confederate Government*.[7] Authors writing for *Confederate Veteran* magazine sometimes used the phrase well into the early 1900s,[8] and in 1898, at the Eighth Annual Meeting and Reunion of the United Confederate Veterans (the forerunner of today's Sons of Confederate Veterans), the following resolution was proposed: that from then on the Great War of 1861 was to be designated "the Civil War Between the States."[9]

A WORD ON EARLY AMERICAN MATERIAL

☛ In order to preserve the authentic historicity of the Revolutionary and Civil War periods I have retained the original spellings, formatting, and punctuation of the early Americans I quote. These include such items as British-English spellings, long-running paragraphs, obsolete words, and various literary devices peculiar to the time. Bracketed words within quotes are my additions and clarifications, while italicized words within quotes are (where indicated) my emphasis.

☛ ENTRIES: DATES, SPELLING, & AUTHORS

In some cases the authors of my various entries are unknown, which I mark as such. However, in the case of material from *Confederate Veteran*, the "unknown" writer is usually the editor, Sumner Archibald Cunningham (the founder of the magazine), or one of his staff members.

As most of my source material here is from *Confederate Veteran*, which began in 1893, chapters from this year forward are longer and more in depth. This is true, in particular, of the years 1893, 1894, and 1895, which I paid special attention to since they were closest to the Civil War years, when recollections tended to be clearer and more accurate. Needless to say, the dates ascribed to many of my entries are arbitrary, confused, and often unknown. In such cases I placed them where I felt they were best suited. Where articles and entries lacked a title, I created them, and in some instances edited or "improved" existing ones for clarification purposes.

Where only the last name of an individual is known, in the Index I add their title (e.g., Captain or Dr.) or marital status (e.g., Miss), where known, for ease of research.

Though this title is nearly 600 pages long, it would have been many times longer if I had included every noteworthy Confederate officer, sketch, and memory that I came across in my research. As this is simply impossible in a general commercial work of this nature, I chose a cross section of material that I personally found of interest—from the mundane to the sublime—and which I felt would be of interest to my readers.

As the editor I have done my best to catch errors in the original material, but, 120 to 150 years after the fact it is not always clear which words and names are actually errors. And though I have left the original text untouched (only giving into the temptation to add my own comments on occasion), the one area in which I have allowed myself free reign is in the spelling of proper names. There were, for example, numerous men surnamed Stewart, Steuart, and Stuart associated with the War, and these surnames are often haphazardly interchanged, for example, when Confederate General James Ewell Brown ("Jeb") Stuart is erroneously called Jeb Stewart. To avoid the nightmarish complications such disorder would have caused myself as well as my readers, I have simply corrected these spelling mistakes whenever and wherever possible.

As was the European-American custom at the time, many people did not write out their first or middle names, but instead used initials, adding to the difficulties for the modern day researcher.

A caveat: naturally, 30 to 50 years after the War, memories began to cloud. This means that the reader will inevitably come across errors (such as word spellings, dates of battles, names, etc.) in the texts of the men and women I have included here. These are minor in nature, however, and do not affect the overall significance of *Rise Up and Call Them Blessed*. In fact, as a Southern historian I consider this material more than accurate and informative enough to form the basis for an authentic "Civil War" history, which is exactly what this book is intended to be—undefiled by nefarious, unclean South-hating hands.

PRESENTISM

☛ As a historian I view *presentism* (judging the past according to present day mores and customs) as the enemy of authentic history. And this is precisely why the Left employs it in its ongoing war against traditional American, conservative, and Christian values. By looking at history through the lens of modern day beliefs, they are able to distort, revise, and reshape the past into a false narrative that fits their ideological agenda: the liberalization *and* Northernization of America, the enlargement and further centralization of the national government, and total control of American political, economic, and social power, the same agenda that Lincoln championed.

Judging our ancestors by our own standards is unfair, unjust, misleading, and unethical.

This book rejects presentism and replaces it with what I call *historicalism*: judging our ancestors based on the values of their own time. To get the most from this work the reader is invited to reject presentism as well. In this way—along with casting aside preconceived notions and the fake "history" churned out by our left-wing education system—the truth in this work will be most readily ascertained and absorbed.

LEARN MORE

☛ Lincoln's War on the American people and the Constitution can never be fully understood without a thorough knowledge of the South's perspective. As this book is only meant to be a brief introductory guide to these topics, one cannot hope to learn the complete story here. For those who are interested in additional material from Dixie's viewpoint, please see my comprehensive histories listed on page 2.

Keep Your Body, Mind, & Spirit Vibrating at Their Highest Level

YOU CAN DO SO BY READING THE BOOKS OF

SEA RAVEN PRESS

There is nothing that will so perfectly keep your body, mind, and spirit in a healthy condition as to think wisely and positively. Hence you should not only read this book, but also the other books that we offer. They will quicken your physical, mental, and spiritual vibrations, enabling you to maintain a position in society as a healthy erudite person.

KEEP YOURSELF WELL-INFORMED!

The well-informed person is always at the head of the procession, while the ignorant, the lazy, and the unthoughtful hang onto the rear. If you are a Spiritual man or woman, do yourself a great favor: read Sea Raven Press books and stay well posted on the Truth. It is almost criminal for one to remain in ignorance while the opportunity to gain knowledge is open to all at a nominal price.

We invite you to visit our Webstore for a wide selection of wholesome, family-friendly, well-researched, educational books for all ages. You will be glad you did!

Five-Star Books & Gifts From the Heart of the American South

SeaRavenPress.com

INTRODUCTION

MOST PEOPLE ARE NOT FAMILIAR with the real American "Civil War," for as Walt Whitman once opined, "the real war will never get in the books." But the only reason it "never got in the books" is because it has been aggressively suppressed by the victors: Left-wing South-haters. Thankfully, this 150 year old, highly politicized, anti-intellectual trend is finally coming to an end.

For those who got their Civil War "history" from school, mainstream books, or the Liberal media, *Rise Up and Call Them Blessed* will be a life-altering experience. For it is filled, not with the Northern-slanted, cherry picked words of progressive, biased, modern historians whose only purpose is to disseminate anti-South propaganda, but with the words of men and women who actually lived through the conflict; many who also survived "the Second Civil War on the South": the far more severe period deceptively known as "Reconstruction" (1865-1877).

These eyewitness accounts, which I label "tributes to the Confederate soldier," are factual Victorian testimonies concerning what took place in the years spanning 1861 to 1901. Their words—unlike the 21st-Century writer, who is separated from the War by a century and a half—derive from first-hand experience. Many of the men whose writings I have collected fought and bled on countless "Civil War" battlefields, suffering every privation and horror imaginable, and some quite unimaginable. A large proportion of my women writers watched their husbands, fathers, brothers, sons, and sweethearts march off into the haze of cannon smoke (one out of four who were never seen again), while Yankee troops abused them, forced them (along with their children) out onto the streets, then pillaged and burned their homes to the ground.

These are the kinds of eyewitness accounts that make up much of the "real war" that has been wholly ignored in our mainstream history books—books comprised of distortions, alterations, redactions, and even wholesale myths, lies, and inventions. What is their purpose? The same purpose all fake military history has: to demonize and humiliate the loser while covering up the many crimes committed by the victor.

To make this real war experience as rich, complete, and historically interesting *and* accurate as possible, I have included the words of men and women, European-Americans and African-Americans, slaves and free blacks, Southerners and Northerners, Confederate soldiers and Union soldiers, privates and generals, surgeons and prisoners, upper class and lower class, educated and unschooled, Conservatives and Liberals, sectionalists and nationalists; nearly the entire spectrum of American Victorian society. Amid this diverse mixture one will find not only an assortment of North-hating Southerners and South-hating Northerners, but also examples of the North-loving Southerner ("scallywag") and the South-loving Northerner ("Copperhead")—offering a true "slice of life" image of the views held at the time.

As 99 percent of these individuals were not historians or even writers, but soldiers and ordinary civilians, the reader will inevitably come across the occasional semantical error. This is to be expected and is usually nothing more than faulty memory accessed decades after the War, or improper education. For example, many of my 19th-Century contributors refer to the United States of America, and sometimes also the Confederate States of America, as "nations." As I have repeatedly shown in my other works, the Founding Fathers of both the U.S.A. and the C.S.A. rejected the idea of a national government,[10] quite consciously forming confederacies, or more accurately, "confederate republics," as George Washington, Alexander Hamilton, St. George Tucker, and numerous other Founders called the U.S.[11]

If we were a nation (as Liberals have long falsely claimed us to be), there would be no such thing as states' rights, for the states would not be individual sovereigns, "little republics," as Thomas Jefferson styled them, or "distinct nations," as John Jay referred to them.[12] Most significantly, there would be no Ninth and Tenth Amendments, those all-important clauses in the Bill of Rights that carefully delineate the powers of the federal government and those of the states. In a true nation the federal government, or national government as it would be called, would possess all available powers while the states would possess few or none.

Our political reality is the opposite, however. The American colonies seceded from Great Britain based on the idea that "governments are instituted among men, deriving their just powers from the consent of the governed."[13] Thus the Tenth Amendment reads:

The powers not delegated to the United States by the Constitution, nor prohibited by it to the States, are reserved to the States respectively, or to the people.[14]

As long as "the people" possess all of the many powers reserved to them—as the Bill of Rights permanently guarantees—we will remain a confederate republic, not a nation.

In the tragic event that the Tenth Amendment is one day overturned and we do become a nation, we will no longer be the United States of America, a *voluntary union of independent conservative republics* (as the Founders intended). We will become the "Soviet States of America," an *involuntary nation of dependent socialist republics* (as Liberals intend).[15]

Another mistaken idea that sometimes appears in the words of the writers and speakers I have included here is that the Southern Cause was a failure, a "Lost Cause," in Victorian parlance.

The Southern Cause was not lost, and it will never be lost. Why? Because the Southern Cause was an *idea*, and ideas cannot be destroyed; not by bayonets, pistols, or cannon, or any other method—either physical or non-physical. This

idea, the one the Confederate armies fought for, was, in essence, the political theory of *conservatism*, with small government Conservative Jefferson Davis as its leader. Against this were the Union armies, led by big government Liberal Abraham Lincoln, who fought for the political theory of *liberalism* (note that in the 1860s the platforms of the two major parties were reversed from what they are today).[16] As is obvious, these two concepts—which naturally morph into two opposing forces or political parties—are inherent in human nature, have been with us since the beginning of politics (in ancient societies), and are just as vital and active today as they were 3,000 years ago, or 150 years ago.[17]

The Southern Cause, conservatism, was not "lost" then. It was merely temporarily prevented from attaining power between 1861 and 1865. Proof that the Conservative Cause was not lost is that 20 years after the War ended, New Yorker Grover Cleveland became president of the U.S., the first Conservative (then known as a "Democrat") to be elected since the War began in 1861.[18] Thus it would be more accurate to say that though the Liberals won the military war in 1865, they lost the political war in 1885. And they lost it again in the 2016 election. As I write these words, Conservatives are in full control of all three of our governmental branches: the executive, the legislative, and the judicial.[19]

Clearly, the Southern Cause is very much alive to this day. Instead of Confederate soldiers, however, it is now being carried forward by their political descendants: Conservatives, who have founded scores of traditionalist, constitutionalist, and nationalist groups like the Tea Party, the Alt.-Right, Sons of the Confederate Veterans, United Daughters of the Confederacy, Order of Confederate Rose, the National Rifle Association, the John Birch Society, and many others. There is no such thing as the "Lost Cause" in authentic American Civil War history, and those who use this phrase evince a basic misunderstanding of both history and politics.

Though some of my 19th- and early 20th-Century sources—culled from letters, speeches, reminiscences, personal observations, anecdotes, stories, and official reports (military and civilian)—are indeed misinformed on these two topics, it was important to me to incorporate them into the narrative in order to provide as broad an overview as possible on how the Confederate soldier was perceived during the Victorian Era.

While my writers were sometimes confounded by semantics, they suffered no confusion whatever about the larger issue of the day; namely, Lincoln's War, from the Southern state secessions that preceded it to the Northern "Reconstruction" that succeeded it. As eyewitnesses and even participants in these events, they are, without question, the most highly qualified authorities on the conflict. This is, after all, exactly why they have been disregarded and slandered by the Left. And this is precisely why I am bringing their long neglected words back into the light of day.

The significance of preserving their experiences, views, and thoughts cannot be overemphasized. Among other things, the 19th-Century individuals in this book will objectively answer the following vital questions:

- What were the real causes that led up to the War?
- For what cause did the South fight specifically?
- For what cause did the North fight specifically?
- What was the real reason the South seceded?
- Why did the North choose to use force to try and prevent secession?
- What part, if any, did slavery play in launching the War?
- Who was the real Robert E. Lee, Stonewall Jackson, and Nathan Bedford Forrest (among many others), and why will the South (as well as every true

Conservative and American patriot) always honor and love them?
- What is the attitude of the South since the close of the War?
- What is the attitude of the North since the close of the War?

Victorians responded to these questions in a way that no modern writer possibly can, for they themselves lived the answers.

My early American contributors often go into great detail on a wide variety of war-related topics, and in doing so, debunk the illogical views, mean-spirited falsehoods, and Alice-in-Wonderland fairy tales fabricated by enemies of Dixie. From them you will learn, for instance:

- Why Abraham Lincoln's son, Robert Todd Lincoln, Secretary of War under President James Garfield, gave former Confederate soldiers living in Chicago, Illinois, permission to take over a plot of ground and erect a Confederate monument on it.
- Why President Theodore Roosevelt, who approved of the pro-South magazine *Confederate Veteran* (and also read it), heartily praised not only Confederate General Robert E. Lee, but *all* Confederate soldiers.
- Why President William McKinley spoke kindly of the Southern people and proclaimed that it was "the duty of the United States to take care of the graves of the Confederate dead."
- Why Union General Ulysses S. Grant so looked up to Stonewall Jackson that he once told a Southerner: "I can understand fully the admiration your people have for him."
- Why Union General William T. Sherman said of Nathan Bedford Forrest, "I must confess he excited my admiration," and why Union General Philip H. Sheridan pronounced him "one of the most remarkable men produced by the war on either side."

Such facts of history reveal how displaced today's "hatred for all things Confederate" movement is, how uninformed the average person is regarding authentic American history, and the extreme measures the Left has gone to in order to bury the truth beneath a mountain of purposefully deceptive propaganda.

Yet, for those who think that the debasement of our Confederate soldiers, the banning of the Confederate Flag, the defacement and removal of Confederate monuments, as well as South-loathing and South-shaming in general, are modern phenomena, our Victorian ancestors will rapidly disabuse you of this notion. As will become evident, the North's massive "Civil War" smear campaign against the South began the day the first Southern state seceded on December 20, 1860, after which endless streams of both misinformation and disinformation began immediately pouring forth out of Washington.

What follows is just one example of what many Yankees thought about the Confederacy and her military men in 1896, nearly 125 years ago. The writer is Henry M. Boies of Scranton, Pennsylvania:

> . . . as the South itself has professed to accept the issue of the war as a final settlement of the questions on which it was waged, and as that decision was that they were in the wrong, they certainly must logically recognize the fact that the men who fomented and plotted and organized this terrible affliction of our country while wearing its uniform ought not to be held up to the admiration of the coming generations as equally worthy of honor and imitation with the great defenders of our common country. Whatever their affection and enthusiasm for the distinguished leaders whom they followed in their error, they certainly cannot wish their sons to learn that treason is as honorable as loyalty to the Republic; but that is the only lesson which grand monuments to Davis and Lee can teach. How absurd the suggestion of flying an American flag over them! They would never think of proposing to do it. But ought public structures [that is, Confederate monuments] to be erected in this country over which our [U.S.] flag cannot fly?
>
>
>
> It seems to me that our forgiving disposition [that is, the North's] has lapsed almost into an unconsciousness of the guilt of treason, which is the gravest of political crimes.
>
> It is high time . . . that every patriot and lover of his country [Boies is referring here to other Liberals], began to lift up his voice and dip his pen in fire to arouse the public sense of horror at treason and rebellion, "lest the Republic come to harm." It would be far better if the South would put up a monument here and there to Lincoln and Grant, who, they are willing to acknowledge, saved them all they have left, than to obtrusively multiply affront to the nation by this superfluous aggrandizement of the arch-traitors Davis and Lee. However much they may love and revere them, they certainly cannot wish their descendants to imitate them.[20]

Boies' remarks reveal not only the cruelty, stupidity, intolerance, insensitivity, and ruthlessness that drove Lincoln and his Liberal backers to illegally invade a constitutionally-formed foreign country, the *Confederate States of America* (named after one of the nicknames for the early U.S.A.),[21] but also a wholesale ignorance of why the South seceded in the first place: decades of Northern meddling, maltreatment, and harassment, as well as uncountable constitutional abuses. As Lyon G. Tyler (son of President John Tyler) put it:

> The war was nothing more than the outcome of a tyranny exerted for seventy-two years by the North over vital interests of the South.[22]

The men and women whose words I have included in this book absolutely confirm this statement, leaving no doubt as to why the South seceded, why her sons fought, and why her daughters sacrificed. Not to "preserve slavery" or "destroy the Union" (laughable and irrational reasons from any perspective), but to preserve the original conservative government of the Founding Fathers—which Liberal Lincoln had promised to undermine, demolish, and replace.[23]

In doing so, my Victorian writers reveal why America's Confederate soldiers should be honored in every town, public square, park, and city hall for the rest of time. This book, which I have chosen to begin and end with the words of America's greatest Conservative, Jefferson Davis, will greatly aid in justifying that honor.

Lochlainn Seabrook
Nashville, Tennessee, USA
November 2017

Shall we carelessly allow our children to be taught any kind of fables fabricated by any kind of persons, and to receive into their minds opinions contrary to those we judge they ought to have when they are grown up?

PLATO

CHAPTER 1

1861

☛ ADDRESS BEFORE THE CONFEDERATE CONGRESS

Gentlemen of Congress:—It is my pleasing duty to announce to you that the Constitution framed for the establishment of a permanent government of the Confederate States of America has been ratified by the several conventions of each of those States which were referred to to inaugurate the said Government in its full proportions and upon its own substantial basis of the popular will.

It only remains that elections should be held for the designation of the officers to administer it.

There is every reason to believe that at no distant day other States, identical in political principles and community of interests with those which you represent, will join this Confederacy, giving to its typical constellation increased splendor—to *its government of free, equal and sovereign States*, a wider sphere of usefulness, and to the friends of *constitutional liberty a greater security* for its harmonious and perpetual existence.

It was not, however, for the purpose of making this announcement that I have deemed it my duty to convoke you at an earlier day than that fixed by yourselves for your meeting.

The declaration of war made against this Confederacy, by Abraham Lincoln, President of the United States, in his proclamation, issued on the 15th day of the present month, renders it necessary, in my judgement, that you should convene at the earliest practicable moment to devise the measures necessary for the defence of the country. . . .

We protest solemnly, in the face of mankind, that *we desire peace at any sacrifice, save that of honor.* In independence *we seek no conquest, no* aggrandizement, no cession of any kind from the States with which we have lately confederated. All we ask is to be let alone—that those who never held power over us shall not now attempt our subjugation by arms. This we will, we must resist, to the direst extremity.

Jefferson Davis, C.S.A.

The moment that this pretense is abandoned, the sword will drop from our grasp, and we shall be ready to enter into treaties of amity and commerce that cannot but be mutually beneficial.

So long as this pretension is maintained, with a firm reliance on that Divine Power which covers with its protection the just cause, we will continue to struggle for our inherent right to freedom, independence, and self-government.[24] — PRESIDENT JEFFERSON DAVIS (April 29, 1861)

☛ BEAUREGARD'S TRIBUTE TO HIS TROOPS AT FT. SUMTER
Headquarters Provisional Army, C.S.A., Charleston, S.C., April 17, 1861.

Hon. Leroy Pope Walker, Secretary of War, Montgomery, Ala.:

I have the honor to transmit by Col. R. A. Pryor, one of my aides (who like the others was quite indefatigable and fearless in conveying my orders, in an open boat, from these headquarters to the batteries during the bombardment), a general report of the attack of the 12th instant on Fort Sumter. This report would have been sent sooner if my other pressing duties had permitted me to devote my time to it, while the presence of the enemy's fleet still led us to expect an attack along the coast at any moment. A more detailed account will be sent forward as soon as the returns of the commanders of batteries shall have reached this office. The great difficulty I will labor under will be to do full justice to all when so much zeal, energy, and gallantry were displayed by officers and soldiers in the execution of my orders. I wish, however, to record two incidents, which will illustrate the feelings that animated all here.

Whilst the barracks in Fort Sumter were in a blaze, and the interior of the work appeared untenable from the heat and from the fire of our batteries (at about which period I sent three of my aides to offer assistance in the name of the Confederate States), whenever the guns of Fort Sumter would fire upon Fort Moultrie the men occupying Cummings Point batteries (Palmetto Guard, Captain [George B.] Cuthbert) at each shot would cheer [Union Major Robert] Anderson for his gallantry, although themselves still firing upon him, and when on the 15th instant he left the harbor on the steamer *Isabel* the soldiers of the batteries on Cummings Point lined the beach, silent, and with heads uncovered, while Anderson and his command passed before them, and expressions of scorn at the apparent cowardice of the [Union] fleet in not even attempting to rescue so gallant an officer and his command were upon the lips of all.

Pierre G. T. Beauregard, C.S.A.

With such material for an army, if properly disciplined, I would consider myself almost invincible against any forces not too greatly superior.

The fire of those barracks was only put out on the 15th instant, p.m., after great exertions by the gallant fire companies of this city, who were at their pumps night and day, although aware that close by them was a magazine filled with thirty thousand pounds of powder, with a shot-hole through the wall of its anteroom.

I am now removing the tottering walls of the buildings within, and clearing away all the rubbish, etc., from the interior of the work, so as to render it still more formidable than it was before it was attacked.

In one or two days I will send forward to you photographs taken at different points of sight, from which you can clearly understand the condition of the fort within when first occupied by us. I have the honor to be, very respectfully, your obedient servant — PIERRE G. T. BEAUREGARD (Brigadier-General, Commanding)[25]

☛ COL. EARL VAN DORN PRAISES HIS TROOPS
Headquarters Troops in Texas. General Orders, No. 5, San Antonio, Tex., May13, 1861.

It is the pleasing duty of the colonel commanding to thank the volunteer troops of Texas for the valuable services they have again rendered to the Confederate States. Being called upon at short notice to take the field, they responded with that promptness which proved how high is the military spirit of the State, and how ready her people are to seize up arms in defense of her honor and in vindication of their rights. It was not the wish of the volunteers of Texas, however, to fight against those troops of the United States who had been defending their frontiers for years, and who found themselves on their soil in the attitude of enemies only because of political changes which they did nothing to bring about, many of whom had been personally endeared to them by long association and by their gallant deeds (well remembered) as their old comrades in the war with Mexico. With the true spirit of brave men who know how to appreciate a soldiers honor, they marshaled in such numbers before them that the rugged necessities of war might be accomplished without bloodshed and without the loss of reputation to their gallant opponents. There was no exultation over the surrender of the troops of the old Eighth Infantry [U.S.A.]. This would not be the case were the volunteers of Texas called out, under arms, to contend with an invading force sent against them from the North; far from it. There would then be no regrets, no affection, and no disparity of numbers, and death to the foe and victory after the fight would be the object and the aim of every true Texan.

Earl Van Dorn, C.S.A.

Colonel Van Dorn feels proud of the command the President [Jefferson Davis] has assigned him. . . [and he] is also indebted to the gentlemen who did him the honor to serve on his staff for the occasion: Col. P. N. Luckett, Judge F. Tate, Judge T. J. Devine, General James Willie, Capt. P. P. Shea, Dr. Fretwell, Capt. W. T. Mechling, Messrs. R. A. Howard, J. T. Ward, D. E. Tessier, Maj. T. G. Howard, and Dr. H. P. Howard, and especially to Col. J. A. Wilcox, and Capt. J. F. Minter, and Lieut. J. P. Major, C. S. Army, for the happy manner in which they executed their delicate mission to the commanding officer of the United States troops. — By order of Col. EARL VAN DORN (W. T. Mechling, Captain, and Acting Assistant Adjutant-General)[26]

CHAPTER 2

1862

☛ GALLANT TENNESSEAN KILLED NEAR RICHMOND

Among the noble brave who fell in the recent battles near Richmond, perhaps no one deserves more honorable mention than Lieut. John C. Shackleford, of the First Tennessee Regiment, who fell on Friday, the 27th of June, while gallantly leading his regiment in the first charge at Gaines' Mills. Col. Shackleford was in the battle of Seven Pines, and also commanded his regiment in the fight at Ellison's Mills on Thursday before the battle in which he fell. In every action, though but twenty-six years of age, he showed himself to possess in an eminent degree the qualities of a good commander; to wit, coolness, self-possession, and bravery. So gallantly did he demean himself upon the field in the thickest of the fight that the soldiers would often exclaim: "Surely Col. Shackleford's nerves are steel!" When shot

he was waving his sword above his head and cheering his men on, but so thick and terrible was the leaden storm that our men were ordered to retreat. A soldier offered to take him off the field, but he said: "No: it is no use; take care of yourself." He was universally popular, and was the favorite of his own regiment. The First Tennessee will ever cherish his memory with the most grateful recollections, he was a most ardent and enthusiastic devotee to the southern cause, was among the first to respond to his country's call, and was in the service of the Confederate

States in Virginia before his native State had seceded from the old Union. With him love of the Confederacy was a passion, and he seemed to but carry his life in his hand, that he might throw it upon the altar of his own loved native South whenever her interest demanded it. His devotedly affectionate parents, brothers and sisters, are sadly bereaved in the loss of so noble, gifted, and promising a son and brother, but may they be consoled in the reflection that he died at his post, in the full discharge of his whole duty, and now fills a hero's grave.[27] — RICHMOND ENQUIRER (July 17)

🖝 FORREST'S ENGAGEMENT AT SACRAMENTO, KENTUCKY

Headquarters Hopkinsville, Ky., January 8, 1862.

Lieutenant: I have the honor to transmit herewith, for the information of the major-general, the official report of Col. Nathan B. Forrest of his brilliant and dashing affair at Sacramento on the 28th ultimo [December 1861].

The report of Colonel Forrest is a modest recital of one of the most brilliant and successful cavalry engagements which the present war has witnessed, and gives a favorable omen of what that arm of our service will do in future on a more extended scale.

The loss of the enemy, it will be seen, is estimated by Colonel Forrest at 65 killed and 35 wounded and prisoners, and from private and unofficial sources I learn that the number is not overestimated. Our own loss was but 2 killed, but in the death of Capt. C. E. Meriwether, who fell while gallantly leading his command into action, the country and the service have sustained a loss which I most deeply deplore. A brave and chivalrous gentleman, I esteemed him as one of the very best officers of his rank in the service. Colonel Forrest pays what I doubt not is a well-merited tribute to the gallantry and good conduct of his officers and men generally and specially. For the skill, courage, and energy displayed by Colonel Forrest he is entitled to the highest praise, and I take great pleasure in calling the attention of the general

Nathan Bedford Forrest, C.S.A.

commanding and of the Government to his services. I am assured by officers and men that throughout the entire engagement he was conspicuous for the most daring courage; always in advance of his command. He was at one time engaged in a hand-to-hand conflict with 4 of the enemy, 3 of whom he killed, dismounting and making a prisoner of the fourth. The other field officers, Lieutenant-Colonel [James W.] Starnes and Major [David Campbell] Kelley, by their coolness, courage, and promptitude, contributed largely to the success of the day. I have the honor to be, lieutenant, respectfully.[28] — BRIG. GEN. CHARLES CLARK (Brigadier-General, Commanding, C.S.A.)

☛ ENGAGEMENT AT SECESSIONVILLE, SOUTH CAROLINA
Report of Lieut. Col. J. McEnery, Fourth Louisiana Battalion, Secessionville, James Island, S.C., June 20, 1862:

Captain Mallory P. King, Assistant Adjutant-General: I have the honor to submit the following report of the part taken in the battle of the 16th instant near Secessionville by my battalion: A little after dawn on the morning of the 16th instant Colonel [J.] Hagood, commanding First Regiment South Carolina Volunteers, came in person to my quarters, about 2.5 miles distant from this place, and ordered me to have my battalion under arms and march immediately to the Secessionville battery, at which place an engagement with the enemy was being had. With promptness the battalion was formed, and the march, at double-quick, was begun in the direction of Secessionville. When [we] arrived at the first cross-roads some little delay ensued arising from my ignorance of the road leading to Secessionville. After the lapse of a few moments I was assured as to the right road, and instantly the battalion was moved off at double-quick for the scene of action.

Arriving at Secessionville, I was informed that the enemy in force were advancing on the right of the battery on the opposite side of the marsh, directly up the marsh to the bridge. I hastened my command at a run through an open ground to the woods on the marsh. In crossing this open marsh, and while placing the battalion in position on the outer edge of the woods, it was exposed to a terrific fire from the enemy's gunboats, siege battery, fixed batteries, and small-arms. I then ordered the men to advance in the skirt of woods, the better to view the enemy and afford it protection from the incessant fire of the enemy. At this point for half an hour the fire on both sides was indeed terrific. Finally the enemy wavered, fell back, and then began his precipitate retreat on the right and in front. The gallant [Col. T. G.] Lamar being struck down, and being the senior officer present I caused an incessant volley of grape and canister to be poured into the broken and retreating columns of the enemy until they passed beyond view. Colonel [S. D.] Goodlett, my senior officer, arriving about 12 p.m., assumed command.

I cannot speak in terms of too high praise of the coolness, bravery, and gallantry of the officers and men of my little command. I went into the action with 250 men and succeeded in putting to route twice that force of the enemy on the right. I think that this force of the enemy would undoubtedly have completely flanked the battery but for our timely arrival. The small band of brave men in the fort, exhausted and broken down in their almost superhuman exertions in repelling the foe in front, must have been unequal to the task of successfully engaging the enemy in front and on the right. . . . I am, captain, your obedient servant.[29] — J. MCENERY (Lieutenant-Colonel, Comdg, Fourth Louisiana Battalion)

CHAPTER 3

1863

☛ ACTION NEAR THE WHITE SULPHUR SPRINGS
Report of Maj. R. Augustus Bailey, Twenty-second Virginia Infantry, August 29, 1863.

Lieutenant Noyes Rand, Acting Assistant Adjutant-General: I have the honor to make the following report of the part taken by the Twenty-second Virginia Regiment in the action of August 26 and 27, near the White Sulphur Springs: In obedience to an order from Col. George S. Patton, commanding the Confederate forces, the Twenty-second Regiment, consisting of nine companies (Company K being stationed at the Narrows of New River), was formed in line of battle to support and immediately in front of Chapman's battery, with orders to hold the position at all hazards, this being the center of the Confederate lines. The strength of the regiment actually in the fight was about 500, aggregate.

Soon after forming, the following companies, i.e., Companies A, B, E, G, and H, were detached by Lieutenant-Colonel Barbee and deployed as skirmishers on a ridge about 1,000 yards in front of and stretching some distance to the left of the four remaining companies under my charge. The skirmishing companies soon became hotly engaged, holding their ground for some time, stubbornly resisting and beating back the enemy until, being attacked by a much superior force, they were

compelled to fall back on the line. In making this movement Companies H, E, G, B, and a portion of Company A, all under the command of Lieut. Col. A. R. Barbee, took position on the extreme left of the line, with Colonel Derrick. The other portion of Company A fell back to the companies under my command. Of the further action of the four above-mentioned companies I am
unable to speak, as they were not ordered up to my line till the fight was over.

. . . The position assigned my command—an open field, without any protection save such as was afforded by a low rail fence—was much exposed during the entire fight to a heavy fire of musketry and the frequent discharge of grape, shell, and canister, which the enemy threw with great accuracy, in consequence of which we lost heavily the first day.

Notwithstanding the great disadvantages under which they labored, the officers and men acted most nobly, repelling the oft-repeated and daring attempts of the enemy to dislodge them. The commanders of companies and their subaltern officers are entitled to much praise for their coolness under fire and the tenacity with which they held their ground.

The enemy, having signally failed with artillery in all their attempts to drive my command back, brought one regiment up in front, with one more as a support, and commenced a spirited and bold charge on my lines. This may be considered the most critical moment. My ammunition was almost entirely exhausted—few had more than five rounds, many none at all. This caused some to break to the rear, but they were easily rallied by their company officers. The enemy, advancing with loud cheers, made a most desperate assault on our lines. Here the bravery of the troops was conspicuous. Led on by their company officers, they determinedly met the foe and repulsed them in handsome style, driving them in confusion beyond their own lines, killing many, and wounding and capturing the field-officer who headed the charge.

My thanks are due Lieut. E. T. Jackson, acting adjutant, for his prompt execution of orders, and Sergeant-Major Quarrier for his exertions in keeping the men at their post. Too much credit cannot be given Capt. John K. Thompson, acting field-officer, who assisted me much by his coolness and conspicuous gallantry.

While the enemy were vigorously attacking my lines two companies from Derrick's battalion came bravely to our assistance and rendered good service. After this charge was broken we were exposed to a continuous fire of artillery and small-arms till after night-fall. During the night the command was busily engaged preparing for the following day.

At daybreak of the 27th, the enemy opened on us again and kept up a spirited fire until about 11 a.m., when they again attempted to form and charge us; but were whipped, scattered, and driven in disorder back before they could form, and being repulsed along the entire line, retreated hastily from the field.

My command was under fire twelve hours the first day and about five the second. Captured 20 prisoners, among them 1 field-officer, and brought off a good many guns and pistols.

Attached to this report you will find a list of the casualties in this regiment. I have the honor, lieutenant, to remain, very respectfully.[30]
— R. A. BAILEY (Major, Twenty-second Virginia Infantry)

CHAPTER 4

1864

☛ REPORT ON FLORIDA ENGAGEMENT
August 17, 1864, 3 o'clock; Captain W. G. Barth, Assistant Adjutant-General:

I have the honor to report that I had engagement to-day with the cavalry force of the enemy at this place, and by Divine aid the victory was decisive and complete. It lasted about two hours; 140 or 150 prisoners were captured, and will be forwarded this afternoon. Among them were 1 captain, 2 lieutenants, and 1 surgeon, several killed and wounded. Our loss is slight—1 killed and 5 wounded. A 12-pounder howitzer was captured, with horses and fixtures complete; a fine piece. About 100 negroes were re-captured, with three of the enemy's wagons, a considerable number of horses, and other things. They numbered 342, and were the Seventy-fifth Ohio  Regiment, Colonel Harris commanding, and Fourth Massachusetts. This party left Baldwin by Trail Ridge and passed between Waldo and Orange Springs. *They pillaged and thieved everything as they went, stripping the houses.* The whole command would have been captured, but my horses were completely worn down. I pursued them from 5 to 10 miles after the fight, one part going toward Newnansville and the other toward Waldo.

I had with me besides my own command Captain Rou's command of 80 men, from Second Florida Cavalry Regiment, and Captain McElvey, of Fifth Florida Cavalry Battalion, with a detachment of 40 men. I had only about 175 men in the engagement. The officers and men behaved with great gallantry. Lieutenant Bruton, of the artillery, exhibited great coolness and bravery. The march was commenced from Waldo last evening at 9 o'clock in pursuit, and after a most fatiguing march all night they were not overtaken until 8 o'clock this morning. The enemy are reported to have four regiments of colored troops at Starke, and I have them to watch and look after closely. I hope the cavalry will not be so difficult to manage hereafter. I am, captain, your obedient servant.[31] — J. J. DICKISON (Captain, Commanding, Second Florida Cavalry)

Union mortars at Yorktown, VA.

CHAPTER 5

1865

☛ GEN. JOSEPH WHEELER'S FAREWELL TO HIS MEN

Gallant Comrades—You have fought your last fight, your task is done. During a four years' struggle for liberty you have exhibited courage, fortitude, devotion. You are the sole victors of more than two hundred sternly contested fields. You have participated in more than a thousand conflicts of arms. You are heroes, veterans, and patriots. The bones of your comrades mark battle fields upon the soil of Kentucky, Tennessee, Virginia, North and South Carolina, Georgia, Alabama, Mississippi. You have done all that human exertion could accomplish. In bidding you adieu I desire to tender thanks for your gallantry in battle, your fortitude under suffering, and your devotion at all times to the holy cause you have done so much to maintain. I desire also to express my gratitude for the kind feeling you have seen fit to extend toward myself, and to invoke upon you the blessing of our heavenly Father, to whom we must always look for support in the hour of distress. Brethren in the cause of freedom, comrades in arms, I bid you farewell.[32] — MAJOR GEN. JOSEPH WHEELER (April 29)

Joseph Wheeler, C.S.A.

🖙 LAST ORDER OF GEN. ROBERT E. LEE

After four years of arduous service, marked by unsurpassed courage and fortitude, the Army of Northern Virginia has compelled to yield to overwhelming numbers and resources. I need not tell the survivors of so many hard-fought battles, who have remained steadfast to the last, that I have consented to this result from no distrust of them. But feeling that valor and devotion could accomplish nothing that could compensate for the loss that would have attended the continuance of the contest, I determined to avoid the sacrificing those whose past services have endeared them to their countrymen.

By the terms of the agreement officers and men can return to their homes and remain until exchanged. You will take with you the satisfaction that proceeds from the consciousness of duty faithfully performed, and I earnestly pray that a merciful God will extend you his blessing and protection. With an unceasing admiration of your constancy and devotion to your country, and a grateful remembrance of your kind and generous consideration for myself, I bid you an affectionate farewell.[33] — GEN. ROBERT E. LEE (Hdqrs Army of Northern Virginia, April 10, General Order No. 9)

🖙 INCIDENT AT FORT PILLOW

When [Union] Commander Davis took possession of Fort Pillow after its evacuation by the Confederates [in 1864] the following letter was found lying on a table in the officers' quarters:

> Fort Pillow, Tenn. To the first Yankee who reads this: I present this table not as a manifestation of friendship, yet I entertain no personal animosity to him, but because I can't transport it. After six weeks' bombardment, without doing us any harm whatever, I know you will exult over the occupation of this place, but our evacuation will hurt you from another point with disastrous effect. Five millions white [Southern] men fighting to be relieved from oppression will never be conquered by twenty millions actuated by malice and pecuniary gain, mark that. We have the science, energy and vigor, with the help of God, to extricate ourselves from this horrible and unnatural difficulty pressed upon us by the North; the day of retribution is approaching, and will fall upon you deadly as a bolt from heaven; may your sojourn at this place be of few days and full of trouble.[34]

☛ GEN. FORREST'S FAREWELL ADDRESS TO HIS TROOPS

Soldiers, the old campaign has ended, and your commanding general deems this an appropriate occasion to speak of the steadiness and patriotism with which you have borne the hardships of the past year. The marches and labors you have performed during that period will find no parallel in the history of this war.

On the 24th of December, 1863, there were three thousand of you, unorganized and undisciplined, at Jackson, Tenn., only four hundred of whom were armed. You were surrounded by fifteen thousand of the enemy, who were congratulating themselves on your certain capture. You started out with your artillery, wagon trains, and a large number of cattle, which you succeeded in bringing through, since which time you have fought and won the following battles—battles which will enshrine your names in the hearts of your countrymen and live in history an imperishable monument to your prowess: Jacks Creek, Estenaula, Somerville, Okolona, Union City, Paducah, Fort Pillow, Bolivar, Tishomingo Creek, Harrisburg, Hurricane Creek, Memphis, Athens, Sulphur Springs, Pulaski, Carter's Creek, Columbia, and Jacksonville are the fields upon which you have won fadeless immortality. In the recent campaign in Middle Tennessee you sustained the reputation so nobly won. For twenty-six days from the time you left Florence, on the 21st of November to the 26th of December, you were constantly engaged with the enemy, and without a murmur endured the hunger, cold, and labor of the campaign. To sum up in brief your triumphs during the past year, you have fought fifty battles, killed and captured sixteen thousand of the enemy, captured two thousand horses and mules, sixty-seven pieces of artillery, four gun-boats, fourteen transports, twenty barges, three hundred wagons, fifty ambulances, ten thousand stand of small arms, and forty block-houses; and have destroyed thirty-six railroad bridges, two hundred miles of railroad, six engines, one hundred cars, and fifteen million dollars' worth of property. In the accomplishment of this great

Forrest after the War.

work you were occasionally sustained by other troops who joined you in the fight, but your regular number never exceeded five thousand, two thousand of whom have been killed or wounded, while in prisoners you have lost about two hundred.

If your course has been marked by the graves of patriotic heroes who have fallen by your side, it has at the same time been more plainly marked by the blood of the invader. While you sympathize with the friends of the fallen, your sorrows should be appeased by the knowledge that they fell as brave men, battling for all that makes life worth living.

Soldiers, you now rest for a short time from your labors. During the respite prepare for action. Your commanding general is ready to lead you again to the defense of the common cause, and appeals to you by a remembrance of the past career, your desolated homes, your insulted women, and suffering children, and, above all, by the memory of your dead comrades, to yield obedience to discipline, and to buckle on your armor anew for the fight.

Bring with you the soldier's safest armor: a determination to fight while the enemy pollutes your soil, to fight as long as he denies your rights, to fight until independence shall have been achieved, to fight for home,  children, liberty, and all you hold dear. Show to the world the superhuman and sublime spirit with which a people may be inspired when fighting for the inestimable boon of liberty. Be not allured by the siren song of peace, for there can be no peace save upon your separate, independent nationality. You can never again unite with those who have murdered your sons, outraged your helpless families, and with demoniac malice wantonly destroyed your property and now seek to make slaves of you. A proposition of reunion with a people who have avowed their purpose to appropriate the property and to subjugate and annihilate the freemen of the South would stamp with infamy the names of your gallant dead and die living heroes of this war. Be patient, obedient, and earnest, and the day is not far distant when you can return to your homes and live in the full fruition of freedom around the old family altar.[35] — GEN. NATHAN BEDFORD FORREST (May 9)

CHAPTER 6
1866

☛ **APPOMATTOX & ROBERT E. LEE**

There stood the mournful remnants of that once glorious army that had dipped its conquering banners to the crimson tide of eight and twenty sanguinary battles and strewn its heroic slain from the feet of Pennsylvania's mountains to the gates of their own capital city; that had given Manassas to Beauregard and twined the fame on the Seven Pines battles in the laurel wreath of Johnston; that had caused the waters of the Shenandoah eternally to murmur the name of Stonewall Jackson, and, stretching its right arm out to the distant West, had planted victory on the drooping banners of Bragg; that had witnessed four gigantic campaigns, and through all their shifting and tragic scenes, and under all difficulties, trials, toils, and dangers, had remained steadfast and faithful to the last; and, after having witnessed the rising of the Southern constellation as it loomed up brightly on the horizon of war, pursuing to its splendid zenith the fiery path of Mars, now beheld, not unmoved, its declining splendors going down in the gloom of eternal night.

Robert E. Lee, C.S.A.

And he, its illustrious chief, whose lofty plume was ever its rallying point in battle and around whom its affections warmly clustered, now commended it for its past devotions and bade it adieu forever. Slowly and sadly he rode from that mournful field, for his strong sword hung shattered at his side and the cause that he fought for was beneath the foot of power. Few were the eyes that grew not moist at witnessing that departure. It was the agony of a great cause finding expression in the sublime soul of its great defender.

And though that cause be gone, yet will its memory continue to live, and ever honored will be those illustrious names that sacrificed at its altars. And on the scroll of fame no name among the list of eminent worthies will shine with a purer, serener, or more resplendent light than that of Robert Edward Lee. His fame is monumental. His name will be placed alongside those of the great captains of history—[the Duke of] Marlborough and [Marshall] Saxe, of Lilly and Eugene—and as long as the fame of the Southern struggle shall linger in tradition and song so long will his memory be cherished by the descendants of the Southern races, while his character will stand up in the twilight of history like some grand old cathedral, lifting itself in imperishable beauty above the objects of earth, majestic in its vast proportions, awful in its solemn stateliness, sublime in its severe simplicity.[36] — J. QUITMAN MOORE

CHAPTER 7
1879

☛ **MY FIRST MEETING WITH NATHAN BEDFORD FORREST**
In February, 1841, when I was but ten years of age, I remember well a small company of volunteers which marched out of the town of Holly Springs, Mississippi, to the relief of Texas, then threatened by invasion from Mexico. In that little band stood Bedford Forrest, a tall, black-haired, gray-eyed youth, scarce twenty years of age, who then gave the first evidence of the military ardor he possessed. The company saw no fighting, for the danger was over before they arrived, and the men received no pay. Finding themselves in a strange country, without friends or money, Forrest, with the characteristic energy which distinguished him in after life, split rails at fifty cents per hundred and made the money necessary to bring him back to his family and home.[37] — GEN. JAMES R. CHALMERS

James R. Chalmers, C.S.A.

CHAPTER 8

1886

☛ THEODORE ROOSEVELT'S TRIBUTE TO ROBERT E. LEE
No man who is not willing to bear arms and to fight for his rights can give a good reason why he should be entitled to the privilege of living in a free community. The decline of the militant spirit in the Northeast during the first half of this century [19th] was much to be regretted. To it is due more than to any other cause the undoubted average individual inferiority of the Northern compared with the Southern troops—at any rate, at the beginning of the great war of the rebellion. The Southerners, by their whole mode of living, their habits, and their love of outdoor sports, kept up their warlike spirit, while in the North the so-called upper classes developed along the lines of a wealthy and timid bourgeoisie type, measuring everything by a mercantile standard (a peculiarly debasing one, if taken purely by itself), and submitting to be ruled in local affairs by low, foreign mobs, and in national matters by their arrogant Southern kinsmen.

Theodore Roosevelt.

The militant spirit of these last certainly stood them in good stead in the civil war. *The world has never seen better soldiers than those who followed Lee, and their leader will undoubtedly rank, without any exception, as the very greatest of all the great captains that the English-speaking peoples have brought forth; and this although the last and chief of his antagonists may himself claim to stand as the full equal of Marlborough or Wellington.*[38] — THEODORE ROOSEVELT

CHAPTER 9

1887

☞ HEROES OF THE OLD SOUTH

I will tell you, young people, of the South which has passed away, that you may admire and imitate whatever was grand and noble in its history, and reject whatever was wrong and defective. The scandals that have brought shame upon the American name occurred when the old South was out of power. No official from the old South was ever charged with roguery; no great statesman of that period ever corruptly made money out of office. . . .

Confederate monument, Union, WV.

I love to hear the philanthropists praise Mr. Lincoln, and call him the second Washington, for I remember that he was born in Kentucky, and was from first to last, as the *Atlantic Monthly* truly said, "a Southern man in all his characteristics." I love to hear them say that George H. Thomas was the stoutest fighter in the Union army, for I remember that he was born in Virginia. I love to hear of the wonderful deeds of McClellan, Grant, Meade, and Hancock, for if they were such great warriors for crushing with their massive columns the thin lines of the ragged Rebels, what must be said of Lee, the two Johnstons, Beauregard, and Jackson, who held millions at bay for four years with their fragments of shadowy armies? Pile up huge pedestals and surmount them with bronze horses and riders in bronze. *All the Union monuments are eloquent of the prowess of the Rebels and their leaders.*[39] — GEN. DANIEL HARVEY HILL

CHAPTER 10

1891

☛ RECOLLECTIONS OF GENERAL STONEWALL JACKSON

I have to-day, after a lapse of thirty years, a very vivid recollection of his appearance, and how he impressed me.

Dressed in a simple Virginia uniform, apparently about 37 years old, six feet high, medium size, gray eyes that seemed to look through you, light brown hair, and a countenance in which deep benevolence seemed mingled with uncompromising sternness, he impressed me as having about him nothing at all of "the pomp and circumstance" of war, but every element which enters into the skillful leader, and the indomitable, energetic soldier, who was always ready for the fight.

At First Manassas Jackson won the sobriquet of "Stonewall," which has supplanted his proper name, and will cleave to him forever.

Thomas J. "Stonewall" Jackson, C.S.A.

The chivalric and heroic [General Barnard Elliott] Bee, who had been steadily borne back all of the morning, and his little handful of brave fellows nearly swept away by the blue waves which threatened to overwhelm everything before them, rode up to Jackson and exclaimed almost in despair: "General, they are beating us back." "No, sir," said Jackson, his eyes fairly glittering beneath the rim of his old cadet cap, "they shall not beat us back. We will give them the bayonet."

It was then that Bee, about to yield up his noble life, galloped back to the scattered remnant of his command and rallied them by exclaiming: "Here stands Jackson like a stone wall! Rally behind the Virginians! Let us determine to die here and we shall conquer!"

Jackson at the Battle of First Manassas.

And thus was the name of the heroic Bee linked forever with that of "Stonewall"—

"One of the few immortal names,
That were not born to die."

But the soubriquet given was as inappropriate as can be imagined. Jackson was more like a cyclone, a tornado, a hurricane, than a stone wall.

Jackson was accustomed to keep his plans secret from his staff and his higher officers as well as from the people, and once said: "If I can deceive our own people I will be sure to deceive the enemy as to my plans."

It was a very common remark in his corps: "If the Yankees are as ignorant of this move as we are old Jack has them."

His Quick Decision and Crisp Orders: Jackson was noted for the quickness with which he decided what to do, and his short, crisp orders on the battlefield.

I happened to be sitting on my horse near by, when Col. Alexander Swift Pendleton, of Jackson's staff, rode up to Gen. [Jubal Anderson] Early, at Cedar Run, and touching his hat quietly said: "Gen. Jackson sends compliments to Gen. Early and says advance on the enemy and you will be supported by Gen. [Charles Sidney] Winder."

"Gen. Early's compliments to Gen. Jackson and tell him I will do it," was the laconic reply, and thus the battle opened.

On the eve of another battle a staff officer rode up to Jackson and said: "Gen. [Richard Stoddert] Ewell sends his compliments and says he is ready." "Gen. Jackson's compliments to Gen. Ewell and tell him to proceed," was the quiet reply. And soon the noise of the conflict was heard. At Cold Harbor, on the memorable 27th of June, 1861, after he had gotten his corps in position, the great chieftain spent a few moments in earnest prayer, and then said quietly to one of his staff: "Tell Gen. Ewell to drive the enemy." Soon the terrible shock was joined, and he sat quietly on his sorrel sucking a lemon and watching through his glasses the progress of the fight. Presently a staff officer of Gen. Ewell galloped up and exclaimed: "Gen. Ewell says, sir, that it is almost impossible for him to advance further unless the battery

Charles S. Winder, C.S.A.

(pointing to it) is silenced." "Go tell Major [Richard Snowden] Andrews to bring sixteen pieces of artillery to bear on that battery and silence it immediately," was the prompt reply.

Soon the battery was silenced. "Now," he said, "tell Gen. Ewell to drive them," and right nobly did Ewell and his gallant men obey the order. When on his great flank movement at Chancellorsville, Gen. Fitz [i.e., Fitzhugh] Lee sent for him to ascend a hill from which he could view the enemy's position, he merely glanced at it once, when he formed his plan and said quickly to an aide: "Tell my column to cross that road."

Just before he was wounded at Chancellorsville he gave to [Gen.] Ambrose Powell Hill the order, "Press them and cut them off from the United States ford," and as he was borne off the field bleeding, mangled and fainting, he roused himself to give, with something of his old fire, his last order, "Gen. Pendleton, you must hold your position."

His Rigid Discipline: He was very stern and rigid in his discipline, and would not tolerate for a moment the slightest deviation from the letter of his orders. He put Gen. [Richard Brooke] Garnett under arrest for ordering a retreat at Kernstown, although his ammunition was exhausted and his brigade was about to be surrounded, preferred charges against him, and was prosecuting them with utmost rigor when the Chancellorsville campaign opened. He insisted that Gen. Garnett should have held his position with the bayonet; that the enemy would have retreated if he had not, and that under no circumstances should Garnett have fallen back without orders from him (Jackson). After the death of Jackson, Gen. Lee, without further trial of the case, restored Gen. Garnett to the command of his brigade, and this brave soldier fell in the foremost of Pickett's famous charge on the heights of Gettysburg. A brigadier once galloped up to Jackson in the midst of battle, and said: "Gen. Jackson, did you order me to charge that battery?" pointing to it. "Yes, sir. I did. Have you obeyed the order?" "Why, no, general; I thought there must be some mistake. My brigade would be annihilated, literally annihilated, sir, if we should move across

Jackson's monument at Chancellorsville, VA.

that field." "Gen. _____," said Jackson, his eyes flashing fire and his voice and manner betraying excitement and even rage, "I always try to take care of my wounded and bury my dead. Obey that order, sir, and do it at once."

I heard one day, on the Valley campaign, a colloquy between Jackson and a colonel commanding one of his brigades. Jackson said quietly: "I thought, Col. _____, that the orders were for you to move in the rear instead of in the front of Gen. [Arnold] Elzey's brigade this morning."[40]

Arnold Elzey, C.S.A.

"Yes, I know that, general; but my fellows were ready before Elzey's, and I thought it would be bad to keep them waiting, and that it really made no difference anyhow." "I want you to understand, colonel," was the almost fierce reply, "that you must obey my orders first and reason about them afterwards. Consider yourself under arrest, sir, and march to the rear of your brigade." Jackson put Gen. A. P. Hill under arrest (for a cause that was manifestly unjust) on the second Manassas campaign, and he probably put more officers under arrest than all other of our generals combined. There is no doubt that Jackson was sometimes, too severe, and that he was not always just, and yet it would have greatly increased the discipline and efficiency of our service if others of our Confederate leaders had had more of this sternness and severity towards delinquents.

His Attention to Minute Details: He was unceasingly active in giving his personal attention to the minutest details. He had an interview with his quartermaster, his commissary, his ordinance and his medical officer every day, and he was at all times thoroughly familiar with the condition of these departments. It is a remarkable fact that, despite his rapid marches, he rarely ever destroyed any public property, or left so much as a wagon wheel to the enemy.

Not content with simply learning what his maps could teach him of the country and its topography he was accustomed to have frequent interviews with citizens, and to reconnoitre personally the country through which he expected to move, as well as the ground on which he expected to fight. Being called to his quarters one day to give him some information concerning a region with which I had been familiar from boyhood, I soon found out that he knew more about its topography than I did, and I was constrained to say, "Excuse me, General, I have known this section all my life, and thought I knew all about it; but it is evident that you know more about it than I do, and that I can give you no information at all."

Often at night, when the army was wrapped in sleep, he would ride out alone to inspect roads by which, on the morrow he expected to move, to strike the enemy in flank or rear.

After all the crowning glory of Jackson, as it was also of Lee, was his humble, simple-hearted piety, his firm trust in Christ as his personal Savior, his godly walk and conversation, and his life of active effort for the good of others. . . . Suffice it to say, that as I saw him frequently at preaching or at the prayer-meeting drinking in the simple truths of the gospel, heard him lead the devotions of his ragged followers in prayers that I have rarely heard equalled and never surpassed in fervid appropriateness, knew of his active efforts for the spiritual good of the soldiers, and conversed with him on the subject of personal religion, I was fully satisfied that this stern soldier not only deserves a place beside Col. [Franklin] Gardner, and Gen. [Winfield Scott] Hancock, and Capt. [Hedley] Vicars, and other Christian soldiers of the century, but that the world has never seen an uninspired man who deserves higher rank as a true Christian.

An early sketch of Jackson as a U.S. military officer, date unknown.

I recall here just two incidents. In the early spring of 1863 I was one day walking from our camp to a meeting of our chaplains' association, when I heard the clatter of horses' hoofs behind me, and, turning my head, recognized Gen. Jackson riding along as was his frequent custom.

As he came up we saluted, and he asked if I was going to the chaplains' meeting, and, receiving an affirmative response, he at once dismounted and, throwing his bridle over his arm, walked with me about two miles.

Prayer in Stonewall Jackson's camp.

I shall never forget that walk of the humble preacher with the great soldier. Military matters were rarely alluded to, and when I would introduce them he would promptly change the conversation. We talked of the recently organized chaplains' association, and how to make it more efficient; of the need of more chaplains and other preachers in the army, and how to secure them; of the best way of procuring and circulating Bibles and religious literature; of certain officers and men in whose salvation he felt peculiar interest, and for whom he asked that I would join him in special prayer and effort; of the necessity of having chaplains stick to the post of duty even more faithfully than other officers and men, and other kindred topics. And then we got on the subject of personal piety, the obstacles to its growth in the army and the best means of overcoming them, and as he quoted readily, and applied aptly some of the most precious promises of God's word, I almost imagined that I was talking, instead of to this grim son of Mars, to one of the grand old preachers of the olden time who knew nothing about "new theology," but was content to follow implicitly the word of God, and to sing with the spirit and the understanding.

I may now barely allude to his glorious death, the logical sequence to his noble life of simple trust and self-sacrificing toil in the vineyard of the Lord. Cut down in the execution of what he regarded as the most successful military movement of his life, shot by his own men ["friendly fire"], who would have died rather than willingly harmed a button on his old gray coat, his brilliant career ended in the full tide of his ambitions and hopes of future service for the land and cause he loved so well, he could yet calmly say to weeping friends who stood around, "It is all right. I would not have it otherwise if I could. I had hoped to live to serve my country, but it will be infinite gain to be transplanted and live with Christ." And in his delirium, after saving with the old fire of battle, "Pass the infantry rapidly to the front," "Tell A. P. Hill to prepare for action," "Tell Major [Willis Alston] Hawkins to send forward rations for the men," a peaceful smile passed over his placid countenance, and his last words were, "Let us cross over the river and rest under the shade of the trees."

And this great man died! Nay, he did not die! The weary worn marcher went into bivouac—the hero of a hundred battles won his last victory, and went to wear his "crown of rejoicing," his fadeless laurels of honor, and heaven and earth alike have echoed the plaudit:

> "Servant of God, well done;
> Rest from thy loved employ.
> The battle's fought, the victory's won.
> Enter thy Master's joy!"[41] — REV. J. WILLIAM JONES

CHAPTER 11

1892

☞ REMEMBERING CONFEDERATE GEN. AMBROSE P. HILL

I first met Ambrose Powell Hill at his old home in Culpeper, where the bright buttons, lithe figure, and manly bearing of the West Point cadet "at home on furlough" attracted my boyish fancy and excited my boyhood's ambition that I, too, might go to West Point and be a soldier.

Ambrose P. Hill, C.S.A.

It seems but yesterday that I saw in Culpeper and in Washington the young artillery officer whom I so much admired, or when I met him in Culpeper when he had just brought to his old home his bride, the beautiful and accomplished sister of the afterward famous Confederate General, John H. Morgan.

When at Harper's Ferry in the spring of 1861 the Thirteenth Virginia regiment was organized of volunteer companies, who were among the first in Virginia to take the field, and in which I had the high honor of being "high private in the rear rank," it was with great joy that I recognized in the new colonel my old friend A. P. Hill. From that day until the close of his life I watched his brilliant career as he rose through the successive grades of Brigadier General, Major General, and Lieutenant General. Since the war I have studied his history in the light of the official records, and my admiration for the man and the soldier has steadily increased as the years have gone on.

A. P. Hill was one of the most thoroughly accomplished soldiers whom the war produced. Educated at West Point in the palmy days of the Academy, he had graduated with honor, and devoted as he was to his profession he had, as a young artillery officer in the United States Army, earnestly studied the great campaigns of the great soldiers of history, and sought by every other means in his power to perfect himself in all that pertains to the art of war, or the details of the duties of the soldier, he was, therefore, considered by his fellow soldiers as high authority in every thing pertaining to military matters.

When appointed Colonel of the Thirteenth Virginia regiment at Harper's Ferry in the early spring of 1861, he proceeded at once to organize, equip, drill, and discipline his regiment until it was soon pronounced one of the finest in the service. . . .

It was my privilege to see [one day] a number of our leading generals. Our grand old chieftain, R. E. Lee, clad in a uniform of simple gray, and having the bearing of a king of men; Stonewall Jackson, in his dingy uniform, mounted on "Little Sorrel" sucking a lemon and evidently very impatient at the delay in the advance of his column; stern old Ewell, who impressed one as being every inch a soldier; Jeb Stuart, in his fighting jacket, and with the bearing of the "flower of cavaliers," and others who were "winning their spurs." But no soldier whom I saw on that historic day impressed me more than A. P. Hill. Pressed in a fatigue jacket of gray flannel, his felt hat slouched over his noble brow, sitting his horse with easy grace, glancing with his eagle eye along his column as it hurried past him into battle, and yet taking time from his pressing duties to give me a warm grasp of the hand and a cordial greeting as he inquired after "the boys of the old Thirteenth." I was more impressed than ever before with his soldierly bearing, and said to a friend as he rode off, "Little Powell will do his full duty to-day." And right well was this prophecy fulfilled. Encountering the enemy in his strong position and heavy entrenchments near New Cold Harbor about 2 o'clock p.m., Hill bore the brunt of the fight for about two hours until Jackson got into position, and Longstreet went to his assistance, and then bore his full share in the grand charge which swept the field along the whole line of Cold Harbor and Gaines's Mill, capturing fourteen pieces of artillery and many prisoners, and driving the enemy in great confusion from every position. I may not give in detail the further movements of those seven days of carnage and Confederate victory, which raised the siege of Richmond and drove McClellan's splendid army to the cover of his gunboats at Harrison's Landing. . . .

But, alas! the end drew nigh. A. P. Hill had spent a delightful winter at Petersburg, cheered by the presence of his wife and children, but his health was poor and his surgeons had persuaded him to take a "sick furlough" and rest for a season at the house of a relative in Chesterfield County, but he had left strict injunctions with his staff to be notified of any threatened movement, and accordingly on Saturday, the 1st of April, he hastened back to his headquarters, and when his thin line—"stretched until it broke," as General Lee expressed it—was cut in sunder in the early hours of Sunday, April 2, Hill at once galloped to the scene and exerted himself with even more than his accustomed gallantry to re-establish his lines.

Finding this impossible, for the enemy outnumbered him fully five to one, and he had no reserves, he determined to reach and take personal command of the part of his corps which had been cut off, and it was in this brave attempt that he was shot down and instantly killed by a squad of the enemy whose surrender he had demanded.

His body was recovered by a charge of the members of his staff, and the headquarters guard, and was temporarily buried at the home in Chesterfield, whence he came to take command of his corps.

No general orders announced his death, no guard of honor attended his burial; for the grand old army of which he had been so conspicuous a member had taken up its sad march to Appomattox Court-house.

But he has lived in the hearts of his old corps and of loving comrades; he will live in life-speaking bronze that loving hands have reared, and he has passed into history as one of the noblest, truest, grandest soldiers of all the bright galaxy that made the infant Confederacy the admiration of the world, and will extort from posterity an endorsation of the noble sentiment of the English bard—

"No nation rose so white and fair
Or fell so pure of crime."[42] — REV. J. WILLIAM JONES

CHAPTER 12

1893

☛ RECOLLECTIONS OF GENERAL FRANK CHEATHAM

Gen. [Benjamin Franklin "Frank"] Cheatham was always extremely popular with the soldiers. While many a private was repelled by the austere manner of his [own] colonel or brigadier, he would apply to "Mars Frank" for relief against any grievance, assured of immediate attention. For instance, if rations were short, upon the simple statement from a boy soldier, as the general was riding by, he would give the commissary notice that such must not occur again [and] when possible to avoid it.

On [Gen. John Bell] Hood's march into Tennessee, Cheatham was commander of a corps, and yet he was general wagon-master of his command whenever trouble occurred with the train. As the army passed down Sand Mountain, some of the wagons had mired in the valley ahead. The general was making his way down the steep mountain in the darkness, where the men were piled in the roadway asleep. Working his way on patiently for some time, and feeling that he must go on, he exclaimed, "Damn it, boys, you know I don't want to ride over you!"[43]

Benjamin F. Cheatham, C.S.A.

☛ RECOLLECTIONS OF GENERAL ROBERT E. LEE

General Lee was not misled by military politicians. In one of his letters he wrote, "I can conceive of no greater evil than the dissolution of the Union." When he returned to Virginia all his pride and devotion to the army inspired him to remain with it. He was told [by Lincoln] he could have command of the Union Army if he remained. This was a dazzling offer. But he believed that his first duty was to Virginia, and when Virginia called he felt it his duty to answer without regard to personal considerations.[44] — HUGH SMITH THOMPSON

☛ MEMBERS OF THE GALLANT OLD GUARD OF THE CONFEDERACY

Passing, one by one, into the Silent land, the heroic leaders who struggled desperately to save "the lost cause" have been dropping out of mortal ken during the past quarter of a century, until now a very small group is left. Very interesting are the figures which make up the little band, men of hoary hair and faltering step they are now, but their names recall memories of the days when they were active and alert, braving shot and shell on the field and cheerfully bearing privation and hardship in the camp or on the march. In those times, in the cities of the East and the farm houses and homes of the West, their names were execrated, and on the hotly contested border land their approach was dreaded with sinking heart. The new generation which has grown up to manhood since that time has learned to look at them in a more kindly light. Their valor and their devotion are come into recognition; their disappointment and their failure plead for them, and we remember that they, too, are Americans whose prowess does honor to our race.

Busily occupied with business affairs in New Orleans, the last surviving general of the Confederacy, Gen. Pierre Gustave T. Beauregard, still exhibits the untiring, indomitable energy which characterized him during the four years of war. In spite of his seventy-four years, he retains the old pugnacity of his youth and middle age. He does not wield the old weapons, but the man who has the hardihood to cross the old general's path and oppose his plans speedily learns that he has an antagonist who can adapt himself to any mode of warfare, and has lost none of his strategic skill.

The general has a certain right to speak authoritatively, so far as experience can give the right, he having had the honor and the responsibility of opening the ball, by directing the attack on Fort Sumter, and of commanding, in conjunction with Gen. J. E. Johnston, at the battle of Bull Run. The general explains with graphic force how, if that battle had been fought as he planned it, and if he had been permitted, even after the battle had taken place, to add his later plans, he could have "crushed [Union Gen. Robert] Patterson, liberated Maryland, and captured Washington." He surrendered with Gen. J. E. Johnston to Gen. Sherman, in April, 1865.

Jubal A. Early, C.S.A.

Associated with Gen. Beauregard of late years is that other prominent soldier of the South, Gen. Jubal A. Early. The two men are congenial associates, having many characteristics in common. The same dash and impetuosity, the same impatience of contradiction or control, distinguish Early as they do Beauregard, and the same effects are seen in both their lives in numerous and bitter enemies. Gen. Early, who is seventy-six years old, has been a soldier since boyhood, though more than once he has abandoned a martial career for law or business. He had a West Point training, and first smelled powder in the Florida War of 1837. He quitted the army at the close of the war and commenced the practice of law; subsequently he sat in the Virginia Legislature for two years. The outbreak of the Mexican War lured him from the pursuits of peace. He served as a major of volunteers, and acted as Governor of Monterey the last two months of its occupation. He returned to the practice of law when the army was disbanded, and served for ten years as attorney of the commonwealth. He was appointed colonel on the outbreak of the Rebellion, and took part in the battles of Bull Run, Fredericksburg, and Gettysburg. In 1864 he was sent to the Valley of the Shenandoah. There, after a few minor successes, he fought the disastrous battle of Cedar Creek. Six months later, in October, 1864, a still more severe disaster befell him at Waynesboro, where [Union] Gen. [George Armstrong] Custer almost annihilated his command. Lee, who still retained his faith in Early's capacity, was unable to resist the popular feeling in the army against the defeated general, and felt himself obliged to remove him from his command. In his letter relieving him from duty, Lee, with the delicacy of the true gentleman, softened the blow by assuring Early of his own regard, but reminded him that the country and the army would naturally judge by results, and consequently there could be no doubt that his influence would increase the already serious difficulties accumulating in Southwest Virginia. Early at once quitted the army and spent some time in Europe.

A conspicuous figure among the survivors of the great struggle is Gen. Simon Bolivar Buckner, who a few years ago was elected Governor of Kentucky. He was one of the pall-bearers at the funeral of Gen. Grant, whom he always admired and honored. He was the general to whom Grant sent the dispatch which stirred so much enthusiasm in the North early in Grant's career, and which history has immortalized. The North thought it had the right ring, and that the man who wrote it was the man for the hour. The words, which soon became famous, were: "I propose to move immediately upon your works." This was at Fort Donelson. Buckner's two superiors, Officers [John Buchanan] Floyd and [Gideon Johnson] Pillow, had made their escape, when they found the position no longer tenable; but he declared that he would stay with his men and share their fate. He remained, and after the capitulation was sent as a prisoner of war to Boston, Mass., where he was kept until exchanged, six months later. On his return to the field he commanded under [Braxton] Bragg in Tennessee. He fought at Murfreesboro and Chickamauga, and surrendered with E. Kirby Smith at Baton Rouge, in May, 1865. Buckner was another of the West Point graduates, and had also, like so many of his comrades and foes, done gallant service in the Mexican War. He is now sixty-nine years old.

Simon B. Buckner, C.S.A.

Now sitting in the United States Senate for his native State of Georgia, is another brave officer of the southern army, Gen. John Brown Gordon, who has just passed his sixtieth birthday. He bears on his body evidences of his valor in the shape of eight wounds received in battle. He entered the Confederate Army as a captain of infantry, but before the close of the war had risen to the rank of lieutenant general. He was one of the officers who surrendered to Grant at Appomattox.

Last, but not least remembered, of the old chivalric guard of the Confederacy come those sturdy heroes, Stephen D. Lee and Alexander P. Stewart. Gen. Lee now holds a position of responsibility in a university at Starkville, Miss., while Gen. Stewart, who is living quietly at Oxford, Miss., was recently appointed Confederate commissioner on the committee for the construction of a national Cemetery on the site of the old battlefield of Chickamauga, where so many of the sons of the Confederacy fell fighting for the stars and bars.

Stephen D. Lee, C.S.A.

The animosities of the war have long since been buried, and by none more completely than by the men who fought most bravely and sacrificed most in the struggle. The North unites most heartily with the South in recognizing the heroism of the men who fought so gallantly for their convictions. In the closing years of their lives the chieftains of the old Confederacy enjoy the love and honor that is accorded to true soldiers, and when they finally pass away from the scenes of their struggles they will not lie among those who are soon forgotten.[45] — ST. LOUIS *GLOBE DEMOCRAT*

☛ REMARKS AT THE FUNERAL OF GEN. EDMUND KIRBY SMITH
There are times when the reverent silence with which the Church lays her dead to rest may be fitly broken, and this is such a time. There are lives which stand forth conspicuous above their fellows, occupying lofty station or gifted with heroic qualities of soul, or illustrious with great achievement, and in the best way of all these ways—in essential

worth—this was such a life. As the last full General of that Confederacy which is becoming more and more a tender and distant memory, our dear friend in his death closed another generation of men. As one by one the leaders have passed over to the silent shore, some of us have felt that the glory and sadness, the hopes, the memories, the regrets of that sublime but fruitless struggle were concentrated in him, lent new interest to his life, and crowned him with a crown of honor. Surely all that was best and truest and most worthy in that cause which we call "Lost" was imaged forth in this pure and manful and unselfish life. And when the recording angel shall unroll the scroll on which are blazoned the names of those whose lives have been lives of sacrifice for conscience' sake, there will be none that will shine with a purer lustre than that of Kirby Smith. For these qualities of a great soldier were pre-eminent in him—courage, magnanimity, humility, unselfishness, and the fear of God. All the records of chivalry can disclose no truer nor higher attributes of nobleness than these. His Strength was gentleness, his gentleness was strong. Valiant in light, a stranger to tear, a hero in many a conflict, he was yet a little child in the genuineness of his simplicity—the reality of that humility which he learned at the feet of Jesus Christ. The magnanimity of great, majestic souls was his. When he surrendered the war for him was over. No bitter accusations, no vengeful reproach passed his lips. Though it were the very furnace of affliction, the dread anguish of shattered hopes and a career cut short, no darkness of those dark days could dim the cheerfulness of his hope, the constancy of his faith. No temptation of public fame, no attraction of worldly advantage, no opportunity of self-praise, ever wrung from him one harsh or angry

Edmund K. Smith (C.S.A.) with his wife and children.

word in poor and pitiful contention of reviews. Yes, over all and through all and in all the impulses of his nature were that love and fear of God which made his home a Christian home and made his life a Christian life. No stress of financial embarrassment, no privation of those comforts which men hold dear, tempted him for a moment to forget his honor. To toil, even in his age, to suffer and to submit; these were small things to him compared with the sting of conscience. From the day when he deliberately spurned the wealth which his command of the Trans-Mississippi Department placed within his hands to the day—only a few weeks ago—when he refused a princely income as the price of principle, he was always inflexibly and grandly true to what be believed was his honor as a soldier, his duty as a citizen, and his faith as a follower of Jesus Christ. Thus was he brave. Thus was he faithful. Thus was he a good soldier, tried and steadfast, amid the smoke and din and tumult of the blood-stained field. Thus was he a greater soldier on that harder battlefield of life, where those whom we expect to be the bravest too often flinch and fail.

To-day, therefore, those of us who are too young to have known him in the stirring scenes of his military career, but who have learned to love and reverence his character in the peaceful occupation and enjoyment of this place, come with sad hearts and glad devotion to pay tribute to the beauty and the strength of his unique personality. His faith was strong, his hope was buoyant. But above both of these and shining through them was a great and tender human love, of which the apostle [Paul] speaks when he says: "Now abideth faith, hope, charity, these three, but the greatest of these is charity."[46] To us here this was perhaps the most conspicuous quality of his nature. The most devoted of husbands! The most affectionate of fathers! To the trees, the flowers, the rock-ribbed mountain and the starlit sky; to the creatures that crawl and creep and fly and run and leap around us in the living world; to man and brute, nature in all her moods and to nature's God, this man's heart went out in sweet, unselfish joy. God is love.

What nobler tribute to his servant can there be than this? What crown of glory so unfailing! He loved much. He was much loved. And "whether there be prophecies, they shall fail: whether there be tongues, they shall cease; whether there be knowledge it shall vanish away, but love never faileth."[47] — REV. THOMAS F. GAILOR

☛ ADDRESS TO THE UNITED CONFEDERATE VETERANS

Comrades, no argument is needed to secure for those objects your enthusiastic indorsement. They have burdened your thoughts for many years; you have cherished them in sorrow, poverty, and humiliation. In the face of misconstruction you have held them in your hearts with the strength of religious convictions. No misjudgments can defeat your peaceful purposes for the future. Your aspirations have been lifted by the mere force and urgency of surrounding conditions to a plane far above the paltry consideration of partisan triumphs. The honor of the American government, the just powers of the Federal government, the equal rights of States, the integrity of the Constitutional Union, the sanctions of law and the enforcement of order have no class of defenders more true and devoted than the ex-soldiers of the South and their worthy descendants. But you realize *the great truth that a people without the memories of heroic suffering or sacrifice are a people without a history*.

John B. Gordon, C.S.A.

To cherish such memories and recall such a past, whether crowned with success or consecrated in defeat, is to idealize principle and strengthen character, intensify love of country, and convert defeat and disaster into pillars of support for future manhood and noble womanhood. Whether the Southern people, under their changed conditions, may ever hope to witness another civilization which shall equal that which began with their Washington and ended with their Lee, it is certainly true that devotion to their glorious past is not only the surest guarantee of future progress and the holiest bond of unity, but is also the strongest claim they can present to the confidence and respect of the other sections of the Union.

In conclusion, I beg to repeat, in substance at least, a few thoughts recently expressed by me to the State organization, which apply with equal force to this general brotherhood.

It is political in no sense, except so far as the word "political" is a synonym of the word "patriotic." It is a brotherhood over which the genius of philanthropy and patriotism, of truth and of justice, will preside; of philanthropy, because it will succor the disabled, help the needy, strengthen the weak, and cheer the disconsolate; of patriotism, because it will cherish the past glories of the dead Confederacy and transmute them into living inspirations for future service to the living republic; of truth, because it will *seek to gather and preserve as witnesses for history the unimpeachable facts which shall doom falsehood to die that truth may live*; of justice, because it will cultivate National, as well as Southern, fraternity, and will *condemn narrow-mindedness and prejudice and passion*, and cultivate that broader, higher, and nobler sentiment, which would write on the grave of every soldier who fell on our side: "Here lies an American hero, a martyr to the right as his conscience conceived it."

I rejoice that a general organization, too long neglected, has at last been perfected. It is an organization which all honorable men must approve and which Heaven itself will bless. I call upon you, therefore, to organize in every State and community where ex-Confederates may reside, and rally to the support of the high and peaceful objects of the United Confederate Veterans, and move forward until by the power of organization and persistent effort your beneficent and Christian purposes are fully accomplished.[48] — JOHN BROWN GORDON (Commander of the United Confederate Veterans, which later became the Sons of Confederate Veterans)

☛ BATTLE REMINISCENCE

[This is what I remember about my] experience with an Ohio soldier, either of the Sixty-second or Sixty-third Ohio Regiment, July 22, 1864, just at the edge of Decatur, Ga., about six miles from Atlanta. As my command (Muldron's Mississippi Calvary) went into Decatur I saw a wounded Federal in the hot sun, and I halted and asked him if I could do anything for him. He said, "Yes, please give me water and get me out of the sun." I unslung my canteen and gave him half in his own canteen and carried him to the shade. He then pointed to one of our men and said, "That man took my money and knife." I ordered the man to return them to him, which he did, and I said to the Federal that as soon as the battle was over I would have him carried to the field hospital. After the fight was over I went back to see about him, but he had been taken away, and

I do not know anything more of him. He was shot through the right lung, and may have died. My recollection is that he belonged to Badge's corps, as we captured this general's headquarters, with books and papers.[49] — W. A. CAMPBELL

☛ BATTLE REMINISCENCE
[During the War Confederate soldier] Mr. T. J. McGahee, now a citizen of Columbus, Mississippi . . . was wounded in the leg and captured and carried to the Federal hospital, and the surgeon in charge decided to amputate it. McGahee said to the doctor: "I do not want my leg cutoff, I would rather die." But the surgeon said: "I don't care what you want. I am going to cut it off." So McGahee was put on the table and preparations made to cut. McGahee refused to take chloroform, and as the surgeon came up to the table, McGahee, who uses his left hand, gathered all his strength and hit the surgeon a stinging blow in the nose, bringing the blood and knocking him down. As soon as the surgeon could recover from the blow, with an oath he rushed at the man, cut him so badly with the surgeon's knife that he was afraid to operate, and so McGahee was carried back to the hospital, and he has his leg yet. He does not remember the surgeon's name, but no doubt if yet living he will remember this incident well.[50] — W. A. CAMPBELL

☛ BATTLE REMINISCENCE
[Confederate soldier] A. J. Story, of the Eleventh Alabama Regiment, [Cadmus Marcellus] Wilcox's Brigade, Mahone's Division . . . captured a [Union] Capt. W. W. Wadsworth, of Pumell's Legion, Maryland troops, at the Davis Farm battle, seven miles from Petersburg, Va., on the Weldon Railroad. He took his sword and pistol from him and has this sword now. If he knew that Capt. Wadsworth was living, or any of his immediate family, he would return it gladly. The pistol he gave away in Virginia. The sword was given to Capt. Wadsworth by his friends of the Twelfth Ward in Baltimore, so the inscription on the hand of scabbard shows. Mr. Story says as he was going back with his prisoner he met Maj. Crow, of the Ninth Alabama Regiment, and turned him over to the Major, and Capt. Wadsworth handed the Major his watch and purse to take care of, as they were both Masons.[51] — W. A. CAMPBELL

☛ BRIEF BRILLIANT CAREER OF GEN. THOMAS C. HINDMAN

Gen. Thomas Carmichael Hindman [Jr.] was born at Knoxville, Tenn., in 1830. His father, Thomas C. Hindman [Sr.], moved to Mississippi when T. C. Hindman, Jr., was quite young. He and his brother Robert were in school at Princeton when the Mexican war broke out, and they left school to join the army. Their father, in the meantime, had become colonel of the Mississippi Regiment in that war. Young T. C. Hindman, at the age of seventeen, was brevetted second lieutenant for gallantry. In 1856, having moved to Helena, Ark., he made the race for Congress against Dorsey Rice, and was elected as a States' Rights

Thomas C. Hindman Jr., C.S.A.

Democrat [the Conservative party at the time], taking his seat in 1857. During this canvass he and Pat Cleburne, who was his room-mate and bosom friend, were attacked by John Rice, Dorsey Rice, and their brother-in-law, James Marryatt, who shot them from concealment and dangerously wounded both of them. Hindman was wounded very badly in the left side, while Cleburne was shot entirely through. In return James Marryatt was shot dead, and Dorsey Rice and John Rice ran away and left the city. In 1861 Mr. Hindman resigned his seat in Congress to enter the Confederate army. Returning to Arkansas, he raised a legion known as "Hindman's Legion," of which he was elected colonel, he was made brigadier-general at Bowling Green, Ky., in which State he took part in some severe engagements. At the battle of Shiloh he led a division and was dangerously wounded in the first day's fight, and his horse was shot while he was making a charge. He was promoted to the rank of major-general for his conduct at Shiloh. After recovering from his Shiloh wounds he commanded the Trans-Mississippi District, and by his energy and aggressiveness organized and equipped quite an army. He had succeeded in almost clearing the department of Federal forces when he was ordered, at his own request, to the eastern side of the river for more active service. While in Arkansas he commanded the Confederates in the bloody battle of Prairie Grove, where the Federals, though superior in numbers, were defeated and demoralized under Gen. [James G.] Blunt. He commanded a division at the battle of Chickamauga, and was so badly wounded that for several months afterwards he was unable to resume command. When the war closed Gen. Hindman went to the City of Mexico, where he remained for about three years. Returning to Helena he took a very active part in the protection of his people from the carpet-bag element and was assassinated by unknown parties September 28, 1868.[52] — UNKNOWN

☛ TRIBUTE TO GEN. PIERRE G. T. BEAUREGARD
I knew Gen. Beauregard as long and more intimately than any of his old army friends now living, except, probably, Gen. Jubal Early. I knew him before the war, and was his chief quartermaster and confidential staff officer at Manassas from June 1, 1861, until after the battles of Blackburn's Ford and Bull Run, on the 18th and 21st of July, when Gen. Joseph E. Johnston, by virtue of his rank, assumed command. I, of course, was after that was on Gen. Johnston's staff. All this, however, is matter of history. I want to indorse every word found in these resolutions, and to reiterate, if possible, the sentiment that he [Beauregard] was one of the greatest of civilization's soldiers and chieftains. He was a man of matchless ability as a great field commander, and known to be and pronounced one of the greatest military engineers living. His attack on Fort Sumter and his defense of Charleston won for him the admiration not only of the South, but of the European nations. He was not only a great leader, but he was a great organizer, and had the love and confidence of the Southern soldiers, no matter from what part of the South the soldiers came. The mention of his name (Beauregard) on the battlefield would inspire as much enthusiasm as "Napoleon" ever did in the zenith of his glory. I was by his side at Blackburn's Ford and Bull Run unless off executing his

Pierre G. T. Beauregard, C.S.A.

orders. He was a perfect [Joachim] Murat in a charge, he was cool under fire, and his presence everywhere created a shout that made even a soldier quicken his pace in the charge.

I was not only with him in Virginia, but was with him at Corinth after the battle of Shiloh, and had the honor of his presence on two or three occasions at Corinth when I "skirmished" with the enemy. After the fight at Farmington he came up with Gen. Van Dorn and simply said: "Cabell, I am proud of you and your Texans." He could have said nothing that would have given me more pleasure, and I know what was said was fully appreciated by the brave men I commanded.

Gen. Beauregard's manner to his soldiers during the war was such as to win their love and admiration. His career since the war has shown him to be a "modest citizen of tender traits and sensitive honor," of generous and noble impulses always ready and willing to assist with his purse or to encourage with his example and advice the people of the South, whom he loved better than his life. Whether on the tented field or in the councils of State, Gen. Beauregard was always the same brave and true patriot. I not only admired him as a great soldier, but loved him as a brother, and his name and his fame will be cherished by me and mine as long as we are permitted to remain on this side of the great river that we all have to cross.[53] — WILLIAM LEWIS CABELL

☛ CONFEDERATE MEMORIAL DAY—ITS ORIGIN

Confederate Cemetery, Springfield, MO.

It is a matter of history that Mrs. Charles J. Williams, of Columbus, Ga., instituted the beautiful custom of decorating soldiers' graves with flowers, a custom which has been adopted throughout the United States. Mrs. Williams was the daughter of Maj. John Howard, of Milledgeville, Ga., and was a superior woman. She married Maj. C. J. Williams on his return from the Mexican War. As Colonel of the First

Georgia Regulars, of the army in Virginia, he contracted disease, from which he died in 1862, and was buried in Columbus.

Mrs. Williams and her little girl visited his grave every day, and often comforted themselves by wreathing it with flowers. While the mother sat abstractedly thinking of the loved and lost one, the little one would pluck the weeds from the unmarked soldiers' graves near her father's and cover them with flowers, calling them her soldiers' graves.

After a short while the dear little girl was summoned by the angels to join her father. The sorely bereaved mother then took charge of these unknown graves for the child's sake, and as she cared for them thought of the thousands of patriot graves throughout the South, faraway from home and kindred, and in this way the plan was suggested to her of setting apart one day in each year, that love might pay tribute to valor throughout the Southern States. In March, 1866, she addressed a communication to the Columbus *Times*, an extract of which I give:

> We beg the assistance of the press and the ladies throughout the South to aid us in the effort to set apart a certain day to be observed from the Potomac to the Rio Grande, and to be handed down through time as a religious custom of the South, to wreathe the graves of our martyred dead with flowers, and we propose the 26th day of April as the day.

She then wrote to the Soldiers' Aid Societies in every Southern State, and they readily responded and reorganized under the name of Memorial Associations. She lived long enough to see her plan adopted all over the South, and in 1868 throughout the United States. Mrs. Williams died April 15, 1874, and was buried with military honors. On each returning Memorial Day the Columbus military march around her grave, and each deposits a floral offering.

Miss Mary Kennon Jones of Texas, Confederate Maid of Honor.

The Legislature of Georgia, in 1866, set apart the 26th day of April as a legal holiday in obedience to her request. Would that every Southern State observed the same day.[54] — MRS. GEORGE T. FRY

☛ STORY OF FIVE PRIVATES

It was in the early days of '61, just after the pressing call for volunteers rang over the South, that the real shock of contending armies closed in the death-grapple which was to last for four awful years, and when volunteers for the armies of Virginia seemed almost to sign their death warrants as they mustered for the fray. Nothing daunted, the boys of the Confederacy, from Maryland to Texas, rushed forward to the defense of their beloved Southland. With all the chivalry and dauntless courage that has ever marked their race they sprung forward to the contest, and were ever ready to even die when duty called.

When the first regiment from South Carolina (Maxcy Gregg's) was ordered to Virginia, one evening just before leaving Charleston, there assembled in one of the most refined and charming houses in this old city by the sea, a party of young fellow volunteers of this regiment, representatives of some of the best families of this State. They had come to bid adieu to the young ladies of the house, whose brother was one of their number. Their ages ranged from seventeen to nineteen. They were bright, buoyant spirits, with high hopes and noble aspirations, whom even the dangers and uncertainties of the future could not tame.

Confederate vet Thomas W. Colley.

The tender mother and devoted, trembling sisters, filled with sad forebodings that this might be the last meeting for some of them, at least, yet they nerved themselves with fortitude to the terrible ordeal, and not a word was spoken to shake the determination of the young soldiers in the holy cause that called them forth. With firmest faith in the justice of their cause, and that God would do what was just, they surrendered them at their country's call, bade them farewell with sad but hopeful faces, and not until they had gone upon the long, dark journey from which but one ever returned, did they weep over the departure of their loved ones.

The following extract from an address by Charleston's gifted orator, Col. James Armstrong, who was with them in the fight and saw what he relates, will best give the last scene in the bloody drama of which the above sketch gives the first, and which recounts the splendid bearing and the death of four of these five young friends:

> That old Roman, Maxcy Gregg, orders his brigade to charge, and with a yell that awakes the slumbering echoes of meadow and stream, they press irresistably along. The chivalrous Col. A. M. Smith falls mortally wounded, and the blue flag of South Carolina, which he told his men to die by but never let trail, wavers; for the boy hero, James Taylor, who bore it, had his breast fatally pierced by a bullet after being twice fatally wounded. It is for but a moment, for the daring young Shubrick Hayne takes it from his dying grasp, and again it floats on high. Alas! he too, falls to the earth to rise no more. It is now in the hands of the youthful but fearless Alfred Pinckney, but soon it drops from his nerveless grasp as he falls mortally wounded across the body of his friends. Then the fourth, Gadsden Holmes, sprang forward to rescue it, but fell pierced with seven balls before he reached the Flag. It does not touch the earth, for another hero rushes from the ranks of the color company and takes the tailing standard, and again the Palmetto rustles in the breeze held by the stalwart arms of the lion-hearted Dominick Spellman, who bore it through the fight. Many others perished beneath the withering flame, but the column moved victoriously on, and after a most stubborn and bloody resistance the enemy retreated, and the danger that menaced the capital of the Confederacy disappeared with the setting sun.[55] — "PALMETTO"

☛ MORTALLY WOUNDED

Among all the thrilling incidents, hair-breadth escapes and deeds of valor that have been published, I have never seen where any old vet has acknowledged how bad he was scared "durin'" the war, so I come to the front and tell my truthful story. How ignorant we were in the beginning about war! I fully believed I could whip five yanks before breakfast, and was afraid the war would be over before I could try my hand. Whole regiments were armed with long shop-made knives and old "pepperbox" pistols, expecting a hand to hand fight. But to my story. I had served in the Virginia army, had been discharged from injuries received, and had re-inlisted just in time to go through the Georgia campaign under Johnston and Hood. So you can imagine whether I had a chance to kill a yank or not. One of those foggy, gloomy mornings in June, 1864, not far from New Hope Church, I was on videt. All old vets know how perilous the moment the fog would rise, or daylight come. It was similar to turkey-hunting, waiting to see how to shoot. All still. No cheering commands or martial music or rebel yells. A shot up or down the line would ring out and some poor fellow would cross the river. I was hiding behind my pile of rocks in an old field with gun in position. To my right I saw a bright Enfield [rifle] poked around another pile of rocks but a short distance away. Of course I changed position, but only to be in range of another yankee on my left behind his pile of rocks. Imagine the situation. Retreat, I considered, was the better part of valor. On my hands and knees I began to crawl. No shot was fired until I reached an open space some two hundred yards wide, and in the woods was a line of works held by our skirmishers. On I went with all possible speed. How I wished for wings to fly! Zip! zip! the bullets would pass—a thudding sound. I was certainly struck. I glanced down and saw that my pants were red to my boot tops. I could feel the blood in my boots, but no time to make examination. A solid blue line was yelling behind me. Completely faint and exhausted, I rolled over the works only to find my canteen shot through and my [red] sorghum [syrup] all wasted on my pants and in my boots.

Thanks to the God of battle, I have been permitted to live and raise a large family, and will expect to meet many of the old country veterans at Birmingham in July.[56] — "CAMP BEE"

☛ THE HERO OF PICKETT'S OLD BRIGADE

It is the eve before a great battle. The sun is low in the west. A death-like stillness has settled over the two armies—one on Seminary Ridge, the other on Cemetery Hill. It is the battle of Gettysburg. The fight of the first day is over. The Confederates are hopeful, for Gen. [Robert E.] Lee's small army has held in check Gen. [George Gordon] Meade's vast forces. The sun goes down, the hush deepens, the armies slumber, the golden stars come out in the violet skies above. They shine down upon the pale, sweet face of a young soldier. The night is sultry, and the youth sleeps on the uncovered ground. The delicate face has the innocence and infantile purity of a baby's holy countenance. All day the dreaming boy has fought with tiger fearlessness, now he sleeps quietly under the watching stars, and his weary limbs rest in the careless grace of slumber. Beside the sleeping boy is a strong, manly warrior. He does not sleep, but guards the resting youth. A thickly foliaged tree shelters them.

This fair young soldier is the man's wife, but their comrades deem the two father and son. Sleep on, weary soldier, take your brief, unconscious rest, tomorrow's night will find you in eternity! The Gettysburg of your life will have been fought, and you and hundreds of your comrades will have pitched your tents on the camp fields of the great beyond. Ah, child-woman! you have no equal in your heroic devotion. The perils of battle are joys when shared with your heart's idol.

With the first dim streak of light that crosses the blood-stained hilltops commences the cannon's boom. The hollow roar echoes down the valley between Seminary Ridge and Cemetery Hill, then dies far away like the roll of distant thunder. The great battle of Gettysburg rages in fierce fury. In this battle [Confederate General George Edward] Pickett and his division make their charge that renders their names immortal, and gives the historian a chapter of unparalleled heroism. In the fiercest shriek and wildest roar of battle, suddenly the

George E. Pickett, C.S.A.

cannon's thunder dies over the hilltops, the smoke rolls down the valley, a hush solemn as death falls over these vast armies. A small band in Confederate gray goes down the opposite hillside, slowly and calmly. Orderly and straight into the teeth of death they march. They reach the foot of the hill, and are crossing the valley. The silence is yet unbroken. Stern Federal warriors stand awe-stricken, and are thrilled with wonder at sight of this unequalled heroism.

At length the silence is broken. The roar of cannon shake the earth. The boom dies, the smoke clears, and shows a wide gap in that moving wall, but in good order the broken ranks come together. Steadily the brave immortal Pickett and his men march forward, and again the cannons thunder. The smoke drifts away and reveals a wide, wide gap. The ranks move together again, closing the gap. A long line of their gray-clad comrades crosses the valley behind, and the little band moves unfalteringly forward. The cannons again boom. The smoke clears! A wider gap than ever this time, but once more it is closed, and the heroic few move onward. The hearts of brave federal soldiers grow sick at such slaughter. At last Pickett and his survivors reach the hill on which is stationed Gen. Meade's great army. Up the steep side they charge, over the breastworks they go, and back goes the Federal army, but it is only for a time. Pickett's division is slaughtered charging that vast Federal army.

In that charge a flag-bearer in the Confederate ranks is shot. A fair, sweet-faced young soldier raises the old standard. For a moment it floats above the storm of battle. Thick the bayonets gleam, but the youthful hero, with a rigid countenance and unflinching bravery, keeps an eagle eye fixed on the silken banner as it waves in the smoke. A stream of sunlight floods it for a moment, and hallows the ghastly upturned face of the girl soldier as she holds aloft the silken emblem. A sword pierces her, and she falls beside her husband. Both surrender life in this wonderful charge.

The world has heard of Gettysburg and its slaughter, but it has never been told the thrilling but sad story of the young wife who fell beside her husband that day when Pickett's immortal division attempted the impossible.

Many months have passed since then. Burning suns and purple skies have kept their silent watch over the spot where the girl-soldier fell.

Again it is sunset. An old man and his little boy walk over the field where once was fought the great battle. The old man had fought in that battle. He shows his child the area over which Pickett's old brigade had charged. He tells the boy of the sweet-faced flag-bearer, and searching for the place where the young hero fell they find an old flag. Tattered it is and dropping to pieces. It had been embroidered by the fair hands of Virginia women with their own hair. As the young boy raised it he saw underneath two skulls. Through long silent  days and the solemn hush of nights it had been their winding sheet; under burning suns and golden stars it had been their blood-drenched and battle-rent shroud. Digging a hole in the hillside, the Federal veteran wrapped the skulls in the flag and buried them in the calm, sweet hour of the sunset stillness. He had lost two sons in that battle. They had fallen repulsing Pickett's division, but this evening the bitterness dies in the breast of the old Federal soldier. He stands, and watching the sunset his thoughts drift back to that day when he saw the young girl-hero, calm and serene, with her large blue eyes fixed upon the silken banner, unflinching in the shriek and storm of battle. His sword had pierced her. There was no bitterness in his heart now.

Europe has her Joan of Arc, her Charlotte Corday, America her Mollie Pitcher, but the Confederacy has her sweet girl-hero who fell in the charge of Pickett's men at Gettysburg.[57] — MARTHA CAROLINE KELLER

☛ A CONFEDERATE SURGEON'S STORY

If all the striking incidents that occurred to surgeons engaged with the armies in our late war were published the book would contain some of the most interesting incidents of that awful conflict. I write of one that happened near Dumfries, Va., in the winter of 1861-1862. I was surgeon of the 11th Mississippi Regiment, and Dr. Estell of the 1st Tennessee Regiment. One morning we were both ordered to report at the quarters (two miles distant) of a captain of artillery for some professional service, the nature of which was not revealed. Dismounting near his tent, we observed the Captain sitting a few paces from the front of the tent, in company with a lady dressed in deep mourning, a black veil falling over her face. The Captain arose and met us, remarking that a youth was in the tent whom he wished us to examine in order to ascertain if he was diseased, and if so, whether it was organic and likely to have existed long, and then pointed us to the closed door. We entered and found a young man lying on a stretcher, with two soldiers armed and sitting on campstools at his feet. The youth was quite delicate, well dressed and comely. After conversing with him in regard to his age, health, the origin and duration of his complaint, we made a careful physical examination. We found palpable organic affection of the heart, which had existed since his access to puberty, four years before that time. It was one of the clearest cases we have ever seen. Then approaching the couple as they sat in silence, I said, "Captain, the young man is certainly afflicted with organic disease of the heart of long duration, and he ought never to have been enlisted as a soldier." Instantly the lady sprang to her feet, screaming out. "God bless you, you have saved my only child!" and throwing her arms around me she wept for joy. Soon she rushed to the tent where her son lay.

It was a startling mystery to us, but the Captain explained: The boy had enlisted in '61, and from the battle field at Manassas he had deserted and fled to his home. Late in the fall he had been arrested and returned to his command at Dumfries, where he had been tried and was condemned to be shot on the next day after our examination. In the meantime his mother, hearing the news, hastened to the army, and had arrived in time to plead for an examination to prove her son's real condition. The Captain showed us the General's order, which was, "Arrest the sentence and discharge him if the surgeons confirm the mother's statement."[58] — DR. R. H. DALTON

☛ RECOLLECTIONS OF JEFFERSON DAVIS

I have so much love for this grand man, and the glorious cause he and his brave soldiers fought for, that I feel I must add my mite of praise to them, though they do not need it. The heroic struggle of these grand patriots will live in the heart of every true Southerner, and on the pages of the sublimest history ever penned by mortals. I was a resident of Cuba when the unrighteous civil war was forced upon the South, and my mind and strength went out, as it were, to the heroic, self-sacrificing soldiers who were engaged in fighting for our rights with an untold energy, that surprised me. I watched closely the unequal contest, the suffering, the bravery of our people with a yearning sympathy and a fire in my soul that almost consumed me. England played her game of hypocrisy with us, while the Continent [Europe], with irresponsible men, replenished the Northern army. Our soldiers on many fields were outnumbered three or four to one, but in their renewed endurance under the most terrible

Winnie Davis, "Daughter of the Confederacy."

provocations illustrated a heroism that was never equalled on the battle-field. Again, I saw slain, defeated, taken prisoners, led away to suffer and die among their enemies, and the cross weighted me to the earth. At last the end came. Our hero, friend and President, Jefferson Davis, was taken prisoner, shackled and put in a Northern prison, to suffer indignities and slanders heaped on him in venomous hatred, and ridiculed with the most stupendous lies by his captors that the world ever heard. Bear with me; I must speak it out; age gives me the right to do so if not my patriotism.

Mrs. Sarah E. Brewer.

While he was in prison, and indignities were so unjustly put upon our beloved President, I sat in my foreign home with bowed head and folded hands, brooding over the ruin that had been meted out to the Southland by her cruel victorious foes.

After Mr. Davis' release from prison—and thanks to Gen. Grant we owe for his life—he went with his wife to my home in Havana. Worn and pale from prison trials, he was hardly recognizable as the grand, heroic, eagle-eyed leader of forces. With the beautiful climate, the close attention of his charming wife and the many devoted friends that surrounded him, he began slowly to rally to better health, giving us supreme pleasure.

Bear with me a little longer. It is to be expected that old people will take license in speech, and I beg pardon if I have trespassed on forbidden ground, but it is of our "Winnie" [Varina Anne Davis, the daughter of President Davis] I would write. I never believed that she would wed a man from among her father's enemies. She is held so high in our hearts, so honored, so beloved, and I believe in the eternal fitness of things.

In my Havana home I had the pleasure of entertaining many eminent Southerners—[James Murray] Mason, [John] Slidell, Beverly Tucker, E. Kirby Smith, and others less noted but equally true and brave to the cause we espoused.

Our Southland blooms again with thrift and beauty, the same old Southland with its chivalry. Phoenix-like she has risen from her desolation and her ashes without other aid than from her own sons' unflinching, indomitable will and energy. *There is no "new" South. The very term is repugnant. Away with it. We are the same people, have the same interests, the same chivalry and the same patriotism.*

We are determined by our united efforts to build a monument worthy of our beloved leader, our President, that will tower above all others ever built to the memory of man, that coming ages may see how we honored and loved the man who gave his all to establish our Southern Confederacy. May the angels keep watch above his ashes.[59] — MRS. SARAH E. BREWER

☛ TO THE SOLDIERS OF THE SOUTH

The veteran Confederate soldier was a typical gentleman. He was as gentle as a lamb, as brave as a lion, and as ferocious as a tiger when aroused. . . . He was as proud as Lucifer, as retiring as a woman, and withal a hero on the field of battle. "He knelt to no God but high heaven; he asked no friend but his sword."

Members of the United Daughters of the Confederacy, Hot Springs, AR.

The mothers, wives and daughters of the South, from whom we received our being and inspiration, joyed at our successes and wept at our reverses. They cheered us forward with their kisses, tears and smiles, and received us with sobs of bitter anguish when we returned as vanquished heroes. They girded on our armor with the injunction of the Spartan mother, to return with our shields or upon them. They never despaired, never asked forgiveness, never dreamed of surrender. The eyes of many a dying soldier have been moistened by their angelic ministrations. We are orthodox in our religion, orthodox in the belief of the justice of our cause and orthodox in the love of our women.

All that was ever good in us, all the virtues we may now or hereafter possess, had their birth in the spirit of the Old South. We love our memories, we cherish our institutions, and our dead are sacred.[60] — JOHN P. HICKMAN

☛ WHY OUR SOLDIERS FOUGHT

. . . the war was maintained by the defense upon principle, and . . . [our] sagacious [Confederate] leaders were not "fire eaters," as has been basely represented, but patriots who exercised patient intelligence until compelled to use sword and bayonet.[61] — SUMNER A. CUNNINGHAM

George Washington.

☛ THE CAUSES OF THE WAR

We are met in this place to look for the first time on a monument erected by loving hearts in honor, first, of the Confederate dead from this county, whose names adorn yon monument; second, of all Confederate dead, no matter who they are, who have been committed in this county to the keeping of their mother earth.

No more appropriate place for a Confederate monument could have been selected within the valley of Virginia, situated in one of the most beautiful of the counties of Virginia—one that, in proportion to her population and ability, contributed as much of men and means as any other within her confines to the Confederate cause; whose sons attested their valor from Manassas to Appomattox; which, during four years of strife, was the marching ground of friends and foes, and which witnessed "grim visaged war" in all of its glory and in all of its shame.

It was in this county, too, that the great rebel of America, George Washington, developed his young manhood. Over her hills and valleys Daniel Morgan, of our Revolution, strove and roamed. Within this cemetery repose the remains of Edmund [J.] Randolph, one of the authors and defenders of the Constitution of the United States, in defense of which those in whose memory yon monument has been erected died. Within the chapel in this inclosure that great man, Christian and Bishop, William Meade, who loved his State, and all that was true, lovely and honest, and who taught our Robert E. Lee his catechism, reasoned of righteousness, temperance and judgment to come. Around us are the graves of pious fathers and mothers, of idolized wives, devoted brothers and sisters, and precious children, over which have been placed the monuments of love and sorrow. Many of those dead were with us in heart and soul in our conflict, praying for us as we marched through the cold of winter, the heat of summer, and engaged in the strife of battle, and who, when we returned after these four years of struggle, without banners and with crushed hearts by reason of the prostration of the hopes in which we trusted, and the loss of the cause we loved, kept us true to the belief that the Lord God Omnipotent reigneth, and doeth all things well, and taught us to look upward and onward.

Confederate soldiers.

The soldiers in whose honor yon monument was erected were chiefly Virginians but not all. Some were from the Old North State, some from our sister, Tennessee, and some from the land of the cotton plant. Some were dear friends, with whom we of the Second Virginia Infantry and the Clarke Cavalry marched and fought. Mothers, some of them were your sons. Daughters, some of them were your brothers. Comrades, all of them were your fellow-soldiers. No matter where they were born they were with you in heart and soul, and marched under the flag you and they loved.

Twenty-eight years have passed since the close of our civil war. Since then a majority of the adults living in those years have been called home, and almost a new generation has taken their places on the farm and plantation, and in the counting-room, shop and office. Time, I trust, has healed the wounds of war, but with the revolving years the causes and events of that terrible struggle seem to be forgotten, or if not forgotten, considered as unimportant events of history. And even the history of those events, and the causes that led to that struggle, are not set forth fairly and truthfully. *It is stated in books and papers that Southern children read and study that all the blood-shedding and destruction of property of that conflict was because the South rebelled without cause against the best government the world ever saw; that although the Southern soldiers were heroes in the held, skillfully massed and led, they and their leaders were rebels and traitors, who fought to overthrow the Union, and to preserve human slavery, and that their defeat was necessary for free government and the welfare of the human family.*

As a Confederate soldier and as a citizen of Virginia I deny the charge, and denounce it as a calumny. We were not rebels; we did not fight to perpetuate human slavery, but for our rights and privileges under a government established over us by our fathers and in defense of our homes. The South loved the Union. Her interests were identified with it. Her statesmen had aided in its creation and development. Her warriors had fought under its flag, by sea and by land, and shed their blood in its defense. To the South the Union was a temple dedicated to American constitutional liberty [conservatism]—to the principles of a liberty approved by great thinkers and consecrated by the blood of martyrs; a liberty that was designed to protect the individual man in all that was right, and to prohibit him from doing that which was wrong. Not a liberty for one class of people or section of country to prey on any other people or other section. Not a liberty for the majority to invade the rights of the minority, and to use the powers of the government to the aggrandizement of the former and the injury of the latter, but a liberty

Thomas Jefferson.

guaranteeing equality of right and privileges to each section and each State. But when the priests [Liberals] that ministered at the altars of this temple sought to teach new theories of liberty, such as had not been taught by the fathers, and which were destructive of the principles of the Constitution, and fatally injurious to the rights of the States, and especially to the Southern States, then the cotton and sugar Southern States determined to abandon the temple and erect one, where they could worship according to what they understood to be the faith delivered by the fathers, who in the belief of man's capacity for self-government, and in prayer to God, had built our political temple.

In determining to separate, those States thought they were sustained by the teachings of the Declaration of Independence, which declared in immortal words that *"all governments derive their just powers from the consent of the governed,"* that when any form of government becomes destructive of these ends it is the right of the people to alter or abolish it, and to institute a new government, laying its foundations on such principles, and organizing its powers as to them shall seem most likely to effect their safety and happiness. They also thought that *the powers granted to the general government, by virtue of which it alone controlled the States, were delegated powers, which could be revoked at any time by the party delegating.* They read in the resolutions of some of the States adopting the Constitution of the United States *an express reservation of this power.* Our own State, especially when she adopted the Constitution of the United States, declared that *the powers granted to the United States could be resumed when perverted to her injury or oppression.*

Those Southern States believed that the powers granted to the federal government had been used to their injury and oppression, and therefore they decided to abandon the Union. In taking this step, slavery was not the cause, but the occasion of the separation. It might as well be said that tea was the cause of our separation from the government of Great Britain in 1776. The government of Great Britain, prior to that date, claimed the power to tax the colonies, although they were not represented in the parliament. That power the colonies denied; they claimed they were British citizens, and as such were entitled to all the rights of every other citizen of that kingdom; that because separated from the island that contained the capital, they were not less citizens of that kingdom; that it was a principle dear to Britain that no money should be taken from him in the form of taxes except by consent of his representatives, and as they were not represented in parliament England had no right to tax America. Notwithstanding the protests of the people of this country, England taxed America by putting a tax on tea. Hence the Boston tea party, the war of the revolution of 1776 and its results.

The Boston Tea Party, early American conservatism.

The Southern States claimed they had exactly the same right in the Union as the Northern States; that her soldiers had fought in the war for independence, in that of 1812, in the Indian wars and in the Mexican war; that her statesmen had contributed to the adoption of the Constitution of the United States, the development of American institutions and the enlargement of the territory of the Union; that *the common government should be administered for the benefit of all the people, and not to develop one section to the injury of the other sections; not to tend the social and moral views of one part of the country to the disadvantage of another part of it.* They claimed that when the Union was formed slavery existed in all of the States; that it was recognized in the Constitution of the United States, and because it had become unprofitable in one portion of a common country, and therefore had ceased to exist in that section, the slaves of the North having been sold South, the powers of the general government should not be used to the injury of the South.

I would not do justice if I did not state just here that there was a section of people at the South [where the American abolition movement began] and at the North [where American slavery began] in the early days of the republic and since opposed to slavery on moral and economic grounds.[62] . . . *[At] our revolutionary period the anti-slavery sentiment was stronger in Virginia than in New England. Massachusetts was at that time engaged in the slave trade, deriving profit from the use of her ships in that traffic. It was not until after the great difference of opinion between the statesmen of the country as to the powers of the general government that the sectional differences on the subject of slavery became so decided and marked. With the increase of this difference of sentiment as to governmental powers grew the difference on the subject of slavery. In this State, about 1832, there was a most powerful anti-slavery party*, headed by such men as James McDowell, one of the most eloquent and cultured of our Governors, and by Charles J. Faulkner, father of the distinguished United States Senator of that name from West Virginia.

Slave trading in Massachusetts, birthplace of American slavery.

But it was not until the failure of those who claimed large powers for the general government on the subject of a national bank, international [internal] improvements and a protective tariff to obtain control of the government, that the anti-slavery party [Liberals] assumed any considerable importance. A combination was made in the North and Northwest by those who claimed the aforementioned powers for the general government with the anti-slavery men. The combination claimed for the general government, on the subject of slavery—

1. Power to abolish slavery in the District of Columbia.
2. Under the power to regulate commerce, the power to prohibit the carrying of slaves from one slave State to another slave State.
3. The right to prohibit slavery in the territory of the United States.

Black field servants working on a Mississippi cotton plantation in 1832.

You will observe, first, that all of these matters related to slavery, but the principle, under all this claim for power, like that in regard to the taxation of tea, was far deeper than appeared on the surface. It involved the integrity of the Constitution of the United States and the equality of the people of the Southern States.

The District of Columbia contained the capital of the United States. Southern members of Congress came to Washington to discharge their duties, bringing with them their wives and children, and if by hostile legislation their servants—the maids of their wives and the nurses of their children—were to be liberated by act of Congress as soon as they trod the soil of the District, that city was no place for Southern Senators and Representatives.

As to the commerce between the States, as stated before, slaves were recognized as property when the Constitution was adopted. The Constitution of the United States contained a provision for their rendition when they escaped from one State to another; also, for the continuance of the slave trade until 1808. *To interdict the selling of slaves from one State to another would have been, in effect, to deprive the citizens of our Southern States of the right to migrate to another. Also to deprive him of the use of what had been considered property from the foundation of the government.*

To prohibit slavery in the territory of the United States would virtually exclude the Southern citizen of the United States from the common territory. The territory of the United States, about the settlement of which this controversy culminated, was obtained as the result of the war with Mexico, and *to exclude the citizen with his slaves was, in fact, to deliver the territory purchased by the money and by the blood of all to one section of the*

Servants' quarters, Tennessee, 1857.

country, to be organized into such political form as to give political power to one section of the country, and thereby give effect in legislation to all the views of the North on the subject of governmental powers. The South claimed an equality of right in all the territories, in the District of Columbia, and in the trade and commerce of the country, and to deny her rights was practically to make her people hewers of wood and drawers of water to the more prosperous and populous section. *Notwithstanding the objections and even protests of her statesmen and people, the territory acquired from Mexico was organized so as to exclude slavery, and therefore the South from settlement therein. Not only was this done, but a sectional [Liberal] President [Lincoln] was elected by a sectional majority on a sectional platform of party principles.*

The South then seceded, not in a body, but separately. The Constitution of the United States had been adopted by States, each State acting by itself and for itself. Our own State, Virginia, seceded in April, 1861. I would like to tell about the action of the Gulf States, and of the views of their great thinkers and statesmen, but I have not time to do so.

Edmund J. Randolph.

I am sure, however, you will indulge me for a short time, while I recall some things about Virginia, even if I repeat myself, connected with the part she took in the transactions of that period, and in those of our revolutionary days and since, which will present her to you as the grandest figure of any State in the records of time.

In every period of her history Virginia has stood up for the right, as she understood it, against her seeming interest and against power. *Settled by English speaking people, she inherited from them the love of truth and liberty, and devotion to right, that has distinguished the inhabitants of Great Britain from the days of her Alfred to our revolution.* When the clash of opinion arose as to the rights of the British colonies in America, Virginia, against the seeming interest of her people—certainly against that of her leaders—took the side of the weak in favor of the right, and against the strong and wrong. Her Patrick Henry, by his Demosthenean eloquence, moved the hearts of his countrymen to resistance, as the storm moves the sea. Her George Mason, amid the throes of revolution, gave to his State and the world Virginia's great bill of rights and her first constitution—the first written constitution the world ever saw. Her [Thomas] Jefferson, with his pen, recorded in memorable words the rights of a free people and the wrongs of America. Her Washington led the armies of the rebellious colonies to victory, peace and independence. The war over, the colonies that had been united in defense against Great Britain formed a Union [actually a confederation or confederacy], under what are known as the Articles of Confederation.[63] Then, in order to strengthen that Confederation and promote the common welfare, Virginia ceded to the Confederacy all of her magnificent territory northwest of the Ohio River, now the abode of a great population and the center of wealth and political power.

The Articles of Confederation proving inadequate, a convention of the States was called, and that body gave to the world the Constitution of the United States. That instrument was largely the work of Virginia. The convention that formed it was called chiefly through Washington. Her Madison and Edmund [J.] Randolph and Henry Lee, its chief defenders in Virginia, against *the opposition of such men as Patrick Henry, George Mason, Thomas Nelson, Jr., and Richard Henry Lee, who opposed its adoption by their State without amendment, for reasons which, had they been heeded then, would in all probability have averted our civil war*.

Winfield Scott.

Some of the writings and utterances of these distinguished objectors, in the light of recent events, seem to be as prophetic as the words of the great Jewish prophet, Isaiah. The Constitution was adopted, George Washington was made the President of the United States. He put the Federal government in operation, organized the great departments of the government, recommended and approved appropriate legislation, and laid the foundation upon which has been built this great republic. The third President was [Conservative] Thomas Jefferson. Under his administration we obtained from the great Napoleon for $15,000,000 title to the territory known as Louisiana, which comprised not only the State of Louisiana, but Missouri, Arkansas, Iowa, and parts of Nebraska,

Kansas, Minnesota, and the Indian Territory. Jefferson was succeeded by another Virginian, James Madison. Under his administration war was declared against Great Britain, which brought that power to respect our flag and the rights of our sailors. To another Virginia President, John Tyler, are we chiefly indebted for the State of Texas. Although it was annexed during the administration of James K. Polk, yet the credit of its acquisition is due to John Tyler's administration.

After this came another war, in which our Winfield Scott planted the flag of the United States on the halls of the Montezumas, in the city of Mexico, and thereby obtained peace between this country and Mexico; and as a result of that peace all the territory of the United States, bounded by the Mexican frontier on the south, and the Louisiana purchase on the east and north and northwest, and by the Pacific on the west, was added to this country. In the Mexican battles Virginia and the South bore their full part. No sooner was the territory acquired than the controversy arose as to its settlement between the sections of our country; one claiming that it should be kept open and free to the people of all the country, whether the North or the South; the other that it should be dedicated to freedom; that the national soil should be like the enchanted ground of an Eastern story, upon which all that entered, no matter how clad, were immediately arrayed in garments of light and beauty—so every slave, as soon as he trod the national soil with his master, should stand clothed in the robes of freedom. Apparently *this seemed like the earnest protest of the lovers of freedom against slavery, but in reality it was but a scheme to exclude the South from the occupancy of the newly acquired territory.* The student of the political history of the period will discover that *it was not so much opposition, in the decade of 1850-60, to slavery as the desire to get political control of the country, in order that the vast powers of the general government might be yielded to aggrandize one section at the expense of the other. In the furtherance of that scheme it was important to exclude from the newly acquired territory Southern men and their influence in*

John Letcher.

order that the views of the opposite school might take root and obtain power and control. No more effectual method than the exclusion of slavery, and thereby the Southern slaveholder, could have been devised. The Southerner was accustomed to slavery and slave institutions in his home and on his farm and plantation, and if prevented by law from taking his slaves to the territory of the United States he therefore was virtually excluded. He would either have to forego the advantages

William C. Rives, C.S.A.

of purchasing cheap lands or leave his labor and his domestic habits behind him. Therefore *this scheme, however fair to the eye, was in effect a denial to the Southern slaveholder of any participation in the common territory, and was equal to a deed of cession of all that territory to the Northern States. It was the determination of the Northern States to adhere to that policy, by the election of a President pledged to such views, that caused, as heretofore stated, the separation of the Gulf States from the Union.* Virginia, however, did not then secede. Her patriotic Governor, John Letcher, called an extra session of the Legislature to meet January 7th, 1861. That Legislature convened a delegated convention of the people of the State, which assembled at Richmond on the 13th of February, 1861. That convention was composed of some of the most distinguished, *conservative* and *patriotic* citizens of Virginia. Among them Alexander H. H. Stuart, John Janney, Robt. E. Scott, John B. Baldwin, Geo. W. Summers, and your fellow-citizen, Hugh M. Nelson, whose name graces yon monument—all Union men [that is, they loved the Union], as were the majority of that body. That convention chose for its president that eminent citizen of London, John Janney. He belonged to a Quaker family, loved peace and the ways of peace. I doubt not that this had something to do with his selection. It was designed to show that *Virginia was for peace, and not for war.* Previous to that her Legislature had sent a commission composed of four of Virginia's distinguished sons, viz.: John Tyler, Geo. W. Summers, William C. Rives and James A. Seddon, to Washington to attend what was called a Peace Congress, that convened upon her invitation or suggestion. That Congress failed to accomplish any good results. On the 8th of April, 1861, the Virginia convention sent a commission, consisting of William Ballard Preston, A. H. H. Stuart and Geo. W. Randolph, to see President Lincoln and obtain information as to his views, purposes and policy in regard to the seceded States. The report of that committee was not satisfactory. After this the affair of Fort Sumter took place. It fired the Northern heart. President Lincoln called for his army of 75,000 men, and on Virginia for her quota. After this Virginia seceded, she did this chiefly because she was called upon to contribute her share of force to coerce the seceding States. As valuable as the Union was to her, as much as she loved it because of her part in its construction and maintenance, she held it was not an end, but the means to an end—*personal and political liberty, State equality and sovereignty*; that *the Union established by the fathers was one of consent, love and affection, and not of force*; that whether it was wise on the part of the Gulf States to separate was not a matter for her to determine, because in her judgment they clearly had the right to separate, and *those wielding the powers of the government of the United States had not the right to force them back into the Union, and that to force them back into the union, and that to compel them by force to return, would be to trample under foot the teachings and principles of the fathers*, therefore, with sad heart and tearful eyes, she passed, in April, 1861, her ordinance of secession.

John Tyler, C.S.A.

I have made this brief reference to the foregoing facts in regard to Virginia's contributions to the cause of American liberty, and to the Union, and to her course in the early days of 1861, to show how dear to her was the Union, how she yearned for peace, and that *it was not slavery that induced her to separate from the then government of the United States, but her love for the Constitution and the Union, as established by the fathers.*

The record of our State from 1776 to April 17, 1861, is a glorious one. In the history of the States during the sad days between the election of President Lincoln and the war she stands as the sole champion of peace. Were I an artist, and wished to perpetuate on canvas some one scene in Virginia's great history, I would not select the great debate at

Williamsburg, when Patrick Henry uttered those memorable words, "Give me liberty or give me death;" nor George Mason in the act of reporting his bill of rights; nor would I go to Philadelphia and paint the scene in the old Independence Hall, when a Virginia deputy moved that Congress should declare that the united colonies are and of right ought to be free and independent States, absolved from all allegiance to the British crown; nor would I select Thomas Jefferson reporting the Declaration of Independence; nor George Washington receiving the sword of Cornwallis at Yorktown; nor the same great man attesting the Constitution of the United States; nor would I select the execution by Virginia of her deed ceding the northern territory; but I would go to Richmond in the sad days of 1861 and select as my subject John Tyler and his associate Peace Commissioners in the act of leaving for Washington, there, if possible, to effect a peaceful settlement of the pending difficulties, and under my picture I would inscribe the words of the Master: "Blessed are the peacemakers."

Failing in her efforts to secure a settlement of the difficulties, and having been called upon to aid in forcing her sisters of the South back into the Union, Virginia, as stated, seceded, and then joined the Southern Confederacy.

Richard Taylor, C.S.A.

Thereafter her territory became the Flanders of the war. Her ports were blockaded, her capital invested, her buildings were destroyed. Not only her mills that ground the grain for her people, the barns that protected the grain and sheltered her horses and cattle, but some of the very *homes of non-combatant citizens were destroyed by fire*. During all these years of carnage, of suffering and distress, she maintained her ancient renown, and remained as true to her faith and her duty as the [compass] needle to the pole. Her loss was great. Among those that died on her battle-fields was the world-renowned soldier—that man of genius, courage, faith and prayer—Stonewall Jackson, the dashing Ashby, the knightly Stuart, and the gallant Hill. And then other gallant officers and brave men, who fell in the various battles, large and small, from Manassas to Appomattox. . . .

John C. Breckinridge, C.S.A.

But there were a host of others in that conflict whose names, although not on yon monument, are in our hearts.

Virginia's Southern sisters were with her. She stood by them and they by her, and they were worthy of her. I would like to tell, if I had time, of the gallant band from Maryland, who on every field sustained the name and fame of old Maryland; of the Old North State—God bless her—and her [William Dorsey] Pender, [Stephen Dodson] Ramseur, [Robert Frederick] Hoke and others—her sons not only repose in this cemetery, but in every cemetery where the heroes of the Army of Northern Virginia, rest; of Georgia and her gallant [John Brown] Gordon and his braves, who plucked safety from danger on many a battlefield, and won the admiration of all that love the true and the brave; of the troops from Louisiana under [Richard] Taylor, [Harry Thompson] Hays and [Francis Redding Tillou] Nicholls, who won imperishable laurels at Port Republic, Winchester and Gettysburg—men without superiors in courage and dash in the ranks of either army in our war; of [William] Barksdale's Mississippi men and their gallant deeds at Fredericksburg and elsewhere.

And then I should like to go to our Western armies and say something about that great man, Albert Sidney Johnston, who too soon for his country and her needs, on that woeful Sabbath day, May 6th, 1862, gave his life for our cause; and of that great Christian soldier, the friend of our William Meade, Leonidas Polk, and his soldiers and their great deeds; of the great [William Joseph] Hardee, without fear and without ambition; of that thunderbolt of war and superb soldier, [Nathan Bedford] Forrest; of the gifted [John Cabell] Breckinridge and his gallant Kentuckians, who illustrated by deeds on many a battle-field their gallantry and devotion to the lost cause. Comrades and friends, the Southern army was a wonderful army, and not only in Virginia, but elsewhere, did deeds of valor worthy of comparison with any that history records, and justice will be done it by historians in the years to come, for

"Thy scales, Mortality, are just
To all that pass away."

Our peculiar Southern institutions are now of the past, but those who lived under them can point with pride to the men and to the women that have been developed by them. Viewed from a material standpoint, the South was far inferior to its successful rival. No vast accumulation of material capital in corporate or in individual hands appear in her statistics. No great monuments of human art or human labor adorn her scenery. Her rivers, great and small, were allowed to flow in comparative peace to the ocean, and the solitude of her mountains has generally been undisturbed save by the woodsman's axe, the rifle of the hunter, the voice of the herdsman and the peaceful shepherd. And yet, notwithstanding all this comparative indifference to material development, she has produced, men, women and maidens, the peers of the greatest of the descendants of Adam, in the Senate, on the field or in the home circle. This statement as to her children is not to be confined to any period of the history of the South. It was illustrated in the war of the revolution and

Braxton Bragg, C.S.A.

since, and especially during our late civil war. In the late war the Confederate generals achieved great reputation, but in front of them were brave soldiers, supported and encouraged by the counsel, the prayers, sacrifices and example of self-denying mothers, wives and sisters. It was the character, the courage and devotion to their flag of the soldiers of the armies of the South that enabled our generals to work such wonders. The names of these brave private soldiers are not mentioned in history, but they are embalmed in the hearts of their surviving comrades and friends. It was the men so educated, sustained and encouraged that followed [Stonewall] Jackson from Manassas to Chancellorsville; that stormed under [Jubal Anderson] Early the forts and works of Winchester; that stormed the heights of Gettysburg; that fought and died at the Wilderness and Spottsylvania Courthouse and Cold

Harbor; that kept the hosts of Grant out of Petersburg from June, 1864, to April, 1865; that followed Albert Sidney Johnston from Kentucky to Shiloh; that fought under [Braxton] Bragg at Chickamauga; that fronted the armies of Sherman, and that stood with their faces to the foe, often without food or shoes, and did not surrender the sword until it fell from their sides.

But neither patriotism nor courage availed. The cause we loved was lost. My friends, it was not lost because our quarrel was not just; not because our leaders were not skillful and our soldiers brave; but because he who rules above deemed it best it should fail. Said the gifted and eloquent W. C. Breckenridge:

> He who has striven to discover the true secret of human history is often confused by the martyrdoms that seem to be in vain. Human hearts lie thickly strewn along the pathway of time, and brutal heels stain themselves with richest blood as they stride unfeelingly to power. The scaffold and the dungeon, the rack and the stake, the battle-field and the hospital confuse the earnest student who loves God, and he cannot unravel the riddle why such costly sacrifices should be in vain. The mockings and the scourgings, the bonds and imprisonment, the hidings in dens and eaves, the beheadings and burnings with which our human annals are tarnished, and yet glorified, are the mysteries of God's dealings with men. But this we know, that the loftiest of mankind, the most divine of mortals, have been the martyrs whose blood has enriched the world, and from whose graves the most precious harvest has been gathered, and that the seed sown with tears shall be reaped with rejoicing.

Four Southern belles.

Beautiful and sad, but true words. My friends, as I look upon the graves around me, and yon monument, the most comforting thought to me is this: "The Lord God Omnipotent reigneth." God is in history—in all history; was in our history during our war, and although the final result was not according to our desires and hopes, sure am I that the time will come when we will acknowledge that he in mercy and not in wrath afflicted us. I do not know when or how this will appear. Who knows but that *the devotion of the South to the true principles of the constitution* may not in the future cause the fructification of those principles and their growth throughout the land? Who knows but that the example of courage and devotion to duty of our leaders and soldiers, our mothers, wives and sisters, may not hereafter influence the leaders of our whole people to put duty and honor before power and place, and to do and think only of the things that are true, honest and of good report?[64] Who knows but that as a result of the knowledge which each section of our people acquired by the war, of the pluck of the other, and devotion to what each thought was duty, our whole people may be more closely bound together than at any former period of our history, and that hereafter Ephraim will not vex Judah, nor Judah Ephraim?

Human institutions have their uses and their limitations. They are the scaffolding to the building, a means to an end. Although African slavery was not the cause, it was the occasion of our war. It was useful and valuable in its day. It lifted a people who, in the land of their nativity, were savages, out of barbarism and animalism to such a plane of Christian civilization as to qualify them, in the judgment of the Conquerors of the South, to participate in the government of the great republic. What a tribute to the much abused South! What a monument to Southern Christian men and women! Match me if you can out of the record of missions subsequent to the days of the Apostles and the early teachers of Christianity any work among the heathen that can compare with it in results, when viewed from the standpoint of those who have given the African the ballot.

Robert E. Lee, C.S.A.

But in the plan of the Great Ruler, doubtless the time had arrived for African slavery to pass away. So far as we can see, it could not have been gotten rid of in this country except by the means used.[65] *Mr. Lincoln did not by his war proclamation intend to destroy slavery in the States. Its destruction was an evolution of the war—a war measure, consequent upon the events and results of war.*[66]

Moses, the world's great law-giver, commanded his people to teach the laws he had been directed to give them unto their children, in the house and by the wayside, to bind them as a sign upon their hands, and as frontlets between their eyes. *May we not, in imitation of the great law-giver, tell our fathers, mothers, daughters and teachers to teach the children committed to their care and instruction the principles of American liberty, State and national, not as taught by the precept and example of the multitude, but as delivered by the fathers of the republic, and for which our comrades died that fell in battle. To tell and teach them that the dead, in honor of whom this monument has been erected, were not traitors, but true citizens, who gave their lives in defense of the truth, as they understood it, and of their altars and their homes; that Lee, Jackson, ["Jeb"] Stuart, [Turner] Ashby and [Ambrose Powell] Hill, and their soldiers, were not rebels, nor traitors, but patriots, loving God and their fellow-men. and that they did their duty to their country.* Teach them also to look upward to the Great Ruler of all things, truth and untruth, and forward to the duties in life that may be before them; to do their duty as our brave soldiers did; to do it under all circumstances to themselves, to their country and their God—and then come what may, success or failure, they will receive the plaudits of good men, the approval of their own consciences and the approbation of their God.[67] — COL. RICHARD HENRY LEE (at the dedication of the Confederate monument at Old Chapel, in Clarke County, Virginia)

☛ REMINISCENCES OF A MISSISSIPPI BRIGADE

Gen. William Barksdale, of Columbus, Miss., came into the brigade as colonel of the 13th regiment just prior to the battle of Ball's Bluff. The brigade at that time consisted of the 13th, 17th and 18th Mississippi, and the 8th Virginia, commanded respectively by Cols. Barksdale, [Winfield Scott] Featherston, [Erasmus] Burt, and Eppa Hunton. The first two became generals, the third was killed at Ball's Bluff, and the fourth went to Congress a number of years after the war.

Gen. [Nathan George] Evans, of South Carolina, commanded us in that light, and whether it was by accident or grit, or good

William Barksdale, C.S.A.

generalship, or all three combined, I know not, but anyhow we wiped up things so clean, and got so many compliments, both from home and everywhere else, and were so feasted and toasted, and treated so kindly by the good people of Leesburg, we didn't care how long the war lasted.

Richard Griffith, C.S.A.

So when the time came to reorganize at the end of our volunteer term, one year, and ex-Gov. and ex-Senator A. G. Brown, and ex-Congressman O. R. Singleton, both captains of companies in my (the 18th) regiment, told us if we would reorganize immediately they would "wager their heads to brass pins the war would end in sixty days." (B.'s exact words.) They believed it and we believed it, and we "went in for durin'" almost to a man.

Alas, alas! vanity of vanities! Soon we were transferred on stock cars, reeking in mud, to Richmond, and, huddled on a steamer like cattle, took our way to the Peninsula. From the beautiful hills and fertile valleys, the crystal springs and clear, running streams, the fresh baker's bread and clover-fed beef, and the milk and honey of old Louden, to the marshes and lagoons and brackish water of the Warwick! These, with the rancid bacon, the musty corn-meal and rice, and the cool, damp atmosphere, made us realize what war was. About that time, March, 1862, the troops from the different States were brigaded together, and the 8th Virginia was exchanged for the 21st Mississippi, Colonel, afterward General, Benjamin G. Humphreys, commanding.

Winfield S. Featherston, C.S.A.

During the Peninsula campaign, and up to the seven days' fight in front of Richmond, Gen. [Richard] Griffith, of Jackson, Miss., commanded the brigade. On the morning of the battle of Savage Station, while we were driving the enemy before us along the railroad track, he was struck by a shell from one of the enemy's guns—fell from his horse and died in a few hours. A good man, a true patriot, and a gallant officer.

Barksdale—the ranking colonel, Featherston, having been previously promoted and placed in command of another brigade—took immediate command, was promoted to the rank of General in a few days, and continued in command till he fell, leading his men, at Gettysburg. The first verbal command that I recollect of his giving to the brigade as a body, and one that was characteristic of the man, was at Malvern Hill, two days after Savage Station. The enemy had stationed his artillery so as to sweep every spot of the open space, or farm. We had been moved up by a circuitous route into a dense wood bordering on the farm, concealed, as we thought, lying down, some crouched behind trees, all doing our best to keep out of danger till we should be called into action. Every old soldier knows the suspense of such a moment. The only available spot for our own artillery was a small elevated open space a little to our left, and every piece that attempted to unlimber there was knocked up almost before it could be fired, so perfect was their range, and so many were the guns bearing on it. I counted nineteen dead horses in that one place. Then when our artillery was silenced they began to feel for us. At first the shells bursted in the tops of the trees, then a little lower, and down came limbs mingled with pieces of shell. Then they began to burst in our midst, one shell killing and wounding seven men, setting the clothes of one of the latter on fire—a most horrifying sight! It was at this crisis that Gen. Barksdale mounted his horse and yelled, "Attention! This brigade must take that battery." He was a man of whom it could be truthfully said. "Bold as a lion, yet gentle as a lamb." He was not a military man, but was a pure type of genuine southern chivalry, a southern gentleman of the old school. Quick to resent and as quick to forgive; quick to punish disobedience in a subordinate, and as quick to ask forgiveness. Just as far removed from military hauteur as one could imagine. I cite one instance: We were in camp, it was one summer evening. Gen. [Howell] Cobb, of Georgia, his old friend and

Benjamin G. Humphreys, C.S.A.

former fellow-congressman, had dined with him. We were drilling, when the two Generals, arm in arm, coats off, came walking out to look on. It reminded me very forcibly of two farmers in antebellum days taking an afternoon stroll through the farm to look at the crop. We loved Gen. Barksdale, because we knew he was proud of us, and would do anything in his power for our welfare. No truer patriot ever fell on the field of battle.

Gen. [Benjamin Grubb] Humphreys was a West Pointer—was there at the same time with Mr. [Jefferson] Davis, but unlike him, he chose a more peaceful calling, that of a planter in the rich bottom lands of the Mississippi, where he could enjoy the peace and quiet of home life, and indulge in his favorite sport of hunting deer and bear. For the rank he held, and as a commander of infantry, I do not think he had a superior in either army. He possessed all the qualities, both natural and acquired. He won the love of both officers and men by his great kindness. He won their unbounded confidence by his coolness and ability under the most trying circumstances. He was approachable on all occasions. His officers obeyed him implicitly, not because they recognized his right to command them, but because to comply with an order from him was the right thing to do. I cite one instance only to prove the above, and to show what estimate Gen. [James] Longstreet put upon

James Longstreet, C.S.A.

him. At midnight on the 6th of May, 1864, our (Longstreet's) corps was twelve miles from the battle field. It was ordered to get there in the quickest time. We arrived on the ground about sunrise. It happened that our brigade was in front, our regiment leading. As we came up at a double-quick, in marching order, on the plank road, there were in a group, sitting on their horses, the following Generals, Lee, Longstreet, [Elisha Hunt] Rhodes, [Alfred Moore] Scales, [Samuel] McGowan, and, I think, A. P. Hill (am not certain as to the latter). It was an extremely critical moment. Hill's men, who had been engaged the evening before and a portion of the night, were exhausted and outnumbered, and were falling back. Something had to be done, and done quickly. Gen. Lee turned to Longstreet and said, "General, you had better form your line back a half mile and bring it up." Longstreet said, "I think we can form here." Turning to Humphreys he said, "Form your line, General." We had just halted, and were panting like lizards, when Gen. H. straightened himself in his stirrups and said, "Battalion front. By company, right half wheel, double quick, march!" Wounded men and minnie balls were coming through our ranks before we got loaded. The enemy got within a few steps of us in the dense cedar thicket, but we stood it until they began to back, then it was our time to press. Our brigade had done good fighting before, but I thought it reached the climax on that occasion. My own company went in with two officers and thirty-four men, and lost sixteen killed and wounded in a very few minutes.[68] — W. GART JOHNSON

☛ A CONFEDERATE WESTMINSTER ABBEY

As time advances, removing the actors in the tragedy of the Confederacy from the world's stage, and their memory becomes less and less a matter of personal knowledge, and more of tradition, literature and art should be invoked as custodians of their fame.

War is terrible, but never were soldiers endowed with military genius so unpolluted by its demoralizing breath as Davis, Lee, Jackson, Johnston, and many others who have identified their names with the Confederacy. Their deeds and lives we can place without fear of comparison by the brightest episodes in history. Defeat cannot vitiate such virtue and genius as theirs, and for them, and the principles which inspired their valor before all the world, let us ordain fitting sepulture for ashes, fitting monument for a just though lost cause, for genius and virtue an apotheosis. Can these ends be achieved more co-ordinately than by the erection of a Confederate Westminster, so to

Westminster Abbey, London, England.

speak—a national mausoleum at Richmond, our capital, where Davis, Lee and all the heroes of the South should be interred, their individual fame preserved and yet blended in the unity of the Confederacy? It is just that this relation between them and their cause be maintained, for one vivifying principle, *State's rights*, ran through them all, quickening latent genius into flame, and while their individual names were blazoned on the temple of fame, they flashed on the world's horizon as a glorious constellation—the Southern cross, the Southern Confederacy.[69] — NANNIE NUTT

John S. Mosby, C.S.A.

☛ REMEMBERING THE WAR
Gen. [William Tecumseh] Sherman, before he died, was a neighbor of mine. One night I took the General up to the Kilpatrick Grand Army Post [U.S.A.]. On the way back I asked him if he didn't think "Kil" [Union General Hugh Judson Kilpatrick] was a good fighter.

"Splendid," said Sherman, and then he said, "but he was a great boaster, too. Well, he had a right to boast, for he could never boast stronger than he fought."

"One day," continued the General, "Kilpatrick was recounting at Willard's Hotel in Washington his experience in driving back rebel reinforcements at Chancellorsville. Listening to him was a crowd of old soldiers, among whom was [Confederate Colonel John Singleton] Mosby.

"'Why,' said Kilpatrick, 'the woods swarmed with rebels. I had two horses shot under me and—'

"'What did you do then, Kil?' asked [Union General George Armstrong] Custer.

"'Why, I jumped on to a Government mule: a ball knocked me off, but the mule charged right ahead into the rebel ranks. I never knew what became of that mule.'

"'Why, General,' said Mosby, 'I saw that mule. He came right into our lines.'

"'Well, I'm glad to see my words confirmed,' said Kilpatrick, seriously. 'Then you really saw him?'

"'Yes, sure.'"

"'Head shot off?'

"'No, died from mortification [that is, embarrassment].'"

Gen. Sherman always said with pride that the [Union] Army of the Tennessee never retreated. They started in at Memphis and came out at Charleston and Wilmington in a fourth of the time that it took the Army of the Potomac to see-saw back and forth between Washington and Richmond. One day after the war the General said he was talking with a [Union] veteran from the Army of the Potomac. The soldier was describing the big fight of [Union Gen. Joseph] Hooker at Chancellorsville [against the Confederate armies of Lee and Jackson].

"Did the rebels run" asked Sherman.

"Did they run?" repeated the soldier. "Did the rebels run? Great Scott! I should say they did run. Why, General, they run so like thunder that we had to run three miles to keep out of their way; and if we hadn't thrown away our guns they'd run all over us, sure!"[70] — ELI PERKINS

☛ IN OUR FATHER'S HOUSE

The Grand Army Posts [that is, Union veteran camps], in the aggregate led by designing politicians, appear as partisans in politics more to their discredit than is due. Confederate Veteran organizations repudiate politics. Your great captain [Ulysses S. Grant], in accepting the resignation of Gen. Lee, illustrated the sentiments of his best soldiers in refusing that good man's sword, and in telling him that "the boys will need their horses to make crops." Grant never had heart in the radical measures of the administration while Chief Executive. This was given out as a last expression of his life, and kept a secret even from his wife until after he was dead.

True patriots of the two sections are much more in harmony than they think. Unhappily the political victors, by our system of government, wielded so much power that the Union veteran was dashed by the current, and he could not check its tide. Many thousands of the best soldiers who suffered for the flag but refused to ally themselves with these sectional partisans, have been refused any benefits of office through all the decades that have followed. *Many of them have stood as true to principles, however, as the great body of the Southern people.* This element is stronger than it realizes, and the day may yet be predicted when it will be heard.

A letter [from a Union soldier] . . . commends [the South's] "fraternal spirit" . . . Such is [our] spirit. All honor to the bronzed American soldier who acted upon the teachings of his fathers and ours, that "the Union must and shall be preserved." The Confederate soldier must not fail to honor such, and he will not. In paying tribute to their courage and manhood we honor ourselves.

Sumner A. Cunningham, C.S.A.

Resting upon this declaration the bold assertion is made that *the average Southerner is a better patriot than the average Northerner. American soldiers of the Union should accept this, and they might, with fine grace, admit it.* Placing our ancestors on equal footing, and Union veterans will certainly admit as much, they should know that we who suffered greater hardships through the four bitter years of war became more intensely devoted than if we had been paid for our service. *We fought for home and the constitutional principles of our fathers, while they [Yankees] can only claim to have fought for the latter and the Union.*

So far reference is had only to the American sons who volunteered to battle for the Union, and the premises should be accepted. If positions had been reversed the men of the South would have been less ardent than they are and were. Again, this sentiment will be in greater contrast when we remember that *many thousands of foreigners came to America to fight for pay, having not a particle of sentiment. This picture must be depressing to the American soldier who fought for the Union. The ostracism of Southern men through all these years has been bad for the spirit of national pride that we all would like to have.*

The foreign writer of history who goes about our national capital and sees the bronze dedicated to the Union side only will think of our "reconstructed" rather than our "reunited" country. *(These monuments are almost exclusively to officers. In the South the finest monuments are to private soldiers.)* If he crosses over to Arlington on the opposite side of the Potomac, he will witness that the magnificent home of Robert E. Lee, which has been converted into sexton's quarters of a national cemetery, has not even a portrait of that eminent man whom the civilized world delights to honor, and a man whose ancestors, back to the formation of the government, were eminent in its establishment and maintenance.

How long, O brothers of American sires, will you keep silent against these unwise and unpatriotic thing? "We are," indeed, "in our father's house," and "we love our country's flag." We would not if we could substitute another for it. *The "Flag of the Confederacy" is, however, absolutely sacred, and will be forever, yea forever. It is a lost flag, and that should be the term rather than "lost cause." Our cause is not lost. The principles of the government for which we fought are being maintained*, save as to State's rights and slavery. The abolition of the latter is everywhere accepted, and the former is a question of expediency still as much as ever it was.

Constitutional government is the underlying principle for which all good men pray, and for which southern as well as northern men will fight. Do let us all, both North and South, with the issues removed that caused a long "unpleasantness," press forward to our high calling as Americans. Confederate veterans, proud sons of men, you have done and are doing your part well. You will so continue. Nothing can deter you from devotion to the principles impressed by education and grounded in by experience. Continue patient under trial and all will be well in the end.[71] — SUMNER A. CUNNINGHAM

☛ OUR UNKNOWN DEAD

Comrades—The solemn ceremony of Decoration Day has been performed. The few graves, alike of the Confederate and the Union soldiers that rest in our cemetery [in Orlando, Florida], have been decorated with floral offerings, and the cause that so few of Confederate dead sleep where loving kindred can care for them, inclines me to say a few words in regard to the unknown dead.

There is evidence that in the beginning of the late war it was the intention of the Federal Government to concentrate their forces and form two or more grand armies and wage war only on the enlisted troops of the Confederacy, and by sheer power of numbers overwhelm their opponents and end the war by a second Sadowa or Sedan victory.

In this, however, they were not successful. [Yankee Generals George Brinton] McClellan, [John] Pope, [Ambrose Everett] Burnside and [Joseph] Hooker unavailingly encountered Lee, and in the West no great victory was obtained.

During this time the Federal forces were largely increased, and a navy, which in the end numbered four hundred and seventy odd war steamers, was created, manned by thirty-four thousand [Yankee] seamen, and carrying four thousand four hundred and forty guns. This armament was stationed along the Atlantic seaboard, the gulf coast and on the waters of navigable rivers, occupying sounds, inlets, bays and harbors, supporting and protecting, under cover of these guns, large detachments of their land forces, in numbers estimated nearly equal to a third of their troops in service. Now, whatever may primarily have been the object of these many isolated detachments, it soon developed into making raids in the adjacent country, and afforded opportunity to pillage when not met with opposing forces. . . .

From Dalton down to Atlanta, and around that city, there was one continuous conflict for one hundred days, and not a day passed without some troops being engaged, and so the dead were left throughout a hundred miles on either side, resting where they fell. If we turn to the East again we find that Grant crossed the Rapidan May 4, 1864, and taking the direct line to Richmond, immediately the battle of the Wilderness followed, and he announced that he was going "to fight it out on that line if it took all summer." A few days after came the battle of Spottsylvania, and June 1ˢᵗ that of Cold Harbor, where the Federal troops refused to make a second attack.

In these three great and sanguinary battles the commander of the Union force did not meet with success, and so on the first day of summer he left that line and swung around, as McClellan did, to the James River. After Cold Harbor it seems as if there was no desire for another general engagement, and the hammering away mode of war commenced on Lee. On July 18, 1864, President Lincoln called for 500,000 more men, and so the detrition process went on for nine months, mainly on and near the picket line, being in all nearly eleven months and a half, that Lee confronted Grant's hosts of men, and overall this extent of country lay the blue and the gray side by side in death. Devastation, as in the Palatinate, had done its work.

Now, when the war ended the Federal Government, with commendable zeal, very humanely collected most of their dead and had their remains removed to their beautiful cemeteries, and there keep green the sod and fresh the flowers on their graves.

There was no Confederate Government to collect and care for the remains of the Confederate dead. Along the banks of the Father of Waters for more than a thousand miles the inhabitants tread unawares over the unknown graves of those who battled for the South. Along the shores of the Potomac, the Rappahannock and the James, wave the golden harvests on soil enriched by their blood and mouldering dust. From the capes of the Chesapeake adown the stormy Atlantic, and trending around the Gulf, rest thousands of our dead; or go to the heights of Allatoona, to Lookout's lofty peak, or Kennesaw Mountain's top, and you may seek in vain where the dead rest. Time, with the relentless forces of the elements, has obliterated all traces of their graves from human eye; they are known only to Him who can tell where Moses sleeps in "a vale in the land of Moab." So the forgotten are not forgot, the hand that made the thunder's home comes down every spring and paints with bright colors the little wild flowers that grow over their resting places, and they are bright on decoration day. The rosy morn announces first to them that the night is gone, and when the day is past and the landscape veiled with evening's shade, high on the mountain's top the last rays of the setting sun lovingly lingers longest, loth to have the lonely place where the bright-eyed children of the Confederacy rest in death.

Samuel G. French, C.S.A.

And wherefore did they die? *They fell in defense of their homes, their families, their country, and those civil rights arising from that liberty God gave man as a heritage in the beginning. They furnished to their country much that will be noble in history, wonderful in story, tender in song, and a large share of that glory which will claim the admiration of mankind.* We can to-day place no wreaths of immortelles on their unknown graves, yet we can rest assured the echoes of *posterity will render their deeds illustrious.*

And now, as I look back on the past and recall to mind your trials and sufferings—which will be forgotten—I am sure the world will not forget that your valor merited a success which is better now than to have achieved it.[72] — GEN. SAMUEL GIBBS FRENCH

☛ MEMORABLE WORDS OF TWO MEN

The last words of Capt. James Lawrence, as may be seen by the entrance to the old cemetery around Trinity Church, were. "Don't give up the ship," and they remind me of that terrible night at Franklin, Tenn., in November, 1864, where my Confederate Brigadier, O. F. Strahl, just before receiving the first of the three shots that ended his life, said, "Keep firing."

The Carter House, Franklin, TN. (Photo L. Seabrook)

We had captured and were in possession of the enemy's last line of breastworks, at that particular place, but were exposed to a terrific enfilade from a cotton gin across the Columbia turnpike. The deep ditch was nearly filled with our dead, and many of our men had crossed over this last line, after a hand to hand encounter with the stubborn foe. The colors of my regiment were carried beyond it, but had fallen from a lifeless arm and lay between the lines. In addition to the enfilade fire mentioned the enemy was well protected within the walls of a large brick residence, Mr. [Fountain Branch] Carter's, about sixty yards distant. The situation was such that some of our men, posted on the side of the captured embankment, fired while others passed up the loaded guns. Gen. Strahl stood in the ditch and passed up these loaded guns as they were handed him by the men of three lines of battle, who had protection from the front embankment. Those who were tiring fell rapidly as they were exposed to the enfilade and the direct shots, and would become new targets by every flash from their guns, as it was in the night.

Volunteers had ceased to fill the vacant places on the works, and the General had resorted to asking the men about him, "Have you shot any?" When he asked me I made no reply, but arose from where I had been lying and loading, just back of the entrenchment, and on taking position I rested one foot on the pile of my dead comrades that by this time had about filled the ditch and the other on the embankment. It was about one hundred yards to the cotton gin, still occupied by the enemy, and there was only one other to assist me in firing. The well-aimed fire from the enemy had so exhausted our force that I thought we should either try and get away or surrender, and asked my commander what we had better do. His answer was given without hesitation, "Keep firing." I had fired guns then until my shoulder was black from bruises, and the exhaustion had caused my throat, down into my chest, to seem as dry as dust, and I was extremely discouraged. My associate was shot, and, falling against my shoulder, shrieked heavily, and I asked him how he was wounded. Almost simultaneously with the shot that soon ended his groans, I think, another struck the General, who threw up both hands and fell on his face. I thought him dead, but he was not, and replied to my query of the soldier, that he was shot in the neck. He then inquired for Col. [Fountain E. P.] Stafford, that he might turn over the command, and crawled over the dead in the ditch to where Stafford was killed, almost in standing position by the dead around him. Within a few steps of the line of works, as Gen. Strahl was being carried to the rear, one of two other shots proved instantly fatal. I am grateful, now, in being aide to

Otho F. Strahl, C.S.A.

pay this tribute to one of the most gallant men that ever fell in battle.

I have gone, since that memorable night, to the little Episcopal Church at Bolivar, Tenn., where a beautiful memorial window has been dedicated to him.

No nation will ever erect in his honor such a monument as that by Trinity Church to Capt. James Lawrence, and the enemy may never vie with his comrades in his honor, but the beautiful tribute inscribed to Capt. Lawrence could not be re-used better than in setting forth the character of Otho French Strahl.[73] — SUMNER A. CUNNINGHAM

☛ THE PRIVATE SOLDIER OF THE CONFEDERACY

Stirred by a pure love of his country, of his home and fireside, the private soldier rushed to arms for their defense at the first call, regardless of the perils of battle or the hardships of the camp. The wife of his bosom and his beloved children were left to the care of trusted but untried slaves. He came from the halls of learning, from the huts of ignorance, from the counting-room, from the farm; he was a professional man, he was a day laborer, he was rich and he was poor. Regardless of social position or conditions of wealth, animated and inspired by the love of a common cause, they became bands of patriotic brothers, and, shoulder to shoulder, they battled with a heroism the world had not known before, and for four long years they kept the world from overrunning this fair Southland!

Was he only valorous and distinguished as a victorious warrior? Follow him in Stonewall Jackson's campaigns. Mark his patience along the forced marches. Rushed along over hill and through dale, in mud or sand; drenched by rain or scorched by sun; barefooted at times, burdened with twenty-five pounds weight in the shape of musket, accoutrements, ammunition, blanket, etc., his haversack containing a small pone of stale cornbread and a slice or two of rancid bacon, his canteen most of the time empty; aroused from night's sleep or started from day's rest, he obeyed with a willingness and promptness which characterize only the devotee to a sacred cause. . . .

Such were the private soldiers who fought for the South during the bloodiest civil war the world ever knew; and despite the odds of three to one in number of men, and with a skeleton navy, shut in by blockade from foreign aid, they nearly achieved independence. The faith he had in the righteousness of his cause was beyond the imagination of his foe. It made him suffer every ill with composure and cheerfulness.⁷⁴ — CONFEDERATE CAPTAIN B. H. TEAGUE

☛ THOSE WHO WORE THE GRAY
It is noble to care for the graves of men who died for home and country, and woman is true to the trust. The memory of the boys who wore the gray is a sacred inheritance to the South, and it is duty as well as pleasure to honor those who died far from home.⁷⁵ — FLORA ADAMS DARLING

☛ THE CONFEDERATE SECESSION
. . . young men will ask, was not slavery so bad that the Constitution, which shielded it, was rightly violated in order to destroy it? That is the question which has been answered by the roar of artillery in the affirmative. But can that answer by force be justified in the forum of morals? *If solemn compact may be violated in order to destroy what that compact guaranteed, what value is there in a written Constitution?* It only awaits a new fanatical sentiment to justify a new crusade upon its integrity. If the obligation of compact may be impaired or destroyed because of its subject-matter civilization will perish, because it cannot survive the death of good faith or the repudiation of public or private compacts.

Miss Daisy Sims of North Carolina, daughter of a Confederate soldier.

But let me present another view. The crusade not only destroyed slavery, but entailed upon the South a social condition for which the crusaders [abolitionists] suggest no relief, and a condition which seems to be without the hope of peaceful solution. Those who had no interest in the relation have inoculated the South with a social and political disease for which their statesmen have provided no remedy and can find no panacea. These were the issues upon which the Southern States seceded, and defended their imperiled rights with a valor, constancy and fortitude which has made them immortal.

We cannot be placed in the false position of having fought to hold men in slavery. The South never made a free man a slave, and never took from the dark land one human being to shackle him with servitude. The race of Southern men inherited the institution, which was put on us by the cupidity of [Yankee] slave traders against the protests of our [Southern] colonial fathers. Eight millions of Caucasians and four millions of Africans—the first masters, the last slaves. That was the problem we inherited. Shall they remain slaves and how long? or be at once emancipated? and then be put into possession of equal power with the white man to direct a common destiny? Shall our constitutional power, our inherent natural right to regulate this special interest, be wrested from us and vested in aliens to that interest, to be exercised by them to create social and political relations never known in the history of civilized man, and for the right regulation of which no prophecy could forecast a law, and our sad experience has been unable to devise a remedy? *To put it forensically, the South did not plead to the issue of slavery or no slavery, but to the jurisdiction. To create the jurisdiction was to give up self-government.*

If we resisted the government, we defended the Constitution; we supported the sovereignty which ordained the supreme law of the land, though we opposed by force the usurpations of the delegated agent of the sovereignty.

We failed—were defeated—came back to the Union, yes, but to the Union under the Constitution—and though amended—in substance the same old Constitution. The rents in its sacred parchment are healed; the blood-stains are obliterated.

Virginia greets the daughter of North Carolina, a younger sister in this great Union. Let us labor to perpetuate this galaxy of commonwealths, bound by the gravitating forces of commercial, geographical, social and political interests, and of common aspirations, as the inheritors of the free institutions of the Anglo-American race. Let us co-operate to save the Union from the maelstrom of a *centralized* paternalism, and to anchor our liberty and right in the safe harbor of ancient constitutional polity. *God preserve and perpetuate the union of these*

States on the solid rock-bed of the Constitution of our fathers!

Let no censorious criticism suggest a doubt of our faithful devotion to the Constitution and Union of to-day because we honor and revere the patriotism of those who died for the lost cause. The heroic purpose failed; our Confederacy sank beneath the political horizon in clouds which could not blacken history. The sun of the Confederacy lighted them with the effulgence of its own transcendent glory. The fame of its heroes, of their genius for leadership, of their constancy, fortitude, martial prowess and devotion to duty, all Americans will one day claim to be the common heritage of the Union.

Andrew Jackson.

I come from an historic institution that bears the illustrious names of Washington, the spotless hero in victory, and of Lee, the no less spotless hero in defeat. I live near the grave of this most splendid type of the Virginia cavaliers, and of that of Stonewall Jackson, the noblest type of the Scotch-Irish race. I come to Tennessee, two of whose sons, the hero of the Hermitage [Andrew Jackson] and the eminent James K. Polk, were elected Presidents by all the States of the Union; the one whose sturdy arm struck down the giant bank monopoly, the other the no less hateful monopoly of tariff spoliation. President Jackson declared the Union must and shall be preserved—the Union under the written Constitution of the fathers. Both of them were of kindred lineage with heroes of the Confederacy, with Stonewall Jackson and Leonidas Polk, who died as defenders of the lost cause.

Standing reverently near the tombs of your mighty dead, I hesitate not to say that neither would have condemned these Confederate heroes of their blood. The spirits of these Jacksons and these Polks, of Davis and of Lee, of the two Johnstons, and of hundreds of others hovering near us, would join in our fervent aspiration that this and coming generations shall be faithful to the Union and the Constitution, upon which, as their best foundation, liberty and right and justice shall ever securely rest. The living and the dead of the lost Confederacy and of the restored Union, by their devotion to truth and right, call upon us, one and all, to uphold and defend this constitutional Union. With patriotic purpose, despite the breakers which threaten our shipwreck, guided by the chart of the Constitution, and with humble trust in the God of our fathers, let us here and now resolve to remit no effort as citizens of a common country to steer this fleet of American commonwealths into the haven of peace and fraternity, with the noble memories of past achievements, and with united aspirations for the heritage of a common glory among the nations of earth.[76] — JOHN RANDOLPH TUCKER

☛ SAMMY, KEEP YOUR SHIRT ON
On a march at night [Confederate] Gen. [Samuel G.] French's division was moving when those tiresome and exasperating halts occurred so often that the men became worn out with the oft-repeated command to "move up." Gen. French was trying to get his Quartermaster to push the headquarters team to the front, as the enemy was dangerously near in the rear. The men having dropped down by hundreds in the road to sleep it was almost impossible to get a team through without running over the men. Gen. French became impatient and rode forward to see for himself. He began to order the men out of the road with an occasional oath [swear word]. In the midst of his career a thin, sharp voice, just off the road, sang out, "O Sammy, keep your shirt on; don't burn your shirt." The General was furious, and rising up in his stirrups said: "I will give fifty dollars to know the man who said that." It is needless to say he did not find out, but laughter was heard along the line for some distance.[77] — SUMNER A. CUNNINGHAM

☛ REMINISCENCES OF LEE AT GETTYSBURG
It was on the morning of the 3rd of July, 1863, at Gettysburg. On the evening before Hood and McLaws' divisions of Longstreet's corps, on the right wing, had driven the enemy from all his positions on the open plain to the stronghold of Cemetery Ridge. My company C, 18th Mississippi), with others, was occupying the extreme front picket line in direct range of the sharpshooters. We were in the edge of an apple orchard. Adjutant Harmon, of the 13th Mississippi, and I were hugging a pile of rubbish, anything to hide behind, that we had thrown together, when Gens. Lee and Longstreet—on foot, no aids, orderlies or couriers, fifteen or twenty steps apart, field glasses in hand—came walking past

us, stopping now and then to take observations. They were arranging, as we soon found out, for the famous charge of Pickett's division. As Gen. Lee halted in a few feet of us, knowing the imminent danger he was in, one of us said, "Gen. Lee, you are running a very great risk." At that moment the searching minnie [ball] was cutting close to him, showing that he was the mark aimed at. He went on with his observations as calm and serene as if he was viewing a landscape. A few minutes afterward we heard him say to Longstreet, in substance, "Mass your artillery behind that hill," pointing to a ridge just in our rear, "and at the signal bring your

guns to the top of the ridge and turn them loose." It put us to thinking of what would become of us—the picket line. We could not leave our posts; we were in plain view of the enemy, without protection except from small arms; we had no utensils with which to throw up earthworks. We knew the shells from our guns would go over us, but those of the enemy! Well, spades or no spades, we went into that ground quicker than you would think. We were like the fellow after the ground hog, it had to be done. Bayonets, pieces of board, any thing to get out of sight. Two or three to a hole, and we went in like gophers.

That was the grandest and at the same time the most terrible artillery duel I ever witnessed. Think of it. There were sixty-five (I was told) of our own pieces on that one spot, and more on another portion of our line, all firing as fast as they could, and the cannon of the enemy replying. I don't know how long it lasted. When it stopped on our side Picket's division charged! They had to march over us. Doing nothing myself, I had time to look. It was one of the grandest sights ever mortal eyes looked upon. It makes me shudder now, as I see the shells plow through the ranks of that gallant band.[78] — W. GART JOHNSON

☛ A 12-YEAR OLD BOY'S OBSERVATIONS OF GEN. LEE
A few years after Gen. Lee accepted the presidency of the then Washington College [on August 4, 1865], I was sent to be entered in the preparatory department, along with an older brother who was to enter college. The morning after we reached Lexington we repaired to the office of Gen. Lee, situated in the college building, for the purpose of matriculation and receiving instructions as to the duties devolving upon us as students. I entered the office with reverential awe, expecting to see the great warrior, whose fame then encircled the civilized globe, as I had pictured him in my own imagination. Gen. Lee was alone, looking over a paper. He arose as we entered, and received us with a quiet, gentlemanly dignity that was so natural and easy and kind that the feeling of awe left me at the threshold of his door. Gen. Lee had but one manner in his intercourse with men. It was the same to the peasant as to the prince, and the student was received with the easy courtliness that would have been bestowed on the greatest imperial dignitary of Europe.

Robert E. Lee, C.S.A.

When we had registered my brother asked the General for a copy of his rules. Gen. Lee said to him, *"Young gentleman, we have no printed rules. We have but one rule here, and it is that every student must be a gentleman."* I did not, until after years, fully realize the comprehensiveness of his remark, and how completely it covered every essential rule that should govern the conduct and intercourse of men. I do not know that I could define the impression that Gen. Lee left on my mind that morning, for I was so disappointed at not seeing the warrior that my imagination had pictured, that my mind was left in a confused state of inquiry as to whether he was the man whose fame had filled the world. He was so gentle, kind, and almost motherly, in his bearing that I thought there must be some mistake about it. At first glance Gen. Lee's countenance was stern, but the moment his eye met that of his entering guest it beamed with a kindness that at once established easy and friendly relations, but not familiar. The impression he made on me was that he was never familiar with any man.

I saw Gen. Lee every day during the session in chapel (for he never missed a morning service) and passing through the campus to and from his home to his office. He rarely spoke to any one—occasionally would say something to one of the boys as he passed, but never more than a word. After the first morning in his office he never spoke to me but once. He stopped me one morning as I was passing his front gate and asked how I was getting on with my studies. I replied to his inquiry, and that was the end of the conversation. He seemed to avoid contact with men, and *the impression he then made on me, seeing him every day, and which has since clung to me, strengthening the impression then made, was, that he was bowed down with a broken heart. I never saw a sadder expression than Gen. Lee carried during the entire time I was there. It looked as if the sorrow of a whole nation had been collected in his countenance, and as if he was hearing the grief of his whole people. It never left his face*, but was

Lee on his warhorse Traveller.

ever there to keep company with the kindly smile. He impressed me as being the most modest man I ever saw in his contact with men. History records how modestly he wore his honors, but I refer to the characteristic in another sense. I dare say no man ever offered to relate a story of questionable delicacy in his presence. His very bearing and presence produced an atmosphere of purity that would have repelled the attempt. As for any thing like publicity, notoriety or display, it was absolutely painful to him. Col. Ruff, the old gentleman with whom I boarded, told me an anecdote about him that I think worth preserving. Gen. Lee brought with him to Lexington the old iron-gray horse ["Traveller"] that he rode during the war. A few days after he had been there he rode up Main street on his old war horse, and as he passed up the street the citizens cheered him. After passing the ordeal he hurried back to his home near the college, and never again appeared on the streets on horseback. He took his usual afternoon horse-back rides, but ever afterward he rode out back of the Campus. He was incapable of affection. The demonstration was simply offensive to his innate modesty, and doubtless awakened the memories of the past that seemed to weigh continually on his heart. The old iron-gray horse was the privileged character at Gen. Lee's home. He was permitted to remain in the front yard where the grass was greenest and freshest, not withstanding the flowers and shrubbery. Gen. Lee was more demonstrative toward that old companion in battle than seemed to be in his nature in his intercourse with men. I have often seen him, as he would enter his front gate, leave the walk, approach the old horse and caress him for a minute or two before entering his front door, as though they bore a common grief in their memory of the past.[79] — JOHN B. COLYAR

Washington and Lee University, Lexington, VA.

☛ JUBAL A. EARLY & HIS CAMPAIGNS

In the *Confederate Veteran* for February [1893] there appears an article from the St. Louis *Globe-Democrat* that does great injustice to General Early, one of the grandest soldiers the war produced. This article says:

> In 1864 General Early was sent to the valley of the Shenandoah. There, after a few minor successes, he fought the disastrous battle of Cedar Creek. Six months later—in October, 1864—a still more serious disaster befell him at Waynesboro, where General Custer almost annihilated his command. Lee, who still retained his faith in Early's capacity, was unable to resist the popular feeling in the army against the defeated General, and felt himself obliged to remove him from his command. In his letter relieving him from duty, Lee, with the delicacy of the true gentleman, softened the blow by assuring Early

of his own regard, but reminded him that the country and the army would naturally judge by results, and consequently there could he no doubt that his influence would increase the already serious difficulties accumulating in Southwest Virginia, fairly at once quitted the army and spent some time in Europe.

I do not know why General Early was relieved from duty in Southwest Virginia and General [John] Echols put in his place. This I do know, that neither General Lee, nor any other soldier in the army ever doubted the capacity of General Early as an officer and soldier. General Early was sent on the valley campaign for the purpose of drawing Federal troops from in front of Richmond. He succeeded in doing this, and the campaign of Early through the valley was a great success. He drew at least one-third of Grant's army from in front of Richmond. Before the disastrous battle of Cedar Creek spoken of,

Jubal A. Early, C.S.A.

General Early defeated Gen. Lew [Lewis] Wallace, with 12,000 men, at Monacacy, Md. Early had under him four divisions of infantry and one of cavalry—two divisions, forming Breckinridge's corps, under Generals Gordon and [John Austin] Wharton, and one under General [Stephen Dodson] Ramseur and one under General [Henry] Heth. The division of cavalry was under General [Lunsford Lindsay] Lomax. In the battle of Monocacy only one division of infantry was engaged—that of General Gordon, from Breckinridge's corps. I do not know how many men were in this division at that time, but do not think there were over 3000. Later on, in September—the 20th, I think—Early fought the battle of Winchester. He had in this battle, all told, not over 5,000 infantry and 2,000 cavalry. The troops engaged were the corps of Breckinridge—two divisions under Gordon and Wharton; the division of Heth, and the division of Ramseur. These four divisions constituted his infantry force. The cavalry consisted of two divisions, one under Fitzhugh Lee and the other under Lomax. The battle of Winchester began a little after daylight, on the Berryville pike, one mile from Winchester, and lasted all day, our lines not giving way till dusk. When the battle began Ramseur, with his division, was just a mile out from Winchester on the Berryville pike. He was attacked in force a little after daylight. Wharton's division of Breckinridge's corps was seven miles out from Winchester, at a place called Brucetown. Gordon's division of Breckinridge's corps was at Bunker Hill, fourteen miles from Winchester, and Heth's division was at Martinsburg, twenty-four miles from Winchester. As I said above, the battle began in front of Ramseur. The divisions of Wharton, Gordon and Heth were double-quicked to his support as soon as possible, Heth not arriving until about 6'clock. On that day Early fought (from about daylight until dark) the whole of [Philip H.] Sheridan's army, numbering about 30,000 infantry and 10,000 cavalry. Our losses in this battle were heavy. We retreated that night to Fisher's mill, arriving there about daylight. Several days after our arrival at Fisher's mill General Breckinridge was ordered to his old department of Southwest Virginia, leaving his two divisions with Early. Sheridan followed Early up the valley and defeated him at Cedar Creek. A week or ten days after the battle of Cedar Creek Sheridan again defeated Early at Waynesboro. Now, Sheridan had in these two battles a big army; Early had a very small force, not over 3,000 men at the outside. Could he be expected to defeat this large army of Sheridan's with a very small force of not, as I said above, over 3,000 men? The three battles of Winchester, Cedar Creek and Waynesboro were all fought within a month, and not six months apart, as this article says.

Henry Heth, C.S.A.

General Breckinridge, I think, was made Secretary of War very late in the fall of 1864. I will not be sure as to dates, but think it was even later than this, probably not until January or February, 1865, that General Breckinridge left the department of Southwest Virginia for Richmond. General Early was appointed in his place, but was soon afterward relieved from duty and General Echols put in command of the department. I do not pretend to know why General Early was relieved and General Echols appointed, but do not think that the valley campaign and the battles of Cedar Creek and Waynesboro had anything to do with his removal from the command of the department of Southwest Virginia. I do not think General Early ever left the South for Europe until after the war. I do not know, however, where he went when he left the department of Southwest Virginia. That General Early was one of the greatest soldiers of the war no one who saw him during the war can doubt. Even if there was any truth in the article written for the *Globe-Democrat* I think it should have remained unwritten.

John Echols, C.S.A.

In conclusion, [I] will say that if Early's campaign in the valley had not been successful Richmond would probably have fallen in June, 1864, instead of April, 1865. That General Lee's object in ordering Early to the valley, and to make a demonstration against Washington and Baltimore was to draw Grant's troops from his front there can be no doubt. If General Early had failed in drawing these troops from Grant's army, then this correspondent of the *Globe-Democrat* might have been right, General Early was relieved, why I do not know. He is a grand old man, and all Confederates should look up to him and admire him.[80] — JAMES B. CLAY (staff of Gen. Breckinridge)

☛ A CHARACTERISTIC CONFEDERATE
Capt. J. Warren Hudson died in Selma on the morning of the 5th of July, 1893, aged 62 years. He came from Virginia when a youth, and took position among the young business men of Alabama. When war was declared, he was of the first to enlist, and was soon promoted to a captaincy in the famous fourth. Every officer and man was his personal friend. Industry, urbanity and unselfishness were his prominent characteristics throughout his life. He was never idle, and yet he was never so tired from ceaseless toil but that he found opportunity to attend the sick and bury the dead, he always had a smile and tender words and open purse for the distressed. He ascribed all to his Savior, and during the most severe pain his heart was thankful.[81] — SELMA, ALABAMA *MIRROR*

☛ HOW THEY STOOD PICKET UNDER FORREST

One day in 1864 orders came to the regiment for a detail for scout and picket duty, and the instructions accompanying the orders were for the detail to proceed along a certain road until the enemy was discovered, then stop, hold him in check if possible, but under all circumstances to inform the General of the whereabouts and strength of the enemy. All know that when "old Bedford" [Nathan Bedford Forrest] issued orders he intended them to be obeyed, and promptly, too. So worn out as the men were it was not long before the party, under command of Lieut. Garner, started on what might prove a wild goose chase, and was just as likely to prove a tiger hunt, with lots of tiger in it. Of one thing the men were sure, they would go until they found the enemy if he was on that road.

Every old soldier knows that on such expeditions he always picked out a mate. One of the men, Burns, a youngster in point of years, but an old soldier, and one of the best that Forrest had, picked out Dick Townsend for his chum. Townsend was riding a gray, almost white, horse. This part of it Burns did not like at all, but decided he would rather risk Townsend with a white horse than any other man there, with a less objectionably colored horse. But I'll let Burns tell the rest.

We had ridden ten or twelve miles, when, just after dark, we came up to an old fellow's house and asked him if there were any yanks about, and he told us that they were camped just across the creek about half a mile ahead. We went on quietly, keeping a good lookout, and sure enough, when we got near the creek we could hear dogs barking. They always had dogs about their camps; why, we never could tell, unless it was because the negroes followed them and the dogs followed the negroes. At any rate, the dogs were always there. We halted, and could distinctly hear them talking; and after listening long enough to be sure that we had accomplished our mission, we fell back down the road about a quarter [mile] and put out a picket. It came Townsend's and my turn to go on late, and we went to the top of the hill with a lot of orders, mostly "nots"—namely, not to talk, not to smoke, not to make the least noise, and not to shoot, if possible to avoid it, and not, under any circumstances, to dismount, but to sit quietly on our horses and watch. I do not know how long I had been there when I got so sleepy it seemed to me I should fall off of my horse. I leaned over, and in a whisper asked Townsend if he was sleepy too. He said he was nearly dead. Finally, we could stand it no longer, and got down off our horses and began walking back and forth in front of them as far as the halters would let us, but this didn't do any good. Looking around I saw that the road was raised—that is, it was higher than the ground on either side of it. I told Townsend that I was going to sit down on the ground and rest. We both sat down, putting our feet in the ditch. There were plenty of weeds growing close up to the side of the road. I leaned over and put my head down on my hands as they rested on my gun. I did not  expect nor intend to go to sleep, but I was completely fagged out. I don't know how long I had been in the position described when something passed by through the weeds with a whisk, a whisk that waked me instantly. It was right under my nose when I saw it, and I tell you the truth when I say it nearly scared the life out of me. It scared me so bad I yelled, "Hellfire, what's that?" as loud as I could, and then I saw it was nothing but a coon. Almost instantly we were on our horses listening, but the yanks never heard a word, or if they did they made no sign. As soon as we found we hadn't alarmed them we got to laughing, and really after the scare was over it was about as funny an adventure as any that happened to me during the war. It shows how little it takes to scare a fellow almost to death when he is tired out and expecting to be scared anyhow. Just before day we withdrew, but Townsend and I laughed all day over that terrible fright.[82] — "SCOUT"

☛ FATE OF TWO FLAGS

The younger generation can hardly realize the horrors of war. They listen to the stories of the battles, of how the bullets flew and the men dropped one by one, but still they fail to realize the deadly execution of

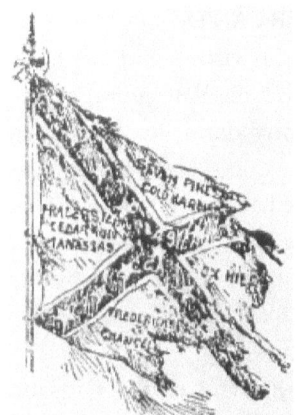

Confederate flag of the Forty-Ninth Georgia Infantry.

the minie-ball or the shot from a squirrel rifle.

The post of honor, as well of danger, in a battle is that of the color guard. Attached to the right center company of a regiment, the guard is composed of a sergeant and seven corporals, whose duty it is to carry the colors, and as the colors are most frequently the point of attack it makes them the place of danger, for to lose them is a disgrace, to capture them an honor. In victory they were the salient point of the enemy's attack in their attempts to dislodge the victors, regain their lost ground and capture the colors. In the repulse of a charge they were the rallying point of those who came out with their lives.

As an illustration of how dangerous is the position of a color guard, and how badly a flag can be riddled with bullets, I present you with two specimens, one flag from each army. The first is the battle flag of the Forty-ninth Georgia Infantry. The spearhead is lashed to the staff with a piece of rope—bullet-embedded in the staff. The flag is inscribed with the names of the battles in which it was borne—Frazier's Farm, Cedar Run, Manassas, Fredericksburg, Chancellorsville, Seven Pines, Mechanicsville, Cold Harbor, Ox Hill, Harper's Ferry, Shepherdstown.

The second flag is that of the Second Wisconsin Infantry, of the famous Iron Brigade. It bears no device except the name of the regiment. This regiment, according to *Fox's Regimental Losses in the Civil War*, sustained the greatest percentage of loss of any in the entire Union army—19.7 per cent—and the brigade to which it belonged, according to its numbers, the heaviest of any of the war, the regimental loss being 238, and the brigade loss, 1,131. These two flags were indeed where the bullets fell the thickest.[83] — C. H. SMART

Union flag of the Second Wisconsin Infantry.

☛ "WELL-DONE, GOOD & FAITHFUL SERVANTS"

If the Confederate soldier was a hero in war, his virtues and manhood shone transcendent in peace. Returning to his desolate home or the charred remains of what was once the family domicile, broken in fortune, often in health, or suffering from wounds, he gathered his dependents around him, faced the future as he had faced his enemies in battle, and betook himself again to the struggle for existence. In spite of all the unfavorable conditions and the heavy burdens imposed by the [Liberal Yankee] Government, [here now in 1893] he has again become the astonishment of the civilization of his age.

These are the worthy sons of the sires who wrested this fair land from the despot's hand [Great Britain] and made the Federal Government rich and powerful and illustrious by their genius, patriotism and statesmanship, and inaugurated and maintained that higher order of civilization which began with our Washington and ended with our Lee. And if ever a similar era is to be restored to mankind it will be by the sons of soldiers of the lost cause, who inherit the qualities of head and heart of their patriot fathers.

Comrades, the history of the war is yet to be written, and in that future volume, when truth shall have been eliminated from error, the Confederate soldier will stand out in bold relief the peer of the battle-scarred veteran of the Roman phalanx with his hundred wounds in front, aye, worthy to wear upon his breast the red cross of the Legion of Honor, and in all the attributes of magnificent manhood prouder than the sceptered king upon his throne.

My brethren, *we have no apologies to make for our devotion to the lost cause.* So long as the kindling of life in our bosoms remain we will cherish its sacred memories, hallowed by the blood of our comrades who sleep beneath the shade of the trees on the banks of every river from Appomattox to the Rio Grande. And you, my friends, who have passed through this baptism of blood, and survived this tearful ordeal of fire, you, a small remnant of that patriot army which now sleeps on fame's eternal camping ground, you, who have met to-day to shake hands again, renew your former friendship and take steps to perpetuate the memories and preserve for future generations every name that belongs to the high roll of fame, and bequeath it as a rich legacy to your children, to every one of you, comrades, I would say, all hail! Some of you are full of years, and all of you covered with martial glory as with a mantle of light. If I cannot hail you as victors in the final outcome of the war, the world hails you as chiefest among its heroes. As we marched years ago, shoulder to shoulder, under the battle flag, and witnessed the harvest of death beneath us, so we to-day, by the blessing of heaven, march hand in hand under the banner of peace, acknowledging our allegiance to God, yielding obedience to law, and favoring such methods as tend to the prosperity of our country, the maintenance of law and order, and the elevation and refinement of society.

 As our ranks grow thinner and thinner, and when at length the last old Confederate is detailed for duty in the grand army above, and when we meet to answer the last roll call, may we hear the eternal fiat. Well done, good and faithful servant, soldier of the lost cause, soldier of the cross, enter thou into the joy of thy Lord![84] — CAPT. R. W. MINUS

☛ THE CONFEDERATE UNIFORM, AS TOLD BY A YANK
It is not generally known that the Confederate uniform was designed at West Point. It happened in this way: I was an instructor of artillery at the academy from May 1, 1859, to September, 1860. My quarters were in the east tower of the cadet barracks. [Soon-to-be-Confederate] Gen. Simon B. Buckner, who was Adjutant General of Kentucky, came here for the purpose of obtaining a new uniform for the troops of that State. We agreed that the handsomest uniform was the cadet gray. He and I worked on it for several days. I remember suggesting to him that there was a good opening in one of the [U.S.] departments for a relative of his, and that he received the information very coldly. Buckner went South, and the uniform we had decided upon became that of the Confederate army.[85] — UNION GEN. RUFUS SAXTON

☛ CONFEDERATE DEFIANCE
There was a fine illustration of Confederate independence, yet obedience, on the return of the Thirty-seventh North Carolina to their homes at the close of the war. They were in and on top of box cars, when the burden to one was breaking in the top and threatening serious disaster. Comrades in the car braced the roof, in a measure, and managed to stop the train. The conductor and engineer went back to the broken car and ordered the men to get down, but they guyed and

ridiculed the railroaders. The Federal officer in charge, who was riding in a passenger car, was appealed to, and he ordered the men to get down, but with like result. The hardy Confederates were defiant to the last. It was reckless of them to take such peril on their own account, but they were accustomed to peril, and there seemed to be a fascination in it to them. When their own commander, Colonel Johnson, realized the situation he said, "Come down, boys!" That was enough. In quicker time than it could be written they got off the broken car.

This story recalls a day in February, 1862, when my regiment was en route to St. Louis on the way to prison from Fort Donelson. That bitter, bitter cold weather will not be forgotten by those who suffered. The steamboats were making very poor headway against blocks of ice, large as houses. The 2,100 prisoners on the *Empress*, with but a single stove to warm by, quickly went to the south side, and very soon they careened the boat. Its  captain, fearing an explosion by the water running out of one side of the boiler, appealed to the men, urging that their lives were in peril, and begged them to move to the other side; but it was of no perceptible benefit. I remember that my only dread was the thought of going down into cold water. There was no dread of death. Our suffering had made us careless of life.[86] — UNKNOWN

☞ THE NAME OF LEE

Fellow citizens of the old commonwealth of Virginia, I come from the fair domain of the mother of statesmen and of Presidents! I come from the valley of the Shenandoah, the daughter of the stars. There the river flows, whispering the name of Lee, Lee, Lee. There the rivulets, flowing down the mountain sides to join the sweeping to the sea, whisper the name of Lee, Lee, Lee. And the northern plain, scarred by the fiery feet of the "god of war," look up to the blue canopy of heaven above and softly whispers the name of Lee, Lee, Lee.

I come from the eastern shore, where old ocean rolls in upon the land, and sun and sand and breeze and shore make glad the eye and heart, and when I ask what are the wild waves saying, the answer comes, Lee, Lee, Lee.

And so to-day, when I ask whose hand has been the guiding hand, whose spirit the controlling spirit, whose the heroic example that has brought the South up out of the valley of despair, out upon the fields of prosperity, enabling her to go forward seeking larger fields of success, greater realms of happiness, reply comes echoing down the corridors of time the name Lee, Lee, Lee.[87] — VIRGINIA SENATOR JOHN W. DANIEL

☛ THE EXAMPLE OF ROBERT E. LEE

. . . after the war, when the fact was established that Gen. Lee would not be molested by the Government, business proposals went to him from every direction—offers of light duties and large salaries. Some enthusiastic friends wanted him to take a European trip. All of these propositions he courteously but positively refused. It has been said that upon one occasion one of the General's daughters said to the committee, "You people don't offer father what he wants. If you will do that he will accept it." "What is it?" was the unanimous response. The answer was,

"work." The inspiration given by the daughter of Lee at that time was the power that has lifted the South up out of her rags and poverty, and is fast preparing her to assume her original position in the government—that is, providing largely over sixty per cent of the [entire country's] revenue.

It was not the paltry donation of twenty-five dollars by the "chief ruler" [Lincoln] of the nation that enabled Charleston to clear away the debris and rebuild her shattered walls caused by the shaking earth, it was the musical sound echoing down from Rockbridge's crown, work, work, work. It was not the loan of a few hundred tents and the gift of a few boxes of drugs that enabled the citizens to dispel the malaria, drive out the "black angel of death," and make Memphis one of the healthiest as well as one of the thriftiest of cities, it was the noble example set by Lee.

Persecuted by carpet-bagism, plundered by legislation, swept by cyclone and flood, scourged by disease and death, the South has come forth from the crucible unsullied and unspotted, and stands to day not only the peer but far outrivals all of her Anglo-Saxon sisters in all of the attributes that go to make man a law-abiding, country-loving and God-honoring subject.[88] — SUMNER A. CUNNINGHAM

☛ CAREER & FATE OF GEN. LLOYD TILGHMAN

During the memorable campaigns, extending from the construction and defense of Forts Henry and Donelson to the final investment of Vicksburg, but few Confederate generals were more prominent and more popular in the Western army than was Gen. Lloyd Tilghman, of Paducah, Ky. As a West Point educated soldier and officer, his ability and bravery were soon recognized. His skill and efficiency in the construction and his heroic defense of Fort Henry—especially on the 6th of February, 1862—marked him as an able commander and a brave man. In command of the troops in the fort only, and when the unequal attack came on the land forces made good their escape, but the brave Tilghman held the fort until nearly half his gunners were either killed or wounded. And when the victorious [Union] Commodore [Andrew Hull] Foote, with his armada of seven gunboats, took possession of Fort Henry he had as prisoners of war General Tilghman and staff and sixty men. But with this began a prominent career of General Tilghman. He did not remain a prisoner but a few months, and was exchanged most probably for an officer of equal rank captured by the Confederates at the battle of Shiloh. At all events, in the fall of 1862 he rejoined the Army of the West, then in North Mississippi, and was put in command of the First brigade of

Lloyd Tilghman, C.S.A.

[William Wing] Loring's division. At the battle of Corinth, Miss., he took a prominent part. Then in all the operations of that Mississippi army, first under command of General [Earl] Van Dorn, and then General [John Clifford] Pemberton, our General Tilghman bore a conspicuous part, up to the time of his death on the 16th of May, 1863. During the retreat of the army from Holly Springs to Grenada, Tilghman's brigade was assigned the responsible position of rear-guard, and repeatedly gave battle to and held in check the advancing forces of General Grant. It was during these days of trying service that General Tilghman had the misfortune to incur the displeasure of General Pemberton, and which that General continued to cherish, with jealous hatred added, up to the very day that the brave Tilghman was killed.

Bombardment of Fort Henry.

With these memories so prominent and distinct to the writer of these lines, it has always been a matter of regret that so little has been known and said of the faithful and gallant services, although short, of that grand specimen of the Southern soldier, and that so little notice of his death upon the battle-field has ever been given. So far as is known by the writer, no authentic or fair statement of the death of General Tilghman has been published, and this sketch is given in the hope that a fuller and more worthy notice of his services and his death may be given by some one better informed and more competent to the task.

Gen. Lloyd Tilghman was killed between 4 and 5 o'clock, on the evening of the 16th of May, 1863, on the battle-field of Baker's Creek, or Champion Hill. General Loring's division occupied the right of Pemberton's line; Tilghman's brigade, composed of two Mississippi regiments (15th and 22nd), 1st Louisiana, Rayburn's (Miss.) battalion and McLendon's battery, afterward known as Merrin's (Miss.) battery, occupied the extreme right. The first guns of that memorable battle were fired into this brigade early in the morning, but almost immediately the heavy fighting drifted to the left of our line.

John C. Pemberton, C.S.A.

For hours the enemy seemed to be in full force, and ready to advance upon us. [John Stevens] Bowen's division having been driven from its position, our division dropped back to keep in alignment with Bowen's, and soon after this, which was then sometime after midday, the enemy advanced in force, and was there held in check by Loring's division until night came on. After repulsing the enemy's first assault they threw forward their line of sharpshooters, and with their artillery on the main line, kept up the fight until dark. About 200 yards to the front, and a little to the left of our battery, there was a large farm house and a row of plantation cabins. These cabins were taken possession of by the enemy's sharpshooters, and they were picking our men off rapidly. General Tilghman directed the gun-sergeant to train his gun, a 12-pound howitzer, and dislodge the enemy from the cabins. He dismounted from his horse and gave some directions about sighting the gun. While this was being done a shell from one of the enemy's guns on the line exploded about fifty feet to the front. A ragged fragment of this shell struck the General in the breast, passing entirely through him and killing the horse of his Adjutant a little farther to the rear. His death occurred, of course, very soon, and his remains were carried to the rear. That night they were started to Vicksburg, accompanied by his personal staff and his son, Lloyd

Tilghman, Jr., and the next evening they were buried in the city cemetery in Vicksburg.

One more brief item, and I leave the subject for some abler pen. The dislike and jealous treatment of [by] General Pemberton, to which I have alluded, annoyed General Tilghman very much all the spring of 1863. General Loring was the close friend of General Tilghman, and stood as a breakwater between the two men. But on the 15th of May, the day before the battle of Baker's Creek, and not two hours in advance of the fulsome order to "prepare to meet the enemy," came an order from General Pemberton relieving General Tilghman of his command, and directing the senior Colonel of the brigade to take its command.

Here was a pretty kettle of fish. The whole army right close up, face to face, with Grant's army, twice or three times as strong, and our officers all in a stew.

General Loring again cut the Gordeon knot. The next morning, even after the enemy had disturbed our early repast, this one-armed General rode squarely up to the pompous Pemberton and, in language more forcible than elegant, more caustic than clever, informed the "General Commanding that unless he then and there revoked the order of the day before in reference to General Tilghman that he might dispense with his (Loring's) services for that day's

William W. Loring, C.S.A.

battle." And then it was that an order was hastily written—on the pummel of a saddle, I believe—restoring General Tilghman to his command, and to one more day's faithful, brave service for the Confederacy, and before the sun went down on that day he yielded up his life for the cause he believed just and holy.

It is a well-known fact of history that in the terrific bombardment of Fort Henry by Commodore Foote, with his flotilla of seven gun-boats, and after a large number of the gunners within the Fort had been killed, either by the enemy or the explosion of two heavy guns of our own, that General Tilghman assisted with his own hands in manning the guns of the fort. So is it also true that the last act of this brave man was to sight a field gun, and direct the cutting of a shell fuse, so as to do the best execution upon the invaders of his country.[89] — F. W. M.

☛ AN EXPERT SHARPSHOOTER

During the war, when the Federal troops occupied Franklin, Tenn., a [Union] picket force was kept on the Carter's Creek pike, about two and a half miles out, at the head of Campbell's lane. A Confederate scout and sharpshooter, who rode a gray horse and carried a long gun on his shoulder, was in the habit of coming from the west of the pike across the fields and quietly getting in shooting range and firing on the picket and then [would] dash away across the country, making his escape. On at least one occasion one of the [Union] pickets was shot from his horse, as the lady, who was then a little girl, tells me. She says the picket in every instance fled to the town, and soon a [Yankee] company would come out to the pike looking for the rebels. These attacks of this one rebel occurred frequently, and the [Confederate] family in the brick cottage got in the habit of looking out for the soldier on the gray horse. Some years after the war a son of this family was in Arkansas, and by chance met this soldier who rode the gray horse, and he took delight in telling of his adventures with the Federal picket on the Carter's Creek pike near Franklin.[90] — W. A. C.

☛ GEN. EDMUND KIRBY SMITH'S CAMPAIGN IN KENTUCKY

[The following are] the recollections of a boy soldier of the Confederacy as to the Kentucky campaign of General Kirby Smith. July, 1862, the army of General Bragg was transferred from Tupelo, Miss., to Chattanooga by rail, and after a day or so at the latter place, the famous old "Granite" Brigade, commanded by Gen. Patrick R. Cleburne, of which I was a member, along with the brigade of Gen. Preston Smith, were sent to Knoxville, Tenn., where we first saw our new commander. A short time was spent in cooking rations and storing our camp equipage, for on that campaign we bivouacked under the blue sky. Cleburne's Brigade consisted of the Second, Fifth, Thirty-fifth and Forty-eighth Tennessee Infantry and the Fifteenth Arkansas. Smith's Brigade consisted of five Tennessee regiments, both brigades being commanded by General Cleburne as a division, together with Churchill's

Division, embracing the brigades of Ecton and McNair, the former consisting of Arkansas troops, while the latter hailed from the Lone Star State. These four brigades commenced their toilsome march from Knoxville about August 1st, and nothing of interest transpired until we reached the Cumberland Mountains at Wheeler's Gap. When we were making the ascent the horse of Adjutant Fowler, of the Second Tennessee, got into a bees nest and rushed through the brigade riderless, over sleeping men, almost stampeding both the Second and Forty-eighth Regiments.

Preston Smith, C.S.A.

We passed rapidly to the rear of Cumberland Gap to assist Stevenson's Division in defeating the garrison there, but we nearly starved ourselves in that sterile mountainous region. From here we marched toward Lexington to be within striking distance of the main army under General Bragg. At Barboursville we were joined by three cavalry regiments—First Georgia, First Louisiana and Fourth Tennessee (Starnes'). At London, Ky., our cavalry captured a part of Houck's Second Tennessee federal Infantry. From there we passed on to Big Hill and camped. We had just stacked arms when Metcalfe's and Munday's cavalry regiments had the temerity to charge into our camp, but one fusillade from the first battalion of the Forty-eighth put to inglorious flight all that we did not unhorse. Next morning we marched about five miles up the pike toward Richmond, when we filed to the right in an open field and formed in line of battle, our battery passing up the hill in front. We moved the Forty-eighth, my regiment, in its immediate rear and to support it, and in quick time the first of the three engagements that constituted the battle of Richmond, Ky., was on, and the loud mouthed dogs of war were unleashed. Our battery was soon engaged with two six-gun batteries of the enemy, and right nobly did they sustain themselves. One after another was being carried to the rear disabled and torn by shot and shell until their Captain called for volunteers from our regiment to supply their places. Just then a young man from a farm near by came upon the field and asked to be assigned to duty. Col. Ben Hill, Brigade Commander, sent him forward to the battery. In a little while

Edmund K. Smith, C.S.A.

he dropped back with an ounce Scharpnel ball imbedded in his shoulder, but the gallant boy would not leave the field until ordered to the rear by Colonel Nixon. Looking back to the rear on an eminence I saw General Smith and staff, and wondered why he would hold us there where we could not strike a blow and be punished by exploding shell. General Cleburne was shot square in the mouth that cost him several of his teeth, and Col. Lucius E. Polk, our subsequent commander, was as wild as a march hare from a wound in the top of his head. But our grand commander's strategy showed itself. A wild, tumultuous yell, a crash of musketry, and Preston Smith's Brigade had taken them in flank. Here Colonel Fitzgerald, of the One Hundred and Fifty-fourth Tennessee, fell, and then brave old Ben Hill in loud tones shouted, "Forward! double quick!" and right eagerly did our command rush forward and down the hill to join in the battle with our comrades on the right. Just as we reached the pike a full volley of cannister from one of the enemy's batteries went above our heads, sounding like an immense covey of birds on wing. Our skirmishers' well aimed rifles on their cannoneers were effective, and their rout was soon complete. For four miles we gave chase, skirmishing with their rearguard until we reached Zion Church. There they formed for fight, but a determined rush by the old Forty-eighth, supported on the left by the Second and on the right by the Thirty-fifth, caused them to leave their position precipitately, and then again we took up the chase. On the outskirts of the town, through the cemetery, a contiguous cornfield and a grove of walnut trees, [Union General William] "Bull" Nelson, who had arrived with his division and what remained of [Mahlon Dickerson] Manson's and Krauft's commands, deployed to receive us. We quickly formed our lines and moved on the cemetery, and in twenty minutes one hundred and forty men of the Second and one hundred and twenty-eight of the Forty-eighth were killed and wounded. They bore the brunt of the battle. It was here the peerless Dick Butler, commander of the Second Tennessee, adored by his regiment and beloved by the whole brigade, gave up his life for the cause he loved so well. In ascending the hill to the cemetery a grape-shot struck Colonel Nixon in the left Breast, smashing his watch and striking a copy of the Testament in his breast pocket, which saved his life; our old commander, a veteran from Mexico, staggered a few paces backward, plunged forward on his hands, but struggling to his knees, loud above the din of battle shouted, "Forward, Forty-eighth!" Over into the cemetery we went. Here I plainly saw General Nelson trying to rally his men. But they could not withstand our onslaught, and pell-mell, without alignment, they rushed into the streets of Richmond, closely pursued by the victorious Confederates. At the outer edge of the town they were confronted by our cavalry and Ecton's Arkansans, when they threw down their arms and in a body surrendered. The fruits of our victory were nearly seven thousand prisoners, as many small arms, sixteen pieces of artillery and two Brigadier-Generals. This battle occurred August 30, which was a very hot day.[91] — ROBERT M. FRIERSON

☛ MAGNIFICENT CONFEDERATE FIGHTING

As one advances in the study of the battle of Chickamauga he must, at every step, become more and more impressed with the magnificence of the Confederate fighting. Since the first assertion that Chickamauga was for both sides the bloodiest battle of the war, in proportion to numbers and the time of the engagement, and that it far outranked in the percentage of killed and wounded any of the battles of modern Europe, there has been an industrious searching of records, both of our own war and of recent famous foreign campaigns, to test the accuracy of the claims made for Chickamauga. But the further the investigation has proceeded, and it is now sufficiently completed to allow general results to be stated with certainty, the more clearly the truth of the first assertion has been made to appear. It is not strange, therefore, that the discussions of the past year, which have served to dispel so many of the misapprehensions which clouded the public mind in regard to this battle, and dwarfed it in the history of the country, should have created such widespread interest in its real history, and raised it at once to the very front rank of our most notable engagements.

The marvel of German fighting in the great battle of Mars la Tour was performed by the 3rd Westphalian regiment. It suffered the heaviest loss in the German army during the Franco-Prussian war. It went into the battle 3,000 strong, and its loss was 49.4 per cent. There was nothing in the campaigns of which this formed a part which exceeded these figures, and they became famous throughout the German army.

And yet in our war there were over sixty regiments whose losses exceeded this, seventeen of them just above sixty per cent, and quite a number ranged from seventy to eighty per cent. There were over a score of regiments on each side at Chickamauga whose loss exceeded that of the Westphalian regiment.

But the object of this letter is more particularly to set forth the character of the splendid fighting performed by every portion of Bragg's army on this noted field in Georgia.

The battle of Saturday opened in front of General [John Milton] Brannan, on the extreme Confederate right, and here a brigade of Forrest's cavalry, dismounted, assisted almost immediately by Confederate infantry, assaulted the Union lines. As they were driven back by an overwhelming fire they were continuously reinforced for nearly four hours. The battle was continuous and constantly at short range. In fact, it was a distinguished feature of the whole two days' battle that most of the fighting was at close range, much of it hand to hand, with the bayonet and clubbed muskets. Forrest's men in front of Brannan

Edward C. Walthall, C.S.A.

assaulted time and again, marching up into the very faces of the Union infantry, and in their final effort came on four lines deep, with their hats drawn down over their faces, and bending forward against the storm of lead as men face the elements. The rapid fire of long and well-trained infantry seemed to have no effect upon these veterans, and it was not until they had marched up into the line of fire of batteries, which, with double-shotted canister, enfiladed their ranks at a murderous range, that their advance was checked. Even here they stood and fought with desperation. [Matthew Duncan] Ector and [Claudius Charles] Wilson of [William Henry Talbot] Walker's division, and [Edward Cary] Walthall and [Daniel Chevillette] Govan of [St. John Richardson] Liddell's, all marching to the assistance of those contending in this hell of battle, became, in turn, as hotly engaged themselves in front of [Absalom] Baird, and for hours on this portion of the field the scene just described on the extreme Confederate right was repeated for all of these brigades. At the first onset Walthall and Govan drove their lines over the flank of the regular brigade and captured its battery, only to be themselves pushed back again almost at the point of the bayonet, and so shattered from their own courageous exposure at short range as to be practically put out of the fight for several hours. Nothing could exceed the valor of these troops. There was nothing in the way of desperate fighting either of infantry or artillery which they were not called upon to face. And they did face it with a courage seldom equalled, and which it was impossible to surpass.

. . . [Benjamin Franklin] Cheatham, moving to the support of Walker, turned on Johnson with irresistible fore, and drove him well backward toward the LaFayette road, when Palmer arriving on [Richard W.] Johnson's right, these two divisions, acting in concert, drove Cheatham back a mile, and badly shattered his entire command. Next came [John Bell] Hood with [Evander McIvor] Law and Bushrod [Rust] Johnson's divisions and one brigade of [William] Preston's, and these grappled with [Jefferson Columbus] Davis, Wood and Sheridan along lines of battle that at times were scarcely two musket lengths apart, and thus till sundown this contest raged in the thick woods between the LaFayette road and the Chickamauga, each line bending backward as the other delivered its heaviest blows, and as if gathering strength by the recoil, in almost every instance, rushing forward again to sway the opposite backward in turn. There was no general stampede on either side at any point of the first day's battle, but weight of lines and weight of metal, and the momentum of blows vigorously delivered controlled the result at every point.

Henry D. Clayton, C.S.A.

Late in the evening Saturday, when the fighting on the flanks had well nigh ceased, came [Alexander Peter] Stewart's division of [William Brimage] Bate's, [Henry DeLamar] Clayton's and [John Calvin] Brown's brigades, pounding its way past the flanks of two Union divisions, and, doubling back the flank of a third, they penetrated beyond the LaFayette road. Before its brave career was checked it had well nigh divided the Union line. It is easy to see that over all this extended area of bitter and continuous fighting the loss must have been terrific. The figures to be presented below will make the character of this fighting, to which reference has thus been made in most inadequate terms, more clearly understood. But stubborn, terrific and deadly as was the Confederate fighting of Saturday, it became but ordinary performance when compared with the marvellous exhibition of courage and endurance which were exhibited in that army on Sunday before the Union breastworks about the Kelley farm, and upon the slopes of Snodgrass Hill and the Horseshoe Ridge.

The Union line about the Kelley farm was established on the crest of a low ridge sheltered by heavy woods, and the troops were protected in their position by a low breastwork of logs and rails varying from two to four feet in height. Time and again from 10 o'clock till 2, the whole right wing of the Confederate army rolled its lines in on the slight works in continual breakers, only to be shattered and driven back as the waves of the waves of the ocean go to pieces on the beach; brigade after brigade dashed themselves against the salient of this low work, to be shattered and broken, and to retire with a loss so great that after 2 o'clock, and throughout most of the afternoon, the right wing of the Confederate line had so much weakened itself by its brilliant, tremendous, and yet ineffective fighting as to be practically incapable of further effort until much time had been consumed in reorganization. But even this fighting, persistent and marvellous as it had been, was surpassed by the wonderful assaults of Longstreet's wing throughout the afternoon upon the ridges held by Wood, Brannan and [James Blair] Steedman.

Benjamin H. Helm, C.S.A.

Thomas C. Hindman Jr. and his children.

For an hour after the break took place in the Union line on Sunday the entire Confederate army was assaulting the Union position. Breckinridge's division, with [Benjamin Hardin] Helm, Adams and [Marcellus Augustus] Stovall, was turning the Union left and had moved far into its rear, but Helm's brigade, striking the salient of Baird's position, had been effectually shattered, its commander killed and some of his regiments almost annihilated. [States Rights] Gist and [Alfred Holt] Colquitt of Walker's had fought with the same fierceness and the same want of success. Stewart, in front of Reynolds and Brannan, with his three magnificent brigades of Bate, Clayton and Brown, had pushed into the very face of the Union line, but still found themselves unable to carry the low works before them. At the same time Law's division of Longstreet had rushed upon the front of Harker, moving across open ground and under heavy enfilading fire of Frank Smith's regiment battery, and up almost to the muzzles of the infantry's rifles. In this movement Kershaw supported Hood and thus the Union troops on the right had the full view and full experience of the fighting of Longstreet's veterans, Bushrod [Rust] Johnson in front of Brannan, [Thomas Carmichael] Hindman before Steedman, with Preston's strong brigades as a reserve, alternately assisting on one point and then on another of the ridge—all these covered its long slope almost continuously from noon till dark with the lines of assaulting columns. The splendor of such fighting as this is enhanced many fold by the fact that from the beginning to the end it was unsuccessful. Ordinary soldiers can be carried forward in battle so long as success attends their movement, but a test of manhood, of soldierly ability, of courage and endurance, which it is difficult to measure and which cannot be overestimated, comes when through a long

States R. Gist, C.S.A.

afternoon, assault after assault, seemingly in overwhelming numbers, has failed and when the whole line of each succeeding advance and retreat is thickly strewn with dead and wounded and all the terrible wreck of battle.

To say that in the face of such experiences the Confederate lines were rallied quickly after every repulse and brought forward again to new and ever vigorous assaults over slopes thus covered with horrors, is to all that can be said in praise of the valor of the officers who directed and the soldiers who executed these marvellous storming parties.

Bushrod R. Johnson, C.S.A.

Turning to the figures of loss in independent commands, they will be found to show that this praise of the Confederate fighting is in no sense exaggerated. In truth, language cannot exaggerate it. . . .

No ordinary comment could emphasize the story of valor and endurance which such figures tell. And while it is impossible for those [Yanks] who fought to save [that is, destroy] the Union[92] to look with any more complacency upon the cause in defense of which such heroism as this was displayed, men everywhere must admire such exhibitions of manhood and no American can fail to cherish a certain degree of pride in the fact that men of his own race and nation were equal to such endeavors on the battle-fields.[93] — *CINCINNATI COMMERCIAL GAZETTE*

☛ POINT LOOKOUT PRISON REMINISCENCES

Albert W. Traylor was a private in Company E, 21st Va. Infantry, Terry's Brigade, Gordon's Division, A. N. V., stationed at Camp Ewell, and was captured before Petersburg on March 25, 1865, when Gordon made a brilliant but unsuccessful assault against the enemy's right. He was imprisoned at Point Lookout and held there for seventy-two days after the surrender at Appomattox, his parole bearing date June 21, 1865.

The number of prisoners taken exceeded, perhaps, 1,500. Officers and privates were separated, and after the usual formalities of marching from one headquarters to another to be listed, counted, weighed and prepared for shipment, which proceeding consumed the entire day, the privates were all loaded in and upon box and flat cars and taken to City Point, where they were that night herded in a pen, like so many cattle, and in the morning given a cup of coffee and a piece of bread a each, marched on board a boat and shipped to Point Lookout.

This cape, or promontory, is situated at the mouth of the Potomac, having that river on the south and west, and Chesapeake Bay on the east. The area of this prison comprised probably twenty-five acres, inclosed by a strong plank fence about sixteen feet high, with a guard walk or parapet. It was used as a prison during the greater part of the war, and had, as he understood at the time of his imprisonment more than twenty thousand inmates, who were lodged in tents that covered the entire inclosure except the passageways, or "streets," as they were called, seven men being quartered in an "A" tent, which occupied a space of seven square feet. The tents were without floors, no straw was provided, and unless a prisoner was so fortunate as to have saved his blanket or oilcloth he was obliged to sleep on the bare ground. They were set apart by divisions, like the wards of a city, and the daily routine consisted of roll-call about six o'clock, a pint tin cup of coffee, and about half a loaf of baker's bread, which was of excellent quality, with a raw piece of codfish or mackerel served to each prisoner as they marched in divisions by the "cookhouse" about eight or nine o'clock, and the same tin cup of pea or bean soup, with the same quantity of bread, and a small piece of corn beef or salt pork, similarly served, about one or two o'clock. This constituted a day's "rations," and while it never was, perhaps, satisfactory, it was so much better, and, for the most part, so much more than they had for some time previously been able to secure in the army camps, that the murmuring was not so great as might have been expected, and no man suffered for food. Maj. A. J. Brady, of the United States Army, was then Provost Marshal or Commandant of the prison, and is especially remembered by Mr. Traylor as a man of good temper and kind heart. His tribute to his character was indeed a glowing one, and he concluded by saying that it would even yet afford him pleasure to go to any inconvenience to do him honor, if alive, or to do reverence to his memory, if dead, adding that Major Brady's consideration in the treatment of the unfortunates there imprisoned did more than any other one thing to prepare him for acceptance in proper spirit the results of the war.

Religious services were conducted by the men in some part of the prison almost daily, and by ministers from Baltimore and Washington on Sundays. Thousands were baptized by immersion in the Chesapeake Bay. A thriving business was done by some of those for whom the food allowance was unsatisfactory, in washing the clothing of their fellows, the pay being a part of the rations of the one served. Petty thefts of rations, etc., were common and fisticuffs frequent, but the punishments were never harsh or severe.[94] — SUMNER A. CUNNINGHAM

☛ FIRST CAPTURE OF FEDERALS AT SEA

At the meeting of Columbia County Camp No. 150, Confederate Veterans, at Lake City, Fla., on the 17th of August, the name was changed to E. A. Perry Camp, in honor of the late Governor [Edward Aylesworth] Perry, who so bravely commanded the Florida brigade in the Army of Northern Virginia.

. . . This camp has the original flag presented to the Columbia Rifles, in 1861, under which the first capture of Federals was made by Confederates on the sea. The capture was made off Cedar Keys, July 3, 1861, [Union] Lieutenant Seldon and Eighth Marines. The old flag was left at home by the company after a regimental flag for the Second Florida was obtained. Funds are being raised for the [Jefferson] Davis monument, and to purchase the Confederate Home in Jacksonville.[95] — SUMNER A. CUNNINGHAM

☛ A CONFEDERATE PRISONER TAKES ON A UNION GENERAL

[Union General Ambrose E. Burnside] had dismounted and was seated on a camp-stool, and was surrounded by [U.S.] negro guards. The [Confederate] prisoners were halted at the line of guards, and the officer in charge announced to the General that they had captured the colonel of a regiment, many officers and men, three flags, and several pieces of artillery. Rising from his seat General Burnside approached us, and addressing me, inquired what regiment I commanded, and being informed that it was a Tennessee regiment, he asked from what part of the state. "From East Tennessee," I replied. With an expression of astonishment, General Burnside said, "It is very strange that you should  be fighting us when three-fourths of the people of East Tennessee are on our side." Feeling the rebuke unjust and unbecoming an officer of his rank and position, I replied, with as much spirit as I dare manifest, "Well, General, we have the satisfaction of knowing, that if three-fourths of our people are on your side, that the respectable people are on our side." At this the General flew into a rage of passion and railed at me, "You are a liar, you are a liar, sir, and you know it." I replied, "General, I am a prisoner and you have the power to abuse me as you please, but as to respectability that is a matter of opinion. We regard no man respectable who deserts his county and takes up arms against his own people." To this General Burnside replied, "I've been in East Tennessee, I was at Knoxville, I know those people, and when you say that such men as Andrew Johnson, [William Gannaway] Brownlow, [Elisha] Baxter, [Oliver Perry] Temple, [John] Netherland and others are not respectable, you lie, sir, and you will have to answer for it." At this point I expected he would order me shot by his negro guards, but he continued. "Not to any human power, but to a higher power." With a feeling of relief I answered, "O, General, I am ready to take that responsibility." "Take him on, take him on," the General shouted to our guards, and thence we were marched some two or three miles toward City Point . . .[96] — COL. ABRAM FULKERSON

☛ A CONFEDERATE RESPONSE TO YANKEE LIES
[In the following brief essay a Confederate defends Dixie against the common and typically mean-spirited Yankee refrain that "the Civil War has civilized the South where all was crimes and fetters." L.S.]

The South planned first the co-operation and consolidation of the [American] Colonies; Patrick Henry sounded the key note of Independence; Thomas Jefferson wrote the Declaration; a Southern

Colony emblazoned first on her standard, " Virginia for Constitutional Liberty." A Southerner [Washington] led the armies of the Revolution to victory, and it was Southern intellect and patriotism [mainly that of James Madison] that planned the Federal Constitution, and finally brought about consolidation. To the South is due that Texas is not now a hostile government; that Louisiana is not a French republic, and that the majestic Mississippi is all in our own land. The old South led in the council chamber, in the field, and to battle. *How can the Northern people bring charges so infamous against such a record of loyalty and patriotism?*

The South was not responsible for slavery nor eager for its perpetuation. The first nation on the civilized globe to protest against it as monstrous was a Southern Colony. Virginia twenty-three times protested to the [British] Crown in public acts of her Assembly, and in 1778 passed a law absolutely forbidding the further importation of slaves.

On the other hand, slavery received its first legislative sanction by the Commonwealth of Massachusetts.

The prohibition of the slave trade was finally brought about through the influence of President Jefferson and the active efforts of the Virginians.

The North led with plans of gradual emancipation, because slavery was not profitable there; but in the South as well, societies for abolition and colonization were organized. Naturally the South moved slowly, for to her people the problem was a vital one, the number of slaves in Virginia alone being seven times as great as in the entire North. . .

Civil war was the result. The North had the backing of the resources and sentiment of the world, besides overwhelming odds in battle; and *for four years the South baffled an army that could have withstood the universe.*

The war left the South exhausted to the last degree. The ragged, half-starved Confederate soldier, crushed with defeat, returned to his once happy and beautiful home to find his house in ruins, his farm devastated, his slaves free, his stock killed, his barns empty, his trade destroyed, and his money worthless.

The North took advantage of this helpless condition, and under the euphemism of reconstruction made an attempt to destroy the South. She was dismembered, disfranchised, denationalized, and turned into military provinces. Besides the war having rendered to the torch and sword three billion dollars' worth of property, she has been robbed from her poverty of a billion dollars in twenty years to pension Northern soldiers. [Pro-South Virginian and President Woodrow Wilson's Ambassador to Italy] *Thomas Nelson Page is reported to have made this* strong statement: *"It was intended that the South should be no more."* But God called her forth with the old spirit; she resumed her youth like the eagle, fixed her gaze upon the sun, and once more spreading her pinions, lifted herself for another flight.

Steps must be taken to preserve from oblivion, or worse, from misrepresentation, a civilization which produced, as its natural fruit, Washington and Jefferson, Lee and Jackson. Their stories must be told and their deeds must be sung through the ages—not what its enemies thought it to be, but what in truth it was.

Thomas N. Page.

We are not willing to be handed down to the coming generation as a race of slave-drivers and traitors. So let the North lay aside her prejudice and hatred, and seek the truth instead. She should reveal that the [Southern] Cavalier, as well as the [Northern] Puritan, was on the continent from the earliest days, and has been the most conspicuous element in its progress and its freedom. She should admit that the South has a heart of feeling and honor, and is worthy of justice.[97] — ARTHUR MARSHALL

☛ HOW MARYLAND "REBELS" VIEWED THE WAR IN 1893

We have no ex-Confederate societies, but several large, strong, and active Confederate societies. We have never mixed in any manner with the other side—have no joint reunions, no joint banquets, no decoration or memorial days in common. In fact, we do not mix, we go our way and they go theirs, and we find we gain more respect by so doing. We do not belong to that class of Confederates that *believed* [past tense] they were right. *We knew we were right in 1861, we knew we were right when the war closed, and we know today that we were right.*[98] — WILLIAM H. POPE

☛ CHARGE ON FORT SANDERS AT KNOXVILLE

In November, 1863, Longstreet, with the two divisions (Hood's and McLaws') which he had brought with him from Virginia to aid Bragg in the battle of Chickamauga, left the vicinity of Chattanooga for Knoxville, where we were to meet again our old friend and former opponent, General Burnside, of Fredericksburg fame.

We marched through the country, and crossed the Tennessee River at the little town of Loudon. From there to Knoxville we had to contest every foot of the way with [Union] Col. Frank Woolford's Kentucky cavalry. They had long range repeating rifles. Besides, they were hard fighters—so hard that when we got in sight of the city we had to double team on them with both infantry and artillery before we could run them in.

John B. Magruder, C.S.A.

We succeeded, but there stood Fort Sanders in all its terror, looming up on the horizon, right in our path. It bristled with cannon, and was well supported by infantry inside and out. But something had to be done, and there was little time to parley. True, we had Burnside shut up in the city, but Sherman with another army was coming in our rear. We had either to take the fort, or move on to greener pastures. You see the dilemma. In front of the fort a deep moat, abatis, wires stretched, rifle pits, vidette holes, and all kinds of impediments to obstruct our approach. Of course, we privates knew nothing of what was going on in the minds of the generals (good thing, I reckon), but we didn't have to wait long.

So much in reference to the whole command. Now for the part taken by our brigade.

We had two young colonels in the brigade. [Kennon] McElroy of the Thirteenth Mississippi, as brave and as gallant an officer as ever drew sword. I had known him at the University of Mississippi. As a soldier, in style and manner, he reminded me of what the old West Pointers used to say of our General [John Bankhead] Magruder when he was a cadet there, "a beau ideal." The other was [John C.] Fizer of the Seventeenth, just as good and true.

On the night of the 29th of November, about dark, General Humphreys sent us orders to prepare for action. The orders ran about thus: "The Eighteenth and Twenty-first Regiments will charge and take all the pickets between our front and the fort at midnight. At daylight in the morning, the Thirteenth and Seventeenth will charge over you and

William T. Wofford, C.S.A.

take the fort." He said he selected the two young colonels that they might win new laurels. We of the Eighteenth and Twenty-first didn't raise any howling objection to it, either. Our orders were for each captain to select a man to carry the picks and spades of the company with which to hide ourselves in the ground when we got near enough to the fort. Of course there were other troops—[Joseph Brevard] Kershaw's South Carolina on our right, and [William Tatum] Wofford's Georgia on our left—preparing for the same thing; but being only a captain in the line, I tell what I saw and know.

The hour of twelve came. We were at the appointed place, drawn up in skirmish line, so that as we neared the fort we would not crowd each other by concentration. The stars shone brightly and the ground was freezing rapidly. My only lieutenant was sick in camp, but I walked along the line and told the boys to meet me on the other side of those yankee picket lines under that fort, and it would be all right. I am thus particular, because it was the only real night charge we ever made.

At the command we moved forward through brush, briers, and thorns, in the face of the picket firing, capturing or driving all the pickets into the fort, and getting pretty close to the fort itself. Then came the fun, if there is any fun in such things. I called for my pick and spade man, and true to his trust here was my faithful Irishman, Pat Burns, with his arms full of the implements, in addition to his fighting accoutrements. The line was marked the full length of the regiment for our earth work. Then you ought to have seen the fire fly out of those rocks. The enemy in the fort, only a few rods off, tried to depress their guns so as to shell us, but every shell went over our heads, and served only to add increased zest to the work. We had to get into that ground before day, and we did.

We had accomplished our part of the contract, and were prepared to hold the position taken, and being so close to the fort, we could aid our assaulting friends from the rear, till they passed over us, by picking off the gunners in the fort.

At the dawn of day up came the two gallant regiments, steady and determined. Fizer of the Seventeenth, with a hatchet buckled on to his sword belt, with which he had vowed beforehand to cut down the tall flag-staff on top of the fort, and McElroy of the Thirteenth, the very picture of chivalry, were at the head of their respective regiments. They moved quietly till they passed over us and our embankment, then with the rebel yell they rushed for the fort. It was as grand a charge as I ever saw, but success was impossible under the circumstances, and ought to have been foreseen before the attempt was made.

The assaulting force was composed of regiments from different brigades, with no general officer in immediate command. These regiments, instead of moving on parallel lines till they enveloped the fort, began to converge from the start; so when they got to the deep ditch or moat at the base of the fort, they were in the condition of Napoleon's Old Guard at the battle of Waterloo, when they came to the sunken road of Ohain. They knew nothing of it till they came suddenly upon it; hence, they rushed headlong into it. There was no help for it. Companies and regiments were so mixed and jumbled it was utterly impossible for the officers to tell their men from others. It was in the midst of this confusion that Colonel McElroy got back out of the ditch and asked a Georgia colonel on his left to move his regiment further to the left, in order to make room for his Mississippi regiment. The Georgia colonel (I forget his name), a brave and good man, questioned the right of an officer of his own rank to command him. Neither knew which ranked the other. They were discussing the matter in pretty sharp terms, when they were both shot down in their tracks. Lieutenant-Colonel O'Brien of the Thirteenth, a brother-in-law of Gov. W. G. Brownlow, was captured. Major George Donald, of the same regiment, another old college mate, narrowly escaped with his life, by running the gauntlet of the "whistling minies" from the fort to our embankment.

In the meantime Colonel Fizer had had a little better success. True to his purpose, with hatchet in hand, he had climbed to the top of the parapet, and was making for the flag-staff, when a ball shattered his arm, and he rolled back into the ditch. Many more tried the same thing, and I think a few got over, but never to return. A close inspection showed the face of the fort too steep to climb.

It was a short, but one of the most desperate struggles of the war, and deserved better success. Had either one of the brigades, Kershaw's, Humphreys' or Wofford's, tried it, I shall always think it could have been taken.[99] — W. GART JOHNSON

☛ FORT SUMTER—CAREER OF COL. ALFRED MOORE RHETT
Alfred Moore Rhett, born in Beaufort, S.C., October 18, 1829, was the second child of Senator Robert Barnwell Rhett. In his youth he was singularly attractive by his amiability and gay, bright spirits. In unselfishness he was ever conspicuous; at the same time his coolness and utter fearlessness in danger were already his striking characteristics. He graduated at Harvard University in July, 1851. On the last day of December, 1860, he was commissioned First Lieutenant Company B Battalion, South Carolina Artillery. April 12-13, 1861, he was in command of the Sumter Battery, in Fort Moultrie. His guns were most ably handled,

Battle of Fort Sumter.

and on the second day they fired the officers' quarters in Sumter with forty rounds of red-hot shot, forcing [Union] Major [Robert] Anderson to evacuate the fort. Rhett's company was then transferred to Sumter, and on April 18th he was promoted to Captain, and was in command of the work.

Colonel Rhett commanded at Fort Sumter April 7, 1863, when [Union] Admiral [Samuel Francis] Dupont made the great naval attack in Charleston Harbor. He had a garrison of five hundred officers and men of the regular artillery which had been raised to a regiment. At the opening of the tremendous engagement Colonel Rhett ordered the regimental band to the ramparts to greet the enemy with [the song] "Dixie." He himself stood upon the southeast angle of the fort, nearest the fleet, and had the flags of the Confederacy, his State and regiment raised and saluted by thirteen guns. During this engagement forty guns in Sumter were in use, and in two hours and forty-five minutes the battle was fought and won. The great "Ironsides" and fleet of Monitors withdrew signally defeated. One of them sank the next morning by the Morris Island shore. The ships had been struck five hundred and twenty times by the guns from the Confederate fortifications. The guns and mortars of Sumter were hotly engaged after this day and night against [Union] General [Quincy Adams] Gillmore in his efforts to take Morris Island, who in his report characterized the fire from Sumter as "accurate and destructive." When Gillmore finally established his breaching batteries four hundred yards from Sumter, with the declared intention of destroying the work, Colonel Rhett said, "Gillmore will silence us, but I will fight the fort low down." Then began that most terrible bombardment, lasting from April 17th until September 2nd, in which time 6,828 shot and shell, of size and destructive qualities hitherto unknown in the annals of war, were hurled upon Fort Sumter. There were no earthworks at this time within the walls, which in the after bombardments gave great protection to the garrison. There was therefore no place of safety, and the immense walls were crushed in and fell, the great guns were dismounted and disabled, some being pitched backward

Interior of Ft. Sumter during bombing.

from the top of the high parapet to the parade ground below. The shaking and jarring, the hideous noise, the continual danger, never ceasing day or night, Fort Sumter became a ruin, with not one gun left with which to fight. Colonel Rhett was strongly recommended by General Beauregard, and was promoted to the command of a brigade, the command to include the Fort Sumter garrison. His headquarters were then in Charleston, but he visited Fort Sumter nearly every day. He was almost constantly under fire, giving anxious attention to the work being carried on there for the protection of the garrison.

After the evacuation of Charleston, in General [William Joseph]

Hardee's march to North Carolina, Colonel Rhett commanded the rear guard, which consisted of the First Regiment South Carolina Artillery, the First South Carolina Infantry, Lucas' Battalion Artillery, and Maj. A. Barnet Rhett's Battalion of Field Artillery.

In the battle of Averysboro Colonel Rhett was taken prisoner. Both his Adjutant and his staff officer were sick, and he rode forward alone into the woods and in rain and fog to seek [Wade] Hampton's command, which he wished to support his left flank. A squad of Federal cavalry which had lost their way and got into the Confederate lines, being enveloped in waterproof cloaks, were mistaken by him for some of Hampton's men, and he rode straight up to them. They covered him at once with their carbines, and he became their prisoner. He was carried to Fort Delaware, and was only released in August, 1865.

Colonel Rhett was a "magnificent disciplinarian." Strict, but always just, he won the affection and confidence of the men and officers under his command. He exercised a constant care of his men, never uselessly exposing them, though unhesitatingly exposing himself to danger and sparing himself no fatigue.[100] —UNKNOWN

☞ VIVID REMINISCENCES OF FRANKLIN

I participated in [the battle of Franklin II, November 30, 1864] as a private soldier in Twenty-fourth Tennessee, the right regiment of Gen. Strahl's Brigade. Gen. [Samuel Gibbs] French is correct as to [William Wing] Loring commanding the right division of Stewart's Corps, and being on the extreme right of the line during the engagement. It was Gen. [Mark Perrin] Lowrey, of [Patrick R.] Cleburne's Division, whom you heard make a speech to his brigade. . .

Cleburne's left dressed on the right, and [John Calvin] Brown's right on the left of the [Columbia] pike. Gen. Edward Johnson's Division of [Stephen Dill] Lee's Corps marched just in rear of [Benjamin Franklin] Cheatham's Corps, and if Lee was at the head of his command you were doubtless correct as to Gen. [John Bell] Hood addressing Gen. Lee. It is true Lee was at Columbia the day before, but the head of his command was at Rutherford Creek the next morning, only six miles south of Spring Hill, and Lee himself could have been on the ground. The two Mississippi brigades of Edward Johnson's Division, Lee's Corps, made a gallant and heroic charge on the left of Brown's line between sundown and dark, and were repulsed with heavy loss, as was manifested by the numbers of their dead left on the ground. There was but one Confederate battery engaged until after dark. It was Bledsoe's, from Missouri, which moved down the pike with Strahl's Brigade. After losing their horses they pushed their guns forward by hand. The Federal line of battle on their right, and Confederate left of the Columbia pike, was much longer than on their left, or Confederate right of said pike, which was the cause of so much lapping of the Southern troops on the right, and why so many troops of different divisions assailed the enemy at and around the old gin-house.

Carter's gin-house at Franklin.

The pike being Cleburne's left guide, as he advanced his division obliquely to the right, lapping the corps of Gens. [Alexander Peter] Stewart, Cleburne, [Edward Cary] Walthall, and French. These divisions, all assailed the works at that point. To the credit of Brown's Tennessee Division, with Gist's Brigade of South Carolina and Georgia troops, be it said, they assailed the Federal works without lapping, and drove the enemy from their main line of ditches. The two right brigades of his division, [George Washington] Gordon's and Strahl's, although heavily pressed from both flanks from an enfilading fire, never once yielded the advantage gained. The Federal troops were withdrawn from their extreme right and placed in front of these two brigades. In that part of the line the heavy night fighting was done. While the greater number of the Confederate dead lay in front and near the gin-house, the Federal dead were thickest around the Carter house in front of these two brigades. Strahl's Brigade was composed of the Nineteenth, Twenty-fourth, and Forty-first consolidated Tennessee regiments. Lieut. Col. S. F. Shannon, of the Twenty-fourth, was severely wounded in the neck from the top of the Federal works.

Imagine the dangerous position of those troops while fighting large odds in front with great masses of the enemy on their right side in the same line of works! These men held their position without flinching until the enemy were all gone. I myself lay so close to a Federal battery that every time it fired I could feel the heat. I remember having seen Gen. Strahl in the works when we first reached them. He was assisting one of the Nineteenth Tennessee in climbing over. Those who went over had to be helped. The works were much

McGavock Confederate Cemetery, Franklin, TN.

higher on this part of the line than on the right and around the gin-house. He afterward moved to the left, and I saw him no more. . . Gen. French tells us that his Missouri Brigade lost sixty-five per cent. It was a small brigade, and has one hundred and thirty men buried at McGavock Cemetery at this place. I endeavored, just a year ago, to mark the positions held by the various troops, and line of Federal ditches in this battle, and the points where the various Generals were killed, and stationed posts to designate these places. I am satisfied there is some inaccuracy . . . . [The spot where] Gen. [John] Adams [fell] is marked some eighty yards to the right of the gin-house . . .[101] — B. T. ROBERTS

☛ AT THE YANKEES' JOHNSON'S ISLAND PRISON

It was in the fall of 1863, I think, when the boys [of the Fourteenth Tennessee Regiment, C.S.A.] were worn in body and soul with the weariness of prison life. One day a regiment of Ohio volunteers were marched out amid much elation and beating of drums. Their bright new uniforms, fluttering flags, and glistening guns made a sad contrast to the boys inside the walls, who with a curiosity born of a long-continued monotony, called out to them and asked them where they were going.

It was in the days when the daring [Confederate Gen.] John [Hunt] Morgan had just escaped from the weary toils of the Columbus penitentiary, and had again with his undaunted spirit gotten together his famous command and was harassing the yankees; and the boys had a sly notion of what was up; so when the answer was hurled back at them, in a preconceived triumphal derision, "We are going to catch John Morgan and bring him back." It was truly an inspiring sight to behold the gorgeousness and brilliancy of their departure, yet already in our mind's eye we had bridged the lapse of time and beheld their triumphal return.

John H. Morgan, C.S.A.

. . . Of all the dilapidated, broken down sets of men ever seen, these [returning Yankees] surely were the worst. They appeared as if a "cyclone had struck them." From what had been the exultant departure, their dejected return made a pleasing contrast to the boys, and excited to no little degree their risibilities. We called to them as they passed, and inquired kindly after the health of Gen. John Morgan, but to none of our questions would they respond. I happened to notice a guard who I knew belonged to these Ohio volunteers. I asked him about their trip after General Morgan. To my inquiry, with an oath [expletive], he said: "Why, man, before we knew we were in his vicinity, he had us surrounded and captured us all at once; and then began the greatest race "for fun" that you ever saw. He made us lay down our guns, and ran us up and down the country for ten or twelves miles, until we were completely worn out, and our clothes torn and covered with mud and dirt; and then giving us our parole, turned our faces toward home and told us to "git," and we "got."[102] — B. F. WILSON JR.

☛ THRILLING ADVENTURES OF CAPT. JOHN NORRIS

Capt. John S. Norris, of Henderson, Ky., a gallant Confederate soldier of the civil war, served as Lieutenant as well as Captain under General [John Hunt] Morgan, and was one of the officers, prisoners of war, selected for retaliation by the Federals, and kept prisoner at Johnson's Island for several months, and on starvation rations, both at that place and in Nashville, Tenn. He was one of the first to enlist when war was declared, and one of the bravest of military leaders. His heroism and daring endurance will ever be remembered by those who survive him. During the battle near Murfreesboro, Tenn., three horses were shot [out from] under him in one day. At the time the cruel and barbarous law was issued that any soldier found in the boundaries of Kentucky should be instantly shot down, without quarter, yet such was his devotion to his family that he would go through these difficulties and dangers at the peril of his life for the pleasure of seeing them but a few hours, and upon one occasion was known to have walked from Nashville, Tenn., to Henderson, Ky., a distance of about 150 miles.

Captain Norris was fond of relating adventures and anecdotes pertaining to the war, recalling with great accuracy the stirring scenes through which he passed with the "boys in gray;" and would often tell with pride the pathetic story of the heroism exhibited in his eldest daughter, a wee tottling of barely three years, who, on beholding from the window the [Union] troops advancing, apparently to take him prisoner, pressed her little hands firmly against the door, exclaiming confidently, "Papa, I'll hold the door." This was during an occasion when he was on parole.

He was a man of strong prejudice, and as high honor. Unselfishness and courtesy were his predominant characteristics; these, combined with his engaging social qualities, attracted the personal friendship, confidence and respect of all those who came within the sphere of his immediate association; and he would often speak with appreciation of the kindly consideration, politeness and respect tendered him under all circumstances at the hands of the Federals, even though they made an exception in his favor.

About six months before the close of the war he was compelled to resign his charge, and was granted a discharge from further service, on account of ill health—neuralgia in its worst form, brought on by exposure from camping on the damp ground, in consequence of which he suffered much during the remaining years of his life. Honored, respected and beloved by all, he passed away from this world in January, 1875, in the forty-fifth year of his age. How large a majority of the loyal patriots and comrades whom we knew and loved are now on the other side, but "to live in hearts we leave behind is not to die."[103] — A FRIEND

☛ A BRIEF SKETCH OF GEN. ROBERT E. LEE

Robert E. Lee, C.S.A.

The son of "Light Horse Harry Lee" [Henry Lee III] of the [American] Revolution, and descended from a long line of illustrious ancestors who played conspicuous parts in English history, a careful genealogist has traced his ancestry back to King Robert the Bruce.

But Robert Edward Lee needs no royal lineage to fix his place in history, or account for his stainless character and noble deeds, for he was himself a born leader, a very King of Men, and derives no lustre from even royal ancestry.

So bright, cheerful and manly as a boy he met so fully his obligations at school and home that his widowed mother exclaimed, when he was leaving for the Military Academy at West Point, "How can I do without Robert? He is both son and daughter to me."

He passed through the academy and graduated second in a brilliant class without ever receiving a single demerit. Of the bright galaxy of American officers in the Mexican war, no other won greater fame, or performed more distinguished service. He was covered with "brevets" for "gallant and meritorious service," and General [Winfield] Scott did not hesitate to speak of him as "the very best soldier I ever saw in the field."

In 1852 he became Superintendent of the Military Academy at West Point, and introduced a number of changes, and reforms which abundantly showed his capacity as Superintendent of the Academy, and manager of young men.

In 1855 the famous "Second Cavalry" Regiment was formed, and Hon. Jefferson Davis, then [U.S.] Secretary of War appointed to it that splendid corps of officers among whom were Albert Sidney Johnston, Colonel; Robert Edward Lee, Lieutenant Colonel; Geo. H. Thomas, and Wm. J. Hardee, Majors; Earl Van Dorn, John B. Hood, E. Kirby Smith, [George] Stoneman, and others, Captains; and Fitzhugh Lee, and others, Lieutenants.

Happening at home on furlough he was sent to Harper's Ferry to command the Marines who captured John Brown who was then "firing the first gun" of the great war that was to follow.

In March 1861 he came from his regiment on the frontier of Texas, in obedience to orders summoning him to Washington, and was made full Colonel of Cavalry. General Scott and other friends used all of their influence to induce him to "stand by the old flag," and he was offered [by Lincoln] the supreme command of the Federal army in the field. But although not a secessionist, and ardently attached to the Union, and the old flag and saying emphatically, "If the millions of slaves in the South were mine I would free them with a stroke of the pen to avert this war," he promptly replied to Mr. Lincoln's messenger, the elder Blair [Francis Preston Blair], "I cannot bear arms against my state, my home, my children." He went at once to General Scott, told him his decision, resisted all of his entreaties, and the next day wrote his famous letter of resignation.

Samuel Cooper, C. S. A.

He was made Commander-in-Chief of the Virginia forces by the "Virginia Convention," and afterward full General in the Confederate Army, Gens. Sidney Johnston and [Samuel] Cooper ranking him. His services in organizing the new levees (in the West Virginia campaign, where the failure was due to causes beyond his control), and in preparing the seacoast fortifications of South Carolina and Georgia for the magnificent defense they afterward made, were all invaluable, but may not be detailed here.

When Gen. Joseph E. Johnston was wounded at Seven Pines the last of May, 1862, and Gen. Lee put in command of the Army of Northern Virginia, the situation was perilous in the extreme. McClellan, with

105,000 men, was strongly fortified within sight of the spires of Richmond, with 10,000 more men at Fortress Monroe, and McDowell's column of 40,000 which was to have moved down from Fredericksburg, only detained by the brilliant "valley campaign" of Stonewall Jackson. Lee's plans were soon formed and brilliantly executed. Sending [Jeb] Stuart on his famous "ride around McClellan," he secured the information he wanted as to the enemy's position, ordered Jackson to join him, concentrated other troops which swelled his numbers to 78,000 (the largest army he ever commanded) and then, by a series of splendid maneuvers and brilliant victories, forced McClellan to cower under the cover of his gunboats at Harrison's Landing, defeated John Pope on the plains of Manassas, drove his army into the fortifications at Washington, and sent him to fight Indians in the West, and persecute gallant Fitz John Porter at Washington. Then followed the advance into Maryland, the capture of Harper's Ferry, the battle of Sharpsburg, where Lee, with 33,000 men, defeated every effort of McClellan's 87,000 to drive him from the field; and the battle of first Fredericksburg, where those plains were made forever historic as "Burnside's slaughter pen."

In May, 1863, Lee, with 52,000 men, won over Hooker's 132,000 the splendid victory of Chancellorsville, attacking Hooker in his entrenchments and driving him pell-mell across the river. Then followed the Pennsylvania campaign, in which Lee captured [Robert Huston] Milroy's garrison, artillery, wagons, and immense supplies at Winchester, and with 62,000 men fought [George Gordon] Meade's 105,000 at Gettysburg, where he won a decided victory on the first day, gained important advantages on the second day, and was defeated on the third day, only because (as he always believed and said to his intimate friends) of the failure of Longstreet to carry out his orders.

In the campaign of 1864 Gen. Grant had more than 275,000 men in four converging columns (in Southwestern Virginia, the Valley, Culpeper, and up the James), which set out simultaneously to capture Richmond, and the world never saw armies more splendidly equipped. To oppose this mighty host Gen. Lee could muster, all told, during the campaign, scarce 75,000 men, destitute of everything save the heroic courage and patient endurance of as true soldiers as history records. The result of the summer campaign was that after losing more men than Lee had Grant sat down to the siege of Petersburg—a position which he might have taken at first without firing a shot or losing a man—while Lee made his lines impregnable to a direct assault, and sent Early's Corps to defeat [David] Hunter and threaten Washington. He had outgeneraled Grant at every point and defeated him in every battle. Then followed the siege of Petersburg and that slow process of "attrition" by which Lee's army was reduced to 33,000 half-starved men to hold over forty miles of breastworks, and the thin lines were stretched until they broke, the retreat to Appomattox begun, and 7,800 ragged, starved heroes stacked their bright muskets, parked their blackened guns [that is, cannon] (nearly every piece wrested from the enemy in battle—two of them that very morning), and yielded to the "overwhelming numbers and resources" which surrounded them.

Lee and Jackson on the battlefield.

But grand as he was in war, Lee was even grander in peace. Refusing every offer of pecuniary assistance, he only sought a place for honest work, and accepted the Presidency of Washington College, Lexington, Va., where, as he expressed it, he "could teach young men to do their duty in life." He was only spared to fill this position five years, but even that brief time (I do not hesitate to declare from personal observation and careful study) he proved himself the greatest college president this country ever produced. It was my privilege to follow his standard during the war, and to see something of him during those stirring days, but my prouder privilege to know him intimately during the five years of his life in Lexington, and to have had free access to his private letters and papers. I speak, then, from careful personal observation and full study of his character and career, when *I unhesitatingly pronounce him not only the greatest soldier but the noblest gentleman, the truest patriot, the purest man that ever figured in American history. And far above all this, he was one of the humblest, sincerest, most consecrated Christians whom I ever met.* Taking Christ as his personal Savior, and fully trusting in him alone for salvation, he was a constant reader and student of God's word, a man of prayer, an earnest and efficient worker for the salvation of others, "an Israelite indeed, in whom there was no guile," who lived and died in the service of the Great Captain, and now wears his glittering crown.

> That crown with fadeless glories bright,
> Which shall new luster boast
> When victors' wreaths and monarchs' gems
> Shall blend in common dust.[104] — REV. J. WILLIAM JONES

Lee leading a charge.

☛ TRIBUTE TO ROBERT E. LEE

When the future historian shall come to survey the character of Lee, he will find it rising like a huge mountain above the undulating plain of humanity, and he must lift his eyes high toward heaven to catch its summit. Gen. Lee possessed every virtue of the other great commanders without their vices. He was a foe without hate, a friend without treachery, a soldier without cruelty, and a victim without murmuring. He was a public officer without vices, a private citizen without wrong, a neighbor without reproach, a Christian without hypocrisy, and a man without guile. He was Caesar without his ambition, Frederick without his tyranny, Napoleon without his selfishness, and Washington without his reward. He was obedient to authority as a servant, and royal in authority as a true king. He was gentle as woman in life, modest and pure as a virgin in thought, watchful as a Roman vestal in duty, submissive to law as Socrates, and grand in battle as Archilles![105] — SENATOR BENJAMIN HARVEY HILL

☞ THE SOUTH'S GREAT BATTLE ABBEY
Gather the sacred dust
    Of the warriors tried and true,
Who bore the flag of a nation's trust
And fell in a cause, though lost, still just,
    And died for me and you.

As a nation progresses in civilization and enlightenment, so will its reverence for its dead be shown. As far back as the days of Edward the Confessor we find the germ of a national burying ground for England in the beginning of Westminster Abbey. In that spot, dear to the hearts of all in whose veins runs the blood of the Anglo-Saxon, lie entombed the greatest and best that Englishmen as well as Americans hold dear. The tomb of the monarch, statesman, poet, priest and soldier lie there, and no spot of that green island is so dear to the hearts of her people as that which contains the graves of her honored dead.

Westminster Abbey, burial site for many of England's greatest heros and heroines.

It is the pride and glory of every Frenchman to point to that spot made sacred by the resting place of the great Napoleon. And to no day in their history do they point with greater tenderness than to that on which all that is mortal of the great world conqueror was deposited beneath the lilies of his much-loved country.

Egypt, once the seat of the world's civilization, had the tombs of her Pharaohs. Scotland, brought home the heart of Robert Bruce and reverently entombed it in Melrose Abbey. And so carefully did Spain preserve the haughty figure and stern lineaments of the Cid Campeador, that at one time when the enemies of his country were about to prevail over her armies the body of the stern old warrior placed in front of the host he had once led to victory spread confusion and dismay throughout the ranks of the foe. It is to this principle of reverence for the dead and their last resting places that we owe the deathless spirit of patriotism, that spirit which makes a man love his country next to his God, and bids him welcome death in preference to dishonor.

Melrose Abbey: Scottish model for a Confederate battle abbey.

The love of country itself is not more deeply intertwined with the most sacred feelings of the human heart than that love which makes a shrine of patriot graves. It is this feeling which for nearly one hundred years has caused the hearts of Americans to turn reverently to that spot on the gently flowing Potomac, made holy by the grave of the father [George Washington] of his country. And it is that feeling which caused the South, only a few short months ago to witness the most solemn pageant that ever wound over her flower-decked hills and perfumed valleys. No spectacle of the closing years of the nineteenth century is more imposing than that of carrying the dead chieftain of the Confederacy [Robert E. Lee] back to the spot where the most stirring scenes in the great four years' drama were enacted—that drama in which he was the most conspicuous figure, and which ended so tragically at Appomattox.

Le Pantheon, Paris, France, the final resting place of many notable figures.

And henceforth to all true Southern hearts, what Melrose Abbey is to Scotland, Westminster to England, and the glorious Pantheon to France, will be that silent city of the dead where Jefferson Davis sleeps among 12,000 of his comrades, heroes of the lost cause. At last the South has her Battle Abbey, and though she may not gather within it all who laid down their lives for love of her, the tomb of her chieftain will, in the slowly revolving years, be looked upon as the representative tomb of that cause for which men poured out their life's best blood.

Listen to the South, weeping for them still, her forgotten braves. Louisiana, who rocked him so tenderly to her heart, fanning his brow with the perfumed breath of her orange groves. And Mississippi, how she wept to give up her favorite son, the one who, above all others, has shed luster on her name. The soft swell of the Gulf bursts like a sob from her bosom, the mighty, roll of the Father of Waters joins in the sad refrain, and pointing to the green covered mounds at Shiloh and Vicksburg, and a hundred other well fought fields, she cried in tones tremulous with sadness:

> List, sons, your watch is long,
> The soldier's guard was brief;
> Whilst right is right and wrong is wrong
> You may not seek relief.
>
> Go, wearing the gray of grief,
> Go, watch o'er the dead in gray,
> Go, guard the private and the chief,
> And sentinel his clay.

Virginia, the grand old mother of the South, has gathered to her bosom the mightiest of the sons of valor. In the shadow of her lofty mountain pines sleeps Robert E. Lee, the kingliest soul that ever drew sword in the cause of truth and justice. In her arms also nestles the lofty Christian hero, Stonewall Jackson, who murmured when dying, "Let us cross over the river and rest under the shade of the trees." Here, too, sleeps the Prince Rupert of Southern cavaliers, [Jeb] Stuart, the gay and gifted cavalryman, one of Stonewall's band in life, and sleeping

Albert S. Johnston, C.S.A.

under the same green cover-lid in death. And what pen could describe in fitting terms the numberless green hillocks whose only designation are the mystic letters, "C.S.A." How wonderful, how passing strange, that those letters, so proudly, so fondly worn and cherished once, should now represent only the shadow of an empire. What deeds of sacrifice, of valor, and of honor wrought for them, "C.S.A." It was no shadow to those who followed Lee, and the Johnstons, and Stonewall Jackson, and Bedford Forrest, for four long and bloody years. It was no shadow to those who, dying, blessed it with their latest breath, believing that victory, like an overshadowing halo, had crowned the offering of their lives. It was no shadow, that which floated over valiant armies, wasted at last by disease, hardships, and death, overpowered by armies recruited from the world's enlisting grounds; and it is no shadow to us to whom it is committed to treasure up the memory of those who died for us, who threw themselves, for the sake of Fatherland, into the imminent deadly breach, and instead of victory found a grave. Shall not those graves be sacred to Southern hearts?

> We care not whence they came,
> Dear in their lifeless clay.
> Whether unknown or known to fame,
> Their cause and country still the same,
> They died wearing the gray.[106] — CAMILLE WILLIAMS

☛ JOHNNY REB: THE TYPICAL CONFEDERATE SOLDIER

Nearly thirty-three years have passed since the alarm of war called from their peaceful pursuits the citizens who were to make name and fame as Confederate soldiers. The stirring scenes and the dreadful carnage of a memorable conflict have been removed by the lapse of time into the hazy past, and a new generation, however ready it may be to honor those who fought the battles of the South, is likely to form its idea of their appearance from the conventional military type. The Confederate soldier was not an ordinary soldier, either in appearance or character. . . . [thus] I will undertake to draw a portrait of him as he really appeared in the hard service of privation and danger.

A face browned by exposure and heavily bearded, or for some weeks unshaven, begrimed with dust and sweat, and marked here and there with the darker stains of powder—a face whose stolid and even

"Johnny Reb."

melancholy composure is easily broken into ripples of good humor or quickly flushed in the fervor and abandon of the charge; a frame tough and sinewy, and trained by hardship to surprising powers of endurance; a form, the shapeliness of which is hidden by its encumberments, suggesting in its careless and unaffected pose a languorous indisposition to exertion, yet a latent, lion-like strength and a terrible energy of action when aroused. Around the upper part of the face is a fringe of unkempt hair, and above this an old wool hat, worn and weather beaten, the flaccid brim of which falls limp upon the shoulders behind, and is folded back in front against the elongated and crumpled crown. Over a soiled shirt, which is unbuttoned and buttonless at the collar, is a ragged gray jacket that does not reach to the hips, with sleeves some inches too short. Below this trousers of a nondescript color, without form and almost void, are held in place by a leather belt, to which is attached the cartridge box that rests behind the right hip, and the bayonet scabbard which dangles on the left. Just above the ankles each trouser leg is tied closely to the limb— a la Zouave—and beneath reaches of dirty socks disappear in a pair of badly used and curiously contorted shoes. Between the jacket and the waistband of the trousers, or the supporting belt, there appears a puffy display of cotton shirt which works out further with every hitch made by Johnny in his effort to keep his pantaloons in place. Across his body from his left shoulder there is a roll of threadbare blanket, the ends tied together resting on or falling below the right hip. This blanket is Johnny's bed. Whenever he arises he takes up his bed and walks. Within this roll is a shirt, his only extra article of clothing. In action the blanket roll is thrown further back, and the cartridge box is drawn forward, frequently in front of the body. From the right shoulder, across the body, pass two straps, one cloth the other leather, making a cross with blanket roll on breast and back. These straps support respectively a greasy cloth haversack and a flannel-covered canteen, captured from the yankees. Attached to the haversack strap is a tin cup, while in addition to some other odds and ends of camp trumpery, there hangs over his back a frying pan, an invaluable utensil with which the soldier would be loth to part.

With his trusty gun in hand—an Enfield rifle, also captured from the enemy and substituted for the old flint-lock musket or the shot-gun with which he was originally armed—Johnny Reb, thus imperfectly sketched, stands in his shreds and patches a marvelous ensemble—picturesque, grotesque, unique—the model citizen soldier, the military hero of the nineteenth century. There is none of the tinsel or the trappings of the professional about him. From an esthetic military point of view he must appear a sorry looking soldier, but Johnny is not one of your dress parade soldiers, he doesn't care a copper whether anybody likes his looks or not. *He is the most independent soldier that ever belonged to an organized army. He has respect for authority, and he cheerfully submits to discipline, because he sees the necessity of organization to effect the best results, but he maintains his individual autonomy, as it were, and never surrenders his sense of personal pride and responsibility. He is thoroughly tractable if properly officered, and is always ready to obey necessary orders, but he is quick to resent any official incivility, and is a high private who feels, and is, every inch as good as a General.*  He may appear ludicrous enough on a display occasion of the holiday pomp and splendor of war, but place him where duty calls, in the imminent deadly breach or the perilous charge, and none in all the armies of the earth can claim a higher rank or prouder record. He may be outre and ill-fashioned in dress, but he has sublimated his poverty and rags. The worn and faded gray jacket, glorified by valor and stained with the life blood of its wearer, becomes, in its immortality of association, a more splendid vestment than mail of medieval knight or the rarest robe of royalty. That old, weather-beaten slouched hat, seen as the ages will see it, with its halo of fire, through the smoke of battle, is a kinglier covering than a crown. *Half clad, half armed, often half fed, without money and without price, the Confederate soldier fought against the resources of the world. When at last his flag was furled and his arms were grounded in defeat, the cause for which he had struggled was lost, but he had won the fadeless victory of soldiership.*[107] — G. H. BASKETTE

☛ TRIBUTE TO A BOY SOLDIER
[William "Billy" Youree of Company K, Second Tennessee Regiment Infantry, C.S.A.] . . . was a puny, sallow, undeveloped youth when he came to us at Corinth, seemingly too weak to handle a musket or endure

a march, but he never missed a battle, I think, in which we were engaged. Although he was frequently sick he never shirked a duty nor asked a favor. He did his duty like the strongest. Indeed, his death was caused by his dogged persistence in remaining at the front when he was totally unfit for service. When we crossed the Chattahoochee [River] after the hard and trying Dalton campaign, Billy was so broken down and unfit for service that I ordered him to the hospital. To my surprise he came back to the company in a day or two, and when I remonstrated with him he simply said he "would rather stay with the boys." We were then on the skirmish line at Peachtree Creek, and that day our flank was turned by two brigades of the enemy who emerged from a pine thicket in a few paces to the left of the line. It was a run for life. Being detained by my duties somewhat, I was the last to get started. In a short while I came across the poor fellow in much distress because he was unable to run. I could only bid him do the best he could, and with a bitter pang I passed on, leaving him to his fate. In a few moments I was wounded, but managed to get back to the main line. We never learned his fate until the war was over and it was ascertained that he had not been a prisoner. Then there could be no doubt with us all but his poor old mother, in the absence of positive knowledge, refused to believe him dead, and to the day of her death clung to the hope that her darling boy would return to her.

Billy Youree was a model character. He had none of the vices of camp. His Bible was his constant companion, and his morals pure; indeed, he shamed us all by his example of patient, uncomplaining fortitude under the most trying circumstances, though he was but a weak, pitiful-looking, undeveloped boy. When at his grave yesterday morning tears burst from my eyes and a fervent "thank God" from my lips that the lost had been found, though it was but the bones of the dear little fellow.[108] — E. L. DRAKE

☛ A PLEA FOR HISTORY

I hope it may never he said of the South that she has ceased to appreciate the sacrifices of her men or the patient endurance of her women in her hour of darkness and need.

I saw the widow yield to her country her eldest born, on whom she leaned to manage her estate; then another and another son in quick succession until her baby boy of sixteen was called.

I saw the wife bid good-bye to the husband, and draw close to her breast the little ones who depended on him for bread, and looking aloft cry, "God pity us."

How fondly do I remember the contending emotions of fervent patriotism, love, and pride in my own heart as I saw my young husband start to the front arrayed in the suit of gray which my willing hands had woven, cut and made, he who was mine, now yielded to God and his country.

Wives, mothers, daughters, and sweethearts of Confederate soldiers.

Shall the South ever forget these things? Never! Sweep away the dust of time! Let nothing dim their luster! As Rizpah, in sacred writ, stood guard over the bodies of the dead whom she might not bury, and drove away the vultures which would have fed on their bodies, so *we will resist and drive away the unholy touch of every harpy who would drag down in the dust the sacred memories of the past.* It ennobles us to write of noble deeds. It enkindles in our breasts the sacred flame of heroism, and the hovering spirits of our dead heroes shall inspire us to emulation.[109] — MARTHA MOSS NORTHEN (wife of Georgia Governor William Jonathan Northen)

☛ SEVERE DISCIPLINE IN THE CONFEDERATE ARMY

While Joe E. Johnston's army was near Dalton, after the fall of Missionary Ridge, Gen. P. R. Cleburne's division was camped out on the Spring Place road. Pickets from the division were detailed every morning and mounted by Major Dickson, Cleburne's Inspector General. The Major was very exacting. He would order the men to stand at right dress at shoulder arms while he instructed the commissioned and non-commissioned officers. The men would frequently change positions a little for comfort, and whenever he saw any of them do so he would order them out of line and put them on extra duty at headquarters. This severity became an annoyance to all of the division, until it was common for four or five hundred men to go out to see the ridiculous performance.

A crisis came one morning when General Cleburne and his Adjutant went out to see the Major's performances. He had his men to right dress at shoulder arms and open ranks, and commenced his instructions to the officers as usual. As soon as this happened Adjutant General Buck left General Cleburne and went to the Major, said something to him, and returned to where General Cleburne was. The Major in the meantime was instructing as usual. General Cleburne then commanded in a loud, clear voice, "Major Dickson, bring the men to order arms while you give those instructions not in the book." The old rebel yell was given with a hearty good will.

For a long time after this when Major Dickson would come by the command some one would halloo out, "Who gave the instructions not in the book?" "Major Dickson!" would be the answer in chorus by nearly every one in hearing distance. The last time the writer ever heard it thrown into the Major's face General Cleburne was with him, and the General said, "Boys, I don't believe I would worry him any more, as he is sorry of it."[110] — A CONFEDERATE VET

☛ PICKET DUTY ON LOOKOUT MOUNTAIN

Just before the great battle at Chickamauga I was stationed, with a little squad, to watch the movement of the enemy not far away in the valley below. One day a foraging party of the enemy came in sight with thirty or forty wagons and about one regiment of infantry. All of the wagons but seven passed on, when the regiment halted and stacked arms, and the men were soon busily engaged in gathering a field of corn. General M. happened on the mountain that day and gave his consent for us to go down and give them battle. Every available man of our seventeen all told was soon in line, and going down a narrow trail we soon reached the creek below, where we deployed as skirmishers the full length of the field in order to get all under fire at once. At length the order was given, "Fire." You ought to have seen them—drivers dismounted, left their teams, and all rushed pell mell through the corn to where the guns were stacked. Overjoyed at our victory we were soon across the creek busily engaged with the mules and wagons that had been left behind in the stampede. We had captured thirty-five mules and six wagons, one mule having been killed in the fray and one team escaped. The arrangement on leaving the summit was for General M. to act as signal corps. One gun fired indicated fight; two guns, retreat, and every man for himself. All were as busy as bees trying to force the mules across the creek. The bank was steep, and they not inclined to take it, when, to our surprise, the signal to fight was heard. All were in a moment of time ready for battle, waiting breathless for the approach of the enemy. The keen ring of the rifle was again heard from the mountain top. "There, boys, that means run. Kill the mules before you go." They were soon dispatched. Then came the retreat in dead earnest, and every man was for himself. Such scrambling to find some safe place among the cliffs and under the laurel bushes. Soon we were in safety high up on the mountain side from where every movement of the enemy below could be plainly seen. The commander, a gallant fellow, mounted and coming to battle in fine style, skirmishers deployed and moving to the front cautiously to locate the position of the attacking party. When within range of our Enfield rifles we opened fire on them again, and continued it. They marched bravely forward until within a few hundred yards of our retreat, halted, then poured one solid volley into the rocky side of old Lookout; faced about seemingly in disgust, and marched away in the direction the train had gone, leaving, as they doubtless thought, thirty-six mules and six wagons to the mercy of the Johnny Rebs. When fully satisfied that they were gone, we crept, one by one, from our hiding places (without the loss of a man), again crossed the creek, re-entered the field, filled the wagons with corn stalks and burned them. Four mules escaped unhurt, which we carried triumphantly to the mountain top. This is my experience as picket on Lookout Mountain.[111] — JOE (Company G, Ninth Tennessee Infantry)

☞ TRIBUTE TO HOOD BY A UNION SOLDIER

John B. Hood, C.S.A.

. . . I was somewhat surprised, and may say pained, during my recent trip South, to note the disposition among soldiers of the late Confederate Army to criticise and disparage the merits of [Confederate] Gen. [John Bell] Hood. That he made mistakes no unprejudiced student of the war between the States will deny, but that he was possessed of some of the best qualities that belong to great military commanders is equally indisputable. As between the General and his critics touching the battle of Franklin, my sympathies are entirely with the former; while my admiration for the splendid valor exhibited by his heroic legions on that bloody field is not diminished by the fact that they were Americans all, and that to day the survivors would fight as desperately for the "stars and stripes" as they did on that November day twenty-nine years ago for the "stars and bars." Franklin, from the Confederate standpoint of view, must ever remain one of the saddest tragedies of the civil war; on the other hand, there were in that battle possibilities to the Confederate cause, and that came near being realized, scarcely second to those of any other in the great conflict. Had Hood won—and he came within an ace of it—and reaped the legitimate fruits of his victory, the verdict of history would have been reversed, and William Tecumseh Sherman, who took the flower of his army and with it made an unobstructed march to the sea, leaving but a remnant to contend against a foe that had taxed his every resource from Chattanooga to Atlanta, would have been called at the close as at the beginning of the war, "Crazy Sherman." No individual, not even Hood himself, had so much at stake in the fight at Franklin as the hero of the "march to the sea."[112] — WASHINGTON GARDNER (Union veteran from Michigan)

☛ STORY OF AN OLD BROKEN PISTOL
I was with Gen. [Richard] Dick Taylor, not far from the Mississippi River. News had reached him that a "cotton thief" was at a certain place buying cotton and shipping it North. I was ordered to go and capture and bring him in. I went alone, and as I was approaching the house where he was reported to be staying, I saw him going from it as fast as his horse could carry him. I gave chase and finally overtook and captured him. He had only a few dollars in money on his person, and in a pair of saddle-bags there were only an old broken pistol and a shirt. I took him to headquarters. What become of him I never learned. My story is about the old pistol, which I appropriated. On examining it I deemed it of  no value, and gave it to the children of a female cousin who lived in that section, and whose house I more than once visited. At the close of the war I called there, and seeing the pistol I said to her, I will take this home with me as a trophy of the war. She readily assented, and I put it in my pocket.

My wife and children were at the home of my father in Franklin County, Mo., about forty miles from St. Louis. On reaching them I gave my children the pistol as a souvenir of the war, and it became a plaything for them indoors and out, and was often laying out in the weather. After a few years my father had a sale of his household effects, and the pistol was thrown into a box of old bits of iron, and was sold with them. A year or so later I was at the house of the purchaser and saw the weapon. A desire to possess it again came upon me. I gave its history and asked for it, and it was given me. I took it to my then home in St. Louis, and again it became a toy for my children. One day one of them came to me with the pistol and a splinter of wood in it, saying, "There is something in here." I took the splinter, pressed it in, and discovered there was something soft in the barrel. I called on my wife for a hairpin, formed a sort of screw and succeeded in drawing out a roll of greenback notes. There were six one hundred dollar bills and four ten dollar bills [the equivalent of about $10,000 in 2017], and the only sign of damage was rust marks from the pistol barrel on the outside of the roll. It then became manifest why the captured cotton buyer carried that old broken pistol in his saddle-bags.[113] — J. W. C.

CHAPTER 13

1894

☛ BRIEF SKETCH OF NATHAN BEDFORD FORREST

Born in Bedford County, Tenn., July 13, 1821; died at Memphis, Tenn., October, 29, 1877. He removed to Hernando, Miss., in 1842, and was a planter until 1852, when he removed to Memphis.

General Forrest was one of the most remarkable men developed by the war. In fighting he was the Stonewall Jackson of the West. United States Senator John W. Daniel, of Virginia, in his great speech as orator for the United Confederate Veterans, at their reunion in New Orleans, in April, 1892, said: "Forrest, the 'Wizard of the Saddle,' oh what genius was in that wonderful man! He felt the field as Blind Tom [Thomas Wiggins] touches the keys of a piano.[114] 'War means killing,' he said, 'and the way to kill is to get there first with the most men.' There is military science—Napoleon, Stonewall and Lee—in a nutshell. He was not taught at West Point, but he gave lessons to West Point." Erroneous statements have been published, even in Encyclopedias, concerning his [so-called] illiteracy.

Nathan B. Forrest, C.S.A.

His lovely Christian wife [Mary Ann, née Montgomery] died in Memphis only a year or two since. Of his family now living there are Captain William [Montgomery] Forrest and his three children—Mary E., [Nathan] Bedford [II], and William.[115] — UNKNOWN

☛ BRIEF SKETCH OF BENJAMIN FRANKLIN CHEATHAM

Born in Nashville, October 20, 1820; died September 4, 1886. He served as Captain of Volunteers in the Mexican War, and distinguished himself in the severest battles there. On returning from Mexico he was appointed Major General of the Tennessee Militia.

In the Confederate service he was at once made Brigadier General, and soon afterward a Major General. He was in many fierce battles, and always was the pride of his soldiers. In the Hood Campaign he commanded one of the three Corps.

"Mars Frank" was the familiar term under which any private soldier would address him, who hesitated to ask the same things of their regimental commanders. After the war he engaged in farming, and when he died was Postmaster at Nashville. The honor and affection in which he was held was verified by his having "the largest funeral that has ever been held in Nashville." The procession was more than a mile in length. His faithful, lovely wife [Anna Bell, née Robertson] "crossed over the river" not long after him. Their five children—three sons and two daughters are all doing well, and live in a good home at Nashville, provided by their parents.[116] — UNKNOWN

The children of Benjamin F. Cheatham, C.S.A.

☛ A WAR WAIF IN THE C.S. ARMY

I enlisted as a private in the Second Louisiana Volunteers in 1861. My first real soldiering was on the Yorktown Peninsula, in Virginia. While there, or at Suffolk (I forget which), there strolled into camp a young boy, scarcely over 10 or 12 years of age, who attached himself to one of the neighboring regiments. Who he was, or where he came from, I cannot now recall. He was looked upon as "no man's child," and as such found genial fellowship among the soldiers. I soon realized that he was a cosmopolitan, and at home anywhere, for I next saw him the pet of the

First South Carolina Volunteers. How long he stayed with them I cannot say. It was fully a year before I saw him again. His small form and boyish face were a great contrast to the men among whom he mingled. I remember then how odd it seemed to see that lad in a camp, but he was truly "the child of the regiment." After we had fallen back to Richmond, and after those terrible seven days' of battle, the army was reorganized and the troops brigaded by States, so I lost sight of our Carolina neighbors, and also the boy.

At the second battle of Manassas, on the 29th of August, 1862, our brigade ([William Edwin] Starke's—poor fellow, he fell at Sharpsburg), was lying in the woods nearly opposite that "terrible deep cut" when the dripping, spattering fire of the Yankee skirmishers drove in our out-lookers (as "Old Jack" [Stonewall Jackson] didn't have a counter skirmish line), the cry "F-o-r-w-a-r-d" rang along our lines, and we advanced and ran almost into the Yankees, who, giving us a deadly volley, fell back rapidly across a field and into the woods beyond, where a battery, supported by a swarm of troops, was posted. Nothing checked us. Under a withering fire of minnies and canister we pressed on, Bradley T. Johnson, riding ahead, with his sword  run through his hat, waving us on, until we waved him out of our line of line. When we arrived within about one hundred yards of the battery the line was halted, and under this raking fire the alignment was corrected, and the men "right dressed" to be shot down.

I have thought often since, that the command of halt, under such a fire might have been heroic, but it certainly was not wise. However, not a man faltered. Again, "Forward!" and we drove straight for the guns. Just then I felt a thud, a biting, a twist around and fell. A minnie had struck my pocket Bible edgewise, and passing nearly through the New Testament part, dug a trench across my left side into the flesh. With the blood spurting from the wound I started rearward, while our boys—brave fellows—went up and over the battery, scattering its supports like chaff. As I struggled back over the field, the dead and the wounded, blue and gray alike, lying around, I heard a great rumbling on my left and turned and saw that our guns were plunging to the front, under lash and shout, to seize the hills whence to pour shot into the then retreating foe. I can see them now tumbling, bouncing, and surging to gain that front. What else did I see? So close I could nearly touch him, the little boy sitting on the limber of one of the pieces [cannon], his eyes aflame, his hat waving, his treble voice shouting excitedly, and his whole being lit up and aglow with the terrible magnetism of battle, cheering on the line. That was the last that I saw of him. He passed on and was lost in the cloud and smoke of the field, but the memory of that inspiring scene will never fade.[117] — A. L. SLACK

☞ CLEBURNE'S BRIGADE AT SHILOH

[Here is a] brief account of Shiloh as I saw it, being a private in the Twenty-third Tennessee Regiment (Pat Cleburne's Brigade). On the morning of April 6, 1862, when the entire line moved forward, our brigade had to face a battery of twelve guns; eight 20-pound rifles (brass), and four 12-pound Napoleon guns. We were ordered to halt and lie down in a deep ravine while the battery was shelling our position at a fearful rate. Just in our front was a ridge, a peach orchard, and the Federal encampment. General Cleburne told us to prepare for a charge. Soon it was ordered and we moved forward at double-quick, passed through the encampment, down the slope on the north side of the ridge near to a branch. Here a line of infantry rose up and poured such a destructive volley into our ranks that we recoiled and fell back to the first ravine. Here we rallied, and General Cleburne came to us again and said, "Boys, don't be discouraged; that is not the first charge that was ever repulsed; fix bayonets and give them steel." Then he ordered, "Forward! Charge!" We leaped forward with a deafening cheer and drove the infantry out of the ravine, but firing from the battery and a line of infantry was so heavy just in rear of the battery that we again fell back, with great loss, but soon reformed, and were ready for the third charge,

Patrick R. Cleburne, C.S.A.

when a Louisiana brigade was brought up to our support. Another charge was ordered and we moved forward over the dead and wounded, this time to reach the goal that had cost the lives of many of our best men. But the struggle was not yet over for the battery, as the boys in blue fired some of the guns when we were within ten feet of their muzzles. Here we had a hand-to-hand contest over the guns, but we were triumphant, and this fine battery of twelve guns was ours. Cleburne's Brigade was composed of the Seventeenth, Twenty-third and Twenty-fourth Tennessee and First Arkansas Regiments.

I cannot close . . . without saying that the [Union] men of this battery were the bravest men we ever had to deal with. They were worthy of our steel, not one of them surrendered with a whole hide. They had been in the United States service for twenty years. If this should fall into the hands of any soldier, on either side in this charge, I would be glad to correspond with him.[118] — J. A. WHEELER

☛ FEASTING & FIGHTING WITH FORREST

The following incident is but a remnant of the spice-box that, like pride, had a fall, or rather a more expeditious send-off during Gen. Forrest's raid on Paducah, Ky.: Maj. Thompson led an attack on Fort Anderson, a huge affair, surrounding the Marine Hospital. Close by and overlooking the fort was the two-story brick building of Dr. Bassett. Some six or eight young Kentuckians, among whom were the Douglas and Meriwether boys, thought that this house presented some fine strategic points of value, both as a commissary department and "shooting-box"; the big 32-pounders in the fort could not be handled with any degree of safety if any party of sharp-shooters should happen to occupy the upper story. Accompanied by their Captain, the house was at once taken possession of, and Mrs. Bassett, delighted with the visit of the "Southern boys," made at once extensive preparations for their comfort. The large dining table was taken up-stairs, for the greater convenience of her guests, and heaped with all the delicacies and good things that the house, cellar or pantry afforded. And nobly did the famished defenders of a lost cause respond to the tempting viand. The battle had now begun in earnest, and "the boys," with their mouths full, sent their unerring missiles amid the enemy's cannoniers, to their utter discomfort and demoralization. The huge thirty-two in front of the house could not be fired. Every time a head appeared it was promptly scalped. The boys enjoyed the fun immensely, and divided their time between "shootin' an' eatin'." After many failures, one artilleryman succeeded in pulling the lanyard, and a storm of grape and canister whistled through the house, without, however, touching the boys or the "vittels." Douglas remarked that this was the best place to fight in he had ever struck, and as long as the ammunition on the table held out he was willing [to paraphrase General Grant] "to fight it out on that line if it took all summer."

The enemy made great efforts to reload the gun, but every time a man appeared a whistling messenger, laden with "pie," stopped the performance. It had become intensely interesting and amusing on one side, and exceedingly dangerous on the other. The enemy soon realized the state of affairs, and took all available means to dislodge the sharp-shooters. The trouble was that the little band in the "Bassett house"

Forrest leading a charge on the Yanks.

had command of nearly every gun in the fort, and not only stopped proceedings against themselves, but hampered and annoyed the gunners on the opposite side, so as to prevent anything more than straggling shots, that did little or no execution. The gunboats, however, made active demonstrations in favor of the fort, and one of the shells, intended no doubt for the Bassett house, cut Maj. Thompson in two. But the end was nearer than "the boys" imagined. An unlucky shell from the enemy, striking a little lower, hit the edge of the table and made a promiscuous mingling of china, wood, meat, iron, vegetables, glassware and pie, the "tout ensemble" of a well-regulated dinner-table. It beat a "bull in the china-shop." To see the beautiful walls plastered with pie, and the blackberry jam and preserves dripping mournfully from the ceiling was just a little too much for them. "Boys," said Meriwether, "let's go." The Captain tearfully removed a lump of plum jelly from his eye and said, "You're right." The defenders having left, the enemy immediately riddled the house with solid shot and grape, making a complete wreck of the noble building.

Confederate battery, Pensacola, FL., 1861.

Meeting a refugee from the fort some months afterward, and regaling him with the narrative above stated, he remarked that he was one who tried to work that gun, and escaped the "rebel bullets;" "but," says he, "I smelt the patching!" "How was that?" I answered. "Well, they sent ball right under my nose, taking off a part of my mustache."[119] —
WILLIAM R. ST. CLAIR

☛ AN UNINFORMED YANKEE WOMAN

A young lady of Rock Island, Illinois, was deploring the treatment of Union soldiers in Southern prisons to a Confederate when he asked her to remember that with all the advantages of the Union side in medicine, clothing and food, the percentage of deaths was greater among Confederates in Northern prisons.[120] She was astounded at the remark and said, "Did we have your men in prison?" She had been reared close to the place that many gallant Southerners laid down their lives, and yet had no conception that these deplorable conditions ever existed but on one side.[121] — SUMNER A. CUNNINGHAM

☛ VICISSITUDES OF A PRIVATE SOLDIER

I give you a short history of my soldier life. I was raised in Hardeman County, Tenn., went to Texas in 1859, and was there when the racket commenced between the States. I volunteered in the fourth Texas Cavalry, served seven months, when we were dismounted. Was at Corinth under Generals Van Dorn and Price; thence to Tupelo; thence to Chattanooga, and from there into Kentucky under General Kirby Smith. With 6,000 men he whipped [William] "Bull" Nelson at Richmond with 18,000 men. Out of thirty cannon we got twenty-nine of them, only leaving him one to salute his friends with when he got to Cincinnati, where we stopped running him. I fought at Perryville, was captured and paroled. I then came down here where I was raised. After awhile General Forrest came along, and I went with him for a spell, until the report got circulated in camps that he was going to send all old soldiers back to their old commands at twenty-five dollars per head. I told the boys that I was not for sale, and so one of the darkest rainy nights I ever saw a lot of us ran away, and going down a long red hill south of Jackson, Tenn., one fellow's nag fell down and swapped ends. He got up, felt about for his horse, and got hold of his tail. He said, "Boys, my mare has broke her neck," and it was true. I then went back to the Tennessee Army at Dalton, Ga., and on to Atlanta. Then around Sherman and on to Nashville by way of Franklin. I was in General French's Division, Stewart's Corps, after General [Leonidas] Polk was killed. That occurred June 14, 1864. We did not stay at Nashville; we left there and went south between Nashville and the Tennessee River. On the 25th day of December I gave a fellow $15 for a plug and a half of tobacco. We crossed the Tennessee River and went into Mississippi, and thence to Mobile, Ala. I was in siege there for two weeks. We left for Meridian, Miss., and there we blowed the hounds off.[122] — J. W. JOHNSON

☛ FATHER RYAN TO GENERAL BUTLER
When [Union] Gen. [Benjamin Franklin] Butler was in command at New Orleans during the rebellion, he was informed that [Confederate] Father [Abram Joseph] Ryan, priest and poet, had been expressing rebellious sentiments, and had said he would even refuse to hold funeral service for a dead yankee. Gen. Butler sent for him in haste, and began roundly scolding him for expressing such un-Christian and rebellious sentiments. "General," the wily priest answered, "you have been misinformed; I would be pleased to conduct funeral services for all the yankee officers and men in New Orleans."[123] — DICK REID

Abram J. Ryan, C.S.A.

☛ A SKETCH OF STONEWALL JACKSON
Gen. Thomas Jonathan "Stonewall" Jackson was the most picturesque figure in the war. In him there were two men in one; he united qualities that are not only alien to each other, but that seem almost incompatible—military genius of the highest order with a religious fervor that bordered on fanaticism; a union of the soldier and the saint, for which we must go back to the time of [Oliver] Cromwell. In the great operations of war he was silent and uncommunicative; wrapping himself in his reserve as in a military cloak; asking no advice; forming his own plans, which those nearest to him could not penetrate and hardly dared to conjecture, and were disclosed even to his military family only when he gave his orders for the march and the battle. While the world saw only the soldier with a coat of mail over his breast, those who knew him best saw under it a great human heart.[124] — HENRY M. FIELD

☛ MY MEMORY OF STONEWALL JACKSON

General Thomas Jonathan Jackson and I entered the Virginia Military Institute the same year, 1851, he as a professor and I as a cadet. That quiet, polite and dignified new professor, twice brevetted for gallantry in the Mexican War, soon impressed that corps of high-toned but mischievous young Virginians as being a man of intense individuality of character. He was conscientious and fearless in the discharge of every duty and strictly just in all his intentions.

Stonewall Jackson, C.S.A.

In his class room and at artillery drill he always, in a few but polite words accompanied with that well-known military salute, turned the laugh on all cadets who ventured a joke at his expense, and no excuses were ever rendered for the reports subsequently read at parade, the result of their youthful indiscretion.

While in camp I was visited by my sister, and during her stay at the Rockbridge Alum Professor Jackson was exceedingly polite and deferential. She was deeply impressed by his delicate and gentlemanly attention and kindness to her—a young girl just from school—and it was through her that I first learned to honor the then unknown hero for his chivalrous bearing in the presence of women.

The outbreak of hostilities brought to this modest professor his opportunity to show the world that he was a very great soldier—that he possessed an instinctive genius for war of an amazing brilliancy that could not long be concealed. His conclusions, and their tremendous results when reduced to practice, never appeared to be reached through ordinary intellectual processes, but by instantaneous inspiration.

He knew that his ragged and often starving soldiers idolized him and had most implicit confidence in him, and yet he never courted public demonstrations of any kind. However, his presence on the march and on the battle-field always created the greatest enthusiasm. I often noticed that when cheered on the march he would simply lift his cap in recognition of the shout and immediately spur his Old Sorrel to get by as soon as possible. At Cedar Run, when he appeared in my front after we had driven the enemy, my men greeted him with one of their wild rebel yells, and when it had subsided many called out: "Let General Jackson tell us what he wishes done and we will do it." In recognition of such great enthusiasm on the battle-field he simply bared his head and said not a word.

This great soldier was pure and clean as ever man was; he was both a lover and doer of truth. Of the slightest equivocation or of any conscious indirection he was absolutely incapable. In this respect he measured others by his own standard and, as I well know, he expected every man, and more especially every officer, to perform his whole duty without evasion or neglect or failure.[125] — GEN. JAMES HENRY LANE

☛ A SKETCH OF GENERAL BRADLEY T. JOHNSON

Bradley T. Johnson, C.S.A.

Gen. Bradley Tyler Johnson, Baltimore, President of the Confederate Association in the state of Maryland, began service as Captain of Company A, First Regiment of Infantry. He was promoted to Major, June 17, 1861; to Lieutenant Colonel, July 21, at the battle of Manassas; to Colonel, March 18, 1862; and to Brigadier General, June 28 1862. His gallantry was conspicuous in the hardest trials, Stonewall Jackson's report of the Valley Campaign says: "In a short time the Fifty-eighth Virginia became engaged with a Pennsylvania regiment called the 'Bucktails,' when Colonel Johnson, of the First Maryland Regiment, coming up during the hottest period of the fire, charged gallantly into its flank and drove the enemy with heavy loss from the field, and captured Lieut. Colonel Kane, commanding." General Johnson is at the head of the Confederate Association of Maryland, and has done much in time and money for its maintenance.[126] — SUMNER A. CUNNINGHAM

☛ THE CONFEDERATE DEFEAT AT NASHVILLE

The situation of the [Confederate] army in front of Nashville [December 15-16, 1864] was extraordinary. We were on a range of hills near the Granny White pike, and so situated that for more than a mile to our

Battle of Nashville monument, Nashville, TN. (Photo L. Seabrook)

extreme left the overwhelming forces of the enemy could be seen pressing our flank in so that each private soldier could see for himself that our only avenue for retreat would soon be cut off. The Federal army overwhelmed us. My personal experience is as vivid as anything in life. Our line was broken only a few yards to my right, and the prospect of getting out was so hopeless that my immediate companions refused to undertake to retreat, and remained there to surrender. I had gone about a hundred yards, when I stopped and, turning upon a handsome young Federal, was about to fire upon him and stopped, with the sentiment that he was too brave to be killed, and just then he "pulled down" [shot] on one of our fellows, when with quick, careful aim I fired once more for my home and native land.

That awful, awful day! Hood's army was crushed at Franklin [November 30, 1864], and his soldiers, in going on and on, suffering all that is possible, did it almost without hope; but they would have died a thousand deaths rather than be untrue. No apologies are offered for the rout from before Nashville. No braver and truer men ever existed, and the remnant yet alive care not for the record of that day. They realize that man is not omnipotent.[127] — SUMNER A. CUNNINGHAM

☛ SUMNER A. CUNNINGHAM: BOY SOLDIER

I am a native Tennessean, was a volunteer soldier in the Forty-first Tennessee Infantry. I did my whole duty. I don't remember an engagement with the enemy in which any soldier or officer went farther than I did, except at Franklin, where a few got over the last entrenchment, but I did more effective fighting from the embankment. In the battle of Jonesboro, where we faced two lines of infantry behind breastworks, one above the other, on a hill in the woods, the most awful firing of small arms that I ever heard, I had advanced beyond all my fellows, not realizing that they had fallen back. On seeing that I was within about seventy yards of a thousand men, each of whom could have killed me in a twinkling, I saw near me Lieut. W. S. Bearden, commander of his company, standing by a small tree, the blood pouring from a hole in his trousers above the knee. I assisted in his support to the rear, and went in again, leaving others to care for him.

Sumner A. Cunningham, C.S.A.

I never held a commission, but was Corporal, First Sergeant, and served as Sergeant Major of my regiment. Once I was ordered to wear a sword and take command of two companies in an important task. There was no boy soldier in the command better known, perhaps, and to these veterans I submit for testimony. Because I was "so small, and a good soldier," by special favor of my Colonel, J. D. Tillman, now a banker and lawyer at Fayetteville, Tenn,. I was permitted to carry a short Enfield rifle. However, it was an effective gun—it was submerged in blood at Franklin. I was faithful through the war, and if I ever fail murder me, cover me in a ditch and mark not the spot.[128] — SUMNER A. CUNNINGHAM

☛ THE ALL-AMERICAN SOUTH IN 1894
The war ended twenty-eight years ago, but it is still the habit of the North to think of the people of the States which attempted to secede as enemies of the Union and of the Constitution. . . . [Thus] it will be said, admitting that the South is American, and has preserved the Anglo-Saxon traits, nevertheless a war was necessary to keep her in the Union. . . .

The excellence of the American Union is in the principles upon which it is established—that is to say, in the Constitution. Surely no man will say that it is more important to preserve the physical integrity of the Union than the principles of the Constitution. We claim for the South, in the war between the states, absolute good faith. Whether she was right or wrong, the impartial judgment of the future will fairly determine. I affirm that the South has been, from the first, absolutely faithful to the principles of the Constitution, as she in good faith construed it. Let me indicate briefly the extent of her participation in the formation of the Constitution and the establishment of the Republic. *It is correctly said by a Southern statesman that the Constitution was "adopted and promulgated by a convention in which Southern influences predominated."*

Virginia did lead the movement for the establishment of the Constitution, and the reader who wishes to know the extent of the influence of George Washington, of Virginia, in this movement, is referred to the pages of John Fiske, of New England. [John] Rutledge and [Charles Cotesworth] Pinckney, of South Carolina, were the most important contributors to the form, as to the substance, of the Constitution, with the exception of James Madison, of Virginia, who justly bears the name of "Father of the Constitution." The Bill of Rights is mainly the work of Thomas Jefferson.

Charles C. Pinckney.

During the first century of our national life Southern statesmen held the Presidency and shaped the policy of the Government. They acquired Florida, and extended our domain to the Rio Grande and to the Pacific. The Constitution was first construed by John Marshall, of Virginia. The school of strict constructionists, which made a fetish of the Constitution, was founded and supported by Southern men. When the Southern Confederacy was formed [in 1861] it adopted as organic law the old [U.S.] Constitution, unchanged in any essential respect.

There is no fact nor logic which can prove that the South ever deviated from her fealty to the Constitution, or ever shed a drop of blood except in defense of its principles as she construed it.

The war construed the Constitution, and the South has in good faith and unreservedly accepted every legitimate result of the war. No man who is honest and who is adequately informed will say that her people are not absolutely loyal to the Union and the Constitution. *I go further,* and affirm that in the troubles which the future is sure to bring, the principles and the institutions of American liberty will find their most loyal and steadfast support in the twelve millions of Southern Anglo-Saxon Americans.[129] — SUMNER A. CUNNINGHAM

☛ TOUCHING INCIDENT DURING THE VIRGINIA CAMPAIGN
As the last assaulting column of blue approached [us], Capt. John P. Rains, commander of our company (A), was patting me on the shoulder and repeatedly saying as I loaded my Springfield rifle as rapidly as possible, "Give 'em hell Needham; give 'em hell!" Suddenly . . . [a Union] officer, mounted on a fine, swift horse, came at a racing run along the plank road from the yankee lines, and it seemed that I was the first one to notice him, and I called to the boys to "shoot the man on the horse," at the same time firing obliquely toward him. The gallant fellow reeled and fell a corpse on the hard plank of the road. After the battle was over, and we returned to the bloody ground where we made the stand, Captain Rains, I and others went to where the dead officer lay, whom Captain Rains recognized as a schoolmate of his at the Philadelphia Law School. The gallant Captain burst into tears over the fate of his old-time friend. He was [U.S.] Colonel of a Pennsylvania regiment, but I have forgotten his name. Several of the boys fired at the same time, so none of us knew who sent the fatal ball, and I am glad of it.[130] — NEEDHAM B. HOGAN

☛ SKETCH OF GEN. WILLIAM L. CABELL
Gen. William Lewis Cabell was born in Danville, Va., Jan. 1. 1827. He was the third child of Gen. Benj. W. S. and Sarah Eppes Cabell, who lived to see seven sons and two daughters grown, six sons held prominent positions in the Confederate Army. The seventh, Dr. Powhattan Cabell, died from the effect of an arrow wound received in Florida just before the Confederate War began.

Gen. Cabell entered the Military Academy at West Point in June, 1846, graduating in 1850. He entered the United States Army as Second Lieutenant, and was assigned to the 7th Infantry. In June, 1855, he was promoted to First Lieutenant and made Regimental Quartermaster of that regiment. In March, 1858, he was made Captain in the Quartermaster's Department and ordered on duty on Gen. Pessifer F.

Smith's Staff, who was then in command of the Utah Expedition. After Gen. Smith's death [U.S.] Gen. [William Selby] Harney assumed command, and Capt. Cabell remained on Gen. Harney's staff until the close of the expedition, when he was ordered to rebuild Fort Kearney. In the spring of 1859 he was ordered to Fort Arbuckle in the Chickasaw Nation, and in the fall of that year to build a new post about 100 miles west of Arbuckle, high up on the Washita River in the Indian country.

When the war became inevitable Capt. Cabell repaired to Fort Smith, Ark., and from there went to Little Rock and offered his services to the Governor of the State. On receipt of a telegram from President Davis he went to Montgomery. Ala., then the Confederate Capital. Capt. Cabell reached Montgomery April 19th, where he found the acceptance of his resignation from the United States Army, signed by President Lincoln.

He was at once commissioned as Major under the Confederate Government, and under orders from President Davis left on April 21st for Richmond to organize the Quartermaster Commissary and Ordnance Departments. He remained in Richmond attending to all these duties until June 1, 1861, when he was ordered to Manassas to report to Gen. Beauregard as Chief Quartermaster of the Army of the Potomac.

After the battles of the 18th and 19th of July Gen. Joseph E. Johnston assumed command and Major Cabell served on his staff until January 15, 1862, when he was relieved and ordered to report to Gen.

William L. Cabell, C.S.A.

Albert Sidney Johnston, then in command of the Army of the West. He was assigned to Gen. Van Dorn in the Trans-Mississippi Department, with headquarters then at Jacksonport, Ark.

He was next promoted to the rank of Brigadier General, and assigned to command of all the troops on White River, where he held the enemy in check until after the battle of Elk Horn, March 6th and 7th. After that battle the army was transferred to the east side of the Mississippi. The removal of this army, which included [Sterling] Price's Missouri and [Ben] McCulloch's Arkansas, Louisiana and Texas troops, and his own command, devolved on Gen. Cabell, and was performed within a single week from points along White River.

Van Dorn's Army continued, after reaching Memphis, to Corinth, and Gen Cabell was assigned to a Texas brigade with an Arkansas regiment attached. He commanded this brigade in several engagements around Farmington and Corinth, and commanded the rear of Van Dorn's Army on the retreat from Corinth to Tupelo.

Gen. Bragg's Army was ordered to Kentucky, and Gen. Cabell was transferred to an Arkansas brigade, which he commanded in the battles of Iuka and Saltillo in September, and at Corinth on October 2 and 3, 1862, also at Hatchie Bridge on the 4th of October. He was wounded leading the charge of his brigade on the breastworks at Corinth, and also at Hatchie Bridge, which disabled him from command. What was left of his command was temporarily assigned to the 1st Missouri Brigade under Gen. [John Calvin] Brown. He was ordered to the Trans-Mississippi Department to recuperate and inspect the Staff Departments of that army.

When sufficiently recovered for duty in the field he was, February, 1863, placed in command of all the forces in Northwest Arkansas, with instructions to augment his command by recruits from every part of the State. He was very successful, and organized one of the largest cavalry brigades west of the Mississippi. He commanded this brigade in more than twenty battles. On the raid into Missouri under Gen. Price he was captured in the open field near Mine Creek in October, 1864, and was taken to Johnson Island (in Lake Erie), and later to Fort Warren near Boston, until released August 28, 1865.

Grover Cleveland.

Gen. Cabell went from Boston to New York, and thence to Austin, Texas. He subsequently lived at Fort Smith, Ark., and engaged in the practice of law until he moved to Dallas, Texas, in December, 1872. He was Chairman of the Democratic [then the Conservative party] Executive Committee in Arkansas, and Chairman of the Arkansas Democratic delegation that went to the Baltimore Convention which [bizarrely] nominated [socialist] Horace Greeley for the Presidency. He was four times elected Mayor of Dallas; was a delegate from the State of Texas to the Convention that nominated Mr. [Samuel Jones] Tilden in St. Louis and President [Grover] Cleveland at Chicago in 1S84 and 1892. He served as U.S. Marshal under President Cleveland's first administration.

[As of 1894] Gen. Cabell is Lieutenant General of the Association of United Confederate Veterans, commanding the Trans-Mississippi Department, embracing all the country west of the Mississippi River. He is ever zealous in forwarding their interests. Gen. Cabell married the daughter of Maj. Elias Rector, of Arkansas, a woman of great intelligence and courage, and noted for her ready wit. During the war she followed her husband and did much to relieve the sick and wounded. Her name was "Shingo," an Indian name, meaning "Little Bird," and the soldiers thought no name so sweet or more appropriate as she came from near or far to answer their cries for aid when in distress. His oldest son Hen. K. Cabell, was Deputy U.S. Marshal under his father, and is now Sheriff of Dallas County, Texas, being the youngest man ever elected to that office in the county. Three other sons, all noble boys, and one married daughter, Mrs. J. R. Currie, whose husband is a Mississippian, form his household and share his love for the South, and prize her noble and wonderful history.[131] — SUMNER A. CUNNINGHAM

☛ SKETCH OF GEN. STEPHEN DILL LEE

Stephen D. Lee, C.S.A.

Born at Charleston, S.C., September 22, 1833. Graduated at West Point, in 1854. In the United States Army until South Carolina seceded when he resigned in 1861. He was one of the officers who carried Beauregard's demand for the surrender of Fort Sumter, and afterward the order to open fire on the fort. He was Captain of Artillery, Hampton's Legion, in Virginia, then Major, Lieutenant Colonel and Colonel of artillery, and was in the battles of the Peninsular campaign from Yorktown to Richmond, Seven Pines, Savage's Station and Malvern Hill. He did gallant service also in the battles of Second Manassas and Sharpsburg. He was promoted to Brigadier General and sent from Virginia to Mississippi and commanded batteries and garrison of Vicksburg under Gen. M. L. [Martin Luther] Smith. He defeated Sherman at Chickasaw Bayou, in the winter of 1862 and 1863. Three horses were shot from under him at Baker's Creek. After the siege of Vicksburg he was made Major General to command all the cavalry in Mississippi, Alabama, East Louisiana and West Tennessee. He was again promoted to Lieutenant General and placed in command of that department. He organized cavalry regiments, confronted Sherman's army of 30,000 men with his cavalry force of 2,500 men from Vicksburg to Meridian, fought with General Forrest the battle of Harrisburg, Miss., against A. J. [Andrew Jackson] Smith's army, where the odds were 5,000 against 16,000 Federals. The latter withdrew toward Memphis.

Rippavilla Plantation, Spring Hill, TN., on Columbia Pike, where Hood and his officers breakfasted the morning after the disastrous Battle of Spring Hill. (Photo L. Seabrook)

Later he was assigned to command of Hood's Corps, Army of Tennessee, before Atlanta, and was in the battles of 28th of July and also at Jonesboro. He was with Hood in his Tennessee campaign, his corps was left at Columbia with two divisions, artillery and wagon trains of the army, while Hood made his flank movement at Spring Hill, arrived at Franklin in time to take part with one division in that terrible battle, having marched from Columbia after the balance of the army had reached Spring Hill; was in the battles around Nashville, and repulsed the enemy in his assault on Overton Hill, which was held until the left and center of our army was driven back in disorder. He covered retreat of the army, after its disastrous rout, his corps being the only one with organization intact. Daring the next day after the rout, he presented a defiant front, repulsing every effort of Wilson's cavalry, from early dawn to 10 o'clock at night. So successful was this persistence that little or no effort was made for battle afterward. On the second day of the battle, a rear guard was organized under the command of Generals Walthall and Forrest, the latter having arrived from Murfreesboro, but the pursuit was feeble after the first day, no fight of consequence occurred, and Hood was allowed to recross the Tennessee River. Gen. Lee was severely wounded while with the rear guard in the afternoon of the day after the rout. He surrendered with his corps, under Gen. J. E. Johnston, in North Carolina.

Since the war Gen. Lee has been a planter, and President of the Mississippi Agricultural and Mechanical College, which position he now holds. He has represented his county and district in the State Senate, and was a member of the convention which framed the Constitution of his State. He was sixty years of age September 1893. He is the third officer in rank of living Confederates, Generals Longstreet and A. P. Stewart having older commissions.[132] — SUMNER A. CUNNINGHAM

☛ SKETCH OF THE GALLANT JOHN PELHAM

He was of "Kentucky stock," but born in Alabama, September 7, 1838. The London *Times* said he excelled any man of his age, on either side, in the great conflict.

Young Pelham was at West Point, and would have received his commission [in the U.S. army] in a week, but he resigned and came South to enlist for his section. As a cadet he had dash and soldierly bearing. He always walked straight as a "bee line," and never looked back, no matter how much noise the other cadets made in his rear. He was considered the best athlete at West Point, and was noted for fencing and boxing. . . .

At Cold Harbor he advanced one gun a third of a mile to the front, and for more than an hour it was the only gun on the Confederate left firing, drawing the attention of a whole Federal battery, until Stuart said to Stonewall Jackson: "General, all your artillery on the left is idle; nobody is firing except Pelham." After the battle the warm pressure of Jackson's hand told how well he had demeaned himself. Shortly after this Pelham drove a gunboat from the "White House" with one gun. He again received the thanks of Stonewall at second Manassas, where he thrust his guns forward almost into the enemy's columns, and used them with bloody effect. During this fight Jackson said to Stuart, pointing to the young artillerist at his guns: "General, if you have another Pelham, give him to me." He was then twenty-three years old.

John Pelham, C.S.A.

In the bloody repulse at Shepardstown his guns roared for hours. It was in this gory track that an instance occurred which illustrates his courage. He was with one gun far in advance of the others, when the enemy almost reached him, and Stuart ordered him to retire; but he begged successfully to be allowed to remain a little longer, but his cannoneers "scampered away" and left him alone. He loaded the piece and fired almost in the face of the enemy surging forward like a great billow; and then, mounting one of the lead horses, began to gallop away with the cannon, but had not proceeded far when the horse was shot from under him. Quickly cutting the traces, to be free from the dead animal, he mounted another, and it, too, was shot down immediately. He escaped with the gun only after a third horse had been shot.

At Sharpsburg he commanded nearly all the artillery on the Confederate left, and rent the blue lines with shot and shell. . . .

Amid shot and shell he had opened the great battle of Fredericksburg, and had become immortal. He was a Major of artillery then. His commission as Lieutenant Colonel was issued soon after, and only waited confirmation when he was killed at Kelly's Ford, on the Rappahannock [River], March 17, 1863. He had gone to visit some ladies in Culpeper County, when he heard the cannonading and hurried to the scene. His artillery had not come up, but he galloped to a regiment that was wavering, and shouted: "Forward, boys! forward to victory and glory!" and at that moment was struck by the fragment of a shell that penetrated the brain, and he died shortly after midnight.

Gen. Stuart telegraphed to Hon. J. L. M. Curry, at present trustee of the great Peabody Fund, who then represented Pelham's Alabama district in the Confederate Congress: "The noble, the chivalric, 'the gallant Pelham' is no more. He was killed in action yesterday. His remains will be sent to you to-day. How much he was beloved, appreciated and admired let the tears of agony we shed and the gloom of mourning throughout my command bear witness. His loss is irreparable."

His remains were taken to Richmond, and lay in state at the Capitol, viewed by thousands. He was buried at Jacksonville, Ala., amid the scenes of his childhood. Gen. Stuart's general order to the division, announcing his death, concluded: "His eyes had glanced over every battlefield of this army from the first Manassas to the moment of his death; and, with a single exception, he was a brilliant actor in all. The memory of 'the gallant Pelham' his many virtues, his noble nature and purity of character are a sacred legacy in the hearts of all who knew him. His record was bright and spotless, and his career brilliant and successful."

He was calmly and recklessly brave, and saw men torn to pieces around him without emotion, "because his heart and eye were upon the stern work he was performing." Such is the brief but resplendent career of the "boy artillerist."[133] — JOHN D. RENFROE

Confederate Veterans Home in Maryland, 1894.

☛ HOME FOR FEMALE CONFEDERATES IN CHARLESTON

This "oldest" of Homes for Confederates is in its twenty-seventh year. It is for women only, the mothers, widows and daughters of Confederate soldiers. It was founded and has been managed by women. It has housed hundreds of widows and educated nearly a thousand daughters of Confederate soldiers. The association owns a valuable and extensive building, formerly the Carolina Hotel, on Broad street. At its twenty-sixth anniversary meeting, January 30th, a gift of twenty thousand dollars was announced from Baltimore. The gift is the finer because the name of the donor is withheld.[134] — SUMNER A. CUNNINGHAM

☛ THE CAREER OF THE C.S.S. *MERRIMAC*

Having been one of the *Merrimac's* [Confederate] officers, and with her during her whole career, I am somewhat familiar with her history. On March 8, 1862, the *Merrimac*, with ten guns, destroyed the [U.S.S.] *Cumberland*, twenty-four guns; [U.S.S.] *Congress*, fifty guns; riddled the [U.S.S.] *Minnesota*, forty-eight guns, and put to flight the [U.S.S.] *St. Lawrence*, fifty guns, and [U.S.S.] *Roanoke*, forty-eight guns. In the encounter with the [U.S.S.] *Monitor* on the following day, after a fearful combat of five hours, when they were frequently only a few yards apart, the *Merrimac* having only shell, which were not effective against the iron turret of the *Monitor*, succeeded in dislodging her pilot-house and blinding and otherwise disabling her commander. The *Monitor* then hauled over the bar into shallow water, where the *Merrimac* could not follow her. The *Merrimac* returned to Norfolk and went into the dock for repairs, two of her guns having had their muzzles shot off, her armor considerably damaged, her prow wrenched off, and her steam pipes and smoke stack completely riddled.

U.S.S. frigate *Cumberland*.

On the 11th of April the *Merrimac* returned to Hampton Roads. The *Monitor* was plainly in sight, together with the iron battery, *Naugatuck,* and other war ships. Seeing no disposition upon their part to engage, the *Merrimac*, to provoke them, sent in two of her tenders, the [C.S.S.] *Jamestown* and [C.S.S.] *Raleigh*, and they cut out and brought away one brig and two schooners in plain sight of the Federal fleet and of the French war ship *Gapendi*, and of the British Corvette *Rinaldo*.

On the 8th of May following, while the *Merrimac* was at the Gasport Navy Yard, a tremendous fire was opened upon the battery at Sewell's Point by the ironclads *Monitor* and [U.S.S.] *Naugatuck*, and the United States steamers *Susquehanna*, seventeen guns; *Dacotah*, six guns; *Seminole*, five guns, and *San Jacinto*, twelve guns. The *Merrimac* immediately got under way and proceeded to the scene of conflict, regarding the attack as an invitation to come out and fight. Upon getting in full view of the situation, we saw just beyond the attacking squadron the [U.S.S.] flag ship *Minnesota*, forty-eight guns; *Cayuga*, six guns; *Jamestown*, twenty two guns; *St. Lawrence*, fifty guns, and the powerful steamers *Vanderbilt, Baltimore, Illinois* and *Asago*, especially arranged and equipped for running the *Merrimac* down. The *Merrimac* continued on at full speed, and when within about a mile of the nearest vessel, they all, with one accord, got under way and ran below Fortress Monroe.

The two-gun U.S.S. *Monitor* (foreground), the ten-gun C.S.S. *Merrimac* (background).

The *Merrimac* continued the pursuit until the shots from the [island of] Rip Raps (Fort Wool) were flying away beyond her. She steamed slowly about the [Hampton] Roads until nearly dark, and then returned to her anchorage.

The above facts are matters of record. I challenge any one to show by any authentic record or statement that the *Merrimac* was ever defeated, that she ever declined an engagement, regardless of the number or strength of her adversaries, or that she ever lost an opportunity to bring on an engagement if possible. . . . no ship ever did as much to revolutionize naval warfare and to rebuild the navies of the world.[135] — H. B. LITTLEPAGE

☛ SKETCH OF STANLEY S. CRITTENDEN
Maj. Gen. Stanley S. Crittenden, commanding the Division of South Carolina, United Confederate Veterans, is a native of his State, and is sixty-three years old. His father, Dr. John Crittenden, was one of the early settlers of Greenville. His grandfather, Nathaniel Crittenden, of Connecticut, was a Lieutenant, and one of six brothers in the Continental Army. The mother of Gen. Crittenden was Miss Stanley, a member of that well known family in the old North State, he was educated in Greenville and at Elizabeth, N.J.

Stanley S. Crittenden, C.S.A.

In 1855 Gen. Crittenden married Miss Eliza E. Lynch, of Virginia, who died in 1868, leaving one son and three daughters. He afterward married Mrs. C. A. Bedell, of Columbia, S.C., a lady eminent for her culture.

Gen. Crittenden was a planter. He volunteered at the first call for troops, and was elected First Lieutenant of a company that became part of the 4th South Carolina regiment under Col. J. B. E. Sloan, and participated prominently in the first battle of Manassas. This regiment and Wheat's battalion, forming Evans' brigade, on our extreme left, commenced the great battle and held the hosts of the enemy in check for two hours before being reinforced. The regiment suffered severely in killed and wounded. The day after this battle Lieut. Crittenden received the appointment of Adjutant in place of the gallant Samuel D. Wilkes, of Anderson, who was killed.

In the great battle of Seven Pines, in May, 1862, when many of this gallant regiment were killed, Adjt. Crittenden was wounded by a minie ball in the left breast while in front of his command. During his absence because of this wound Gov. [Francis Wilkinson] Pickens appointed him Lieutenant Colonel of the 4th Regiment of Reserves then forming for the defense of the Carolina Coast. At the expiration of this service on the coast he volunteered as a private in Gen. [Martin Witherspoon] Gary's mounted regiment, [Wade] Hampton's famous legion, for service around Richmond. He also served on the staff of [Confederate] Gen. [Martin Witherspoon] Gary.

After the war Gen. Crittenden returned to planting, but for ten years served in his State Legislature as Representative and as Senator. He was Postmaster at Greenville four years during Mr. [Grover] Cleveland's first administration. He succeeds Gen. Ellison Capers, now Assistant Bishop of South Carolina, and has devoted much time and attention to the interests of the brotherhood [the U.C.V.], and the number of Camps has increased from six to more than thirty. He hopes to meet the representatives of at least fifty Camps of United Confederate Veterans from the Palmetto State at Birmingham.[136] — SUMNER A. CUNNINGHAM

☛ WAR REMINISCENCES—MOTHER OF THE CONFEDERACY
The venerable Mrs. Sallie Chapman Gordon-Law, of Memphis, Tenn., dedicates some "Reminiscences of the War of the Sixties" to her children, grandchildren and friends, in a neat pamphlet of sixteen pages. Although "Mother of the Confederacy," she still lives to testify in behalf of a people who dared perform their duty as they saw it, regardless of cost, comfort or life.

The story she tells concisely begins with woman's work for our armies in Memphis. Every day but Sunday the women met and sewed for the private soldiers. When her own son went home from school, threw down his books and said, "Mother, I have enlisted for the war," she replied, "You did right, my son."

In the narrative she says: "My home has ever been in the Sunny South; my paternal ancestors, the Gordons of Virginia, my mother's, the Kings of South Carolina, were all rebels of the first revolution; my father, Chapman Gordon (in his teens), with two elder brothers, Nat and Charles, fought in the battle at King's Mountain, and through the entire war.

"My mother's father, too old for the [American Revolutionary] war, sent all his sons and sons-in-law. They fought in and belonged to the command of Generals [Francis] Marion and [Thomas] Sumpter. My second brother, Wyley J. Gordon, was an officer in the U. S. Army, in the War of 1812. My brother, Gen. George W. Gordon, of Columbia, Tennessee, with three sons, fought in the Confederate Army of 1861. My nephew, Gen. John B. Gordon, whose record for valor and heroic deeds is too well known to call for comment, with his three brothers, all fought in the Confederate Army. My nephew, Maj. Augustus Gordon, was killed at the age of twenty-one, while leading a charge at Chancellorsville, Virginia. My brothers, Charles' grandsons and Harvey's sons, were in the Confederate Army. My cousin, Gen. James B. Gordon, of North Carolina, was killed at Brandy Station, near Richmond, in Confederate service. And I know of over thirty brave, heroic privates of my kindred who belonged to the war of the 'Sixties.'

Mrs. Sallie Chapman Gordon-Law of Memphis, TN, known as "the Mother of the Confederacy."

". . . After the battle of Shiloh, many of the wounded were brought to our hospital. I carried many articles of clothing, etc., beyond the lines to our soldiers.

"In our hospital at Memphis, we had domestic wines, lemons, pickles, clothing, and I proposed taking them to our sick soldiers at Columbus, Kentucky. I had large boxes packed and carried them to the hospital there. I made the second trip a few weeks later with more supplies for the sick. The morning after my arrival the battle of Belmont came off. We were on the steamer *Prince*, at breakfast, when Capt. Butler came in, saying: 'Ladies, finish your breakfast, but the yankees are landing their gunboats above.' We jumped up and ran out on the guards and saw the wildest confusion—soldiers running to and fro to get ready for the battle; then the cannonading commenced from the Federal gunboats, with Confederate artillery from the high bluffs. The cannonading was sublimely grand. My own dear boy was there in Gen. Cheatham's command, marching out to battle. It was a grand, victorious battle for us.

". . . The steamer *Prince*, on which we were staying, carried over many wounded Confederates, and among them the brave, heroic Gen. William H. Jackson, whom it was our privilege to nurse and attend. He was dreadfully wounded, and that night many officers came in to see him, Dr. Bell, Surgeon, from Memphis, among the number. Young Dr. Yandel came in, and Dr. Bell said to him, 'Yandel, I want you to go and detail so many men (I forgot the number), with buckets of water, and go to the battlefield and give those wounded and dying men water.' I went to Gen. [Leonidas] Polk and got an order to have four yankee surgeons taken out of prison to go to the battlefield to attend their wounded, and every one of them refused to go, but ours went.

George W. Gordon, C.S.A.

". . . Standing in the pilot-house with us was a young girl who had gone up to see her brother. She had always lived in Cincinnati with an aunt, her mother being dead and father and brother living in Memphis; when the war commenced her father had gone and brought her home. Young Star had enlisted in the same company with my son. All the way going up on the boat she had been defending the Union; and while the battle was raging, and the musketry mowing down thousands, with tears streaming down her face, she said, 'Oh I wish I had a gun. Oh! for a gun!' 'What do you want with a gun, Alice?' 'To kill the yankees.'

"After the battle was over I went to the hospital to see if I could do anything for the wounded. I was invited in to see the apparently mortally wounded Federal officer, Col. Dorrity. At sight of the wounded man I lost sight of the enemy of my country. I made a glass of lemonade and fed him with a spoon, as one arm was cut off and the other paralyzed. I said to him, 'Col. Dorrity, have you a wife?' He replied, 'Yes, at Cape Girardeau.' At that moment Col. Bethel, Gen. Polk's Adjutant, came in, and I said to him, 'Col. Bethel, will you please take my compliments to Gen. Polk and ask him, as a special favor, to let Col. Dorrity's wife be sent for.' He left immediately, and a courier and a flag of truce were sent for her, by order of the magnanimous, heroic Gen. Polk. At two o'clock P.M. the next day, the wife of the prostrate, paralyzed, wounded husband, was with him.

"The morning after the battle of Belmont, I called at [Confederate] Gen. [Gideon Johnson] Pillow's office, on business, when a little boy came in with a message. He was dressed up in Confederate uniform, with a military cap. I asked, 'Why, my little boy, what are you doing here?' He said, very modestly, 'I belong to the army.' 'What can you do here?' 'Well, yesterday I was on the battle-field, and got down in a sink hole, when I saw a yankee with his gun pointed right at my Colonel, and I fired away and killed him—now, that is what I am doing here.' 'How old are you?' 'Twelve years old.' 'Where were your father and mother to let you come here?'

Gideon J. Pillow, C.S.A.

'Oh! I ran away, and am staying at my uncle's tent, and if you don't believe I killed the yank, come with me and see his watch.' He said to Gen. Pillow, 'Now, I want a furlough to go home and see my father and mother'. . . . He got it.

"After the Federals occupied Memphis, I heard that my dear brother, George W. Gordon, a prisoner from Johnson's Island, was on a boat anchored out in the Mississippi River, very ill. I walked up and down the river bank from nine till five, trying to get permission to go to see him. At last I met Col. Oaks, a Federal officer, who politely said he would send me in a skiff, and I was taken by two Federal soldiers. On reaching the boat, it was filled by Confederate officers, prisoners from Johnson's

Island, bound for Vicksburg to be exchanged. I found my brother very ill, so ill I remained with him that night, and Col. Johnson, an elegant gentleman from Kentucky, proffered his berth to me, he sleeping on a blanket in the cabin. . . . I left for Vicksburg next day to nurse and attend to him, driven by a ten year old grandson; but when I arrived at Mrs. Vernon's, sixty miles from Memphis, I heard the sad news that he had died in ten minutes after landing at Vicksburg.

". . . My noble, patriotic brother, the Christian soldier, tried to lead souls to Christ. Regularly, night and morning, he had prayers, and invited all who were disposed to attend.

Meeting of the United Daughters of the Confederacy, 1897.

"Our hospitals all broken up, I felt I must seek a new field in which to work. In our Southern Mothers' treasury was $2,500 in Confederate money, and, with the aid of Mrs. W. S. Pickett, we laid it all out for quinine, morphine and opium, and I carried it into the Confederacy, on my person, distributing it in the hospitals at LaGrange, Ga., and there I had the compliment of having a hospital called for me (The Law Hospital), which many Surgeons and old soldiers still recollect.

"Miss Anna Hardee, [Confederate] General [William Joseph] Hardee's daughter, went the rounds daily with me. We made egg-nogg every day for the pneumonia and typhoid patients, and carried coffee to sick patients. . . .

"While at Columbus, Ga., I heard of the terrible destitution of the soldiers at Dalton, Ga., in Gen. J. E. Johnston's division. Thousands of soldiers were having to sit up all night round a log fire, for want of blankets. I was so greatly troubled to hear of the great suffering of the brave heroes who were standing like a "stone wall" between the women and children of the South and the enemy, that after a sleepless night, I went directly to a Ladies' Aid Society, where a number of patriotic women of Columbus, Ga. were at work for the soldiers. I told what I had heard of the suffering, for want of blankets, by the soldiers, and made an appeal to them for aid, telling them if they would furnish the blankets, I would go in person to Dalton and distribute them to the soldiers. With generous liberality, boxes of good things—chicken, ham, sausage, butter, pickles, bread and cake were packed, and I carried them to our Memphis soldier boys at the time I did the blankets.

"On Christmas night I left for Dalton, accompanied by the noble, patriotic President of that Aid Society, Mrs. Robt. Carter. At Atlanta my boxes had to be rechecked to Dalton. I met Dr. LaGree, of New Orleans, who proposed to telegraph Dr. John Erskine to meet us on our arrival at Dalton, at three o'clock in the morning, and he did so.

". . . At Dalton I sent a note to Gen. Hardee, Gen. Johnston being absent, telling him my mission. He came immediately. A courier and carriage were sent to us, and our first visit was to the old 154th Regiment, Gen. Preston Smith's. That night we had quite a levee of Officers. Gen. Hardee said that he had in his division fifteen hundred men without a blanket; Gen. [Thomas Carmichael] Hindman, one thousand; Gen. Cheatham, hundreds; and many other divisions in a similar condition. Gen. Pat Cleburne said socks were a luxury his men did not know; he had not had a pair on for five months.

"That evening a wagon was sent, with twenty soldiers, to receive the blankets I had brought. The boxes had been opened by order of Dr. Erskine; and I distributed the blankets and clothing to those who needed them.

". . . I then returned to Columbus, wrote and published in the papers what I had seen and heard at Dalton, of the great need of blankets for the Confederate soldiers, and made another appeal to that Ladies' Aid Society for more blankets. And they again nobly responded to my request, and went to work with zeal unprecedented, working night and day, taking the last blanket from their beds, cutting up carpets and lining them. I went out and in one hour I collected twenty-five hundred dollars from the business houses, and laid it out in the Columbus factories for jeans and coarse cloth. The women and children worked night and day, and in ten days I returned to the army in Dalton with seven large dry goods boxes, one each for Tennessee, Kentucky, Mississippi, Louisiana, Arkansas, Missouri, and Texas, all packed with five hundred and thirty blankets and coverings, and sixteen hundred pairs of socks, for the soldiers. I then went up to Tunnel Hill where Gen. Cleburne had his division; we rode on sacks of corn, for a freight train carried the Arkansas box to his soldiers. Had the boxes opened at the General's quarters, and as he was very soon to make a speech to his men on re-enlisting, said the box of blankets would do more than anything he could say, showing them the interest the women at home felt in them. But for the generous aid of the noble, patriotic women of Columbus, Ga., I would have been powerless to take those needed stores of blankets and socks to our suffering soldiers.

"After the second effort by the ladies of Columbus, and expecting to make the second trip with blankets, I wrote to Gen. Johnston of my intention, and asked him to send me an escort to Dalton. The difficulty in having to travel with so many boxes, and they to be transferred at Atlanta, was hazardous and annoying. Gen. Johnston sent the escort immediately and we left again for the seat of war, this time accompanied by three ladies, Mrs. Sallie Wilkins, my niece, and a daughter and granddaughter of Gov. [John] Forsythe. We were invited to dine with Generals Johnston, Hindman, [Alfred] Cumming and others, and my escort to dinner at Gen. Cumming's was the Rev. Dr. Stiles. We had four o'clock Confederate dinners, and were always sent for by the Adjutant of the General with whom we were to dine, with a carriage, and always escorted by Dr.

John. Gen. J. C. Brown gave a party in honor of my lady friends. His headquarters were out about two miles in a large eight room brick house. The rooms were handsomely draped with Confederate flags, with a splendid band of music in the wide hall. There the Episcopal Bishop and the Presbyterian Rebel woman stood on the same platform under the Confederate flag. Gen. Johnston ordered a grand parade—thirty thousand brave, tattered troops—in honor of my mission to his soldiers. Mrs. Johnston invited me to take a seat in her carriage.

". . . My poor services to my struggling, bleeding country I know was only a drop in the ocean of that gigantic, cruel civil war. Still, for all those years of the 'Sixties,' they were most cheerfully, lovingly, and gratuitously given. In all my trips with supplies for the soldiers, I paid all my own expenses, never asking or receiving so much as a railroad pass or ticket. No, no; my whole heart and thoughts and deepest sympathies were all absorbed in the destiny of my people. For that just cause I would have died, could that sacrifice have brought peace, instead of a surrender, in which all was lost, save honor.

Young Confederate ladies, Lebanon, TN, 1899.

"Could I write all the incidents of my war record of the 'Sixties' a book could not contain them—the many reminiscences of those sad, gloomy, sorrowful years of terror and gloom. Perhaps at fifty years I might have accomplished it, but now, at eighty-seven years, I feel inadequate to the task; still, memories of suffering, blood, and tears at the bedside of the wounded, dying soldier, is indelibly stamped on my memory, and will probably last until the dreams of this fitful, checkered life are over, and I am transported to that 'House of many mansions,' prepared for all who love and serve God. I have had the honor of being called the 'Mother of the Confederacy,' a compliment I esteem higher than any that could be conferred upon me."[137] — MRS. SALLIE CHAPMAN GORDON-LAW

☛ SKETCH OF GEN. JUBAL A. EARLY

The fall down some steps by the Lynchburg, Va., postoffice, February 16th, was the cause of Gen. Jubal Anderson Early's death. It was pitiable to see that the gallant old hero was so dazed by the fall as to object to leaving the carriage on arriving home, saying it was not his home. He was taken out in a wheel chair several days in succession, but he died in two weeks.

Gen. Early was born in Franklin County, Virginia, November 4. 1816. His father, Jacob Early, was a farmer, his mother a Miss Hairston, who inherited a large number of slaves.

While Early was a student at West Point he and [future Yankee General] Joe Hooker, who made high reputation in the battles for the Union, had a difficulty that grew out of a debate in which Early excepted to Hooker's speech upon "the atrocities of slavery." Early was a Whig [the Liberal party of that day] of the old school, and defeated a candidate "who advocated disruption of the Union" in the memorable convention of 1861. He was the extreme member of the convention in favor of the Union, and the last to sign the secession ordinance, and then entered upon the journal his special reasons for concurring. . . .

Jubal A. Early, C.S.A.

Dr. J. William Jones, Chaplain of the University of Virginia, writes: But now that he has "passed over to the great majority," let us forget his faults [gambling] and remember his great ability, his stern patriotism, his unpurchasable integrity, his love for truth, his hatred of skulking "during or since the war," his unwavering devotion to the land and cause he loved so well, and his able defense of the truth of Confederate history, and manly vindication of the name and fame of our Confederate leaders and people.

Robert E. Lee, C.S.A.

As a soldier, he was unquestionably one of the ablest men we had. His service in command of Ewell's old division at First Fredericksburg, Second Fredericksburg, Gettysburg, and the campaign of 1864, from the Rapidan to Cold Harbor, and the ability with which he handled A. P. Hill's corps when in temporary command of it at Spottsylvania Court House, during the sickness of Gen. Hill, gave the army and the people the highest opinion of his ability as a soldier, and there was no surprise when it was announced that Gen. Lee had put him in command of Ewell's corps (the old "Stonewall" corps), and had sent him to meet Hunter at Lynchburg.

If Gen. Early had fallen at Cold Harbor in June, 1864, or in front of Washington, July 8th, he would unquestionably have gone down to history as one of the ablest generals of the Confederacy. The subsequent disasters in the Valley did dim his fame, for the time at least, but when the future historian comes to scan all of the facts, he will do justice to this able and sturdy soldier.

Gen. Lee always spoke in high terms of Early's "ability, zeal, and devotion to the cause," and of "the fidelity and energy with which he always supported his (Lee's) efforts, and the courage and devotion he manifested in the service of the country."

Upon several occasions I heard President Davis speak of Gen. Early as among the ablest soldiers whom the war produced, and there can be but little doubt that this will be the calm verdict of history.[138] — SUMNER A. CUNNINGHAM

☛ HUMBLE TRIBUTE TO CAPT. E. T. SMYTHE

The following incidents illustrate the love and between Captain E. T. Smythe of Anniston, Ala., and the privates of his company. Ours was Company C., Fifth Alabama Battalion. In November, 1861 (before the battalion was organized) our company was ordered from Richmond to Yorktown. We traveled by rail to West Point, where we went aboard an open top schooner on the York River. A Virginia winter was upon us in full blast, rain and sleet, making the weather extremely disagreeable. We reached Yorktown just at nightfall. The wind was blowing at a furious rate, and the waves were so high that we found it impossible to land, and were forced to cast anchor at a safe distance from the shore. We were without shelter, food or fire, and the elements fairly raged. After anchor was cast the Captain of the boat came around and invited Captain Smythe into his cabin for supper, but he very politely expressed his

Confederate guns.

thanks for the invitation, saying his men had nothing to eat, and he would fare just as they did, and although the Captain of the boat and many of us urged him, we could not induce him to change his mind, or to take even a cup of coffee, while his men were without food. I have known him, when weary and worn with marching, to positively decline the cordial, urgent appeals by superior officers to ride, those officials proposing to walk themselves.

In the winter of 1861 we were in winter quarters on the banks of the Potomac near Dumfries. One Sunday, when the ground was covered with snow to the depth of about eighteen inches, a requisition was made upon Capt. Smythe for a detail from his company to assist in building a stable for the horse of Adjutant O. Hooper. When the requisition was made and Capt. Smythe was informed of the purpose, he said to the Sergeant, "Tell Capt. Hooper my men do not build stables on Sunday. It is not a military necessity, and I do not allow them imposed upon in that way."[139] — M. T. LEDBETTER

☛ FORREST'S CAPTURE OF WOOLFORD

I belonged to Forrest's old brigade, Company A, 11th Tennessee Cavalry. After the battle of Chickamauga we were camped at Cleveland, Tenn., and [Union Colonel Frank] Woolford at Philadelphia, eight miles south of Loudon. We started one morning, and rode all day and all night. The next morning we surrounded Woolford. He was ready for "the fun." The 11th was in line behind the artillery, the 4th in our rear, the 8th on our right, the 9th and 10th on the road between Philadelphia and Loudon to cut off their retreat. Forrest hadn't occupied a road running west, and when it got too hot for the boys in blue they started west. Forrest saw the gap, and ordered our regiment (the 11th) to dash across the road. It was about half a mile from us. At the same time the 4th took our place in the line. We got in about 200 yards of the road when Col. [Daniel W.] Holman ordered my company (A) and Company B to charge. We went at them like wild men, firing our revolvers, and with the old Confederate yell we went through their line, still shooting and yelling, Col. Holman at the same time coming down on the other side of the road. They whirled back for town. With the old 11th Tennessee still after them, they rushed through Philadelphia for Loudon. Here they met the 9th and 10th. The only thing they could do was to surrender. We got 500 prisoners, 7 pieces of artillery, 82 wagons, 600 stand of small arms, with all of their camp equipage. This was before the siege at Knoxville. Longstreet was then on his march from Chattanooga. He came up in a few days. Then we drove them into Knoxville, where we cut their line in two. After the battle I saw some dead yanks in the branch [river] and pulled some of them out.[140] — GEORGE W. YOUNGBLOOD

Nathan B. Forrest, C.S.A.

☛ NEED OF U.S. HISTORY FROM THE SOUTHERN VIEW

One of the pressing needs of our whole country is a history of the United States, for schools and for popular use, written from the Southern standpoint. We do not want a prejudiced, partisan account of our political and social life, and of our civil war, but a clear, vivid story of the difficulties, efforts and growth of our people, in the light of those great ideas and principles which controlled the actions of Southern statesmen from the origin of the Republic.

Hitherto Northern men have written the history, and naturally in the light of Northern ideas and principles. Of course our great civil war has been treated as a "wicked and causeless rebellion," as a war stirred up by a few ambitious spirits for personal ends, and for the maintenance and extension of the institution of slavery. Our children are taught to believe that we were rebels and traitors against "the best government the world ever saw." *Now, a movement so widespread, so nearly unanimous, and which called forth the enthusiastic devotion and heroic efforts of millions of people for four years, is not causeless. But the causes lie far back in our history. The contest was between two different conceptions of the nature of our government. The Southern people made their desperate struggle to maintain the government which they believed its founders established.* When they were defeated they accepted in good faith the government as it now is, and are loyal to it, *but they do not believe that it is the government according to the idea of the framers of the Constitution.* It may turn out to be better. Certainly they have no idea of trying to establish by force their idea old State's rights. But *they will always contend that they fought for the Constitutional rights of the people, as originally guaranteed to them.*

Confederate Memorial Hall, New Orleans, LA, 1894.

Now, the histories written by Southern men, as far as I have seen, do not set forth clearly the idea and purpose which animated the South in all the years before 1860, when it controlled the government. Our historians are usually content to give our side of the civil war, with some of the causes that led up to it; but for all the period preceding that fearful contest they differ little from Northern writers.

James H. McNeilly, C.S.A.

How few of our children know that Jamestown, Virginia, was settled before the Pilgrim Fathers came to this country, or that the vast domain which forms four-fifths of the United States was won by Southern men, or that slavery was forced upon this country by England, seconded by New England, or that in 1860 one-tenth of the slaves were communicants in churches.

What we need is a history of the country from the beginning, which shall show *the wonderful part the South had in its conquest and development, and the patriotic spirit and great sacrifices made by the South for the Union.* It can only be written by one in thorough sympathy with the ideas of the South, as well as a with thorough knowledge of the great facts of history.

The history of this country to the close of the civil war is not the "History of the Rise and Fall of the Slave Power," as Vice President [Henry] Wilson wrote it,[141] but the history of *the overthrow of the Constitution as it was originally adopted.* While giving hearty devotion to the government as it now is, and while laboring to make it a glory and a blessing to the world, *we yet owe it to our ancestors, and to our dead, to show in history that government, as we believe it was intended by its [Conservative] framers [known today as "limited government"], and as it made such wonderful progress under our administration of it until the [Liberals'] opposing idea ["big government"] triumphed.*

Upon our Confederate veterans lies the duty of securing this vindication of their cause from the facts of all our past history. We owe it to our fathers, to ourselves and to our children that *the history of our common country should not he left to be told by those who are out of sympathy with our spirit and principles, and so are unable to do justice to our motives or actions; and who therefore fail to record the glorious part we had in winning and developing the country, and fail to understand the meaning of the heroic struggle we made, not to preserve slavery, but to preserve our rights under the Constitution.*[142] — REV. JAMES H. MCNEILLY

ESCAPE IN A DUGOUT CANOE

While on a scout in King and Queen Counties, being pursued by a detachment of Federal cavalry, we took to the woods, and dodging down the banks of the Rappahannock [River], found a dugout concealed in some bushes, but no paddles. Tearing clap-boards off the roof of a deserted house close by, "Sandy," Guedron Coleman (one of the Roswell troopers), and myself shoved the canoe into the river and pulled away for Port Royal, but before we had gotten two hundred yards out the yanks rode up and ordered us back. "Sandy," who was in the stern, passed me his "Enfield" [rifle]—we were all paddling for dear life with the clap-board paddles, and kneeling down at that—with "Cap., you do the shooting, Coleman will load and I will paddle." No thought of surrender there. I had to do the firing lying on my back. Coleman loaded kneeling, while "Sandy" and the current that we had just struck carried us to the other side. It was rather ticklish work—"Sandy" said he had to "shift his quid to balance the boat;" but my firing made them dismount and take to cover, and that gave us time to get farther off. We always thought I hit one, as they dismounted almost as soon as I fired and hurriedly moved their horses back from the bank. All honor to the Confederate soldier who, like "Sandy" Guedron, always did his duty.[143]
— F. E. EVE

THE CAUSES OF THE WAR

[This reunion] revives many hallowed memories of the past. It calls up the memory of the days when husbands separated from wives and children; when sons separated from fathers and mothers, brothers and sisters; when loving and loved ones left their homes to enter the armies of the Confederacy, with hearts proudly responding to the calls of patriotism, and aching for those who were left at home. It calls to mind the forming of military organizations, and their march to the seat of war, buoyant with hope under bright new banners, in the presence of smiles which came through tears, the waving of handkerchiefs, the silent prayer of hope and love, and the soulful good-bye—God bless you. It calls to mind the long marches, the scenes around the camp fires, and anxious preparations for battle. It brings before the mind anew the panorama of battle. It calls up the memories of first Manassas, of Seven Pines, of the seven days in front of Richmond, of Fredericksburg, of Second Manassas, of Sharpsburg, of Gettysburg. It reminds us of Fort Donelson, of Shiloh and Corinth, of Chickamauga, of Lookout Mountain, of Elkhorn, of Vicksburg, of Stone's River, of Atlanta, of Murfreesboro, of Franklin, where Pat Cleburne and other heroes fell, and of a hundred other fields on which Confederate skill and courage and constancy were displayed. It causes a renewal of our admiration and love for such great Captains as Robert E. Lee, Stonewall Jackson, [Albert] Sidney Johnston, Joseph E. Johnston, Beauregard, Bragg, Longstreet, Hood, Kirby Smith, Gordon, Cleburne, Polk, Price, Breckinridge, [Hiram Bronson] Granbury, Randall, [William Read] Scurry, Ector, Cabell, [Lawrence Sullivan] Ross, [Thomas Neville] Waul, Ben McCulloch, John Gregg, Tom Green, W. H. F. and Fitzhugh Lee, J. E. B. Stuart, Forrest, Wheeler, and a hundred other heroic leaders in the lost cause.

Cameron N. Biscoe, C.S.A.

Great as was the ability and courage and purity of our Generals, who deservedly achieved a world-wide fame, and proud as we were and are of their characters and virtues, we turn with still greater pride and holier reverence, if such a thing be possible, to the memory of the subaltern officers and private soldiers who, for four weary years of privation, suffering, carnage and death, carried the banners of the Confederacy and offered their lives on the altar of their country's liberty; because they served and suffered without the incentive of office and rank, animated solely by their love of home, country and liberty, and their devotion to a cause dearer to them than life. *There were features in the struggle of the Confederacy which must hold their place in history as long as the admiration of genius and courage and virtue shall survive.*

. . . Of late years we occasionally hear the inquiry as to what caused this great war, with all its sacrifices of life and property. Sometimes the inquiry is made by those seeking information, . . . others make it in order to belittle those who were engaged in it. *A struggle which cost hundreds of thousands of valuable lives, and by which many billions of money was spent and property sacrificed, could hardly have been engaged in without a sufficient cause. And those who assume that it was not, only show their own ignorance of the history of our country.* Without raising the question as to who was right and who wrong in that struggle, I think our children should know why their fathers engaged in so great a war.

During colonial times in this country the political authorities of Great Britain, Spain and France, and the Dutch merchants planted African slavery in all the North American colonies. At the time of the declaration of American independence, 1776, African slavery existed in all of the thirteen colonies. At the date of the adoption of the Federal Constitution, 1787, African slavery existed in all of the States except one. The commercial reason for the planting of African slavery in this country was no doubt stimulated by the hope of ease and gain. It was at the same time justified by the church on the ground that the negroes were taken from a condition of heathenish barbarism and cannibalism and brought to where they could be taught the arts of civilization and industry, and where they could be instructed in the doctrines and practices of the Christian religion. I am not discussing the question now as to whether this practice and these views were correct; I am only telling you what was done and thought to be right by our ancestors and by the great governments of the world.

When the Constitution of the United States, the compact of union, was adopted it recognized the right of property in African slaves. The trade was still being carried on, and the Constitution of the United States provided that it should not be prohibited by Congress prior to the year 1808, twenty years after the adoption of the Constitution. It also provided that slaves escaping from one State into another should not be discharged from service or labor, but should be delivered to their owners. There were differences of opinion as to the rightfulness of slavery among the men who formed the Constitution. Subsequently, and before 1861, *a number of Northern States, where slave labor was not profitable, abolished that institution [not immediately, but by gradual emancipation].*[144] And by degrees a strong prejudice grew up against slavery: first among philanthropists and religionists; and then, in a number of States, it became a political question. The agitation of this question was not at first entirely sectional, but it became so subsequently. Its agitation, as early as 1820, threatened the perpetuity of the Union, and it continued until it caused bloodshed in Kansas, also the invasion of Virginia by John Brown and his deluded followers for the purpose of inaugurating civil and servile war in that State. When he was executed for his crimes Northern churches were draped in mourning, and their bells tolled in sympathy for him and sorrow for his fate.

In the Thirty-fifth [U.S.] Congress [1857-1859], when the agitation was threatening the peace of the country, *thirty odd propositions of compromise were made, for the purpose of averting the danger of disunion; all of these without exception were made either by Southern members or Northern Democratic [then Conservative] members, and every one of these propositions was received by the Republican [then Liberal] members with hooting and expressions of derision. The Southern members [Conservatives] were often told that they had to submit to the will of the majority. The Constitution was denounced by some of the agitators [that is, Liberals] as "a league with hell and a covenant with death," and the agitators claimed that there was a "higher law"* [today known as "social justice"] *than the Constitution.*

In the campaign of 1860 the Republicans [then the Liberal party] nominated as their anti-slavery ticket *both their candidates for President and Vice President from the Northern States*; a thing which had not occurred before that time, except in the election of General [Andrew] Jackson as President and Mr. Calhoun as Vice-President, both from Southern States, in 1828, when there was no sectional issue. In 1832 the peace of the country, if not the integrity of the Union, was threatened

John C. Calhoun.

on the question of the revenue policy of the government, which led to the steps taken by South Carolina to nullify the acts of Congress [known as "nullification"] by which duties on imports and for the protection of home industries were levied in a way which it was believed did not bear equally on the different parts of the country, and which was believed to involve a violation of the Constitution.

Thomas Jefferson.

Both these were questions which came up under the broader and greater question of the proper construction of the Constitution of the United States. In the Federal Convention of 1787, which framed the Constitution of the United States, the question as to the character of the government we were to have, and of the powers which were to be conferred on it, and in the conventions of the States, which ratified the Constitution, were very ably discussed, some of the [Liberal] members in each preferring a strong Federal Government, and others [Conservatives], jealous of the rights of the States and more solicitous for the liberties of the people, preferring a government with limited powers.

The States represented in the Federal Convention were each free, sovereign and independent. The Constitution formed by that convention and ratified by the States conferred on the government, so formed, certain specified and limited powers necessary to enable it to conduct our foreign and Federal relations, reserving to the States respectively and to the people all the powers not so delegated. The question was discussed in the convention as to what should be done in case of disagreement between the Federal Government and one or more of the States. A proposition was made by [Liberal] Alexander Hamilton to confer on the Federal Government power to coerce refractory States; and was voted down. So this power was not expressly given by the Constitution, nor embraced in the powers given.

During President Washington's administration, the first under the Constitution, the question as to whether the Constitution should be *strictly construed*, so as to preserve the reserved rights of the States [Conservative], or should receive a *latitudinous construction* looking to strengthening the government beyond the powers delegated by it [Liberal], was sharply made between [Conservative] Thomas Jefferson, the Secretary of State, contending for its strict construction, and [Liberal] Alexander Hamilton, contending for a broader construction.

During the administration of the elder [John] Adams [a Liberal] the Congress, with the approval of the President, passed what is known in the history of the times as the Alien and Sedition laws. The strict constructionists, under the lead of Mr. Jefferson, denied the constitutionality of these laws, and charged that they endangered the liberty of the citizens. *Upon this issue the American people agreed with Mr. Jefferson and elected him President in the year 1800, and again in 1804.*

In the year 1793 the legislature of Kentucky, and in the year 1799 the legislature of Virginia, passed resolutions denouncing the Alien and Sedition laws as violative of the Constitution, as dangerous to liberty, and asserted the right of the States to protect themselves against unconstitutional laws and acts of the Federal Government. And in these resolutions they asserted the right of the States to protect the people against the unconstitutional acts and arbitrary power of the Federal Government, that they were the judges of their rights and remedies, but that this power was not to be exercised by them except in extreme cases when there was no other remedy.

Under this issue what was known as the Federal party [then the Liberal party] went out of power and out of existence. And under this, as under the doctrine of the then Republican [Conservative] party, which afterwards became the Democratic [Conservative] party,¹⁴⁵ Mr. Jefferson [Conservative], Mr. Madison [Conservative]

James Monroe.

and Mr. Monroe [Conservative] successively held the office of President of the United States for twenty-four consecutive years. It was always the doctrine of the Democratic [then Conservative] party, down to 1860, and was specifically endorsed by its national conventions in several canvasses for President and Vice-President preceding the war.

I am not saying whether this is or is not the doctrine of the Democratic party now [as of the writing of this piece, 1894, the Democratic Party was still Conservative];¹⁴⁶ I am only reciting these facts to show the opinions which prevailed before the war between the States, and in a large measure guided the people of the Southern States when they passed their ordinances of secession. *They believed a public opinion had been created in the Northern States which threatened the peace of the country and the rights of the people. They believed the constitution of the United States had ceased to be a shield for their protection, also that their safety and welfare made it necessary for them to withdraw from the Union, and to form a government friendly to their people, and under which their rights would be secured to them.*

They were in part led to this conclusion by the facts I have stated and because the people of the Northern States had repudiated the provisions of the Constitution, and of the acts of Congress which were intended to protect them in the enjoyment of their local social and domestic institutions, and which were intended to protect three thousand million dollars of property in slaves; also that they had repudiated a decision of the Supreme Court of the United States which affirmed the doctrine of the Constitution and laws of Congress on this subject; that some of the Northern States had passed laws forbidding their authorities and people from aiding to execute the provisions of the Constitution and laws requiring the rendition of fugitive slaves.

King George III.

These things and others of like character caused the Southern States to attempt to withdraw from the Union. And the principles I have called to view, and the facts I have referred to, led to the great war which cost so much blood and treasure. These principles and events are answers to the new generation as to why their fathers gave their services, their property, and their lives in that war; why brave men fought and died, and why holy men, and pure and noble women prayed for its success; why senators and representatives in Congress, and officers of the army and navy surrendered their offices and emoluments and abandoned a condition of peace and security and offered their fortunes and their lives in so unequal a contest; and why the people at large in these States, with remarkable unanimity, staked every earthly thing which was precious and dear to them, in so unequal a war, rather than submit to the degradation of living under a violated Constitution and laws, and being compelled to accept only such rights in the Union as might be accorded to them by the grace of hostile popular majority.

Some persons, who were specially wise after the war [sarcasm], say we had better have compromised than have accepted battle with such a preponderance of population and wealth and the power of an organized government against us. *Can any one point to an instance in history where principles of such magnitude, and property of such value, were settled by compromise?* As well have asked why our revolutionary fathers did not compromise with King George [III]. It was one of those cases which, under all the circumstances, could only be settled by an appeal to the god of battles. And those who think a settlement could have been made by a compromise certainly cannot have been familiar with the facts which led to the war.

[Socialist New Yorker] Horace Greeley, in the preface to his history of what he calls the rebellion, said: "The war might have been brought on a little earlier, or it might have been postponed to a little later date, but sooner or later it was inevitable." And he spoke the truth. It is unreasonable to assume that statesmen, philanthropists, citizens in the ordinary peaceful walks of life, the ministers of religion, and the women of the country, would needlessly and without provocation have consented to engage in a war of such magnitude, and that, too, when numbers, the materi4als of war, and a powerful organized government, were to be encountered by people without a general government, without an army, without a navy, and without a treasury. *I do not believe that any people in any age ever entered into a war with higher or purer or holier purposes; nor do I believe that any people in the world's history ever displayed more patriotism or made greater sacrifices, or exhibited greater endurance and courage than the soldiers and people of the Confederate States.*

You will all understand that in making these statements I am not

A Confederate generals' war council (l-r): Beauregard, Polk, Breckinridge, Johnston, Bragg, Hardee.

doing so to renew the passions and prejudices of the war, or to question the patriotism of the men who fought for the Union. I doubt not that their patriotism was as pure and their belief that they were in the right was as strong as ours. I am discussing these things as facts of history, which if not kept in view by our people might make posterity question the patriotism and virtue of the noble men who fought in that war, and of the pure women who worked and prayed for their success.

Jefferson Davis, C.S.A.

No one can feel more gratification that the war is ended and that peace and fraternal good will are restored between the people North and South, than I. And I can meet and greet the soldier who wore the blue as a friend and a brother, and am glad that many of them have made their homes among us. We are now under the same government and flag; we have the same laws and language; we read the same Bible and worship the same God; we are the same people, with the same hopes, aspirations, and destiny.

One of the proudest memories of that great war is of the conduct of the women of the Confederacy, who willingly gave their fathers and husbands and brothers to the service of the Confederacy. In very many cases they took upon themselves the burden of supporting their families, both aged parents and children, by their own labor. And in the struggles to take care of home affairs they would spin and weave, and knit, and make up garments for their loved ones both at home and in the ranks of the army. They denied themselves the ordinary comforts and the necessaries of life in order to help supply the army, to take care of the sick and wounded soldiers, and to feed and clothe such as were in their reach. Many good women—who before the war were only engaged in such indoor and delicate employments as the customs of the country had assigned to women—in the absence of the male members of their families in the army, in order to support their families, planted and cultivated and gathered the necessary field crops, chopped and hauled wood, fed and attended the stock; cheerfully performing such duties as their part of the sacrifices necessary to achieve *the independence of the Confederacy*. If time permitted this might be illustrated by many striking instances of the grand heroism of our women, a moral heroism even greater and grander than that of the soldier who fell in the excitement of battle. I mention one such instance, as told me by Governor [John] Letcher, of Virginia, during the war. He had visited his home at Staunton, and returning had stopped at the house of an old friend. Seeing none but the good lady at home he inquired for the balance of the family. Her reply was that her husband, her husband's father, and her ten sons were in the same company in the army. He said to her that having been accustomed to have a large family around her she must feel very lonely. This noble matron replied, "Yes, it is very hard to be alone, but if I had ten more sons they should all be in the army." *Can any one be surprised that a country, whose women were capable of such sacrifices, and sufferings willingly endured, and devotion to and prayers for their country's cause, should have prolonged the struggle for independence after its army had been reduced by casualties in battle and otherwise to a mere skeleton, whose money had been depreciated until it had but little purchasing power, whose soldiers were half naked, with barely food to sustain life, and whose country had been desolated by the ravages of war?*

Confederate veterans, 1899.

The world's history can hardly show an instance in which such courage and constancy and devotion have been shown by both men and women in the face of so powerful an enemy. And I predict that in the not distant future, some [Thomas Babington] Macaulay will be found who will do justice to their patriotism, and skill, and courage, and that the citizens of all parts of the Union, North and South, will feel a just pride in the fact that such men and women and their descendants form a part of the population of this great Republic; as we of the South shall feel a just pride in being citizens of a country which produced at Davis and a Lincoln, a Lee and a Grant, a Stonewall Jackson . . . and their respective compatriots.

With all our pride on account of the qualities exhibited by our people during the war, perhaps the most striking illustration of their capacity for *self-government* is shown by their conduct since it ended. Their country desolated by the war; their wealth and resources exhausted; tens of thousands of their best men filling honorable graves on the fields of battle; their social and domestic institutions destroyed; their local governments annulled under the policy of reconstruction; denied the blessings of civil government; the military made paramount to the civil authorities; the right of the writ of *habeas corpus* suspended; arrests without affidavits of guilt and without warrant; citizens liable to be tried by drum head military courts; [Liberal] freedmen's bureaus established everywhere, under the control of the military and a set of lawless camp followers of the army, stimulating the negroes to hostility to the [Conservative Southern] whites; with an alien race made dominant who were unused to the exercise of the duties of citizenship, and unqualified for self-government, with no security for his, person, or property. Overwhelmed by all these calamities, that the people should have been able to reorganize society, and to re-establish civil government, revive

Confederate monument, Franklin, TN. (Photo L. Seabrook)

the ordinary industries of the country; and, in less than thirty years, reach the condition of general prosperity which now prevails throughout the Southern States, furnishes the strongest possible proof of the capacity of our people for the preservation of social order and self-government, and cannot fail to secure for them the good opinion of the civilized world.

I wish to say something about reunions, like the present, of the soldiers of both the Southern and the Northern armies. Some persons object to them because they fear the effect will be to revive and perpetuate the passions and prejudices of the war. I think this is a mistaken view. That they cause a revival of the memories of the war is true. But it does not necessarily follow that such meetings will revive the passions and prejudices of the war. *Many instances have occurred in both the South and the North in which the soldiers of the two sides have met together, and in fraternal kindness recounted the triumphs and glories of their respective armies, those of the one side feeling that those of the other were entitled to their respect, and all feeling that they were now fellow citizens and brethren.*

John H. Reagan, C.S.A.

That war will go down in history as one of the great wars of the world—the officers distinguished for skill and the soldiers distinguished for courage rarely equalled in ancient or modern times. As long as patriotism and love of country and admiration for skill and courage survive, the memory of the achievements on both sides will gratify American pride, and stimulate American patriotism and valor.

A people without a history cannot command respect. One of the offices of history is to perpetuate achievements in the arts, in the sciences, in arms, in government, and in religion, and so to cultivate the love of country and the glory of a people.

Whatever lingering prejudices may still exist, preventing any of the people of either side from doing justice to the memory and motives of those on the other side, must in a few more decades entirely give way, and then the sons and daughters of the late Confederates will be proud of the valor and achievements of the Federal officers and soldiers, and the sons and daughters of those who served in the Federal armies will be equally proud of the achievements of the late Confederates. And each side, in my judgment, does well to perpetuate the remembrance of the virtues, the skill, the courage, and the achievements of its statesmen, its generals, its soldiers and its noble women.[147] — JOHN H. REAGAN (at this time the only surviving member of the original Confederate cabinet)

Sam Davis monument, Pulaski, TN. (Photo L. Seabrook)

☞ SAM DAVIS, THE HERO MARTYR

It is not of the words of a statesman, nor of the deeds of a great general, but of the actions and death of a noble Southern hero that I beg you to listen to. A short time before the battle of Mission Ridge Gen. Bragg had planned a campaign through Tennessee into Kentucky. It was important to know the exact strength of the Federal forces occupying the sections through which he was to pass. For this information, which had been promised by a Federal officer at Nashville, a courier was to be sent. This perilous undertaking, to pass through a country swarming with Federal soldiers, required a man of the coolest courage and unflinching devotion to duty. Sam Davis, of Coleman's Scouts, a youth of nineteen years, was chosen for the hazardous journey. He went dressed in his gray, and accomplished his task, but on his return was taken prisoner near Pulaski, Tenn. A search of his person revealed the important papers he carried, and from their accuracy and minuteness of detail it was at once suspected that he had secured them from a Federal officer of the engineering department. It was highly important to detect the name of the traitor, and to that end Davis was questioned. His answers were straightforward. Frankly admitting that he had received the papers as suspected, he firmly declined to give the name of the officer. The commander pressed him, offering him pardon and safe return into his lines, or would subject him to trial by court martial, to result in death on the gallows. He was unmoved, and stoutly refused to sell his friend. A commission being appointed, he was tried, found guilty, and sentenced to be hanged as a spy Friday, November 23, 1863, in the town of Pulaski. When his fate was made known to him he expressed some surprise at its harshness (being dressed in his army colors and wearing his Confederate arms when captured—[it is obvious that] he was no spy), but he showed not the least fear or weakness—nor the quiver of a muscle. In writing to his mother he realized full well the end. Death was certain. These are his words to her:

> "Dear Mother—how painful it is to write to you that I have got to die to-morrow morning. I will die hanged by the Federals. Mother, do not grieve for me. I must bid you goodbye for evermore. Mother, I do not hate to die. Give my love to all. Tell the children all to be good."

Memorial gathering, at the home of Sam Davis, Smyrna, TN, 1890s.

A nobler heart never beat! Think of his grief-stricken mother as she read those lines. The simplicity, the sincerity expressed in them illustrates his character. Directly after writing this he was again visited by the Chaplain, but he remained firm not to reveal the confidence given him. At the time appointed for his execution, seated on his coffin, his arms pinioned at his back, he was driven to the scaffold which had been erected on an elevation overlooking the town. He saw the soldiers move the coffin from the wagon, and, turning to the commander, inquired how long he had to live. "Just fifteen minutes," was the reply. Then, without a tremor or the slightest change of countenance, he said, "The rest of the battles will have to be fought without me."

As he ascended the steps of the scaffold in company with the

Chaplain, after committing a few keepsakes to a friend, his mind evidently turned back to his home. Familiar scenes and trying recollections thronged upon him. He recalled his dear mother as she bade him farewell at the gate, giving to him her treasured Bible, asking God to take care of her precious boy. He saw his father, his frame trembling with emotion as he took his hand and said, "My son, go and fight for our Southland, and, if need be, die in her cause;" and no doubt he recalled the tender words of his dearest one as they knelt at the altar and vowed to be all and all to each other. At this moment a messenger, dispatched in hast from headquarters, arrived at the scaffold. It was the last offer of pardon. He was told that such fate might he avoided by giving the name of the officer from whom he had the treasonable documents. Though standing upon the brink of eternity, he turned upon the messenger and, with a glowing indignation, said, "No! I would die thousand deaths first. I will never betray the confidence reposed in me." After a short prayer the black cap was drawn over his head and he stepped upon the trap, and with the calmness of a philosopher, the sternness of a patriot, the sincerity and courage of a Christian martyr, paid the severe penalty of unswerving devotion to duty and honor.

Far and wide his death was mourned. His executioners wept. The common soldiery stigmatized the deed as a cruel assassination. Among his own lines his comrades resolved to erect a monument to mark the resting place of one who deserved the title of Marshal [Michel] Ney, "the bravest of the brave."

Noble Sam Davis was admired by his enemies and loved by his friends. No one ever awakened greater sympathy. His youth, his courage, his coolness under the trying circumstances, endeared him to all. Even now, after the lapse of twenty-nine years, at the mention of his name to a comrade or friend, a tender sympathy causes the tear to rise unbidden to the eye. He was a martyr to what he conceived to be his duty.[148] — J. M. KING JR.

☛ HONORING THE PRIVATE SOLDIER

I am not one of those who, clinging to the old superstition that the will of heaven is revealed in the immediate results of "trial by combat," fancy that right must always be on the side of might, and speak of Appomattox as a judgment of God. I do not forget that a [Alexander V.] Suwaroff triumphed, and a [Tadeusz A. B.] Kosciuszko fell; that a Nero wielded a sceptre of empire, and a Paul was beheaded; that a Herod was crowned, and a Christ was crucified; and, *instead of accepting the defeat of the South as a divine verdict against her, I regard it as but another instance of "truth on the scaffold, and wrong on the throne."*

Appomattox was a triumph of the physically stronger in a conflict between the representatives of two essentially different civilizations, and antagonistic ideas of government. On one side in that conflict was the South, led by the descendants of the Cavaliers, who, with all their faults, had inherited from a long line of ancestors a manly contempt for moral littleness, a high sense of honor, a lofty regard for plighted faith, *a strong tendency to conservatism, a profound respect for law and order, and an unfaltering loyalty to constitutional government.*

But, it was not to perpetuate slavery that they fought. The impartial student of the events leading up to the civil war cannot fail to perceive that, in the words of Mr. Davis, "to whatever extent the question of slavery may have served as an occasion, it was far from being the cause of the conflict." That conflict was the bloody culmination of a controversy which had been raging for more than a generation, and the true issue in which, as far as it pertained to slavery, was sharply stated by the Hon. Samuel A. Foot, of Connecticut, when, referring to the debate of the admission of Missouri to the sisterhood of States, he said: "*The Missouri question did not involve the question of freedom or slavery, but merely whether slaves now in the country may be permitted to reside in the proposed new State, and whether Congress or Missouri possessed the power to decide.*" And from that day down to 1861, when the war-clouds burst in fury upon our land, *the real question in regard to slavery was not whether it should continue in the South, but whether the Southern man should be permitted to take his slaves, originally purchased almost exclusively from Northern slave-traders, into the territory, which was the common property of the country, and there, without interference from the general Government, have an equal voice with his Northern brother in determining the domestic policy of the new State. The question was not whether the negro should*

Patrick Henry.

be freed or held in servitude, but whether the white man of the South should have the same privileges enjoyed by the white man of the North. It was not the desire to hold others in bondage, but the desire to maintain their own rights that actuated the Southern people throughout the conflict. . . .

That Union was dear to the Southern people, but the Union which the men of the South loved, and which they were willing to make concessions and sacrifices to perpetuate, *was that formed by the fathers*, to establish justice, insure domestic tranquillity, provide for the common defense, promote the general welfare, and secure the blessings of liberty. *It was a fraternal federation of sovereign States, guaranteeing equal rights to all, and leaving each free to regulate its domestic affairs in its own way.* It was a Union in which, in reference to questions of foreign policy, every citizen would echo the sentiment expressed by Patrick Henry, when, after Concord and Lexington, in a message to Massachusetts, he said: "I am not a Virginian, I am an American;" and yet it was a Union in which, in reference to questions of domestic policy, *every citizen, like that same great orator and patriot, would recognize the right of his own State to his highest allegiance. It was a Union in which the people of each State would enjoy the blessings of local self-government, and find in home rule a safeguard against any possible attempt of the Federal power to interfere with their peculiar interests.*

. . . Virginia, Mother of States and statesmen and warriors, who had given away an empire for the public good, whose pen had written the Declaration of Independence, whose sword had flashed in front of the American army in the war of independence, and whose wisdom and patriotism had been chiefly instrumental in giving the country the Constitution of the Union—Virginia, foreseeing that her bosom would become the theater of war, with its attendant horrors, nobly chose to suffer rather than become an accomplice in *the proposed outrage upon constitutional liberty*. With a generosity and magnanimity of soul rarely equaled and never surpassed in the history of nations, she placed herself in the path of the invader, practically saying: "Before you can touch the rights of my Southern sisters you must cut your way to them through my heart."

From the Potomac to the Gulf, from the Atlantic to the Rio Grande, the sons of the South sprang to arms. From stately mansion and humble cottage, from the workshop and from the farm, from the storeroom and from the study, from every neighborhood and vocation of life, *with unanimity almost unparalleled, they rallied for the defense of the land they loved, and of what, in their inmost souls, they felt to be their sacred and inalienable birthright.*

They were true-hearted patriots, worthy to rank with the noblest souls that ever battled for freedom. They fought for home and country, and to maintain the fundamental principle of all free government that the right to govern arises from and coexistent with the consent of the governed.

And if patient self-denial and cheerful self-sacrifice and unquailing fortitude and unfaltering devotion to country and unwavering loyalty to duty and dauntless courage in defense of the right make heroism, the men whom we honor to-day, and whom we would not have our children forget, were sublime heroes. History has no more illustrious page than that which tells of their achievements. *Poorly equipped, poorly clad, poorly fed, and virtually without pay, they confronted at least three times their number of as well equipped, well clothed, well fed, and well paid soldiers as ever marched to battle; wrested from them a series of*  *victories unsurpassed in brilliancy; and for four years, stormy with the red blasts of war, successfully resisted all their power.* In dangers and hardships that "tried men's souls," the defenders of the South were tried, and always found "true as tempered steel." Laboring under disadvantages which even their friends can never fully appreciate; supplementing their scanty rations with weeds and grasses; their bare feet oftentimes pressing the frozen ground or blistered on the burning highway; their garments as tattered as the battle-torn banners that they bore, they bravely fought on for the cause they loved, and sealed their devotion to it with their blood.

. . . In intelligence and thought they were, from training and association, far above the average soldiery of the world. *Notwithstanding all that has been said about the illiteracy of the South, I believe that no country* ever had a larger percentage of intelligent and thinking men in the ranks of its army. Thousands of them were highly educated, cultured, refined, and in every way qualified to command. Sitting on the brow of the mountain overlooking the winding Shenandoah, and the little town of Strasburg, and the beautiful valley stretching away toward Winchester, and, at that time, dark with the blue columns of Federal soldiery, a Louisiana private, idly talking of what he would do were he in command, gave me almost every detail of the plan, which, afterward perceived and executed by the commanding officer, carried confusion and defeat to the Federals. Had the need arisen, as in the case of the Theban army at Thessaly, more than one [Theban General] Epaminondas might have been found serving as a private in the Confederate ranks.

And I believe that *no army was ever composed of men more thoroughly imbued with moral principle. As a rule, they were men who recognized the obligations to be just and honest and merciful, and to respect the rights of others, even in the time of war. Never flinching from conflict with armed foemen, their moral training and disposition forbade them to make war upon the weak and defenseless. To their everlasting honor stands the fact in that their march through the enemy's country, they left no fields wantonly laid waste, no families cruelly robbed of subsistence, no homes ruthlessly violated.* "In no case," says an English writer, "had the Pennsylvanians to complain of personal injury, or even discourtesy at the hands of those whose homes they had burned, whose families they had insulted, robbed, and tormented. Even the tardy destruction of Chambersburg was an act of regular, limited, and righteous reprisal." The Pennsylvania farmer, whose words were reported by a Northern correspondent, paid to the Southern troops no more than a merited tribute, when he said of them: *"I must say, they acted like gentlemen; and, their cause aside, I would rather have forty thousand rebels quartered on my premises than one thousand Union troops."* And they acted like gentlemen not merely because the order of their commanding General required them so to act, but because *the spirit within themselves was in harmony with, and responded to, that order.*

It was Jackson's line of Virginians, rather than Jackson himself, that resembled a stone wall standing on the plains of Manassas, while the storm of battle hissed and hurtled and thundered around them; and if I mention the name of Jackson rather than that of the ruddy-faced boy who fell, pierced through the brain, and who was buried on one of Virginia's hills, in a lonely grave, over which to-day the tangled wild weeds are growing, it is not because one was more heroic than the other, but because Jackson, by his greater prominence, more fully embodies before the eyes of the world the *patriotism and courage and heroism* that glowed no less brightly and steadily in the heart of the beardless boy. These noble qualities, possessed by both, and displayed by as his ability and position permitted, bind them together in my thought, not as officer and private, but as fellow-soldiers and brother patriots. Exalted virtue, like deepest sham, ever obliterates rank, and brings men into a common brotherhood.

As my mind recalls the persons and events of those years in which the Confederacy struggled for life, there rises before me the majestic figure of the great Southern chief—the peerless soldier and the stainless gentleman; the soldier who was cool, calm, and self-possessed in the presence of every danger, and who, with marvelous foresight and skill, planned masterly campaigns, directed the march of war, ruled the storm of battle, and guided his men to victory on many a well-fought field; the gentleman who was as pure as a falling snow-flake, as gentle as an evening zephyr, as tender as the smile of a flower, and as patient as  the rock-ribbed mountains. I need not name him, for his name is written in ever-enduring letters on the heart of the South, and honored throughout the civilized world. Around him I see a company of intrepid leaders whose achievements have surrounded their names with a glory which outshines the luster of coronets and crowns. I would not pluck one leaf from the laurel with which they are garlanded. I would, if I could, lift to a still higher note and sing in still loftier strains the paeans that are chanted in their praise. But I see, also, the men whom these Captains led—men unswerving in their devotion to a noble purpose; self-forgetful in their fidelity to what they saw to be right, and sublimely self-denying and self-sacrificing in their adherence to the cause they espoused; *men who loved their country with a love stronger than a love of life*, and, with no thought of compensation beyond that country's freedom and honor and safety, bravely toiled and suffered and endured, and *gave their bodies to be torn by shot and shell, and poured out their blood like water to the thirsty ground*; I see the private soldiers and sailors of the Confederacy, and, with uncovered head and profoundest reverence, I bow before those dauntless heroes, feeling that, if the greatest suffering with the least hope of reward is worthy of the highest honor, they deserve to stand shoulder to shoulder with Lee and his Lieutenants in the brotherhood of glory.

The heroic soul greets all heroes as kindred spirits, whether they are found fighting by its side or leveling lance against it. It is the narrow, ungenerous, and selfish soul that can find nothing to admire in the courage, devotion, and heroism of its enemies. . . . In the world's life, wrong has often triumphed for a season. There have been many times of oppression, where human rights were trampled in the dust by despotic power, and the hopes of men seemed dead. But *the student of history will find that every chaos has been followed by a cosmos. The agony and sweat and tears and blood of every age have brought forth a new and better era.* . . .

And reasoning from what has been to what shall be, I believe that *not in vain were the battles, and not in vain was the fall of those who battled and fell under the banner of the Confederacy*. Having, by their glorious deeds, woven a crown of laurel for the brow of the South, that drew to her the admiring mind of the world, by their fall they entwined in that crown the cypress leaves that drew to her the sympathizing heart of the world. *The land in which we live is dearer to our hearts since it has been hallowed by their sacrifices and watered by their blood. Though dead, they speak, admonishing us to prove ourselves worthy of kinship with them, by being heroes in peace as they were heroes in war.*

In our country "the war-drum throbs no longer, and the battle-flags are furled." The quiet stars that, thirty years ago, looked down on sentineled camps of armed men, resting for the morrow's conflict . . . now look down, night after night, on quiet homes, where the sleepers, disturbed by no call to arms, peacefully slumber until singing birds wake them to the bloodless labors of a new-born day. Fields that, thirty years ago, were clouded by the smoke of battles, and trampled by charging thousands, and torn by the hoof-beats of the war-horse, and plowed by the shot of cannon, and drenched with the blood of the dead and mangled men, are now enriched by tillage, and contributing their fruits to nourish the life and increase the prosperity of the people. "Peace folds her wings o'er hill and valley." But peace, as well as war, demands of us high devotion and unswerving loyalty. If, with peace, we have decay of patriotism and loss of virtue and the triumph of private over public interests, and the sacrifice of law and justice to secure partisan ends; if, with peace, we have the accumulation of wealth at the cost of the country's welfare and the honest manhood of its citizens, our peace must prove but the downward path to the ruin in which so many nations, once great and prosperous, have been swallowed up. Better far the desiccations and horrors of war than such peace."[149] — REV. R. C. CAVE

☛ REMEMBERING GEN. WILLIAM HICKS "RED" JACKSON
Next after the name of Thomas Jonathan "Stonewall" Jackson in the memorandum of Confederate commanders published by the United States Government is that of William H. Jackson, who is recorded as commanding a cavalry division under Gen. S. D. Lee, in the department of Mississippi and East Louisiana.

William H. Jackson, C.S.A.

As second in command of the United Confederate Veterans a brief sketch of him will be read with the greater interest by [those are] . . . not familiar with his important career since as well as during the war.

Gen. Jackson's parents were both of Virginia, but he was born at Paris, Tenn., in 1835. His only brother, Judge Howell E. Jackson, is an ex-United States Senator, and is now a member of the Supreme Court of the United States.

A West Point graduate of the class of 1856, he entered the regular army and was in the service of "Uncle Sam," on the Western frontier in 1861, when he resigned and in company with Col. Crittenden, of Kentucky, and Maj. Longstreet he returned to his native State and was made at once captain of an artillery company.

While leading an infantry charge in the battle of Belmont, Mo., he received a bullet which he has since carried. He was made colonel and brigadier general in quick succession, and then succeeded to the command of Forrest's old division, with the Texas brigade added. At the close of the war Gen. Jackson was made commissioner by [Richard] Dick Taylor for the parole of prisoners at Gainesville, Ala.

To these brief notes of his military career we add his remarks on accepting the honor conferred upon him at the Birmingham reunion: "I have eschewed politics so far as never to seek or hold any political office, but *I appreciate more highly my selection to this high office to which you have called me than I would to have been Governor of the State of Tennessee or even to be President of the United States. I prize it above any honor that could be offered by citizens of America.*"

Gen. Jackson's remarkable career since the war, and he is now in the zenith of importance as a citizen, will be read with interest by comrades and by the public. He and his brother, Judge Jackson, married the two daughters of Gen. William Giles Harding, who lived near Nashville. Gen. Jackson took charge of the well-known Belle Meade estate as the venerable Harding became infirm of age. Belle Meade is entitled to the pride of its owner and of the country. It is located west of the city.

Belle Meade Plantation house, Nashville, TN. (Photo L. Seabrook)

The residence is about six miles by the Harding Pike, and it has been in the Harding family since about 1800. The acreage is 5,300. All the outer lines are of stone fencing, thirty-five miles in all, which cost one dollar a running yard to build it.

The place is noted for its thoroughbred horses. The figures will stagger credulity, and yet they are accurate. The yearlings sold at the annual sales at Belle Meade from 1875 to 1893 inclusive brought in the aggregate $615,000. And these colts have realized for their owners on the American turf $2,777,000 [the equivalent of about $63 million in 2017].

One horse, Iroquois, is now regarded the most remarkable horse in the world. He is the only American-bred horse that ever won the three great events of England: the Derby, the St. Leger, and Prince of Wales stakes. It is a source of gratification to Americans, and causes their great pride in Iroquois, that being American he has achieved such victories on English soil, and has demonstrated the fact that an American horse that can win the English Derby is as successful a sire as the English horse that wins the English Derby. Iroquois is so successful a sire that ten of his produce sold in 1892 for an average of $8,500 each [about $231,000 each today], or $85,000 cash for the ten [$2.4 million today].

Belle Meade's carriage house. (Photo L. Seabrook)

One of the luxuries worthy of note, among the many that are not used, is a park of 500 acres, in which hundreds of deer roam as free as if in an unlimited forest.

The success of Gen. Jackson in building up Belle Meade to its present renowned reputation is evidently due to the very liberal outlay of money for the best stock and for the best improvements, the General subscribing to the idea that "nothing short of the best in anything will prove an eminent success."

Gen. Jackson has steadily become more and more interested in public matters. He is the father of the "farmer movement" in this country, having organised at an Exposition here the first National Farmers' Congress ever held in America. And he held the position as President of that Congress for several years.

He also organized the first agricultural paper in this part of the country, the *Rural Sun*, favoring the idea that "agricultural journals, like almanacs, should be calculated for the latitude they are designed to serve."

He is at present President of the Nashville Gaslight Company. He is the President of the Electric Railway, which was recently purchased for over a million dollars and reorganized.[150] — SUMNER A. CUNNINGHAM

☛ BRAVE & TRUE SOUTHERN MEN & WOMEN

Who among us cannot remember some fair-haired boy who threw away books and toys to take up arms in our cause? His life had been like a summer day all genial and sunshine, but when the struggle came his hot blood ran wildly through his veins, his pure, young heart beat high noble hopes, and forgetting all the ties at home he breathed a fervent prayer for those he loved and marched to fields of strife. And when the battle raged at a furious height we have marked his steady step and watched with pride his steadfast eye as he walked in the path of death, with the smoke curled up from the crimson field, and have found him foremost among the dead, his brave heart stilled forever!

But far grander than the faith and fortitude and courage of our men was the calm endurance of our heroic women. Where under the sun can be found daughters of any land who were more tenderly guarded, more kindly revered, and more indulged than the women of the South? Every wish gratified, every hope realized, every want supplied, they were nursed as delicate flowers that a rude wind would blight and a want of care destroy; and yet, how brave and enduring they were! They saw father and son, husband and brother go forth, and they were proud that they went. The doting mother gave her heart's pride to the cause with many a secret pang, but not a murmur of complaint. The devoted wife, whose existence was interwoven as it were with that of her manly lord, would see him go with a sorrow too sacred for us to know, and yet she would not bid him stay. The

Miss Mary Connally, Confederate Maid of Honor, 1894.

maiden, all youth and tenderness and love, would twine her snowy arms about her brother's neck and weep until her heart would almost break; and she, too, would have him go. Freely would she have given her pure, young life to shield him from the slightest harm; but she knew that he was brave and true, and she would rather have him die a thousand deaths than he should bear a coward's name or falter in a noble cause.

And so, throughout the length and breadth of the entire South, the greatest sacrifices that brave hearts ever made were offered up by our devoted women. They saw those they loved go forth to battle and die, and, although they felt it hard and terrible to bear, they nerved themselves for every blow and proved equal to every trial.

They will never tell and we can never know how many dreary hours of the silent night they spent in the agony of their hidden grief, praying for those who were battling far away or who, perhaps, were lying dead beneath Virginia snows.

Who of us did not believe that the faith and fortitude, courage and devotion of our people would give to our arms success complete and most triumphant? And yet, now when we look back to those four years, we are amazed to know that we suffered so much and endured so long.

In that fatal but most glorious struggle great deeds were done, which in after years history will proudly record and of which poets will be pleased to sing. Impartial men will write of the bleeding feet, the scanty rations and wasted forms, of the toil and trouble, care and sorrow of our noble braves; and they will tell how, forgetful of every pain and pang, they courted danger as a thing of sport, and fought as though it was a boon to die on their native soil for their native rights. And history will tell of warriors such as the world has rarely known.

Confederate battery, TN, 1861.

As long as valor and genius are revered his memory will be green in our land and we shall look back to his blameless life and splendid achievements with hearts overflowing with gratitude and love.[151] —
COL. GEORGE TUPPER

☛ THE PRIVATE

The private soldier never made a mistake. He was always foremost in battle, always in the right place.[152] — W. L. STEPHENS

☛ WHY HE WOULD BE A CONFEDERATE

[What follows is] . . . a pathetic story of a little Southerner with his mother in a Brooklyn, New York, theater, when the play was *Held by the Enemy*.

During a brief intermission he asked: "What did the yankees fight for, mother?"

"For the Union, darling," was the answer.

Just then the curtain fell, and the orchestra struck up "Marching through Georgia." An expression filled with memories, brought up by the air, swept over the sad face of the mother.

After a brief pause the little fellow asked: "What did the Confederates fight for, mother?"

The second question was hardly asked before the music changed, and the ever-thrilling strains of *Home, Sweet Home* flooded the house with its depth of untold melody and pathos.

"Do you hear what they are playing?" she whispered. That is what the Confederates fought for, darling."

Then he asked quite eagerly: "Did they fight for their homes?"

"Yes, dear; they fought for their homes."

Was it the touch of sorrow in the mother's voice? Was it the pathos of the soft, sweet notes of *Home, Sweet Home*? Or was it the intuition of right? No matter. The little boy looked up at his mother with adoring eyes, burst into a flood of tears, and, clasping his arms around her protectingly, sobbed out: "O mother, I will be a Confederate!"

The mother's tears mingled silently with those of her true-hearted boy as she pressed him to her heart and repeated softly: "Yes, they stood for home and honor; yes, they fought for freedom's name."[153] — SUMNER A. CUNNINGHAM

☛ LAST DAYS OF THE ARMY OF TENNESSEE

"Halt! camp at full distance, unload your guns, stack them, and rest at ease."

At this all field officers seemed to retire into the thick woods that surrounded us to hide their faces for a time, and left us to draw full rations from our imaginations. We looked and listened in the death-like silence for an answer to our hungry thoughts. We saw our guns left without a guard; our cannon was left alone in open ground. No picket had been put out to herald the approach of our enemies, who had been following us for two days. We listened closely and expectantly for orders to build breastworks, but no orders came. We sat and dreamed. We walked around. What was happening in that once jubilant army? Now it was so still. Only the neigh of hungry horses broke the death-like silence. In this awful stillness and stupor the trees, the shadows, seemed to sigh "Death, Death."

The stillness is broken as if by magic! The thunder-tones of the enemy's cannon, familiar, oft repeated, echo over hill and dale, and through the woodland, on the right and on the left, behind us. We rush to our posts and wait for orders to fall into line. We listen for the bugle and breathlessly wait for the long roll, but no bugle sounds, and no orders to fall in. . . .

We see the field officers as they ride slowly about and seem to be dreaming. When one is asked to explain what this awful suspense means, he only answers, "I don't know; but something will be known to-night on dress parade." The suspense only increases as time passes until dress parade is called. Each eager to be first, a line is formed in less time than ever before. All are ready and

Lee after the surrender, April 9, 1865.

eager to hear, yet afraid to hear. The Adjutant walks out in front of the line, but he looks downcast. His walk, his features tell that unwelcome news or some evil forebodings await us. When he pulls from his pocket a piece of brown paper, he says: "Soldiers, this is hard to read; not because it is not well written, but because of what it contains." His voice is husky as he reads: 'Robt. E. Lee has surrendered, and we are now entering a ten days armistice.' That's all. Officers return your companies to their respective quarters."

Ah, yes! The cannon that have thundered all day is the rejoicing of the enemy! Will we also have to give up? If so, where will we be carried? What is the end? Will we go home to see the dear ones that we have not seen in so long? Will we ever know whether they are yet alive, or will we, must we, fill the prisons of the conquerors? "Yes;" "No;" is answered. In this strain we are left until the thunder tones of Lincoln's death resound from end to end of our army. Ten thousand men join Joe Wheeler to cut through the enemy and try to escape to Texas. But soon the order, declared a hopeless undertaking, is cancelled. . . .

We made out our muster rolls and drew our rations. Joe Johnston issued to us the thirty thousand dollars in silver that Jefferson Davis had given him for his services to the Confederacy.

We started home without even seeing the United States Army, with our colors floating in the breeze, not knowing yet that it was a conquered banner. Then, as we did pass outside the enemy's line, our sad faces received sympathy from the "boys in blue," and bidding them a comrade's farewell, we marched on homeward. But, oh, the heartaches on that march.[154] — J. T. C.

☛ BRIEF NOTES OF JOHN MORGAN'S RAID

One of the most extraordinary expeditions of the war was the raid of Gen. John Hunt Morgan through Kentucky, Indiana, and Ohio. One of his soldiers writes:

Our entire command consisted of about one thousand five hundred men, all brave and resolute, well armed and mounted, and eager for the race. [Confederate] Gen. Basil [Wilson] Duke and Col. Dick Morgan were in the van, Capt. McFarland, of the Second Kentucky Cavalry, being the senior captain and acting as major. From Burksville we proceeded on through Columbia, Campbellsville, and Lebanon, where the command fought from early dawn till late in the evening, putting to route the enemy and capturing many of them and destroying the government property. Thence to Springfield and Bardstown, whence the Yankees trailed their banners and fled at the sight of the stars and bars; thence through Bloomington, Garnettsville, to Brandenburg, on the Ohio River, where the command captured two steamboats and one-half of the command were crossed over to fight out and disperse about one thousand men ensconced in a wheatfield on the Indiana side, while the other half were engaged with two gunboats that had come down the river to prevent the crossing.

Gen. Morgan had brought his artillery to bear on them, and in the engagement one of the gunboats was badly crippled, while the other had to assist it to save the crew, and they skedaddled up the river. The army all crossed over to a man, and the enemy in the wheatfield were captured and dispersed; all prisoners being paroled.

John H. Morgan, C.S.A.

Being on the Indiana side, strict orders were given to keep in line and have no straggling. They moved on to Corydon, where the enemy, made up of citizens and soldiers, had the foolhardiness to send out a flag of truce and demand an immediate surrender, but it was promptly returned with the order to surrender at once or the town would be torn to pieces with shot and shell.

They surrendered without much fighting. About one thousand two hundred were captured, and a large amount of government stores were destroyed. The command proceeded to Palmyra, where a short fight took place and more government stores were destroyed. Occasionally some parties would cheer the command; they were evidently Southern sympathizers. This, however, was in the Hoosier, but not in the Buckeye State. The command moved on to Canton, where more prisoners were taken and more property destroyed; thence to New Philadelphia, with more prisoners and a skirmish. In fact the command was never out of the sound of arms or the flash of gunpowder.

The command had fighting and skirmishing through the towns of New Boston, New Baltimore, Williamsburg, Sardinia, Winchester, Jacksonville, Locust Grove, Jasper, Packville, Beaver, Jackson, Butland, Chester, and Buffington's Island. Here it attempted to cross the Ohio River in the face of all the gunboats on the river and forty thousand cavalry and citizens, and held them in check for three hours, when Gen. Basil Duke and half of the command were taken prisoners and sent down the river to Cincinnati. *There the people, it is said, treated them to all manner of abuse they could devise. The little boys were allowed to spit in their faces.*

From there they were sent to Camp Morton, Ind., where they were stripped, their clothes searched, and not as much as a button left them.

At Buffington's Island Gen. Morgan and the other half of the command cut their way through the Yankee files and went on till the 26th of July, passing through the following towns in Ohio: Portland, Harrisonville, Nelsonville, Cumberland, Greenville, Washington, Moorefield, Smithland, New Alexandria, Richmond, Springfield, Mechanicsville, West Point, and Salineville. Near the last place Gen. Morgan and his brother, Col. Morgan, were captured with the rest of the command, the chief officers being sent to the penitentiary at Columbus, Oh., and the rest of the command to Camp Chase, receiving the same treatment as the others. The General and his part of the command were in about ten miles of the Pennsylvania line, fighting all the way.

The number of towns passed through in the raid was fifty-two in all—nine in Kentucky, fourteen in Indiana, and twenty-nine in Ohio.[155]
— ONE OF MORGAN'S MEN

☛ THE WAR WAS NOT A "REBELLION"!
Let me add my earnest and hearty protest against calling our war the "Rebellion." It was not a rebellion, and we were not rebels or traitors. George Washington was a rebel because he fought against properly constituted and legal authority, and if he had failed he would probably have been tried as a rebel, and executed as a traitor. But Jefferson Davis was no rebel when he led the great struggle to maintain proper authority, to uphold law and constitution; and when the Federal Government held him as a prisoner they never dared to bring him to trial, because they knew, under the advice of [U.S.] Justice [Salmon Portland] Chase and the ablest lawyers at the North, that they could never convict him of treason under the Constitution and laws of the United States.

I remember that one day down at Beauvoir [Davis' Mississippi home], several years before his death, the grand old chief of the Confederacy said to me alluding to this question:

Rebellion indeed! How can a sovereign State rebel? You might as well say that Germany rebelled against France, or that France, who was overwhelmed in the conflict, rebelled against Germany, as to say that the sovereign States of the Confederacy rebelled against the North or the government. O that they had dared give me the trial I so much coveted, and for which I so earnestly begged, in order that I might have opportunity to vindicate my people and their cause before the world and at the bar of history! They knew that I would have been triumphantly acquitted, and our people purged of all taint of treason, and they never dared to bring my case to trial.

Jefferson Davis, C.S.A.

Is it not time, then, for those people to cease talking about treason and rebellion, and to stop their insults in calling us rebels? *If there were any rebels in that contest, they were north of the Potomac and the Ohio—the men who trampled under foot the Constitution of our country and the liberties bequeathed us by our fathers.*

Gen. Lee always spoke of the war as the "great struggle for Constitutional freedom," and that is a truthful and distinctive title which I prefer. "The War Between the States" was the title given by Alexander H. Stephens, and is a good one. "Confederate War" would do, but that implies that we made the war, which, of course, we did not, our policy being peace. The "War of Coercion," or the "War against State Sovereignty" would express it; but the "Rebellion," never.[156] — REV. J. WILLIAM JONES

☛ DAUGHTERS OF THE CONFEDERACY

Portsmouth, Va., the city which sent to the field more Confederate soldiers than it had qualified voters, held memorial exercises over the dust of its fallen soldiers on the 25th of May, 1894.

There was an outpouring of the good people to participate in and witness the grand annual tribute of decorating the graves of the dead heroes with flowers.

The loveliest feature of all was thirteen little girls, daughters of Confederate soldiers who are members of Stonewall Camp, robed in spotless white, each ornamented with a miniature Confederate flag, and each hatband lettered with the name of one of the Confederate States, and with a beautiful bouquet in each right hand, marching to the soldiers' burial lot in

Proud Confederate girls, 1900.

the cemetery, through the open ranks of Confederate veterans and armed soldiers, led by a little boy bearing a silk banner on which was inscribed: "Daughters of the Confederacy."

They gracefully deposited their flowers on the graves of the known and unknown alike, and then passed on for the soldiers to close up and fire their salute. Such a testimonial of love is worthy of perpetual custom at the annual gathering in memory of our dead all over the South.

The "Daughters of the Confederacy" at Portsmouth are Clara Ashton, Willie Ashton, Carrie Barlow, Etta Beatan, Florence Hawkes, Marie Hume, Fannie Langhorne, Mary Nash, Janie Peters, Mary Peters, Fannie Slater, Jennie Watts, and Winnie Watts.[157] — SUMNER A. CUNNINGHAM

☛ CONFEDERATE SNOWBALL BATTLE AT DALTON

It was in the spring of 1864, about the 22nd of March; a heavy snow had fallen during the night; the hills and valleys were covered with the flaky white. Joe Johnston's army was in winter quarters at Dalton, Ga. Two regiments of infantry were camped near each other, and in a spirit of fun began in somewhat military order to throw snowballs at each other. The effect was electrical, boyhood frolics were renewed, and the air was full of flying snowballs. Brigades and divisions were soon involved, and such a scene was never before witnessed on earth. Many thousands of men were engaged in a snowball battle. It began early in the morning; generals, colonels, captains, and privates were all mixed up. Private soldiers became commanders and the generals were simply privates, and the usual conditions were reversed. The boys had captured the generals' horses and swords, and were galloping through the flying snowballs giving orders and whooping things up generally. Verbal orders to different portions of the field were sent on flying steeds.

Confederate "Battle of the Snowballs," Dalton, GA, March 1864.

Gen. Patrick Cleburne was noted for his strict discipline, and whenever he caught a straggler from any regiment in the army he would make him carry a fence rail. Well, the boys had captured "Old Pat," when some fellow yelled out: "Arrest that soldier, and make him carry a fence rail." The surgeon of our regiment was calm and even tempered, but would get out of patience with a lot of whining fellows who would report on the sick list day after day. The doctor would look at his tongue, feel his pulse, and say: "Well, there is not much the matter with him; just put him on light duty." They captured the old doctor, and a soldier had hold of each leg, another his head, and others his arms, and as he was brought in as terribly wounded, Fred Domin ran to him, felt his pulse, looked wise, and said: "Well, there is not much the matter with him; just put him on light duty." This same doctor was noted for having had the same affliction as the soldier who complained. If a man went to him with the toothache, he would say: "Shucks, that's nothing; I've had the toothache a thousand times." One day Kenan Hill got a bug in his ear and went to the doctor, hallooing in great agony. The doctor

Sam R. Watkins, C.S.A.

said: "O shucks, that's nothing; I've had a thousand bugs in my ears." One day a soldier got a nail in his foot, and the doctor said: "O shucks, that's nothing; I've had a nail in my foot a thousand times." The doctor had one of his eyes nearly knocked out by a snowball, when Fred Domin ran up to him again, and said: "O shucks, that's nothing; I've had my eye knocked out a thousand times." There was a great deal of this kind of fun and take-off in imitation of some general or other officer, but we were kept too busy throwing snowballs to take it all in at the time. Infantry boys would capture cannon and caissons, and take the horses from the artillery and go dashing through the crowd. They would also hitch to the caissons and dash off somewhere else. This snowball battle lasted all day.[158] — SAMUEL RUSH WATKINS

☛ SOUTH-HATING IN 1894

Not a single Southern historian has presented our cause in its true light. Even Mr. [Alexander H.] Stephens wrote more in a spirit of apology than of justification, and we have sat supinely by and waited for an Englishman to, in part, vindicate us. For *this lack of self-assertion*, it has been said that we were justified by reason of the conciliatory spirit of the North toward us, both in sentiment and practice, and particularly the latter.

It has been urged that the *Northern people* have come amongst us and, in part, built up our waste places. Granting this, who have been the recipients of the gains? Our lands have been sold in many instances for $2.50 per acre that are now worth $500 dollars per acre. In almost all instances the principal office is in some *Northern city* and the principal officers, who get the profits of these investments, live in Northern cities. Thus the profits derived from the so-called "building up of waste places" do us no good. Our lands have been "boomed" by *Northern people*, who always secured their interests on the ground floor. They have bought our lands at wholesale, sold them to us at retail, and the profits have gone *north*. Thus, we have had the Palace Car Brigade superseding the carpetbaggers. Of course there have been honorable exceptions, but these have been the rule. Up to the first inauguration of [Conservative] Mr. [Grover] Cleveland hardly a public office in the government of any prominence was given to the South. Our ministers to foreign courts were all taken from the *North*, and thus foreign sentiment was manufactured against us, and the tide of immigration and capital turned from our doors.

Rutherford B. Hayes.

With all that has been said about [Liberal] President [Rutherford B.] Hayes, his was the first inaugural address after the war that did not vilify the South. He was the first President after the war to recognize the South, and this only in a limited way. And for even this he was ostracised by his former admirers and almost utterly ignored and forgotten by them. I do not hold with those who believe that he was ostracised by reason of his having been the recipient of a stolen Presidency. I do not believe that those who committed the theft so far repented of their action as to have ignored Mr. Hayes because he accepted the result of their action; but it was because they [Liberals] could not use him as a tool, as they had former Presidents, and as they have subsequently. In 1892, twenty-seven years after the war, we find that out of nearly one hundred officers in and attached to [Liberal] Mr. [Benjamin] Harrison's Cabinet, with salaries ranging from $4,000 to $8,000, one was from Mississippi, two from Missouri, and the remainder from the *North*.

Northern histories have been published and distributed in all parts of the world, in which we have been portrayed as "traitors guilty of treason," "rebels" and "murderers." At every meeting of the Grand Army [U.S.] this is repeated; at every unveiling the same is true. *Their press in daily concert heaps upon us slanderous vituperations commensurate with the mental power of the writer to express, and in all this we have acquiesced.*

I do not hold to retaliation as a rule, and certainly do not at the sacrifice of any principle; but when retaliation is the only means of vindicating a correct principle, then I say retaliate.

Confederate heroes.

Thirty years of acquiescence have proved fruitless, and we have impliedly admitted, by acquiescence at least, for the time that our fathers were "traitors guilty of treason," were "rebels," and that we now are "murderers.". . . I have heard a great deal about the recuperative power of the South, derived from *Northern assistance*. I rejoice at this, but what is all this worth if it is to be received at the sacrifice of those principles which go to make men and nations great?

I would abhor that condition which would even give me a dollar with its hand and slander me with its tongue. So let it be understood that *unless they let us alone we will in the future reply in kind*. Let [all pro-South views] . . . be the groundwork of the sentiment that whatever may have been the past, henceforth *if you slander us we will retaliate;* henceforth we will play the part of the lion instead of the cur; henceforth we will assert our manhood at least; and if this be treason, you must make the most of it you can. We do not court controversy, but simply ask to be let alone. We are willing to coöperate in sentiment and practice with Maine and Texas alike. We have acquiesced for thirty years. We think this is enough; and, to be plain about it, in the future we propose to give you as good as you send on this line, and the sooner you find this out the better it will be for all.[159] — MARTIN WILLIAMS

☛ THEY GAVE THEIR LIVES FOR HOME & COUNTRY
. . . For what more important purpose are we here than to honor the Confederate dead and to publicly proclaim that their memory is cherished in the hearts of our people? . . . these men gave their lives for their homes and their country; and if this be true, then there must have been some great principle or wrong involved in the issue, because *men*

will not peril their lives and fortunes for an abstraction nor die for a metaphor.

We were *a peaceful and quiet people, practicing the courtesies of an age that is past, and rose in arms only when our homes were threatened with invasion*; and in doing so we did but exercise the first law of nature, an instinctive law that pervades all life. To have acted otherwise we would have lost self-respect, been untrue to ourselves, unworthy of our homes, false to our country, irreverent to God, who created man in his own image, conferring a nobility—a title above all created by the breath of man.

But I will pass on to the second part of the sentiment, which expresses *the hope that "the memory of the Confederate dead may rest securely in the hearts of the Southern people."*

I know of no better way to establish how deep-seated in the heart of the present generation is the respect for the Confederate dead than to illustrate it by some recent events; and before I do this I wish you to bear in mind that there is a tendency in men to condemn and to abandon their agents and leaders who have failed, and thereby blasted the hopes of their supporters and followers—whether in private enterprises or in military affairs—notwithstanding their labor and devotion to duty. *The masses only look at results. If this test be applied to the Southern people, it will be found that they have ever been true to their leaders, alike in adversity as in prosperity; and this establishes their character as men, just as the field of battle has stamped their character as soldiers; and combined we have the highest known type of manhood.*

This adherence of the Southern people to their leaders is illustrated in their devotion to the memory of Davis, Lee, Johnston, Jackson, Stuart, Pelham, and others.

Behold the Confederacy dissolved! Its chieftain captured, a prisoner in irons; accused of treason, murder, inhumanity to prisoners; the unreasoning mass, impatient ignorance, *a partisan press*, blatant politicians, one and all clamoring for his death more vehemently than did the demoniacal mob at the tribunal of Pontius Pilate! In all this his people did not forsake him. You know the verdict. All the world held him guiltless, the manacles dropped from his wrists, he became a wanderer, homeless.

In after years he [Jefferson Davis] found a shelter by the side of the sea, and there detraction followed him. With trenchant pen he successfully defended himself and his people until, with age, it fell from his trembling hand; and when it became known that his eyes were closed on all earthly scenes and that all the glory of this world had been exchanged for those promised in the prophetic vision of revelation, the voice of lamentation was heard alike in costly mansion and lowly hut, while sorrow, like an eclipse of the sun, overshadowed the land.

Jefferson Davis, C.S.A.

Many of you may remember *the honors shown his remains as they were carried from New Orleans to Richmond, how cities contended for the privilege of guarding them; and the final ceremonies at his grave, where every head was bowed in silence so profound that the gentle heart of the South was heard throbbing at the door of his tomb.*

I was introduced to Mr. Davis late in the evening of February 23, 1847, when I was placed by Gen. Taylor, Col. May, Dr. Hitchcock, and others, in a common baggage wagon between two wounded men and carried from the hacienda of Buena Vista to Saltillo. One of these men was Col. Jefferson Davis, and the other was Lieut. Pickett, of Illinois. So my acquaintance with Mr. Davis runs back over forty years. I think he combined in a high degree the three great qualities of soldier, orator, and statesman. *His life was pure, and nothing could swerve him from the path of honor. From the continued assaults of a nation of enemies more bitter even than that of the English people against the character of Napoleon, he arose triumphant, and has left a notable instance of a man, while living, obtaining a victory over error and silencing the tongue of slander.*

Surely his memory "rests securely in the hearts of the Southern people."

. . . The Confederate dead, in its largest sense, means the men who carried the musket. They met the first shock of battle and bore the brunt of the fight, and went down to death in the front ranks. *The world does not know and comprehend the true character of the Confederate soldier.* Mainly they were men of education, thoughtful, self-reliant, at home neighbors and friends. Each knew his right and left hand comrade—knew they could be depended on not to desert him or abandon a position given them. This individuality of the soldier and fidelity to his comrade beside him gave repose and confidence to the line, confidence to the officers, and strength to our army beyond mere numbers. They were not a heterogeneous mass of humanity from all nations, serving for pay, for bounty, for pensions and spoils [as in the Union army]. The census report shows that little wee Rhode Island has a foreign born population nearly equal to seven of the Southern States. There were more negro soldiers in the Union army than Gen. Lee ever mustered on any field of battle, and Massachusetts recruited some of her regiments in South Carolina and Georgia with negro slaves. [Note: Gen. French neglects to mention, or is unaware, that five times as many African-Americans fought for the Confederacy than for the Union. L.S.[160]]

The cause for which so many Confederate soldiers perished is not lost. It still lives in the autonomy of the States as they now manage home affairs. Appomattox shattered the Confederacy; but it was not a judicial tribunal to determine the rights of the State under the Constitution. All honor then to the private soldier who died that his cause might live. The Confederate Government was only an adjunct to organize defense. It perished.

Sons of Confederate soldiers, cherish the memory of your fathers. You are citizens of a great republic—the one country on which the eyes of distant peoples are turned and their hopes centered. There is no nobility here created by government, but there is a craving for distinction in many ways. One is wealth; others are seen in the formation of such societies as the Society of the Colonial Wars, Society of the Cincinnati, Sons of the Revolution, Aztec Club, Grand Army of the Republic, Association of the United Confederate Veterans, and many others. It is a pride of ancestry and a distinction to be a member of some of these societies. You should all become members of the Association of the Sons of the Confederate Veterans. It is a distinction that will be more highly prized with age.

I have only referred to the part borne by the men during the war. I have been in the hospital where wealth and beauty nursed the wounded, and I have heard the dying soldier sing the song of life, but, like the dying swan's, the last notes were the sweetest as they blessed the women who nursed them. I have seen the dying dolphin on the deck of a ship change his somber colors for the bright hues of the rainbow, and I have seen the dying soldier's face illumined with the dawn of heaven as he said: "Tell them at home I give my life for them." I am not unmindful, ladies, of the power you possess and can exercise in preserving the true story of the war and the memory of the Confederate soldiers. *Tell the true story to your children.* If you do not, your nurses will tell them theirs. They will walk with your little ones to the national cemeteries, and the children will ask: "What are all these white stones for?" The answer is: "They mark the graves of the Union soldiers killed during the war." "Who killed them?" And then follows the stories of the war from the lips of the nurse, and thus every stone also becomes a monument to some unknown Confederate, by perpetuating his memory.

It was woman that instituted [Confederate] Decoration Day, and, as it is immediately connected with the pleasing duty of preserving the memory of the soldiers of the South, I am sure you will annually meet and place floral tributes on the graves of those that rest in our cemeteries, whether of the blue or the gray. You were a potent factor in the war, and the world knows but little of your labors or the sacrifices that you made. Where the strength of man fails, you can lead with a single hair.[161] — GEN. SAMUEL G. FRENCH

Samuel G. French, C.S.A.

☛ KNIGHTS OF DIXIE: PRESERVING TRUE SOUTHERN HISTORY
[This] . . . is the first regularly organized effort to preserve the war and pioneer records of *the Southland*, to encourage the study of Southern history, to teach the children and young people of the South what it has done for itself and *what it has done to make and preserve us as a nation, to correct the willful and malicious errors of history and preserve the true history of the struggles of the South from 1770 to 1865, and since.* It designs to unite in one social and fraternal organization the men and women of the Southland and enables them to *point with pride to what they and their ancestors have achieved.* In view of our Centennial, now is a most auspicious time for organizing such a society. The headquarters of the Knights of Dixie are at Little Rock, Ark. This truly Southern order is rapidly growing and becoming popular in the South. It now has lodges actively working in nine States. There is a fine lodge, N. B. Forrest No.

1, in Memphis, with one of Gen. Forrest's Staff as Commander, and another one will soon be organized. There should be at least two active, prosperous lodges in Nashville, and wherever there is a Bivouac or Camp there should be a lodge of the Knights of Dixie.[162] — P. C. W.

☛ A NOTABLE COLORED VETERAN

One of the best-known freedmen in Columbia, S.C., is old "Uncle" William Rose, who has been messenger for the Governor's office under every Democratic [then the Conservative party] administration since 1876. . . . He is now eighty years of age, but is still active and vigorous enough to be at his post of duty every day, and *nothing delights him more than to take part in any Confederate demonstration.*

William Rose was born in Charleston in 1813, and was a slave of the Barrett family of that city. He was brought to Columbia when only twelve years old, and was taught the trades of carpenter and tinner. In his younger days *he went out to the Florida War as a drummer in Capt. Elmore's company, the Richland Volunteers*, an organization which is still in existence, and which has made a proud record for itself in three wars. Subsequently *he went through the Mexican War as a servant for Capt. (afterwards Col.) Butler, of the famous Palmetto Regiment.*

But the service in which he takes the greatest pride was that in the days of the Confederacy. He was the body servant of that distinguished Carolinian, Gen. Maxcy Gregg, and as soon as he heard that his beloved master had fallen on the field at Fredricksburg he rushed to his side as fast as a horse could take him, and remained with him until the end came. His description of the death of Gen. Gregg, of his reconciliation with Stonewall Jackson, and his

Two of the 1 million blacks who served—in one capacity or another—in the Confederate military.

heroic last message to the Governor of South Carolina are pathetic in the extreme and are never related by the old man without emotion.

William saw [Grover] Cleveland inaugurated, and was present at the unveiling of the soldiers' monument at Richmond, and at the recent grand Confederate reunion at Birmingham. From the latter he returned laden with badges which he cherishes as souvenirs of the occasion.

For sixty years he has been identified with the Richland Volunteers, and they never parade without him. About two years ago he presented a gold medal to the company, which is now shot for as an annual prize. *He never forgets [Confederate] Memorial Day, and no 10th of May has passed by since the close of the war without some tribute from him [being] . . . placed on the Gregg monument at Elmwood. Recently he has been given a small pension by the United States for services in the Florida War.*

Old "Uncle" William is of a class fast passing away. They will not have successors, but *all the world may witness benefactors in Southern whites until the last of them crosses the "dark river."*[63] — C. M. DOUGLAS

☛ THE INVENTION OF TORPEDOES

During the Seminole Indian War in Florida, in April, 1840, Capt. [Gabriel James] Rains, then of the Seventh U. S. Infantry, was stationed at Fort Micanopy, Fla., about twenty-five miles from Fort King. His men were so waylaid and killed that it became dangerous to walk even around the fort. Desperate diseases require desperate remedies, and as the preservation of the lives of his command required it, the following was resorted to by Capt. Rains: The clothing of the last victim of the Indians was made to cover a torpedo invented by him. A day or two elapsed, when early one night the loud, booming sound of the torpedo was heard, betraying the approach of an enemy. Capt. Rains with a squad of men went to the spot, and upon investigation found that the Indians, in removing the clothes, to which the torpedo was attached by a wire, had exploded the torpedo. Yells were heard in the neighboring woods, but whether the

Gabriel J. Rains, C.S.A.

explosion proved fatal to any of the Indians is not known. From this time on Capt. Rains was continually experimenting with torpedoes of his own manufacture.

Upon the breaking out of the Civil War he resigned his position as lieutenant colonel of the Fifth U. S. Infantry, and was made at once a brigadier general in the Confederate army.

A barrel torpedo, one of the many types of "infernal machines" used by the Confederacy.

Soon after the battle of Seven Points, in which he took an active part, Gen. Robert E. Lee sent for Gen. Rains and told him that the enemy had upward of one hundred vessels in the James River and he thought they were about to make an advance that way upon Richmond, and expressed confidence that if any man could stop them he could, and asked him to undertake it. This is from his diary: "Observing that the ironclads were invulnerable to the cannon of all caliber we were using, and were really masters of rivers and harbors, I determined that it required submarine inventions to checkmate and conquer them, and on the James River, opposite Drury's Bluff, I made and placed the first submarine torpedo, the primogenitor and predecessor of all such inventions."

Gen. Rains was placed in charge of the entire submarine defenses for the coast and harbors of the Southern States, and personally supervised the laying of torpedoes in the harbors of Charleston, Richmond, and Mobile. In Charleston Harbor there were laid one hundred and twenty-three torpedoes, which prevented the capture and probable conflagration of that city.

There were fifty-eight vessels sunk and destroyed by torpedoes during the war, many of them of large size. As has been well said, "the invention of the torpedo has entirely changed modern warfare," and Gen. Rains's daughter is proud that her father, a Southern man, was the first to invent and utilize such a valuable means of defense.[164] — A DAUGHTER OF GEN. GABRIEL J. RAINS

👉 GREETING FROM A UNION SOLDIER

Mr. President, Gentlemen of the [Confederate] Third Regimental Association of Georgia: A private [Union] soldier who carried a gun, who was the least of all the men who surround you tonight, is to tell you what you have already learned in your intercourse with the members of the Hawkins Zouave Association [Union] of this city: that we are glad to see you, and take great pleasure in bidding you a most cordial welcome to this the thirtieth anniversary of the organization of the Ninth N.Y. Vols. (Hawkins Zouaves).

We most kindly appreciate the hospitality shown our representatives who visited you one year ago last August—who returned declaring that Georgia grapes and water melons were not only large, but delicious, and were given by the men of the old Third Georgia with lavish hands at Fort Valley, thus manifesting your cordiality and regard for the boys (now old men) of the Hawkins Zouaves, for which we are sincerely thankful.

It is very pleasant to have the opportunity to grasp the friendly hand of those who thought so diametrically opposite thirty years ago. It proves that time not only heals, but cools the blood, gives more mature judgment, enabling each to overlook the past, and while we do not claim to forget those dark hours in our life, nor withdraw

Clark Wright, U.S.A.

an iota, nor impugn the motives or sincerity of an opponent, we can each forgive, and while we let the dead past bury its dead, rejoice in the sunshine of the present, that brings comfort and happiness to all parts of our native land as we remember above and over all else we are American citizens. As such this remnant of Hawkins Zouaves sit down and break bread with, and most gladly greet the survivors of the gallant Third Regiment of Georgia.

And while the professional politician may rave about the rights of the South, or the rights of the North, we calmly step aside from these noisy windmills of both sections to clasp the hand of these brave heroic men of the South, and bid them a joyful welcome to the metropolis of the Empire State of New York.

Honored as we are, by the presence of men who fought in the ranks (the true heroes of every war) and by others who commanded regiments and brigades, yet above and over even these we acknowledge ourselves especially honored by the ladies of the different households of our guests, who, with father, husband, brother, relative, favor us with their presence in New York on this festive occasion.

There are several remarkable parallels incident in the history of the two regiments whose representatives gather around this board. Both were organized in April, 1861; both were composed largely of very young men, who were impressed with the righteousness of the cause they represented, and feeling sure they were right, dared those causes to maintain.

The fortunes of war brought these regiments repeatedly face to face, time after time in most deadly strife, and while each did its best, as soon as the battle ceased humanity took the place of conflict, and the wounded and distressed were cared for without regard to the color of their clothes, whether it was blue or gray, or gray or blue. Few regiments of that great war lost a larger per cent of those engaged, yet neither of them lost a stand of colors, nor were the colors touched by hostile hand; and although the flags of both have been shot into tatters, there is still enough left of each for the survivors of these regiments to annually gather around and show our regard for one another and our love for those who fell fighting beneath their folds.[165] — REV. CLARK WRIGHT (of the Ninth New York Volunteers, U.S.A.)

☛ HE GOT HIS OWN TURKEY

When [Union] Gen. [Benjamin Henry] Grierson made his famous raid from Memphis to West Point, Miss., I was at home on a short leave of absence from the army, to secure better horses. I had succeeded in purchasing two, one for my trusty [black] army servant, Wesley. A Federal raid was expected, and Wesley was on the lookout. While at breakfast pistol shots were heard toward the village, I saw Wesley coming at full speed, and a squad of Federals behind him. As quickly as possible I hurried to the barn for my horse, and just had time to mount as my wife reached me through the back yard with my carbine, pistol, and overcoat. Wesley, and then the Federals, dashed by me as I wheeled my horse behind a negro cabin and dashed away in the open plantation.

The Federals soon halted and commenced to plunder my home, but Wesley saw and followed me. When out of range I halted and deliberately took in the situation. I could see my wife on the gallery pleading for valuables that they were appropriating, and in the yard a large drove of turkeys were being rounded up; a huge smoke from the kitchen chimney told that the cooks had been put to work. A mile away I could see the heavy column advancing—ten thousand mounted men—determined upon devastating that rich region of country between Okolona and West Point, on the Mobile and Ohio Railroad. Imagine my feelings with my young and tender wife in the hands of a ruthless enemy. The true soldier I did not fear, but these were plunderers of the worst order. For safety, I went to the woods the balance of the day. By night I had become desperate, and decided to brave all danger to learn what had been done at home. I had no fear of capture, and *all confidence in my servant Wesley, who had been with me the two years, faithful in all things. He could have had his freedom any day. He had often been in the Federal camp. At one time he captured and brought back the body servant of our colonel, who had deserted and gone to the enemy with his best horse. A book should be written on the Southern army servants, who, in devotion to their master, would go even where the battle raged, carry his bleeding body from the field, and guard it to his far-off home.*

But to my story. As we rode out into that large prairie, we had a scene that no pen can picture. It was one long, lurid flame, made by the conflagration of hundreds of palatial homes, barns, and corn pens, for miles along the railroad. I reached the vicinity of my home easily without contact with the Federals. I was glad to see that the house was spared the torch, but the large plantation fence was a ring of fire. Part of the army was encamped there. As I neared my home the fires had burned low, and thousands in blue were wrapped in their blankets dreaming of home. I evaded their pickets by a large ditch as deep as a man on horseback, which ran through the farm in the direction of the home building. Reaching the gin house, we dismounted a short distance from my residence, and led our horses inside the old log pick room. I sent Wesley to learn the situation, and report as soon as possible. He divested himself of all military apparel, so that he might be taken for one of the home negroes if seen by the Federals. It seemed he would never return. About midnight all seemed quiet and still. Wesley finally returned from the opposite direction unexpectedly. He told almost breathlessly that Miss Laura was all right. He said she was then sitting by the fire knitting. Our two little ones and their grandpa were on a lounge in her room asleep.  All the other rooms were full of soldiers, who were asleep. A back door from my wife's room faced the gin house where we were secreted, and as the picket fence had been burned, nothing prevented me from reaching the door on horseback. I hastily mounted and told Wesley to follow, and rode quietly as possible to the door of my wife's room. The door was partly opened, and I was face to face with my wife. She threw up her hands and whispered: "Have you come to surrender?" I told her no, but to see her, and learn how she had been treated. Except that *she had been robbed of all valuables*, she had been treated respectfully. The guard at the hall door, ordered to keep all out of her room, was then asleep. I leaned over and kissed her good-bye. When asked if I was hungry, Wesley answered. She said that there was under a large pot on the kitchen table the last turkey, ready cooked, but that there was no bread. Handing my bridle to Wesley, I peeped through a crack of the old log kitchen. All was still. On the floor were several Federals asleep. I gently opened the door, reached the pot, quietly took the turkey by the leg and handed it to Wesley. I thus kissed my wife, and off we went in darkness. I learned afterwards that the next morning inquiry was made as to "who got that turkey." She proudly informed the yanks that her husband had been at home and had taken it for his supper. In a few days I joined Gen. Forrest and had the great pleasure of helping to drive the Federals from my own yard, and capturing one who had appropriated the pair of woolen gloves that my wife was knitting the night I got the turkey.[166] — T. M. DANIEL

☛ BRAVE LITTLE PATRIOT REWARDED

The clouds of war and desolation hung over the land. The long-dreaded enemy had come. A large number of Federal troops, "vandals" we called them in those days, had encamped on the outskirts of a Virginia village in the heart of the lovely valley of the Shenandoah.

For several days following their coming the excitement among the citizens was intense.

After a time, nervous mothers who had kept ceaseless watch over their little ones, as if fearful of their being captured and made prisoners of war, relaxed their vigilance and allowed them their usual liberty to roam.

The children, glad of a release from unusual restraint, and realizing that the dreadful yankees showed no craving to gobble up little folks, soon gained courage to go about the camp and watch proceedings.

One day one of the officers, among a group of lounging soldiers, noticed the children hanging around, and thinking to have a little amusement out of the young rebels, called them to him. Some of them took fright and ran away, but the rest reluctantly drew near, with faces more expressive of anxious wondering than pleasure at finding themselves in such close proximity to the foe.

After talking with them for awhile, the colonel said he wanted to know whether they were loyal to the Union or not, whether they were yankees or rebels in feeling, promising that the little girl who gave the best answer should have a nice present. "What shall it be? What do you want above all other things?" he asked.

This was a difficult question for the little Confederates, to whom the possession of a new toy or book was beyond their wildest dreams—yea, and to whom even a new calico dress would be a rare luxury.

After much whispered consultation with each other, it was announced with perfect seriousness that the majority wanted a hoop skirt more than anything else in all the world, though a few decided in favor of "a pair of store-bought stockings that ain't homemade."

Then they formed into line ready to give their answers. But poor little rebels! Partly through an eager longing for the present, but more through fear of giving offense to the big soldiers, all but one of them turned traitor. Each one in the primmest little speech declared her loyalty to the United States. Then the colonel, seeing one little tot standing aloof and keeping silent, a shy-looking little thing with bare feet and a faded, tattered dress, called her into the line. "Come up, little one! Are you a rebel or a yankee?"

Her cheeks glowed and her bright eyes flashed under the limp, old sunbonnet as her answer came in no uncertain accents, "I'm secesh;" then, raising her voice, "I'll live secesh and I'll die secesh!" ending almost in a scream. This outburst was received by the soldiers with hearty cheers for "Little Secesh, the brave Little Secesh!" and none were more enthusiastic than the colonel, who hastened to declare her the victor.

Then, taking her on his shoulder, he carried her in triumph to the village, followed by the crestfallen little traitors, where he bestowed upon "Little Secesh" a pretty and useful present.[167] — UNKNOWN

☛ THE SOUTHERN CAUSE & ITS HISTORY

. . . the Confederate cause . . . is the cause of human freedom under constitutional guarantees as proclaimed in the Declaration of Independence by Jefferson, adopted by the American Constitutional Congress July 4, 1776, and also embodied in the Constitution of the United States.

The Confederate Government was not a revolt against the Government of the United States, but a protest against the abuse of that government as established by the patriots of 1776. It did not abrogate a single well defined principle of the Declaration of Independence, nor of the Constitution framed in pursuance thereto by the founders of the government; but under the most solemn vows and pledges of life, liberty, and sacred honor proclaimed anew these principles in their protest against their abuse and against the perversion of the powers of the government by

Confederate monument, Huntington, WV.

a sectional party which had assumed the reins of government by a mere technicality of law, and in opposition to the popular will of the people expressed at the ballot box by a majority of two hundred and fifty thousand votes.

Following the precept and example of the fathers and founders of the republic, the Confederate States, while thus protesting against the prostitution of the delegated powers of the government to sectional and partisan purposes, embodied these same principles in their Constitution, which the fathers had incorporated in the original compact.

It is not the purpose of this article to enumerate these principles, nor to attempt to exemplify them in the practice of the government from 1789 to 1861. This is the province of history, and every patriotic citizen should be acquainted with the rise, progress, and development of these principles in the body politic as the years have rolled on since their inception on this continent. A true history of these principles and their development under constitutional governments in America is the demand of the age. *The school histories of the United States, compiled and written by partisan [anti-South] authors and forced upon the people by Northern school trusts, are little else than a propagandism of their fanatical dogmas and distorted deductions from a temporary triumph of military power of the many over the legitimate resistance of the patriotic few. . . . [The facts will] . . . prove an antidote to the false teachings of ordinary school histories.*[168] — A. M. BURNEY

☛ HEROIC & PATRIOTIC MARYLANDERS

We come of game stock. I never saw a Marylander who was a coward. I want posterity to consider us as sound-headed as well as warm-hearted, and I want them to understand that our course in leaving our native State was dictated by reason as well as by enthusiasm, that we were perfectly right in doing as we did, and were actuated by the highest motives of intelligent patriotism. That we failed was no fault of ours. We did our full duty, and we will die in the conviction that if we had it to do over we should do just as we did then, only more efficiently, as experience has shown us how to do.

When Great Britain acknowledged the independence of the States, she recognized each by name as an independent and sovereign State. Maryland was as sovereign as England or France.

These sovereign States formed a government to protect their liberty and independence, but they never gave up the right to change their form of government at their pleasure. It was to be a government of equal States and equal laws, but each State must of necessity be the sole and final judge as to when she would require other guarantee and protection of the liberty of the people.

The institution of slavery is the organization of labor in all primitive societies. It always has been so and always will be so.[169] It is one of the great forces by which savage races are civilized and civilized people subdue nature and develop arts, science, and thought. It was the basic institution of the American colonization. New England enslaved the Indians. We never did. But African savages were civilized here, and civilized by the control of the civilized race—its religion, its morals, and its measures. There never has been an equal number of Africans as highly developed as that portion of the race living in America, and this development was the result of American servitude.

The habit of control and the practice of masterdom made the Southern man reliant, positive, and forceful. He controlled the formative period of the new society. He formed the Union under the Constitution, and he directed the policy of the Union for the first seventy years of its existence. His power was the logical result of the institution by which he was formed. His whole energy was directed to the art of governing. The assertion of intellectual predominance and the exhibition of material power in the South produced irritation, envy, and ill will. For thirty years prior to 1860 the North had been gradually making up its mind for the overthrow of the predominance in the South. . . .

When, therefore, in 1861, the issue was presented to the Marylander whether he should stand by, in base ease and inglorious safety, while his blood and kin in Virginia were dying like men, resisting the invasion of their homes and the subjugation of their liberties, he hesitated not a moment, and with the kiss of his mother and the blessing of his father he flew to the assistance of Virginia.

In the Maryland line there were not twenty men who had any property interest in slavery. There was not a man who sought promotion or advantage of fortune. They went to stand by their friends in trouble, to defend rights inherited *from free ancestors.* Those of us who were of mature age had distinct ideas of policy and of the future. *We believed that the interests of Maryland required that she should become one of the Confederate States. We did not believe she would be safe in the hands of the lawless democracy of the North. We knew that our people had the same feelings, and that we fully and fairly represented them; and we knew that the only way to secure that future union was to hold for the State a representation in the armies of the South.*

With that purpose firmly fixed in my mind, I refused to accept a commission of lieutenant colonel from the Governor of Virginia, and was mustered into the army of the Confederate States as captain. And never in that glorious epoch and fiery trial did we cease to maintain a Maryland organization, under a Maryland flag, in the army of the Confederate States. Gen. George Hume Steuart, Capt. George Thomas, and the rest were earnest, faithful, and devoted to this end, and we succeeded in writing the name of the State on the brightest pages of American history. *The existence of the Maryland Line of the Army of Northern Virginia is not recorded on a single page of the archives of Maryland. Not a single honor decorates our gallant comrades; not a recognition of the self-sacrifice, devotion, and chivalry of the Maryland Confederate has ever been made by the powers that have controlled Maryland for thirty-four years. But these men were the best soldiers she has ever had. They fought more battles, won more glory, achieved more victories than the old line of the Revolution.*

George H. Steuart, C.S.A.

Within a few years you have seen insurrections of labor in the States put down by troops. There were more soldiers at Homestead than Washington had for the defense of Philadelphia, and more at the railroad strike the same summer in New York than defended that city from Sir William Howe. In future government will be controlled by the property class—that is, the large property class—and they will control the paid military force.

But an end comes to all that, as it did in Rome and Egypt and Assyria, and in France in 1793, and is coming in Germany to-day. Like causes produce like effects, and logic is eternal and inexorable, and *when anarchy with red riot rules the cities of the North their people will call on the Confederates to save them.*[170] — GEN. BRADLEY TYLER JOHNSON

☛ WHY OUR CONFEDERATE SOLDIERS DID NOT DIE IN VAIN

1. They vindicated the character and quality of the civilization in which they were trained. *For years the life, customs, manners, and institutions of the Southern States had been abused, misrepresented, and ridiculed. The people were denounced as effeminate and brutal, haughty in manners and loose in morals. Their conservatism was regarded as stupidity, their home-loving and home-keeping as narrow provincialism, their hospitality as ostentation, their chivalry as bombast, and their religion as an immoral superstition. But those four years of deadly strife, in which the whole world was held at bay, in which were wrought deeds of daring and magnanimity almost unparalleled in history, taught all the world the strength of character, the firmness of purpose, the long-enduring hardihood of nature, the noble manhood, the gracious womanhood that had been nurtured under a system which had been so grossly slandered.*  Since the war, one of the ablest opponents of the South and her principles, while sharply criticising the manners of the Southern leaders, has borne honorable testimony to their character. The Hon. James G. Blaine, in his recollections of *Twenty Years in Congress*, says: "They were, almost without exception, men of high integrity, especially and jealously careful of the public money. They guarded the treasury against every attempt at extravagance, and against every form of corruption." What a contrast to the dishonesty and rapacity which too often now regard official position as an opportunity for public plunder. Those men may well shame the sordid greed and pitiful ambition of the mass of pettifogging politicians of to-day. These were the men of the old

South—of the old order, which has "given place to the new," and which the fledglings of a new day decry and ridicule. The blood of one of these men of the "Old South," shed on yonder fateful field, was richer than the life current of the whole race of sneering, money-seeking, materialistic apostles of the "new" South [scallywags]. There is indeed a new South, that inherits the traditions and builds upon the foundations and glories in the deeds of the old, that looks forward with generous hope, but also looks back with reverent fondness. Surely that old order has been splendidly vindicated, when it can present as its consummate crown and flower that manliest of men, "pure as light, and stainless as a star," Robert Edward Lee.

2. They revealed and developed the latent powers and capacities of the South and its people. Thrown without preparation into the midst of a war to tax the energies of the mightiest, the exigency demanded not only wise statesmanship and military ability, but also the discovery and utilizing of all material resources, the creation of new industries, and the invention of new appliances. The people rose to the height of the great occasion, became aware of the possibilities that lay in the field and forest and stream, in mountain and mine. They manifested marvelous skill in invention, laying under contribution nature's hidden forces for our help. They who before were a nation of planters and farmers, living retired lives of cultured ease, pastoral peace, or rustic toil, became artisans, builders, manufacturers, financiers, and seamen. Inventing new devices, building ships to revolutionize naval warfare, forging arms, sailing the seas, digging into the depths of the earth, they brought forth the treasures of land and sea and sky to minister to their need. Just as oftentimes a man, in some great emergency, becomes aware of what is in him, and in a moment becomes a giant in strength and faculty; so the Southern people, in those four years of war came to themselves and sprang forth, not by slow process of growth, but by the sudden answer to the call of Providence, to a full realization of the splendid possibilities of achievement in their reach. The great development which has come to the South, bringing varied industries, abounding prosperity, and increasing wealth, is not the result of an infusion of foreign life, but is the outcome of her efforts to carry on the war, and to maintain her cause against a power which closed every port of hers, and shut her up to dependence on her own strength under God.

3. These men achieved a finished testimony, a consistent record against mere materialism in politics or in social life. They proclaimed to all men everywhere, and to the end of time, that there are things more valuable than ease or comfort; that duty's voice must be heeded at any cost. In an age when everything tends to be measured by money values; when "the jingling of the guinea helps the hurt that wounded honor feels," when bodily comfort is the end sought, when self-sacrifice is considered Quixotism—in such a time it is a grand success to make a record, ample, complete, consistent of devotion to duty, which does not count the cost, which shrinks not at any sacrifice, which prefers death to dishonor, which chooses truth defeated rather than profit successful, "right upon the scaffold rather than wrong upon the throne." The story of these men's sacrifices and sufferings, of the wondrous struggle they made, will become one of the world's cherished possessions. These men made history, and wrought a work that shall endure in the spiritual upbuilding of our people. They set forth in time's clearest light a lofty ideal to stimulate the efforts of those who shall come after us. In memory of such devotion, in the presence of such high ideals the sordid spirit of greed shall stand abashed, blushing at its own unworthiness.

4. These [Conservative Southern] men effected a stay of the tide of centralization in our government [that is, liberalism]. The protest they made before mankind, and sealed with their blood, was against the [socialist] destruction of the States [and their rights and sovereignty], and against the omnipotence of the Federal Government ["big government"]. And that protest will be more and more heeded as the passions of war pass away. Each State will be henceforth more secure in her alienable right to her local government and her individual development. *The fight was one that had to do with the very separate existence of all the States, North as well as South.*

The failure to try Jefferson Davis, when he wished above all things to be tried, marked the beginning of a reaction. The courts were more free from the sway of passion, and they saw that in trying Mr.

Jefferson Davis, C.S.A.

Davis they would be putting a sovereign State on trial; for he only obeyed his State; and the courts realized their lack of jurisdiction. Since then, there has been more and more carefulness in guarding the rights of States. While it is true that secession will not again be tried as a remedy for wrongs done a State,[171] it is safe to say that the general government will hesitate long before it uses force to coerce a State of this Union. These men have shown the terrible cost of the attempt to destroy the equality and sovereignty of the States.

Thus the men who fought the war to its bitter end, and laid down their lives or their arms in defeat, were not dishonored. Out of the wreck of their hopes and purposes they saved these grand results. Their civilization was vindicated, their material capacities and resources were revealed, their testimony to the sacredness and worth of honor and duty was finished and sealed; respect for the sovereign right of the States of the Union was fixed on a firmer basis.[172] — REV. JAMES H. MCNEILLY

Leonidas Polk, C.S.A.

☛ QUICK WIT OF BISHOP POLK

About dark, shortly after the arrival of Liddell's brigade, I observed a body of men whom I believed to be Confederates standing at an angle to this brigade and firing, obliquely at the newly arrived [Confederate] troops. "Dear me," said I, "this is very sad. It must be stopped." So I turned round, but could find none of my young men, who were about on various messages. I determined to ride up myself and settle the matter. I cantered up to the colonel of the regiment, asked him in angry tones what he meant by shooting at his friends, and ordered him to cease doing so at once. "I don't think there can be any mistake about it," he said, with some surprise. "I am sure they are the enemy." "Enemy!" I said. "Why, I have only just left them myself. Cease firing, sir! What is your name, sir?" "My name is Colonel _____, of the _____; and pray, sir, who are you?" Then for the first time, I saw to my astonishment that he was a Federal, and that I was in the rear of the Federal lines. I knew there was no hope but in brazening it out, my dark blouse and the increasing obscurity befriending me, so I approached quite close to him, shook my fist in his face, and said: "I'll soon show you who I am. Cease firing at once!" I then turned my horse and cantered slowly down the line, shouting in an authoritative manner to the Federals to cease firing.[173] — GEN. LEONIDAS POLK

☛ MEMORY OF A CONFEDERATE BOY SAILOR
In spring of 1861 I was attending school in Mobile, Ala., and was "marker" for the Gulf City Guards, Company B, Capt. John E. Curran. Returning from school one afternoon, Capt. Curran said, "Hurry, Jere; get on your uniform and come to the armory." I found the company

ready to march, and "fell in" with my gun and flag. We marched to the wharf, and boarded the tug *Gunison*, and steamed down the bay. From hearing the men talk I learned the expedition was for the capture of the [Yankee] ship *Danube*, then lying at anchor off Fort Morgan. We steamed alongside, and the soldiers commenced boarding, I along with the others. I had read bloody stories about boarding ships, and began to feel anxious and was inclined to hold back, but seeing the others climbing the ladders, I slung my gun to a shoulder, with the flag sticking in its muzzle, and started up the ladder. Just as I got over the side of the ship, I saw a [Union] sailor standing on deck, right where I would have to land, with a big pike or something of the kind in his hand, and taking for granted he would attack me, I climbed right up to the masthead and from the crosstrees looked on. There was no fight. The captain of the ship surrendered. The stars and stripes were hauled down, and the stars and bars run up, and soon everything was calm and peaceful. I received my share of the prize money some months after.[174] — JERE S. WHITE

☛ REUNION OF FORREST'S ESCORT

The annual reunions of Forrest's Escort are events of unusual interest, because the personal intimacy of the members has been maintained through the three decades that have intervened. Besides, they have the pride of having done "more hard fighting than did the escort of any other general in the war."

The exercises at the beautiful Cumberland Park, near Nashville, were exceedingly pleasant. Particular reference is made to this fact as suggestive. At reunions of particular commands, when the attendance is only from one hundred to four or five times as many, and when social chats rather than formal speeches are indulged in, the pleasure and profit are greater. If Camps and Bivouacs would have reunions along with business meetings more frequently, the results would be very happy. Their wives and daughters would prepare luncheons and the sons would imbibe the spirit of the fathers in heroic and patriotic achievement.

On this occasion the peculiar characteristics of Forrest were a theme. Terrible as was the man in battle, he manifested much more faith in prayer than may be supposed from his general reputation. He would digress from command in trying ordeals to ask: "Chaplain, are you praying?"[175] — SUMNER A. CUNNINGHAM

☛ MAIDENS DISGUISED AS YANKEES

I was a member of Company D, Seventh Regiment, Virginia Cavalry, Captain Sommers' Company in Col. Turner Ashby's Regiment. I went one night in company with a comrade to call on some young ladies, and as the country at that time was infested with the boys in blue, we agreed to stand guard alternately while the other fellow went in and chatted the young ladies, and I noticed, too, that my comrade was very willing for me to take the first turn in the house, although he acknowledged he was as hungry as a wolf. I was very much in love with one of the young ladies of the house, and I thought that she reciprocated. When I walked into the house my best girl met me at the door, and took me into the parlor. I asked the question, "Where are your sisters?" She said they had gone to a neighbor's to stay all night. I was pleased with that, for, as my comrade's best girl was gone, he would not object to standing guard all the time.

"Now, Ben," said my lady love, "I have been looking for you to drop in tonight, and I have ready the nicest supper I could prepare; so just give me those cumbersome pistols, that you may eat with some pleasure."

I had left my saber on my saddle. "No, I thank you, Miss Nannie. I cannot part with my pistols: there are too many yanks around here." But her bright eyes and lovely smiles disarmed me. She just wanted "to have the honor of holding them" while I ate supper, but she slipped my pistols in a sideboard drawer and turned the key on them. As I finished a good supper two blue coats opened a door on one side of me, and two entered by another door behind me, and all four of them leveled their pistols at

me and commanded me to surrender. To make the matter more real, my girl threw herself on her knees at my feet, put up her hands to the yankees, and begged pitiously for them not to shoot me, and one of the bluecoats said: "Well, Miss, for your sake we will not shoot him, but you must be responsible for his good behavior while we eat our supper." Then one of them said: "Your arms, sir, quick!" I explained that I was already disarmed. One of them leveled a pistol at me and said: "No fooling now, Johnny; give up your arms." And then Miss Nannie said: "O Mr. Yankee, please do not shoot him! I will get his arms for you."

And off to the sideboard she flew to get my arms. During this stage performance my comrade stood on the outside on the gallery looking through the window. I saw that he was shaking his sides with laughter, and in a second it occurred to me that I was not being taken prisoner by real yankees, so I made a break for him, running over the yankees; but he knew what was coming, and jumped off the gallery, and hid. By the time I got back to the dining room the yankees had disappeared, and my best girl met me with a smile and said: "Forgive me, Ben; the girls forced me into this." I told her she had better take to the stage, for it was the best "forced" performance I had ever witnessed. The yankees were her sisters and a young lady neighbor, who had dressed themselves up in Yankee uniforms and laid a trap to capture me. I very coolly told my best girl that she could have made the capture without any assistance whatever.

There is but one of those girls living to-day, and my comrade too has crossed over the river, but many persons yet living in Page Valley remember it well, for it was many a long day before I heard the last of it. The boys used to try to tease me about the matter. I would turn them away with the remark that I would not give a cent for a soldier who would not surrender to four pretty girls. He was no soldier if he did not surrender. Many hundreds of miles separate me now from those lovely valleys where for four long years I followed Stonewall Jackson, J. E. B. Stuart, and Gen. Thomas Lafayette Rosser, through all those stirring scenes, yet anything written of those days and occurrences in those valleys deeply interests me.[176] — B. D. GUICE

☛ SKETCH OF GEN. ABRAHAM BUFORD

The late General Abe Buford was born in Woodford County, Ky., January 20, 1820. He was a graduate of West Point in the class of 1841, and was appointed second lieutenant of dragoons in May, 1842. He served in the Mexican war, and for distinguished bravery at Buena Vista he was breveted a captain. In 1854 he retired from the service. In the summer of 1862 he offered his services to the Confederate Government, and was commissioned a brigadier general of cavalry and served in the Army of Tennessee. In 1864 he organized a brigade, consisting of the Third, Seventh, and Eighth Kentucky Regiments of

Abraham Buford, C.S.A.

mounted infantry, and was assigned to the division of Forrest. He was badly wounded on Hood's retreat from Nashville in 1864, and surrendered at Gainesville, Ala., in May, 1865. Gen. Buford died in Danville, Ind., June 9, 1894.[177] — SUMNER A. CUNNINGHAM

☛ CARING FOR THE WOUNDED AT IUKA
I was on Gen. Price's Staff, Assistant Medical Director to Dr. T. D. Wooten, now of Austin, Tex., when he made the fight at Iuka, Miss. As our army had to retreat before Grant's, and then [Union Gen. William Starke] Rosecrans' army, I was ordered by Dr. Wooten to take charge of our wounded, which I did and remained until the battle at Corinth was fought, about a month later, I think. Having finished with my hospitals, I went down under a flag of truce, and was permitted to go in. The fight was still going on out at Blackland and cannon booming. When I got to Corinth, I found our wounded scattered over the fields and woods, and only one Confederate did I see under a tent or in a room, and that was Col. Boone, of Mississippi, with an amputated thigh. Gen. Forrest having cut the railroad north, the Federal army had but few tents and but little outfit.

I went to Gen. Grant's Medical Director and asked if arrangements could be made to move the Confederate wounded to Iuka, and told him I could procure good rooms and fine water there. The terms were presented through Grant's Medical Director and accepted, and were ratified by Gens. Grant and Price—viz., that the railroads be declared neutral ground for one mile either way. Gen. Price detailed a battalion of cavalry to guard the railroads, and Gen. Grant sent the wounded and supplies to Iuka. There were thirty-six surgeons and assistant surgeons, if I remember correctly, and among the leading ones I remember Dr. Don Roberts, from Missouri; Dr. Needlett's two brothers, from St. Louis, Mo. (the younger one was my clerk and assistant, and since the war has held the Chair of Anatomy in the St. Louis Medical College; the older went to Mobile); Dr. Felton, of Mississippi; Dr. Davis; and others now forgotten.

After getting the wounded and sick together and getting them to Iuka, the surgeons held a meeting, nominated me as head, under the neutrality cartel, as I would call it. The citizens were permitted to come and go free from molestation, and *their property, in negroes,* horses and other things, *was protected*. In a few days we had our wounded well clothed and fed. Two or three hundred wounded had nothing but blankets to cover them, their clothing having been cut off and thrown away full of _____. I think we had as many as 2,000 or 3,000 sick and wounded. We remained there three or four months, when Gen. Price sent his train of quartermaster wagons with clothing. I had gone in debt seven thousand dollars for supplies, issuing my receipt. He sent me six thousand dollars, and I paid the remainder. I sent my account to Richmond for my services and deficit in money expended, amounting to some seventeen hundred dollars, and have never heard from it since.

Many will remember the facts above related, and I think it was owing to the kind treatment given the officers and men at Iuka by Dr. Wooten and the Medical Director of the Federals that enabled me to effect the arrangements which resulted so happily for our [Confederate] soldiers, and for this Dr. Wooten will ever have my kindest consideration. Afterwards I noticed that this plan was adopted around Richmond and many other places.[178] — DR. J. C. ROBERTS

James Madison.

☛ WHAT TO NAME THE "CIVIL WAR"
The founders of constitutional government in America differed essentially in their theories, and the government established has been aptly termed "a government of checks and balances." The Revolutionary patriots had grave reason for placing limitations around the Federal power. They had seen and felt the encroachments of a throne.

It was owing to the jealousy of a centralized government that the first experiment (1776–1789) failed. By the [U.S.] Constitution of 1789 the Federal arm was strengthened; still, what concessions were made by the States, or what implied powers were delegated to the Federal Government, at the time and subsequently, became the subject of frequent and hot disputes. The Virginia and Kentucky Resolutions asserted the constitutional right of a State to resist or oppose legislation by Congress which was palpably pernicious. This historic controversy marks the closing scenes of the eighteenth century.

Again in 1814 the maritime interests of New England met in convention at Hartford, at a time when the power of the young republic was measured on land and ocean against the military power of Great Britain, and so alarming was the [secessionist] attitude of New England that Maj. [Thomas S.] Jessup was ordered with his regiment to Hartford, holding, no one knows what, secret orders from the Executive. Again, in another form we see the assertion of the [secession] principle in 1832, when South Carolina, standing within the Union, began to arm its citizens to resist the mandates of the Federal courts, and Andrew Jackson, a Carolinian, on the part of the government, declared that he would put a halter around the neck of the first man who should shed the blood of an officer of the United States in the execution of Federal process. It cannot be questioned that the quarrels of 1798–99, 1814, 1832 grew in intensity until 1861. Thus we see that two great principles were at issue: the one known as Federal unity [liberal], the other as State sovereignty [conservative]. The last named ultimately divided into two schools of opinion in the South, State rights and Southern rights: the former asserting for the States rights exercised by the general government, and especially claiming that the allegiance of the citizens to the State was primary to the claim of the general government; the latter (Southern rights) asserting this and going further to proclaim the constitutional right of a State to peaceable secession. It was the assertion of this doctrine which culminated in the scenes of 1860–61, when State after State withdrew from the Union, calling their citizens to their defense, and putting upon each citizen the grim alternative of bearing arms against the home or general government.

We come now to a proper designation of the greatest conflict of constitutional history, which the act of secession inaugurated.

From the standpoint of the Union the war had one of two defined and evident meanings: It was a war of emancipation, or a war to determine the alleged constitutional right of secession. *That it was not a war of emancipation was expressly and repeatedly disclaimed by Lincoln and the Federal Congress in 1861, while rallying to the flag the power of the Union. It was true that emancipation was the happy exigence of war, but that it was such primarily was disclaimed in emphatic language.* The term coercion, which seems confusing to some, was simply the armed assertion of the principle of Federal unity, denying the constitutional right of secession, holding such an ordinance null and void, and asserting the duty of the Government to execute Federal process in all the States, including the seceded territory. The War of Secession, or a war to perpetuate the Union, would seem to describe the coercive policy to the Federal administration.

As to the action of the South . . . it was not a war of rebellion. The Southern States claimed to act by lawful authority. In seceding they did not ask war, but peace, and protested their constitutional right to peaceably withdraw from the Union as a right reserved in the creation of the government—reviving the quarrels, and citing as precedents 1798–99, 1814, 1832.

I have more fully developed another paper, from which I quote: "It was in the interest of security and peace that the Southern States renounced allegiance to the Federal Government and resumed their sovereign functions as States, believing the welfare and happiness of the citizens to be imperiled by longer continuance in the Federal Union." It should be clear that so far as the South was concerned, the Civil War was a "War of Secession," or a war waged by the South in the assertion and belief of such political right.

The "War of Rebellion" is objectionable, as it offends. On the other hand, "War of Secession" is suggestive, terse, and significant. The real meaning is embalmed in these words: a war waged by the Federal Government against the asserted right of a State to peaceably, or forcibly secede from the Union, the South maintaining the right as a constitutional franchise; the administration disputing the claim, and holding an ordinance of secession to be null and void.[179] — S. D. MCCORMICK

☛ A CONFEDERATE MONUMENT IN CHICAGO

On last Decoration Day there was sent to us ten boxes of flowers from Texas, and several from our personal friends in other States of the South. The monument is a thing of beauty and will last forever.

Under the auspices of Robert T. Lincoln, President Lincoln's son, the Confederate Monument at Chicago, IL, was dedicated on May 30, 1895; 100,000 people attended.

I would like to say . . . that if the remarks that I have heard made by the multitude of [Yankee] visitors to the monument were heard by every [former Confederate] . . . they would feel different as to the prejudice that is supposed to exist in the North against those who wore the gray. I heard one old battle scarred Grand Army of the Republic veteran say, standing at the base of the monument: "That is worthy of a brave and chivalrous people, as the people of the South proved themselves to be."

Chicago is proud of the ex-Confederates who have become citizens of the city. It should be remembered that it was a son [Robert Todd Lincoln] of Abe Lincoln who, as Secretary of War [in the early 1880s], gave our association the permission to take charge of and improve the lot and erect the monument. There are many ex-Confederates living in Chicago who have never identified themselves with us in this effort, fearing that it would interfere with their business relations with the people, and they have so expressed themselves to me. However, those of us who have never sought to conceal our connection with the "lost cause" have been more honored and respected by all, and have been time and again invited to banquets given by the Grand Army [U.S.A.] of the Republic Camps in this city.

To illustrate a case in point, I will state that four years ago I was persuaded to run for State Legislature in my district, and the Grand Army Camp of 283 members gave me their solid support.[180] — THEO NOEL (a former Texas Confederate soldier living in Chicago, Illinois)

☞ SKETCH OF COL. SAMUEL JONES RIDLEY

Samuel Jones Ridley was a native of Tennessee, a successful planter in Madison County, Miss., when the war broke out. At the organization of the first regiment of light artillery, he enlisted, March 22, 1862, and became captain of Company A, an eight-gun battery of 230 men. I think he received the unanimous vote of the company. He was forty years of age when he enlisted; dark complexion, gray eyes, and six feet three inches in height. He was a splendid specimen of manhood, a typical Southern planter and gentleman. I was his first orderly sergeant, and sustained that intimate relation to him until promoted to the adjutancy of the regiment. He was loved and respected by every member of the battery. He was killed at the battle of Baker's Creek (or Champion Hill), and was personally directing the firing of his guns when he was shot down. He remained on the hill after the infantry support had retired, when he and several of his men went down under the terrible fire of the enemy.

During the session of the Interstate Dairyman's Convention in this city several years ago, [Union] Col. Curtis, of Wisconsin, was my guest, and in the course of some conversation about war times I learned that it was his command that captured the battery. He described the conduct of the captain as most heroic, and said that he would like much to know his name. He was certainly surprised and gratified when I gave him the desired information.

Capt. Ridley was not promoted, as his daughter has heard, but he doubtless would have been had he survived the battle of Baker's Creek. His name and his memory will be cherished by every member of the old battery until they shall be ordered to meet him on the camping grounds of life eternal.[181] — COL. J. L. POWERS

☛ A BEAUTIFUL REPLY BY MR. DAVIS

While President Jefferson Davis was preparing his *History of the Rise and Fall of the Confederate States*, he made a visit to the home of Hon. Henry Leovy, at Pass Christian, Miss. He went to pay a friendly visit to the family and to get some papers he had left with Mrs. Leovy and her sisters, the Misses Monroe, daughters of Judge Thomas Monroe, who had been exiled from Kentucky on account of his Southern sympathies.

Judge Monroe's family were refugees in Abbeville, S.C., at the time Mr. Davis passed through there, on his way South, after the fall of Richmond. With these friends he left a collection of very valuable papers, including letters from Gen. Lee and other prominent Confederate officials. When Mrs. Leovy brought out the papers and a Confederate battle flag and the model of a gun invented by Mr. Davis, while he was Secretary of War, under the United States Government, Mr. Davis took the battle flag, and as he held that in one hand and the gun in the other, he seemed to stand the representative at once of the United States and the Confederate States governments. As he gave the history of the flag, the memory of the war, in which Mrs. Leovy had lost three brothers, and during which her father had been banished from his Kentucky home and she from New Orleans, and the *True Delta*, a paper owned by her husband, had been [illegally] confiscated, rushed over her with such force and vividness as to cause tears to flow down her cheeks and her to exclaim: "Mr. Davis, I have not gotten over the war yet! I believe the ladies were worse rebels than the men, anyhow!"

Jefferson Davis, C.S.A.

"Better patriots, madam," was the energetic and instantaneous reply from the man who had served faithfully in the army and Congress of the United States, and then, believing that the States were sovereign, and that sovereigns could not rebel and that his allegiance was due, first to his State, served his State and country with equal fidelity and ability, when Mississippi had become a member of the Confederate States Government. *It is well for our children to remember that their fathers never admitted that they were rebels and traitors, and to know that, though Mr. Davis* was arrested on the charge of treason, no attempt was ever made to prove the charge, because lawyers knew it could not be sustained.[182] — REV. W. C. CLARK

☛ REMINISCENCES OF A YANKEE SURGEON

I notice that the lapse of thirty years has not extinguished the friendship and attachments that were so often formed between patriots who were foes in battle. Soon after the battle of Stone's River, in which I participated, and in which I lost all of my surgical instruments by having my  three ambulances captured early Wednesday morning, I was placed in charge of a [Union] prison hospital at Nashville. This hospital was on Cherry Street, South Nashville. This hospital was for the sick and wounded Confederates and the sick of the Union army who were under arrest for the violation of military discipline. The position I occupied as surgeon of the hospital gave me the opportunity of making many acquaintances, especially among ladies who thronged the hospital daily to see and inquire about relatives and friends. I well remember some who took an active part in administering to the wants of their sick and wounded friends. They were Misses Cartright, Payne, McEwen, Aline McCall, Leonora Hamilton, and Sallie Edmundson.

I also became acquainted with many [Confederate] prisoner soldiers, most of whose names I do not remember and who, on taking leave of the hospital, did so with evidence of sincere friendship that is not seen in parting with ordinary friends. I remember well Chaplain C. M. Hutton, Third Alabama (home, Clinton, Ala.); Maj. Jones, Twenty eighth Mississippi, captured at Franklin (before the battle); and Capt. King, of Louisiana. There was a young [Confederate] cavalryman in the hospital a long time who was shot through both feet, whose home was in Columbia. I forget his name. Miss McEwen came often to see him. I got him paroled and sent home. I remember he was taken to the provost marshal's in a spring wagon, not being able to sit up in a buggy. Col. McEwen went with us to the Capitol. I will relate an incident connected with this hospital. A young [Confederate] lady came from Gallatin to see her brother, who was wounded. She called at the hospital early Sunday morning without a pass from our medical director. My orders were positive not to allow any one to go upstairs without a pass, but she insisted on going up. I told her I could not allow her to do so; that if I had any discretion, she would not have to ask the second time. She broke down and wept bitterly. I remembered that I had never received an order not to allow any one to come down stairs, and sent for her brother to come down to my room. At the battle of Stone's River, on Friday night about midnight there was a wounded Confederate officer brought to the field operating tent in which I was engaged as assistant surgeon, and he was laid just outside the tent. After many hours, Dr. Walton, of Kentucky, who was in charge, said to us: "We will not do any more work to-night." Just then we heard an exclamation from this officer, and I insisted that he be brought in and his wounds dressed. This was done, and he asked me if his wounds were fatal. I told him that the chances were greatly against him. He was shot through the chest and through the leg. He was carried to a shed near by and laid on some unbailed cotton. I gave him some water and brandy. The night was very cold; I got an order for a pair of blankets and placed them over him and told him that I would see him in the morning, but I failed, as he was sent to Nashville very early. He was Capt. Peter Bramlett, Second Kentucky Infantry [C.S.A.]. Ten days later I saw his death announced in a Nashville paper. Mrs. Payne, who was a frequent visitor at the hospital, wanted to have a friend of hers paroled and taken to her home, and related to me that she had cared for several Confederate soldiers, one of whom was Capt. Bramlett, who had died at her house. She said that when he was about to die she concluded to remove the coarse blankets and replace them with neater ones; that he caught her hand and said: "No, do not remove those blankets, for they saved my life at Stone's River. They were placed over me that cold night by the hand of an enemy, but a brother. You may come across him sometime; and if you should, tell him I died under the blankets he placed over me that night." She sent them to his parents in Paris, Ky.[183] — UNION DR. F. G. HICKMAN

☛ I BORROWED TROUSERS FROM A NEGRO

Rising generations should have some idea of the straitened circumstances of a Confederate soldier. I was wounded near Atlanta, July 22, 1864, and sent to a hospital in the woods, in tents near Forsythe. On arriving at the hospital, I was divested of all my wearing apparel, and the hospital authorities gave me a receipt for my wardrobe, consisting of pants, one roundabout coat, hat, shoes, and shirt and drawers. I was taken from this hospital of tents in the woods to the college hospital at Forsythe, where I remained several months and endured three courses of gangrene. From the college I was sent to Macon and from there to a "college"

hospital, the Cuthbert. After several months at Cuthbert, when I had gotten almost well, the nurse brought me a pair of crutches and would come to my room occasionally to practice me in learning how to use them, so he concluded after awhile that I had learned enough about them to risk myself out on the ground. So he brought in my knapsack; but lo! to my surprise and sorrow, on opening it, I found I was entirely destitute of pants. Some good fellow, in the rounds I had taken, had confiscated the only trousers that I possessed in the world. I didn't have a cent, and I couldn't draw any. What was I to do? The little town we were in had some fifteen hundred wounded and disabled soldiers then, but I could learn of none who had more than one pair of pants, and I couldn't get out to beg the good citizens, and what should I do? For about nine months I had been confined to my bunk and room, and now I was physically unable to paddle my own canoe. I was almost heart-sick, and had well-nigh given up ever getting another pair, when a negro boy named Byrd, serving his young master, Ridley Jackson, in an open-hearted way, proposed to lend me a pair until I could do better. I gladly accepted, put the negro's pants on, and felt as big as a king. I was soon out on the ground, down in town, at the depot, at the Alhambra, and around generally. But alas! my joy was soon ended. After I had worn the pants five or six days, my benefactor came to me one morning just after I had donned his trousers, and said to me that he had just received orders to go to the front, and unless I could pay him three dollars and twenty cents for his pants he would have to ask me to vacate and turn them over to him. With a heavy and sorrowful heart I gave them up and stretched myself out on my bunk, where I mused over the trials and tribulations of a Confederate soldier.[184] — UNKNOWN

☛ SKETCH OF DANIEL DECATUR EMMETT

The heart of every Southerner thrills when he hears the stirring strains of the famous battle hymn of the Confederacy, "Dixie," and no one lived in this country during war times who was not familiar with its sentiment and its music; yet to-day there are very few people who know the name of the writer, and that he is now living and in his old age is dependent on the generosity of others for support. Uncle Dan Emmett, the old time minstrel, in his day and generation one of the leading lights and greatest favorites on the American stage, the author of this immortal song, is to-day quietly spending the evening of his life in the retiracy of a humble home in the outskirts of Mt. Vernon, Oh.

Daniel D. Emmett.

Here in this quiet little Ohio city Uncle Dan was born seventy-nine years ago, on October 29, 1815. He was christened Daniel Decatur Emmett, by his parents, who were Southern people. His father marched to Mt. Vernon in 1812 from Detroit, being one of sixty riflemen.

Young Emmett learned the printer's trade on the Mt. Vernon *Gazette*, and in three years rose from the position of "devil" to foreman. He was of a roving disposition, however, and enlisted in the United States army. His father was displeased at this performance, and had him discharged for being under age.

Early in boyhood Dan displayed decided musical talent. Before he had reached the age of fifteen he had composed several quaint negro melodies. He finally joined a circus and traveled with different companies for eighteen years as a band musician.

In 1859 he wrote his most famous song. He was then a member of Bryant Brothers' minstrels, of New York. One night Jerry Bryant asked

Dan to write him a "hurrah walk around." That was on Saturday night, and Mr. Bryant wanted the piece ready for Monday morning's rehearsal. The song was written Sunday, rehearsed all day Monday, and sung that evening. It proved to be a great success for several years, but when the war broke out the company was forbidden to use it, and the band was hissed [by Yankees] when they attempted to play it.

In the South it was different. Its popularity rapidly increased until it became the war song of the Confederacy. All through the war, when two opposing armies lay encamped near each other and the Union bands would strike up "Yankee Doodle," or "Star-spangled Banner," the Confederates would always respond with "Dixie."

"Dan Emmett's Famous Walk Around" has been revived by a New York road company this season. Uncle Dan wrote many negro melodies, jigs, reels, hoe downs, and songs; but "Dixie" was his most famous composition. Among the most popular of his other songs were: "Dan Tucker," "Old Aunt Sally," "Gumbo," "Sound de Horn," "Gwine ober de Mountain," and "I'm Gwine Back to Dixie."

He has appeared during the past year at several entertainments in Mt. Vernon, and is tranquilly awaiting the fall of the last drop scene.[185]
— ANDREW CARLISLE CARSON

CHAPTER 14

1895

☛ HOW A VIRGINIA GIRL SAVED LEE'S ARMY

In front of Petersburg, in the early spring of 1865, every soldier of average intelligence knew that Gen. Lee was only waiting for the end to come, and wondering how the new born Confederacy was to die. But we were certain that it would "die game."

One evening late in March, Gen. A. P. Hill sent for me and said his impressions were that Grant was preparing for a general forward movement, and that Gen. Lee should have accurate information as to his

movement. He desired me to take as many men as I thought I would need, and get inside the enemy's lines as soon as we could, obtain all possible information, returning one man at a time as we gained it, and that I must get information regardless of danger. Early next morning, with three companions, I had reached a point in rear of Grant's vast army where we could conceal ourselves during the day. My hope was that the next night we could reach a place near Cabin Point where we thought we could certainly get in through the enemy's picket lines.

During frequent scouts in that direction I had become acquainted with a family (the head of which was in the army), consisting of mother, two daughters aged about twenty and eighteen, and a son about twelve years. They were poor but intensely Southern. Their humble log cabin was always open with genuine Virginia hospitality, and especially to a soldier in gray. We had often used the boy, by sending him inside the

Federal lines with a basket of pies, for which he would ask a dollar each. We priced them high to prevent his selling out too soon. He was a very remarkable boy, and soon "caught on" so he could go all through the army. Those old-fashioned, "half-moon" Virginia pies were quite a factor in the secret service of the Army of Northern Virginia. The eighteen-year-old daughter was really the head of the family.

It was to this place we were hurrying, when about two o'clock the second night out, on a broad, sandy road, now little used on account of the position of the armies, the quick ear of our scouts caught the sound of a rapidly approaching horse. We had hardly concealed ourselves when the horse and rider had reached us. With a bound like wildcats, Jackson and Bond had the horse thrown back on his haunches. Instantly a bright pistol flashed in Jackson's face, but I had already grasped the wrist and the bullet went singing through the air. Reuben Boon took the pistol from the small hand, and she cried out, "Would you murder a woman?" I replied, "What are you doing here alone at this hour?" "This is [the] Captain, and the very man I am looking for!"  It was the younger daughter of the family above mentioned. In lifting her from her saddle, I found her to be thoroughly wet and shivering with cold. We wrapped her closely in the folds of two army blankets, and I gave her some whisky from a small flask given me by Gen. A. P. Hill before starting. She soon became quite comfortable, and seated at the foot of a large pine tree, though far from home and with four men whom she only knew as rough soldiers, without a particle of trepidation, in a clear voice she told us that on the day before her family had observed unusual activity in the army. The young brother went out and soon returned to inform them that the whole Army of the Potomac [U.S.A.] was already on a forward movement. The plan was clear to turn Lee's right at Five Forks and Dinwiddie Court House. With Sheridan then to force his way to the South Side Railroad, and there cut off Lee's retreat, then by a general forward movement, the effort would be made to destroy his army. The young lady said that her mother prayed for quick means to inform Gen. Lee, and watched anxiously for some scout to come along. She astonished her mother by telling her she was going that night to give the Confederates information. She kissed her mother goodbye, and mounting their only horse, she sped away in the darkness to give her countrymen, over thirty miles away, the news. She explained that in fording a creek about twelve miles back, her horse fell in water waist deep. She kept her pistol dry, leading the horse out. Again, about seven miles back, a "Halt" rang out, and a minnie ball passed over her head.

We were astonished at the important news and the wonderful action of this remarkable Virginia girl. I told her that we must get this news to our army as soon as possible. She said the men could go, that surely one of them might get through, and added: "I want you to see me home, Captain." I decided to take her home, and had lifted the then helpless girl on her horse, when, after a warm clasp of the hand with each scout and a "God-speed and protect you," she turned to go. I also bade them farewell, with an admonition to let nothing stop them until Gen. Hill was informed of the situation. They started for our army, while I went in an opposite direction to deliver to her mother the grandest heroine history has ever recorded.

I instructed her to stay from four to six rods in my rear [approximately 100 feet], and let this distance separate us unless she wanted to speak with me.

The gray of dawn was beginning when we reached the vicinity of her home. Concealing her in a pine thicket near, I quietly as possible approached the house. Looking through a crack between the logs, I saw the mother and sister sitting by the fire. Their pale, anxious faces told the tale. No sleep had come to them through that long night of anxiety. "Thank God! thank God!" was the only reply that the mother could make when told of her daughter's safety. I lifted her from her horse, but she could not walk a step. When clasped in her mother's arms, she fainted as if dead. Her tired nature was exhausted and the reaction had come.

Two cups of genuine strong coffee and a good breakfast somewhat restored me after thirty-six hours without rest or sleep. I bade farewell to this grand heroine and good family, and with their prayers following me, I started on the perilous journey to Lee's lines.

Grant's entire army was on the move. The usual routes were

blocked. Several times I ran upon them. Once a regiment of cavalry forced me into a creek with nothing but my nose above water and head under drift. I had to remain until they crossed within a hundred feet of me. Another time that day I lay under a culvert almost buried in mud while a brigade of infantry and a battalion of artillery passed over it. Late that night I got into the promised land to find Lee's entire army ready for battle.

Reaching Gen. A. P. Hill's quarters, I found him up and dressed. I gave him such additional information as I had gained. He told me one of the scouts had been captured, but two arrived safe, with the information. In less than an hour after they reported, couriers were dashing in every direction, and in five hours the army was in line of battle. Bushrod Johnson and Pickett had been sent to Five Forks and Dinwiddie Court House, and reached there before Sheridan.

By the patriotic courage of this young woman, Lee met Grant at every point, and but for her the surrender would have been at Petersburg, and there would have been no Appomattox.

I have never heard of this noble Virginia family since that eventful night. Nor have I seen but one of the three scouts. Jackson lives in Oklahoma. The others I have never heard from. I suppose they have gone to join Hill, Stonewall, [James Jay] Archer, and Lee.[186] — UNKNOWN

☛ OUR CONFEDERATE VETERAN ANCESTORS & THE UNION

Andrew Jackson.

Argument is effective, upon the review of history, that *the most loyal friends of the Union, until the actual outbreak in 1861, were the Southern people*.

No greater claim is made than for the proportion the South bore in the [American] Revolution. It is but natural that foreigners could not become as loyal as those whose ancestors fought under Washington. Remember the words of [Southerner] Andrew Jackson: "The Union, it must and shall be preserved." Kentucky stood by her motto "United we stand, divided we fall," in remaining neutral. This theme was taught by the firesides and in the schools of those who espoused the cause of the South in our great war. Now and then expressions are given by those who suffered for the principle of State Rights, that must seem strange to those whose training has been since the war, but the theme of their ancestors was that the Union of the States be maintained, it was argued as policy, however, rather than principle. *The right to withdraw from the compact had never been questioned, hence the greater fear that the Sovereign States would do it. The plea of the South during the childhood of those who made the best Confederate soldiers was that the Union be perpetuated, so when they actually went to war under a different flag, the provocation was such as to make them desperate. Confederates honor the memory of ancestors who fought under Washington, whether they went from New Jersey, Vermont or South Carolina.*[187] — SUMNER A. CUNNINGHAM

☛ INSIDE THE LINES AT FRANKLIN
I was a pupil in the old Franklin Female Institute—the alma mater of so many brilliant women, the mothers and grandmothers of the present generation. Nashville owes a debt of gratitude to at least two of its graduates, Misses Fannie and Martha O'Bryan.

At the time of these reminiscences, Miss Walker (now Mrs. J. P. Hanner), was the principal. The pupils numbered about 175, and as wide awake set of Southern girls as could be found.

While we were trying to concentrate our minds on our books one ear was always open to the varied sounds of the fife and the rattle of drums, the clatter of horses' hoofs, and the electrifying notes of the bugle. We were allowed always to run to the front gate to see soldiers pass. If they were "our boys," we waved our bonnets and handkerchiefs—if they were yankees, and we watched [Union Gen. Don Carlos] Buell's army of thousands pass, we looked and felt dismayed.

On an ever memorable day, the 30th of November [1864], we assembled at school as usual. Our teachers' faces looked unusually serious that morning. The Federal couriers were dashing hither and thither. The officers were gathering in squads, and the cavalry, with swords and sabres clanking, were driving their spurs into their horses' flanks and galloping out to first one picket post and then another on the roads leading south and southwest of town. The bell called us in the chapel. We were told to take our books and go home, as there was every indication that we would be in the midst of a battle that day.

At four o'clock that afternoon I stood in our front door and heard musketry in the neighborhood of Col. Carter's [house] on the Columbia pike. To this day I can recall the feeling of sickening dread that came over me. As the evening wore on, the firing became more frequent, and nearer and louder; then the cannon began to roar from the fort.

The Battle of Franklin II, November 30, 1864.

My father realizing that we were in range of the guns from both armies told us to run down into the cellar. We hastily threw a change of clothing into a bundle and obeyed at once. My mother, who never knew what fear meant in her life, was a little reluctant to go and leave the upper part of the house to the "tender mercies" of soldiers, but she finally joined us in the basement. A few minutes later there was a crash! and down came a deluge of dust and gravel. The usually placid face of our old black mammy, now thoroughly frightened, appeared on the scene. She said a cannon ball had torn a hole in the side of the meat house and broken her wash kettle to pieces. She left the supper on the stove and fled precipitately into the cellar.

After that, the only way we could get anything to eat was by sending a guard, who was in the yard, to the kitchen after it. The patter of the bullets on the blinds was anything but soothing. The incessant booming of cannon and the rattle of the guns continued until midnight, then the firing gradually ceased; we, of course, were in ignorance of who was in possession of the place, but all the while hoping and praying that it might be our boys.

About one o'clock [A.M.] we thought the town was being reduced to ashes, but it turned out to be the burning of the Odd Fellows Hall on the square. About four o'clock we heard the tramping of feet and the sound of voices. Our hearts jumped into our mouths, and what joy when we learned that our own soldiers were in possession of the town! We first learned it from the men who carried Col. Sam Shannon, who had been wounded, to his sister's house, our next door neighbor. Our men were in possession of the town! We didn't "stand on ceremonies" getting out of the cellar. Our doors were thrown wide open, and in a few minutes a big fire was burning in the parlor. The first man to enter was Gen. William [Brimage] Bate, all bespattered with mud and blackened with powder, but a grand and

John Adams, C.S.A.

glorious soldier under it all. I will not attempt to picture the meeting between him and my father, who had been a life-long friend. Next came Gen. Thomas Benton Smith, with the impersonation of a chivalric, gallant soldier, wearing under the mud and dirt his recent hard-earned honors. Poor fellow, how short lived were his joys! A cruel sabre cut at Nashville [a few weeks later] forever dethroned his reason, and he is now in a Tennessee Asylum for the insane.

Space fails me to mention the long list of friends who came that day and received our warmest welcome. I shall mention what a reproof my sisters received from some of their soldier sweethearts. An uncle of ours, who made his home in New York city, during the previous summer had my sisters to visit him, and, of course, they replenished their wardrobes while there. On the morning after the battle they wanted to compliment their soldier friends by "looking their best," so they put on their prettiest dresses. The soldiers were so unaccustomed to seeing stylish new dresses, that they actually doubted their loyalty, thought they should have on homespun dresses instead of "store clothes."

In the afternoon, December 1st, some of us went to the battlefield, to give water and wine to the wounded. All of us carried cups from which to refresh the thirsty. Horrors! what sights that met our girlish eyes! The dead and wounded lined the Columbia pike for the distance of a mile. In Mrs. Sykes' yard, Gen. Hood sat talking with some of his staff officers. I didn't look upon him as a hero, because nothing had been accomplished that could benefit us.

As we approached Col. Carter's house, we could scarcely walk without stepping on dead or dying men. We could hear the cries of the wounded, of which Col. Carter's house was full to overflowing. As I entered the front door, I heard a poor fellow giving his sympathetic comrades a dying message for his loved ones at home. We went through the hall, and were shown into a little room where a soft light revealed all that was mortal of the gifted young genius, Theodrick ["Tod"] Carter, who under the pseudonym of "Mint Julep," wrote such delightful letters to the Chattanooga *Rebel*. Bending over him, begging for just one word of recognition, was his faithful and heartbroken sister. The night before the battle he had taken supper at Mr. Green Neely's (the father of our postmaster), and was in a perfect ecstacy of joy at the thought of seeing his family on the morrow, from whom he had been separated so long. But alas! when the morrow came, that active, brilliant brain had been pierced by one of the enemy's bullets; he was carried home and ministered to by those faithful sisters, and died, I think, without ever

Carter House, Franklin, TN.

having spoken a word.

From this sad scene, we passed on to a locust thicket, and [dead] men in every conceivable position could be seen, some with their fingers on the triggers, and death struck them so suddenly they didn't move. Past the thicket we saw trenches dug to receive as many as ten bodies. On the left of the pike, around the old gin house, men and horses were lying so thick that we could not walk. Gen. [John] Adams' horse was lying stark and stiff upon the breastworks. Ambulances were being filled with the wounded as fast as possible, and the whole town was turned into a hospital.

Instead of saying lessons at school the day after the battle, I watched the wounded men being carried in.

Our house was full as could be; from morning until night we made bandages and scraped linen lint with which to dress the wounds, besides making jellies and soups with which to nourish them.

The times were not without their romances. Only a short time afterward a handsome young Missouri surgeon, in charge of one of the hospitals, married one of our most prominent young ladies. Another Missourian, who was wounded here, and was so popular with the girls, married also. A young soldier who was an artist, met on the field one of our young ladies, who was also of an artistic turn of mind, and the year following they were married.[188] — FRANCES (last name unknown)

☛ NO APOLOGIES FROM FORREST'S MEN
Thank God, I have never met one of the regiment who had apology to make for the part he took in that war.[189] — CAPT. J. C. BLANTON (a member of Forrest's old regiment)

☛ THE OLD WAR SONGS & BALLADS
In the last early autumn I visited a little village of eight or ten families. My friend lived upon a hill at whose feet lay a lovely valley. In our Southern clime our evening's were spent on the broad verandas constructed for every passing breeze to refresh us, and thus this family gathered after tea for chat, and for song.

On a particular evening a banjo and two guitars were brought out, while a sweet mellow alto, two sopranos, and a round full basso formed our band. We sang the new songs and many of the old, when some one in the party said, "Do you all remember the old war song "Maryland?" My answer came with the chords of a sweet guitar, and out into the stillness of the quiet night our voices went forth in the song. Then sprang out of our childhood's memory the grand old song of "Dixie," after which followed the "Bonnie Blue Flag," and the "Home Spun Dress," the music and words of which were as fresh as when my childish voice rose in song so many years ago. When we had finished we were all enthused with memories of the war, and those who were younger in our circle wanted to know this and that of the songs and the war.

Away down South in Dixie . . .

The next morning those of the older villagers told us the ballads wafted across the valley were clearly and distinctly heard and, opening their windows, they listened with sadness and tears to the songs sung over the grave of our dear dead Confederacy. It would not do for us to sing those songs now as we did then; hearts would be too sadly reminded of dear ones gone, and of a past so sacred to every Southerner. We should, however, *never forget to teach these songs to our children. Let them understand, even in song, our cause.* To me the Southern songs of our great war are the sweetest I ever heard. I learned to love them as a child and I will love them until I die.[190] — LUCY MCRAE WALTON

☛ REMINISCENCES OF THE WILDERNESS CAMPAIGN

The Wilderness is a peculiar country. It is slightly undulating, but nothing that side of the Rapidan attains the dignity of a hill. There was very little cleared land in 1864. Some sections were so thickly studded with pines that a man could not ride through them, and the scrub oaks were as thick. When I was there recently I found that in the thirty years the largest of the oaks had been cut into railroad crossties. Two roads lead from Orange C. H. to Fredericksburg; one the plank road, the other of dirt. Their divergence extends about three miles. The Germania Ford road, leading from Culpeper C. H. [Court House] to Fredericksburg, intersects the dirt road at Wilderness Farm, two and a half miles east of the Wilderness battleground. This is the road on which Gen. Grant's army reached the Wilderness, and I saw the little valley on the road, near which still stand the two oak trees under which Gen. Grant pitched his tent and had his headquarters during the battle. The hospital tent where Gen. Stonewall Jackson had his arm amputated, was about two hundred yards in the rear of that spot. About six hundred yards to the rear is the plank road near Parker's store, which was the right of Gen. Lee's army, and near by is Tapp's Old Field, where Gens. Longstreet and [Gouverneur Kemble] Warren were so hotly engaged on May 5th. A Virginia quartz stone, near the plank road, marks the spot where a Texas Ranger, of Gen. Longstreet's corps, caught Gen. Lee's horse by the bridle and bade him go to the rear.

In following the line of Gen. Grant's breastworks on the Brock road, I came to the old furnace road from Chancellorsville, which intersects it, and was the route Stonewall Jackson took to get in rear of the army at Chancellorsville. We left the Twenty-Third Georgia Regiment here to protect his flank, and they were captured. "Old Jack" had his men pile their knapsacks in the road, as he found they would impede them in the march and charge. This is about two and a half miles east of where Gen. Grant's headquarters were on May 5, 1864. There is a monument at the spot where Gen. Jackson was mortally wounded in Chancellorsville fight. I stood with uncovered head at this sacred spot.

John B. Gordon, C.S.A.

During the battle, just as our pickets were being driven in, [Union] Gen. [John] Sedgwick charged us in three columns with the 146th N.Y. Zouaves, commanded by Maj. Gilbert, who was killed and his regiment nearly annihilated. A battery of our artillery had been placed on our right, near the edge of the field, and was charged with grape and cannister, and as fast as the front column was mowed down, another would take its place, but our scattered line could not stop the onslaught, and on they came to our line and soon we would all have been captured, but for the arrival of Gen. [John Brown] Gordon. When recruited, we charged the enemy across the field to the Wilderness on the other side. Near by Gen. Grant had his artillery on the old dirt road, and two pieces were on the left of the road in the excavation of an old gold mine.

In this engagement, my cousin, W. T. Norvell, was killed by my side, and my friend Robert Early, was also killed. Hon. John W. Daniel was severely wounded. I had been a schoolmate of Daniel and Early in Lynchburg, and spoke to both of them during the engagement. Our loss was very heavy, but Gen. Grant's was much larger, for his men were in three columns and exposed to the open field. Next morning over 1,100 of his army were dead.

On May 6th there was fighting on the extreme right and left, but it was quiet in front except now and then sharpshooters would fire at us from the trees. We expected an attack constantly, and were diligent in digging and throwing up breastworks. This "digging" was done with the bayonet, and the dirt thrown up with tin plates. In this section of the Wilderness is found quartz in large quantities, and before the war quite a number of gold mines were operated and much gold found, hence these pits.

Edward Johnson, C.S.A.

The morning of the seventh dawned upon us and yet no attack. The 1,100 dead were still on the field near our lines, and we had to bury them. While doing so, our scouts reported that Gen. Grant was moving by our left flank toward Spottsylvania, and we had to drop our spades and move by right flank in order to intercept him. The distance to Spottsylvania C. H. [Court House] was some sixteen miles. On the march, May 8th and 9th, we had many skirmishes, and on the evening of the 10th, Gen. Gordon was quite heavily engaged. We passed in his rear while the fight was going on and reached what was afterward the bloody angle on that night, May 10th. The night was dark, the woods were dense, and the angle, which was much in the shape of a horseshoe, was formed by our engineering corps voicing to one another. We did not sleep any that night, but worked like beavers with our bayonets and tin plates. By noon of the 11th our trenches were five and a half feet deep, with pine logs resting in front and on top of the embankment, with sufficient space to shoot through. There was a cold, drizzling rain all day of the 11th and through the night, and we were in these muddy trenches. The rain rendered many of the guns useless.

About daylight of May 12, while it was still raining, Gen. [Winfield Scott] Hancock attacked us in two columns, and while my division (Gen. Edward Johnson's) of 1,100 men was resisting the attack in front, Gen. Thomas Francis Meagher, commanding an Irish brigade, broke on our left and took us in the rear, capturing our entire division. We jumped over the breastworks and went through the lines we had just been fighting, and I think there were about three guards to each prisoner. The boys wished to get out of the fracas, but when we reached a point about a mile in rear of Gen. Grant's army, the line was reorganized and the guard reduced to about one for three prisoners. I advised Gen. Johnson and Col. Norvell Cobbs to take off their rank and go with me in the prison as private soldiers, but they did not heed the advice, and were afterwards sent to Charleston under our fire and given a quart of meal a day. They marched us seventeen miles that day through the drizzle and mud. We met 25,000 fresh troops en route from Washington City to reinforce Gen. Grant. They guyed us all day. "Hello, Johnny Rebs, you naked and starved traitors; we are going to send you up to Uncle Sam, so you can be clothed and fed."

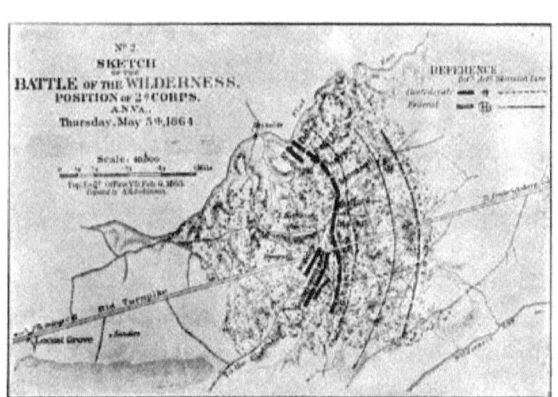
Map of the Battle of the Wilderness, May 5-7, 1864.

On the march we heard the most terrific firing from musketry and cannon. From the bloody angle floated the stars and stripes, and then were twice replaced with the stars and bars. At night fall Gen. Lee was in possession of the bloody angle, but at a great sacrifice. The trenches were piled to overflowing with the killed of both armies, and the dead were strewn thick all around. Some idea of the severity of the conflict may be gained from the stump of a hickory tree now at the Smithsonian Institute. It is about eighteen inches in diameter, and was cut down by minie balls. It hung a while by the bark and outer lining, till a stiff breeze toppled it over. Close by is a monument erected to Gen. Sedgewick near the spot he fell. After nearly thirty-one years the trenches are grown up with oak and pine, thirty to forty feet high. What a fearful campaign from the 5th of May to the 12th, when over 4,000 men fell, and in the seven days with nothing to eat but cornbread, and very little sleep! How changed was Palmer's Field! Where I saw the 1,100 dead, is now grown up a wilderness of pines, so dense the sun cannot penetrate.[191] — MARCUS B. TONEY

☛ SHARPSHOOTING IN LEE'S ARMY

After Gen. Lee had raised the siege of Richmond in 1862, and began playing chess with [Union] Gen. McClellan in the open country, he found the necessity for a closer knowledge of his enemy. His cavalry and scouts gave him a general idea of the movements of his antagonist, but the information was frequently several days old, and counterchanges were often made of which he was ignorant.

More especially did he need constant information from his immediate front to prevent surprises from quick action by his antagonist. He found Gen. McClellan so wiry a foe that it became absolutely necessary to have more accurate data as to his daily movements than his valued scouts and cavalry could bring him from the rear or inside the Federal camps. He found it essential to locate their front line

Confederate sharpshooter.

and its strength, to know whether it was a strong skirmish line making a demonstration, or a line of battle preparing for action. He was able to gain some information from skirmishers sent out to feel the enemy's position, but found it not exactly what he wanted. Profiting by his experience with skirmishers, he had sharpshooters organized in a few brigades. These proved so efficient that rapidly every division was equipped with a corps. These soon became a necessary adjunct and a fixture throughout his entire army.

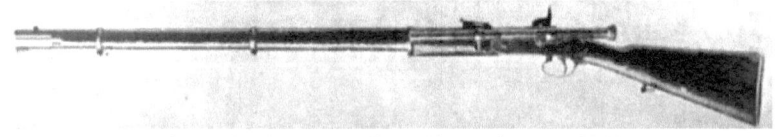

Whitworth rifle fitted with Davidson telescope, 1861.

Officers were selected to command them for their peculiar fitness for this important and dangerous branch of the service. As Gen. A. P. Hill once remarked: "Sharpshooters, like fiddlers, are born and not made." An officer from each regiment, usually a lieutenant, was selected to command the detail from his own regiment, and an officer from the brigade was selected as captain to command the battalion. They were drilled in all the fancy and skirmish drills, in long range and accurate firing. Gen. Lee ordered an abundance of ammunition and the best arms in the service for them. Men distinguished for undoubted courage, with intelligence and perfect self-possession in dangerous places, who could stand any amount of physical wear, severe duty, and strict discipline, were selected. Owing to the peculiarly dangerous nature of their calling, they were instructed in drill to take advantage of every tree, stump, or inequality in the surface, and were not required to preserve perfect alignment when moving to the front.

Early in 1864 blockade runners succeeded in bringing to Wilmington, N.C., two Whitworth rifles, with ammunition. Quite a scramble took place for these guns. [James Jay] Archer's Tennessee Brigade finally got one, and Hood's Texan's, the other. The one to the sharpshooters of Archer's Brigade was assigned to Thomas R. Jackson, and many bluecoats bit the dust at long range from his unerring aim. The one to the Texans was used with deadly effect and credit to the

"Lone Star State."

The first campaign proved, as in everything else, the excellent judgment of Gen. Lee. The sharpshooters were indeed the eyes and the ears of the army. Ever alert and watchful, they caught, and reported each important incident occurring. In the top of a tree with a glass, or crawling on his face close to an unsuspecting picket, counting flags or tents, or watching a moving column to ascertain its destination, was his constant occupation. Something would attract his attention, and perhaps an hour later, would find him four or five miles to the right or left, working out the problem.

Gen. Lee was informed of every move by some fleet-footed sharpshooter, while others were before, or behind moving columns of the enemy, and like sleuth hounds, never lost sight of them. A number developed into valuable scouts, and often, in case of necessity, penetrated to the very heart of the Federal Army. But for the watchful sharpshooters, Gen. Lee could never have met every advance of Gen. Grant in the memorable campaign from Germania to the Appomattox. So annoying were they, and so accurate their information, that Gen. Grant issued a special order concerning them. By their bold bluffs they often delayed the advance of the enemy until Gen. Lee could bring up troops. When an attack was decided upon, they were sent forward to clear off every obstacle to the enemy's line of battle, taking places with their command in the charge.

The fatality was fearful, and their depleted ranks had to be constantly recruited. There was, however, a bright side to their lives. They bore the relation to the army that a drummer does to the wholesale trade in business.

They always had a fund of good humor at hand. In their exposed positions, games of draw poker were often played. The new jokes generally originated with the sharpshooters. When it was quiet along the lines they became well acquainted with the fellows on the other side, swapping tobacco for coffee, or, perhaps, the best poker hand would take the pot. An underground railway was established by them with the Federal pickets opposite. Many letters found their way to anxious parents by this means, and many a coy maiden's heart was made glad by news from her bold soldier lover passed across the lines by the sharpshooters. Strong friendships were sometimes formed between men on opposing lines, and not one instance of treachery, either personal or to their respective armies did I ever know. The night was never too dark or the storm too fierce for them to hesitate when called on. They could go to sleep in a minute, and were so well trained that they could wake at any moment.[192] — SUMNER A. CUNNINGHAM

☛ SOUTH-HATING IN NEW YORK IN 1895

When the American publishers took the liberty of issuing an edition of *The Meditations of Marcus Aurelius*, translated by the classical English scholar, George Long, they took the further liberty of dedicating the book to Mr. Emmerson. Mr. Long was informed of this by admirers in this country, and with the next edition of his book, published in England, he wrote a preface in which he expressed in noblest language his [positive] opinion of Gen. Lee. A gentleman in Baltimore seeing a copy of the "Meditations" containing the preface with this tribute to the Southern Chieftain, and wishing to possess the book, ordered a copy from a New York house. When it came he was surprised to find the book mutilated, the pages containing the preface having been cut out. He went to New York, called on the bookseller, and asked for *The Meditations of Marcus Aurelius*. The young salesman referred him to an elder man, who found a copy and handed it to the gentleman. He turned to the front page and saw that that copy also had been mutilated; the leaves containing the preface were gone. He inquired the reason, and the man curtly replied that he knew nothing about it. Further inquiry elicited the fact that the leaves were not cut out in this country, it having been done in England before the books were sent here. The gentleman learned the name of the publisher in England, and wrote to him. In reply he said he had orders from the New York firm to cut out the leaves containing the preface before shipping the books to America, as the tribute to Gen. Lee would injure the sale of the book in this country.[193]
— UNKNOWN

Robert E. Lee, C.S.A.

☛ GEN. FORREST AMONG CIVILIANS

Every living soldier of Forrest's West Tennessee Cavalry remembers the Sixth Tennessee Federal regiment, commanded by [Union war criminal] Col. F. H. [Fielding Hurst], of Purdy, McNairy County, Tennessee, a [criminalistic] regiment of cavalry unknown to fame by any gallant deeds or meritorious conduct on the battlefield, and one which the war records of the rebellion alone have preserved from merited oblivion.

It may be truthfully said of this [Yankee] regiment that it did more plundering, burning, robbing, and running and less fighting, than any regiment in the Federal army, Fifth Tennessee Federal Cavalry only excepted.

Nathan B. Forrest, C.S.A.

On one of Forrest's campaigns, from Mississippi into West Tennessee, and soon after leaving Corinth, he learned that Hurst and his regiment had evacuated Purdy, and that before leaving they had laid in ashes the homes of absent Confederate soldiers, also those of a number of citizens who were known to be in sympathy with the South.

Wilson's Sixteenth Regiment, of our command, and Newsom's, also, were composed of men from McNairy and adjoining counties, and Forrest knew that unless timely steps were taken to prevent it there would be trouble when he reached Purdy.

When within a few miles of that place he directed me to take a sergeant and five men from his escort, dash on into Purdy, and place a guard around the residence of Col. Hurst.

On entering the town, blackened walls, lone chimneys, and charred remains of buildings gave abundant evidence of Hurst's cowardly vandalism. Learning from a citizen that his residence was in the suburbs, and directly on our line of march to Jackson, we were soon at its front. Dismounting and entering the portico of his dwelling, I tapped lightly on the door with the hilt of my saber. In a moment or so it was opened by a lady, when I asked, "Is this Mrs. Col. Hurst?" She tremblingly answered, "Yes, sir."

I noticed her agitation, also that on opening the door her countenance quickly changed, manifesting on the instant both surprise and alarm.

Hastening to relieve her apprehensions, I said, "We are not here to harm you, but have been sent for your protection. Although Gen. Forrest has not reached Purdy, he is aware of the ruin and devastation caused by your husband's regiment, and has sent me in advance of his troops to place a guard around your house. This guard is from his own escort, and will remain with you until all of our command has passed, and I assure you that neither your family or anything about your premises will be disturbed or molested."

Giving the officer of the guard instructions, I turned to her, and was in the act of raising my cap before mounting my horse, when, brushing away tears she could no longer repress, she said, "Please, sir, say to Gen. Forrest, for me, that this (referring to the guard) is more than I had any right to expect of him, and that I thank him from my heart for this unexpected kindness. I shall gratefully remember it and shall always believe him to be as generous as he is brave."

Returning to the town, I rejoined the General [Forrest] as he was entering the public square, where he halted and was soon surrounded by citizens of the place, among them the venerable father of Col. D. M. Wisdom, of our command, who said, "You see, General, the marks of Col. Hurst's last visit to our town, and you are also aware that a large number of our citizens are Union people, and they are greatly alarmed for fear of retaliation on the part of your command."

Forrest's reply was characteristic and stripped of his habitual way of emphasizing matters: "I do not blame my men for being exasperated, and especially those whose homes have been laid in ashes, for desiring to revenge such cowardly wrongs, but I have placed a guard around the home of Hurst, and others need feel no uneasiness. Orders have been issued to my command that no Union citizen of this town must be insulted, much less harmed, and this order was accompanied by my personal request that it be obeyed to the letter, and I am sure no soldier of my command will disobey the one, or disregard the other. Of one thing, however, the Union friends of Hurst and his cowardly regiment of Tennessee renegades may rely upon. If we ever are so fortunate as to find them just once in my front, I will wipe them off the face of the earth. They are a disgrace to the Federal army, to the State, and to humanity."

Ever after this, whenever it was known that Forrest was on the move, that command stood not on the order of its going. They well knew that whenever they confronted Forrest there would be a long account to settle.

During my service as a staff-officer of Gen. Forrest from October, to the surrender, he fought every [Union] cavalry commander and much of the infantry of the army of the Cumberland [U.S.A.], also that of the Mississippi Generals [Hugh Judson] Kilpatrick, [David Sloane] Stanley, [John Grant] Mitchell, Wilder, [Edward Moody] McCook, and [Robert H. G.] Minty, of the former, and [Benjamin Henry] Grierson, [Edward] Hatch, [Joseph Anthony] Mower, [Gouverneur Kemble] Warren, and Winslow, of the latter, yet for none of these commanders do we cherish the slightest feeling of either disrespect or resentment. I bear cheerful testimony now to the dash, the gallantry and soldierly bearing of these [Yankee] officers, and regret that for the credit of the State of Tennessee, the names of Hurst and [Union Gen. William Sooy] Smith [an accomplice] cannot be added to the list. Truth forbids it, for we never met them where they should have been—at the front.

Before the war they were men of prominence, both of them lawyers of recognized ability. When our army was forced out of Tennessee they had regiments of cavalry ostensibly to fight for the Union,

Charles W. Anderson, C.S.A.

yet history and the *Records of the War of the Rebellion* fail to show their participation in a single battle of any note, nor in all the reports of Federal army commanders have I been able, so far, to find one word of commendation of either of them.

Retribution, as marked as it is just, always follows the cowardly and vindictive use or abuse of power. Shirking both danger and duty on the field, they hounded, plundered, arrested, abused and insulted a helpless and defenseless people, and as a consequence, both have long since sunk into obscurity, despised and execrated by thousands who suffered from their cruel deeds, unrelieved by a single brave or noble act on the battlefield or off of it.[194] — MAJ. CHARLES W. ANDERSON

☛ TRIBUTES TO GEN. BRAXTON BRAGG
. . . Gen. Bragg's career as a Commander of armies, and his intimate personal and official relations with President Davis, influenced the promotion or the degradation of many general officers. Every expression, therefore, of Gen. Bragg concerning individuals was a subject of comment, favorable or otherwise, as he seemed to regard the applicant for promotion. He was "industry personified." While commanding in the field he was always officially accessible, but could rarely be approached socially.

Members of his staff, cognizant of his severe and continuous mental and physical labors, were afraid he would not take nutriment enough to sustain life.

Braxton Bragg, C.S.A.

They would often send his meals to his desk and urge him to eat them there. He was a pattern of sobriety, and had not the slightest epicurean proclivity. His dispatches and all of his official papers, written by himself, were well to the point, and models of clearness and conciseness.

None who approached appealing for justice, pleading for mercy, or asking a favor, ever went from his presence unheard. He would not allow needless interruptions. His prompt dismissal from his presence of all parties when their business was completed often offended even those whose requests had been granted.

Referring to the unhappy state of the army after the battle of Chickamauga, the arrest of certain Generals for failure to obey orders, and then the petition of a dozen of them to President Davis that the Commanding General be relieved, induced a volunteer official conference with him by [myself] Dr. Stout.

Under these conditions, Rev. C. D. Elliott, of Nashville, Tenn., who was widely known, and intimate with generals and private soldiers, in speaking with the Medical Director, said: "Ah! when passing about the many headquarters, I heard little else than discussions about the chances of promotion of various parties, and in some circles, nothing but the abuse of poor old Bragg. But whenever, or wherever I have seen him, I have found him hard at work—night and day—always laboring for the cause, thinking not of self-indulgence or personal ease, but living hard. He is respected and loved by the private soldier. He is eminently a just and, I believe, a consecrated Christian man. . . . He never praises; he never permits himself to be praised or flattered. If he only had suavity of manner commensurate with his self-denying patriotism and untiring industry, what a grandly successful man he would be!"

Gen. Braxton Bragg was born in Warrenton, N.C., in 1815. He was one of the thirty-seven graduates from West Point, and appointed Lieutenant of Artillery. He served in the Seminole war, and was ordered to Texas just before the war began in Mexico. He distinguished himself in the hard battle of Buena Vista. Col. Jefferson Davis also won distinction there.

He was made a Brigadier-General on entering the Confederate Army; in less than a year he was a full General, and in command of the Department of Tennessee. When he had attained to the command of this army, he issued orders in expressive language against breaches of discipline, and required strictest conformity to his orders by officers as well as men. He had a soldier court martialed and shot for reckless disregard of orders in firing his gun on retreat, and it was reported, to the General's detriment, that he had the soldier shot for killing a chicken. In fact, the man violated orders repeatedly by firing his gun, and had finally [accidentally] shot a negro child.

After being superseded by Joseph E. Johnston, Gen. Bragg went to Richmond and remained to confer with the President about military movements.

Mr. Davis evidently never lost faith in his ability, and nobody ever questioned his patriotism.

President Davis being dissatisfied with the retreat by Gen. Johnston, was inclined to supersede him, but Bragg opposed it. Mr. Davis sent him there, when he reported that Johnston's only reply as to his movements was that he would be "governed by the movements of the enemy." Bragg so telegraphed Mr. Davis, and requested that no change be made until he could see him in person, but in spite of this "the return flash over the wire relieved Johnston and put Hood in Command." This information was direct from Gen. Bragg to the author [Stout]. After the war, having been reduced to poverty, Gen. Bragg went to New Orleans and secured employment in his profession as Civil Engineer, but *he lost his position soon through carpetbag domination*. He afterward had charge of improvements in Mobile harbor. He lost his position there because he would not approve certain methods of expenditure by the general government, as he believed them detrimental to the interests of the city.

The tribute concludes with some pathetic [that is, sad] illustrations of Gen. Bragg's sympathy for his fellow man concerning the wounded soldiers whom he left on the battlefield at Murfreesboro. An account is given by Dr. A. J. Foard, who was at the time Medical Director of his army. Dr. Foard stated: "The General was alone, pacing the floor, every gesture indicating great mental agony. At length, turning towards me with tears flowing down his cheeks, he said: 'Doctor, I intend to evacuate Murfreesboro, and have sent for you to consult as to what we had best do for our poor wounded men who cannot be removed.' It was decided to put Dr. W. B. Avent in charge, which suggestion relieved the General perceptibly." Again, when Dr. Stout was in Richmond, April, 1864, Gen. Bragg was talking with him about Federal prisoners at Andersonville. He said: "If the direction of Medical officers falls to you, do see that the poor fellows are supplied with good physicians and surgeons. They are entitled to the most humane treatment at our hands."

A story of the lives of our Generals in charge of departments will convince the soldier who simply had to obey orders, and then was freed from responsibility, that he had the better time of the two. Why, *the private soldier had no more responsibility than did his slaves in the olden time.*[195]

— DR. H. S. STOUT (and Sumner A. Cunningham)

☛ THE GIRL WHO PILOTED FORREST

It was Emma Sansom, a courageous girl in a home remote from other habitations on Black Creek, a stream with perilous fords near Rome, Ga., who volunteered to go with the Confederates when in hot pursuit of Gen. [Able Delos] Streight at the time of his capture. She heard Gen.

Emma Sansom.

Forrest express intense concern about fording the stream, and as her father and brothers were away in the war, she wanted to do "some service" herself, and importuned her mother, who objected, but yielded when that "wizard of the saddle," as perhaps no other could have done, thrilled her with his need for a guide at once. It is said that she asked Gen. Forrest on the way to let her ride in front, as she might be some protection to him against the bullets. The young girl had no thought that it would give her fame beyond all that she had ever done or could hope to do, and that she was mounting behind the General who was fast upon making the most noted captures of the war, save only those great events when our main armies surrendered from sheer exhaustion in 1865.

Miss Sansom married in her mature years, but has long since crossed another dark stream, and may have conferred with General Forrest, who has done likewise, but who had previously made peace with all his enemies.[196] — SUMNER A. CUNNINGHAM

☛ SKETCH OF GEN. WILLIAM JOSEPH HARDEE

William J. Hardee was born in Camden county, Georgia, in November, 1815. Graduated from the U.S. Military Academy in July, 1838; was made a Second Lieutenant of the Second Cavalry, and promoted to First Lieutenant in 1839. He served in the Florida war in 1840, when he was sent by the Government to Europe as a member of a Military Commission to study the organization of foreign armies for the benefit of the United States Army. He was made a Captain in 1844, and served on frontier duty until the war with Mexico, in 1846. He was in many severe engagements during that war. At La Hoya he was brevetted Major for gallant and meritorious conduct. He was promoted twice for gallantry, and was one of the original members of the famous "Aztec Club."

In 1853, he was selected by the Secretary of War [Jefferson Davis], because of his professional accomplishments, to compile a system of infantry tactics, which was completed and adopted for the United States Army, March 29th, 1855. He was then sent as Commandant to the U.S. Military Academy (1856), where "Hardee's Tactics" was then introduced. He remained at West Point until January, 1861, when he resigned, and cast his lot with the Southern Confederacy.

Mr. Davis tendered him the position of Adjutant General of the Confederate Army, but he declined it for service in the field. He was a Colonel at Fort Morgan, Brigadier General in Arkansas, Division Commander under Albert Sidney Johnston, and at the battle of Shiloh commanded the first line of attack. He was wounded, but was made a Major General for bravery on that field. At the battle of Perryville, Oct. 8th, 1862, he was made a Lieutenant General. At the battle of Murfreesboro, the Commander, Gen. Bragg, especially commended him in orders "for skill, valor, and ability."

William J. Hardee, C.S.A.

He commanded the right wing of the Confederate Army at the battle of Missionary Ridge, which battle was fought against his advice, and [Union] Gen. [George H.] Thomas declared that he was "the most efficient General the Confederacy had on that field." Subsequently, the maneuvers of his troops near Cassville, and his masterly retreat in echelon of Divisions, so won the admiration of Gen. Thomas that he mentioned both movements in highly complimentary terms.

When Sherman marched down to the Sea, Hardee was in command at Savannah, ever breasting the storm, calling for more troops, alas! no longer possible! He withdrew his forces, first to Charleston, then to Columbia. He punished the enemy effectively at Averysboro on the 16th of March, 1865, and a few days later, he led, in the battle of Bentonville, the last charge that was made by our war-worn soldiers, and his only son, sixteen years old, was among the last to fall.

Gen. Hardee was called "Old Reliable," and a historian has said that he was second only to Stonewall Jackson. It is recorded that "he was the only Lieut. General who personally inspected the arms and accoutrements of each soldier in his Corps." Gen. Johnston said that "he was more capable of commanding twenty thousand men in battle than any other Confederate General." He was an accomplished soldier, stern and exacting as a disciplinarian, but thoroughly understood his profession, and possessed the rare ability of estimating military operations at their true value. He was both a teacher and an organizer, inspired his men with confidence, and was conspicuously cool, courageous, and calculating on the field of battle.

He was a man of affairs, of talent, and industry; and temperate in his habits. He is remembered by those who visited the Military Academy while he was Commandant for his soldierly bearing, and pleasing address. He was eminently a social man, and very fond of society.

Gen. Hardee died on the 6th of November, 1873, in Wytheville, Va. His remains were removed to Selma, Ala., his home after the war. The funeral procession was the largest ever assembled in Alabama, and many of his old army friends, of both armies, joined in tributes to his memory as "an earnest friend, a genial companion, and a brave soldier."[197] — N. R. CHAMBLISS

☛ CONFEDERATE MEMORIAL DAY ADDRESS, 1895

Clement A. Evans, C.S.A.

We are here on this holy anniversary occasion to publicly declare to mankind and to God our steadfast devotion and undying gratitude to the brave men who fought and died for us, to commemorate in praise and song, in tears and prayers, their heroic deeds and sufferings, and to testify anew our unvarying faith in the purity, patriotism and philanthropy of their motives and purposes.

Gen. [Clement A.] Evans in his beautiful address said if he could crystalize the best spirits of human history, the rarest devotion to conviction of every age, and the tenderest memories of the bravest struggles that ever involved the sacrifice of life, he would blend them all in one hallowed offering: *"To the Memory of Our Confederate Dead!"*

Then he said: "I crave for this moment the genius which no living man possesses to declare in speech the thought and feeling, the faith and hope, the budding glory and the aftergloom which this scene is designed to celebrate. It is the pathetic [sad] quality of this memorial which makes it so sublime as to exceed all eulogy. Here is no artificial magnificence, no pride, nor pomp, no grand array, no royalty lying in state. But in their stead the hush of human passion, the plaintive melody which memory softly chants, and the gentle tread of thoughts taking step to the music of muffled grief. . . .

"O, Southern womanhood! When your gentle nature stirred you to establish this memorial, you gave a holy meaning to love of country; you placed a costly crown upon the virtue of valor, and offered to the patriotic manhood the unusual opportunity to refresh itself at a fount of manly honor! In the endowment of this ceremony by your wealth of everlasting love, you have unconsciously surpassed your own design, for as this day shall break from age to age it will have a tongue to tell in memorial of you that this tender respect for manly heroism sprang first from woman's heart!

Third National Confederate Flag.

"The sword's arbitrament settled whatever can be settled in the great human disputation by force of arms, and no more than that. The triumphs of power take no trophies save those which Might wrenches from the grasp of the weak. The results of war never make changes in human rights. The whole American people were left, at the termination of the Southern struggle, the holders still of all the rights which the fathers of our country pronounced inseparable from free government, inalienable by monarchs or majorities, and indestructible by military force. To declare otherwise would degrade the victorious armies of the Union more than the vanquished veterans of the South. Therefore, this statement must be accepted to escape the alternative conclusion that coercion of the South was a conspiracy of unpatriotic politicians to destroy the old constitution and blood-bought liberties of our country.

". . . No one will wonder at the honor paid to these vanquished men who understands *the real spirit of the South*, and knows the character of its soldiery. Romance has found in them and their career a mine of real story richer than fancy can create. The gray jacket woven in the loom at home, cut and made by a mother's hand, blessed with her prayers, her kisses and her tears, as she fitted it to the form of her martial son—that gray jacket which grew so greasy and tattered with wear—that jacket which showed at last the rude rent through which the fatal bullet sped—aye, it covered, my countrymen, the heart of a man as valiant as Rupert, as chivalrous as Saladin, as true to love of liberty as Bruce, who gave his heart for Scotland, and Warren, the protopatriot who fell at Bunker Hill for freedom."

> They marched all day through cold and heat,
> They marked the ground with bleeding feet,
> They hungered, fought—died! 'Twas sweet
> To march and famish, bleed and die. The noble band
> With much to love, loved most their Southern land![198] — COL. DUPONT GUERRY

☛ SKETCH OF GEN. HENRY EUSTACE MCCULLOCH

One of the most popular veterans in the western part of Dixie was the late Gen. Henry McCulloch, of Texas, who died March 12, 1895.

He was a native of Rutherford county, Tenn. His father, Major Alexander McCulloch, who was Aid de Camp to Gen. Coffee, under "Old Hickory" [Andrew Jackson], was a Virginian.

Gen. McCulloch was educated in Tennessee, but in his young manhood went to Texas (1837). He was elected Sheriff of Guadalupe county in 1843; a member of the Texas Legislature in 1853, and two years later, a State Senator. He served as United States Marshal from 1859, until Texas seceded from the Union. In the war with Mexico, 1846-8, he was Captain of a company of Texas Rangers.

In 1861, he was made Colonel by the Texas Legislature, and by the Confederate Government. He promptly secured the surrender of fortifications in Northwest Texas. In August of that year, he was made Brigadier-General, and organized troops for a campaign in Arkansas and Missouri. He served in important capacities throughout the war.

The *Seguin Anchor* pays this tribute to him: "Away back, when defenseless women and children in the primitive homes of Texas called for protection, Henry McCulloch was found on horseback facing the red man. Before our cities were built, before our railroads and telegraph wires were stretched, when the line of advancing civilization was east of the Mississippi, the McCullochs were fighting in defense of the homes of the western pioneers, and the impress of their strong characters was upon hundreds of young men who grew up at that period. . . The unfortunate and desolated Confederacy did not have a more faithful and consecrated soldier. Distinguished and merited honors fell to his lot, and were freely bestowed by his admiring comrades. His time, his money, his influence, and the martial spirit that was in him, all went for the support and defense of that which seemed a righteous and sacred cause in his sight, and in the sight of the people whom he served. After the war his manly, civic virtues shone as resplendent as his deeds on the field of battle."[199] — SUMNER A. CUNNINGHAM

☛ MILITARY CHARACTER OF GEN. FORREST
No soldier of modern times so forcibly impressed his singular and magnetic individuality upon all surroundings as did Gen. Nathan Bedford Forrest. Naturally great, nature's God designed him for the accomplishment of great purposes. He was untutored in the arts and sciences, and unlearned in the strategy of war as taught by theory, he followed in battle no chartered precept, but relied always upon the unerring dictates of his own great reason. Possessed of a native strategy all his own, he cared for no chartered precedent. He based his combinations and dispositions of troops on the topographical and geographical surroundings. So great was the almost resistless force of his individual magnetism that he impressed every man in his command with the firm conviction that victory would perch upon his standard ere the battle was fought, and no leader was ever followed to battle with blinder confidence on the part of his soldiery. Having passed through all official grades to that of Lieutenant General, he commanded when the war

closed a cavalry corps of twenty thousand men trained to fight wherever and whenever they met the enemy. In moral elan and efficiency as veteran soldiery, they were not inferior to the "Old Guard" of the First Napoleon. Under his leadership and direction the infantry and cavalry arms of the service were combined in one body, which he fought either on foot or horse as the topography of the country and the character of the enemy required, and he moved his large body of horses from place to place with a rapidity never before equalled, and with an ever abiding confidence that the day would be won. He shirked no responsibility however great, and was actuated in all he did by no purpose other than the good of his country. He commanded not only the respect and confidence of his troops, but also that of the citizens of all the states in which he operated. The greatness of his soul manifested itself on all occasions. He never seemed to value his life in a worthy cause. He was ever at the front, and was thereby enabled to detect the first waver of the foe and take advantage of it. Cowardice in either officers or men he thoroughly despised, while few general

Nathan B. Forrest, C.S.A.

officers honored the brave man in the private's jacket as he did. There were privates in his old regiment and in his escort for whom he had as much respect, and whom he treated with as much consideration, as he did regimental commanders. No more knightly soul than his ever lived on this earth. In battle it was his greatest pleasure, sabre in hand, to seek hand to hand personal encounter with some foeman more daring than his comrades, and few there were who, thus engaged, escaped his terrible blade.

    Loving his native South as the child loves the mother from whose gentle breast it draws its life, there was no sacrifice which he deemed too great to make in her service. Subordinated for the first two years of the war to the direction of his inferiors, he bore this indignity uncomplainingly, setting an example to officers and men worthy of their highest and best emulation. Serving in battle often next to his person, although but a boy, I enjoyed his friendship and confidence to an extent perhaps not bestowed by any other general officer on a private. I know that God never made a man who regretted more sincerely an injustice done to either officer or soldier, and that he suffered most keenly from the consciousness of it, also that he was ever ready to make the most generous reparation. During the first years of the war he was greatly hampered by the military authorities of the Confederate government. The President himself attached too great importance to training of the United States Military Academy. It was only in the last year of the war that Mr. Davis was pleased to recognize the great ability of Forrest and to assign him to high command. Then it was that the country received the benefit of his genius. Like Jackson, he was a soldier of the school Napoleonic, originating his own plans and carrying them out in his own way; like Jackson, he fought battles and won victories. In Mississippi, Alabama, Tennessee, and Kentucky, the theater of his operations, he met his enemy and destroyed him, as did Jackson in the valley of Virginia. The student of military history will search in vain for a figure more worthy of his enthusiastic admiration.[200] — HARRY W. RHODES

GEN. N. B. FORREST IN 1864

In the light of history there stands out in clear relief the figure of Lieutenant-General Nathan Bedford Forrest, the most remarkable man our Civil War developed, and the greatest fighter of which the world has an authentic record. Endowed with a physical frame which resisted fatigue and exposure, a muscular organization developed into athletic proportions by reason of the hard manual labor necessity compelled him to perform from the earliest years of boyhood until he was a man, he possessed that quality of mind which never entertained the fear of personal disaster, nor in the flurry of hand-to-hand combat, nor the excitement or confusion of battle, lost for an instant the calm appreciation of what was transpiring. Quick to perceive in the rapidly shifting scenes of battle the opportunity for a fatal blow, he struck as the lightning flashes, blinding and withering. Before his sudden onslaught, to waver was rout; and in his tireless and unrelenting pursuit, rout became panic.

Without education and absolutely without any knowledge of war gleaned from the study of what others had accomplished, he evolved and put into execution the tactics and the strategy of the most famous generals in history. In his terse phraseology: "The way to whip 'em, is to get there first with the most men," and although his greatest victories were won with forces numerically inferior, he so fought his men that where he struck, he was equal to or stronger than his adversary. He realized the value of boldness even when akin to rashness, and, when possible, he attacked notwithstanding the disparity of numbers. When the enemy was about to charge, or was charging, his rule was to go at them at once. He knew that the excitement of a forward movement inspired even the timid with courage; while to stand in the open to receive the thundering onslaught of a cavalry charge, was a severe test of the courage of the bravest, and demoralizing to the timid. The active defensive was in him an intuition. Moreover, he fought his artillery as if they were shot-guns, charging right up to the opposing lines, their double-shotted contents at short range dealing death and disaster. Although his soldiers were called "mounted infantry" and "Forrest's Cavalry," they were neither infantry nor cavalry. There was not a bayonet in his command, and early in the war the sabre was discarded for the repeating pistol. They fought on horse or foot to suit the conditions.

Forrest's cavalry chasing down Yanks.

It is probable that not a regiment he commanded could have made a correct tactical maneuver on foot in action; and beyond the formation by fours and the evolution into line for the charge, the cavalry manual was practically obsolete. With the men he led, strict discipline was impossible; and yet they fought with the steadiness of trained veterans, under the wonderful influence of one who inspired the timid with courage, and the brave with the spirit of emulation.

He said, "War means fighting, and fighting means killing," and when the enemy were not hunting him, he was hunting for them. Ever in the thickest of the fray, it is a marvel that he lived to see the war end. If ever man had a charmed life, such was his. The missile of the assassin, the gun and sabre of the open and honorable foe, turned from their mortal purpose. He was on over one hundred different occasions under fire, and these include the bloody and hotly contested battles of Fort Donelson, Shiloh, Chickamauga, Franklin, and Nashville. "Twenty-seven horses were shot under him," states Gen. James R. Chalmers; and a famous writer, himself a soldier, (Lieut. Gen. Richard Taylor), says: "I doubt if any commander since the days of lion-hearted Richard has killed so many of his enemies as Forrest." His word of command as he led the charge, was, "Forward, men, and mix with them!" Though torn with bullets, and hacked in countless places with the sabre, or hurled from his horse in death struggle of the melée, his life was spared to serve to the end the cause which no man better served than he. . . I consider General Forrest the most wonderful man in the history of our Civil War, and am sure everybody in the South and every Confederate soldier should be glad of an opportunity to do something toward perpetuating his marvelous achievements."[201] — DR. JOHN ALLAN WYETH

Forrest as a young man.

☛ TRIBUTE TO GEN. JOHN CALVIN BROWN

John C. Brown was born in Giles county, Jan. 6, 1827. On the side of both father and mother, he was of Scotch-Irish descent, and was one of a family of nine children. His father was a farmer in moderate circumstances and gave to his son a preparatory school education, finishing with graduating at Jackson College, Columbia, about the time that his older brother, Neill S. Brown, was a central figure in state and national politics, defeating Aaron V. Brown for governor in 1847, and afterward taking an active part in the election of President Zachary Taylor, who appointed him Minister to Russia.

John C. Brown began the practice of law in 1848, and continued in it until 1859. Then, being in poor health he visited the East, making a tour of Great Britain, the continent, Egypt, and the Holy Land. In 1860, he was elector on the [John] Bell and [Edward] Everett ticket. *The election of Mr. Lincoln to the Presidency and the secession of the southern states brought on the Civil War.*

John C. Brown entered the service of his state as a private, and was elected at once captain of his company, and immediately thereafter, colonel of the Third Tennessee Infantry Regiment.

John C. Brown, C.S.A.

At Fort Donelson he was in command of a brigade as senior colonel, and took an active part in its defense. He was captured and sent to Fort Warren; was exchanged in 1862, when he was promoted to Brig.-Gen. and assigned to duty with Gen. Bragg. He participated in the battles of Perryville, and other places in Kentucky. He was afterward with Gen. Joe E. Johnston in the Georgia campaign, and engaged in the battles of Chickamauga, Missionary Ridge, that hundred days fighting between Dalton and Jonesborough, and all the engagements incident to the retreat. He was promoted to Major General; was wounded at Franklin, which finished his military career.

At the close of the war he returned to the practice of law at Pulaski, and continued in active labor until 1870, when elected a member of the Constitutional Convention, of which he was made chairman. In 1870, he was elected Governor; and in 1872, was re-elected to that office. His administration of state affairs as the Executive, was upon a vigilant business basis. He reduced the bonded debt of the state from forty-three to twenty million of dollars, besides paying some three millions of its floating debt.

In 1876, he was elected vice president of the Texas Pacific Railway; and under him the great transcontinental route was built. In 1881, he was appointed general solicitor and attorney for the entire Gould system

of railroads west of the Mississippi River. In 1885, he was made receiver of the Texas Pacific Railroad; and under him it was rebuilt and thoroughly reconstructed. Then in 1888, he was elected its president. In 1889, was elected president of the Tennessee Coal, Iron and Railroad Co.

He died on August 17, 1889, and was interred at Pulaski, Tenn., among the people he loved so well and who honored him so highly. A life size statue stands on a commanding spot in Maplewood cemetery presenting a lifelike figure of him in his soldier's garb, with his hand upon his sword, his head bowed, and his gaze to the South, that he served so faithfully and loved with such ardent devotion.

As a student, he was ambitious, quick, active, and studious; as a lawyer, he stood in the front rank. He was in no sense a case lawyer; but thoroughly versed in its general principles, especially as they affected the history, policy and business interests of the state. He was not an orator, but a man of much force before a jury or an audience. His personal presence was majestic and commanding. I have seen him in many assemblies of distinguished men, and he was ever the center of observation. He was a born leader; in private life an honest and just man, broad-minded, full of charity and toleration. He never spoke harshly of even an enemy in his absence. I knew him intimately; and in his most confidential mood, no word of bitterness ever escaped his lips. But he was quick to resent an affront, and to maintain his right. As a soldier he was a strict disciplinarian, firm but kind, always ready, friendly, and he knew no such word as fear. His officers and men loved and respected him.[202] — JOHN S. WILKES

☛ OVER CONFEDERATE GRAVES

. . . Nowhere, methinks, save in our land, and never save in our time has a people [like we in the South] busied itself to preserve the memory of its defeat. Why is this? . . . Strange spectacle, and yet not strange! *We were conquered, but our cause was just. We were fallen, but not dishonored. Our efforts had failed, but they had made the world ring with our praises. We had the irreparable and the irrecoverable to lament: to blush for, nothing.*

But this answer, considered sufficient then, has ceased to satisfy. The reasons then given were negative in their nature—sufficient, perhaps, to explain why for a season we were not ashamed to keep alive the memory of our failure, but inadequate to account for the continued survival of an active living spirit, which at the end of thirty long years still refuses to die.

I think I find the true reason in my own heart, and I believe I would seek it successfully in yours, indeed, strange as the declaration may sound to some, that great war was fought on the part of the South more on a sentiment than any other war in all history. *We went to war not for conquest, not for glory, not to escape oppression. But a proud and high-spirited people flew to arms to defend what they considered their sacred right, from high handed and presumptuous interference, albeit the right itself was little better than an abstraction. Nothing sordid mingled with our motives. No vulgar ambition stained our high resolve. No selfishness tainted our lofty aspirations. We embraced the cause in the spirit of lovers.* True lovers all were we—and what true lover ever loved less because the grave had closed over the dear and radiant form?

Confederate monument.

And so we—we at least, who as men and women inhaled the true spirit of that momentous time—come together on these occasions not only with the fresh new flowers in our hands, but with the old memories in our thoughts and the old, but ever fresh, lover spirit in our hearts, and seek to make these occasions not unworthy of the cause we loved unselfishly and of these its sleeping defenders.[203] — JOSEPH B. CUMMING

👉 SECOND DAY AT CHANCELLORSVILLE

After driving the enemy some distance, they ran against a heavy line behind splendid works. Retiring behind a low ridge, we rested while Pelham peppered them with his horse artillery. When the artillery duel was over, Capt. Oliver Foster and I were standing off to the right, when

Gen. Lee approached and asked whose troops these were. Capt. Foster answered that it was Archer's brigade, and pointed out the General. With a soldier's curiosity, we followed to hear what he would say to Gen. Archer. After salutations. Gen. [James Jay] Archer explained how his troops had driven the enemy for a mile until they struck the strong entrenched line on the hill, which they did not carry. Gen. Lee looked steadily for some minutes at the strong line on the hill, then turning to Gen. Archer, said in a businesslike way: "General, if you will move your brigade to the front about half way to that ravine, then make a left wheel move in that direction until your right is opposite that clump of trees, then right wheel again and strike *those people* [Lee's term for Yankees] in the front, you will drive them out. They will not bother you much until your last movement."

Archer maneuvered his little brigade beautifully and everything moved like clock work until the right wheel came. The Seventh Tennessee on the right, instead of wheeling, went into their works "on right into line." Hal Manson, (now of Rockwall, Texas), was the first man I saw go in. He never stopped until he stood on top of their works on the other side, waving his hat to the boys to come on. In five minutes he was worrying John Henlin for some of his rations. "Old Bones" knew who carried the biggest haversack. How the other regiments got in I never knew, but it is told that when Col. Newt George, commanding the First Tennessee, and on the extreme left, saw the other regiments going in and driving the Yankees pell-mell from their front, he could not wait for the regular right wheel, but yelled out, "Get in there endways, if you can't get in any other way. Don't you see the other regiments all going in?" No man ever accused Col. George of timidity in battle.

James J. Archer, C.S.A.

The enemy fired but few rounds when the Tennesseans commenced to pour in on them, but their few rounds cost some of the best blood of the South. I recall only now Harry Wingo, Maj. Smith, of the Alabama battalion, and Capt. Thompson, the latter a brother of Mrs. Geo. B.

Guild, wife of Nashville's present popular Mayor [George Blackmore Guild].

That everything happened just as Gen. Lee said it would is one of the reasons that made him the world's greatest general.²⁰⁴ — CAPT. F. S. HARRIS

☞ PRAISE FROM UNION PRISONERS FOR THEIR CONFEDERATE CAPTORS

Gentlemen: The officers of the United States Army, now held as prisoners of war in Columbia, S.C., being about to return to their homes after their captivity of several months, deem it appropriate and due to you to express their grateful feelings for the uniform kindness and consideration with which they and all the prisoners of war have been treated while in Columbia, S.C.

It gives the undersigned (a committee appointed unanimously on behalf of the officers) the greatest pleasure to bear testimony to the care you have exercised to deprive our imprisonment of as many as possible of its unpleasant parts, and in all respects to render our situation as comfortable as was in your power, and we feel that whatever enjoyment we have received while under your charge has been wholly owing to yourselves. During our incarceration as many privileges as were consistent with our safekeeping have been allowed us by you and those who constituted our guard. Whilst occupying the peculiar relations towards you that we have during the past two months, you have exhibited the traits of true soldiers in being just and considerate to those placed in your power; and the recollections of all the manliness and courtesy shown us by you and the Rebel Guard will constitute pleasant moments in our future lives. We earnestly hope that we may meet again under more favorable auspices, when our intercourse may be free and unrestrained and when we can associate together in all the relations of life as men and brothers.²⁰⁵ — COMMITTEE OF UNION OFFICERS

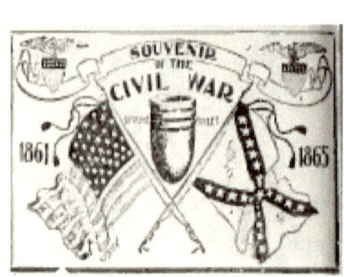
Civil War souvenir, 1890s.

☛ LEE, HIS MEN, & THE SOUTHERN CAUSE

[The Confederate soldier characterized] a type of manhood that the world never saw before and will never know again.

Stripped of all coloring, all prejudice, the real question involved in the "Lost Cause" was a struggle, a death grapple, over the construction of constitutional rights as established, vindicated and bequeathed by the fathers. Viewed from this standpoint, what an immortality Appomattox becomes!

Richmond abandoned, the executive officers of the Confederacy on the retreat, and left without one solitary adviser, the great commander [Robert E. Lee] balanced the odds and alone in the night watches formed his plans only in view of his responsibility to his people, to his conscience and his God.

To look upon him was a vision; to touch his hand was a sacrament; to hear him was a benediction.

On that sad morning he surrendered his army with all of its munitions of war. The great questions involved in the struggle were the integrity of his people and the honor of his soldiers.

Robert E. Lee, C.S.A.

Behind that grand old warrior stood the small remnant of weather-beaten survivors of the Army of Northern Virginia, which had so long confronted Grant's large army, "clamoring" for extermination [of the South], and behind all that the adverse sentiment and active prejudice of the outside world. "Few and faint, yet fearless still" they stood, ready at the word to charge on to slaughter and to death.

Never before was there presented such overwhelming odds. Never before did balance hold such tremendous issues. Solitary and alone, anomalous, majestic, immortal, unrivalled in all the past, unapproachable in all the future, that occasion stands pre-eminent, sublime, the cynosure of all generations.

Tattered and torn, broken and barefoot, despairing of success, yet resolute and defiant in conviction, powerless in strength yet invincible in principle and conscience, that little remnant gathered round its matchless idol as he stood presenting to the universe the concluding act in the splendid pageant of the "Lost Cause."—the vanquished dictating terms to the victor; the "old guard," surrounded on all sides, beleaguered beyond all escape, demanding and achieving honorable recognition and triumphant vindication for the living and the dead for whom it stood sponsor.

Alas! tho' coming generations will not again look upon the like, because the world in all coming time will never again behold such a contest for principle by men who, "holding their consciences unmixed with guile, stood amid all conjunctures true to themselves, their country and their God." *To us is left the heritage of unsullied and impregnable honor.*

Their's no Judas kiss, their's no traitor's promise, and the pledge so given and so vouched, albeit wrung from them in their weakness, has been fulfilled in the gross and in the detail, to the last syllable and the last letter.[206] — AN EAST TENNESSEAN

George Washington.

☛ SOUTHERN PATRIOTISM

The sacrifices made by the Confederate soldier put the question of motive beyond cavil. There never was a time between Fort Sumter and Appomattox, when, even in the death struggle, the Confederate soldier did not feel that he was fighting for his country—for the legal right to local self-government under the existing constitution made by his fathers. And he never doubted the right to claim for the South an equal share of glory won, and sacrifices made by revolutionary ancestry. He remembered with pride that the first declaration for colonial independence was made at the South, in Mecklenburg, N.C.; that Thomas Jefferson, a Southern man, wrote the Declaration of Independence adopted by our fathers. He remembered that Patrick Henry, another Southern man, when doubt and hesitation had paralyzed the popular heart, raised the battle cry, "Give me liberty, or give me death," and aroused all patriots to decision and action. He also remembered that George Washington, a Southern man, led the army to final victory securing liberty to American colonies; and that when the turning point of the struggle came, Southern heroes from this valley, at King's Mountain, after the misfortune at Camden, turned the tide of war, and were the initial that led to the climax of victory at Yorktown. Such assured historic facts nerved the Confederate on to deeds of valor, and made him a willing sacrifice to his convictions.

The history of our country from 1789 to 1860—shows that the patriotism of the South was prolific, of great civil achievements, by which the country grew in power and in wealth, until it became the wonder of the nineteenth century.

History sustains the South in the claim that all the territory brought into the United States government has been by gift from Southern states, or acquired by Southern policy, except Alaska, and that every state in the Union has been carved out of that territory, excepting two—Vermont and Maine. It is a historical fact that every foot of territory secured to the United States, after the treaty with England on the close of the Revolutionary War, was signed by Southern presidents, except that small portion known as the Gadsden Treaty, signed by President [Franklin] Pierce.

John Tyler.

. . . Old Virginia passed the title to the five original Northwestern states. Old Virginia also gave title to Kentucky. North Carolina gave the United States title to Tennessee. The next acquisition was the Louisiana Purchase by President Jefferson, from France, carrying with it all the remaining territory to the geographical point where the tide in the Northwest flows to the Pacific Ocean. Then Florida, with certain rights in Oregon, was purchased from Spain by President [James] Monroe. President [John] Tyler signed the treaty with Texas. President [James Knox] Polk signed that with Mexico for California, New Mexico and Arizona.

And singular to say that the treaty with Russia by which Alaska was secured, although negotiated for under Mr. Lincoln's administration, the final treaty was signed by President Andrew Johnson, a Southern man. *So, with the exception named, the treaties that brought every foot of territory added to the United States were signed by Southern presidents, in conformity with*

Southern policy. The South felt that she had done a full share to the extension of our country, and felt sensitive at the proposed denial of her rights.

But "there is a divinity that shapes our ends, rough-hew them how we will"—and it seems the war was inevitable. When our patriotic fathers, by way of compromise, planted certain seeds in our political garden, they proved to be seeds of discord, and after our variable political sunshine, clouds and rains, for three quarters of a century, they at last germinated and blossomed into blood. The process was slow, but sure, just as with the little snowflake that falls on the crag in the Alps, and becomes the nucleus of the mighty avalanche when a little sunbeam falls on it, and melts and loosens its hold, the avalanche tumbles, crashing and thundering into the vale below. So did the causes, created with the best intention by our fathers, become the nuclei, which accumulated into mighty proportions, and the avalanche of war came thundering and crashing through the land.

Andrew Johnson.

Feeling that their constitutional rights were imperiled, and that they could not be as equals in the government, and having failed, after repeated efforts, to further compromise and reconcile essential differences, eleven of the Southern states, asserting their primary rights as sovereign states, each acting for itself and on its own responsibility, formally and peaceably withdrew from the Union, each placing itself just as it was before entering into the compact of union.

This was not done in anger, nor in indecent haste, but with proper grace and dignity, overcast with sorrow. The time of so doing extended from December, 1860, to June, 1861. Each seceding state, from natural sympathy and common interest, aligned itself alongside of those that had preceded it; and, after the fashion of the original formation of the Union, they united their fortunes and made common cause. Three other border states, Kentucky, Missouri and Maryland, hesitated in the attempt to join their seceding sisters, and finally remained in the Union [though portions of Kentucky and Missouri finally did secede], while numbers of individuals and organized commands, following their convictions, promptly and bravely left their homes in these states and united their destinies with the land of the South.

Believing in the justice and righteousness of their cause, and to maintain their constitutional rights, and undaunted by such obstacles, the eleven seceded states organized what is known as "The Confederate States" [taken from one of the earlier names given to the U.S.A.].[207]

. . . *These Confederate states were organized and established as a separate government, and moved to its chosen capital—Richmond, Va.* I use the term "established" significantly. This organized government, by constitutional designation, gave itself the name of "The Confederate States," having a government for four years—years of battle and of blood—and it was organized after the fashion of the one established by our [Founding] fathers. It had, in fact, all the machinery and paraphernalia of a thoroughly organized and equipped government.

Confederate White House, Richmond, VA.

It had its national flag and a patriotic and gallant army to defend it. That flag emblemed its nationality and waved over Confederate armies that guarded its citadel defiantly for four years. *It was defensive and not offensive war. The Confederates asked to be let alone—only that.*

. . . *To disestablish it, it required 2,759,059 gallant and well equipped Federal soldiers four years, fighting hundreds of battles with a loss of more than half a million men and at a cost in money of four or five billions of dollars.*

It is a historic fact that President Lincoln formally called through all sources for *2,759,059 men* for military service.

. . . It is also a historic fact, obtained from the best available data at my command, that the Confederate States had on their army rolls from first to last, during our four years' strife, in round numbers, less than 600,000 men.

When truthful writers come to understand such facts, can it be believed that they will speak of it as a "mere rebellion," and not as the greatest of civil wars?

The word "rebel," while intended as a word of reproach, created no alarm among Confederates. They recognized the fact that wherever you find in history a struggle for liberty, the word "liberty" is preceded by the word "rebel"—as in the struggle of our own revolutionary fathers for independence.

The political theory held at the South—that our Union was a compact—evidenced by the Federal constitution, of which the Federal government was the creature, and the states the creator, the former the agent, the latter the principal, may or may not have been the true theory of our confederation, but it was unquestionably the conscientious conviction of our people, our statesmen and our states.

It was a theory of wise men which secured the liberty of local government without weakening the central power for public defense; it left domestic affairs to the care of those most interested in all that relates to home, while it intrusted foreign relations to the watchful care of the general government as the agent of all the states. Capable of extension throughout the continent, it has already extended from ocean to ocean, from lake to gulf, securing the largest liberty to each constituent state, and yet uniting the will and power of the whole for the common defense of all— "Distinct as the billows, yet one as the sea."[208] — WILLIAM B. BATE

☛ DARING CONFEDERATES IN THE WAR

E. C. De Jarnett was a private in Company F, Twelfth Texas Cavalry, Parsons Brigade, and in 1864 was in Rapids Parish, La., during [Union General Nathaniel Prentiss] Banks' retreat down Red River after the battles of Mansfield and Pleasant Hill, La. One day, just after dinner, the Federals were burning and plundering sugar houses across Bayou Rapids from us. De Jarnett crossed the bayou by swimming his horse, and went about a mile in an open field to see and learn what he could about the enemy. When about a mile from the bayou, in plain view of our picket stand, he encountered a man on horseback, dressed in citizen's clothing. Thinking he recognized the man as an acquaintance, De Jarnett noticed him very little, [for] his attention was directed to about twenty-five or thirty Federals who were up the bayou about a half mile distant. As the man approached within a few feet, De Jarnett spoke to him and asked what command he belonged to. The man replied that he was a Federal soldier, and, at the same time presenting his pistol, ordered De Jarnett to surrender, and as the latter could not get at his pair of holsters, he caught hold of the Yankee's pistol and they had a hand to hand fight for it. At last the pistol was dropped to the ground, and De Jarnett pulled one of his pistols, which was in turn caught by the enemy as he was in the act of firing, and the Yankee shoved it so it only shot off the hind tree of his saddle. The Yankee at once let go the weapon, when De Jarnett hit him over the head and knocked him from his horse. During this hand to hand fight, the detachment of Yankees came running to the rescue of their comrade, and De Jarnett made for the bayou where we were, and it was indeed a race for life, as more than a score of the enemy were after him, firing as fast as they could. He beat them to the bayou by about one hundred yards, and plunged his horse in and swam over to our side. Our picket in the meantime engaged the fire of the pursuers. You can judge De Jarnett's  surprise when he reached the water, and on looking around, saw the [riderless] horse he had knocked the man from close behind him. It jumped in the water and swam safely to our side. De Jarnett's prize consisted not only of the horse, which was a very valuable one, but a fine pair of pistols and soldier's baggage. I think De Jarnett still lives in this state.

On another occasion, shortly after this, we had a small skirmish with the enemy, six or eight miles northwest of Alexandria, La., on Bayou Rapids. The enemy drove us back and then retreated toward Alexandria. A Lieutenant of our regiment was ordered to take ten men and place out our picket for the night on a certain ditch that ran through a sugar cane field. The ditch was about seven feet deep, and was over grown with cane briars and weeds. On reaching the ditch about dusk, the Lieutenant ordered one of his men, William P. Love, noted for his personal bravery and presence of mind, to go across the ditch on foot and see if he could locate the enemy's picket. The night was dark, and as Love went forward, he missed the vidette picket of the enemy, but located the reserved picket. On returning, he came upon the vidette, who promptly ordered him to halt, but as Love was coming from the direction of the Federal picket the vidette thought he was one of his own men. Love came up to the picket, who was on the ground holding his horse by the bridle, and before the vidette knew what he was about, Love caught him by the throat and called to our Lieutenant, who was still on our side of the ditch, to come over and help him. The Yankee reserve picket heard the noise and at once came to the vidette's relief, getting there before our men could cross the ditch. It was so dark no one could fire a gun for fear of hitting his friend. As the Yankee picket surrounded Love and the vidette, who were having a hand to hand fight, Love suddenly threw the vidette to the ground, mounted his horse and fled. When and where he crossed the ditch he never knew, as it was so dark he could not see it, but he rode the vidette's horse safely in to camp. Love died soon after the war in Robertson County, Texas. A braver man never lived.[209] — A. J. BURLESON

☛ THE CONFEDERATE FLAG

Some Grand Army men [Yankees] from different sections were talking about "Old Glory" [the Union or U.S. Flag] on public school buildings; when asked if they meant to imply that as a demand of the Southern people specially, they seriously seemed surprised when informed that at the South there was a suspicion that it was to have those who had battled against the Stars and Stripes made to realize its supremacy and to understand it as a symbol of power, when all asserted that it referred to foreign elements in the North who did not respect the flag and did not even want their children to study the English language. *They said it is never a question with them about respect for the national flag in the South, and they judge correctly.*

Our people respect the national flag, but they have not yet the genuine affection for it that they had before the great war to establish constitutional liberty in the rights of States.

Still, they cheerfully march under and revere it, and if anybody, from any section, casts a slur upon it, Southern blood would dash into boiling heat. If any man, whatever his station, should actually show discourtesy to our national flag or the soldiers of the United States army when there is the slightest suspicion of disloyalty to our republican government, he would find the South a very unhealthy section. *Anarchy will never get a hold in the South while the Confederate soldier element predominates.*

But *there is a devotion to the Confederate flag that is as strong as the love of sympathetic humanity. There is nothing in this world that could induce the Southern people to surrender their affection for it. The God of ensigns never witnessed among His creatures a devotion more after divinity than those who suffered willingly under its pure folds. It went down without [any] other stain than the blood of martyrs.*

The survivors of that noble army who followed in the flash and smoke of battle remember how their brothers by their sides, with prayers upon their lips for the right, whether or not of their choice, fell dead by shot and shell while pressing on to victory—or death. They know that life is short, and they believe in the eternity beyond; they yearn for good government and will make sacrifice of ease and money without stint for its maintenance, but they do not think enough of any government, nor of life itself, to surrender their respect for that most sacred emblem in the world. There is but one flag and there is to be but one, but *the children, and children's children, of those who were true Confederate soldiers will respect that flag as long as parental influence exists.*

Veterans of the United States army, who are proud of being Americans, can well afford to want the Confederate Flag as emblematic of the strongest patriotism and the highest type of chivalry that the human race has ever known.

President [Grover] Cleveland never did a nobler thing than to suggest that Confederate flags, which had been captured by Union soldiers, be turned over by the United State Government to the States from which they served.[210] — SUMNER A. CUNNINGHAM

☛ SKETCH OF GEN. THOMAS NEVILLE WAUL

Gen. Thomas Neville Waul, of Texas, is a native of South Carolina, born near Statesburg, January 5, 1813, and was an only child. His mother died when he was an infant. His grandfathers on both sides were soldiers of the [American] Revolution.

The death of his father, his own ill health and straitened circumstances induced young Waul to leave the South Carolina College before graduating. He declined to take any part of the small patrimony, giving all to his stepmother. He went west on horseback, stopping at Florence, Ala., where he, at the age of seventeen, was made principal of a school. At the end of a year, with strong credentials, he went on to Vicksburg, Miss., where he met S. S. Prentiss. The two became fast friends, and young Waul studied law in his office. He made such progress in the law that he was licensed to practice before the Supreme Court of his State while yet a minor. He resided afterward at Yazoo City, and then at Grenada, where he married Miss Mary Simmons, of Georgia. He succeeded in the law and became active in politics. He was elected to the first Confederate Congress from Texas, but declined a re-election, having determined to go in the field. He then raised "Waul's Legion" of 2,000 men.

Thomas N. Waul, C.S.A.

In the siege of Vicksburg, Col. Waul won promotion, and was made Brig.-Gen., after his exchange. In the battles of Mansfield and Pleasant Hill, La., he so distinguished himself that he was given the command of Walker's division, after Gen. [John George] Walker was wounded, and later of all the troops in the field. In the battle of Saline, or Jenkins Ferry, hard fought in the mud with muskets and bayonets, it being impossible to use artillery, two Texas Generals were killed, and Gen. Waul, the other, was severely wounded.

After the war, Gen. Waul having lost his property along with his people, he resumed the practice of law. He served as a member of the Constitutional Convention of Texas, but has refrained from political life, except in a few instances. His merits for Commander of the Trans-Mississippi Department of United Confederate Veterans were pressed with great zeal at Houston.[211] — SUMNER A. CUNNINGHAM

☛ TEST OF COURAGE FOR A SOLDIER
Near nightfall on the 6th of May, 1864, the second day of the fighting in the Wilderness at Spottsylvania, the General (Jeb Stuart) desired to ascertain whether or not the line of Federal earthworks in his front had been abandoned. Gen. Stuart sent to Maj. Dangerfield, whose regiment was close by, for a man who would "'perform a hazardous duty." Private Jim O'Mera was selected and reported to Gen. Stuart. In reply to his salutation, Gen. Stuart simply said, "You see that line of earthworks; I want to know if it is manned. Ride within seventy yards of it, then turn to the left and gallop parallel with it to the end of the line. If the enemy is there, ride rapidly and they will shoot behind you." Jim simply replied, "All right, Gin'ral, I know it," with an appreciative gesture. Jim rode within seventy yards of the works and started on his run, parallel with the line. The works being well manned, were immediately illuminated by a terrific fusillade. It did not swerve Jim, however. When he had gone half the length of the line a bullet went through his horse's nose midway between the eye and the nostril. Jim then stopped his horse, unslung his carbine, and with as much deliberation as if aiming at a squirrel, he fired upon the enemy. He then spurred his horse and ran parallel with the line to the end; then hurried to Gen. Stuart, who had watched the wonderful feat, saluted and reported: "They'er thar yit, Gin'ral."[212] — MAJ. F. A. DANGERFIELD

☛ MIGHT, NOT GOD, WINS WARS
. . . Since the days of Abraham there has not been recorded a single instance where right ruled the contests and battles between contending nations; might and not right has prevailed in all ages and with all people. Homer has adorned his poetry by assuming that the gods took sides in the battle between the Greeks and Trojans, yet looking to the truth of history *there is no proof that the Ruler of the universe has ever taken sides in a battle between men. Better soldiers with better arms, more skillfully commanded may conquer superior numbers, but all things being equal, victory, as a rule, is with the heaviest battalions. . . There is no such thing as abstract right in the affairs of nations as*

recorded in history; power has been the universal rule and is the rule now with England and all other nations.

. . . Secession without war is a peaceable revolution and a revolution with war is a forcible secession. *Our ancestors seceded from England; they preferred peace, but war came; they triumphed and are now applauded by the world as patriots, wise statesmen and great warriors.* If they had failed they would be recorded in history as rebels and traitors. Great Britain had the right in 1776 to subdue her seceding colonies but did not have the might, and she has the same right to-day, and if she had the power would doubtless be as ready to take possession of these United States as she was to occupy Egypt.

Some people say that through the device of loans and bonds that our people are as much or more her slaves than if Queen Victoria and the Parliament made our laws. *Secession in one sense was right in 1861, and is right now . . . No moral wrong or dishonorable conduct attaches to the advocates of secession; it was simply a military mistake. . . There may be glory and fame but there is little wisdom in fighting a battle with overwhelming odds against you.*

The South was conquered; African slavery was the pretext [Note: not according to Davis, Lee, Lincoln, or Grant. L.S.],[213] but the same principle that ruled Philip, Alexander, William the Conqueror, Timour the Tartar, Napoleon and other conquerors dominated the Northern mind. *To reduce the proud slaveholder to a level with the negro was the ruling idea with the abolitionist, but Northern politicians had other motives for the crusade of slander and abuse which they preached against the South. Their purpose was to transfer the offices and control of the Government from Southern to Northern men. The war accomplished these purposes, and in addition thereto has made slaves of the people to bond holders, bankers, corporations, millionaire speculators and hungry creditors for debts, public and private, so large that no human wisdom can tell the day when they can be paid, if ever paid. It is written of conquerors: "Where his carnage and his conquest cease He makes a solitude and calls it peace."*

Texas seceded from Mexico, and if left to fight her own battles unaided, it is probable that Mexico would have subdued her; the armies of the United States came to her relief and fought the battles of Palo Alto, Monterey Buena Vista, Vera Cruz, Cero Gordo, Contreras, Churubusco, Molino Del Rey, Chetultezpec, and captured the city, and thus, by military power established the right of Texas to secede. For these services to Texas thus rendered, the United States obtained from Mexico, territory of incalculable value.

Massachusetts had a strong party for secession in 1812 [and 1814-1815], and has a perfect right to secede to-day, but before doing so she ought to be sure that she has the might to maintain by military power her independence if the other states resist.[214] — COL. JOHN H. SAVAGE

CHAPTER 15

1896

Fitzhugh Lee, C.S.A.

☛ LEE FAMILY HUMOR
[The following . . .] is a good illustration of the love the Confederate soldiers bore toward Gen. Robert E. Lee. As it is well known, Gen. Fitzhugh Lee [Robert's nephew] was at the head of the cavalry, and these were much envied by the infantry men, who had to walk through the mud and dust.

After Gen. Robert E. Lee had surrendered, Gen. Fitzhugh Lee rode away from Appomattox. While riding through a lane he met an old North Carolina soldier.

"Ho, there," cried General Lee, "where are you going?"

"I've been off on a furlough, and am now going back to join Gen. Bob Lee," replied the soldier.

"You needn't go back, but [you] can throw your gun away and return home, for Lee's surrendered."

"Lee's surrendered?"

"That's what I said," said General Lee.

"It must have been that damned Fitz Lee, then. Rob Lee would never surrender," and the old soldier put on a look of contempt and walked on.[215] — GEN. FITZHUGH LEE

☛ SKETCH OF NATHAN BEDFORD FORREST

Lieutenant-General N. B. Forrest, who was my immediate commander during the first year of the war, if not *the greatest military genius*, was certainly the greatest revolutionary leader on our side. He was restrained by no knowledge of law or constitution; he was embarrassed by no preconceived ideas of military science. His favorite maxim was: "War means fighting, and fighting means killing." Without the slightest knowledge of them, he seemed by instinct to adopt the tactics of the masters of military art.

. . . On December 28th, 1861, Forrest, with 300 men, met the enemy for the first time, about 450 strong, near Sacramento, Ky. This fight deserves special notice, not only because of its success and the confidence inspired in the raw Confederate cavalry, but because it displayed at once the chief characteristics and natural tactics which were subsequently more fully developed and made Forrest famous as a cavalry leader. He had marched his command twenty miles that day when he found a fresh trail where the enemy's cavalry had passed. Putting his command at a gallop, he traveled ten miles further before he struck the rear guard. His own command was badly scattered, not half up with him, but without halting he rushed headlong at them, leading the charge himself. When he had driven the rear guard on to the main body, and

One of the 27 horses killed under Forrest.

they turned on him with superior force, he quickly dismounted his men and held the enemy in check until his command came up, and ordered them to attack in flank and rear. This movement was successful, and the retreat of the Federals soon began. Quickly mounting his men, he commenced one of his terrible pursuits, fighting hand to hand with pistol and sword, killing one and wounding two himself, continuing this for miles, and leaving the road dotted with living and dead.

. . . [Confederate] Major David Campbell Kelley, who then for the first time saw his superior under fire, describing the wonderful change that took place in his appearance, says: "His face flushed until he bore a striking resemblance to a painted Indian warrior, and his eyes, usually so mild in their expression, flashed with the intense glare of the panther about to spring on its prey. In fact, he looked as little like the Forrest of our mess-table as the storm of December resembles the quiet of June."

General [James Ronald] Chalmers relates: "Some of the notable points in Forrest's manner of fighting, were (1) reckless courage in making the attack, a rule he invariably followed and which tended to intimidate his adversary; (2) the quick dismounting of his men to fight, showing that he regarded horses mainly as a rapid means of transportation for his troops; (3) his intuitive adoption of the flank attack, so demoralizing to the enemy even in an open field, and so much more so when made, as Forrest often did, under cover of woods which concealed the weakness of the attacking party; (4) his fierce and untiring pursuit, which so often changed retreat into rout and made victory complete; (5) following, without knowing it,

Forrest's men rounding up the Yankee criminals at Ft. Pillow.

[Charles James] Napier's precept of the art of war, he was always in front making personal observations. This practice brought him in many personal conflicts and exposed him to constant danger, and he had 27 horses killed and wounded under him in battle. This practice led to imitation by his general officers, and at Hart's cross-roads, the day before the battle of Franklin [November 30, 1864], I witnessed Forrest with two division and three brigade commanders, all on the skirmish line.

"At Shiloh, Forrest, without orders from any superior officer, had pushed his scouts to the river and discovered that reinforcements of the enemy were coming. I was then in command of an infantry brigade, which by some oversight had not received the order to retreat; about midnight, Forrest awoke me, inquiring for Generals Beauregard, Bragg and Hardee, and when I could not tell him, he said in profane but prophetic language, 'If the enemy come on us in the morning, we will be whipped like hell.' He carried this information to headquarters and, with military genius, suggested a renewal at once of our attack; but the unlettered colonel was ordered back to his regiment."

. . . I recall an anecdote strikingly illustrative of the esteem in which Forrest was held by the people, and he always told it on himself with great delight. When Bragg was retreating from Tennessee, Forrest was among the last of the rear guard. An old lady ran out of her house to the gate as he was passing, and urged him to turn back and fight. As he rode on without stopping, she shook her fist at him and cried, "Oh! you great, big, cowardly rascal! I only wish old Forrest were here; he would make you fight!"

. . . One of the greatest secrets of Forrest's success was his perfect system of scouts. He kept reliable scouts all around him and at great distances and often, even days in advance, he was informed of movements that were about to be made.

. . . Near West Point, (1864) Forrest soon came up to where I was standing on the causeway, leading to the bridge, and, as it was the first time I had ever been with him in a fight, I watched him closely. His manner was nervous, impatient and imperious. He asked me what the enemy were doing, and I gave him the report just received from Colonel Duff, in command of the pickets. He said sharply. "Well, I will go and see myself." He started across the bridge, which was about thirty yards long and then being raked by the enemy's fire. This struck me at the time as a needless and somewhat braggadocio exposure of himself, and I followed him to see what he would do. When he reached the other bank, the fire of the enemy was very heavy and our men were falling back, one running without hat or gun. In an instant Forrest seized and threw him to the ground, and, while the bullets were whistling around him, administered a severe thrashing with a brush of wood.

General Joseph E. Johnston said if Forrest had been an educated soldier, no other Confederate general would have been heard of.

Dr. John B. Cowan, of Tullahoma, Tenn., who was chief surgeon to Forrest's Cavalry during the war, and was intimately associated with Forrest, says that at the battle of Okalona, where Forrest's brother Jeffrey was killed, his grief was overpowering when he realized that the brother whom he idolized, and who, being a posthumous child, had been tenderly reared and carefully educated by the elder brother, was mortally wounded. Although the Federals were in flight with Forrest pursuing, he seemed for a moment to forget the great responsibility of his position as a commander, in the agony of this sudden affliction. He dismounted, picked up his dying brother and held him in his arms as he would a child, until his lifeblood was spent. The wound was of such a character that surgical relief was impossible, and he bled to death within a few minutes. The rough soldier kissed his dead brother tenderly, with tears streaming from his eyes, laid him gently upon the ground, took one last look, and then his expression of grief gave way to one of almost ferocity; he sprang to his horse, shouting to [Jacob] Gaus, his bugler, "Blow the charge!" and swept ahead of his men in the direction of the retreating enemy. Dr. Cowan followed as close behind him as he could keep in the pursuit, and the faithful escort were well up with their great leader. Half a mile or so down the road they suddenly came upon the enemy, who had determined upon a stand. A piece of artillery was placed to sweep the road by which they must approach, and the Federals, dismounted, had taken a strong position on either side of the road. As soon as they were observed, the Federals fired upon them, and Dr. Cowan remonstrated with the General for thus exposing himself. Forrest remarked, "Doctor, if you are uneasy, you can ride out of range;" and the General continued in this position, making a careful survey of the enemy's position. His horse was killed under him, and he mounted another, belonging to one of the escort who had just then ridden up.

John B. Cowan, C.S.A.

While Forrest was riding a little further on, on the side of a little eminence, this horse was also killed. Satisfied with the reconnaissance, which had only occupied a few minutes, he drew his saber and shouted to the escort, "Move up!" This plucky body of sixty men followed with equal bravery their daring and now reckless leader.

It seemed to me then that the General, maddened by grief at the loss of his favorite brother, wanted to go with him. It was only the matter of a moment when the General and his escort were mixed up with the Federals in a fearful melée. I put the spurs to my horse, ran back in the direction from which we had come to hurry up help, met Colonel [Robert] McCulloch with a portion of his Missouri regiment, and said to him, "Colonel, for God's sake hurry down the road as fast as you can. The General and his escort are down there in a hand to hand fight, and I am afraid he will be killed before you can get there!" Forrest slew three men with his sword in this terrible fight before the Federals yielded and fled from the field.

Forrest as a Memphis alderman, 1850.

General Richard Taylor, who later in the war was placed in command of the department in which Forrest operated, says in his book, *Destruction and Reconstruction*, "Some months before the time of our first meeting . . . he had defeated [Union Gen. Samuel Davis] Sturgis at Tishimingo, and he soon repeated his defeat of General Grant at Okolona.

"Okolona was fought on an open plain, and Forrest had no advantage of position to compensate for great inferiority of numbers, but it is remarkable that he employed the tactics of Frederick [the Great] at [the battles of] Leuthen and Zorndorf, though he had never heard these names. Indeed, *his tactics deserve the closest study of military men*. When asked to what he attributed his success in so many actions, he replied, 'I got there first with the most men.' I doubt if any commander since the time of lion-hearted Richard, has killed so many of his foes as Forrest. His word of command was unique, 'Move up, and mix with 'em!' While cutting down many a foe with long-reaching arm, his keen eye watched the whole fight and guided him to the weak spot. Yet, he was a tender-hearted, kindly man. *The accusations of his enemies that he murdered his prisoners at Fort Pillow and elsewhere are absolutely false. These negroes told me of Forrest's kindness to them.*"

A reunion of Forrest's soldiers, both white and black, Lynchburg, TN, c. 1920s.

In the closing campaign at Selma, in April, 1865, General Taylor says: "Forrest ordered his brigades to the Catawba crossing, leading one in person. He was a host in himself, and a dangerous adversary to meet at any reasonable odds. With one brigade, Forrest was in [Union Gen. James Harrison] Wilson's path; he fought as if the world depended on his arm, and sent to advise me of the deception practiced on two of his brigades, hoping to stop the enemy if he could with the third, the absence of which he could not account for. After Selma fell, he appeared horse and man covered with blood, and announced the enemy at his heels, and that I must move at once to escape capture. I felt anxious about him, but he said he was unhurt and would cut his way through."

If Forrest was terrible and relentless in battle, he was by nature gentle, tender and affectionate. His love for children was very strong. My personal friend, Colonel R. B. Kyle, of Gadsden, on the 25th of June 1895, gave me in writing the following personal reminiscence of the great soldier: "About May 7th, 1863, as Forrest was returning from the capture of Streight, at Rome, he stayed all night at my house. Forrest's terrific pursuit of Streight, and the capture of his large command with a force only one-third as numerous as the enemy, had, of course, filled the country through which Streight had passed with the idea that Forrest was a tremendous fighter, and gave me the impression that his mind would be occupied only with things concerning the war; but the only thing that seemed to concern him while in my house for almost a day and all night, was my little two-year-old boy, to whom he took a great fancy, holding him on his lap and carrying him around the place in his arms. The little child showed great fondness for him and loved to stay with him. The next day, when Forrest rode away in the direction of Guntersville, he took the little fellow two or three miles on the road with him, holding him on the saddle in front of him, and I rode along with Forrest this distance in order to bring the child home to his mother. He kissed the little fellow tenderly as he bade him good-bye and, turning to me, said, 'My God, Kyle, this is worth living for!'

John A. Wyeth, C.S.A.

"I again met Forrest in the fall of 1863 on board a train en route to Montgomery. Ala., to meet President Davis, with whom he had some correspondence, and who had asked Forrest to come to Montgomery, as he wanted to see him personally. We renewed our acquaintance, and in conversation he told me he would not serve longer under Bragg. He said that he [Bragg] was not competent to command any army; that the army had whipped the Federals badly at Chickamauga, and that he, with his command, had followed them almost to the suburbs of Chattanooga; that they were demoralized, and could have been captured, and that he rode back himself, after sending couriers and getting unfavorable replies, and found General Bragg asleep. He urged that they move on in pursuit of the enemy at once, as their capture was certain. Bragg asked how he could move an army without supplies, as his men had exhausted them. Forrest's reply was, 'General Bragg, we can get all the supplies our army needs in Chattanooga.' Bragg made no reply, and Forrest rode away disgusted."[216] — DR. JOHN ALLAN WYETH

☛ SOUTHERN SENTIMENT

The South again having entered the Union, surrendered all that was claimed of her. To the new Amendments of the Constitution she is as loyal as she was to the old. In fact, the Constitution finds its true defenders from this section. It is as much our Union and our flag as it ever was. Brave soldiers will spring forward from this section as quickly as from any other to defend it against foreign foe.

Isham G. Harris, C.S.A.

Tennessee is to-day as much an integral part of this Union as Vermont, and is just as proud of our great Republic; yet the Governor of this State was quite right when he told the Governor of that, at the dedication of Chickamauga Park, *we would certainly teach our children that in the great struggle—in which thousands gave up their lives at Chickamauga and elsewhere—we fought for the right.* And our war Governor [Isham Green Harris] was right in his reply when President Lincoln, on the 15th of April, 1861, called upon the Governors of the several States for militia—75,000 in the aggregate—to suppress "certain combinations" in the seceding States. [Said Gov. Harris:] "Tennessee will not furnish a single man for coercion, but 50,000, if necessary, for the defense of our rights or those of our Southern brethren."

Yet, I think all resentment against the North on the part of the people of the South died with the closing of the war. Having submitted their cause to the arbitrament of the sword, and the decision being against them, they quietly submitted. In place of this, there was a warm feeling of friendship for the Northern soldier who had fought so bravely for a restoration of the Union.[217]

On the contrary, I think a hatred of the South began at the North

Henry Wirz, C.S.A.

only with the close of the war.[218] Else, why the hanging of the helpless man [Confederate Captain Henry] Wirz, for not feeding sufficiently the prisoners of war that were refused exchange by their own people, when our own soldiers were starving? Why the hanging of poor, *innocent* Mrs. [Mary] Surratt? *Why the order commanding every rebel soldier to cut off the buttons from his old gray jacket? Why the manacling and chaining of Jefferson Davis in a casemate of a fort from which there could be no possibility of escape? And yet they dared not submit the question of his treason to the courts!*

What a commentary it would have been—after fighting four years to make treason odious, after destroying the South—to find there had been no treason!

Why such expressions from representative men of the North like this from Henry Ward Beecher, who said in a sermon: *"Those who suffered in the South were not martyrs in a good cause, but convicts in a bad one,"* and *"who shall comfort them that sit by dishonored graves?"*

Why should our brothers at the North approve the attempt by the old fanatic, John Brown, to massacre the slave holders of Virginia with the help of their slaves? Why do they eulogize him as the noblest of heroes? Why should the conquered South have been subjected to the bitterness of reconstruction, her people refused the privilege of the ballot, and the heel of the ignorant negro placed upon the neck of the proudest people of all America? Why should the [U.S.] Secretary of State [William H. Seward] have informed the Pan-American Congress that there was nothing worth visiting south of the Potomac River?

It has been said that the injured one can always forgive, but that he who maliciously wounds another can never forgive his victim.

The writer saw armed Federal soldiers guarding the graves of the few Confederate

Mary E. Surratt.

soldiers buried in a corner at Arlington, on the 30th of May, 1868, to prevent the Southern ladies from placing flowers on their graves.

Is there any one in the whole South who can understand the wild frenzy and rabid utterances of a Governor of a Western State at the prospect of a return of some old flags to certain organizations in the South—who wished them as souvenirs—twenty years after the war was over? Why is it that partisan school books and histories must be continually written, filled with such falsehoods, when the authors could easily discover the truth if they desired it?

Confederate heroes.

Why should continual effort be made to impress the seeker after truth with a belief that the South attempted to destroy the government by making war upon it, when that South attempted peaceably to secede from a contract after the conditions were broken?

. . . The children of the North are still taught the silly old lie of Jefferson Davis' capture in women's clothes. That it has been disproved again and again, by his actual captors, and never had any basis except a waterproof cloak, seems of no consequence.

A prominent statesman, afterwards a candidate for the Presidency, declared on the floor of the House of Representatives that the Southern leaders in the war were more cruel than the Duke of Alba [Fernando Álvarez de Toledo] in the Lowlands, and further stated that he fully realized the awfulness of such a charge.

He knew, of course, that there were fewer deaths and more prisoners in the South, more deaths and fewer prisoners at the North; that food and medicine was scarce in the former, and plentiful in the latter. He thought the horrible lie would be useful politically.

I have never seen a solitary instance, in the Northern so-called histories, of a battle in which the Union army was defeated but what the relative strength of the two armies was falsely given.

. . . We must not forget the glorious memories of the Old South. The "business interest" must not be allowed to destroy all sentiment.

Enterprise and thrift are well enough, but there are some signs in this desire for an exchange of old ideas for the new that seem but *taking the false for the true*. The old time Southerner, with all of his exaggerated pride and pompous manner, was a man of unflinching probity and would not lie nor steal.

Some of the financial agents of the New Regime can do both. The defaulting trustee, the "promoter" and the tramp, unheard of under the old dispensation, are very much in evidence under the new.

And the old time hospitality of the South! It is going too. Perhaps there is none of this characteristic mark of the dear old days left—so illustrative of a warm, unselfish heart—save in portions of old Virginia and the Carolinas.

. . . There is something better than wealth, something dearer than success. *Let us cultivate and renew the virtues of the Old South*, while we gather from our Northern brethren whatever they can give us that may be of present use. And *let us ever keep fresh in our hearts proud recollections of the patient endurance, the indomitable resolution, and the matchless heroism of the Rebels of 1776 and 1861.*

There will come a time when justice will be done Southern song, Southern sentiment, and Southern heroism. Wise statesmen will yet arise who will realize, as Charles Sumner did, that since the Union has been restored, it is not the part of the patriotic lover of that Union to attempt to perpetuate by emblem, device, or statute the fact that one part of the country had subjugated another part, that brothers of the same race had once been engaged in bloody Civil War. . . . Can there be any doubt that the future will do full justice to the South's heroic struggle, her brave soldiery, and her great Captain?[219]
— DANIEL BOND

☛ CONFEDERATE INDIAN SOLDIERS

In May, 1861, [Christian mystic and Confederate] Gen. Albert Pike came as Commissioner from the Confederate States Government authorized to make treaties with the Southern Indians. At first [Cherokee] Chief

[John] Ross refused and insisted on his nation remaining neutral, and would not allow enlistment of Cherokee troops into the Confederate service. [Cherokee leader] Stand Watie had, however, in a quiet way enlisted a regiment in readiness to join the Confederates. John Ross was evidently holding off for further development. This was before the battle of Springfield, on Wilson's Creek, as the Yankees called it. Success crowning our arms there, Ross hastened to treat with Gen. Pike and agreed to put in the Confederate service a regiment to be armed and equipped by the Confederacy, and he did so. In making that treaty he would allow none of the leaders of the Ridge party to take part in it.

Albert Pike, C.S.A.

Previous to this Gen. Ben McCulloch authorized Capt. John Miller and myself to raise an independent company to serve for three months. We were known as the Dixie Rangers and we were to occupy the neutral land in part of the Territory and Southern Kansas. In that company served the afterwards noted William Quantrell, about whom I will, at some future time, take occasion to say something, to correct stories abou this death, etc. I will only say here that, when you knew Quantrell, you knew a kind-hearted man, an intrepid soldier and a gentleman of whose friendship I was, and am, proud.

The Third Louisiana Regiment came up to us. Many of us saw that Regiment under fire at Springfield and Pea Ridge, where it made its mark as well as at other points, wherever it served, in fact. When that Regiment left us after the Pea Ridge fight, our Indians were distressed, and to the end of the war they never ceased to regret the separation from them of the Third Louisiana.

At the expiration of their three months' term of service the Dixie Rangers were disbanded, and nearly all, myself included, joined Company K., First Cherokee Regiment, Capt. Thompson Mayes, a brother of the late principal Chief Joel B. Mayes. Capt. Mayes was a man of superior education and a fine officer. This was Colonel Watie's pet company. There was but the one company in the First Cherokee Regiment, composed of and officered by Indians. In the other companies whites and Indians were mixed as well among the officers as in the ranks, and it worked well and smoothly. In the Choctaw regiments some companies were either all whites or all Indians, which caused more or less friction and jarring. But the plan had been adopted by Col. D. N. Cooper and could not well be changed.

Many of Col. Watie's Regiment took part in the battle of Springfield, but went there with his permission as individuals and not as an organized body.

A number of Missourians came to us and took part in the fight. Some came unarmed and others armed with their shotguns and rifles. Among them was an old, lean and lank Baptist preacher with a Flintlock rifle about seven feet long. He would kneel on one knee, take deliberate aim, and say: "May the Lord have mercy on that poor critter's soul," and pull the trigger. Then he would get up, reload, get down on one knee again and repeat his prayer, fire. I stood and looked at him fire five or six times, and I believe he made every bullet count.

Stand Watie, C.S.A.

Very little was done between that fight and the battle of Pea Ridge, except a fight that took place in December, 1861, between our Cherokees and the forces of [Chief] Opothleoholo, the leader of the so-called Loyal Creeks, Seminoles, Wichitas, Kickapoos and Delawares. The weather was extremely cold. We found Opothleoholo occupying a strong position in the mountains near Chustenola. We commenced driving them from the start, captured their baggage and papers, and followed them for three days up into Kansas to the big bend of Arkansas River. The Pin Regiment [made up of members of a secret and violent organization known as the Ketowah Society] came up the second day, but took no part in the fight. Many of the enemy were killed. Here and there we would strike [capture] bunches of their squaws huddled together. These we sent back to our camp and fed. In their flight they had thrown away their infants, which were frozen stiff. Altogether it was a sickening sight.

After this, nothing worth noting took place until we were ordered to Pea Ridge, where the Cherokees distinguished themselves capturing a battery. Here one of the Yankee artillerymen was lying stretched out, face down, between two of the pieces apparently dead. One of our full blood Cherokees took out his knife, got his fingers in the Yankee's hair and cut out and jerked off a scalp about the size of a dollar. Thus resurrected, Mr. Yank got him on his legs in a hurry, and "he ran like a quarter horse," not a gun was fired after him, but a yell went up: "Go it, Yank, we have a lock of your hair." This scalping business, however, brought on more or less correspondence between opposing commandery, and our Indians were strictly ordered to keep their fingers out of white men's hair, leaving it optional with them to take such mementoes from other Indians or let it alone.

At this time we were in the Department of Arkansas, first under Gen. [Theophilus Hunter] Holmes and next under Gen. [Thomas Carmichael] Hindman. We were then put into a department of our own, called the Indian Department, and under Gen. [William] Steele. Colonels Cooper and Watie were made Brigadier-Generals. Gen. Watie had the command of the First Indian Brigade, consisting of the First and Second Cherokee Regiments, commanded respectively by Colonels .T. M. Bell and W. P. Adair, Scales' Battalion, Major J. A. Scales and Quantrell's Battalion, the latter the most of the time on detached service in Missouri and Kansas.

The Second Indian Brigade, Gen. Cooper, was composed of two Choctaw regiments and the Chickasaw Battalion.

The Third Brigade consisted of First Creek Regiment, Col. D. N. McIntosh, and the Second Creek, Col. Chilly McIntosh, and the Seminole Regiment. Col. John Juniper, and commanded by Brig-Gen. Sam Checoti.

In the summer of 1862, I was sent out West to enlist for the Confederacy, and succeeded in raising one battalion of Osages, Major

Broke Arm, one large company of Caddoes and Arrapahoes, Capt. George Washington, and one company of Comanches, Capt. Esopah or Esc Habbe, their Chief. All of these reported to Gen. Watie and were of good service to us, as they rambled between Kansas and the Texas Panhandle and prevented any invasion from Kansas, which otherwise would undoubtedly have taken place. After the Pea Ridge fight, Gen. Price's Missourians and the Third Louisiana Regiment were ordered east of the Mississippi River, and we were left to ourselves, all Indians, except Wills' Battalion and a Texas infantry regiment, which were stationed at our depot of supplies and saw no fighting.

In the summer of 1862, Chief Ross and the Pin Regiment deserted to the Yankees. From that on we saw no rest, and hardly a week passed but what bushwhacking engagements between us and the Northern Indians and Yankees took place. Early in the spring of 1863 the military authorities in Kansas conceived the idea of returning the Northern refugee Cherokees to their homes in time to plant a crop. They had furnished them with horses, seeds and necessary agricultural implements, and they came escorted by Gen. Blount, commanding Kansas troops, and Col. Phillips, commanding the old Pin Regiment. But Gen. Watie did not propose to let them alone. We routed them from settlement to settlement and they, together with Col. Phillips Regiment, had to shut themselves up in Fort Gibson. We were quite beholden to the Yankees for the supplies thus furnished by them, which mostly fell into our hands.

John Ross.

[Confederate] Gen. Samuel Bell Maxey now took command of the Department. He was the Indians' idol. His free and easy manner suited them exactly; besides, he was a fighter and kept us moving. When Red River Banks [a nickname for Union Gen. Nathaniel Prentiss Banks] started on his expedition, which terminated at Mansfield, Federal Gen. Steele was to move out from Little Rock, and [Union] Gen. [John Milton] Thayer from Fort Smith, to join Banks in Texas. The greater part of our Indians were waiting for Thayer to come out from Fort Smith, but he concluded best not to show himself and he acted wisely, for our boys were spoiling for a fight. Part of the Indians commanded by

Gen. Maxey met Steele at Poison Springs, captured his train, and sent two Negro regiments to the happy hunting grounds. We followed Steele on his retreat to Saline River, where we fought in mud and water, belly deep to our horses, and felt very much relieved when Parsons' Brigade of Missourians, who had force-marched it from Mansfield, came up in double quick, and one of them called out: "Stand aside, you critter companies, and let us at them." Well, we critter companies stood aside, and Parsons' men went at them sure enough.

I must pass over numerous small engagements we had with the Northern Indians. They gave us the most trouble. Had we not had them to fight, we would have had a comparatively easy time of it. But they knew the country as well as we did and took advantage of that knowledge. Their losses, however exceeded ours.

Samuel B. Maxey, C.S.A.

Among our captures from the enemy, I will mention one steamboat loaded with dry-goods, near Webber's Falls, for Fort Gibson, and a train of about 200 wagons loaded principally with ready made clothing, on Cabin Creek, Cherokee Nation.

The last winter of the war, Gen. Maxey was ordered to Texas, Gen. [Douglas Hancock] Cooper took command of the Indian Department, and Gen. Watie of the Indian Division. This was the first time that we saw some rest for a little over a month, when we had gone into winter quarters near Red River in Choctaw Nation.

About a year previous to this, messengers had been sent to the Western and Northwestern Indians to meet us in Council at Walnut Springs. The object of this council was, first, to make peace between the different tribes. The next programme was for these tribes, thus united, to invade Kansas from the north and west, whilst we would meet them from the south, and leave but a greasy spot of Kansas. We had, during that winter, prepared a number of pack-saddles, as we would not be encumbered with a train. Unfortunately, Gen. Lee's surrender took place but a short time before the meeting of this Council. Hence, we thought best to confine the proceedings to peace-making between the Indians, and I have heard of no war between them from then until now. Tribes from Idaho, Dakota and Montana were present. It was, perhaps, the largest Indian Council that ever met.

The disbanding of the Indian troops took place in April, 1865. The Choctaws, Chickasaws, Creeks and Seminoles returned to their respective homes, which had not been desolated. With the Southern Cherokees it was different. Their houses had been burned, their stock  stolen and driven into Kansas. Many of them who, at the outbreak of the war, counted their stock of horses and cattle by the thousands, could barely raise a pony to go home on. Their country was now in possession of the Federals and Pins, and they were therefore compelled to remain as refuges in the Choctaw Nation and keep up a quasi military organization until after the meeting of the United States Commissioners and Southern Tribes of Indians at Fort Smith, in June, 1865, when peace was declared.

I have thus endeavored to give a mere outline of the campaign in the Indian Territory. But I cannot conclude this hasty and incomplete sketch with out words of praise to our Indian allies, especially the Cherokees, under their able leader, Stand Watie, and our Seminoles, under that good man and strict disciplinarian, Col. John Juniper.[220] — THOMAS F. ANDERSON

☛ FIRST EXPERIENCES IN BATTLE
On the morning of June 25, 1862, the twenty-fifth North Carolina Regiment left Richmond for the scene of action, all anxious to see a real live, wild Yankee. We had orders to report to [Confederate] Gen.

[Benjamin] Huger, who was stationed on a road leading to Richmond in the direction of what was then known as White Oak Swamps or Seven Pines. We passed the general headquarters before we knew it, and as soon as the mistake was discovered, our Colonel, Henry M. Rutledge, returned to report, leaving Lieut. Col. Samuel C. Bryson in charge, who moved the regiment some distance, halted and stacked arms. He had hardly broken ranks when a courier came dashing from the front with orders from Gen. [Ambrose Ransom] Wright, who commanded a Division composed principally of Georgians and Louisianians, to bring the first troops he found, and he unhesitatingly delivered the order to Col. Bryson, who ordered us to take arms and load. He then moved us down the road in the direction of a brisk rattle of musketry. We soon began to meet men with bloody heads, broken arms, and otherwise variously wounded, the sight of which caused some of us to feel shaky about the knees. Some of the boys, feeling encumbered, delayed not in divesting themselves of such things as a deck of cards,

Benjamin Huger, C.S.A.

which, upon being pitched out, would display all manner of faces and make a fellow feel like he had played the deuce. "Hurry up!" we hear from the front; "Double quick!" came from our leader; occasionally fizz, or zip! or "What was that?" Couriers and horsemen were darting in all directions; the very elements seemed filled with excitement. The order was to form line of battle on the left of the road, which was nicely done by right of company to the front. Soon we saw an officer come dashing through the pines, his long beard, parted in the middle, blowing back over his shoulders. He called out, "Where is the commander of this regiment?" "I am he," was the answer of Col. Bryson. "Move your men forward, Colonel," was the order given. Col. Bryson unsheathed his sabre, stepped to the front and gave the command, "Forward, boys!" When we had gone about one hundred yards we came to the edge of an old field, on the opposite side of which we could see the Yankees coming. Col. Bryson gave the command, "Steady! Front rank, kneel!

Aim! Fire!" A tremendous crash of musketry was heard for miles away. This was the only fire our regiment ever made by command.

We soon discovered the blue coats did not stand, but hastily disappeared. By this time Col. Rutledge had joined us. He deployed companies A and B, and sent us to the front to ascertain the enemy's position. We moved forward into a dense huckleberry thicket. Part of us got lost and were caught between two fires. We called it a hot time notwithstanding that we felt chilly and almost wished the war was over. We had been sent out to ascertain where the Yankees were, but we now thought it proper to find where our friends were, and with an improved double-quick got back to the regiment.

It was not long before the Yankees charged, but we held our ground. They made several attempts, but were as often beaten back. During one of our moves, Col. Bryson was walking backward in front of the regiment when his heel came in contact with a dead man; his legs misunderstood him and he fell sprawling. The Colonel thought himself killed, but on looking around and seeing a dead Yankee he got up, apparently satisfied. About this time a real Johnny Reb exclamation came from the ranks: "Look out, Colonel, how you fall; you might hit a rock or snag and get hurt."

Our Major was John W. Frances, a large fat man. He enjoyed being with the skirmishers and amused himself by firing his Colt's repeating rifle. It was enjoyable to hear him complain that he "believed the Yankees wanted to get him shot or they would have 'fit' in the woods where the trees growed bigger."

Late in the afternoon one of the enemy's batteries moved up and was shelling our men on the right. A detachment was sent out from our regiment to sharpshoot them, which caused them to bring their guns to bear upon us and we suffered considerably from their shell and grape. Finally, by the aid of an extra battery of our own, we succeeded in driving them off the field. When night came we were relieved, and rejoined our own (Ransom's) Brigade. On our way out we met the long bearded officer, Gen. Wright. He called for Col. Rutledge, who was on foot, wearing a roundabout jacket and carrying an Enfield rifle. His boyish appearance won the admiration of the General, who paid the highest compliment to him and his regiment for their day's service.

We had next a sad duty to perform for those who could no longer

be with the regiment. Part were placed upon stretchers and borne where they could be cared for, but sadder than this was the work of assigning others to their final resting place. Never do we hear rehearsed the "Burial of Sir John Moore" without thinking of that night, and hearing the distant guns that told of something to come on the morrow.[221] —
JAMES REESE

☛ A LITTLE SOUTHERN GIRL REMEMBERS HER GRANDFATHER

She was a tiny maid of three, but she sat upright on the cushioned seat of the well-filled passenger coach with a certain majesty and grace that pleased the more thoughtful travelers, who stopped now and then to hear her quaint, childish prattle. She was unconscious of any interest she had awakened, and told story after story of her home, dolls, playmates, and games to the lady with whom she was traveling. Then she grew confidential and climbed into her companion's lap, and this gave a place at their sides to the gentleman who wished to join them a moment later. The tiny bit of precious humanity noticed, in her quick, intelligent, sympathetic way, that an empty sleeve hung at the gentleman's right side, but she looked out of the window, apparently lost in thought.

Frank Gailor, C.S.A.

After a while she spoke, but her eyes seemed still to regard the passing scene: "My farver's farver was in the war, and one day, when they had a battle, he saw ever and ever and ever so many poor men, who had little chillun at home, killed wite there before his eyes; and they was bewied wite there, and nobody could tell their names, and their little chillun never could see them any more." She never seemed to see the empty sleeve, but the gentleman was conscious she had done so, and that the dear little mind had tenderly grasped the truth, that he was one of those who had been "in the war," and that his arm had been left with the unnamed dead on some battlefield—maybe the one where her "farver's farver" had fought. As he rose to leave the train he kissed the child, and the little one's companion saw a tear on his furrowed cheek.

The "farver's farver" [referred to by the little Southern girl, was her own grandfather] Major Frank Gailor . . . killed in battle at 29 years of age . . . [and considered] one of truest and bravest men whose deeds shed lustre on the fame of Memphis.[222] — SUMNER A. CUNNINGHAM

☞ IMPORTANCE OF HONORING OUR CONFEDERATE PAST
[Confederate veterans and their descendants live] . . . in obedience to the divine command: "Honor thy father and thy mother." Respect for the virtues of our progenitors is the surest road to that epitome of all virtues, self-respect, in itself the cause and the result of virtue. Our object can best be told in the words of the South's sweetest singer: It is to perpetuate "the story of the glory of the men who wore the gray."

Daily the beloved and revered forms of those who bravely bore their part in the South's great struggle are passing from our view to "rest under the shade of the trees" with Lee and Stonewall Jackson. With the characteristic modesty of true merit they die, for the most part, with their lips sealed as to the mighty deeds in which they bore their share. Too rarely have their pens preserved in lasting form the record of their swords. The story of their lives, replete with inspiration to nerve the hearts of generations yet unborn, is retained only in fragmentary form in the minds of their children. Material that would adorn forever the pages of history, of poetry and of romance is daily swallowed up in the grave. In so far as we can prevent it, this must no longer be.

The true historian must have a heart as well as a head. His heart must beat in unison with the feelings of the people whose history he traces: in sympathy he must be one of them. If this subtle unity of feeling be lacking, the labors of the historian degenerate into a mere dry-as-dust chronicle. The soul of history has fled, and only the dull facts, the mere corpse, remain.

The so-called histories used in our schools teem with misstatements as to the facts, and with false conclusions; while matters of opinion are stated as facts, and the youthful mind is perverted by being deprived of the opportunity of judging for itself. Hence we have acquired the habit of acquiescing in silence instead of meeting misrepresentation by prompt challenge and sturdy denial, backed by logical argument.[223] — JULIAN L. WELLS

☛ SOUTH-HATING IN CONNECTICUT, 1896

Robert E. Lee, C.S.A.

The Christian Advocate, connectional organ of the M. E. Church, South, tells how Rev. Mr. Twichell "Tore a passion to tatters" because some of the students of Yale College, New Haven, Conn., had [lovingly] planted a piece of ivy procured from the grave of Gen. Robert E. Lee. Rev. Newman Smyth endorsed . . . [Twichell's intolerant] protest in a speech.

The [pro-South] *Advocate* says: "They [Yankees] are slow to learn the lesson of charity. At a time when even a Republican [by 1896 a Conservative] National Convention has forgotten to say a word about the war, they are still seeking to tarnish the names of the great men who led the South, in the terrible times of our civil strife."

We [Southerners] speak with full knowledge of the facts when we say that there is no pulpit [that is, no Christian church] below the Ohio in which a minister would dare to assail the memory of Lincoln or Grant. The people simply would not tolerate it. The feeling among us is that every great American belongs to the whole country, and is entitled to be honored accordingly. And yet the South is reckoned [by many Northerners as] narrow and provincial!

As to Robert E. Lee, his fame is secure. The English speaking race has produced no loftier character. His father—the famous "Light-Horse Harry"—wrote of him while he was still a boy: "Robert was always good." From his youth to his venerable old age he was never guilty of speaking an unclean word nor of performing an ignoble deed. Modest, unpretentious, magnanimous, he is worthy to be linked in memory with that other lofty Virginian who led the Continental armies to victory.

In contrast to the above, the following brief [mean-spirited] note is given [by the Connecticut Yanks]: "It shows what the attitude of Tennessee is to the man who carried on the war against the South."[224] — SUMNER A. CUNNINGHAM

☛ NAVAL BATTLE ON MEXICAN COAST

Possibly one of the fiercest, yet sublimely beautiful, battles that was fought during the Confederate War was a naval engagement between four small crafts on the side of the Confederacy, and three large frigates of war on the Northern side, which occurred on the morning of April 4th, 1862, in the Mississippi Sound, full abreast of Biloxi.

The C.S.S. *Carondolet*,

The morning was very dark but clear, and the waters of the Gulf of Mexico were as calm and quiet as they were ever known to be; in fact, so pacific that the flashes of the great guns would glisten over their surface at a distance of eleven miles, like flashes of wicked, vivid lightning, while the roaring of the guns and ricocheting whiz of cannon balls awakened the inhabitants of the pretty towns of Pascagoula, Biloxi, Mississippi City, Pass Christian and Shieldsboro, or Bay St. Louis, as it is familiarly called.

In all lists of engagements of the war that the writer has yet seen, this one is omitted, and it seems that historians have never been made aware that such an one ever occurred. The vessels of the Confederacy that were engaged were the *Bienville*, *Carondolet*, *White Cloud* and *Arrow*, all from the Port of New Orleans; and they steamed out of Lake Pontchartrain, past Fort Pike, down the Rigolets and out into the Sound. This passage was made April 2nd, and on the 3rd the vessels were manned in the Bay of St. Louis by volunteers from the ranks of the Infantry that was scattered along the coast. These men received only a few hours drilling in heavy artillery, and only the naval officers aboard understood how to manipulate the big guns. The United States had the *Hartford*, *New London* and the famous historical *Kearsarge* on duty at the Ship Island, which was the Gulf Station of the United States Navy. This island is the largest of the group known as the Chandeleur Islands, which lay about fourteen miles south of the mainland of Mississippi.

Scattered along the coast, at the five little towns named above, was

[Confederate] Colonel John B. Deason's Third Regiment of Mississippi Infantry, which was deployed in two Companies at each point for the purpose of guarding the coast. All along near the Gulf shore and through these towns runs the New Orleans and Mobile Shell Road, and at each village long benches line either side of it, and these are shaded by large, fine magnolia trees. Of course, after the "Baby waker" [a large gun] sounded in this naval battle, all the soldiers left the camp and went close upon the sandy shores of the Gulf where they could see the fight and hear the roar of the cannon as they belched forth their fiery streaks in a sure enough combat. The long rows of benches were soon occupied by both soldiers and civilians. About half past 3 o'clock on this beautiful morning, these vessels lined up for battle began letting go the heavy broadsides, and from 4 o'clock until daylight the fusillade kept up incessantly. Very frequently to those on shore it seemed as if all seven vessels were bunched inside of ten acres of water, and their evolutions as the fight progressed could be outlined by the stream of blazes from the big guns, the sounds of which would seem to roll leisurely east and west clear along the coast.

The C.S.S. *Alabama* and the U.S.S. *Kearsarge*, June 19, 1864.

When daylight came on, the four Confederate vessels came into Pass Christian, where it was ascertained that all of them had been severely pierced with cannon balls and heavy shells, but the [C.S.S.] *White Cloud*, a big side-wheeler that had formerly been a passenger and freight steamer on the Mississippi River, was the worse splintered. The [C.S.S.] *Bienville*, *Carondolet* and *Arrow* were built with lower and upper works, and on the old "walking beam" pattern. Six men were killed and fourteen wounded on the Confederate side. The loss on the Federal side was greater, for the [U.S.S.] *New London* was sunk in about fifteen feet of water and was badly listed towards the course of Ship Island; and it was reported by men on oyster sloops that twelve men were killed on the Federal fleet while twenty-two were wounded. The [U.S.S.] *Hartford* and *Kearsarge* each received many wounds, but, so far as known, the Confederate authorities never got an authentic report of the killed or wounded on board of either. It is well remembered that the Federals never tried that little "Mosquito fleet" again, even if it was manned by the "very rawest" kind of material from the Confederate ranks. In point of beauty this engagement certainly was the finest of all that occurred, either on land or water, during the five years of the greatest war the world ever knew.[225] — TOM HALL

U.S.S. *Kearsarge.*

☛ STONEWALL JACKSON & FORREST

The growth of military fame in the great struggle of the Confederacy for independence gives renewed prominence, continually, to Stonewall Jackson and to Nathan Bedford Forrest. It is now prophesied by [confederate veterans] . . . that some artist will blend their likenesses and that they will be classed in history as the two most wonderful Commanders of men in battle that is of record to this time. Their achievements become more and more thrilling to the student of military annals.

Loyally obedient to their superiors in rank, ordinarily—when in the midst of battle, each acted as if Supreme Commander and it seems that each had the sagacity to discern the motions even of the opposing Commanders.

Jackson would spend much of the night in prayer and in reconnoitering, so that in the morning of battle, plans were already perfected and "Forward," or "By flank," were the orders without hesitation.

Stonewall Jackson, C.S.A.

Forrest, with perhaps less study of the situation, determined to "get there first"—and to kill or capture the enemy. Forrest was not as considerate of a Higher Power as Jackson during the war period. He was not a West Pointer, but he possessed that innate gallantry which was ever conspicuous in consideration for women and children. When the great war was over and all of his black hair was silvered, his heart, too, was subdued; and he was diligent in behalf of that higher order of manhood toward the Unseen Cause that had spared him through so many battles wherein horses, almost by the score, were killed under him, and many of his fellow men died in his presence.[226] — SUMNER A. CUNNINGHAM

☛ SKETCH OF GEN. OTHO FRENCH STRAHL

Otho French Strahl, a native of Ohio, had removed to the South and was practicing law at Dyersburg, Tenn., when the war of 1861-1865 began. He enlisted promptly in the Confederate Army, was soon promoted to the command of his Regiment, the Fourth Tennessee Infantry, and then to Brigadier General, holding that position when killed at [the Battle of] Franklin, Nov. 30, 1864.

Gen. Strahl was a model character, and it was said of him that in all the war he was never known to use language unsuited to the presence of ladies.

[I] . . . was a boy soldier in his Brigade—Forty-first Tennessee—and was so thrilled with his noble record on that last eventful day and night, when his gallant Commander gave his life for the Confederate cause, that he went on the sacred pilgrimage, a few years ago, to a Kansas ranch to see a sister, Mrs. Sigler, and tell her of his last hours.

There he . . . saw a memoranda and letters from the General's trunk. Mr. Sigler, although a Northwesterner, manifested much interest, and with pride produced the General's beautiful gray uniform coat, with its collar decorated in wreathed stars.

In reply to a remark of surprise that Gen. Strahl [born in the Midwest] should have been so zealous to his death for the Confederacy, his sister said that both of his grandmothers were Southern women.

The correspondence and further comment will be read with interest, especially by all who were familiar with the awful carnage at Franklin. Bishop Chas. Todd Quintard, who was Chaplain to the First Tennessee Infantry, and has ever been zealous in behalf of Southern people, writes: "I am glad to know that you have a photograph of Gen. Strahl, and pictures of the cotton gin and the Carter House. I have a table made from the wood of the cotton gin. The day on which the battle of Franklin was fought Gen. Strahl presented me a beautiful mare, named Lady Polk. His inspector, Lieutenant John Marsh, as he bade me adieu, threw his arms about me and gave me a farewell kiss. My intercourse with these two men was of a most sacred character. Marsh had been fearfully wounded at the battle of Chickamauga. I had watched over him on the field and in the hospital. On the 22nd of February I had baptized him in Gilmer Hospital near Marietta; and he was confirmed by Bishop Elliott, of Georgia, on the day following. To both I had broken that bread which came down from heaven. John Marsh was knit to me by the tenderest ties of friendship. There was in him what [3rd Earl of] Shaftsbury [Anthony Ashley-Cooper] calls the 'most natural beauty in the world,' honesty and moral truth—honesty that was firm and upright. 'He would not flatter Neptune for his trident, or Jove for his power to thunder.'

Otho F. Strahl, C.S.A.

"Gen. Strahl I baptized on the 20th of April, and I presented him for Confirmation to the Right Rev. Stephen Elliott. The following is from the report of Bishop Elliott: . . . 'The day of Strahl's death was to me a most pathetic one. He evidently felt that the approaching battle was to be his last—with many tender words he bade me farewell. I kept the mare he gave me through the war. Afterward I sold her and with the proceeds of the sale I erected a memorial window in St. James Church, Bolivar, to his dear memory and that of his Inspector, John Marsh. I need not say how sacred these memories are.'"

[I] . . . read the above with moistened eyes. It is a coincidence like special providence that these two faces, Strahl and Marsh, were indelibly impressed upon [me] in that awful charge at Franklin—[my] position being right guide to the Brigade, [I] was near Strahl in the fatal advance; and was pained at the extreme sadness in Strahl's face. He was surprised, too, that his General went in the battle on foot. Lieut. Marsh, who formerly belonged to the Artillery, and with a stiff arm from the battle of Chickamauga, always wore an artillery jacket—was on his white horse in advance of the line of battle up to within about three hundred yards of the breastworks. There was in his face an indescribable expression—while animated and rather playful, there was mingled in its heroic action evidence that he felt he was on the brink of eternity. But he wavered not and rode on and on until rider and horse lay dead before us, terribly mangled with bullets. How strange that these reminiscences come to the writer to be recorded for the entire Southland so many years after the event![227] — SUMNER A. CUNNINGHAM

☛ DEATH OF THREE CONFEDERATE HEROES

[Of the countless thousands of Confederate heroes, here are] three others who were [illegally] shot by the invaders. They are W. T. "Billy," Green, Tom Brown and Bill Davis, all soldiers, but dubbed "bushwhackers." They were captured three or four miles from Lynchburg, Tenn., and shot without the formality of even a "drum head" court-martial. They were a trio of the bravest martyrs that ever took up arms in defense of home. They were not shooting at the enemy, but were endeavoring to get away from them. Davis and Green were on one horse when captured. Davis was shot and Green had surrendered when a Federal officer came rushing up, exclaiming to his subordinate: "Shoot the damned bushwhacker. Why did you let him surrender?" Whereupon Green sprang like a young lion upon the Federal, wrenched his pistol from his grasp and shot him down, when the Federals literally riddled him with bullets. Davis and Brown died equally as brave, but without such desperate resistance.[228] — FELIX MOTLOW

☛ CAMPAIGNING UNDER DIFFICULTIES

One of the toughest sieges that any squad of skirmishers went through in the entire Civil War was that during the winter of '62 and '63, along Deer Creek Pass in Mississippi. The work was against the Federal gunboats, and the Confederates were compelled to remain in water from shoe to knee deep all of Christmas week, and for about two weeks on either side of it. One of the greatest vicissitudes was in finding room enough to lie down at night without being in water, and another was in getting food of any kind. For over five weeks the writer was on this skirmish line, and during most of this time subsisted on corn that was toasted on the cob as best it could be done at a fire surrounded entirely by water. It was very trying, and at times the soldier felt as if he would like for a friendly minie ball to stray along and take the top of his head off.

One sunny Sunday I remember well, when private Swazey came hurrying down the levee that we were lying behind watching for a Yankee head to pop up on a big gunboat, and, short of breath, exclaimed: "Say, boys, come go with me quick. There is a bear in that clump of trees; I saw it go in just now." The clump of trees he referred to was surrounded by water, and was the only land visible except the levee that we were on, but the water through which it was necessary to pass to reach it was not over waist deep, and four of us hurriedly went with Swazey. We soon reached the highland island, and then deployed so we could close in on bruin and be sure not to miss him. Slowly each of us crept into the thicket, and for a time all were sure that poor Swazey was mistaken in his vision, and finally we were about to give up in dispair, for by that time we had all hoped to get some kind of fresh meat, bear or no bear. While we were "guying" him on the subject, and at a moment when I was about to rise to resume my way back to my post of duty, my eye caught sight of a very small bear sure enough, then, quicker than a twinkle, my old trusted Enfield resounded the glad tidings to my comrades that bruin was ours. We quickly cut its throat, and in less than ten minutes had it swinging from a limb, skinning it. The animal was very poor, for, like ourselves,

it had had nothing to eat for many days. We were not to be bluffed at its condition, however, for as soon as it was skinned and quartered we were on our way back to line, anticipating what a good time we would soon have eating it. We had no way to cook it, however, and in order to eat it at all, we were compelled to cut in small slices and dry it over the fire. We managed to save a canteen of grease each, even as it was but had an awful job in doing it. These canteens of grease every man saved until after we were recalled to our regimental quarters, Jan. 6, 1863, at Snyder's Bluff, a few miles back of Vicksburg, on the Yazoo River. We carried them to Fort Pemberton, and from there to Chickasaw Bayou, where we went through a regular six day skirmish battle, and it was after this that we went into camp on Snyder's Bluff, where at last we got to mix our bear grease with meal and eat it. The battle of Chicksasaw Bayou was one of the hardest prolonged engagements of the war, and while our forces were on duty in water all the time, the Yankees got fresh men from off their transports every day, and all but their skirmishers were on board their boats at night. It was a terrible ordeal for us, and our men were carried out of the bog sick, in long lines every day, until our force was reduced to 284 sound soldiers—your correspondent was one of them—and was one of nine only in his regiment to answer roll call ready for duty on January 7th, 1863.

Union gunboat, circa 1863.

One thing that benefited the sharpshooters along Deer Creek Pass, however, was the target practice we got in shooting the sights off the big guns on the gunboats. Every sunny day we could see the brass shine a mile off, and whenever we were sure one could be "tripped" the crack of an Enfield would ring merrily over the water, and away would fly a valuable piece of Yankee property. Once in a while the top of a man's head would rise above the bulkhead and a body shot would be received by an unfortunate Yank that chanced to show up above what we called the "dead" line. Whenever we killed a man, the gunboats would line up and shell the surrounding territory, sometimes for an hour before ceasing; and while this was going on, we skirmishers would simply lie down behind the levee and often go to sleep under the music of the big Yankee guns. To have them waste all their valuable ammunition was "nuts" for us. In the entire five weeks that our squad was fighting gunboats only three of us were hurt, and they were caught by a big limb that a Yankee shell knocked off a tree.[229] — TOM HALL

☛ DARING DEEDS OF FORREST'S STAFF & ESCORT

Robert A. Hatcher, C.S.A.

[What was our most impetuous dash in battle?] My mind readily reverts to the final scene when we touted the enemy at Chickamauga, thirty-three years ago. On Sunday, September 20, 1863, Stewart's Division occupied the right of the left wing commanded by Gen. Longstreet. A staff officer informed Gen. Stewart that the whole of the left would attack exactly at five o'clock. The Federals in our front were covered by log breastworks; and, although we had been fighting desperately Friday and Saturday and until then, the old division, with Gens. Bate, Brown and Clayton in conjunction with our detached Gen. Bushrod Johnson commanding a division, responded as precipitately as if just entering the fray. They leaped the barricades, broke the Federal lines into confusion and soon got them muddled. Stewart's staff and escort, animated and flushed with the excitement of the dawning victory, led by Maj. Robert Anthony Hatcher, Adjt. General, the brigade staffs joining in, dashed into the Fourth Brigade of regulars, cut them half in two apparently, and in this way we were instrumental in capturing four or five hundred prisoners.

In the excitement a Federal officer shot at Lieut. Terry Cahal, but the pommel of his saddle bow caught it and saved him, and in the twinkling of an eye one of the escort brought his adversary down. Oh! the scene was of thrilling animation, impetuosity, and dash! Gen. Stewart had ordered Maj. J. W. Eldridge to bring up the reserved Eufaula Battery. I can hear Eldridge's stentorian voice now: "Bring up the Eufaula Battery! forward! double quick! march!" Here she came a tumbling and Darden's, in conjunction with Humphrey's and Dawson's Batteries, already in action, administered with effect farewell shots to a badly defeated foe. It was a vividly memorable occasion. The sun of Chickamauga was setting gloriously; the sable curtain of night was rolling down; "Hallelujah! 'tis done!" permeated the hearts of Bragg's Army, when that old Rebel yell seemed really to shake the earth, peal over the hill tops, ring through the gorges, and hasten the footsteps of [Union Gen.] Rosecrans' stampeded army. Then began the concentration of Generals at our point, and when hand shaking and congratulations were the order of the day. Gens. Longstreet, Stewart, McLaws, Buckner, Bushrod Johnson, Bate, Clayton, Brown, and others were present. I felt like thanking God— I did thank Him, not only for the glorious victory, but that I was spared the storm of shot and shell through the long, bloody battle.

Maj. Anderson, in rejoinder, after a moment's reflection, said: "I witnessed a most blood curdling venture at Paducah, Ky., in March, 1864. We had [Tyree Harris] Bell's and [Abraham] Buford's Brigades of Cavalry with us and had determined to try and take the city, let the boys get some good clothes and get back, knowing that we could not hold it. By Gen. Forrest's order, a few of the staff took nineteen of the escort and dashed through the city to the wharf. Two [Union] gunboats were there, the *Peosta* and the *Paw Paw*. The *Peosta* steamed down to get in range of our command, but the *Paw Paw* opened on our

Alexander P. Stewart, C.S.A.

William B. Bate, C.S.A.

squad with shot and shell. We took shelter behind and in the houses and peppered her deck, and penetrated her portholes until she set sail and steamed away, allowing us to burn ninety bales of cotton. While some of our men were engaged in destroying the cotton, the first thing we knew of being nearly cutoff was a peremptory order from Gen. Forrest to "Get out of there!" The Federals were coming in different directions and scattered our squad. One of the staff was cut off entirely and, on entering a street, his only hope was to charge two cavalrymen. Like Richard, he had set his life upon a cast and concluded that he would stand the hazard of the die [dice]. He did so, and, when at close quarters, one Sir Knight dropped from his horse, severely wounded. A hand to hand encounter followed with the other, who at last broke and ran. The officer followed at his heels and threw at him one empty pistol. Thinking the fire exhausted, the Yankee suddenly wheeled on the Rebel, who then fired the two reserved cartridges from his other navy [pistol], but with no apparent effect. The Yankee also emptied his pistol at the officer. They then drew sabers; the tug of war had fairly come, swords gleamed in the sunlight and, like trained gladiators, the death struggle between them began. The Yankee must have been a skilled swordsman; the Rebel was not, but somehow parried his blows, struck him in the side of the neck, dropped him in the middle of the street and got away."

After detailing this thrilling encounter, Maj. Anderson grew eloquent over the many hair-breadth escapes and startling adventures of *Gen. Forrest, who is believed to have been the greatest cavalry commander the world has ever known*; he had the dash of a Murat, the determination of a Combronne. He recurred to the scene the day after the Chickamauga battle, when Forrest fought his way to Missionary Ridge, climbed a tree and saw Chattanooga blocked with retreating soldiers, the streets impacted with wheels, the pontoon bridge broken, and everything a tumultuary mass. He directed his Adjutant to dispatch Gen. Bragg to let him go into Chattanooga, that "every hour lost was the loss of a thousand men." The army, however, was allowed to lay in torpor which was depressing. Had Forrest been permitted to make the dash Bragg's Army would doubtless have captured or annihilated the Army of the Cumberland.[230] — CHARLES W. ANDERSON

👉 A WISE LITTLE GIRL FROM NASHVILLE

In a seminary of this city a few years ago, a little girl [Mary L. Morris] came to her history teacher one morning and told her she didn't intend to study Mr. [Thomas Wentworth] Higginson's *History [of the United States]* any more, that she had burnt her book up, for "it made the Yankees win all the battles." The other little girls in the class who were daughters of old soldiers burned their books, too, and there was no history class. [The United Confederate Veterans] . . . heard of it and passed resolutions of approval, and the news papers throughout the South noticed it in the most complimentary manner. From Arkansas came a most flattering paper, signed with 500 names, telling these little girls that, innocently, they dared to take the first step toward writing a history that would do justice to the South.[231] — SUMNER A. CUNNINGHAM

👉 GALLANTRY OF A STAFF OFFICER

At the opening of the bloody battle of Franklin, Tenn., there occurred the most thrilling act of bravery I ever witnessed. I belonged to the famous "Whitworth Rifles" detachment of long range sharpshooters of Cheatham's grand old Division. This Division was the front one of Hood's army in the advance from Spring Hill to Franklin. Our position on the march was always in front of the Division, and we were thus the advance of our army. The Federals were tardy in their retreat when in a few miles of Franklin, but our detachment was commanded by that veteran master of skirmish line tactics, the hard-fighting Lieutenant John M. Ozanne, and, by tactics peculiar to our arm of the service, we maneuvered every Federal soldier into their works with but a single shot. We took position on Merrill's hill, a high, rocky, sparsely wooded elevation about twelve hundred yards south of the Carter house, and the line of battle commenced forming back at the Winstead hills, a mile or more to our rear.

Soon the Federal artillery began firing all along our front, throwing their shells high over our heads at the line of battle as it formed in our rear. As soon as possible we trained our guns on the Federal gunners, which we could then see through the embrasures in their second line of earthworks. After a while our skirmish line, composed of men about five or six yards apart, in single line, advanced to the attack. Over the ridge they came and down the slope of the hill they went into the level valley below, with step as proud and knightly as though they were princes of the whole earth.

Several hundred yards in advance of the foot of the hill was the first Federal line of earthworks running from the Columbia pike to the west and several hundred yards long. When the skirmish line passed our position on the north apex of the hill, I was forcibly struck with the very peculiar appearance of the officer in command. His eyes seemed strangely brilliant as the fire of battle blazed in them, his ruddy face seemed all aglow with intrepid valor, while a halo of martial glory seemed to surround him as down the slope he went, with horse at full speed, riding as gracefully and as chivalrously as a knight of old. Soon they had reached a position in easy rifle range of the Federal works, and I supposed the officer would halt and wait till the line of battle came up to reinforce him.

He did not do so, but took position in front of the line and at full speed dashed from one end of his line to the other, encouraging his men by his daring and dash. About this time I became convinced that he was going to charge the line of Federal works with his skirmish line, and although Federal shells and thousands of minie balls from sharpshooters all along their second line of earthworks were whizzing near me, I was so thrilled and entranced that I ceased firing and stood still in order to take in the whole of the impending

Joseph Vaulx, C.S.A.

tragedy. Instead of resisting the onset of the skirmish line, the Federals gave up their works without firing a shot and, seeing his advantage, the intrepid commander pressed his skirmish line forward in quick time and gained on the Federals, so that about the time the last of them scaled their works, the skirmish line got into the ditch in front. This saved the skirmish line from a withering fire which would have been given them but for the retreating Federals.

This officer was Major Joseph Vaulx, now of Nashville, who was on Major-General Frank Cheatham's staff. . . . Long may Major Vaulx live to wear in peace the knightly wreath he that day so gallantly snatched from the gory brow of grim visaged war.[232] — I. N. SHANNON

☛ SKETCH OF GEN. JOSEPH EGGLESTON JOHNSTON

Ardent admiration for that great military genius and Southern leader, Gen. Joseph E. Johnston, prompts this . . . [essay,] and to ask if any steps have been taken to raise a monument to his name and fame. Such would be the pride of his soldiers yet living, and a reminder to coming generations of the distinguished service of this truly great man in the cause of Southern independence.

Gen. Jos. E. Johnston was regarded by many of our ablest military critics as pre-eminently the greatest military genius and strategist the war produced on either side. In stating this, I do not wish to clip one sprig from the chaplet of fame of the immortal Lee and his great Lieutenants, Longstreet, Jackson, Gordon and others.

Joseph E. Johnston, C.S.A.

Gen. Jos. E. Johnston was prominent in several wars, and the ranking officer in the United States Army at the breaking out of the great war with the exception of Gen. [Winfield] Scott, and was regarded as a very genius in the art of war.

It was he who, at the early beginning of the struggle, when so much stress and importance was placed upon the holding of Harper's Ferry, told the Confederate officials that "Harper's Ferry was untenable when an opposing force commanded Maryland Heights." Stonewall Jackson's marvelous tactics afterwards, resulting in the capture of that stronghold with its garrison of 11,000 men, arms, munitions of war, etc., proved the correctness of his great foresight into military strategy.

It was Gen. Jos. E. Johnston who performed that first great military move on the chess board of war, in eluding [Union Gen. Robert]

Patterson in the valley and, by a masterly retreat, joining Gen. Beauregard in time to win the first great battle of the war—Manassas—defeating Gen. McDowell's plan of invasion, which is conceded by all military men to have been a great and most brilliantly conceived plan on the part of the Federal commander. Many of our military men thought, had not Gen. Johnston been wounded at Seven Pines, the battle of Malvern Hill would never have been fought and that useless slaughter would have been avoided; not that Gen. Lee failed in driving them back, but he was not acquainted with the topography of the country as well as Gen. Johnston, and did not know Gen. Johnston's plan of attack. Besides, at that

Victor Moreau.

time, the army did not have that unbounded confidence in Gen. Lee that he afterwards gained, and never lost. He had been unsuccessful in his early campaign in Western Virginia, and it has always been a question, would McClellan ever have retreated as safely as he did if Gen. Johnston had remained in command.

It was Gen. Johnston who advised against the fortifying and holding an army inactive, cooped up at Vicksburg, and foretold it would meet with the fate of the Austrian Army and Gen. [Karl] Mack [von Leiberich] at Ulm in that memorable campaign of the great Napoleon in 1805. And even after Gen. Grant's crossing of the Mississippi River below Vicksburg at Bruinsburg, the army might have been saved if Gen. Pemberton had not positively disobeyed Gen. Johnston's orders in not withdrawing the army from the trap and, uniting with his little nucleus of an army at Jackson, meeting Grant in open field.

Again, after this great disaster, the fall of Vicksburg and loss of the army, as predicted, Gen. Johnston was put at the head of the army in that memorable Atlanta campaign, which was so ably conducted, from the time of his falling back from Buzzard Roost to his supersedure by Hood at Atlanta, as to rank equal to, or surpass, [Victor] Moreau's celebrated retreat through the Black Forest. With less than 40,000 fighting men, Gen. Johnston confronted and baffled Gen. Sherman with over 100,000, and, although his enemies said he was too slow, too much of a Fabian policy, and he would not fight, had he been let alone he would eventually have whipped Sherman, as many think. With his small army it was certainly the part of a good general and military wisdom to make Sherman attack him in fortified positions (where he did not flank) and lose three or four to one.

Again, after that rash attack of Gen. Hood's and that most disastrous of any campaigns into Tennessee and the dreadful slaughter at Franklin, Gen. Johnston was again called to take the remains (a mere remnant) of that once grand army, now fleeing panic stricken, and confront Gen. Sherman, defeating him in his last battle at Averysboro, N.C., and, to crown his last acts, out-generaled Sherman in diplomacy by securing terms in the final surrender that the United States Government would not ratify, and Gen. Grant was sent to close the negotiations.

Napoleon I.

Gen. McClellan on one occasion was asked his opinion of Gen. Johnston, and he said: "Gen. Johnston could plan a campaign and fight a battle equal to the great Napoleon," and the writer heard a distinguished General of Sherman's Army say: "As soon as Gen. Sherman knew Hood was in command he said, 'I will whip that army. Atlanta is mine,' and changed his whole plan of tactics." It was a sad fact that Gen. Johnston was not in accord with our great chief, and Mr. Davis seemed prejudiced and kept him handicapped.

All I have herein stated is history and, while lengthy, it was necessary, and if it will be any incentive to active steps in raising a monument not only over Gen. Johnston's grave, but one grand and imposing structure, commensurate with the man and his eminent abilities, in the city of Richmond, in his beloved native Virginia that he so ably defended, I will feel my effort is not lost.²³³ — GEORGE F. ROZELL

☛ APPEAL FOR TRUE SOUTHERN HISTORY

It is a matter of transcendent importance that Southern children shall be taught the truth as it relates to Southern history from the earliest settlement of this country to the present time.

There has been, and is, culpable neglect of this vital subject by Southern parents and teachers. In consequence of this neglect, *Southern children have not only been kept in ignorance of the achievements of Southern men and women in literature, science, art, statesmanship and generalship, and, indeed, in every branch of human activity that has advanced civilization, but much of the literature and history taught in our public schools does the South injustice by omission of important facts, or wrong by the perversion of history.*

Think of the South—that section which, for the first sixty-four years of our national life, furnished the Presidents for fifty-two years, most of the Cabinet Officers, and the Chief Justices from 1801 to 1861—classed, as has been done by the *Encyclopedia Britannica*, as a semi-barbarous people saved only by Northern civilization! And *we make so few protests against these misrepresentations that the outside world has come to believe and repeat them, to our injury. The boys and girls of the South should be taught the true history of the South.*

The South has too long been indifferent to the character of the education that her children receive in the public schools.

Your committee earnestly recommends, therefore, that R. E. Lee Camp, No. 58, United Confederate Veterans, of Jacksonville, Fla., shall *make every proper effort to eliminate from the curriculum of our public schools every book that, by omission of essential facts, or by perversion and distortion of the truths of history, does injustice and wrong to the ancestors of Southern youths.*

And we cordially invite the co-operation of every camp of Confederate Veterans in this State, those of other States, and of all persons who are interested, that *justice shall be done to the people of every section of this great country.*

The report was unanimously adopted, it being: Resolved, That this report be published in the Jacksonville papers, and that the papers throughout the State be requested to copy it; that copies be sent to each United Confederate Veterans Camp in this State and to each member of the Historical Committee of the United Confederate Veterans, and to R. E. Lee Camp at Richmond, Va., and to the official organ of the United Confederate Veterans, published at Nashville, Tenn.

Resolved, also, That this Committee be continued and instructed to bring this matter before the next Legislature of this State.[234] — THE COMMITTEE ON ERRONEOUS SCHOOL HISTORIES, ROBERT E. LEE CAMP, UCV, JACKSONVILLE FLORIDA

☛ SOUTHERN MOTHERS

What a flood of memories come surging at the name "Southern Mothers!" And who were the Southern Mothers? Bands of devoted women who gave themselves wholly for love of their own cherished Southern country. Young and old—the gray haired matron, the young mother, and others to whom the sweet name of mother had never been lisped by baby lips—all alike enlisted under this sacred banner.

Their first work was making the uniforms in which to clothe their brave defenders. Day after day, week after week, these little hands of women met at different houses, and with nimble fingers, but saddened hearts, they fashioned the garments to make comfortable their soldier boys. Next came the nursing of the sick, for many of our men, unaccustomed to hardships of any kind, could not stand the severities of camp life, and were sent to the Southern Mothers to be nursed back to health or laid to rest in Elmwood. Then came the wounded to be cared for. After the battles of Belmont and Shiloh the wounded, both friend and foe, claimed and received the kind ministries of the Southern Mothers. When the tide of war had swept past our doors, and left so many of these Southern Mothers within the enemy's lines, they could only suffer and pray; for no one who did not pass through those fearful years can imagine the sorrow of friends left behind, longing as they did, for news from the front, with only uncertain rumors to relieve their fearful anxiety.

Ah, those days are numbered with the past, and where are the Southern Mothers? Nearly all have entered into rest, the few who remain—grandmothers now—with gray hair and faltering step, will soon join their sisters in a land of peace. To their daughters, they have a legacy to bequeath—The Confederate Memorial, a legacy of duty—to them we commit the sacred trust of keeping green the memory of the brave men and women who lived and suffered through those trying years. *The South has a history to preserve, a history which they are proud to give to the world, and the names of Davis, Lee, Jackson, the Johnstons, Polk and hosts of others, should never pass into oblivion, but be handed down from mother to daughter for the generations to come.*[235] — MRS. RALPH WORMELEY

CHAPTER 16

☛ HEROIC MISSISSIPPIANS AT LOOKOUT MOUNTAIN
When the "Yanks" advanced on us in three lines of battle, we had but one thin line and no reserve, as a good portion of the Brigade had been captured early in the morning while on picket duty by Lookout Creek, where the pickets had been carrying on a friendly exchange of papers, tobacco, coffee, etc.

Walthall's Brigade extended from the perpendicular cliffs near the top down the rugged mountainside, north, toward the Tennessee River; and as the ground was covered with large rocks, we were afforded fair protection, except from the artillery, which played on us incessantly from Moccasin Point across the river.

As the enemy would advance and drive us from one position, we would fall back a short distance, reform, get positions behind the rocks, and give it to them again. Many of our boys were captured that day on account of our line holding its position until the enemy were so near that it was almost certain death to run. This was one of the few times in battle that it took a braver man to run than it did to stand; because those who remained behind the rocks could surrender in safety, and those who ran would draw the fire of the heavy Yankee line. It was near the noted Craven House that our line was formed, when the blue coats crowded us, and came very close before our line gave way. Just as we started to fall back, the color bearer, who had bravely carried our regimental flag through many hot places, fell dead. One of the other boys, seeing this, turned back and grasped the colors, when he, too, went down, and fell across the former with the color staff under him. By this time the enemy was almost upon the flag, when a gallant youth from south Mississippi (I wish I could recall his name)—turned back and running to within a few steps of the enemy's line, seized the colors, breaking the staff off short, and ran after his regiment, waving the flag and hallooing at the top of his voice. It appeared that the entire Yankee line was shooting at him, but he soon regained his regiment and, with the short flag staff in his hand, mounted a large rock and waved it as high as he could reach, at the same time calling out that old saying so familiar to soldier boys: "Rally round the flag, boys," which they were very prompt to do. The boys loved that old flag better after that than ever before.

That night we were relieved by other troops, and the little handful of us that was left was moved down into the valley, and there, in the shadow of Lookout Mountain that dim moonlight night, that little short flag staff was stuck in the ground, and the boys crowded around it with saddened hearts and recounted the eventful and dangerous scenes of the day, some telling where Tom, Jack or Jim had fallen and others had surrendered. Many of them showed where minie balls had cut their hats, coats or blankets. The meeting at that flag was one never to be forgotten, and many of us joined hands around it and pledged that no "Yank" should ever lay hands on it without passing over our dead bodies, and they never did. Strong men unused to tears, although accustomed to the cruel scenes of war, cried like children.

The next day the colors were fastened to a hickory pole and were carried triumphantly until the crisis came, and then the little remnant that was left of the Twenty-seventh Mississippi followed that flag down the Mountain in perfect good order, while other regiments left the Ridge in disorder.[236] — J. W. SIMMONS

☛ THE LAST TIME I SAW GENERAL FORREST
It was at the battle of Dixie Station, or Ebenezer Church, in Alabama, April 1, 1865. The artillery, [John Watson] Morton's Battery, I think, occupied the big road leading from Montevallo to Selma, the Eighth Kentucky on the left and the Third Kentucky on the right of the battery. About forty or fifty of [Union Gen. James Harrison] Wilson's Command charged over the battery and attacked General Forrest and Staff a short distance in the rear of the guns. Forrest was cut across the face with a saber and his horse shot in several places so that he died that evening. Forrest stuck his saber through the man killing him upon the spot. When

the hand-to-hand contest was over Forrest rode up in the rear of our regiment, the blood dripping from his saber, and said: "Boys, I have bloodied this old blade again, and the first man that runs I will stick it through him." A private standing near me (regret that I have forgotten his name) turned upon the General and said with indignation: "General Forrest, I give you to understand that this is the Eighth Kentucky. We are not running stock." General Forrest made a most polite bow and said: "I beg your pardon, gentlemen. I did not know the regiment when I spoke." In a few minutes we were into it heavily, and, as Forrest fell back, about sixty of us were surrounded and captured on the field. The next day was the battle of Selma, the last battle of Forrest's Cavalry.[237] — REVEREND E. C. FAULKNER

Forrest equestrian monument.

☛ NORTHERN ATTACK, SOUTHERN RESPONSE
Elite, a society periodical of Chicago, contained an editorial recently under the caption "Time to Call Off 'Dixie,'" in which it argued: The song is sectional, and its tendency is to keep alive the lost cause. The "Star-spangled Banner," "Hail, Columbia," etc., are not sectional. Let us drop "Dixie" for good and set the bands to playing national airs. Why do Northern people, go out of their way to conciliate Southern folks? They always do. At the convention of Sons and Daughters of the American Revolution, if a delegate's name from Connecticut was called, it aroused no enthusiasm; but let a name from Georgia be announced, and the house immediately found its hands. These societies are pledged to treat the war of the rebellion as if it had never occurred, so their action cannot be explained on the ninety and nine who went not astray and the rejoicing over the one wanderer basis. By all means let all be cordial and kind, but let the bands stop playing "Dixie" and the people stop playing toady.

A Southern Woman's Answer to *Elite*: *True merit rarely goes without recognition. We, as Southern people, glory in this "tendency to keep alive the sentiment of the lost cause." Why not: Have we anything of which to be ashamed? True, defeat was ours, but it was brought about not through any lack of bravery, gallantry, or patriotism for what we believe to be right because of its being guaranteed by the Constitution of the United States. The record of Confederate soldiers is without a parallel in history, and, as time goes on, instead of being classed as traitors, their many gallant deeds and loyal hearts will be appreciated for their true worth, and their names go down in history as heroes true to every trust.*

Miss Birnie Cunningham, Confederate Maiden.

"Time to call off 'Dixie?'" No! "In Dixie's land, we'll take our stand. *We'll live and die by Dixie."*

It is not that we love the "Star-spangled Banner" less, but "Dixie" will always be absolutely sacred to Southern hearts. For around "Dixie" twine our fondest memories and dearest associations. "Dixie" went with our loved ones through all the perils of war, and in their darkest hours of strife "Dixie's" bright, sweet strain cheered the boys on.

Why, then, should we call off "Dixie"? Its strains are melodious and edifying. Rather call off "Marching through Georgia," which reminds one of naught save cruelty and ruin, and in whose bars there is no music.

Why is it that the lady of the South receives the recognition of any convention in which she participates? It is simply that a true Southern woman stands out in any company and shows by every word and deed her superiority. She realizes her true worth, and others are bound to recognize it. We agree that it is time to put a stop to "toadyism," but let the bands continue to play "Dixie," and may its strains continue to send a thrill of joy and pride to the heart of every true Southerner for generations to come![238] — "HALCYON"

☛ GEN. GRANT ON STONEWALL JACKSON, 1864

While our people [Union troops] were putting up the tents and making preparations for supper, Gen. Grant strolled over to a house near by, owned by a Mr. Chandler, and sat down on the porch. I accompanied him. In a few minutes a lady came to the door, and was surprised to find that the visitor was the general-in-chief. He was always particularly civil to ladies, and he rose to his feet at once, took off his hat, and made a courteous bow. She was ladylike and polite in her behavior, and she and the General soon became engaged in a pleasant talk. Her conversation was exceedingly entertaining. She said, among other things: "This house has witnessed some sad scenes. One of our greatest generals died here just a year ago: Gen. Jackson, Stonewall Jackson, of blessed memory."

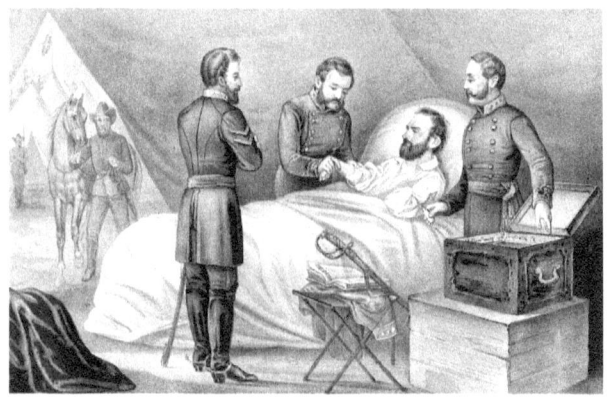

Death of Stonewall Jackson, May 10, 1863.

"Indeed?" remarked Gen. Grant. "He and I were at West Point together for a year, and we served in the same army in Mexico."

"Then you must have known how good and great he was," said the lady.

"O yes," replied the General. "He was a sterling, manly cadet, and enjoyed the respect of every one who knew him. He was always of a religious turn of mind and a plodding, hard-working student. His standing was at first very low in his class, but by his indomitable energy he managed to graduate quite high. He was a gallant soldier and a Christian gentleman, and I can understand fully the admiration your people have for him."[239] — UNION GEN. HORACE PORTER

☛ LEE & DAVIS
Robert F. Lee's name will be monumental, and will be placed by the side of the great captains of history; and as long as the fame of the Southern

struggle shall linger in tradition or in song will his memory be cherished by the descendants of the Southern race; while on the scroll of fame no name will shine with a purer, serener, or a more resplendent light than that of Robert F. Lee.

> No braver sword led braver band,
> Nor braver bled for a better land;
> Or better band had cause so grand,
> Or cause a chief like Lee.

Jefferson Davis lives in my memory as one who, dying without a nation or name, stands as grand a man as ever lived in the tide of times. Great in victory, but greater in defeat; great as described through the red haze of war, but greater as contemplated through the clear air of peace; great as a general, but greater as a man—behold him! a character which, if not perfect, conceals its imperfections by the effulgence of its virtues, even as the sun conceals the spots upon his dazzling disk.[240] — F. W. MERRIN

☛ FORREST'S RAID ON PADUCAH

It had long been the desire of the Third, Seventh, and Eighth Kentucky Regiments of Buford's Brigade, Loring's Division, to be horse soldiers, and various attempts had been made for a transfer, but not until March, 1864, did success crown our efforts. After retreating across the State of Mississippi to Demopolis, Ala., orders were received for those three regiments to report to Gen. N. B. Forrest.

We left Demopolis and marched to Gainesville, where orders were received from Gen. Forrest to halt and wait for horses. As soon as horses were provided we moved to Tibbe Station and joined the command. W. W. Faulkner's Regiment and Jesse Forrest's Battalion were brigaded with us, under command of Col. A. P. Thompson. We were here joined by Gen. Abe Buford, who was unwilling to separate from the Kentucky regiments, and had, at his request, been transferred to Forrest, and was given a division composed of the brigades of Thompson and Tyree Bell.

The march to Kentucky was begun as soon as the division was organized. Our horses were all old hacks, and so weak that for many days we walked fifteen minutes of every hour to give them a rest. When we reached Tennessee, where we could get rough forage, our horses improved so rapidly that we were enabled to make longer marches and ride all of the time. On the night of March 24 we camped eight miles from Mayfield, Ky., and on the morning of the 25th, after inspection, we moved on to Mayfield.

At Mayfield ten men of Company D, Third Kentucky, were detailed, under command of Lieut. Jarrett, to go in advance with Col. A. P. Thompson. Nothing of importance occurred until within three miles of Paducah, when Sergt. Rosencranz, who was two hundred yards in advance, beckoned us from the top of a hill to come on, firing his pistol at the same time at a squad of Federal cavalry coming up the other side of the hill. When we reached the top of the hill the Federals were out of

sight. We followed on to the fair grounds, where we halted and waited for the command. Gen. Buford coming up with the division, we moved into the town, capturing pickets as we advanced. A considerable squad was taken where we crossed Broadway. Thompson's Brigade was found between Broadway and Trimble Street, about one-half mile from the fort, where we sat on our horses and waited for the enemy, who we could see marching on the streets to get into the fort. The men clamored to be led against them while outside, but as the object of the raid was for medical supplies, and not for fight or prisoners, no movement was permitted until they were safely housed, when the Kentucky Brigade dismounted and moved on the fort, driving in and killing skirmishers as we advanced. While we moved on the fort and kept the enemy employed, [Union] Gen. [Don Carlos] Buell was ransacking the town for medical supplies and surgical instruments.

We moved in line of battle across the commons until the houses were reached, when the different regiments moved in column down the streets—the Third Kentucky on the south side of Trimble Street to the west side of the fort, the Seventh and Eighth Kentucky on our left to the north side, and Faulkner's Regiment and Forrest's Battalion on our right to the south side of the fort. Col. Thompson remained with the Third Kentucky, and when in about three hundred feet of the fort the head of the column was turned into an alley between Fifth and Sixth Streets, in the rear of Robert Crow's house. Col. Thompson had halted, and his horse stood across the street, his head to the south and his front feet in the street gutter. The Colonel held his cap in his right hand above his head when he was struck by a shell, which exploded as it struck him, literally tearing him to pieces and the saddle off his horse. Col. Thompson's flesh and blood fell on the men near him. I was within ten feet of him when he was struck, and my old gray Confederate hat was covered with his blood; a large piece of flesh fell on the shoulder of my file leader, John Stockdale. Although Col. Thompson was surrounded by his staff and couriers, only he was hit.

As soon as we got in position in the alley we opened with a volley. The top of the works was black with [Yankee] heads; our first volley cleared them. At the crack of our guns a cloud of dust arose from the top of the works. After the first volley we fired at will.

Col. Ed Crossland, of the Seventh Kentucky, upon whom the command of the brigade devolved after the death of Col. Thompson, came into the alley on foot, and had just ordered us to fall back behind Long's tobacco factory, one hundred and fifty yards distant, when he was struck in the right thigh by a rifle-ball. After we had fallen back Gen. Forrest sent in a demand for the surrender of the fort. On the enemy declining to surrender, we were ordered to advance in squads as sharpshooters and silence the guns. Lieut. Jarrett, with nine men, took a position protected by a frame cottage, and we held our corner down. Our gun was never loaded after we got in position until the enemy succeeded in bringing to bear on us a gun from some other part of the fort. The ball came through the house and I was knocked down. As I fell I heard Lieut. Jarrett order the squad to get out. I don't know how long I was down, but when I got up all were gone. I followed, and, finding a good position behind a coal pile, I lay down beside Capt. Crit Edwards, telling him that I was hurt. He examined me, and said: "You are not shot." It was a great relief to me to have the assurance that I was not hurt, for I was struck on the left jaw, and thought my jaw all gone. We did not again advance on the fort, but lay where we were until ordered to our horses.

Some of the men who were not satisfied took such positions as were most favorable for sharpshooting, to pick off the men in the fort. A number were in the second story of Long's brick stemmery. This building was being used by  the Federals as a hospital, and many sick were in the main part of the building. Our men were all in the L. The Federals shelled the building, killing some of their own men. One of our men, Ed Moss, Company D, Third Kentucky, was killed, and his remains were burned in the building on the morning of the 26th, when the Federals burned that end of the town. About sundown we fell back to our horses, and remained there in line until after nightfall. Company D, Third Kentucky, was from Paducah, and after the fighting was over we visited our homes. I found my father, mother, and children, with a number of the neighbors, in the cellar at home, where they were amply protected from shot and shell.

We bivouacked on the night of the 25th six miles from Paducah on the Mayfield road, and on the morning of the 26th the Kentucky Brigade was disbanded, to enable them to visit their homes, with orders to assemble at Mayfield April 1.

In accounts published in Northern papers it was said: "The Confederates charged the fort, and were repulsed with heavy loss." The facts are that we did not approach nearer than one square (about one hundred yards), and there never was an order or an intimation of an intention to charge the fort. The official report of Thompson's Brigade showed our loss to be thirteen killed and wounded, four of them from Company D, Third Kentucky. We had a battery of four mountain Howitzers, which was placed on the river bank and popped away at the gun-boats. It is doubtful if the balls reached halfway; but they made a noise, and it looked like fighting. One artilleryman was killed on Broadway while cutting down a telegraph pole. It was never our intention to attempt the capture of the fort; we accomplished all we aimed. We had entire possession of the town, and held it as long as suited us.[241] — J. V. GREIF

🖛 HEROES OF THE GREAT WAR

The magnificent pageantry of the grand funeral cortege that recently escorted the body of Gen. Grant to the tomb erected by a grateful nation and prepared by loving hands for his final resting place will take a prominent place in history. How the old warrior would have rejoiced could he have seen the soldiers who had followed and those who had so bravely opposed him in that four years' conflict moving together with silent, reverent step to do homage to his memory—the blue and the gray, true soldiers, brave men!

Did not the martial music and the booming cannon carry back the memories of those veterans to the days of Belmont, Donelson, Shiloh, Vicksburg, Chattanooga, the Wilderness, Cold Harbor, Spottsylvania, Petersburg, and Richmond?

Those who have never been soldiers in battle, who have never seen their opponents advance with their long lines dotted from flank to flank with waving standards, at first men dropping here and there, then, as they draw nearer, falling at every step, then the shout, the charge, the struggle, the carnage, sometimes victory, but sometimes also broken lines, repulse, and finally retreat, leaving a field strewn with wounded, dying, and dead—those who have never passed through such scenes cannot understand the feeling of brave men for those whose prowess they have felt and whose courage they have witnessed.

The armies which met in battle from 1861 to 1865 were mostly composed of the best people of our land. They offered their lives to their cause from the highest motives of patriotic devotion. The same spirit actuated them that moved their patriotic fathers in the Revolution of 1776.

Soldiers of such opposing armies are not enemies. The word enemy does not express the attitude such men hold toward each other. They met and fought with a courage and a determination without parallel in history, but it was not in a spirit of anger; it was in the fulfillment of duty. The courage, fortitude, and resolution of the combatants of both armies made it the most sanguinary and terrific war that had ever employed the arm of the soldier or engaged the pen of the historian; but as between the soldiers who fought each other so fiercely there was not, and never had been, and from the nature of things never could be, any of the despicable feeling known as hatred.

Such soldiers entertain no feelings of revenge or malice or bloodthirstiness. Their fathers had marched, fought, and triumphed under the same banner for more than a century. They had seen their country from one of the weakest become one of the most powerful on the face of the earth. They had seen our possessions and population expand from the Atlantic to the Pacific, and whether duty called upon them to enlist under the stars and stripes of the Union or under the stars and bars of the Confederacy, they felt the same pride in the glorious progress of American development and civilization.

Such men go beyond this. Not only do they feel no enmity, but it gives them pleasure to attest their admiration for chivalry and virtue wherever found, and they delight to do honor to brave opponents who have offered life and fortune in a struggle for principle, honor, and liberty. . . .

The published reports of the battles of the Wilderness and Spottsylvania, May 5-12, which might be properly classed as one battle, tell us that the Federal casualties were greater than the loss in killed and wounded in all the battles of our wars since our forefathers landed on these shores and laid the foundation upon which our government is based. . . .

At Shiloh the Confederate killed and wounded were one-third of the army. At Murfreesboro the killed and wounded of Rosecrans were twenty-one per cent, and Bragg's killed and wounded were twenty-eight per cent. At Chickamauga Bragg's killed and wounded were thirty-four per cent of his entire army, and Rosecrans' killed and wounded were sixteen per cent. . . .

When we seek for the causes of the great conflict of 1861-65 we must look beyond such incidents as the sympathy with the negro inflamed by *Uncle Tom's Cabin*; beyond the John Brown raid; beyond the Dred Scott Decision; beyond the Wilmot Proviso; beyond the Missouri Compromise; beyond the constitutional constructions and the questions of rights in the territories. *We must look back to the differences, dissensions, and controversies which existed between and*

Dred Scott and his wife Harriet.

divided our forefathers centuries ago.

The Puritans landed in Massachusetts, Connecticut, and other Northern colonies. The Huguenot, the Catholic, and the Cavalier settled in the colonies of the South. All brought with them their distinct views, passions, and prejudices, the outgrowth of dissimilar education and association. The colonies thus established were largely impressed with the characteristics of their founders. Two centuries did not obliterate the differences between these two classes of settlers, but in some localities only marked and intensified them. Antagonisms were softened by the trials of the seven years' struggle of the Revolution, again by the war of 1812, and still again by our triumphant campaign on the plains of Mexico; but the fruits of the Mexican conquest *gradually generated conditions fertile in elements of discord and distrust that finally developed into a struggle for supremacy and power.* Mistaken philanthropy and prejudice of the one against the institutions of the other, a sectional triumph in the national elections, bold threats of the infringement of constitutional rights, the conviction on the part of the Southern States that their only safety was in separation, and finally the organization of armies, both North and South, were events which transpired in such rapid succession that before the consequences could be realized the clash of arms was heard and men connected by the dearest social, marriage, and family ties were arrayed against one another in battle. . . .

Richard S. Ewell, C.S.A.

The leading actors in those stirring events have passed away. Grant, McClellan, Sherman, Sheridan, Thomas Meade, [John] Sedgwick, and [Henry Wager] Halleck of the one side, and Lee, Jackson, Bragg, the Johnstons, Beauregard, Hill, [James Patton] Anderson, and [Richard Stoddert] Ewell of the other, have crossed the dark river and await the coming of the war-worn veterans—their comrades.

May we not imagine that the brave heroes who rest under the shade of the trees meet each comrade as he joins the bivouac of the dead?[242] —
GEN. JOSEPH WHEELER

☛ MEMORIES OF GEN. NATHAN BEDFORD FORREST

If one should examine current history and biography to obtain a correct estimate of Gen. Forrest's life and character, only the bitterest disappointment would result. A central figure in the great martial drama of the war between the states, as can be plainly seen in the multitude of reports and dispatches penned during the contest by the leading commanders of both armies, he has been neglected in a marvelous degree since its close by the busy so-called historians and biographers, in accordance with their own peculiar views.

David C. Kelley (left), Forrest (right).

In some . . . volumes he is dismissed with slight mention; in others, as, for instance, a certain encyclopedia of American biography, he is pictured as an "illiterate cutthroat and butcher." And even in a leading school history, printed in the South and used in most of the educational institutions in this community, we find in the whole book only this historical tribute to the man whom Gen. Sheridan pronounced one of the most remarkable produced by the war on either side: "N. B. Forrest and John Morgan—famous for their raids in the West." And this the man whom Lord [Garnet Joseph] Wolseley, the commander of the British Army, thought worthy the careful study of great soldiers, and to whose military career and skill he paid, in a long analytical article, a glowing tribute.

Only in a little volume entitled, *Campaigns of Forrest and Forrest's Cavalry*, published in 1867, by Gen. Thomas Jordan and J. P. Pryor, is there a fairly correct statement of Forrest's military career; and this book was written by gentlemen entirely capable, but who were not eyewitnesses of the great cavalry leader's achievements, and therefore loses greatly in graphic detail and description.

I therefore feel it to be a sacred duty of those who are familiar with any part of his career to contribute while still living their mites to rescue the story of this remarkable man from oblivion. The late lamented Maj. [Gilbert Vincent] Rambaut, of Forrest's Staff, had undertaken this task for the Confederate Historical Association, of Memphis, but was cut off after his second article by an untimely death—a mishap greatly to be deplored, as he was an accomplished and accurate writer and a companion of the noted general throughout the war.

But to revert to my subject. Few people except advanced in life and who had met Forrest before his death, which occurred nearly twenty years ago, have a correct idea of his personal appearance and distinguished presence; and of these few, only those who have seen him in battle have any adequate conception of the heroic mold and fiery energy of this equestrian son of Mars. Tall beyond his fellows, of herculean build, broad shoulders surmounted by a massive head,

Gideon J. Pillow, C.S.A.

dark gray hair, keen gray eyes, which blazed when lighted with the fire of battle, he was instantly recognized, even by strangers, as the commander of his army, and was as well known by sight to Federal as to Confederate soldiers. His face was peculiarly intellectual and his features strongly marked, the expanding nostrils and massive jaw indicating impetuous energy and of overwhelming will power.

In the company of other distinguished officers he showed to the greatest advantage. Grave, dignified, unobtrusive, he was ever alert, and, when his opinion was asked, the lightning was not quicker. His ideas were tersely, lucidly, and briefly delivered, and he at once relapsed into silence. He never resorted to argument. His manner, while respectful, was almost imperious at such moments. The incident at Fort Donelson is richly illustrative of the character of the man under such circumstances. He, then a colonel of cavalry, being called upon by the council of war for an opinion, pointed out that it was the duty of the three generals to withdraw their commands by a road which he indicated, instead of surrendering them to the enemy; and, his advice being rejected, he curtly told them that he would rather that the bones of his men should bleach on the hills than to surrender them. He strode from the room to withdraw his command from the fort by the route indicated, which he successfully accomplished without losing a man.

But to the rank and file Forrest was a delight. He was absolutely approachable at all times to the humblest soldier. When not absorbed in thought or engaged in combat he indulged constantly in playful familiarity and exchange of badinage with his men, as did also the great Napoleon. No general officer ever dreamed of taking liberties with his hair-trigger temper. No private soldier in his ranks ever hesitated for an instant to jest him about any trivial matter or to guy him about his personal appearance or unusual actions, even in battle.

On one occasion, at Richland Creek, Tenn., when the enemy's artillery was hurling shells like handfuls of marbles about us, the General coolly dismounted and stepped behind the only tree in the vicinity, a movement which all of us longed to make, but dared not in his presence. One of the men said to him: "Come out from behind that tree, General. That isn't fair; we haven't got trees." "No, but you only wish you had," laughingly replied Forrest. "You only want me out to get my place."

On another occasion, at Mount Carmel, Gen. Forrest dismounted under a hot fire of musketry, and sat down on a rock, an example which was quickly followed by the writer, who was attending him, and who took care to get down on the opposite side of his horse from the enemy. The General, who had begun feeding his warhorse, "King Philip," with some blades of fodder he found there, turned, and, observing my point of vantage, playfully said, "You had better get on the other side of that horse, bud, and stop the bullets. Horses are lots scarcer than men out here"—a suggestion, by the way, that was not followed.

But there were two liberties which no one, private or general, ever attempted to take with Forrest. One was to disobey his orders, and the other to abandon the field in the presence of the enemy. Either of these breaches of soldierly conduct instantly brought down upon the offender a wrath that was truly frightful. On one occasion he seized a piece of brushwood and thrashed an officer whom he detected running away from the field almost to the point of taking his life.

Col. David C. Kelley, major of his first regiment, wrote: "The command found that it was his single will, impervious to argument, appeal, or threat, which was ever to be the governing impulse in their movements. Everything necessary to supply their wants, to make them comfortable, he was quick to do, save to change his plans, to which everything had to bend. New men naturally grumbled and were dissatisfied in the execution, but when the work was achieved they were soon reconciled by the pride they felt in the achievement."

Gen. Forrest always exhibited the profoundest regard for religion. Col. Kelley, then and still a preacher, relates that Gen. (then colonel) Forrest and himself were intimately associated in camp for the first year or more of the war, tenting together, during which time Col. Kelley continued his lifelong habit of holding morning and evening prayers. These services Gen. Forrest always reverently attended, though not at the time a member of any Church. However, he became a very devout member of the Cumberland Presbyterian Church some years after the war.

Forrest's staff.

After returning from his successful expedition into West Tennessee, in May, 1864, he immediately issued the following most unusual General Order No. 44:

> Headquarters Forrest's Cavalry Department, Tupelo, May 14, 1864. The major-general commanding, devoutly grateful to the providence of Almighty God, so signally vouchsafed to his command during the recent campaign in West Tennessee, and deeply penetrated with a sense of our dependence upon the mercy of God in the present crisis of our beloved country, requests that military duties be so far suspended that divine service may be attended at 10 a.m. on to-morrow by the whole command. Divine service will be held at these headquarters, to which all soldiers who are disposed to do so are kindly invited. Come one, come all. Chaplains in the ministrations of the gospel are

requested to remember our personal preservation with thanksgiving, and especially to beseech the throne of God for aid in this our country's hour of need. By order of Maj.-Gen. Forrest. Warren H. Brand, Acting Assistant Adj.-Gen.

To ladies Forrest was instinctively knightly and deferential. A man of singular purity of life and absolutely temperate, he held woman in the highest regard, and lavished a degree of affection upon his devoted wife altogether unusual in a man of his fiery temperament. Only under peculiar circumstances did he seem to become oblivious of the presence of ladies, and that was during those fits of intense absorption in thought into which he so often lapsed when working out the great military problems which engaged his attention. On these occasions his staff discreetly withdrew to a distance and left him undisturbed. As soon as he had arranged matters in his mind he would rejoin his staff and at once proceed to chaff them in a vein of pleasantry. Once, while thus absorbed on a railroad car, as related by Maj. Rambaut, a lady, against the protest of the staff, insisted on going back and interviewing him. In a moment the stately dame returned in a towering rage, declaring that the General was not a man, but a bear. A few moments later he came forward, and with deft politeness not only pacified, but captivated the offended matron. Presently, struck by a peculiarity of his appearance, she suddenly asked: "General, why is it that your hair is so much grayer than your beard?" As if with some faint recollection of his recent misbehavior, he quaintly replied: "I don't know, madam, unless it be that my mouth is always shut when my head is working."

On another occasion, as related by the venerable Mrs. John McGavock [Caroline "Carrie" née Winder], of Franklin, during the storm of the great battle there, Gen. Forrest rode rapidly up to her door, where she had gone to meet him, and, without so much as seeming to notice that she was there, strode by her into the hall, up the stairway, and out on the balcony, where he gazed intently through his glass for ten minutes at the enemy's position, and then returned in the same way to his horse, without paying the slightest attention to her presence, and rode rapidly away.

But another incident, related by Col. D. C. Kelley, vividly exhibits Gen. Forrest in another mood. When campaigning with his regiment in the vicinity of Fort Donelson the men captured some Federals who were known as bushwhackers by our men, as they operated in the country where they enlisted. The wife of one of these prisoners, seeing her husband in captivity, rushed out to where Col. Forrest was standing and, falling on her knees, appealed to him for his release. Col. Kelley witnessed this incident from a distance, and, observing the woman spring from the ground and clap her hands, questioned Col. Forrest about the unusual scene when he came up. The Colonel replied with rather unsteady voice: "They can have their husbands if I've got them—that is, if they will make them behave."

Forrest's signature.

When in camp Forrest's restless mind was ever busy with the details of organization. Nothing escaped his attention, and no one, since the days of Napoleon, could more quickly equip an army or form a powerful military force out of raw recruits. In speaking of this marvelous power of organizing his raw West Tennessee volunteers later in the war, Gen. Thomas Jordan says: "In that short time (sixty days) he had been able to imbue them with his ardent, indomitable spirit and mold them into the most formidable instruments in his hands for his manner of making war."

Another characteristic of the man was his boundless fertility of resource when in close places. On one occasion, on crossing the Tennessee River, he found himself in a rough, rocky country, with unshod horses. At once he was at a standstill, for the horses could not march on the sharp rocks, and there was no material with which to make shoes. Encamping for the night, he at once sent details throughout the country to bring in all the old wagon and buggy tires that could be found at the farmhouses and barns around. Putting his smiths to work with this material, by morning he had all his horses splendidly shod and resumed the march without delay.

On another occasion, when on his rapid march of one hundred miles to attack Memphis, in August, 1864, he learned, when nearing Coldwater River, that the stream was out of its banks and that no bridge or ferry existed. Without apparent hesitation details were made, with instructions to scatter through the country, take up the heavy plank floors of the ginhouses, and meet him at the river with the planks, which the troopers carried on their horses. He then hurried forward with some axmen, felled the telegraph poles near by and the large trees on the river bank, and, rolling the logs in the stream, secured them with such ropes as he had, supplemented with grapevines, and, laying the planks first as stringers and then across, soon had a substantial floating bridge ready, over which his command marched with scarcely a halt when they arrived.

In battle Forrest was the very genius of war. Habitually riding a large gray horse, "King Philip," of great spirit, his towering form was seen everywhere on the field. At the investment of Murfreesboro, in December, 1864, it was the writer's fortune to witness one of those characteristic but unconscious displays of martial heroism by Gen. Forrest of surpassing grandeur. He had posted a division of infantry to meet a daring sortie of the Federal garrison, and, taking a cavalry brigade, had sought the enemy's rear. Learning that the infantry had given way, he came bounding back on his grand horse, and, pausing a moment, rose in his stirrups to survey the scene. Then, throwing off his military cape, his saber flashed in the air, and, seizing a flag, he plunged, with blazing eyes, into the mass of fleeing men, right under the awful fire of the enemy's guns, staying the stampede by sheer force of will power, and rider and horse presenting a picture in the terrible tragedy [that was] . . . worth all the perils of the battle to have witnessed.

In war he was always aggressive, never waiting to receive an attack, but, after a rapid personal reconnaissance, invariably hurling his whole command on the enemy. He seemed at all times imbued with "that fierce fever of the steel, the guilty madness warriors feel," even to the point of unreasoning rashness. But there was method in his madness, and no charge was ever made by Forrest that was not justified by the outcome.

It is stated that he was one hundred and seventy-nine times personally under fire in his four years of service, and it was rare that he suffered a check, never a defeat. His constant successes against almost incredible odds inspired his men with unbounded confidence in him, and he was thus enabled to hurl his unquestioning brigades like thunderbolts upon his less active enemy, and always with disastrous results to the latter. Nor was this all. Without training, but by instinct a very master of the art of war, he was quick to see an enemy's vulnerable point, and concentrating with marvelous rapidity would strike the deadly blow before his opponent could correct the mistake. Brice's Cross Roads, or Guntown, was a type of one of his battles. Having but three thousand and two hundred cavalry, and his enemy, [Samuel Davis] Sturgis, moving on the rich stores of grain about Tupelo with eight thousand and three hundred men, of which five thousand were infantry, Forrest, who was watching on the flank, observed that Sturgis' Army was marching in a straggling column of eight or ten miles in length along a narrow, muddy

road, and impeded with enormous wagon trains. Quickly conceiving his plan of action, Forrest galloped his command to the head of the Federal column, and, concentrating in front of the enemy's first brigade, a cavalry force about fifteen hundred strong, by a common impulsion threw his whole command upon it and crushed it before help arrived. Attacking in turn the succeeding brigades of cavalry and infantry as they arrived and took position—the latter so exhausted by a double-quick march for miles in the mud under a hot June sun that they could not at once begin the fight—they were successively crushed, and by 3 p.m., after five hours' fighting, the whole mighty host of Sturgis was a defeated and flying rabble, run down and captured by hundreds as they scattered. So great was the terror inspired by the furious energy of their pursuer that the Federal commanders report that the flying fragment of infantry covered the entire distance to Collierville, Tenn., ninety miles, in a little over forty hours, leaving all their trains and artillery and more than one-third of their force dead, wounded, or captured, in Forrest's hands. *No such annihilating overthrow overtook any other command of either army during the war.*

But it is not my purpose to describe Forrest's battles in detail, and

I will present only a brief synopsis of his military career. Gen. Forrest joined the Confederate army June 14, 1861, at Memphis, as a private soldier in Capt. Josiah White's Tennessee Mounted Rifles, afterwards Company D, Seventh Tennessee Cavalry. His career as a private soldier was uneventful for about a month, but was rendered notable among his comrades by his constant and lucid criticism of the current military movements of the great armies. Having been authorized, in July, 1861, by Gov. [Isham Green] Harris, of Tennessee, to raise a command, he at once went to work, and by October had, with characteristic energy, raised a battalion, and soon after a regiment, of which he was elected colonel.

With this regiment of dare-devils he soon became famous, and at Fort Donelson, Shiloh, and Murfreesboro, where he earned his promotion, he gained a distinction never before enjoyed by an American cavalry commander. As a brigadier-general, he rose rapidly in public esteem, gaining great distinction at Chickamauga, and, during the [Able Delos] Streight raid, capturing that daring Federal commander and eighteen hundred men with less than three hundred of his own troopers.

But it was in his characteristic operations in Tennessee, on the enemy's lines of communication—destroying railroads, capturing blockhouses and garrisons, with thousands of prisoners and hundreds of wagons, teams, etc.—that he became the terror of the Federal generals. "If I could only match him," wrote Gen. Sherman, "with a man of equal energy and sagacity, all my troubles would end."

However, it was only when Forrest was given a cavalry department with the rank of major-general, his district embracing North Mississippi and West Tennessee, that he attained the utmost splendor of his renown. Here he was made guardian of the granary of the Confederacy, the rich prairie lands of Eastern Mississippi and Central Alabama. Having a domain without troops, he rode straightway with a small force through the enveloping Federal lines into West Tennessee, and, collecting several thousand hardy young volunteers, mostly well-grown boys, he mustered them in a few weeks into that famous band which, with some veteran troops collected together, is now known to history as Forrest's Cavalry.

The Federal commander at Memphis, [Stephen Augustus] Hurlbut, who had thousands of men guarding the railroad from Memphis to Corinth, was superseded by [Union] Gen. [Cadwallader Colden]

Washburn because of his failure to prevent Forrest's movement into and return from West Tennessee with his recruits and supplies. In February Gen. Washburn sent Gen. William Sooy Smith, with a powerful force of seven thousand men, to find Forrest and punish him for his impertinence, and, incidentally, to destroy the great grain stores about Okolona. Forrest fell upon him with his new recruits, about three thousand strong, at Okolona and Prairie Mound, and utterly routed his great host, driving it back to Memphis. In return Gen. Forrest rode again into West Tennessee, penetrating to the Ohio River and capturing Fort Pillow, Union City, and other points, with their garrisons.

After his return, in June, Gen. Sturgis, with eighty-five hundred men, marched against the grain fields in Eastern Mississippi, and at Brice's Cross Roads, or Guntown, was fallen upon by Forrest and annihilated, losing more than one-third of his force with all his artillery and equipage.

Sturgis was followed in turn by [Union] Gen. Andrew J. Smith, with fourteen thousand men, who, after a terrible battle with Forrest at Harrisburg, near Tupelo, July 14, returned hastily to Memphis. Enraged by his defeat, Gen. Smith reorganized at Memphis and started again, in August, by way of Oxford, with a powerful army. Forrest, with his exhausted command, was unable to check this army by force, and resorted to strategy. Leaving half his force under Gen. [James Ronald] Chalmers in front of Smith at Oxford, he rode with the remainder, less than two thousand men, by way of Panola—one hundred miles, in less than sixty hours—to Memphis, capturing the city, and almost capturing Gen. Washburn, getting his uniform, hat, boots, and papers in the residence, No. 104 Union Street, the doughty General escaping down an alley in his night clothes. This caused Gen. Hurlbut to remark, as related by Gen. Chalmers: "There it goes again. They removed me because I could not keep Forrest out of West Tennessee, while Washburn can't keep him out of his bedroom."

James R. Chalmers, C.S.A.

The movement, however, as Gen. Forrest anticipated, resulted in the rapid retreat of Gen. Smith again to Memphis. Then for a period Forrest, gathering his forces, roamed at will over Middle Tennessee, destroying the Federal railroad lines and trains and capturing garrisons; and, though finally enveloped by thousands of the enemy, escaping across the Tennessee River with rich spoil. Then, riding leisurely down the west brink of that stream to Johnsonville, more than one hundred miles, he destroyed the enemy's great depot of supplies there, with more than six million dollars' worth of property and their gunboat fleet—"a feat of arms," wrote Gen. Sherman, "which I must confess excited my admiration."

Hood leading his men through a burning woods.

Next followed perhaps the grandest achievement of Forrest's military career. Gen. Hood had moved on Nashville, fighting his way to the Tennessee capital, with Forrest in advance, and had rashly risked a battle with a foe outnumbering him two and one-half to one, and been defeated, his army, for the first time in its history was routed and disorganized. Halting at Columbia, he sent for Gen. Forrest and appointed him commander of his little, hastily formed rear guard. There were two thousand infantry, picked men, and fifteen hundred cavalry, but every man was a hero. With these Forrest calmly undertook to hold in check the victorious Federal army of nearly seventy thousand men, and so he did. Backward, step by step, from Columbia to the Tennessee River, for eight days and nights, did Forrest and his Spartan band hold back the eager enemy, while Hood's routed columns gathered at and crossed over the river.

In vain did the great blue masses essay to break over this slender barrier and get at Hood, by crushing whom they could speedily end the war in the West. Forrest's mailed hand was everywhere, and struck sturdy, deadly blows, which paralyzed every effort of their advance guard to break through his lines. The weather was bitter cold and the sleet came down, while the roads were streams of freezing water; but the ragged, barefoot heroes and their grand leader never faltered. The enemy were delayed until Hood's last men and wagons were across the river, and finally the little rear guard, cut and slashed and weather-beaten, crossed at midnight with their indomitable leader, to rest in safety beyond. *This masterly achievement has only its parallel in the heroic [Michel] Ney, who covered Napoleon's beaten columns in the retreat from Russia.*

Such was the great leader whom Memphis gave to the Confederate army.

And now one word about duty. Out in beautiful Elmwood, with only a plain circlet of marble to mark the spot, sleep the remains of this great soldier. No marble shaft there points to heaven, with scroll or tablet to tell the passer-by: "Here rests a hero." Only a sprig of oak carved on the circle tells of his fame. Thoughtless thousands, in whose interest and for whose benefit his mighty deeds were done, pass daily to and fro about this city without giving a thought to his history or a tribute to his fame. O shame upon our people! If we cannot, like the appreciative Roman populace, bring his statue to stand in our beautiful square, I urge that at least in the great Battle Abbey about to be erected, Memphis build into the wall a tablet that will rescue from oblivion the name and fame of *the greatest cavalry leader perhaps that the world has ever seen.*[243] — J. P. YOUNG

☛ CHRIST IN THE CONFEDERATE ARMY

On the threshold of [our Confederate reunion] . . . it has occurred to me that it would not be inappropriate to express not only our admiration for the patriotism of these men, but our appreciation of the Christian faith and fortitude which thousands of them so nobly illustrated amid all the temptations, privations, and perils of the protracted struggle through which they passed.

We will neither deify nor canonize our dead comrades, but simply commemorate with grateful hearts and reverent spirits their manly deeds and resplendent virtues. We should honor them not only because they deserve it, but for the ennobling effects of it upon ourselves and our posterity.

My countrymen, we can do more than bury our fallen heroes. We can praise them and claim for them the homage and admiration of the world. We can make annual pilgrimages to their graves and cover with earth's loveliest and sweetest flowers the sod beneath which their ashes sleep. We can record their names on towering monuments of imperishable stone, and celebrate their valorous deeds in the rapturous effusions of immortal song.

Confederate Battle Flag with star-filled St. Andrew's Cross.

I am sometimes confronted by a cold-hearted, self-seeking, mammon-worshiping man who wants to know what good will come to us from keeping alive such sentiments. He wants to know how much these reunions of the veterans at the North and veterans at the South, and these memorial orations, sermons, and songs, and this multiplication of monuments will advance the material interests of the country. He wants to know how many debts they will pay, how many factories and railroads they will build, and how much new capital they will bring to our cities and towns. My reply is that *the poorest, weakest, and meanest country on God's footstool is the country without sentiment. A nation without sentiment is a nation without character, without virtue, without power, without aspiration, and without self-respect.*

Patriotism, in its last analysis, is the love of one spot or section of earth more than any other. The late Gov. [John] Winthrop, of Massachusetts, in one of the greatest orations of his life, said: "I am a New Englander, and I am bound by the strongest ties of affection and blood to assert and vindicate here and elsewhere the just renown of New England's sons." You may call that sectionalism, but I call it patriotism. *All honor to the man who, while he upholds his nation's flag and stands ready to shed his heart's blood in defer every inch of her soil, loves his own section of that nation more than any other section, his own state more than any other state, his own neighborhood more than any other neighborhood, and his own home more than any other home. That sentiment deserves and will receive die unqualified endorsement of every truly patriotic mind.*

This is not the occasion to discuss the issues upon which the two great sections of this country went to war with each other. It is enough to say that the people of both sections believed they were right, and from the beginning to the end of the struggle fought for what they believed to be the best interest of their country. They submitted their differences to the arbitrament of war. The decision of that tribunal has been rendered, and every honorable and patriotic citizen of the republic on either side of Mason's and Dixon's line will stand by and uphold it to the last extremity. . . .

I have it directly from the lips of the man who was the instrument which God honored more than any other in that glorious work that there were more than fifteen thousand conversions in the Army of Northern Virginia. These wonderful displays of divine grace among the soldiers of the South were not confined to the army commanded by Robert F. Lee. Revivals attended the faithful preaching of the gospel in almost every regiment that fought under Bragg and Breckinridge and Kirby Smith. Thousands of brave men in these armies who had publicly professed Christ proved by their meekness and patience in suffering, and by their joy in death, that their professions were not spurious. I recall the case of Lewis Minor Coleman, a gallant young officer, who received his mortal wound at Fredericksburg. For more than three months his sufferings seemed to be all that any mortal could possibly bear, yet it was endured with the utmost patience and resignation. When convinced that there was no hope of recovery, he was more than patient; he was happy; he was jubilant. He said to friends weeping at his bedside: "Tell Gen. Lee and Gen. Jackson they know how Christian soldiers can fight, but I wish they could be here that they might see how one of them can die." When his sinking pulse indicated the speedy termination of his sufferings, his brother bent over him and said: "Lewis, you are dying." His response was: "Come, Lord Jesus! O come quickly."

. . . The history of this century will contain nothing along the line of Christian philanthropy more beautiful than some of the deeds of our Confederate soldiers. Permit me to refer to an incident which furnishes a very signal illustration of the grace of Christian magnanimity: Richard Kirtland was a sergeant in the Second Regiment of South Carolina Volunteers. The day after the great battle of Fredericksburg [Confederate Gen. Joseph Brevard] Kershaw's Brigade occupied the road at the foot of Marye's Hill. The ground about Marye's house was the scene of the desperate struggle which occurred the day before. One hundred and fifty yards in front of the road, the stone facing of which constituted the celebrated stone wall, lay [Gen. George] Sykes' division of the United States Army. Between these troops and Kershaw's command a skirmish fight was continued through the entire day. The ground between the lines was literally covered with dead and dying Federal soldiers. All day long the wounded were crying, "Water! water! water!" In the afternoon Serg. Kirtland went to the headquarters of Gen. Kershaw, and, with an expression which betokened the deepest emotion, said: "General, all through last night and to-day I have been hearing those poor, wounded Federals out there cry for water. I can stand it no longer. Let me go and give them water." "Don't you know," replied the General, "that you would get a bullet through you the moment you stepped over that wall?" "Yes, sir," he answered, "but if you will let me, I'm willing to try it." After some reflection the General said: "Kirtland, I ought not to allow you to take this risk, but the spirit that moves you is so noble I can not refuse. Go, and may God protect you." Not only with curiosity, but with painful anxiety, did his comrades watch this brave man as he climbed the wall and proceeded upon his mission of mercy. Unharmed and untouched, he reached the nearest sufferer. He knelt beside him, tenderly raised the drooping head, rested it gently on

Chandler House, Guineys Station, VA, where Stonewall Jackson died.

his noble breast, and poured the cooling, life-reviving fluid down the parched throat. This done, he laid him carefully down, placed his knapsack under his head, straightened his broken limbs, spread his overcoat over him, replaced his empty canteen with a full one, and turned to another sufferer. By this time his conduct was well understood by both sides, and all danger was over. For an hour and a half did this ministering angel pursue his work of mercy, and ceased not until he had relieved all on that part of the battle-field. He returned to his post unhurt. How sweetly did the hero sleep that night beneath God's stars! I have told this story in Gen. Kershaw's own words. I challenge the world to find anything in the annals of our race more Christlike and more worthy of the admiration of men and angels.

Veterans, in the few years that remain to us let it be our constant endeavor to emulate the virtues of these men. Let us follow them as they followed Christ, so that when life's battles are over we may sleep serenely, and in the morning of the resurrection awake to answer the roll call of those who fought the good fight and were faithful unto death.

There was nothing that did more to promote the growth of Christian feeling and rectitude in the Confederate army than the spirit and bearing of its leaders. Never did an army march into battle officered by men more loyal to Christ than Stonewall Jackson, Robert E. Lee, and many of their subordinates. Who can calculate the power of Jackson's religious influence upon the men whom he led to battle? Gen. Ewell was so impressed by it that he was heard to say: "If that be religion, I must have it." After making a profession of faith in Christ, he confessed that his rebellious heart and will had been conquered by the power of Jackson's godly life.

Never did the angels of God descend from their starry heights to hover over a more touching scene than Stonewall Jackson's death or to catch from human lips language more beautiful and significant than his dying words: "Let us cross over the river and rest in the shade of the trees."

Though dead, he yet speaketh. The sun has gone down, but there still lingers a blaze of glory on every mountain peak, and the clouds that hover about the scene of his departure are turned to amber and gold.

No eulogy that my poor feeble lips could pronounce would be worthy of the exalted character and deathless fame of Robert E. Lee. All the great virtues were harmoniously and beautifully blended in him, making an almost perfect man.[244] — REVEREND J. B. HAWTHORNE

☛ SWAPPING HORSES IN MID-STREAM

[What follows is] . . . a most wonderful exhibition of presence of mind and instantaneous action in the presence of great danger an act of Col. Sid Cunningham, of Gen. John H. Morgan's command, during the Ohio raid. It was when the attempt was made to escape from the Buckeye State into Virginia by swimming the Ohio River. The river at that point was about half a mile wide and very deep. A long string of [Confederate] cavalrymen extended entirely across the stream, generally in twos, each encouraging his gallant steed. Col. Cunningham and a comrade were swimming their horses side by side, Cunningham being on the lower side and in midstream, when a Federal gunboat hove in sight around a bend in the river, and without ceremony fired a shell into the swimming column, shooting off the head of Cunningham's horse and killing his comrade. Cunningham grabbed the dead man's horse by the mane and held on like grim death, while the noble steed bore him safely across to the Virginia shore.[245] — SUMNER A. CUNNINGHAM

☛ TRIBUTE FROM A YANKEE SOLDIER

During the Atlanta campaign, in 1864, after a hard battle on the 10th of June, near Kennesaw Mountain, the contending parties struggled until darkness covered the mountains, a kindly mantle covering the dead and dying boys in blue and in gray.

Some thousands of us, yet alive, lay there helpless until near morning, when searching parties, under cover of darkness, moved us to the rear. With us was carried back to the field hospital a young Confederate soldier, mortally wounded, and suffering great agony, being shot through the bowels with a Minie ball, and he was laid on a cot adjoining mine. He was intelligent and educated. The long campaigns in which he had been engaged had reduced his wardrobe to a low ebb, but through the torn and tattered raiment shone the reflection of the gentleman.

In mortal agony, low moans would escape his faltering lips; and, recovering himself and turning to me, he would apologize for having disturbed me. At every request I made for the attendant to bring him some relief he turned gratefully to me with a gentle "Thank you;" for every cup of water or dose of medicine administered the kindly "Thank you" followed.

Knowing that his time for this earth was short, he gave me his name, company, and regiment, and requested that I communicate with his people if I should ever have the opportunity. But before giving their names and addresses he became flighty, and his mind evidently wandered back to his home in Tennessee. Again he lived over the old home life among his kindred and friends, he walked along the shady paths and over the old fields; again he tasted the cold water, which he dipped up with the old gourd as it flowed over the rocks in the dear old spring-house; once more he romped with his sisters and talked with them of father and mother in heaven. Then his mind would revert to the war, would dwell upon the gathering gloom that was spreading over his dear Southland, would picture in feeling terms the loss of some brave comrade and the suffering borne by those who had been brought up in luxury; but for himself no sigh nor complaint ever escaped him. Again, becoming a suppliant at the throne of grace, he thanked his Heavenly Father that it was his fortune to have fallen into the hands of those whom he had looked upon as enemies, but who, in his adversity, had proved to be friends. He fervently implored God to be a father to his orphan sisters and protect them in the days to come. In feeling supplication he asked the Great Ruler to bless his beloved land and the rulers thereof, and prayed that the days of danger and trouble would soon end in peace.

Thus the moments slipped away, and during the dark hours of night his soul went back to his God. Thus passed from my presence through the portals of heaven the immortal spirit of William Hugh Parks, Company K, Twelfth Tennessee, C.S.A.

At my request young Parks was buried in a shady nook in a grave separate and apart from all others, and his lonely resting-place marked. I also mapped the vicinity, so that his place of burial could be found in the future should his friends be discovered. In 1869 his remains were disinterred, and now rest with his comrades in the Confederate cemetery at Marietta, Ga.

Time passed on, and in the spring of 1865 the war was virtually over; and the government, not being able to patch me up for any further use, turned me adrift, a physical wreck, to begin life anew. I endeavored to forget the scenes of those four dark years, and I put as far away from me as was possible all remembrance of those sad times, till one day, several years after, I came across one of my war-time diaries. It brought to mind my promise to the dying Confederate. I wrote letters to a dozen post-offices in Tennessee, but could learn nothing. I resolved to try another method, and advertised in the newspapers of Memphis and Nashville. In a few days letters began coming thick and fast from comrades, friends, and relatives. No word had ever reached them concerning his fate. From these letters I learned that young Parks's home had been at Humboldt, Tenn., and that his two sisters, Mrs. M. P. McIntosh and Mrs. S. E. Northway (now of Waverly Place, Nashville), lived there. A correspondence followed with one of these sisters that continued through several months, and I received some beautiful letters expressive of gratitude in the most devoted Christian spirit for the small service I had rendered.[246] — UNION SOLDIER G. H. BLAKESLEE

☛ ADVENTURES WITH GENERAL FORREST

Early in June, 1861, Gov. Isham G. Harris, of Tennessee, commissioned Nathan Bedford Forrest, of Memphis, colonel, and directed him to raise a regiment of cavalry in Kentucky for the Confederacy. At that time the neutrality law was strictly in force in that state. It was full of Northern detectives and recruiting officers for the Federal army, but Forrest went immediately to Elizabethtown and there learned that a company was being raised for the South in Meade and Breckinridge Counties under Capt. [Frank] Overton. Forrest went there, saw Overton and others of the company, and arranged with them to join him. There were about a hundred of them, all splendidly mounted, but without guns. Notifying these men to go quietly and singly to Nolin, near Elizabethtown, at a certain time, he took four or five of the company and went to Louisville, where he bought about three hundred Colt's navy pistols, a hundred cavalry saddles, bridles, etc., complete equipment for his men. He then went on to Shelby County. En route he heard of my father as a noted Rebel, and went to our house to stay overnight. I was attending a military drill with a local company to which I belonged, and as I rode up home, dressed in my new uniform, I saw my father and a splendid-looking man in serious conversation in the front yard. I was introduced to Col. Forrest and told that he was recruiting soldiers, and, as I had already determined to go out, he wished me to go with him.

The next morning I drove Col. Forrest to a Democratic [then the Conservative party] meeting near Christiansburg, where we met several boys to whom I introduced him. Six, including myself, agreed to meet him at a livery stable in Louisville. Our little crowd, comprised of William Maddox, Gamaliel Harris, William and John Lilly, Young Howard, and myself—none of us over eighteen—arrived at our meeting-point about dark of the day following, and Col. Forrest soon had us all busy carrying coffee-sacks filled with navy pistols, bundles and packages of saddlery and cavalry equipments on our shoulders for a distance of about two squares [about 200 yards], until we had filled four wagons, which occupied us until about midnight. When all was ready we started slowly and cautiously out the Elizabethtown turnpike, with two men in advance of the wagons, four immediately following, and four, including Col. Forrest, a short distance in the rear.

When we had gotten five or six miles out of the city one of the rear-guard came galloping up and reported that the Louisville mounted police were after us. This news came from a friend whom Col. Forrest had left in the city to watch police headquarters until we got a safe distance away. The wagons were hurried up and rattled away with the two guards in advance, making much noise, and we formed across the pike to await the charge of the police. This was my first line of battle. After waiting some twenty minutes, the wagons having a good start, and still hearing nothing, we moved on. We heard afterwards as a fact that they did follow us for about five miles. We arrived safely at Nolin that evening, after having driven over forty miles.

During that evening and night Capt. Overton's company, called the "Boone Rangers," arrived. Two Colt's navy pistols, a saber, saddle, bridle, etc., were immediately issued to each man, and being splendidly mounted, it was the finest military display I had ever seen. I thought that with that company, armed and equipped as it was, it was foolishness to march South to organize. We ought to go back, take Louisville, and then Cincinnati, and I felt that the war would last no time with the Boone Rangers in the field. We then, of course, defied state authorities and marched boldly through Elizabethtown, Munfordville, Bowling Green, and Russellville on to Clarksville, where we sent our horses by dirt road and we went by rail to Memphis.

We went into camp at the old fair-grounds, Memphis, and drilled every day. While there several other companies joined us: Capt. May, with a Memphis company; a company from Texas; Maj. [David C.] Kelley, with a company from Huntsville, Ala.

In the fall we went by boat to Columbus, Ky., arriving there just after the battle of Belmont. We then marched across the country to Fort Henry and on to Hopkinsville, Ky., where we went into winter quarters. We scouted and fought gun-boats on the Cumberland River many times during that fall.

While stationed at Hopkinsville our company, with another of our regiment, with three days' rations, moved out on the Princeton road under command of that brave and gallant officer, Maj. D. C. Kelley, and on to Princeton, Ky., where we went into camp for the night. The next morning we marched out on the Ford's Ferry road. Ford's Ferry was on the Ohio River a few miles above Smithland, where about ten thousand

Federals were encamped. The little town of about a dozen houses was at the foot of a rocky hill or mountain, with a flat area about two hundred yards wide between that and the river. We arrived at the top of this hill overlooking the river and town about nine o'clock at night. Detachments were detailed and instructed in their specific duties. Silence was the order; no one was to speak above a whisper. It was very dark. A Federal transport, loaded to the guards with army stores, was tied up at the town landing. This was our game, and we had a long train of wagons with us to be loaded from the transport. A gun-boat lay about seventy-five yards out in the stream, with its frowning guns covering the transport. About a hundred yards higher up there was another gun-boat in full view. After the council, each squad understanding explicitly its instructions, we were marched to the foot of the hill and dismounted, number fours holding horses. Quickly but quietly we moved to the bank of the river, about twenty paces from the transport, and lay flat on the ground, while five men, under command of Maj. Kelley, boarded the transport, closely supported by fifteen more. Not a word was spoken. All nature seemed as still as death. Some went below and others to the office of the middle deck of the transport. Pistols were drawn at the heads of officers and employees, who were told that silence and strict obedience only would insure their lives, that to speak one word was certain death. The captain of the boat was ordered to put his men to work immediately loading our wagons. About two o'clock the last of the wagons moved slowly up the hill and over the top, and then we put the torch to the transport. In three

minutes the place was as light as day. At that time several small boats were seen to shoot out from the sides of the gunboat. They were allowed to come on within twenty feet of the shore, whin Maj. Kelley said: "Now let them have it boys!" We gave them a volley and fell back to our horses, mounted, and rode slowly up the long hill. Soon both gunboats opened on us and shelled the town, but did us no harm. Some of the wagons were overloaded and stuck in the mud, and as a consequence the road was strewn with bacon, coffee, salt, etc., from Ford's Ferry to Princeton.

This was one of the most brilliant feats of the war, and if there has ever been a line in print about it I have not seen it. When we got back to the camp at Hopkinsville we were the proudest boys in the army. Nothing else was talked about until the next raid. Every fellow had to tell his envious comrade who was not in it his own particular experience. As will be seen, we were many miles in the rear of the Federal army with a small troop and heavily encumbered with a wagon train. Had they been at all on the alert, they might have cut us off and captured us. The Yankees frequently cut off more than they wanted of that crowd, but, like the boy that caught the bee, let them go again.

One evening, shortly after this, we were all lying in camp playing poker and writing love-letters, when suddenly "boots and saddles" rang out on the quiet air. Then there was a general hustling, and in another minute came the order: "Mount and fall in. Company A, quick!" Nothing was said about rations, as was usual on starting on a scout, so we all knew that this meant something unusual was to take place. Every man hustled to get into line. The sick recovered instantly. Forrest had received information that the noted Federal, Col. Jackson, with his crack Kentucky regiment, was scouting in the vicinity of Greenville, about forty miles away. We had scouted five hundred miles to meet that regiment, without success, and now was our chance, but only our commander knew what we were to do or where we were going. We got in line in the shortest possible time, and were off on the Greenville road at a brisk walk. Soon it began to rain and then to freeze. We went on to Pond River and camped for the night, starting again at daylight. At Greenville we got the first news of the enemy, who were reported several hours ahead on the road to Calhoun, on Green River, where ten thousand of the Federal army were encamped. We moved on at a brisk pace, and after a while we passed a house where several ladies, much excited, waved their handkerchiefs, and told us that the enemy were an hour ahead. Here we struck a trot and moved on as fast as our jaded horses could carry us. Directly we heard a shot in front, and then several shots in succession. "Come on, boys: the advance guard has struck them." Then we started in a gallop, and soon passed a couple of prisoners captured by the advance-guard, one of them wounded and both bloody and muddy; a little farther on a loose horse, full rigged, and close by a bluecoat stuck in the mud; then several bluecoats in the same fix. But no one stopped to take charge of a prisoner at this stage of the game. The ride from here on was like a fox-chase, the best mounted men in front, regardless of order or organization. On we went through the little town of Sacramento, where every window and door was full of excited people waving their handkerchiefs. Finally the Federal rear-guard, under Capt. Bacon, found time, as he thought, to make a stand, and formed one company on the crest of a hill at the end of a lane through which we had to pass; but our boys never checked up. They went right on into them in a confused heap, every man firing and fighting in his own way as fast as they came up. Some of the officers made an effort to form a line, but there was little order in it. The enemy broke after one volley. It was said that Col. Forrest personally killed three men in this engagement. Our boys killed eighteen and captured about thirty altogether. This was our first land fight. We had fought gunboats before, but this was our first chance to "mix," as Col. Forrest used to say; and then we were the worst worn-out and the hungriest crowd in the Confederacy, but we had no difficulty in getting all we wanted to eat at that time in Kentucky. Great piles of biscuits, fried chicken, and ham were brought into the picket posts by the citizens, and the best part of it was that the girls generally brought it to us and remained to see us eat and hear what we had to say. We got back to camp with our prisoners, and then there was more talk and much regret too, for the gallant Capt. Ned Meriwether had fallen in this engagement. He was very popular, and his life alone made it a costly victory.

Our encampment continued at Hopkinsville, but we were constantly on the go, fighting gunboats on the Cumberland and watching the Federal armies on Green River and the Ohio, until we were ordered to Fort Donelson, about February 1, 1862.[247] — CHARLES W. BUTTON

☛ HE WAS A HERO, IF A PAUPER
In the battle of Gettysburg a stalwart [Confederate] lad from Darlington, S.C., was bravely advancing in the face of a hot fire when a shot tore off his first finger. An officer ordered him to the rear. "No, sir," was his reply; "they will call me a coward if I go back for that." A moment later a piece of shell took his arm off clear and clean above the elbow. A comrade caught him, and the poor fellow said: "I will go back now, but I would rather lose my arm than to be called a coward."

Two weeks ago there was a death in the poorhouse. The bed was hard, the walls bare, the wan face cold and still, while across the breast was pinned the armless sleeve of a pauper's coat. The heroic soul of Henry Miller had winged its flight to God, far beyond the reach of want and ingratitude.[248] — HON. J. L. MCLAURIN

☛ SCENE ON THE MANASSAS BATTLE-FIELD
When the first battle of Manassas was over and the Federal army, routed, were retreating in great disorder, I beheld a scene I shall never forget. It was the carrying of the body of [Confederate] Col. Charles F. Fisher, Sixth North Carolina Regiment, from the battle-field.

A rider on horseback bore the body, cold and stiff in death. He held it carefully and tenderly in front of his saddle and carried him away from the field of carnage, where he had fallen while leading his regiment to victory.

He was doubtless carried to his beloved state for interment.

The Second Tennessee Regiment, William B. Bate, colonel, and the other regiments of Holmes's Brigade, having been held in reserve on the right of our army, were ordered forward when the battle was most severe, near the Henry House.

It was very hot and dusty, and the movement was at double-quick in the rear of artillery and under a heavy artillery fire from the enemy. Just as we came upon the field of action and in full view of the enemy the Federal lines broke and the battle was won.[249] — T. P. WEAKLEY

☛ A WOMAN'S EARLY RECOLLECTIONS OF GEN. LEE

I have been asked by a dear, young, patriotic friend to open the room of memory, and to give some recollections of our beloved Southern hero, Gen. R. E. Lee.

It was in the early days of my wifehood, my husband [Mr. Moses] was at the nearest port, and during his absence the terrible [hurricane] disaster of Last Island occurred [August 10, 1856], and our sea-girt home resounded with the roar of the angry gulf, which was dashing its waters all around us as if greedy for more prey. The commander of the fort kindly sent down conveyances to take us and what household goods we needed to a place of safety, which we found in the enclosure of the fort. It was a pleasant place just outside the town, its parade-ground forming a square, by two sides of which were pretty cottages—the office and soldiers' quarters. Among the officers, attracting attention even then among them, was [then U.S.] Col. Lee, the courteous, stately gentleman, the ideal that Addison has left us of the "fine old English gentleman"; nor need this comparison give offense when we remember the ancestry of our much-loved General, and that the type again lived in the chivalrous Southern gentleman.

Col. Lee was of commanding presence, but with a tenderness of manner often seen in a physician who fights with death, and in a brave man who may be called at any time to encounter it. In spite of his grand look, however, and military bearing, there was a gleam of mischief and tease in him. Not long after our acquaintance New-year was ushered in—a day that every one in the little town tried to keep in the old-fashioned, hospitable way.

Robert E. Lee in the 1850s.

I might tell you of my struggles to make my table presentable in a frontier town, where nothing could be hired, nothing borrowed, and hardly anything bought, and in a nearly empty house; but I at last succeeded, and was scarcely dressed, and not yet out to do the honors of the day, when Col. Lee called to wish me a happy New-year; and now, as each year carries me farther off from that pleasant greeting, I still recall our General, with eyes brimming over with mischief, teasing me and threatening to let all the garrison know how late Capt. M.'s wife was dressing, and that she was not even ready when he called. He came to wish me goodby some weeks later. I had been obliged to vacate my former lodgings, as the owner of the house needed it, and a very steep flight of stairs led to our apartments, up to which his genial presence appeared with: "How high up in the world you've got!"

Many a time have I looked up to his statue in our Crescent City [New Orleans] and felt that his words have fallen with prophetical meaning on himself; that figure of bronze on the shaft of white, as if 'twere emblematical of that strength of character which raised him in its purity above the level of mankind.[250] — MRS. M. MOSES

☛ BATTLE OF FRANKLIN RECALLED
I witnessed an example of nerve at the battle of Franklin which takes rank with the most notable of thousands during the war. Gen. Thomas M. Scott, of Louisiana, the adjutant-general of his brigade, the writer, and several other wounded officers of the staff and line, were quartered at the McGavock home [Carnton Plantation] after the battle. I recall the agony of Col. W. S. Nelson, of the Twelfth Louisiana, as he lay dying, torn to pieces by a discharge of grape and canister at close range. "My poor wife and child! my poor wife and child! O my God! can you not get the surgeons to administer some drug that will relieve me of this torture?" I did try, though my appeals were in vain. I could imagine what he suffered as the cold perspiration gathered in knots on his brow, and, of course, knew that death was inevitable.

Carnton Plantation, Franklin, TN. (Photo L. Seabrook)

The case of immediate reference here, however, was that of a Capt. Jones, from Grenada, Miss. He was lying on the floor. One of his thighs had been shattered by a cannon-ball; the bone of the other had been laid bare by a like discharge. One of his arms was also shattered and, as I recall it, one of his hands had been torn away. He was the worst wounded man I ever saw, except that no vital organs had been lacerated, as in the case of Col. Nelson and others. At Capt. Jones's side knelt Dr. George C. Phillips, of Lexington, Miss., the manly surgeon of the Twenty-Second Mississippi, ministering to his wounds. "Captain, it would subject you to useless pain to amputate your leg," said the tender-hearted young surgeon. "The wound is fatal, or would be by amputation."

"You are right, Doctor," replied Capt. Jones; "but I don't intend to have that leg cut off, and I don't intend to die. I want to hold on to what is left of me. Why, bless your soul!" he added, holding up his shattered hand, as a smile passed over his face, "there is enough left of me to make a first-class cavalryman."

This was said in reference to the old joke which infantry soldiers good-naturedly were used to getting off on the brave riders of the Confederacy.

I do not know what finally became of Capt. Jones. I have heard that his fractured leg grew together after a fashion, and that he was living several years ago.[251] — C. E. MERRILL

☛ GEN. JOHN H. MORGAN'S WAR-HORSE

Did you ever hear of Black Bess, Gen. John Morgan's fine mare? One day after our army had fallen back from Nashville, on retreat to Shiloh, Morgan's squadron made its appearance in the enemy's rear, passing Old Jefferson, between Nashville and Murfreesboro. Morgan, the ubiquitous raider, the dashing horseman, had dropped from the sky, like a meteor, with his squadron. He stopped for a time, and citizens rushed out to greet them. An orderly was leading an animal that all eyes centered upon. She was trim and perfect—not like a racer, not as bulky as a trotter, nor as swaggy in get-up as a pacer, but of a combination that made her a paragon of beauty. She was an animal given to Col. Morgan by some admirer from his native Kentucky, and they called her Black Bess. She was to bear the dashing Rebel chieftain through many dangerous places. There was gossip in every mouth about his daring feats. I looked and lingered upon Black Bess and the part she was to play in her master's career.

In reporting how she impressed me I employ Hardy Crier's description of his famous horse Gray Eagle. He said that he drove Gray Eagle through the streets of Gallatin, and the high and low stopped to watch his action. He stopped on the square, and a crowd collected, among them a deaf-and-dumb man, who critically examined the horse, and in a moment of utter abstraction took out his slate and pencil and wrote the words "Magnificent! magnificent!" and handed it around to the crowd. This was my idea of Black Bess. Every bone, joint, and tendon of the body, from head to foot, seemed molded to beauty. A flowing mane and tail, eyes like an eagle, color a shining black, height about fifteen hands, compactly built, feet and legs without blemish, and all right on her pasterns—she was as nimble as a cat and as agile as an antelope. My idea of a wild horse of Tartary . . . could not surpass the pattern that Black Bess presented. Quick of action, forceful in style, besides running qualities, a touch on the ear would bring her from a run to a lope, from a lope to a single-foot, from that to a fox-walk. She was as pretty as a fawn, as docile as a lamb, and I imagined her as fleet as a thoroughbred.

Black Bess, Gen. Morgan's horse.

When the squadron left Old Jefferson, on the night of May 4, 1862, they went to Lebanon, eighteen miles. The citizens were enthused. It was a hotbed of Southern sentiment throughout the march, a number of citizens riding all the way to talk to Middle Tennessee soldiers. One of these citizens, Hickman Weakley, our Clerk and Master, was the owner of the "Mountain Slasher Farm," near Jefferson; and, while delighted with friends, his greatest pleasure was to look upon and admire Black Bess. Slasher's colts had reached the acme of Tennessee's boast in saddle-horses, yet nothing he had seen could equal or compare with her. That night in Lebanon kindness to Morgan and his men was so great that his squadron was permitted to camp almost anywhere. The Yankee nation was bewildered with their daring, and the Confederates were tickled. Forsooth the squadron grew careless over triumphs. When least expected, Morgan turned up. No straggling soldiery with the enemy then, for fear of being captured. Telegraph-wires under control of his operator, and upon every tongue would come the query: "Have you heard anything of John Morgan?" At this zenith he had reached Lebanon. The wires were hot with messages to intercept him, and couriers were busy to unite commands. [Union] Gen. [Ebenezer] Dumont with eight hundred came from Nashville; Col. Duffield with a large force from Shelbyville and Murfreesboro, and Col. [Frank] Woolford from Gallatin; truly the Federal cavalry from every adjacent section were after him, for the chiefs in Scotland's mountain fastnesses were not more feared. That night Morgan's men camped in the court-house, livery-stables, and the college campus, and the people were preparing to give them a grand breakfast next morning, when about four o'clock, May 5, two thousand Federal cavalry made a dash, went in with the Confederate pickets, and completely surprised Morgan and his men. The horses were stabled so that the squadron could not reach them. It was at this critical time that Col. Morgan called into requisition Black Bess. Every street was jammed with bluecoats. The dash was so sudden that concert of action was impossible. One hundred and fifty of his men (nearly all) had been taken, and hundreds were after the redoubtable John Morgan himself. He mounted his mare, and, with a few of his men, rode out on the Rome and Carthage pike, pursued by Dumont's cavalry. With Black Bess under rein Morgan began a ride more thrilling than that of McDonald on his celebrated Selim and of a different kind from that of Paul Revere. Gen. Morgan was an expert in firing from his saddle while being pursued; so he waited until the foe got within gunshot, wheeled, and emptied his pistols, and then touched up Black Bess until he could reload. The victors tried for dear life to catch him. The prize would immortalize them. Dumont, with a loss of only six killed and twelve wounded, as shown by his report of the battle of Lebanon in "Records of the Rebellion," would have a triumph sure enough could he catch the cavalier who was bewildering the nation. The run was fifteen miles, but at the end of it Black Bess pricked her ears and champed her bit, as if ready for another fifteen. It was more rapid than [Union Gen. Benjamin Mayberry] Prentiss' fancied ride in a thunder-storm. When Black Bess got to the ferry on the Cumberland River she was full of foam, with expanded nostrils and panting breath; yet, with fire in her eyes, she looked the idol of old Kentucky breeding and her bottom grew better the farther she went. Aye! she was the marvel of her day, and Dick Turpin's Black Bess could not have been her equal.

Black Bess landed John Morgan out of the danger of his enemies and into the embrace of his friends. I have often thought of this fine mare and wondered whether she was shot in battle or captured, recalling how our women prized clippings from her mane or tail.

In this country, before the war, we had the Rattler-Saddlers, the Mountain Slashers, the Travelers, and the Roanokes; since the war, the Hal Pointers, Bonesetters, Little Brown Jugs, McCurdy's Hambletonians, and Lookouts; but for amiability, ease, and grace, nothing, in my mind, has equaled Black Bess, the pride of the old squadron and the idol of John H. Morgan.

John H. Morgan, C.S.A.

In the Army of Tennessee, when John C. Breckinridge, John C. Brown, and E. C. Walthall appeared on horseback, they were mentioned as the handsomest of our generals and the outfit complete; but to see John Morgan in Confederate uniform and mounted on prancing Black Bess, upheaded, animated, apt, and willing, as horse flesh should be, the equipment was simply perfect, the accouterment grand.

I submitted this article to Gen. Basil Duke, Morgan's right arm in war-times, who replied in substance that Black Bess was presented to Col. Morgan by a Mr. Viley, of Woodford County, Ky.; that she was captured at the Cumberland River on this famous run, and that after the war Mr. Viley offered by advertisement a large sum for her or to any one who would give information concerning her. She was sired by Drennon, a famous saddle stock of Kentucky, and her dam was a thoroughbred. Her saddle qualities were superior. About fifteen hands high, she was a model beauty, though a little hard-mouthed. Morgan was much wrought up over her loss.[252] — B. L. RIDLEY

CHAPTER 17

1898

☞ FIGHTING UNDER GEN. FORREST

I was mustered into service September 15, 1861, at Montgomery, Ala. Our company was soon ordered to Memphis, Tenn., and camped about four miles out of town with a squad of cavalry commanded by N. B. Forrest, who told us that he had orders to raise a regiment, and we joined it. He had us drilled every day for about a month, during which time several other companies joined. There were five companies each from Alabama and Tennessee, and known as Forrest's Cavalry; later it was "Forrest's Old Regiment."

Our four days' siege at Fort Donelson and the way Forrest brought us out when the fort was surrendered proved our merit as soldiers and his generalship.

During that campaign I was one of twenty-five men selected to go down on the north and east side of Cumberland River, under Capt. Bradshaw, as independent mounted rangers, to watch the movements of the Federals. On Saturday night, February 15, 1862, we reached the ferry on the opposite side of the river from Fort Donelson, and tried to get the ferryman to put us across the river into the fort, but he refused to do so; and it was lucky for us. About four o'clock Sunday morning a man came to our camp, awoke us, and said that Fort Donelson had surrendered, and that we must flee for safety. We mounted, and left for Nashville and farther south.

In the battle of Shiloh we did hard fighting. After that Maj. D. C. Kelley took about two hundred men and, leaving Corinth, went near the Tennessee River to find out about the enemy. When we found them he attacked them, although they were about eighteen thousand strong. In a short time part of the command was completely cut off. Coot Maxwell, F. M. McKenzie, and I were the last to leave the battle-ground. Maj. Kelley told us that we were cut off and to make our way out. He sprang off on his big sorrel horse, and we followed. We were shot at, but escaped unhurt. Maj. Kelley would fight with us when there was fighting to do, and then preach to us at leisure hours. He was a good and brave man.

We fell back from Corinth to Tupelo, where we reorganized and enlisted for four years or during the war. We were then ordered to Guntersville, Ala. During the summer the Federals came up on the opposite side of the Tennessee River and opened fire on Guntersville, across the river, with their artillery. I was ordered to take a posse of men out to a cross-roads south of town (now known as Wyeth City), to keep the enemy from coming into town on that side. The citizens had to leave town during the fight. A lady was brought through my lines who had been struck with a cannon-ball. It was a horrible sight. Our men got on an island in the river with their small guns and drove the enemy back and held the town.

Later on Gen. Bragg started on his march into Kentucky, and we were ordered to Chattanooga, where we were made his advance-guard. Making our way to the front, we drove the Federals into Nashville; then we withdrew, went up the Cumberland River, and forded it, keeping between the two armies until Gen. Bragg got ahead of the enemy, and then we became his rear-guard. We had to keep a sharp lookout day and night and had much skirmishing and some heavy fighting. On one occasion we were crossing Green River at Mumfordville and I was sent with a squad of men a half-mile down the river to guard a ford to keep the Federals from crossing and cutting off our forces at Mumfordville. I held the ford until one regiment crossed the river and opened fire upon us. I was then cut off, if they had known it, but we got back without the loss of a man or a horse. On another occasion, a few miles south of Elizabethtown, Col. [John Austin] Wharton, who was at that time colonel of the Texas Rangers, gave me a posse of men, and told me to hold Red Mills until he released me; and if any Federal troops came down from Elizabethtown, to report to him at once. He took his regiment and fell in with Forrest's Cavalry and went back about a mile and attacked the Federal forces, and held them in check until Gen. Bragg moved on in the direction of Louisville; but when Col. Wharton fell back, instead of returning by the Elizabethtown road, he took the New Haven road, and left me to confront the whole Federal forces. I held my post until a blue streak of Federal soldiers, four deep and half a mile long, marched up to within about two hundred yards of me. Col. Wharton had not sent any orders to me, so I told my men that we would evacuate Red Mills and make our way across the country to New Haven, a distance of about ten miles. Before reaching that point we had added to our squad until there were about seventy-five. We made the trip without loss of men or any damage and joined our old command at New Haven. None of us were ever punished for disobeying Col. Wharton's orders in leaving Red Mills. I never saw him afterward.

When we had reached Bardstown, Col. Forrest, for his gallantry, received orders to go back to Murfreesboro, Tenn., and raise a brigade. We made one day's journey in that direction, passing through Springfield, at which place I spent the last night that I camped out during the war. Sunday, September 28, 1862, we reached Lebanon. On that day and at that place I received a wound in my foot, which caused my leg to be amputated. That was a few days before the battle of Perryville. After I received the wound Forrest stood over me and made a speech, saying that I was one of the first men that joined his regiment at Memphis, and had always been true to him and to our Southern cause; that he had seen me tried in many dangerous conflicts, and always found me at the front. Turning to some ladies who had gathered around me, he said to them: "I am going to call on you to volunteer. Who among you will take this gallant young soldier to your private home and take care of him till he gets well?" Three noble-hearted ladies responded at the same time, claiming me for their guest. Col. Forrest then turned to me, and asked me if I had any money. I told him that I had but very little; and he took from his pocket $25 and gave it to me, saying: "I give you this for your gallantry. It will do to buy your tobacco till you get able to travel; then report to me, and I will give you a furlough home."

Gen. N. B. Forrest was one of the greatest and bravest men in the Southern army. He was a tender-hearted man, though firm in all his commands. The ladies who volunteered to take me to their homes were Mrs. Judge Kavanaugh, Mrs. Hood, and Mrs. Hogue. Mrs. Kavanaugh being the first to send conveyance for me, I went with her. I was placed under Dr. Shuck, who tried faithfully for about a month to save my foot, but failed. Then Drs. Braidy and Morris, of the Northern army, took charge of me and treated me kindly and successfully. On October 24, 1862, my leg was amputated. I remained with Mrs. Judge Kavanaugh till January 14, 1863; then reported to the Federal authorities, who sent me to St. Louis, Mo., and kept me till April. I was very well treated while in the Northern prison, and made friends everywhere I traveled. I was sent from St. Louis to City Point, Va., and exchanged about the 1st of May, 1863. This ended my war career.[253] — JOHN F. FORE

Miss Willie Emily Ray, Confederate Maid of Honor.

☛ THE GLORY OF THE SOUTH

The honor and glory of this great struggle was with the South, and Southern soldiers ought, in justice to themselves and their dead comrades, to preserve the memory of it. While the North and Northern soldiers are inveighing against all manifestation of sectional feeling, they are erecting monuments to their successful leaders and telling the story very much to their credit and to our detriment.

The North had more than four soldiers to one in the South. Its armies were reenforced and assisted by six hundred ships of war, manned by thirty-five thousand sailors. It had unlimited credit, which meant an unlimited supply of money. It had factories to manufacture everything needed to arm and equip, to supply and maintain, its armies and fleets. It had railroads running in every direction for the transportation of its troops. It had intercourse with the whole world, and could draw recruits for its army and navy from it.

The South had none of these advantages, or had them only to a limited

extent. But, notwithstanding all its advantages, it took the North four years to crush the South, and then it did it by a grinding process and without having gained a single decisive victory.[254] — GEN. VINCENT MARMADUKE

☛ TELLING THE TRUTH TO CHILDREN

... it is the duty of every enlightened Southern man to see that the truth—not biased and warped accounts—of the history of the civil war is transmitted to posterity. The nobleness, the chivalry, the self-denial, the bravery, and the tireless endurance of the Confederate soldier should be instilled into every Southern child. No history should be taught them which pictures their ancestors as traitors and rebels. They should understand the great [conservative] principles which were contended for prior to the war, which were settled by the highest tribunal in the country, the Supreme Court, favorably to the [Conservative] South, which the [Liberal] North would not accept, appealing to a "higher law" [which today's Liberals refer to as "social justice"] and which were finally referred to the arbitrament of the sword.

... Southern children ought to know of the imperishable grandeur of Gen. Lee, of the magnificence in battle of Stonewall Jackson and Albert Sydney Johnston, of the daring bravery of Forrest, of Morgan, and of Cheatham. The renown of the Confederate soldier is not told in splendid monuments; it rests in the hearts of the Southern people, and there it must be kept fresh and green forever. They want their children to receive facts. From facts no conclusions can be drawn derogatory to the courage of Southern soldiers or to the genius and military prowess of Southern generals.[255] — THE *NASHVILLE AMERICAN*

☛ SKETCH OF STONEWALL JACKSON

No other man in history can be likened to him. He has oftener been compared with Oliver Cromwell than with any other great soldier. But Cromwell was a great statesman, of far-reaching wisdom; we would be inclined to pronounce Jackson a warrior, pure and simple. Four years of incarceration together at West Point and subsequent service together in the armies of the United States and Confederate States gave me as good opportunities of estimating the mind and nature of Stonewall Jackson as any man has ever enjoyed. I believe Jackson was as fond of me as he ever was of any man of our times. It was for his [second] wife [Mary Anna, née Morrison] to awaken and nurture, and, since his death, to disclose to the world the deep tenderness of that wonderful character, a tenderness never before suspected. In the life and letters of her husband are revelations of affectionate gentleness unknown to any but her.

Jackson at West Point: I entered the military academy at West Point in June, 1842. A week afterward a cadet sergeant passed, escorting a newly arrived cadet to his quarters. The personal appearance of the stranger was so remarkable as to attract the attention of several of us who were standing near and chatting together. Burkett Fry, A. P. Hill, and George Pickett made our group. The new cadet was clad in gray homespun, a wagoner's hat, and large, heavy brogans. Weather-stained saddle-bags were over his shoulders. His sturdy step, cold, bright gray eye, thin, firm lips, caused me to say, "That fellow looks as if he had come to stay," and on the return of the sergeant I asked him who that cadet was. He replied: "Cadet Jackson, of Virginia." Whereupon I at once ascended to his room to show him my interest in him, a fellow countryman in a strange land. He received my courteous advances in a manner so chilling that it caused me to regret having made them, and I joined my companions with criticisms brief and emphatic as to his intellectual endowments.

Oliver Cromwell.

Days and weeks went by with no change in the "snap shot" estimate then imparted. One evening, while Fry and Hill and I were lolling upon our camp bedding, the evening police were going on, and "Cadet Jackson, from Virginia," was upon duty about our tent, when I, desirous again to be affable and playful with our countryman, lifted the tent wall and addressed him with an air of authority and mock sternness, ordering him to be more attentive to his duty. His reply was a look so stern and angry as to let me know that he was doing that job. Whereupon I let that tent wall drop, and became intensely interested in my yellow-back novel. So soon as police was over I arose and girded my loins, saying that I had made Cadet Jackson, of Virginia, angry, and must at once humble myself and explain that I was not really in command of that police detail. I found him at the guard-tent, called him out, and said: "Mr. Jackson, I find that I made a mistake just now in speaking to you in a playful manner, not justified by our slight acquaintance. I regret that I did so."

He replied with his stony look: "That is perfectly satisfactory, sir." Whereupon I returned to my comrades, and informed them that in my opinion "Cadet Jackson, from Virginia, is a jackass," which verdict was unanimously concurred in; and thenceforward nobody in that tent "projected" with that cadet until our four years' course was ended and we were emancipated from the military prison of West Point, for we all liked and respected him.

After our encampment of two months was over we went into barracks, and were arranged in sections alphabetically, and thus it was [future Union Gen. George B.] McClellan and I sat side by side. "Mac" was a great help, and besides he was a little bred-and-born gentleman, only fifteen and a half years old.

"Old Jack," as we called [Gen. Jackson then], hung about the bottom [of the class grade-wise]. At the first January examination all below him were cut off. He was foot [infantry], and probably would have been cut off also, but his teachers observed in him such a determined intention to succeed that they felt sure he would certainly improve; and he did.

Our rooms were small, each with two single bedsteads (iron), a bare, cold floor, and an anthracite grate. "Old Jack," a few minutes before taps, would pile his grate with coal, so as to have a bright, glowing fire when taps sounded and all other lights were out. Then he would lie prone upon the floor, when the light enabled him to study the lesson for the day, and very soon he began to rise in his class; and we all were glad of his success, for cold and undemonstrative as he was, he was absolutely honest and kindly, intensely attentive to his own business; and, as it was, he came to be near the head of our class, the largest that had ever graduated there. We had, altogether, one hundred and sixty-four members—counting those turned back into it—and we graduated sixty after four weary, profitless years (to me).

On returning to Virginia from West Point the boys stopped at Brown's hotel, where "Old Jack" had his first and last [drunken] frolic, to which in long years after his fame had filled the world he dimly alluded, when he said he was too fond of liquor to trust himself to drink it; but poor Dominie's long-pent craving was never slaked any more until his enfeebled frame was laid to rest in a soldier's grave away off in the shadow of the Rockies.

From the moment that Jackson entered upon his duties in the army he evinced that terrible earnestness which was the characteristic of his conduct in battle or in work. During the [Mexican-American] battles in the valley he served as a lieutenant of [John Bankhead] Magruder's Battery and won many distinctions. Having entered the service as a second lieutenant, he was brevetted first lieutenant, captain, and major in one year's field service.

When John Brown made his attempt to arouse insurrection in Virginia Gov. [Henry Alexander] Wise called out the troops of the state and ordered the corps of cadets to be held ready for immediate service. Gen. Smith, superintendent of the corps, promptly obeyed the orders. Maj. Jackson reported at the guard-room ready for the field. Gen. Smith, after giving attention to some matters requiring it, said: "Maj. Jackson, you will remain as you are till further orders." At that moment Maj. Jackson was seated upon a camp-stool in the guard-room with his saber across his knees. Next morning at reveille Gen. Smith repaired to the guardroom and found Jackson sitting on the camp-stool, and said: "Why, Major! why are you here?"

"Because you ordered me to remain here as I was last night, and I have done so."

Mary Anna Jackson, Stonewall's second wife.

Next year he went off to the great war between the states, and won fame at once. Rumors of a great victory came. His wife and friends were anxious for the news. It came by a courier, who spurred in hot haste to his home in Lexington. These were the words: "My subscription to the negro Sunday-school is due. It is fifty cents, which I send by the courier."[256] Nothing more. At the first Manassas [battle] his fame was made when that noble [Confederate] soldier Barnard Bee cried out to his wavering men: "See where Jackson, with his Virginians, stands like a stone wall! Let us form behind them!" After the repulse at Malvern Hill Gen. Lee and other generals were discussing the situation, and what we were to do in the morning. Jackson was lying upon the ground, apparently slumbering, his cap lying over his face. He was aroused and asked his opinion of what was to be done in the morning.

Removing his cap from his face, he said: "They won't be there in the morning." Nor were they.

One morning while marching with his staff he stopped at the door of a farmhouse. A gentle-looking woman was in the porch with a little child at her knee, of whom he requested a drink of water. She promptly handed him a stone jug of cool and fresh water, which he quaffed like a horse. One of his staff asked the good woman to "give me a drink of that water, please." She emptied the pitcher upon the ground, went into the house, and brought out a white pitcher, from which she gave the captain a drink.

"Why did you not give it from the other pitcher?" asked the officer.

"Oh!" she replied, "no man's lips shall ever again drink from that pitcher."

Again, while marching on to some new victory, he halted by a farmhouse, whence a young mother came out into the road with her young child in her arms, and said: "General, won't you bless my child?" He took the little infant in his arms, and, reverently raising it, with uncovered head prayed for God's blessing upon it.

In the battle of Kernstown he was worsted by Gen. [James] Shields (one of the noblest of the Federal commanders), because of the Confederates' ammunition being all exhausted. Gen. Dick Garnett withdrew his troops. Jackson arrested Garnett, one of the truest and highest gentlemen in our army, and held him in arrest until Garnett, by personal influence, procured a trial by court martial. Jackson was the principal witness for the prosecution. The court acquitted Garnett after hearing Jackson's testimony, and only permitted the defense to be spread upon the record on Garnett's demand that after such unusual and conspicuous severity it was his right. Poor Garnett fell in front of his brigade in the great charge at Gettysburg. He was mourned throughout our army, for a braver and gentler gentleman never died in battle.

Stonewall Jackson, age 24.

Jackson Feared No Man: While a professor of the Virginia Military Institute Jackson arrested and caused a distinguished cadet to be dismissed for an infraction of the regulations. That cadet was distinguished as a scholar and soldier. He found himself, after four years of study and scholarly achievements, deprived of the diploma which was the object of his long endeavor. Without it his livelihood was imperiled. He was justly outraged by such harshness, and vowed he would castigate Jackson, and prepared himself to execute that purpose. He was a powerful and daring young man. The friends of both were deeply anxious. Jackson was urged to have him bound over to keep the peace. This would involve his oath that he was in bodily fear of his enemy. He replied: "I will not do it, for it would be false. I do not fear him; I fear no man." Then the superintendent of the academy had to take the oath as required by the law, and have the young man bound over to peace. When the war came on Jackson, upon his own promotion to a corps, had this young fellow made brigadier, and he became one of the most distinguished generals of the war, and is known to-day as one of the ablest men of our state.

Jackson was awkward and uncomfortable to look at upon a horse. In the riding-school at West Point we used to watch him with anxiety when his turn came to cut at the head or leap the bars. He had a rough hand with the bridle, an ungainly seat, and when he would cut at a head upon the ground he seemed in imminent danger of falling headlong from his horse.

About 1850 Jackson was a lieutenant of artillery stationed at Governor's Island, when he was invited to accept the chair of mathematics in the Virginia Military Institute. In those days the government would grant an officer leave of absence for one year to enable him to try such an office before resigning his commission. So he came up to West Point to see McClellan and myself and other comrades before retiring from the army. He was more cordial and affectionate than was usual with him, for he was never demonstrative in his manners, and he was in good spirits, because of his promotion and the compliment paid him.

He informed us, however, of a peculiar malady which troubled him, and complained that one arm and one leg were heavier than the other, and would occasionally raise the arm straight up, as he said to let the blood run back into his body, and so relieve the excessive weight. I have heard that he often did this when marching, and, having become very religious, his men supposed he was praying. I never saw him any more, except at Manassas after the battle, when Gen. Johnston and other officers were congratulating him upon his fine conduct in the battle. These peculiarities have often been cited as evidences of the great genius he possessed.

I have always heard it said that he was an advocate for raising the black flag and showing no mercy to the enemy who were invading our country and destroying our homes; and it has been said that he urged Gen. Lee to assault the enemy in the town of Fredericksburg by night, after their defeat and while they were retreating over the river, and that Gen. Lee refused to do so because of the peril to the people of the town.

Dabney H. Maury, C.S.A.

I have never heard of Jackson evincing any sympathy or gentleness or merciful regard for the wounded enemies he must have seen nor tender emotions of any sort. Therefore the delightful book lately published by his widow is a revelation and surprise. Nothing in all literature can equal the exquisite gentleness and sweetness this book gives us of the stern, stolid, impassible nature, who lavished such tenderness upon the object of his love. To her he unlocks a treasure of rich and pious and loving emotions, which his most intimate friends had never before suspected to exist.[257] — GEN. DABNEY H. MAURY

☛ LUNCH WITH A WAR-GOD ON TOP OF VALLEY MOUNTAIN
I never shall forget the rainy evening while on my return from Mingo Flats I passed [a] . . . tent. [Inside] I saw a fine head and a smiling countenance. I halted, dropped my old musket to a rest, and said to the man . . . "Are you dry? Have you anything to eat?"

"Yes," to both questions was replied, and "Come in, and help yourself" was added.

After enjoying some ham, light bread, and pickle, I said: "I feel good now, and will be going down the mountain. Will you kindly tell me

who you are?"
"Lee is my name."
"What? Not Gen. Robert Lee, our commander?"
"Yes."[258] — HENRY HUNTER SMITH

☛ A MOVING STORY OF PRIVATION
In our old marching days the privations we endured seemed to stimulate the imagination, and the story of our sufferings lost nothing of pathos as the sufferer told it. We had a deep sense of our sacrifices, and often used them to stir the soul of pity in some good woman, so as to add to our rough and scanty rations. Very seldom was a prosperous farmhouse visited by a soldier who had eaten anything in three days, and the look of gaunt, hollow-eyed hunger he could assume would melt the heart of a graven image, and has brought forth many a good dinner from the unsophisticated, who had not learned to distrust the pitiful plea.

One case comes to mind where the tale was so touching that it moved even the soldier himself to tears over his own sad case—at least that was what some of the boys who saw it all reported afterward in the regiment.

After a hard day's march, we went into our camp a little before sundown, and three days' rations of cornbread and bacon were issued to us and stowed away in our haversacks. Near our camp there flowed a beautiful stream, and on its banks were fine farms that seemed to have an abundance of things good to eat. The instinct and the appetite of the men at once told them that it was a good place to replenish rations, and so a number of them, with or without permission, started out to forage, not waiting to lay aside or empty their haversacks.

Pretty soon they came to a farmhouse in which the family were just sitting down to supper. They sent in one of their number to see what could be gotten. This one was very skillful in gaining the good will of any one that sympathized with the "poor soldier." As he walked into the dining-room he saw a great dish of broiled ham, plates of hot biscuits, pitchers of milk, jars of honey, and he also detected the fragrance of "sure-enough" coffee. There were dainties to make his mouth water.

He found the family to consist of a mother, evidently a woman of refinement, and three or four children, while there were plenty of servants. At once he put on his best manner, for he was a gentleman "to the manner born," and in a moment he was invited to supper. He proceeded to make himself agreeable, for he was a delightful converser, and he found that the family were intensely Southern, the father being with Lee, in Virginia. As the farm was rather out of the line of the armies, it had not been visited before by hungry soldiers, and they were glad to see a Confederate. After an extraordinary meal—for our boy was long and "hollow to his heels"—he told the lady that this was his first meal in three days, and asked if she would have three dozen biscuits made for him, with a slice of broiled ham in each. He wanted them for himself and his two messmates, and would pay well for them. She, good and guileless woman, told him that she would gladly do what she could for a Southern soldier, and would not think of taking pay—which was well, as he had "forgotten" his purse. The cook was ordered to prepare the biscuits and ham.

Meanwhile he laid himself out to entertain the lady with the story of our privations. With touching pathos he described the pangs of hunger, and emphasized his own sufferings in contrast with the abundance he had left at home. He painted the weary march and the long and lonely vigil of the sentinel, almost exhausted by his lack of food. So moving was the story that the lady wept and the children sobbed in sympathy. At last the soldier himself was so carried by the pity of it that he shed tears freely over the mournful memory.

Right in the midst of the sad scene the cook came in, bringing the great dish of ham and biscuits, and set it down before the sorrowing soldier. He at once began to take care of it, and, picking up his haversack from his side, he took out pone after pone of corn bread, and then a big "hunk" of bacon, laying them on the table, while their place in his haversack was taken by the more toothsome viands. All the while he went on with the tale of his sufferings.

Directly he noticed that the sobbing had ceased and there was a strange stillness with his weeping auditors. Looking up, he saw the lady gazing at him with an expression of wonder and amusement, while the tears still glistened on her cheeks, and it flashed on him that he had forgotten to empty his haversack before he came in, had forgotten in his anguish of spirit how this fat haversack would discredit his story. His imagination was so vivid that it neglected the facts entirely, and he really believed his own story. He had simply allowed the embellishments to hide the facts, until the facts asserted themselves.

Of course there was no explanation possible. The soldier was too fine an artist to offer one. The lady, fortunately, was gifted with humor, and saw the comedy of the situation. As he waited for her reproaches she broke into the merriest laugh, in which he could only join, a self-revealed fraud. She said he was welcome to the rations, for she had not enjoyed so good a cry in a long time; it was such a relief to her. But she begged that in the future he should not give way to his grief, but try to bear up under his sufferings, and no doubt, when he was again nearly starved, a kind Providence would come to his relief, as in this case. Then she bundled up his bacon and corn bread for him to take with him, for she knew such an appetite would need all it could get.[259] —
UNKNOWN

☛ BULLET IN A TESTAMENT
[My little Bible] . . . was presented to me in November, 1861, at Camp Moore, La., by my captain, J. H. Sutherlin. My company, called the Creoles, belonged to Gen. Randall Lee Gibson's Brigade, and had but one man taken prisoner during the war. I participated in every battle and skirmish in which the regiment was engaged, from the great battle of Shiloh to that at Jonesboro, Ga., August 31, 1864.

In the battle of Chickamauga, September 20, 1863, the first charge in the morning was repulsed. Being a little in advance of the line, I did not know when the order was given to retreat, and on looking around I saw the brigade two or three hundred yards away in full retreat, I only left to hold the line or follow suit, and I followed suit in a turkey trot for twenty or thirty yards, when the music of so much lead caused me to take a tree, but not to climb it, as the boys in blue were looking at me from their line of battle. After resting a few moments I decided to make my escape, even at the risk of my life. On leaving the tree it seemed that they fired a peck of balls at me, only one striking my knapsack on my back, passing through my blanket twenty or thirty times, through two company books, clothing, and entered my Testament, breaking through the back and mashing itself nearly flat. It is in the book now, just where it struck thirty-four years ago. My compliments to the boys in blue, whose aim was so bad.[260] — J. W. ALLEN

☛ SKETCH OF GENERAL JAMES BYRON GORDON

At the commencement of the war [North Carolina] Gov. [John Willis] Ellis issued a call for ten regiments of state troops, to serve for the period of three years or during the war. Of these, eight were infantry, one cavalry, and one artillery. Robert Ransom, afterward major-general, was appointed colonel of the cavalry regiment; Laurence Simmons Baker, afterward brigadier-general, lieutenant-colonel; and James B. Gordon, major. This regiment was known as the First North Carolina Cavalry, and became famous in the cavalry of the Army of Northern Virginia. It was thoroughly drilled and disciplined by Col. Ransom and Lieut.-Col. Baker, both of whom were graduates of West Point, and its efficiency was greatly augmented by the ability and skill of Maj. Gordon, who succeeded to the rank of colonel.

James B. Gordon, C.S.A.

Gen. Gordon was a native of Wilkes County, and a prominent citizen of the state. He had been successful, was a gentleman of wealth and leisure, and at that time a member of the council of state, and he possessed many of the qualifications of a successful soldier. His regiment was first attached to the cavalry brigade of Gen. Wade Hampton, which was composed, in addition to the First and Second South Carolina Cavalry, of Cobb's and Phillips' Legions, as a part of [Jeb] Stuart's Cavalry, Army of Northern Virginia. In the spring of 1863, however, the First North Carolina was united with the Second, Third, Fourth, and Fifth North Carolina Regiments of Cavalry, and formed into a brigade, thereafter known as the North Carolina Cavalry Brigade. Gen. Gordon was then promoted to the rank of brigadier-general, and placed in command.

Gen. Gordon's old regiment was incessantly engaged, as a part of Stuart's Cavalry, in the seven days' battle below Richmond, in the Maryland campaign at Sharpsburg, in the Pennsylvania campaign at Gettysburg, and in numerous cavalry battles in Virginia. In all the operations of the cavalry during these years he had borne a conspicuous part as a brave, daring, and skillful officer. Among the many distinguished cavalry officers from North Carolina he stood at the head.

Gen. Gordon's brigade, from this time till the death of its commander, participated in the principal cavalry battles of the Army of Northern Virginia. A detailed account of these numerous engagements would comprise a history of Stuart's Cavalry.

In May, 1864, while Gen. Lee was confronting Gen. Grant, at Spottsylvania Court-House, [Union] Gen. [Philip H.] Sheridan attempted to capture Richmond by a movement in the rear of Lee's army. He approached within three miles of the city on the Brook turnpike, and was only prevented from taking it by the desperate fighting of Stuart's Cavalry. This fighting cost the life of Gen. Stuart at Yellow Tavern and of Gen. Gordon at Brook Church. Gen. Gordon was ordered to attack Gen. Sheridan in the rear. This movement he performed successfully. While leading his men in action he fell mortally wounded, and died a few days thereafter at the officers' hospital in Richmond.

As a brigade commander Gen. Gordon ranked among the bravest and best. Active, alert, and vigilant, he was never taken by surprise, and was always quick to take advantage of any mistake of his adversary and to meet any emergency. He always led his men in battle, and inspired them by his presence with hope and confidence. His death was a heavy blow to the cavalry arm of the service, and was felt as a personal loss by the members of his brigade, all of whom were warmly attached to him.

Gen. Gordon was tall and well proportioned, his bearing soldierly, and his countenance singularly handsome. Kind-hearted, genial, and generous, he made friends of all with whom he came in contact. His soldierly bearing, his courtly and courteous manners, proclaimed the gentleman that he was, "without fear and without reproach."[261] — HON. KERR CRAIGE.

☞ FAITHFUL BLACK SERVANT "UNCLE" DAVE HATCHER

"Uncle" Dave Hatcher.

Dave's master was James Hatcher, Esq., of Edgefield County, S.C., and Dave, in slavery times, was his "driver"—head man of the plantation when no overseer was employed. Dave had the confidence of the white family, for when the body of the young master was brought home from the terrible battlefield of Chickamauga he mourned with them, for "de only boy had done gin up his life a fitin' fur de Souf." When Dave's fidelity was tested, he stuck by "de nimbly"; and during the reign of terror [Reconstruction], when noble men of the South acquiesced in the doings of the Ku Klux Klan [not related to today's KKK][262] to strike awe and fear to the hearts of the newly enfranchised and their carpetbag leaders, Dave was still faithful and true. When his master was to be arrested as one of the Klan, Dave carried the news to him, having learned of it from other negroes. When secure in his retreat, Dave was the bearer of news, etc., to him from home. This fidelity caused his arrest, and at the headquarters of the Federal garrison he was hung up by the thumbs for a long, long time, that the authorities might extort from him the whereabouts of the fugitive; but they did not know Dave, for he said: "I was jes agwine to die hung up befo' I would tell on 'im." Dave was let down at last and turned loose, but to this day does not like that blue uniform, and wonders why "our young sodger people wear it instid of de gray." Dave still holds his own, has reared a "likely set of chillun," and has acquired a little property. He has forgiven the United States government for its indignity of long ago sufficiently to accept a branch of the Star Mail Route, which he faithfully runs, although his "fumbs are a little bit crooked and weak yit."[263] — CAPT. B. H. TEAGUE

☞ SKETCH OF GEN. TYREE HARRIS BELL

Tyree H. Bell was born September 6, 1815, and was reared in Sumner County, Tenn. In 1858 he moved with his family to Dyer County, same State. At the beginning of the war he raised the first company of volunteers that went from Newbern, in his adopted county, and was elected captain. At Jackson, Tenn., they were organized into the Twelfth Tennessee Infantry, and Capt. Bell was elected its lieutenant. Robert Milton Russell, of Trenton, Tenn., was chosen colonel.

    This regiment fought at Belmont, the first battle in the West at least, and Lieut. Col. Bell was in command of the regiment (Col. Russell being in command of the brigade). Two horses were shot from under Col. Bell in this battle. In the battle of Shiloh he commanded the regiment (as Col. Russell was still in command of the brigade). In this battle, in which his regiment was constantly engaged, he lost three horses, all shot from under him while he escaped unhurt; except that the first horse (that was shot from under him) fell on one of his legs, which lamed him for a short time; but he was soon remounted, and continued through the battle.

Tyree H. Bell, C.S.A.

    In the reorganization of the army at Corinth, Miss., the Twelfth and Forty-Seventh Tennessee Regiments, the latter number becoming obsolete, were consolidated and Bell was elected colonel. He led his command in that famous raid into Kentucky under Kirby Smith, and was in all of the engagements. His regiment fought a brigade at La Vergne, Tenn., and it was also in the great battle of Murfreesboro under his leadership. In the La Vergne fight he completely routed the enemy, capturing many prisoners. After this he was sent as a recruiting officer into West Tennessee, where he raised a brigade of cavalry. With it he reported to Gen. N. B. Forrest in the fall of 1864, and was soon commissioned as brigadier general. From that time he "was with Forrest on every raid and in every battle that was fought during the remainder of the war." Although in many battles, he only received one severe wound. That was in the breast and face, at Pulaski, Tenn., from the explosion of a bombshell. That disabled him for only a few days, when he resumed command again. With that exception he was on duty throughout the entire war, surrendering at Gainesville, Ala., with his brigade, May 14, 1865. In 1875 Col. Bell moved to Fresno County, Cal., with his family, where he now resides, hale and hearty in his eighty-fourth year.[264] — SUMNER A. CUNNINGHAM

☛ THE ORIGIN OF THE CIVIL WAR

... Mr. Lincoln issued his proclamation of 1862-1863 as a war measure for the emancipation of the negroes. *Nobody believed that he had the power to emancipate slaves, but he did it.* As soon as we [in the South] were subjugated, in 1865, they adopted what is called the Thirteenth Amendment. The adoption of this amendment ratified what had been done by Mr. Lincoln, and made constitutional what had been unconstitutional, and abolished slavery in the United States. That was the immediate result of our subjugation. In 1866 they adopted what is called the Fourteenth Amendment to the Constitution, which declares that all persons born or naturalized in the United States, etc. Why did they do it? It was to override the celebrated Dred Scott decision. In that case a free negro had instituted a suit in the courts of the United States in Missouri against a citizen of another State, claiming that he was a free man. The question was whether a free negro was a citizen of the United States. The Supreme Court of the

Roger B. Taney.

United States decided that a free negro was not and never had been regarded as a citizen either of the colonies or of the State previous to the formation of the United States; and, therefore, never could be a citizen of the United States [that is, unless the Constitution were amended]. The Chief Justice [Roger B. Taney] went into the history of the African race in this country. Mr. Sumner and Mr. Seward, in the Senate, denounced this decision [even though it was constitutional at the time]. The North rose up in arms. The [19th-Century] Republican party [organized by Liberals and socialists in 1854, and thus the Liberal party of that day],[265] when it assembled to nominate a candidate, adopted as a part of its platform that the decision of the Supreme Court of the United States was not binding upon the country on such a question. And they would not recognize it. [Big government Liberal] Mr. Lincoln was elected upon that platform, and when he was elected the South thought that as the people of the North had claimed for half a century that the Supreme Court of the United States was the arbiter of this constitutional question, that as they had undertaken to repudiate this decision and elect a President on a platform which repudiated the authority of the United States Supreme Court, and that if there was ever a time to go to war that was the time, they went to war upon it. *That is the origin of the civil war. It was not that Mr. Lincoln was elected upon a free-soil platform, but a platform which repudiated a decision of the United States Supreme Court upon this subject in contradiction to which they had contended for up to that time, simply because it was in favor of the South.* Slaves were after that made citizens, in 1865-66. Then came the last ["Civil War"] amendment [the Fifteenth]: The right of citizens of the United States to vote shall not be denied, etc. They thought they had secured the predominance of the Republican [Liberal] party in the South, because the negroes in many of the States were in the majority. Note: "That the right shall not be abridged on account of race, color, or previous condition of servitude." *The Supreme Court, when this article came up for consideration, said that this did not give anybody the right to vote. It is true, negroes were citizens, but the State could discriminate as to what citizens should or should not vote for any other cause than race, color, or previous servitude. This did not secure to the negroes the right to vote, but merely secured to them that they should not be discriminated against on account of race, color, or servitude.*[266] — DR. C. H. TEBAULT

Confederate blockade runner.

CHAPTER 18

1899

☞ MCGAVOCK CONFEDERATE CEMETERY

One of the most beautiful Confederate cemeteries in the South is that near Franklin, Tenn., in which are buried 1,484 Confederate soldiers. This was done by Col. John [W.] McGavock, an old-time Southern gentleman, whose heart was always overflowing with kindness. His acts of thoughtfulness for the Confederate soldiers will never be forgotten, and to his noble wife [Caroline or "Carrie," née Winder], that true daughter of the Confederacy, we are indebted for a copy of every name and the grave of every soldier buried there.

John W. McGavock.

The beautiful marble headstones were secured through McEwen Bivouac, of which George L. Cowan was chairman and treasurer. The amount necessary to complete these beautiful stones was three thousand dollars—about two dollars for each grave. The committee issued an address to the States who had dead buried there, asking for the amount to complete the work, but only three out of the twelve responded. South Carolina, through the efforts of that Christian soldier, Gen. (afterwards Bishop) [Ellison] Capers, appropriated from the State treasury for that purpose, $125; Mississippi also appropriated out of her treasury $900; and Louisiana's brave sons did not wait for their State to be called on, but the Society of the Army of Tennessee (headquarters at New Orleans) promptly sent

$55, and have since given $50 to repair and repaint the fence. This amount, with about $700 from all sources by the committee, is all that has ever been collected, which leaves about $1,200 yet to raise to put the cemetery out of debt.

McGavock Confederate Cemetery. (Photo L. Seabrook)

The committee announce that if those States who have not yet contributed anything will supply their part—viz., Alabama, with 120 buried there, $260; Arkansas, with 104 buried there, $210; Georgia, with 60 buried there, $140; Missouri, with 130 buried there, $260; and Texas, with 89 buried there, $180, they feel safe in asserting that the cemetery will be put beyond the want of aid from any government. In an appeal the committee say: "Will not the old soldiers take this in hand before they shall have all passed away, and see that the graves of those who laid down their lives for the cause for which all fought are kept green?"

The handsome iron fence was principally secured through contributions personally solicited by Miss M. A. H. Gay, of Decatur, Ga. Confederates buried in McGavock Cemetery are given by States, in addition to those enumerated above, as follows: Mississippi, 424; Tennessee, 230; South Carolina, 51; Louisiana, 19; Kentucky, 6; Florida, 4; North Carolina, 2; unknown, 225.

Ellison Capers, C.S.A.

In addition to their part in this Confederate Cemetery, the Daughters of the Confederacy of Williamson County have decided to erect on the Public Square in Franklin a handsome monument, with appropriate designs about the base, and surmount it with the life-sized figure of a Confederate private soldier, and they cordially invite the cooperation of the public. They are asking one hundred good men to contribute fifteen dollars each for that purpose, and that each volunteer will notify Mrs. W. H. Gillespie, Treasurer (Arlington Hotel), Franklin, Tenn., before April 1 next.

The monument committee are: Mrs. George L. Cowan, Mrs. Newton Cannon, Mrs. W. H. Gillespie, Mrs. Thomas F. Perkins, Mrs. Mary Nichol Britt, Miss Annie Claybrooke.[267] — SUMNER A. CUNNINGHAM

☛ FROM THE UNION SIDE AT FRANKLIN

I have read your [Confederate soldiers'] experiences in the battle of Franklin [II], November 30, 1864, and send you, as near as I can remember, the position of our division, engaged in that battle; also my own experiences. At four o'clock A.M., November 30, by direction of [Union] Gen. [David Sloane] Stanley, the division took up the line of march *en route* from Columbia to Franklin, as the rear guard of the army. The Second and Third Brigades of the Fourth Corps were to march in parallel along the road. Col. [Emerson] Opdyke to move in line of battle in the rear. The enemy began skirmishing with Col. Opdyke early in the morning.

When the division reached Winstead's Hill, two miles south of Franklin, Gen. Stanley gave the order to halt, in order to allow us to get breakfast. Col. Opdyke's brigade was placed in the gap and on the point east of the pike, with a section of artillery, to check the advance of the enemy, who was pursuing us at the time. Col. [John Quincy] Lane's Brigade was placed in position on Col. Opdyke's left; Col. [Joseph] Conrad went into line on the left of Col. Lane; Gen. [Walter Chiles]

Whitaker's Brigade, of the First Division, occupied the heights on the right of the pike. The enemy soon appeared, with a heavy force, and the command was put under arms to be ready to repel an attack.

Quickly after these dispositions were made. I observed the troops of the corps moving toward Franklin, and the command withdrew from its advanced position on the heights and followed on toward town. When within half a mile of town, we received orders to reoccupy the heights and to hold them as long as we could. It was not long before the enemy was moving two heavy columns of infantry against our lines, one by each of the pikes leading into Franklin, one column turning our left flank. We then withdrew and joined the main line of our troops, which surrounded the town. Lane's Brigade and a section of artillery took position on the hills to the right of the pike, about one mile north of Winstead's Hill. He remained skirmishing till

Winstead Hill, Franklin, TN. (Photo L. Seabrook)

his right flank was about to be turned, when he was ordered to leave a heavy line of skirmishers to hold the hill as long as possible, and to withdraw his brigade and take position on the right of the Third Brigade, which had been formed on the left of the [Columbia] pike, about four hundred yards in advance of our main line, at the same time placing a section of artillery on the pike between these two brigades. The commanders of the Second and Third Brigades were ordered to hold their positions lone; enough to develop the force of the enemy, but not to attempt to fight if threatened by the enemy in force. Opdyke's Brigade was destined to have a new experience, that of defending the breastworks against assault. We had assaulted works and had helped build them by the mile, but had never yet had the opportunity to defend one against serious assault. The assault at Franklin was made by two infantry corps and one division of a third corps . . . .

A more determined and persistent effort to carry a position was never made in this or any other war. At the first onset the assaulting troops carried the works at the center, while Opdyke's Brigade charged in the breach, retook the works after a fierce struggle, and held them. Right here was the worst fighting I ever experienced in my life. Many of the enemy [Confederates] were killed inside our lines. The fighting lasted until near midnight, when we abandoned our works and crossed the river, leaving our dead and wounded, losing a great many men through capture. Never did men fight more gallantly.

I was in the front line on that charge, and I never saw the dead lie so thick as I saw them that night—a ghastly sight in the white starlight. It is doubtful if in any battle of modern times there were as many personal encounters as occurred at Franklin. I myself was clubbed over the head with a musket held by a six-foot "Johnny [Reb]," and I saw all kinds of stars for a minute or two. At midnight we started for Nashville.

I would like to hear from any ex-Confederate who was in that battle. I kept a diary while in the service, and, looking it over sometimes, I wonder how I ever managed to get home alive.[268] — E. R. DALEY

☛ GEN. FORREST'S ORDER TO COL. BAXTER SMITH

Baxter Smith, C.S.A.

I write of an incident that occurred during the battle that Forrest had with the Federals at Murfreesboro in 1862. I was at home on sick leave just after the battle of Fishing Creek. My health improving, I joined the Texas Hangers and Morgan's men, who were scouting the country near Nashville and trying to ascertain when [Union] Gen. [Don Carlos] Buell would advance his forces. About fifteen of us young men banded together and made our ways out from Nolensville, Triune, and Sparta, [Tenn.,] and met Gen. Forrest in McMinnville as he was coming down on Murfreesboro with about twelve hundred men. I persuaded the boys to join the battalion of Col. Baxter Smith, then a Major. We soon realized that we had a leader who knew his business. About five miles from Murfreesboro we were halted and ordered to "dismount, fix saddles, and tighten girts." This we did, remounted, and galloped into Murfreesboro just about daylight. The Texas Rangers engaged the Ninth Michigan. Quite a number of Federals collected at the courthouse, and Col. [James Jefferson] Morrison, of the Second Georgia, undertook to dislodge them. Gen. Forrest in the meantime hastily collected six companies, Col. Baxter Smith's four companies being of the command. Gen. Forrest, placing himself at the head of these six companies, moved out about two miles from town to attack the Third Minnesota, about twelve hundred strong. Think of it—three hundred and fifty cavalry charge twelve hundred infantry! The charge was disastrous to us. Our men fell back, and Gen. Forrest raged. The writer's horse was shot in the head, and the blood spurted so freely that he got off, expecting his horse to drop; but realizing his danger, he remounted and rode out safely. Gen. Forrest re-formed his men, rode out in front, and, in a clear, distinct voice, said: "Col. Smith, lead the charge." I shall never forget the impression made on my mind at that moment. Col. Smith had taken Trim. Brown and myself on his staff for the fight, and we had to follow him. Col. Smith tied his bridle reins, and, with sword in one hand and pistol in the other, started out in a gallop, and led his command right on into the midst of the enemy; and it was a hand-to-hand fight for about one hour, until the enemy retreated, leaving all their tents and baggage.

Oaklands Mansion, Battle of Murfreesboro, July 13, 1862. (Photo L. Seabrook)

Gen. Forrest captured the entire Federal force, consisting of about twenty-five hundred or three thousand men, a large quantity of army stores, mules, and wagons. We carried them to McMinnville; paroled the men and sent the officers back South. Gen. Forrest gave the men their [musical] band, and they serenaded us with the good old songs of "Dixie," "Bonnie Blue Flag," "The Girl I Left Behind Me," and other Southern airs.

How our hearts filled with joy and pride when we thought of the victory we had won! Armed with shotguns and any other that we could get, and without artillery, while the enemy had the latest improved Enfield and Springfield rifles and a splendid battery of artillery. The battery that was captured that day was taken and used by Gen. Forrest during the remainder of the war, and was known far and near as the famous Morton Battery, being a regular terror to the enemy. It was commanded by Capt. John W. Morton, of Nashville, Forrest's Chief of Artillery.

God bless the old gray-haired Confederates who have had such hard times in this world of disappointments; and when the great Master sounds the last trumpet, may they all be found with "palms of victory" in their hands, "praising God, from whom all blessings flow."[269] — CAPT. FRANK BATTLE

☛ MEMORY OF GEN. JOSEPH WHEELER

Joseph Wheeler, C.S.A.

The first time I ever saw Gen. Wheeler was when the cavalry were covering Bragg's retreat from Shelbyville to Chattanooga. We were engaged day and night, and for a week our saddles had not been taken from our horses' backs. It was one continuous fight, and the rain fell unceasingly. The artillery of the enemy would, now and then, drive through the thick woods into our pickets and get within fifty yards of our line of battle. This continued until we reached the top of Cumberland Mountain. Except for the snow, I do not think Marshal [Michel] Ney had a harder time holding the Russians in check. They never let up; neither did Wheeler. He sat facing the enemy, with his back to us, and a comrade

J. K. Womack, C.S.A.

called my attention to him, saying: "Look at Gen. Wheeler." "Where?" said I. "There," he answered, pointing out the General. I did not believe such a looking man [a scout] was Gen. Wheeler. He had on hip pants, a checked calico shirt, and neither coat nor vest. With pistol in hand, he was looking forward as though he were hunting for bees, and I wondered if that was really our chief. Suddenly a troop of Federal cavalry galloped over the hill to take a view of the situation, and I was amazed when our chief fired the contents of his pistol at them. Before I could get ready to fire they were gone. I learned to love Gen. Wheeler that day, and as I advance in years my love for him increases. To me he is the greatest man in the United States. Diminutive in size, he is quick in action, generous to a fault, brave as Napoleon, and modest as a woman.[270] — MR. J. K. WOMACK

☛ A CONFEDERATE BOY'S EXPERIENCE IN SEEING A BATTLE
On the eve of the battle of Murfreesboro, December 31, 1862, news reached Unionville that Gen. Bragg would attack the enemy early next morning. In company with several friends I decided to go and see the battle, as I had never been on a battlefield. Before sunrise the next morning we were on the road. Upon reaching the battlefield we were halted by guards whom we flanked, and we pressed on toward the smoke of battle. Near the edge of a small field, where many had fallen, I discovered a saber bayonet stuck up between two dead soldiers, one a Federal and the other a Confederate, lying close together, as if they had been placed in that position and marked with the bayonet for future recognition. I took the bayonet, which I still have, though I have often regretted doing so. Both of these soldiers may have been lost to relatives by my thoughtlessness. We did not reach the line of battle that evening, and at sunset went to the hospital, in a church near the town. Here I saw more horrible sights, if possible, than I had already seen. The groans and cries of suffering soldiers rang long in my ears. One little fellow particularly attracted my attention. "O sir, if you have a sharp knife, please cut this [minie] ball out of my hand! It is nearly killing me. The

surgeon says there is no ball in my hand!" he cried in agony. Dr. B. F. Duggan, of Unionville, happened to come in about that time, and said to the sufferer: "Let me see your hand." "Yes, sir: please help me if you can. Are you a doctor?" "I have dressed many soldiers' wounds," said the doctor, and he soon found the ball and cut it out.

"Lion of the South." Memorial to unknown Confederate soldiers.

Wandering over the battlefield that night, we reached the field hospital of the Twenty-Third Tennessee Regiment. Here I learned that my brother Richard had been wounded that evening, but I could not learn how severely. Early next morning one of our company dismounted, and, divesting a dead Federal soldier of knapsack, pistols, gun, and all accouterments, armed himself as a soldier. When questioned he said: "I am going to fight to-day if the battle opens up." In a short time we were with the Twenty-Third Regiment. We were all mounted, and soon after we arrived the enemy, supposing we were officers, threw some shells at us. The second shell exploded in the trees above our heads. I spent most of the day searching for my fallen brother, but all in vain. He sleeps among the unknown dead. I went home, but returned again the third day to search for some traces of my brother Richard. I met the army on the retreat from Shelbyville, when I gave my basket of rations to the boys and turned sorrowfully homeward.[271] — G. B. MOON

☛ HOW LINCOLN TRICKED DIXIE & LAUNCHED THE WAR
. . . The long-threatened "irrepressible conflict" at length burst upon us when South Carolina, in December, 1860, passed the ordinance of secession, just after the election of Mr. Lincoln. In quick succession followed other States in the beginning of the year 1861. Virginia deliberated long, and seriously debated the question. Her geographical position necessarily made her the battle ground.

Eagerly we watched State after State wheel into line, until finally, April 17, 1861, the ordinance of secession was passed by Virginia. It was precipitated by President Lincoln's call for seventy-five thousand volunteers to suppress the rebellion. This was the death knell of the more conservative element, who vainly strove to stem the current; but when the demand was made on Virginia to furnish her quota of the seventy-five thousand to battle with her sister States, the die was cast, and the grand old State, "the mother of Presidents, the mother of statesmen," took the stand for weal or woe to uphold the rights guaranteed her under the constitution.

The States seceded in the following order: South Carolina, December 20, 1860; Mississippi, January 9, 1861; Florida, January 10; Alabama, January 11; Georgia, January 18; Louisiana, January 26; Texas, March 4; Virginia, April 17; Tennessee, May 6; Arkansas, May 6; North Carolina, May 20.

Startling events followed rapidly the action of South Carolina's secession. December 26 Maj. [Robert] Anderson, commanding United States troops, evacuated Fort Moultrie and occupied Fort Sumter; on the 28th the Confederate authorities seized the government buildings in Charleston. On December 20 John B. Floyd, Secretary of War under President James Buchanan, resigned.

January 3, 1861, the Confederates seized Fort Pulaski, at Savannah, Ga., also the arsenal at Taylorsville, Ga., and Fort Caswell, N.C., all the same day. On January 4 the Confederates seized Fort Morgan, in Mobile Bay. On the 8th Jacob Thompson, Secretary of the Interior, another member of President Buchanan's cabinet, resigned. On the 9th the Confederate forces at Charleston fired upon and drove to sea the steamboat *Star of the West*. On the 11th the Confederate authorities seized the arsenal at Baton Rouge, La.; on the 13th Fort Barancas, Fla., was seized by the Confederates, and the same day the navy yard at Pensacola,

Fla., surrendered to the demands of Gov. [Francis Wilkinson] Pickens. On the 16th a commission from South Carolina in Washington demanded of the President the surrender of Fort Sumter. What were the results? As this "firing on the old flag" was the shibboleth of the Sadducean fanatic, I am going to quote history from an impartial writer, an Englishman of conscientious spirit (Percy Greg), who, writing in perfect fairness and disinterestedness, can be fully relied on.

The notorious *Star of the West*.

The True Story of Sumter: As the new President made a triumphal progress to Washington through the States which had elected him he delivered speeches—brief, indeed, but from their very brevity significant and more than ominous, he admitted at Indianapolis that "the marching [of] an army into South Carolina without the consent of her people and with hostile intentions toward them would be coercion and invasion, but if the United States were merely to recover their forts and property, collect the customs duties and assert the powers which the Federal government claimed, was this coercion or invasion?" Mr. Lincoln knew that he could not recover Fort Moultrie or levy a dollar in Charleston till he had laid the city in ashes. Was that coercion? He knew that thirty thousand men could hardly install a Federal judge in Columbia. Was that invasion? *Such playing with double-edged words—and words that flung fire among flax—would have been ridiculed in a debating society, and was unpardonable in one whose words must affect the action of governments, the motion of armies, and the temper of nations.*

A still more startling sentence followed: "If a State and county were equal in extent of territory and number of inhabitants, in what was the State better than the county? What mysterious right had the State to play tyrant?" He might as well have asked: "Why should Belgium enjoy any privilege denied to Lancashire?" *Was he really ignorant of the leading facts of American history, the first principles of American law, or was the question a claptrap appeal to ignorance and faction? If it meant anything, it suggested a subversion of the existing order, sure to be forcibly resisted by two-thirds of the States and more than half their population. To insinuate revolution, to hint civil war in terms like these, indicates the man as yet unimpressed by responsibility.* Even as a matter of taste, what would be thought of an English statesman who should ostentatiously declare that Scotland was of no more account than Sussex, or put Ireland on a par with Derbyshire? How would such an orator, during an excess of Scotch or Irish feeling, be received in Glasgow or Dublin? No public man, after a similar insult to the excited pride of a free people, could hope to enjoy in any great city a reception agreeable to his dignity, and *Mr. Lincoln was prudently advised to avoid the streets of Baltimore, and to pass through Maryland in a sort of incognito. He was in no danger of such treatment as a Royalist chief justice had undergone from the mob of Boston; the assassination plot devised to explain his evasion was a pure fiction, but it would not have suited the President elect to be hooted through the only Southern city he had to enter.* (Even Mr. Horace Greeley virtually admits that this was all the President had to fear.) *Mr. Lincoln appeared in Washington, to be installed without disturbance or demonstration of hostility on March 4, 1861. His inaugural address maintained his ambiguous attitude, and yet committed him to grave and glaring usurpation.*

Whatever Mr. Lincoln's opinion on the legality of secession, he knew it to be a doubtful problem, on which immeasurably superior lawyers held the Southern view. It was either a subject falling within the reserved powers of the Southern States, as the South held; or, from the Northern standpoint, a question of law to be decided by the Supreme Court. Had the court pronounced against the legality of secession, the action to be taken was a question for Congress. Even the despotic [Andrew] *Jackson had appealed to Congress before threatening South Carolina with a military "enforcement of the law." By proclaiming his intention to "execute the laws," seize forts, and collect taxes within the seceded States, Mr. Lincoln not only decided the question of law in contempt of the proper tribunal, but deprived Congress and the Northern people of their right to decide, coolly and at leisure, whether they would endeavor to reconstruct the Union on the novel principle of compulsion. They elected him on positive and emphatic assurances that his election did not mean separation; they were now cheated out of their opportunity of reconsidering the case under the new light which had done so much to solve and* startle them, while half of them still believed coercive war illegal, and a moiety of the other half abhorred it as foolish and wicked.

At the same time Mr. Lincoln threw his glove into the face of the Southern people. He told them he would act in a manner, which, as the facts stood, meant a war of invasion. Yet he had deprecated the idea of war, and, if his words meant anything, had nullified his own menace by renouncing beforehand the only means of executing it. If, as he declared, he would not place intruders in the Southern customs houses, appoint intrusive judges, marshals, and attorneys, or support them by armed force, he could collect no duties and execute no laws. The inaugural speech, like its predecessors, contradicted itself at every turn. For Republicans [then the Liberal party] of Mr. [Zachariah] Chandler's type the speech meant war. Hesitating conservative [that is, moderate] Unionists inferred with equal justice that it promised to avoid war. Democrats [then the Conservative party] saw that the President had given a pledge which nullified his threats of coercion. The Southern people saw that they had been insulted, but saw that the challenge given in one sentence had been retracted in another. Southern statesmen drew the true conclusion, that the speech meant anything or nothing, and must be interpreted by the temper of the North. But that temper was uncertain. A straightforward speech would have steadied it, would have elicited a cry for war or a peremptory demand for peace, and for that reason Mr. Lincoln and his advisers had been carefully ambiguous.

Francis W. Pickens.

The selection of the [U.S.] Cabinet was significant. The Secretary of State was the chief of the violent Republicans [Liberals] who had countersigned [scallywag Hinton Rowan] Helper's abusive and menacing [anti-South] manifesto [*The Impending Crisis of the South*]. The Treasury was filled by Salmon P. Chase, of Ohio, an abolitionist less desperate than [Charles] Sumner and less scrupulous than Greeley. The War Department was in [the] charge of Simon Cameron, of Pennsylvania, a professional politician, of whom it could only be predicted that he would favor whatever course promised the largest opportunities of lucrative jobbery, the most lavished and the most uncontrollable expenditure.

Every post of importance was given to the North. No State south of the Potomac and Ohio was represented in the [U.S.] Cabinet. [Montgomery] Blair, of Maryland, and [Edward] Bates, of Missouri, were Southerners only as was Lincoln himself, by chance of birth. Their nomination to insignificant posts emphasized the anti-national [actually, the sectional anti-South] character of the [new Left-wing government [under Liberal Lincoln].[272]

Such a Cabinet was another proof of the utterly unparalleled nature of the situation, the anti-Unionist attitude of the victorious [Republican / Liberal] party. Never had a Cabinet consisted solely of Southerners, with an insignificant Pennsylvanian and Indianian stuck into insignificant places. Never had the Union been ruled by a [wholly sectional] party in whose conventions the Northern States were not represented, or which had not received a Northern vote tenfold larger than the whole South had cast for Lincoln.

Peace at any price, so it was peace with honor, was the interest of the Confederacy and the policy of its government. It was fortunate that its President [Jefferson Davis] was at once a soldier and a statesman, thoroughly familiar with the military resources of the North, with the strength of the navy, with the character of Northern politicians. He appreciated the motives which might induce the Republican [Liberal] leaders to precipitate hostilities, and was anxious to avert them if possible; and if not, to throw the whole responsibility visibly and unquestionably upon *the party which had all to gain by war.*

The first important act of his [Davis'] government was to send [peace] commissioners to Washington. Their formal instructions of course looked to the recognition of the Confederate States, the provision to be made for the common debt of the Union, the transfer of the forts still held by Federal troops within Confederate jurisdiction, and the settlement of all reciprocal claims. *The immediate object was the maintenance of peace on the lines of the status quo.*

Mr. [Martin J.] Crawford, the first of the [Confederate peace] commissioners, arrived before President Buchanan retired, but the latter had lost his head amid the incessant menaces and denunciations of the radicals [far left Liberals], more excusably and less completely than his successor. Mr. Lincoln might have been hooted through Baltimore; Mr. Buchanan was reasonably afraid of personal outrage on his homeward road, short as it was, and thought it not unlikely that he would find his modest Pennsylvania country seat in flames. Nothing was done till the new government came into power on March 4, 1861. Mr. [William Henry] Seward refused to receive the [Confederate] commissioners. This was needless discourtesy; the reception of eminent citizens of Southern States in no wise prejudiced the question of whether those States had now become a foreign power. The envoys were men of standing too high to quibble with him on points of etiquette. An informal letter from Mr. Crawford to Mr. [John] Forsythe, a public man of the highest character and station, opened their mission on March 12. Couched in the usual terms of diplomatic courtesy, it was answered by Mr. Seward in a long, argumentative, offensive paper, refusing the requested interview with the President [Lincoln]. Mr. Seward, in a long public life and a subsequent official experience of eight years, showed a statesman's adroitness in discriminating between those whom it was necessary to court and those whom it was safe to insult. The nature of the man was indicated by the story—true or well invented—that he gratuitously told a great English statesman (attending the heir to the Crown on a complimentary visit to the States) that his first act on coming into power would be to quarrel with England. Mr. Seward would never have so blustered before a French statesman or a private Englishman. With like adroitness he kept his letter on March 15 for private display and subsequent publication; and to amuse them till the Northern government was ready to act and the Northern people wrought into a different mood, opened an indirect communication with the Confederate commissioners through Judge [Samuel] Nelson and Judge [John A.] Campbell, of the Supreme Court.

Jefferson Davis' funeral car, New Orleans, LA, December 11, 1889.

The question of [Fort] Sumter was urgent. Mr. Seward knew that without express assurances from Washington the Confederate government could not much longer forbear its reduction. *The judges warned him upon their own authority, supported by that of the Chief Justice [Roger B. Taney], that it would be impossible, without serious violation both of the constitution itself and express congressional statutes, to attempt the coercion of the seceding States; also that the refusal of a recognition to which they held themselves clearly and instantly entitled might lead to irrevocable and very unfortunate incidents.*

The Secretary's tone was such that the judges believed him to be restrained even from recognition rather by the state of public feeling in the North than by his own judgment. However that might be, Mr. Seward's language about Fort Sumter was as explicit as possible. "The evacuation of the fort is as much as the government can bear." This was the immediate and pressing issue. Mr. Seward authorized the judges to say that before a letter could reach Mr. Davis the latter would learn by telegraph that *the order for the evacuation of Fort Sumter had been given*. As for Forts Pinckney and Pensacola no change should be made. Judge Campbell communicated this assurance to the commissioners. They required that the pledge should be reduced to writing. This was done by Judge Campbell; the written statement was approved by Judge Nelson, and the whole transaction reported to Mr. Seward by letter.

In consideration of this express engagement to leave the *status* of Fort Pinckney unaltered and *forthwith to evacuate Sumter*, the Confederates made two concessions of vital moment. They refrained from pressing the demand for recognition—a point on which Mr. Seward showed great personal anxiety, and they forbore to reduce the forts, then clearly in their power.

All this occurred on March 15. Seward's pledge obviously implied that the evacuation of Fort Sumter should be ordered within two or three days. *On the 20th the [Confederate] commissioners learned from [Confederate] Gen. Beauregard, commanding at Charleston, that Sumter had not been evacuated, and that Maj. Anderson was still working on its defenses, a breach of the truce which would have entitled the Confederates to compel an instant surrender. The dispatch was submitted to Mr. Seward by the judges above named. He pleaded that the delay was accidental, and repeated his promise. This assurance was again given in writing to the commissioners by Judge Campbell,*

who again communicated to Mr. Seward in writing what had been said on his behalf. Mr. Seward then repeated, on March 21, his absolute pledge to evacuate Sumter and leave the status quo of Fort Pinckney undisturbed. Meantime Mr. [Gustavus Vasa] Fox, afterwards Assistant Secretary of the [U.S.] navy, had urged upon the government a plan for the violent or surreptitious relief of Fort Sumter. Finding, as he said, the President and Mr. Blair disposed to sanction his plan, Fox proposed a visit to Charleston to ascertain its practicability. By Mr. Lincoln's orders he left Washington on March 19, and reached Charleston *on March 21, the day on which Mr. Seward repeated his promise that the fort should be immediately evacuated.* Mr. Fox recorded that he had obtained from the Governor of South Carolina permission to visit Fort Sumter. How that permission was obtained he was careful not to tell, but that it was given on an understanding that his purpose was pacific there could be no question. What actually passed is told in the Governor's report to the State Legislature. The pass was given "expressly upon the pledge of pacific purpose." *Fox's legal status, then, was that of a spy, liable to be hung on detection. Morally, he and his government in the position of men using a flag of truce to cover a concerted surprise, a crime which the opinion of all nations and the customs of civilized war brand with especial infamy.* A few days later a second spy, Col. [Ward Hill] Lamon, employed by Mr. Lincoln, expressly informed Gov. Pickens that he was sent to arrange the removal of the garrison. He obtained a pass. On his return from Sumter he asked if a war vessel might enter the harbor to remove the garrison. The Governor refused Lincoln's "confidential agent" then suggested an ordinary steamer, to which the other agreed. This transaction was reported by Pickens to the [Confederate peace] commissioners by telegraph.

The commissioners sent the message through Judge Campbell to Mr. Seward, who on the next day (April 1) repudiated Lamon in language which suggested that he had been kept in ignorance of the transaction. Mr. Seward, however, engaged in writing that the government would not undertake attempts to supply Sumter without giving due notice to Governor Pickens. Judge Campbell noted the inconsistency, and asked: "Am I to understand that there has been a change in your former communications?"—i.e., the engagement to evacuate Sumter. "None," replied Mr. Seward.

On April 7, learning that the Federal government was making secret preparations for the naval attack planned by Mr. Fox, the [Confederate] commissioners again addressed Mr. Seward in writing (using the signature of Judge Campbell, since Mr. Seward had throughout refused to communicate with them), directly inquiring whether his assurances were to be relied on. The Secretary replied in writing: "Faith as to Sumter fully kept: wait and see."

At that moment *the secret expedition* was ready, and was expected to reach Charleston within forty-eight hours.

On the morrow after this last explicit pledge, at the moment when the fleet was supposed to be off the harbor, Mr. [Robert S.] Chew (a clerk of Mr. Seward's), accompanied by a certain Capt. Talbot, read to Gov. Pickens and Gen. Beauregard at Charleston a paper said to have been delivered to Chew by President Lincoln on April 6, the day before Mr. Seward's last promise to evacuate the fort, notifying the State government that an attempt would be made to supply Fort Sumter with provisions, and that if not resisted no attempt would be made to throw in men, arms, or ammunition without further notice. *Even had it been properly signed and accredited, the paper was a confession of foul play. It ignored Mr. Seward's solemn and repeated engagements. Its delivery was obviously meant not to give warning, but to cover a surprise; and even its promise, coming from Seward's chief and Fox's employer, was dishonored on its face. The notice was a declaration of war—the dispatch of the expedition the commencement of active hostilities.*

Mr. Lincoln's government thus unquestionably began the war, and by a signal act of treachery. Mr. Seward's first pledge to evacuate Sumter was given March 15; the last, April 7. In the interval the question was discussed in the Cabinet. On March 19 Mr. Lincoln sent Fox to scheme an attack; on the 23rd or 24th he ordered its preparation; on April 6 the fleet had set forth; on the 8th it was expected to enter the harbor; and not till that moment were the Confederate authorities warned that an attack was intended. Even had Mr. Seward's promises been unauthorized, the President [Lincoln] was bound by them until abundant notice had been given of their repudiation. Even on this utterly absurd supposition, the attempted surprise of April 8 was a foul treason. But it is as certain that Mr. Seward dared not and did not act without his chief's full knowledge and sanction as that such an offense would have compelled his immediate dismissal. His retention in the highest Cabinet office and in Lincoln's full confidence suffices to fix the latter with previous cognizance and entire approbation of his pledges. Mr. Lincoln's personal share of responsibility for the false promises, the deliberate and protracted deception, and the treacherous surprise which that deception covered and prepared, is matter neither of importance nor of doubt. For nearly a month the government of which he was the absolute chief were keeping the Confederate government from action by pledges which at the same time they were preparing with all possible energy to violate. This treachery had made the capture of Sumter an immediate necessity. Yet it was not summoned till

Union guns pointed at Fort Sumter.

April 11; and then after long parley Anderson refused to surrender, and was reduced when the enemy's fleet was in sight, by a thirty-six hours' bombardment, wherein, strangely enough, no man on either side was hurt, though casemates, guns, and parapets suffered severely. The Confederates had obviously done their very utmost to postpone or avert hostilities. Mr. Lincoln, Mr. Seward, and their colleagues intentionally and deliberately forced on the collision, determined to leave the government no choice but between surrender at discretion and instant war.

They gained their end. Northern feeling would not sanction an offensive war till every effort at peaceful settlement had been exhausted. Hence it was imperative, if Lincoln's presidency were not to be signalized by the immediate dissolution of the Union and to bring the Republican [Liberal] party into universal odium and contempt, or the Chicago [Liberal] platform to be ignominiously retracted, that the North should be hurried into war on false pretenses. The authors of the collusion, the men who had publicly pledged themselves to peace while secretly preferring war, profited by their own duplicity, and concealed the transactions which had rendered the reduction of Sumter an instant necessity of self-defense. The North was persuaded the South had struck the first blow—"had fired on the uniform," "had insulted the flag." *The imperious self-will of a dictatorial democracy was successfully inflamed to fury*, and from this point it would be as profitable to trace the sequence, the fancies in a fever dream, as to follow *the unreasoning impulses of a deluded people*.

The border States had watched the course of events and understood their significance. They saw that *the Federal government had been the aggressor, and—as they on strong prima facie ground believed, and is now proven—the willful, calculating, treacherous aggressor. They saw through the thin veil thrown over offensive invasion and fratricidal war. Their State pride and their constitutional traditions were outraged by the impertinence which treated sovereign States as "lawless combinations."* From Maryland, Virginia, and North Carolina, from Kentucky and Tennessee, from Missouri and Arkansas, came one unanimous cry of disgust, contempt, and indignation. They adhered to the Union in spite of unnumbered insults and wrongs. But the Union to which they adhered was the Union of Hamilton, Washington, Randolph, and Jefferson; a *voluntary union of sovereign States*, excluding every idea of compulsion. *Forced to choose between secession and coercion, with one voice the border States, Delaware scarcely excepted, refused to join in a war of aggression.* Kentucky proclaimed herself neutral. Missouri followed the same course. Gov. [Thomas Holliday] Hicks, of Maryland, refused to convoke the Legislature or appeal to the people. In so doing he betrayed his trust. It was not for him to decide the course of Maryland, but to obey her will as it should be declared by the sovereign people. . . . *The States which were persuaded or tricked into neutrality found to their cost what Mr. Lincoln's explicit and repeated assurances were worth. Maryland, Kentucky, and Missouri trusted and repented in chains, under a reign of terror.* Virginia, North Carolina, Tennessee, and Arkansas better understood, as events proved, the government they had to deal with, the crisis which its proclamation had created. . . . *The action of Virginia deserves special notice. She, above all, was forced by the Washington government to a cruel alternative. She had no mind to* secede, but it left her no choice. She could reach her sister States only through her side. She must be the accomplice or the first victim, and in the latter case, be the issue of the Northern appeal to the sword what it might, she must inevitably be ruined by the costs. Never since the Athenians abandoned city and country and furnished two-thirds of the fleet which saved the calculating and cowardly Peloponnesions from the same fate, has history recorded so noble, so generous, and so glorious a choice. Unless Maryland should act with instant and most improbable energy, depose her treacherous governor, call a contention, pass an ordinance of secession, and bar the invader's road, all in a few days' time, *Washington would be the headquarters of the enemy's chief army, and the war be waged from first to last on Virginia's soil.* No other Southern State was similarly exposed, and none had so much to lose. [For] Virginia was a rich, civilized, and prosperous country, a land of thriving towns and valuable plantations, of well-tilled and well-stocked farms—"the Flanders of the South."[273] — MAJOR MERCER OTEY

☛ HARD TIMES ON HOOD'S RETREAT

I am . . . a resident of North Missouri, still living in the county where I enlisted in the Confederate service in April, 1861. [What follows is] . . . a short outline of my experience with Hood's army in the winter of 1864, when near [Nashville, Tenn.].

I was a member of the First Missouri Battery—a "shoeless Confederate." On the march to Nashville the Federals made a stand at Columbia, on the north side of Duck River. Our battery was sent with a detachment of cavalry and infantry to cross the river and if possible cut off the enemy. We crossed at Davis' Ferry on a pontoon. We had a very rough country to travel over. The night was so very dark we could not pick our road, and while encountering some of the huge rocks that came in our way broke down one of the wheels on the gun to which I belonged. The fifth wheel, which we kept for such mishaps, would not fit. The darkness of the night and the whizzing of Minies from the enemy's sharpshooters, made us think and act fast. Two men were sent to a farmhouse near by, and took the rear

wheel off an old-fashioned Tennessee wagon, and our damage was soon adjusted. We had many obstacles to overcome during the night, and did not reach the main pike at Spring Hill (the point designated) until daylight November 30, 1864, only to find our game had escaped in the direction of Nashville. After a short rest we pursued them to Franklin, where occurred one of the most bloody battles of the war, in which our company performed its duty in this needless butchery of Confederates. The loss on both sides was very heavy. The next morning we found an artillery wheel, left by the enemy in the streets of Franklin, which was soon put in place of the farmer's wagon wheel, and the pursuit was kept up to within three miles of Nashville. Leaving the main army in front of the city, we were again sent with a detachment five thousand strong, under Forrest, to capture Murfreesboro. After drawing the enemy out of the fortification, as Forrest desired to defeat them on the open field, we lost the day by some of our infantry giving way, and narrowly escaped capture. The weather was cold for the climate, and many of our men were without shoes and thinly clad otherwise. I had on a pair of old boots full of holes, and when marching would frequently stop and empty the gravel that intruded on my toes. When the break in our lines at Nashville occurred we were near Murfreesboro, and our route of exit by the main pike was cut off. After a very circuitous march over some of the roughest country I ever saw, attended by severe hardships, we arrived [back] at Columbia December 19, 1864, and made a junction with the main army. Two days previous to our arrival my old boots had entirely deserted my bleeding feet, and my barefoot track was plainly visible in the snow.

A short time before we arrived at Columbia one of my comrades (Taylor) and I, by permission, crossed the pontoon bridge in advance of the company. Arriving at a livery barn filled with soldiers trying to dry themselves around some smoky fires, I asked if any one in there had a pair of shoes to sell or give away. A boy of about fifteen years standing in the office door said: "Yes. Come in." He produced a pair of half-worn cloth shoes and priced them at fifteen dollars. I gave him a twenty-dollar bill, and while he was out hunting change I spied a pair of heavy leather shoes partly covered up by an old Federal overcoat under a bunk in the corner, and when he returned they were changed from that hiding place to one under a coat of the same color worn by the writer.

The boy soon returned with two ten-dollar bills, and said I could have the shoes for one of them, as he failed to get the change desired. Taylor and I left the barn with a step somewhat faster than we entered. I told Taylor he could have the cloth shoes, as they were about two numbers too large for me. We were both shod. The leather shoes were just my fit. I wonder if the person from whom I took those shoes is living? The shoes did me much good. We had many hardships to undergo the remainder of that retreat. Our company surrendered in North Carolina under Gen. J. E. Johnston, April 26, 1865.[274] — SAM B. DUNLAP

☛ A CONFEDERATE WOMAN FIGHTS A YANKEE GENERAL

Mrs. Andrew Erwin.

During . . . [the Civil War] the English government sent a representative to America to inspect our [Confederate] military tactics. He was a Col. Freemantle, chosen from the Cold Stream Guards, who were selected from the best families to guard the queen's palace. He spent several weeks at [the famous home of my sister, Mrs. Andrew Erwin of Beechwood, Tenn.], and wrote a book called *Six Months in the Confederate States*. In this he mentions the ladies he met there . . . [which included me and my sister]. He liked the South better than the North, and seemed to be one of the family. When there was a lull of hostilities Beechwood was a social center. . . .

In 1863, in order to get away from the Yankees, I went to Huntsville, Ala., but it was from the frying pan into the fire, as the Yankees poured into the city, and *I was arrested a few days later by Gen. [Ormsby MacKnight] Mitchell* (Cincinnati), of geography notoriety. *My offense was having been seen with a tiny Confederate flag in my hand.* My niece, Miss Rosa Turner, and Miss Mathews had played with a grace hoop with one of these flags attached, and the three of us were summoned to his tent. He began his questioning, saying to me: "Don't you know I could send you to Fort La Fayette [the notorious Yankee prison] in five minutes?" I said: "That would be very rapid traveling; I do not know that I could make the trip in that time." I could see a lurking smile in his eyes, and he said: "What is your jail made for, Miss?" I answered: "To put outlawed men in, sir." He then said: "No man, woman, or child shall say in my tent that they are Rebels." I said: "I *am* a Rebel, open and aboveboard. You had better watch that class who are good Rebels when *I* see them and good Federals when *you* see them, when they want favors done. You know where to find me." Said he: "Are you a lady?" "Who doubts it?" I said. "You women get to your homes," he replied. If I had had a pistol I should have shot him. He was a poor, cowardly man—sat all the time behind his desk buying cotton in gold while he paid his soldiers in greenbacks. He never went to the front, but sent the Fourth Ohio and other soldiers to fight his battles. This regiment went out fifteen hundred strong, and at the close of the war there were but fifty left! They were brave men, and we women were wicked enough to count the empty saddles on their return. This Gen. Mitchell had some bad men in his command, and was bad himself. He died of yellow fever on the coast of Charleston.[275] — MISS ROWE C. WEBSTER

Miss Rowe C. Webster.

☛ PATHETIC BURIAL AT MIDNIGHT

The Tennessee army had been retreating before Sherman's hosts all summer. The one hundred days' battle of that memorable campaign had ended. Atlanta had fallen, and Gen. Johnston had been relieved. Gen. Hood had taken command and had made his famous speech, in which he said he was going to advance, and that he believed the army would rather advance on parched corn than to retreat on full rations. Every one in hearing hallooed themselves hoarse in rejoicing over the idea of advancing. "Advance on parched corn" became a common expression in the army, but little did we think it would be a reality, as it did on many occasions before the campaign ended. I remember to have seen men picking up scattered grains of corn where cavalry horses had been fed.

The fatal, though then appreciated, advance was soon made. We had marched a few days in the direction of Tennessee, had left Georgia, and were passing through North Alabama, and my division (Edward

Johnston's) was that day in the rear of the army. I belonged to the division provost guard, whose duty it was to bring up the rear of the army. I was on duty in charge of five men, with instructions to remain one mile in the rear of the army and to allow no one to remain behind. The sun was hot, the lanes were long, and the roads dry and dusty. When the sun was setting that afternoon, as we were passing an old-fashioned farmhouse, a farmer hailed us and said one of our men was in the house dying. We found him to be intelligent-looking, of middle age, and probably five feet eleven inches high. He wore a suit of homemade Confederate gray jeans. An examination of his effects failed to disclose his identity other than that by the Palmetto buttons we supposed that he was from South Carolina. We had no time to lose; dark was soon upon us, and we were very tired from a day's long march. The old farmer showed that he was not a Southern man, but he exhibited a kindly feeling. He allowed us to bury our comrade in his family burying ground, and to make a rude coffin of some planks from his barn. Two of us made the coffin while the others dug a grave, and by the time the poor soldier was dead the preparations for his burial had been completed. It was about one o'clock when one of the boys held a torch and we laid him to rest while a short prayer was said. Then we lay down on the soft grass beside the grave and slept until daylight, when we continued our journey.[276] — COL. J. W. SIMMONS

☛ THE POPE & THE CONFEDERACY
William E. Curtis, in special correspondence to the *Chicago Record*, gives some interesting facts in connection with the attitude of Pope Pius IX, toward the Southern Confederacy. While the pontiff never formally recognized the Southern States as a nation, his correspondence with the authorities at Richmond was highly considerate, and is very interesting.

The belligerency of the Southern States was recognized by Queen Victoria May 13, 1861; Emperor Napoleon [III], of France, did the same on June 10 of that year; the King of the Netherlands, June 16; Queen Isabella, of Spain, June 17; and the Emperor of Brazil, August 1. On October 12, 1862, Pope Pius IX wrote to the archbishops of New York and New Orleans, making an appeal to their "apostolic zeal and their episcopal solicitude for the happiness and welfare of their respective people, exhorting them to make efforts in his (the pope's name, as well as in theirs), for the restoration of peace, the termination of the disastrous civil war then raging in America, and the reestablishment of concord and charitable love throughout the whole country." This letter was of a purely ecclesiastical character, and had designedly no bearing on politics. At the date on which it was written, New Orleans had been captured and [Union] Gen. [Benjamin Franklin] Butler had proclaimed martial law there. The prelates to whom the Pope addressed these letters were Archbishop [John] Hughes, of New York and Archbishop [John Mary] Odin, of New Orleans, both of whom complied with his request and ordered prayers for peace.

John Hughes.

Mr. Curtis quotes extensively from Dr. Jose Ignacio Rodriguez, a most learned diplomatist and a recognized authority on diplomatic history. The latter considers that "the attitude of the two prelates, especially of Archbishop Hughes, who was a personal friend of Mr. [William Henry] Seward, in favor of the preservation of the Union, is a matter of historical and diplomatic record." Archbishop Hughes, in writing on the subject, stated: "If a division of the country should ever take place, the Catholics will have had no voluntary part in bringing about such a calamity." He aided the government substantially when a call was made on the State of New York for militia to sustain the laws; the Sixty-Ninth Regiment was mainly composed of Catholics, and Meagher's Irish Brigade and Cocoran's Legion were subsequently raised. He was also sent to Europe on a diplomatic mission. After the Trent affair, November, 1861, there seemed probability that the European powers would recognize the Confederate States, and at the request of Mr. Seward and Mr. Lincoln, Archbishop Hughes went to Europe to use his influence for the good of the United States. He sailed late in 1861, and returned to America in August, 1862. While there he had a satisfactory interview with Napoleon III, and did successful work in Rome. Letters received from Pius IX. shortly after his return show the effects of the prelate's influence. The contents of those letters were made known to Jefferson Davis sometime afterwards, and he opened correspondence with the Pope, to whom he wrote as follows:

> To His Holiness, Pope Pius IX, Most Venerable Head of the Holy See and Sovereign Pontiff of the Holy Roman Catholic Apostolic Church: The letters addressed by your holiness to the venerable heads of the catholic clergy of New Orleans and New York have been communicated to me, and I have read with emotion the terms in which your holiness has been pleased to express the profound sorrow which *the carnage, ruin, and devastation of the present war, waged by the government of the United States against the States and the people* which have elected me to be their President, have produced in your holiness. I refer to those letters by which your holiness directed the prelates above alluded to and their clergy to exhort the people and the authorities to exercise charity and show love for peace.
>
> I deeply appreciate the Christian charity and sympathy which inspired your holiness when making such an earnest appeal to the venerable clergy of the Catholic Church to work for the reestablishment of peace and concord. It is for this reason that I consider myself bound by duty to assure your holiness, personally in my own name, and in the name of the people of the Confederate States, that we have been very deeply moved in our hearts by the feelings of love and Christian charity which have guided your holiness on this occasion, and to state furthermore that these people, though threatened with cruel oppression and horrible carnage, even in their own individual homes, wish, nevertheless, and so they have always wished with fervor, to see the end of this impious war; that in our prayers to the Heavenly Father we have expressed the same feelings with which your holiness is animated: *that we have no ill will toward our enemies; that we do not covet any possession of theirs; that we struggle against them only to cause them to cease to devastate our country and shed the blood of our people, and that our only desire is to be allowed to live in peace under our institutions and laws which protect everybody, not only in the enjoyment of all temporal rights, but also in the free exercise of religion.*
>
> I pray your holiness to accept from myself and from the people of the Confederate States our sincere thanks for your holiness' efforts in favor of peace. May the Lord prolong the days of your holiness, and keep your holiness in his holy guard! — Jefferson Davis, Pres. of Confederate States.

To this letter Pope Pius IX replied December 8, 1863, as follows:

> Illustrious and Honorable President. Greetings: We have just received, with all proper benevolence, the persons sent by you to deliver to us your letter of the 23rd of September ultimo. We have learned with pleasure through the said persons and through your letter what was the nature of the feelings of joy and gratitude which were excited in you, illustrious and honorable President, when given information about the letters written by us to our venerable brothers, John, Archbishop of New York, and John, Archbishop of New

Orleans, on the 18th of October of the preceding year, wherein we made an earnest appeal to their compassionate feelings and episcopal solicitude, and exhorted them to endeavor, with fervent zeal and in our name, to induce the people of your country to put an end to the disastrous civil war which is raging there, so as to secure for your people the benefits of peace and concord and charitable love for each other.

It has been particularly gratifying to us to be informed that you and your people are animated by the same desires of peace and concord which we in the letters above referred to inculcated in the venerable brothers of ours to whom they were addressed. May God be willing to grant that the other people of America [Yankees], and of the authorities who are at their head [Lincoln and his cabinet], seriously considering what a grave thing civil war is and how much misfortune and wrong it carries with it, should listen to the inspirations of a calmer spirit, and resolutely adopt a policy of peace!

Pius IX.

As to us, we shall never cease to address the most fervent prayers to Almighty God, requesting him to inspire in the whole people a spirit of peace and charity and to free them from the great evils which now afflict them. We pray at the same time to merciful God to bestow upon you the light of his grace, and cause you to be attached to us by a perfect union. Given at St. Peter, Rome, December 3, 1863, the eighteenth of our pontificate. — Pius IX.[277] — SUMNER A. CUNNINGHAM

☛ SLAVE OWNERS IN THE UNION ARMY

The First Regiment, Eastern Shore Maryland Volunteer Infantry, [U.S.A.] was organized at Cambridge, Dorchester County, Md., in the fall of 1861, and was commanded by James Wallace, Esq., an attorney at law and farmer. *He owned nine slaves, and had some of them in camp with him as servants. Capt. John R. Keene, of Company C, also had slaves with him, his father being the owner of about sixty. Other officers of this regiment had slaves in camp with them.* The regiment was organized for home service—at least many of the men were enlisted with this understanding, so that when ordered out of the State into the two counties of Eastern Virginia there was much dissatisfaction. Company A (Capt. John C. Henry, of Cambridge) was mustered out of the Federal service, and many then went South and enlisted in what I believe was the First Maryland Volunteer Infantry of the Confederate army. In the battle of Gettysburg we met and fought this regiment and wounded and captured one of our old men of Company A, who informed us that Capt. Henry and several of our old comrades were directly in our front fighting us. This on the Federal right near the base of Culp's Hill. Previously Company B, when ordered into Delaware, had laid down their guns and refused to do service outside the State, but at Gettysburg they served loyally. Company K, Capt. Littleton Long, also had trouble, and the records show that a large majority of the company was dishonorably discharged. The regiment was never treated by the Federal government as were other Northern regiments. It was held back. *There were so many slaveholders in the command that the enlistment of their servants during the absence of the owners from home, and consequent loss of service, caused great dissatisfaction. The slaves of these loyal men, who lost their property while away from home fighting for the Union, were never paid for*, though a record of each slave is kept at the county seats of Eastern Maryland. *The [U.S.] government [under Lincoln] had agreed to respect the right of property in slaves on the part of owners who remained loyal to the Union*, but nevertheless while away from home fighting for the Union these same slaves were enlisted and freed. I suppose there were similar experiences in regiments of other border States.

Yankee slaves.

Our regiment served three years, and was honorably discharged, many of the men "veteranizing" into the Eleventh Maryland Volunteer Infantry.[278] — JOHN E. RASTALL (Adjutant First Regiment, Eastern Shore Maryland Volunteer Infantry, U.S.A.)

☛ BLESSING FOR GEN. FORREST

The impression prevalent about our great cavalry general does not credit him with much religious sentiment, yet there were many things in his career which showed a deep reverence for genuine religion. One of his most trusted officers was Col. David C. Kelley, a Methodist preacher, who maintained his Christian character consistently all through the war, and who was one of the wariest and most dashing of his subordinate commanders. For Col. Kelley he had the profoundest respect, recognizing his sincere piety as well as his splendid courage.

A little incident told me directly after the war will illustrate the tender side of Gen. Forrest's nature. It was told to me by members of my grandfather's family. My mother's father lived six miles south of the little village of Charlotte, in Dickson County, Tenn., on a farm which was granted to his father for services as captain in the Revolutionary war. He was nearly ninety years old at the beginning of the civil war. Though he had loved the Union devotedly, he deeply regretted that he could not fight for the South. He believed in her cause with all his heart. He had his old rifle cleaned and placed where he could lay his hands on it, should occasion arise for him to use it against an invading foe.

On one of his expeditions into Tennessee—I think it was on the way to Fort Donelson in 1863—Gen. Forrest spent a night at my grandfather's, and, by his considerate attention, won the old man's heart. The next morning, when the General and his personal attendants were

Nathan B. Forrest, C.S.A.

ready to start, the old gentleman, though nearly blind, must needs accompany him part of the way. So, taking his staff in his hand and one of his grandchildren to lead him, he walked along by the General's horse until they came to the main road at the edge of the farm. When the General stopped to bid his host good-by the escort rode on. The old man asked him to get off his horse, which he did. He then asked him to kneel down. Then, laying his hands on the General's head and lifting his sightless eyes to heaven, the old patriarch solemnly invoked the blessing of God on Gen. Forrest, on his men, and on the cause for which he was fighting. The General's face was bathed in tears as he remounted his horse.

In a year my grandfather was laid in his grave, Gen. Forrest lived to win many victories during the war, and afterwards he became a humble Christian. It may be that prayer was one of the influences that kept him safe through many dangers and finally led him to that Saviour in whom the old man trusted.[279] — REV. JAMES H. MCNEILLY

☛ CONFEDERATE MONUMENT, FRANKLIN, TENN.
Dedication of the Franklin (Tenn.) Confederate Monument. — On November 30, 1899, the Franklin Chapter, United Daughters of the Confederacy, will unveil a monument to Confederate soldiers on the Public Square in Franklin, Tenn. For years the good people of Franklin have been working for this monument, and success has at last crowned their efforts. A large gathering of Confederates and friends is expected on this most important occasion.[280] — SUMNER A. CUNNINGHAM

☛ HEROES OF THE EIGHTH ALABAMA INFANTRY

Cadmus M. Wilcox, C.S.A.

On July 3, 1863, [Confederate Gen. Cadmus Marcellus] Wilcox's old brigade supported Pickett's Division in the Gettysburg charge and participated in the fight. I belonged to Company G of the Eleventh Alabama, Wilcox's Brigade. In falling back, early in July, 1863, I came across a Capt. or Lieut. Scott, of the Ninth Alabama, who was badly wounded. Shot and shell were falling around us thick and fast, and he called me to assist him. I first thought he was a Federal, so devoted my attention to other wounded Confederates. The officer still pleaded with me to stop and help him, saying he belonged to the Ninth Alabama. I gave him water and bandaged his wounds, and he suffered intensely, begging me to cut his leg off with my pocketknife. As soon as I got to the line I sent some of his men to him, and he was immediately removed from the field. Capt. or Lieut. Scott will doubtless remember this incident, and myself in connection with it.

I went into the army very young, and served to the end. The badge of honor was bestowed on me at the battle of the Wilderness, and I remember the morning well. Wilcox's Brigade was at the head of the division, had marched early and late, and breakfasted by the light of the morning stars. I think it was [Winfield Scott] Featherston's Mississippi Brigade that had the day before held Gen. Grant in check until Longstreet could get up, but in doing this had given up about two miles of the woods on the plank road a little faster than Gen. Lee liked. Gen. Grant, the new commander of the Army of the Potomac, was "pushing the Rebels on to Richmond" with the belief that he could not be stopped. Gen. Grant had about 120,000 men and Gen. Lee about 55,000. Perhaps the latter was a little uneasy. He was sitting on his horse in the road when the Eleventh Alabama passed, and when Gen. Longstreet rode up to him he said: "Something must be done or the day is lost." Wilcox's Brigade was ordered to the left of the plank road, while Hood's Texas Brigade formed on the right. Both moved forward over the remains of the troops who had borne the brunt of the battle the previous day. Our men took position on the crest of a little ridge in the thick woods, and the sharpshooters were thrown out to meet the victorious enemy. We knew the bluecoats were coming, and every man did his duty bravely. Soon after we were in line we heard the Federals giving the order to forward. Our sharpshooters checked the advance of the enemy, but they were later compelled to fall back to the line. William Berry, a tall vidette, stood up in the rear and fired until shot dead; and my uncle, Joe Shuttlesworth, also stood in the rear and shot over our heads until mortally wounded. As the Yankees advanced our men poured volley after volley into their lines before their hitherto victorious progress could be stayed. Finally they faltered and began to give way; then the yell and charge. We drove them back three miles and recovered all the ground lost the day before.

Next morning Gen. [Micah] Jenkins, of South Carolina, was killed, and Gen. Longstreet wounded [both by friendly fire]; and but for these unfortunate incidents, which stopped the advance for several hours, I have always believed that Gen.

Micah Jenkins, C.S.A.

Grant would have met the fate of his predecessors. The delay gave them time to reform the lines and bring up their reserves. On that morning Gen. [James Samuel] Wadsworth, of the Federals, was killed, and we got his sword, a very handsome one.

The Wilcox Brigade made a fine record at Frazier's Farm, where they captured sixteen of the finest guns in the Federal army. The loss in officers and men was severe and the fighting terrific, many of our most valuable soldiers being killed or wounded.

Joe Shuttleworth, known in the regiment as "Joe Shuck," was a young sharpshooter, weighing about one hundred pounds, with sharp features. He stood up bravely in the rear of his company until he was mortally wounded. He was borne from the field to the hospital. I got permission to see him late in the afternoon, and found him in a dying condition, though he talked cheerfully and told me this story, which was verified by one of the litter bearers: As the ambulance corps was taking him from the battlefield one of the bearers of the litter was wounded and fell, letting his suffering burden fall to the ground. Sitting on his war horse, Traveler, Gen. Lee witnessed the incident with manifest tenderness and sympathy. Lifting his hat, Joe said: "Don't be uneasy. That is the Eleventh Alabama, Wilcox's Brigade, and they are filling the road with dead Yankees." Gen. Lee answered: "I know they are, my brave boy." Just then the Rebel yell burst forth, and Joe said: "I told you so." He died in the hospital that night.[281] — S. W. VANCE

☛ SCHOOL HISTORIES IN THE SOUTH

. . . It was supposed some eighteen months ago that the History Committee of the Grand Camp of Virginia, successful in the efforts of that period, had finished its labors and had no further cause for action or reason for existence. *We imagined that books, hostile to the truth and dishonoring to the dead and living of the South, had been driven from our State, and that with them would go opinions derived from them and of like effect, and therefore debasing to those who held them.*

The actual situation is such that we consider it wise to begin this report with a brief description of our position at home and of the forces arrayed against us. It should serve to guide and concentrate our own action. It ought to secure the vigorous cooperation of all the Confederate camps in the South.

We were in error in supposing our work done. We are not altogether rid of false teachings, whatever may be said of the purposes of our teachers. Because of newly aroused thought, the opinions alluded to are less prevalent than they were; but they are still heard from *young men who, during the last thirty years, have been misled as to the characteristics of our people and the causes of the "war between the sections," from some who, "looking to the future," as they phrase it, foolishly ignore the lessons of the past*, and from others who, thinking themselves impoverished by the war and being greedy of gain, have neither thought nor care for anything nobler. There are a few older men who think that the abandonment of all the principles and convictions of the past is necessary to prove their loyalty to the present. There are some who dare to tell us that "the old days are gone by and are not to be remembered;" that "it is a weakness to recall them with tender emotions." *To these we reply: "Put off the shoes from off your feet, for the place whereon you stand is holy ground." Young or old, these men are few, but they are ours, and their children inherit their errors.*

Those not already aware of it will be surprised to learn that there are teachers in the South—high in position but, as we think, very ignorant of our history—who accept the Northern theory that "slavery was the cause of the war," and must accept the dishonoring consequence that its preservation was our sole object in that struggle—the favorite position of the Northern advocate and the last support of his cause. This position they take in spite of the fact that the quarrel between the North and the South began when slavery existed in all the States. That writers or readers should ignore the proofs of this is surprising. We cite, for instance, Washington's stern order issued to the army before Boston in 1775, promising exemplary punishment to any man who should say or do anything to aggravate what he called "the existing sectional feeling." *For that feeling in that day we cannot find cause in slavery*, for the good people of New England [where American slavery got its start] shared our Southern guiltiness.[282] Nor is it to be explained except as springing from the old jealousy of Puritan and Cavalier, and the resentment of the Virginians against the New Englanders for failing to help them in the Indian war; whence, according to some authorities, the epithet "Yankee" sprang.

At a later day, in 1786, Mr. [John] Jay recommended to Congress that, in exchange for a favorable commercial treaty with Spain, we should yield to her condition that "no American vessel should navigate the Mississippi below the mouth of the Yazoo." New England, caring nothing for the distant Mississippi, supported this narrow and selfish policy; exciting, say contemporary writers, "the fierce indignation of the South, and especially of Virginia, to which State Kentucky then belonged. We quote in substance from Mr. [John] Fiske's [Yankee-biased book] *The Critical Period of American History, 1783-1789*. He recites the fact, but sees no connection between the incident and the sectional war.

John Jay.

So of New England's pursuit of separate interests in 1812, the tariff iniquity of 1828, and the nullification struggle, all of which so intensified the general bad feeling. These are matters of commonest knowledge and the gravest import. They are, nevertheless, ignored by many Northern writers as causes of war. One prominent writer, Mr. Fiske, very briefly mentions the [New England secession movement, which met at the] Hartford convention of 1814. Even our old enemy, Mr. Haines, gives the list in a line print note. *The fact is, these matters do not serve the purpose, as none of them could be depended upon to enlist the sentimental sympathy of the world against the South. Slavery and Southern action thereupon must be, for these historians, the cause of the war.* There are people at home who, with these men, ignore all this history and accept and support their view. We are glad that they are few, but they exist; and, therefore, Virginians do not feel as they did when at the touch of hostile spear the shield of the State rang true: when, at the call of honor, the State of Virginia stepped to the front to stay to the end of the war. For all of us there is cause to fear that our success in suppressing the more flagrant evils has lessened our watchfulness against subtler forms which may prove harder to expel; reason to apprehend that our people of Virginia and other Southern States may sink down into a blind content with *a situation which is still full of danger. If you will look over the lists of books allowed in some of our States, you will amazed. The artifices and corruption that secured their adoption would furnish a curious subject for a student of human nature.*

Here in Virginia our hope is in this Grand Camp, with its allies among the scholars in the State, and in the men upon whom the law has laid the heavy responsibility belonging to our State Board of Education. We are glad to know that these are good men and true; that they have on the whole given the public schools of Virginia by far the best set of books they have ever had. So we are glad to acknowledge the good work they have done for the State, however strongly we may dissent from and protest against some of their conclusions. With respect to the situation abroad, it describes it not unfairly if we say that *the reasons for the existence of our History Committee are, in a modified form, the same that in 1861 brought into existence and moved to action in the armies of the South.*

In the "sectional war" (not the "civil war," for that title accords with the extreme national conception and admits that we were not separate Stares) we were called upon to resist an invasion of soldiers, armed and sent into our country by the concurrent purposes of several fairly distinct [Liberal and socialist] parties then and now existing in the North.²⁸³ *They came seeking our injury and their own profit. A new invasion, with like double purpose, is being prosecuted by the lineal successors of some of these parties. Two of them chiefly concern us and our work. The one came—or sent representatives to the war—bent upon the destruction of our Southern civilization, the eradication of the personal characteristics, opinions, thought, and mode of life which made our men different, antagonistic, and*

Alexander H. H. Stuart.

hateful to them. The other preferred war to the loss of material prosperity, which they apprehended in case the South should attain a position beyond the reach of Northern lawmakers and Northern tax collectors. Mr. Lincoln represented the latter, when, in reply to Mr. John B. Baldwin and Mr. Alexander [Hugh Holmes] Stuart, who—as representatives of the Virginia Convention then in session—urged him to delay the action that opened the war, he [Lincoln] asked, "What is to become of my revenue in New York if there is a ten per cent tariff at Charleston?" The following incident points to the former: *About the year 1850 a distinguished Northern statesman said to a party of Southern Congressmen: "You gentlemen will have to go home and beat your plowshares into swords and your pruning hooks into spears, for the Northern schoolmistresses are training a generation to fight the South."*

No longer concerning ourselves with the sentimental Unionists and honest abolitionists—whose work seems to be over—we still struggle against the two [Liberal anti-South] parties we have described. These exist in their successors to-day—*their successors who strive to control the opinions of our people*, and those who seek to make gain by their association with us.

Cooperating with these and representing motives common to them all is a new form of another party, which has existed since sectionalism had its birth; the party which has always labored to convince the world that the North was altogether right and righteous, and the South wholly and wickedly wrong in the sectional strife. This [Liberal] party [by this time, 1899, the Democrats] is to-day the most distinctly defined and the most dangerous to us. Its chief representatives are the historians against whose work we are especially engaged. We are enlisted against an invasion organized and vigorously prosecuted by all of these people. They are actuated by all the motives we have described, but they have two well-defined (and, as to us, malignant) purposes. One of them is to convince all men, and especially our Southern children, that we were, as Dr. [Jabez Lamar Monroe] Curry expresses their view, "a brave and rash people, deluded by bad men, who attempted in an illegal and wicked manner to overthrow the Union." The other purpose—and for this especially they are laboring—is to have it believed that the Southern soldier, however brave, was actuated by no higher motive than the desire to retain the money value of slave property. They rightly believe that the world, once convinced of this, will hold us degraded rather than worthy of honor, and that our children, instead of reverencing their fathers, will be secretly if not openly ashamed.

They seek to carry out their purposes, not now by the aid of armed soldiers, but through the active employment of energies, agencies, and agents who are as the caterpillar and cankerworm for destructiveness and as the locust for multitude. The whole force of journalists, poets, orators, and writers of all classes is employed in their cause, especially the Northern history makers, whose books have been and are now, to some extent, in the hands of Southern children.

The character of the work has been in greater or less degree such as might have been expected. *By every variety of effort, from direct denunciation to faint praise, by false statement and more subtle suggestion, by sophistry of reasoning and unexpected inference, by every sin of omission and commission, these writers have labored since the close of the war, as their predecessors had done before it, to conceal or pervert the facts of our history.* In the past they have been, to a great extent, successful. Up to the war our people were as unknown as if they had lived on another planet, or known only to be condemned. The world has grown wiser. Therefore these men, hopeless of retaining in the high court of the future the packed juries and prejudiced judges before whom they have heretofore urged their cause against us, gradually despairing of final success in

Thomas B. Macaulay.

distorting facts as touching either the legal aspect of the case or our military history, still retain the hope, and *now bend their energies to the task of convicting us all—leaders and people—of such motives as shall appear to the world and to our children as proof of dishonor, and rob statesman, faithful citizen, and soldier alike of the admiration now justly accorded.*

Hon. J. L. M. Curry has lately stated that *"history as written, if accepted in future years, will consign the South to infamy."* He further observes that *"the conquerors write the histories of all conquered peoples."* Whether or not the records of mankind show this last statement to be true, it is not true that all conquered people have so learned the story of their fathers' deeds; nor can it be shown that the conquerors have habitually sought to force such teachings upon them. Wiser statesman have known, with [British historian Sir Thomas Babington] Macaulay, that *"a people not proud of the deeds of a noble ancestry will never do anything worthy to be remembered by posterity." He is a stupid educator who does not know that a boy ashamed of his father will be a base man. Such a direct attempt to change the character of a people has been almost unknown.*

. . . It is not exactly in point, but it is interesting to note that the schools of France to-day use histories that teach the children how entirely Frenchmen won the American war of independence. Doubtless an instance may be found here and there of compulsory study of the history of a conquest by the conquered people. When occurring, it has been the conqueror's final and, to his mind, most radical expedient, applied by and with relentless force, and with deadly intent to change the minds and characters of the new subjects.

Hunter McGuire, C.S.A.

It remained for these, our Southern States, with this State of Virginia leading and guiding the others (as we fear the record shows), to present the first instance of voluntary submission to this last resort of the crudest conquerors. The history of the human race furnishes no like example of men who, by their own action, have so exposed their children; of men, who, unconstrained, have dishonored the graves and memories of their dead. Our own people have aided and are still aiding, with all the insistence of damned and daily schoolroom iteration, in the work of teaching those malignant falsehoods *to Southern children, in the work of so representing a brave people to the world of to-day and the ages to come. How amazing the folly! How dark the crime!*

This folly or crime, for the State of Virginia, is primarily chargeable to the men who, immediately after the war—when our hearts if not our intellects might have been on guard—brought Northern men and Northern histories into our schools and for years employed them to teach us why and how Southern men fought against the North. *Certain honest efforts have been made to expel these books and their teachings. Differences of opinion should not, and do not, induce us to impugn the motives of faithful men; but we regret that these efforts have not been entirely successful. . . .*[284] — DR. HUNTER MCGUIRE

🡢 WARTIME REMINISCENCES

I joined [Confederate] Capt. J. M. Phillips's company, Eighth Tennessee Cavalry Regiment. I was about seventeen years old. I was just recovering from a spell of measles, which had settled on my lungs, and was scarcely able to ride. It was thought at the time that I would not live very long, but my health began to improve on the rough fare and fresh air of camp life. The first time I even heard the whistle of Yankee bullets was between Readyville and Woodbury, Tenn. A company of the Fourth Ohio Cavalry (regulars) had been for several days making raids out from Readyville toward Woodbury. Our regiment determined to undertake their capture. One morning a little before day, we were ordered to fall in line, and moved quietly down Lock's Creek in platoons of four,  led by Col. Smith. In a little while we came in sight of the pike, and on an elevation to our left I observed a line of blue facing us. We began to fire in the direction of this line, and I had never before heard so many bullets whistle through the air. As soon as the Federals had emptied their guns at us they drew their sabers, formed in single file, and dashed among us. Jack Luck, of our company, a strong man and brave, tried to stop the enemy by physical force, but one stroke of a Federal saber felled him to the ground with blood running from his mouth. They went through our lines like sheep jumping out of a lot one at a time, until I thought they were all gone. "Old Paul" Anderson, talking and cursing through his nose, came galloping up with the other half of the regiment; but he had come too late: the birds had flown. Somehow—I have never known how—some five or six Yankees were captured that day. In this battle Capt. J. M. Phillips was captured. I was told that we pressed the enemy so hard they were forced to leave their prisoners. It was not for want of bravery that Paul Anderson, our lieutenant colonel, was not there in time with his half of the regiment. A cooler or braver man never rode a horse.[285] — ELDER J. K. WOMACK

☛ SKETCH OF GEN. BRYAN GRIMES

Bryan Grimes, major general of the Second Corps, Army of Northern Virginia, was born November 2, 1828, and died August 14, 1880. He graduated at the University of North Carolina in 1848, and led for a time the quiet life of a planter. He was a member of the North Carolina Secession Convention, and was commissioned to rank as follows: Major Fourth North Carolina Regiment of State Troops, May 16, 1861; lieutenant colonel same regiment, May 1, 1862; colonel same regiment, June 19, 1862; brigadier general, May 19, 1864, and major general, February 15, 1865.

He participated in nearly all the battles fought by the Army of Northern Virginia. At Seven Pines, as lieutenant colonel of his (Fourth) regiment, he led probably the bloodiest charge of the war. His horse was killed, and in falling pinioned him to the ground. Upon being extricated, he seized the flag, all the color guards having been killed, and planted it upon the enemy's fortifications. In this charge over three-fourths of his men and every officer except himself were killed or wounded. In 1862 he commanded the "Bloody Fourth," and also from November, 1862, to February, 1863, he temporarily commanded the "Ironsides Brigade." At Cold Harbor Col. Grimes led a victorious charge, carrying the colors on horseback until his horse was killed under him. At Boonsboro, though incapacitated for duty, he had himself placed on his horse, and commanded the regiment until this horse was killed, when he continued on foot until from sheer exhaustion he had to be carried from the field. Gen. Grimes had seven horses killed under him in battle. The first and second days at Chancellorsville Col. Grimes fought his regiment with desperate valor, and on the third day charged his regiment over [the] backs of troops who refused to go forward and crossed bayonets with the enemy. At Chancellorsville the regiment had 46 killed, 157 wounded, and 58 taken prisoners out of 327 officers and men, over sixty-two per cent killed and wounded. Col. Grimes

Bryan Grimes, C.S.A.

Stephen D. Ramseur, C.S.A.

commanded the advance into Pennsylvania, and went on picket duty eight miles from Harrisburg, a point farther north than was reached by any other Confederate regiment. At Gettysburg his regiment, under his command, was the first to enter the town, and drove the enemy to the heights beyond, capturing more prisoners than there were men in his command. On May 12, at Spottsylvania C.H., Col. Grimes led [Stephen Dodson] Ramseur's Brigade, recapturing the Horseshoe and retaking Johnston's lost guns, taking many prisoners and killing more of the enemy than the brigade numbered men. Gen. Lee rode down and thanked him in person, saying that they deserved the thanks of the country; that they had saved his army.

On May 19, near Fredericksburg, Col. Grimes handled the brigade with such efficiency that Gen. [Robert Emmett] Rodes said: "You have saved [Richard Stoddert] Ewell's Corps, and shall be promoted, and your commission shall bear date from this day."

Gen. Grimes shared [Jubal A.] Early's varying fortunes in the Valley, and from Cedar Creek, October 19, 1864, in which battle he had two horses killed under him, he commanded Rodes' Division to the surrender, although he did not receive his commission as major general until February, 1864. On November 22, 1864, Grimes' attenuated division by itself routed four thousand of Sheridan's formidable cavalry. At Petersburg his division held over three miles of the trenches, and at Fort Steadman captured the enemy's works, sending to the rear as prisoners a general and five hundred men. At Remus Salient, on April 5, Grimes' Division successfully held the enemy in check. On the 7th his division recaptured the lines from which [William] Mahone's Division had just been driven. At Appomattox Gen. Grimes, commanding all the infantry, actually engaged the enemy and drove them nearly a mile, taking a great number of prisoners and several pieces of artillery. This was the last effort of the expiring Confederacy.[286] — SUMNER A. CUNNINGHAM

CHAPTER 19

1900

☛ A CONFEDERATE EULOGY

Once again has a comrade been relieved from his post of duty. His battle of life here has been fought. Signaled to join the advance guard, he has gone from us. Martial music of Confederate camps can never again bring him into line with those who remain. He has crossed the fateful river and entered upon other service. He now fronts toward the head of time's great column beyond the "gates ajar." On eternity's roster his name now appears. He has taken his place in the ranks of the countless host moving on and on under the eye of the great Captain of the universe, the Conqueror of death itself. To aspirations born of new surroundings our comrade can well be left, and we salute him in tenderest memory on his onward march through the highways of the garnered nations. His mortal body will have its resting place with us, and as the earth will soon hide it from our sight, let us bury also in oblivion any recollection of his human frailties, commemorating only the virtues of one who was our friend in peace, our comrade in war. This last sad rite performed, let us go hence with courage and confidence to the performance of such other duties as may fall to our lot. Let no vicissitude drive or tempt us to abandon our

Confederate heroes.

post or fail in doing all the good we can while on earth we live, remembering that in a little while we too will be called away, and each of us assigned to our proper place by the Supreme Commander.[287] — COL. J. M. SANDIDGE

☛ HOW WE LEARNED THE POSITION OF THE ENEMY

A few days after the battle of Franklin [November 30, 1864] my regiment was in position . . . resting at Dr. Berry's (new) residence, just outside the city limits of Nashville. One morning Gen. Randall Lee Gibson, our brigade commander, asked me if I knew the position of the Federal troops on Brown's Creek. I was ignorant of any creek by that name, even though it was close by us. One of Dr. Berry's boys (now President of the American National Bank in Nashville) said to me, pointing with his finger: "Colonel, that's Brown's Creek where the railroad bridge crosses." The bridge was about halfway between the lines. I gave orders to cease firing on our side, and without any side arms I waved a handkerchief [temporary truce], which was promptly answered by the Federals. I made my way toward the small bridge, and got ahead of the Federal officer and two men, and took advantage of the time to carefully take in the position of the enemy. On their approach the [Union] officer asked me what I wanted. I told him I wanted "a ball of shoe thread to make a pair of boots" (this was true). He replied: "That is a queer thing for a flag of truce." I thought so myself, but I did not know anything better to say. I promised to pay them in tobacco. The officer said he did not believe that the general would allow him to do that. "Well, let me know to-morrow at noon." We shook hands, and I asked the two [Yankee] cavalrymen what command they belonged to. They replied, "Second Kentucky." I said: "Ah, boys, you should be on

Historical marker, Nashville, TN. (Photo L. Seabrook)

my side." They smiled, and we returned to our respective lines. The information obtained seemed to be sufficient, as Gen. [John Bell] Hood ordered an advance that afternoon and drove the enemy back some distance.[288] — COL. R. H. LINDSAY

☛ SKETCH OF CAPT. JOHN W. MORTON

Although it is as a cavalry general that the name of Forrest is best known, students of his great career from the time he enlisted as a private to when he finished as a major general best appreciate the genius of the man in his wonderful, resourceful versatility in handling men and molding them to his purposes in a great variety of emergencies. When he went into the army his knowledge of things military was less than that of the average volunteer; and yet did there ever live a commander who could take a body of men, as did he, untutored, undrilled, and unskilled, and make them to the enemy's imagination so dreadfully persuasive and, in fact, so terribly effective? His troopers, as horsemen, were the peers of any that ever wielded the saber. Dismounting them, he used them successfully against as hardy infantry as ever met a charge, and taught the military world new lessons in cavalry tactics. He made infantrymen of cavalrymen and cavalrymen of infantrymen with results equally brilliant.

The greatest marvel in Forrest's career, and that which was most surprising to professional military chieftains and critics, was his intuitive comprehension of the value of artillery. He entered the army knowing no more about artillery tactics than a crusader of the Middle Ages; and yet he achieved unprecedented victories with that arm of service that were new revelations of his genius. Keenly observant of the qualities of his men, Gen. Forrest made instant use of any special individual aptness. He never better illustrated the soundness of the judgment that inspired the enthusiastic confidence of his men than in his choice of lieutenants—his brigade commanders, his department chiefs, his staff officers, and particularly in his choice of a chief of artillery. For this vital post he selected, against the young man's modest demurring to be chosen over older officers, John W. Morton, then a delicate stripling. But Morton, a smooth-faced boy, had at Fort Donelson won the praise of the generals commanding and absolutely fought his way into Forrest's special esteem. He went with Forrest, and was given his first battery of guns, captured from the enemy on the West Tennessee raid of 1862.

Thereafter Gen. Forrest not only gave to Capt. Morton implicit confidence, but not infrequently relied upon the judgment of the youthful cannoneer commander as to the best service to be had from his guns. It was immediately after the battle of Chickamauga that Capt. Morton went with Forrest into his Mississippi Department.

The General had referred to the artillery captain as the "little bit of a kid with a big backbone." He had delighted the General by keeping his guns in pace with the swiftest movements of his flying expeditions. Morton's batteries lumbered and thundered where sabers gleamed and carbines and pistols flashed in the headlong charge. His guns were the van of the victorious columns at Brice's Cross Roads, where they went into action with the celerity of the skirmish lines. On the Tennessee River and in the Johnsonville campaign—the most unparalleled performance of our civil or any other war—when Forrest struck a crushing blow at one of Sherman's largest depots of supplies, Morton, with his batteries led the way, and, with Gen. Forrest's approval, selected the positions from which they effected the capture of two gunboats, a heavily laden transport, and destroyed at Johnsonville military stores worth, according to an official Federal report, over $2,500,000, in addition to a fleet of eleven steamers, barges, gunboats, and transports, whose sunken hulls may yet be seen at Johnsonville when the river is low—voiceless but eloquent witnesses of the completest victory and most extraordinary campaign of the war.

John W. Morton, C.S.A.

Forrest's artillery, with Morton ever at their head, was in the van of Hood's advance into Tennessee, and while at Franklin and Nashville the Confederate infantry, despite their utmost valor and sacrifice, were overwhelmed by numbers, Morton and his guns successfully broke up the outposts, destroying railroads and blockhouses of the enemy's outer lines, and then joined the stricken army in time to aid in saving it from annihilation.

When the sad retreat of Hood's bruised and battered battalions made their bleeding way beyond the Tennessee River, Walthall and Forrest, with Morton's artillery, held the swarming hosts of pursuers at bay, and the shells of the never-yielding batteries, until the last pale and bloody regiment was safe on the Southern bank of the river, ever shrieked defiance and hurled destruction into the foremost ranks of outnumbering foes.

And when, at last, the Confederate leaders decided to quit the terribly unequal struggle, whose continuance meant the further desolation of the land they loved—already scarred and blighted by four merciless years of war—there was no organization, of those who wore the gray and furled the stars and bars for the last time, so well equipped and ready for fight as Morton's batteries of guns, all captured from the enemy. Their chief was yet so young at the surrender, that when he went home he took a course at school, pursuing the studies that had been interrupted by the war.[289] — SUMNER A. CUNNINGHAM

☛ ADDRESS AT THE FRANKLIN MONUMENT DEDICATION

Confederate Monument, Franklin, TN. (Photo L. Seabrook)

The occasion which brings you here is one to which we have all looked forward with interest. We are making history to-day. *Future generations will point back with pride to this day—that their fathers and mothers, thirty-five years after the close of one of the bloodiest wars of history, when all passion had subsided, all animosities had been buried, and all sections of our common country were at peace with each other as brothers, had paid this tribute of affection to the memory of their countrymen. A generation has passed, and this is in part the work of a new generation. The corner stone of this monument is love—every rock in its foundation is cemented in love; every stroke of the chisel that worked out its beautiful symmetry was made in love; love, pure and simple, welled up in grateful hearts, as a token of which we transmit this monument* to posterity.

This is the work of the noble women of Williamson County. They are the daughters of those women who near forty years ago gave such impetus to the cause of the Confederacy. Go back in memory to the stirring days of 1861. The women were as active as the men. There was an invading army at our borders; nothing was left to be done but go. The women aroused an enthusiasm that brooked no opposition, and *be it said to the lasting credit of Williamson [County, Tenn.] that she put more men in the field than she had voters.* The wife to her husband, the mother to her boy, the sister to her brother, the maiden to her sweetheart—all said: "Go. God be with you till we meet again! Should the fate of war befall you, and should that banner around which cluster the bright hopes of the Confederacy go down, you shall ever live in the hearts of your countrymen." We saw them go. They were boys, the flower of the land. Amid the hardships and deprivations of camp life, the desolation of the battlefield, they knew that promise would be redeemed, and gathered strength and courage from the fact. That promise has been as sacred with the daughters as it was with the mothers.

Caroline "Carrie" McGavock of Carnton Plantation, Franklin, TN, wife of John W. McGavock, the original owners of the McGavock Confederate Cemetery.

Who first suggested this monument, and that it be placed on the public square? is a question that has been asked. No man or woman can claim the credit. *The sentiment that something should be done to show to coming ages that we who saw and knew the Confederate soldier honored and loved him was spontaneous, and had its origin in no single mind; and upon the idea that a monument to his memory was the proper means we were all unanimous.*

Some at first preferred the beautiful McGavock [Confederate] Cemetery, the gift of that venerable gentleman [the owner John W. McGavock] whose memory is lovingly cherished by every man, woman, and child in Williamson County. The locality, while sacred as the resting place of the hallowed bones of our heroes, was too far removed from daily public contact.

Some preferred the battlefield, in sight of the railroad, that strangers in passing might know that we honor our countrymen. But *we don't build it for strangers; we build it for our children. We teach our children patriotism, to love, honor, and defend the government under which we live; and in recent months children of Confederate soldiers, who revere the government, offered the opportunity, have proven themselves to be worthy sons of honored sires.* And all, with rare exceptions, gradually came to the conclusion that the public square was the place, *that our children might know by daily observation of this monument that their fathers and mothers regarded the Confederate soldier as the grandest character in all history.*

John B. Hood, C.S.A.

History has her heroes from the earliest age. They stand out upon her pages as beacon lights, and have ignited the chivalry in the soul of many a boy. But we did not see them; we read about them. The men who left their homes that they had not seen for four years and followed [Confederate Gen. John Bell] Hood out of Tennessee, when they so plainly saw that the star of the Confederacy had begun to set, were heroes before whom, in our eyes, all others pale into comparative insignificance. The men who followed Lee from Richmond, when they could but see that his Appomattox was near, were men in whose fidelity and valor the gods delight. These men were Southerners, our own countrymen. Some of them were from Williamson County. Some of them are here to-day; some have passed over the river, and are resting under the shades of eternity, awaiting the coming of their comrades, which will be short. These Confederate Veterans are the men we desire to honor. It is an honor to belong to the race that could produce them. Our children should know them, and the richest heritage we have to leave them is that their blood flows through their veins. Such is the sentiment that built this monument and located it where it is.

Contrast for a moment their home-coming in 1865 with that of their sons in 1899—you have just witnessed the latter, in the sentiment of which we all heartily join. Ragged, foot-sore, weary, desolation on all sides, burned cities and homes, wasted fields. There was no trumpet to herald their coming; the sound of their approaching footsteps wasted away in the surrounding stillness. . . . But their countrymen and their countrywomen gave them a greeting worth more than the evanescent, fickle "*Io triumphe*" of the returning conqueror. With a silent, melancholy joy you met them; with outstretched arms and hearts full of love you received them, and showed to them then, as you have shown to the world for the thirty-five years since then, that you were proud of the record they made.

Confederate women, 1899.

Only a few words in regard to the manner in which the money was raised. It is the work of the women of Williamson County. They have commanded the willing services of the men, and we have come and gone at their bidding. The monument fund was started by a few women about fourteen year's ago, and their number was continually increased. By ice cream suppers, concerts, cake walks, etc., from time to time a few dollars were raised. During this period these women devoted much of their attention to raising funds for needy Confederate soldiers, for the Soldiers' Home, McGavock Cemetery, etc. On this account the completion of the monument was deferred, and not for lack of interest in it. They succeeded in raising nearly $500. In 1896 Chapter No. 14. United

Daughters of the Confederacy, was organized at Franklin, of which the most of these women became members. The chapter took charge of the enterprise, and went to work with a determination that saw nothing but success, and you see the result. While our pride in our soldiers is great, it is not greater than that we have in these women. *All praise to the United Daughters of the Confederacy! All praise to the women of Williamson County! It took just such women as we have to make the Confederate soldier what he was.*

Fortifications around Franklin, TN, November 1864.

Donations have come to them from all sources. Democrats, Republicans, Populists, Prohibitionists, vied with each other in their contributions. School children gave their dimes. *Federal soldiers took stock, and this is the gift of all conditions of life, to stand as a monument of the affection of a grateful people.* While many Confederate soldiers have been liberal in their donations, I for one, have thought that we should not require much of them, because this is done not by them, but for them; it is done in their honor.

While history for a season may be colored by the conquerors, and thus shadow the truth, in time it will right itself, and the world will know, as we now know, that *no age or country has ever produced the superior of our countrymen in courage, fidelity, and nobleness of character, and we wish to offer for coming generations our humble testimony of these virtues.*

A monument in honor of the Confederate soldier, or something that will impress my children with the grandeur of his character, has been the burden of my heart ever since I have had children. Now that it is an accomplished fact, no man can be more rejoiced.

On the fateful field of Franklin, in addition to the great fatality in the ranks, there was unprecedented fatality among the officers. They led their men. Six generals, one major general, and five brigadiers dead upon the field, and as many wounded. [Patrick Ronayne] Cleburne, [John] Adams, [John Carpenter] Carter, [Hiram Bronson] Granbury, [States Rights] Gist, and [Otho French] Strahl—*names that will ever be sacred to Southerners, as brave and as heroic as any in all the annals of history.*[290] — J. H. HENDERSON (November 30, 1899)

J. H. Henderson.

☛ THE TRUTH ABOUT SOUTHERN RACE RELATIONS
The following tribute of respect from Leonidas Polk Bivouac, No. 3, and William Henry Trousdale Camp, 495, of Confederate Veterans, truthfully portrays the feeling that exists between the Southern people, especially the Confederate Veterans, and the old and faithful Southern negroes:

Whereas the faithful old negro man, Braxton Bragg, died in Columbia, Tenn., Wednesday morning, January 17, 1900; and whereas Bragg was the body servant of Gen. Braxton Bragg, and was true to his Southern friends and principles through life; therefore be it

Resolved, that a page in our minutes be set apart in honor of Braxton Bragg, the negro, who died here at an advanced age; that our thanks are hereby extended to our comrades, Daughters of the Confederacy, and citizens generally who were so kind to Bragg during life and in his last sickness; also to our comrades who made the funeral arrangements.

The following comrades served as pall bearers: H. A. Brown, H. G. Evans, W. J. Whitthorne, J. T. Williamson, H. L. Hendley, and A. N. Akin. Revs Baker P. Lee and W. T. Ussery, conducted the funeral services. Although the weather was inclement, the funeral was largely attended. The Columbia newspapers . . . are requested to publish these proceedings.[291] — W. A. SMITH, J. M. HODGE, B. S. THOMAS

☛ REUNION OF FORREST'S CAVALRY VETERANS

Confederate Veterans Reunion, Gallatin, TN, 1900.

The reunion of Forrest's Veterans will occur on the battlefield of Brice's Cross Roads June 10. This organization was set on foot during the reunion of Confederate Veterans at Nashville, Tenn., July, 1897. All old soldiers were invited to become members who served at any time, however brief, under the command of Lieut. Gen. Forrest. Membership is conditioned on the simple signature of our muster roll; giving name, address, when you entered the service, and present address. The objects of the organization are memorial, historical, and for the sake of good comradeship. To aid in the erection of an equestrian statue to our great commander, all officers when signing the roll will pay to our quartermaster and roll keeper $2, and all privates $1, membership fee. To each veteran making this payment will be given a medallion with the picture of Gen. Forrest on the obverse side and certificate that he was a soldier with Gen. Forrest on the reverse side. . . .[292] — MAJ. CHARLES W. ANDERSON

☛ THE TRUE CAUSE OF THE WAR OF 1861

Accustomed through sixty years to address public assemblies, I am nevertheless subdued with awe in your presence to-day; for we stand together under the shadow of the past. It is the solemn reverence one might feel in the gloom of Westminster Abbey, surrounded by England's illustrious dead. Indeed, we are here the living representatives of countless comrades, who sleep in lonely cemeteries throughout the land; where perchance a single monumental shaft is the ghostly sentinel keeping watch over the bivouac of the dead. It is five and thirty years since the Confederate war was closed and about thirty-nine years since it was begun, and it is sometimes asked why we should stir the ashes of that ancient feud, why we should not bury the past in its own grave and turn to the living issues of the present and the future. To this question, comrades, we return the answer, with a voice loud as seven thunders: *Because it is history, because it is our history and the history of our dead heroes who shall not go without their fame.* As long there are men who wear the gray they will gather the charred embers of their old camp fires, and in the blaze of these reunions tell the story of the martyrs *who fell in the defense of country and of truth.* Nay, more than this: *It is the story of a strife that marks an epoch in the annals of the American people.*

It is known to every schoolboy in the land that two parties existed at the formation of our government, who could not agree in locating the paramount sovereignty which should decide upon all issues arising between the States themselves—the Federalists [the Liberal party of that day], as they were [wrongly and deceitfully] termed, demanding a strong government, concentrating power in the national administration; the [Conservative] Republicans [known then as the Antifederalists and also the Democratic-Republicans], on the other hand, *contending for the distribution of power among the States,* claiming their original sovereignty among their reserved rights. Both parties were too strong to allow the question to be determined by arbitration or through forensic discussion. *It was therefore permitted to slumber beneath certain ambiguities of expression in the Constitution itself to be settled by the exigencies of the future*—not as an abstract principle, but as an accomplished fact. I need not remind you how this issue was raised in 1832 [during Andrew Jackson's presidency], and was postponed through the conciliatory legislation of that period. Such an issue could not, however, sleep forever. The admission of new States into the Union, with their conflicting interests, must reopen the question and compel its decision. Thus *it arose in our day, leading to the establishment of the Southern Confederacy and to the civil war that followed.*

Fellow-citizens, it is simple folly to suppose that such a spontaneous uprising as that of our people in 1860 and 1861 could be effected through the machinations of politicians alone. A movement so sudden and so vast, instantly swallowing up all minor contentions, would spring only from some great faith deeply planted in the human heart, and for which men were willing to die. Whatever may have been the occasion of the war, the hinge on which it turned was

this old question of State sovereignty as against national supremacy. As there could be no compromise between the two the only resort was an appeal to the law of force. The surrender at Appomattox, when the tattered remnant of Lee's great army stood guard for the last time over Southern liberties and rights, drew the equatorial line dividing between the past and the future of American history. When the will of the strongest, instead of "the consent of the governed," became the base of our national structure, a radical transformation took place. The principle of confederation gave way to that of consolidation, and the American nation emerged out of the American republic. . . .[293]
— REV. B. M. PALMER

B. M. Palmer.

☛ THE SOUTH'S RESPONSE TO NORTHERN INTOLERANCE
[During a speech at a reunion of Confederate and Union Veterans in Atlanta, Georgia, on July 20, 1899, Yankee Commander Gen. Shaw made the following insulting comments to the audience:] "There can be but one idea of American citizenship, one stars and stripes, one bulwark of future national glory, and one line of patriotic teachings for all and by all. In this view the keeping alive of sectional teachings as to the justice and rights of the cause of the South, in the hearts of the children, is all out of order, unwise, unjust, and utterly opposed to the bond by which the great chieftain Lee solemnly bound the cause of the South in his final surrender. I deeply deplore all agencies of this sort, because in honor and in chivalric American manhood and womanhood nothing of this nature should be taught or tolerated for an instant."

[John B. Gordon, former Confederate General, and now Commander-in-Chief of the United Confederate Veterans (U.C.V.), quickly stood up and replied:] "Whatever may have been my record in the past, whatever may now be my love for the South and her traditions, I claim equal loyalty with Gen. Shaw in his love for the Union and his fidelity to the stars and stripes. . . . When I saw the [Confederate] flag I followed and loved go down at Appomattox my heart would have broken but for my faith in God and his overruling providence.

"I love this country. I love every acre of it. In these veins runs the blood of the founders of this republic. My forefathers fought and bled for this country's independence, and I believe no man is more ready to serve it in any emergency than myself. I know that my friend, Gen. Shaw, is equally devoted and true. Every sentence of his eloquent tribute to American manhood, and his every sentiment of loyalty to our fathers' flag, finds an echo in my heart. But when he tells me and my Southern comrades that teaching our children that the cause for which we fought and our comrades died is all wrong, I must earnestly protest. *In the name of the future manhood of the South I protest, what are we to teach them? If we cannot teach them that their fathers were right, it follows that these Southern children must be taught that they were wrong. Are we ready for that? For one I am not ready! I never will be ready to have my children taught that I was wrong, or that the cause of my people was unjust and unholy.* [Here there was one long, continuous yell of approval throughout the large building.]

John B. Gordon, C.S.A.

"O, my [Northern] friends, you were right: but I too was right! *We were fighting over principles that we had inherited from our fathers and our fathers' fathers. We were both right*, and when we meet in that great beyond we shall both hear: 'Well done, thou good and faithful servant.'

"When Alexander Hamilton and Thomas Jefferson each wrote his construction of *the true meaning of the constitution, there was a conflict of opinion utterly irreconcilable. But shall we insist that the children of one or the disciples of the other shall not be taught that he was right? From that day to this the controversy has been waged in conflicting opinions, which Gen. Shaw has inherited on the one side and I on the other, and for these convictions long and* devoutly cherished by each, we were both willing to labor, to fight, and to die.

"The decision made by the arbitrament of war was that . . . there should be on this continent the one great republic and one flag over all forever. But the question of which side was right in the conflict was not settled. No result on the field of battle can ever settle a question of right, and I can no more consent to deny my children the privilege of believing that their father was right than I can consent to write dishonor in my mother's dust."[294] — SUMNER A. CUNNINGHAM

☛ WOMEN'S FORREST STATUE ASSOCIATION

The following are the officers of the Women's Forrest Statue Association: Mrs. T. J. Latham, Chairman of the Executive Committee; Mrs. J. Harvey Mathes, Vice Chairman; Mrs. James M. Greer, Secretary; and Mrs. Charles M. Drew, Treasurer.

To the honor of Tennessee, the Memphis women's organizations have resolved on the erection of a monument to Gen. N. B. Forrest. If ever matchless genius, the most daring courage, indomitable will and marvelous success secured imperishable fame for any hero, surely it belongs to our own "wizard of the saddle." Napoleon said: "In war men are nothing, a man everything." Truly was this exemplified in Gen. Forrest. It is well known that the military genius of Forrest was acknowledged in Europe before it was recognized in America, and that both Gens. Grant and Sherman realized his wonderful capacity before it was appreciated by the Confederate generals. The present generation is the one to claim the privilege of perpetuating in bronze, or marble, the heroic deeds of this son of Tennessee, and now is the time to begin, and this is the year to finish the work.

Young Confederate female supporters.

Mrs. Latham accepted the Presidency of the Tennessee State Division of the United Daughters of the Confederacy, with the pledge and condition that the first work should be for the Forrest monument, believing that with the promised aid of many veterans and camps early success would be achieved.

We confidently appeal to every camp and veteran, and U.D.C. Chapters, and public-spirited citizens, for contributions.

Contributions should be sent to Mrs. C. M. Drew, Treasurer, or to Mrs. J. M. Greer, Secretary of the Women's Forrest Statue Association. The circular is signed by George W. Gordon, Major General Commanding Tennessee Division, U.C.V.[295] — SUMNER A. CUNNINGHAM

☛ ADDRESS OF THOMAS C. CATCHINGS

Comrades, Ladies, and Gentlemen: Once more we have gathered together to pay grateful and loving tribute to the memory of the brave soldiers who went to their death in a vain but heroic struggle. Although more than the full span of a generation has been measured since the star of the Confederacy went out in the gloom of utter and irretrievable defeat, *our remembrance of their supreme sacrifice is tenderly and sacredly cherished.*

The great majority of their comrades who strove and battled with them, and yet who, in the providence of God, were spared their fate, have since crossed over the river to rest with them under the shade of the trees. Their survivors have passed the summit of the mountain, and are fast making their way into the shadows of the valley. *Those of us who with these brave men essayed to establish a separate and independent republic which we hoped would find an abiding place among the nations of the earth have taught our children that no stain of treason or blighted faith or broken vows dims the luster of their fame or soils the escutcheon of their honor. The task will soon be theirs to defend from all imputations of crime the nation which died in its infancy, and yet lived long enough to illustrate all the glories of human endeavor*: which, with all its institutions and circumstances and power, utterly perished from the face of the earth, and yet left behind it *the remembrance of valiant deeds and noble performance, which will be reverentially celebrated in song and story as long as time shall last.*

The great civil war, which was the most stupendous drama of all the ages, did not find its genesis in criminal conspiracy or treasonable design. *The Southern States in withdrawing from the union were exercising a power which had been claimed from the very adoption of the constitution. Indeed, in the early days of the republic, the theory was recognized by American statesmen with substantial unanimity, that the constitution was but a compact between sovereign States entered into for their common welfare; that by this compact they surrendered none of the attributes of sovereignty; that because of this sovereignty, any State could lawfully withdraw from the compact whenever in its judgment its interests required it to do so; that the government created by the constitution was a federation possessing only delegated powers; that it did not possess the power to coerce the action of the States; and that if a State chose to withdraw from the union, it was entitled to do so without control or question.* At the date of his birth the hearts of the American people were yet attuned to the joyous song of newly acquired freedom, and patriotic ardor was still aflame from the remembrance of the great triumph which had crowned their endeavors. The proceedings of the convention which framed the constitution, those of the States in ratifying it, and the luminous disquisitions of Madison, Hamilton, and their contemporaries show that *at that period there was little or no difference of opinion on the subject. I think it may safely be affirmed that if the framers of the constitution had avowed that their purpose was to create a supreme central government which would bind the States beyond all power of revocation, or withdrawal, it would never have been ratified.*

James Madison.

Original Secession Sentiment: *The States of New York, Virginia, and Rhode Island went so far as to insert in their resolutions of ratification the explicit declaration that the powers of government vested by the constitution in the United States of America might be reassumed by them whenever they should deem it necessary to their happiness or to prevent injury or oppression. By this declaration these States interpreted the constitution as admitting the right of secession, for if they had reassumed the power's granted to the United States, they would necessarily have ceased to belong to the union. Their sister States, by admitting them, with this reservation in their acts of ratification, to full copartnership in the*

Union, themselves necessarily recognized the soundness of their interpretation of the constitution.

The Virginia resolutions of 1798, which were written by Mr. Madison, and those of Kentucky of 1798 and 1799, which were written by Mr. Jefferson, *expressly declared that in case of the exercise of powers by the Federal government which had not been granted or delegated to it such acts would be void and of no force, and that the States would have the right to judge for themselves, as well of any infractions as of the mode and measure of redress.* These resolutions announced what is commonly known as the doctrine of nullification, with which it is difficult to agree, since it is impossible to perceive how a State could remain in the Union and not obey its laws. But *they are important as containing the district affirmation that the States were not united on the principle of unlimited submission to their general government, and that it had no powers, and could enforce none, except those which had been delegated to it.* It necessarily followed from the doctrine if these resolutions that *a State* might lawfully secede from the union, since they expressly declared that *it was to judge for itself of the mode and measure of redress.* They were the basis of the campaign of the State rights party [Conservative] in 1800, which elected Mr. [Thomas] Jefferson to the presidency, became a part of its creed, and were approved by a majority of the American people in every presidential election thereafter except two, down to the election of Mr. Lincoln in 1860.

Timothy Pickering.

New England, the Home of Secession: *Col. Timothy Pickering, of Massachusetts, a soldier of the revolution, a member of Gen. Washington's Cabinet, and for many years a representative in Congress, openly advocated the secession of Massachusetts and other Northern States, and the formation by them of a separate confederacy.* In a letter to George Cabot dated January 27, 1804, he said:

> The principles of our revolution point to the remedy—a separation. That this can be accomplished, and without spilling one drop of blood, I have no doubt. . . . I do not believe in the practicability of a long-continued Union. A *Northern confederacy* would unite congenial characters and present a fairer

prospect of public happiness; while the Southern States, having a similarity of habits, might be left to manage their own affairs in their own way. If a separation were to take place, our mutual wants would render a friendly and commercial intercourse inevitable. The Southern States would require the moral protection of the Northern Union, and the products of the former would be important to the navigation and commerce of the latter. . . . *It (meaning the separation) must begin in Massachusetts. The proposition would be welcome in Connecticut, and could we doubt of New Hampshire? But New York must be associated, and how is her concurrence to be obtained? She must be made the center of the confederacy. Vermont and New Hampshire would follow, of course, and Rhode Island of necessity.*"

George Poindexter.

It is evident from this letter of Col. Pickering that *he had every reason to believe that the doctrine for which he contended—the right of the States to secede from the Union—met with approval in the States of Massachusetts, New Hampshire, New York, Vermont, New Jersey, and Rhode Island. And it is also to be observed that he entertained the view, which the South subsequently undertook to put into practical effect, that in case of an irreconcilable disagreement it was not only the right of the States, but their duty, to peaceably separate themselves from the union, and that this right rested upon the principles of the revolution, which had led to the separation of the colonies from Great Britain.* Later on, the acquisition under Mr. Jefferson of the Louisiana purchase, as it is commonly called, was denounced with surpassing bitterness, and the admission into the Union of that part of it which we now know as the State of Louisiana was violently opposed.

Congress Indorsed the Secession Doctrine: Josiah Quincy [III], a distinguished representative in Congress from Massachusetts, said in 1811:

If this bill passes, it is my deliberate opinion that it is virtually a dissolution of this Union; that *it will free the States from their moral obligations*, and, as *it will be the right of all*, so it will be the duty of some definitely to prepare for a separation—*amicably if they can; violently if they must.*

Mr. [George] Poindexter, a Southern man [from Virginia], and a delegate from the Mississippi Territory, excepted to the utterances of the distinguished Northern statesman, and called him to order. His point of order was sustained by the Speaker of the House of Representatives, who ruled that discussion of the dissolution of the union was out of order. From this decision of the Speaker an appeal was taken to the House, and *he was overruled. Here was an open avowal in the House of Representatives by a Northern statesman of the right of secession, and a decision by the House that it was a proper and lawful matter for legislative discussion, and that it could not be ruled out upon a point of order.*

1814 political cartoon attacking Pickering and the Hartford Convention.

Confederate Convention in Connecticut: In 1814 a convention was assembled at the city of Hartford, consisting of delegates elected by the Legislatures of Massachusetts, Rhode Island, and Connecticut, and attended also by representatives from the States of New Hampshire and Vermont. It was convened for the purpose of taking into consideration grievances under which those States were resting, growing out of the war with Great Britain. It has been commonly understood that the chief subject of their consultation was the withdrawal of those States from the Union. *While they did not decide at that time to withdraw from the Union, they very clearly indicated their opinion to be that the right to withdraw existed in the States.* They said:

If the Union be destined to dissolution by reason of the multiplied abuses of bad administration, it should, if possible, be the work of peaceable times and deliberate consent. *Some new form of confederacy should be substituted among those States which shall intend to maintain a Federal relation to each other. Events may prove that the causes of our calamities are deep and permanent. They may be found to proceed not merely from the blindness of prejudice, pride of opinion, violence of party spirit, or the confusion of the times; but they may be traced to implacable combinations of individuals or of States to monopolize power and office, and to trample without remorse upon the rights and interests of commercial sections of the Union. Whenever it shall appear that the causes are radical and permanent, a separation by equitable arrangement will be preferable to an alliance by constraint among nominal friends, but real enemies.*

In 1844 and 1845 the proposition looking to the annexation of Texas, and its admission as a State in the Union, was violently opposed, and attended by threats from the New England States of a dissolution of the Union. In 1844 a resolution was adopted by the Legislature of Massachusetts that "the commonwealth of Massachusetts, faithful to the compact between the people of the United States, according to the plain meaning and intent in which it was understood by them, is sincerely anxious for its preservation; but that *it is determined, as it doubts not the other States are, to submit to undelegated powers in no body of men on earth.*" It further declared that *"the project of the annexation of Texas, unless arrested on the threshold, may tend to drive these States into a dissolution of the Union."* On February 11, 1845, the Legislature of Massachusetts sent to the Congress of the United States a series of resolutions on the same subject, in one of which it was declared that "as the powers of legislation granted in the constitution of the United States to Congress do not embrace a case of the admission of a foreign State or foreign territory by legislation into the Union, such an act of admission would have no binding force whatever on the people of Massachusetts." Here is an express declaration by the great State of Massachusetts that the

State House, Boston, MA. New England attempted secession three times prior to Lincoln's War: circa 1804, 1814, and 1844.

John C. Calhoun.

constitution of the United States was but a compact, that the government created by it was one of delegated powers only, and that if the government should insist upon exercising powers not delegated, its acts would have no binding force on the State. It is the doctrine of nullification pure and simple, combined with the suggestion that the exercise of such undelegated powers might drive the State into a dissolution of the Union.

The settlers on the Mississippi River and its tributaries prior to the Louisiana purchase were greatly harassed and vexed in getting their products to market, by reason of the oppressive restrictions imposed by the Spaniards, who then controlled its outlet. In a remonstrance presented by them to Congress regarding their troubles they declared: "If Congress refuses us effectual protection, if it forsakes us, we will adopt the measures which our safety requires, even if they endanger the peace of the Union and our connection with the other States. *No protection, no allegiance.*"

Clash of the Two Theories: *It will be seen from what I have said that the right of a State to secede had been advocated openly by those of the North as well as those of the South, from the very foundation of the Union. In the beginning the proposition that the constitution was but a compact between the States from which they might withdraw whenever in their judgment their interests made it proper to do so was in no sense sectional. Later on the doctrine was advanced that the effect of the constitution was to bind the States together in an indissoluble union, and thereby create a nation which was dominant and supreme. The ablest men in public life arrayed themselves on the respective sides of this proposition. [John Caldwell] Calhoun [of South Carolina] on the one hand and [Daniel] Webster [of New Hampshire] on the other may be accepted as the greatest champions of the opposing theories. . . . In his early career Calhoun* had believed in and advocated the doctrine of the protective tariff, but some years later became a great champion of the contrary theory. Webster began by avowing his belief in the fallacy of the protective tariff, and ended by becoming one of its ablest advocates. The change of conviction on this great question in the minds of these statesmen was no doubt insensibly occasioned by their commercial and industrial environments. . . . Though political rivals, they were personal friends, and in his obituary address upon the death of Mr. Calhoun, Mr. Webster said of him: "There was nothing groveling or low or meanly selfish that came near the head or the heart of Mr. Calhoun."

The discussion was regarded as a legitimate struggle by the opposing forces to secure the acceptance of the theory of constitutional interpretation for which they respectively contended. But thoughtful men all along perceived that if both sides persisted, if neither would yield, if no middle ground could be found upon which both could stand, the time would surely come when the strife for mastery would find its settlement in another field than that of discussion and debate.

Yankee slavery extended to the Caribbean.

Unfortunately for us, the [Northern] institution of slavery had firmly established itself in the South and had grown and expanded as the country grew. It had come down to us by inheritance [from the Northeastern states],[296] and there seemed nothing left for us save to follow the path which we had trod from the beginning, and eliminate as best we could as many as possible of the evils which we all recognized as inseparable from it. If the institution of slavery was accompanied by the suggestion of moral wrong, *the States of the North were no more blameless than we; for aside from the fact that in the early days their inhabitants were themselves owners of slaves, and had parted with them only when they ceased to be a profitable investment, and then by sale for the best price to be had, the very constitution which they helped us to frame declared it to be lawful, and provided safeguards designed to prevent its destruction.* The thousands of sturdy immigrants who flocked to our shores, being white men and unaccustomed to the institution of slavery, naturally swerved from the South and swelled the population of the States and wide-spreading territories of the North. From time to time efforts were vainly made to preserve by compromise to some extent at least *the balance of power between the slave States of the South and the free States of the North.* "The irrepressible conflict," as Mr. [William H.] Seward called it, soon began to manifest itself in earnest. The bloody strife in Kansas; *the John Brown raid in Virginia, which, if those who planned it were sane, was the most*

John Brown.

infamous crime of the century; the triumph at the presidential election in 1860 of the Republican party [then the Liberal party], which had been born but a few years previous [founded in 1854 by Liberals and socialists],[297] made it plain to all that a supreme crisis had come upon us. Intense and wild excitement swept like a storm over the land. [Liberal] Mr. Lincoln and his adherents protested in vain that, the institution of slavery being lawful under the constitution, no war would be made upon it by his administration, and that the right of the people of the South would in all respects be preserved inviolate. But this could not outweigh the famous and portentous [and purposefully threatening] declaration of this great leader, that the Union could not survive half slave and half free.

The leaders of the Southern States were convinced that the state of affairs could no longer be tolerated. Conventions were called in all of them, when *they resolved that withdrawal from the Union was the only remedy which could put an end to the strife and secure that peace and quiet so essential to their prosperity and safety.* The Southern States, one by one, passed ordinances of secession, and solemnly declared that they were absolved from all further allegiance to the United States. The *New York Tribune* (then as now one of the ablest and most potential Republican [Liberal] journals) *declared that "if the cotton States wished to withdraw from the Union they should be allowed to do so;" that "any attempt to compel them to remain, by force, would be contrary to the principles of the Declaration of Independence and* to the fundamental ideas upon which human liberty is based;" and that "if the Declaration of Independence justified the secession from the British Empire of three millions of subjects in 1776, it was not seen why it would not justify the secession of five millions of Southerners from the Union in 1861."

Secession Not Treason: Let it be remembered and graven on the hearts of our children's children, even unto the end of time, that these ordinances of secession were not enacted in pursuance of a theory, then invented and contrived, as a cloak behind which to conceal rebellion and treason, but that they merely enunciated a doctrine which had been boldly and openly declared to be warranted by the true construction of our constitution from the moment of its promulgation, more than seventy years before. There was no treason or disloyalty in the minds and hearts of our people, nor did they essay the severance of the ties which had so long bound them to the Union without just appreciation of the solemnity of their deed. Not only this, but for many reasons they contemplated the rupture with supreme sadness and regret. They had grown up under the old flag, and had been taught to revere it as the symbol of a great and free and generous government. The policies of that government under which it had achieved a growth and prosperity unparalleled in all history, had been almost wholly shaped by Southern statesmen from the beginning. The immortal leader in the war of the revolution [George Washington], whose matchless powers and masterful nature had made our freedom from British tyranny possible, was a Southern man. His was the controlling spirit in the convention which had framed the constitution, and his influence, more than that of all others, had secured its ratification by the States. He became its first President, and under his administration was laid out the course by which the ship of state had sailed its maiden voyage.

Jefferson, Madison, Monroe, Jackson, Tyler, Polk, and Taylor, all Southern men, were afterwards elevated to the Presidency. Jefferson, as every schoolboy knows, was the author of the immortal Declaration of Independence. Under his administration was negotiated the Louisiana purchase, by which we acquired from France that imperial domain embracing the entire States of Arkansas, Missouri, Iowa, Nebraska,

Zachary Taylor.

James K. Polk.

North Dakota, South Dakota, part of the States of Minnesota, Kansas, Colorado, Montana, Wyoming, Louisiana, all of the Indian Territory, and part of the Oklahoma Territory.

Madison, who did so much to explain and popularize its provisions, has been frequently called the father of the constitution. Under his administration the war of 1812 was fought, in which we achieved such glory upon the seas, and which forever secured our shipping and seamen from the interference of foreign powers.

Monroe promulgated the doctrine which bears his honored name, which has been accepted as a part of international law, and which warned all nations that they would not be allowed to make further acquisitions upon, or intermeddle in any manner whatsoever with, the affairs of the American continent. The wisdom and beneficent purpose of the Monroe doctrine is such that it has become one of our fundamental traditions, to be maintained and enforced at all times, at any cost, whether of blood or treasure. Under his administration was negotiated the cession of the entire Floridas, covering 69,749 square miles, which embraced the present State of Florida and small parts of Louisiana, Mississippi, and Alabama.

Under the administration of President Tyler was negotiated the treaty by which Texas, with 376,931 square miles, was admitted as a State of the Union. Under the administration of President Polk was fought the Mexican War, which added fresh luster to our arms. The great leaders of our forces in that war were Winfield Scott and Zachary Taylor, both Southern men.

President Polk also negotiated the treaty with Mexico, by which we acquired that immense domain which embraces California, Nevada, Utah, Arizona, New Mexico, and parts of Colorado and Wyoming. He also negotiated the treaty with Great Britain by which our title was confirmed to that section of our country, including the States of Oregon, Idaho, Washington, and parts of Montana and Wyoming.

Although [Martin] Van Buren, [Franklin] Pierce, and [James]

Buchanan were Northern men, the policies of their administrations were along the lines which had been laid out by the great Southern Presidents who had preceded them.

The illustrious expounder of the constitution, whose fame as jurist has spread to the uttermost parts of the civilized world, was John Marshall, of Virginia, who for thirty-four years presided as chief justice of the Supreme Court of the United States.

The people of the South contemplated with lofty pride the greatness and glory to which the republic had attained under the leadership and guidance of their statesmen. It was with profound regret that they reached the conclusion that a just regard for their peace and safety demanded of them a severance of their relation with the Union. . . . In those ominous and storm-charged days that ushered in the tremendous struggle between the States, the passages between the contending sections on the floor of Congress reflected the intensity of the times. Replying to the exultant declaration of Senator Seward, of New York, that the power had departed from the South, that the scepter was now taken from her hands, and that henceforth the great North would grasp the power of government, Senator [James Henry] Hammond [of South Carolina] thus eloquently summed up the truth of history:

James H. Hammond.

> Sir: What the [Northern] Senator says is true. The power has passed from our hands into yours. But do not forget it, it cannot be forgotten, it is written upon the brightest pages of history, that we, the slaveholders of the South, took our country in her infancy, and after ruling her for sixty out of seventy years of her existence, we return her to you without a spot upon her honor, matchless in her splendor, incalculable in her power, the pride and admiration of the world. Time will show what you will do with her, but no time can dim our glory or diminish your responsibility.

Our love for the institutions our ancestors had aided in founding, and under which we had met with so much prosperity, was made manifest by the form of government which was immediately provided for the Confederate States of America. *The Confederate constitution, with few amendments, was the same as that of the United States. The administrative features of the new government were practically the same as those of the old. No thought of dictatorship or military supremacy on the one hand, or of lawlessness on the other, entered the minds of any.* True to the principles of the revolution and of the Declaration of Independence, we provided safeguards for personal liberty and local self-government.

During the whole of the long strife, and amidst hardship and privation almost indescribable, law and order were everywhere maintained. The Legislatures of the States assembled and enacted such laws as were from time to time deemed necessary; courts of justice were opened for the enforcement and maintenance of the rights of person and property.

Battle of Brandywine, September 11, 1777.

It has often been said that, having failed to settle by debate the issues which had so long been the subject of contention, the South deliberately appealed to the arbitrament of war. This is a mistaken notion of the view which we entertained of our relations to the Union. Under that view, as I have attempted to explain, the Constitution was but a compact between the States which might be dissolved by them at pleasure. Having exercised the right to withdraw from the Union, which, under their interpretation of the constitution, belonged to them, the Southern States saw no necessity for appealing to the arbitrament of war. And when war came, it was not because they had invited or sought it, but because they had determined to maintain their position, which they believed had absolved them from all allegiance whatever to the United States. We contemplated no war upon the States of the North, but hoped and believed that we would be allowed to set up a government for ourselves, and that the relations between the Confederacy which we established and the United States of America would be such as should subsist between friendly nations.

I need not attempt to describe with what valor and fortitude and heroic endeavor the armies of the South maintained themselves during four weary years of strife and bloodshed. We know, and all the world admits, that *the magnificent leadership of our armies and the splendid courage of our soldiers* have illustrated in the sublimest manner possible the martial spirit of the American people. The twenty-two hundred battles that were fought before our cause went down; the twenty-six hundred thousand men who were needed to conquer us; the pension roll of the government, which contains the names of nearly one million beneficiaries; the beautiful cemeteries where rest the dead heroes of the Union armies; the monuments of marble and bronze erected all over the land to perpetuate the names and fame of their great captains; all these make up a memorial of the skill and prowess and unyielding courage of our people, such as the history of the ages cannot parallel.

The end came as might have been expected. Our resources were so limited in comparison with those of the Northern States that only persistence on their part was needed to bring defeat and disaster to the Southern cause.

When it came we accepted the settlement as final and irrevocable, in so far as the further agitation or advocacy of the right of secession was concerned. No matter what may have been the right or wrong of the contention in 1861, we have admitted since 1865 that the Union is indissoluble [note: today's Confederates, like most of their Victorian Southern ancestors, do not, in any way, "admit" this],[298] and that the allegiance of all the people of this great republic is due primarily and fully to the United States of America. But while admitting this, *we do not and will never concede that the result of the great strife was a decision that our interpretation of the constitution was wrong.* The force of arms may be such as to set a controversy at rest by precluding its further agitation, and that, as to the power of a State to secede, was undoubtedly terminated by the triumph of the Union armies [note: this is technically not true],[299] but *truth is eternal and cannot be destroyed.*

My purpose has simply been to present in a brief and summary manner evidence that *at the beginning of our government State rights was commonly entertained, and that it was then in no sense sectional; that it had not been contrived in secret or expressed in whispers; but was openly and frankly advocated at all times and under all circumstances. The judgment of the impartial historian will never be that in standing for our interpretation of the constitution, even to the extent of maintaining it by force of arms, we made ourselves rebels or traitors.*

When the present generation has passed away, and when calm and impartial inquiry is made into the cause which led up to it, I have an abiding faith that this stigma will be taken from our heroic and devoted people. No man can now be heard to impugn the loyalty of the South. There has never been a moment of time since the surrender at Appomattox when there was the slightest ground for questioning it. We knew, but for long it seemed that others could not understand, that the result had been accepted by us as final and irrevocable. We knew that our destiny thenceforth was to be the same as that of our brethren of the North; and we had no ambition left save to preserve our honor untarnished, to build up the waste places, to restore law and order, to help to bind up the nation's wounds, and to contribute what we could to its greatness and grandeur. *We cherished no animosity against the brave men whose armies had been triumphant, and fondly indulged the hope that the rectitude of our purpose would be recognized.* But this was not to be.

The horrors of the civil war were nothing, dreadful as they were, compared with those which came upon us during the process of reconstruction. The right of franchise [the vote] was conferred upon the negroes of the Southern States, who had no preparation for its exercise, and *they easily became the*

victims of wicked and designing men [Liberals] who came down upon us to consume the little substance which had escaped the ravages of war. No good purpose would be subserved by enumerating the crimes which were committed in the Southern States during that dread period, and that under the form of government. *Let me say, however, that they are not justly to be attributed to the negro race. They were the work of bad white men who preyed upon the superstitions and ignorance of that race, and made it a scapegoat for their own wicked performance.* It may be that under the pressure of our environments at that time some things were done by our people which had better been left undone, but when I reflect upon the enormity of our provocation, I realize that if it had not been for the patience and fortitude displayed by the veterans of the Confederate armies, which had come to them through their years of discipline, *there might, and probably would, have been such anarchy and bloodshed throughout the South as would have shocked the civilized world.* We have before us the gravest social problems with which any people were ever confronted. If the negro belongs to the weaker [that is, less educated in Western terms] race, so much the greater is the duty upon us of the white race, by the lessons of example, to prepare him for the proper discharge of the solemn duties of citizenship.

We must not judge the negro too hastily or too harshly, nor expect him, without that preparation which can come only from the long exercise of those duties, to measure up to the standard which we set for ourselves. If they do not understand now, they will in time, that *they can have no separate foundation for happiness and prosperity*  *from that upon which we build our own; that we must live and struggle side by side, all doing their best to work out a just solution of the problems which confront us; and that this can never be accomplished in a way which would bring the best results, except by the steady and persistent cultivation of peaceable and kindly relations.*

Let us esteem ourselves fortunate that we have survived long enough to witness the total banishment of those asperities which so long existed between the different sections of our country. The mellowing influence of time has softened and cleared the vision of us all. We now see things clearly where once we could not see at all. We now know that *good people are the same everywhere*; that *no section has a monopoly of patriotism or virtue*; that *our people, no matter whence they come, are flesh of one flesh and are inspired by the same lofty courage and noble purpose.*

The chastening of the great war has but strengthened the American people for the work which this mighty nation must do through all the coming ages, for the advancement of civilization, and the uplifting of mankind. No human perception is keen enough to foresee the greatness and splendor which will surely come to us *if we will but be true to the fundamental principles of the Declaration of Independence which constitute the* basis of our institutions. It is given to us, in the province of God, to solve the question, long pondered over and debated, as to whether the people are capable of governing themselves. If those whom we intrust with official power are honest and patriotic; if they recognize that they are trustees charged with grave responsibilities, and that there can be no excess of devotion to public duty—the republic will stand. The solution of the problem rests with the people themselves, and they cannot be too vigilant and persistent in exacting from their public servants that they shall measure up to the highest standard of official life. We of the South cannot escape our just share of the responsibilities of the future, and we would not do so if we could. We are fast passing from under the cloud of suspicion and distrust which has so long cast its cruel shadow upon us. Southern men in the future may justly aspire to the highest positions of public office and trust.

Officers of the C.S. army and navy.

Let us so conduct ourselves that we may win anew the sympathetic confidence of all the people of this great republic. Just pride in the splendid deeds of the Southern statesmen of the past should stimulate us to emulate their example. Prosperity and disorder cannot dwell together. We should, therefore, never grow weary in teaching this great and essential truth. If we would banish disorder, we must reverentially uphold the law. It is far better that wrongdoing should go unwhipped of justice through the weakness of the law than that it should be punished through the strength of lawlessness. We must educate our children. Ignorance is the everlasting foe to progress, and we should make ceaseless war upon it, if we would secure for them a fair measure of the fruits of modern enlightenment. We must not forget that calm judgment and *conservative action* are the surest safeguards of peace and safety, for without them we cannot expect a just observance of the rights and privileges of all.

In conclusion let me remind you that, while contending for the purity of the motives which governed our efforts to separate ourselves from the Union in 1861, we must not fail to concede to those who differed from us the same loyal and elevated purpose which controlled our action.

On public as well as private questions men have always differed, and always will differ. It was a sad misfortune that the controversies between the two sections were such that they could not be settled by peaceful methods. Like ourselves, our brethren of the North gave abundant evidence of the sincerity of their convictions by the boundless expenditure of blood and treasure which they made to save the Union. We harbor against them no feeling of animosity or resentment. *The defeat which came to us was that of brave men, by brave men, and for it we reproach neither ourselves nor them.* And now that it is all over I am sure that none of us would have it otherwise.

Thomas C. Catchings, C.S.A.

The South is far happier, and will be far greater, than it could have been if it had succeeded in separating its fortunes from those of the Northern States.[300] Aside from the fact that the spirit of amity now diffuses its generous influence over the whole land, the Union greatly lessens the burdens of government, and enlarges the opportunities for the peaceful pursuits of private life. The flag of the nation is ours. We take our place under its starry folds, and, whether for weal or woe, will follow and uphold it to the end. Let us now, standing by the graves of our sainted dead, pledge to these reunited States the same passionate devotion which the illustrious statesmen of the South in the early days gave with unstinted measure to *the republic as it was established by the fathers.*[301] — HON. THOMAS CLENDINEN CATCHINGS (served with the Eighteenth Mississippi Infantry, C.S.A.)

☛ THE SOUTH'S STRUGGLE FOR INDEPENDENCE

The history of the world is a history of wars. In the year 1861 began the greatest war of the century, and for four long years the smoke of battle hung like a funereal pall over the fairest land on which the sun shines—the Sunny South. *With a valor and heroism never excelled by any people of any country in any period of the world's history the Southern people met the invaders of their homes. Their courage and constancy deserved success and won the admiration and respect of the civilized world.* The numerous graves in national cemeteries and the astounding length of the pension list with which the country is burdened and accursed give indisputable evidence of the valor and purpose with which they fought. They sought no war: they only sought to secure for themselves and their posterity the measure of happiness and prosperity to which they were entitled. They loved their homes, and found there that happiness, that freedom, more to be desired than fame, power, or wealth. To the Southern man the home is sacred. Its purity and sanctity he values more than he does his life or any other possession. In its defense every other consideration is of secondary importance. The invader who seeks to violate its sacred precincts takes his life in his hands, and is met on its threshold by the grim specter of death.

Who can blame us that we fought? Who can blame us that we met the invader of our homes and our country with arms in hands, and fought until from sheer exhaustion, from losses from death, wounds, capture, and hunger—outnumbered three or four to one—we were overpowered?

I bore a very humble part in that great drama of suffering, blood, and death, but I have never for a single instant felt regret for what I did. . . . The men of the North and the men of the South shoulder to shoulder now follow through flood and field.

> Mid shot and shell and saber stroke,
> Mid the death and hell of battle's smoke,

the flag of the Union, the stars and stripes.

Our cause was just. The record we made is imperishable, and so long as time endures, in every age and in every clime, where valor is honored and heroic deeds of daring and devotion to duty fitly appreciated, the soldiers of the Southern Confederacy will live in song and story the peers of the bravest and proudest in the annals of time.[302] — DR. J. N. BOYD

☛ TRIBUTES TO BLACK CONFEDERATES

While the race problem creates serious concern for the welfare of both races and for the country, it behooves *the Southern people, who are, and ever have been, their best friends*, to be on the alert for opportunities to influence all classes for the general good. [As white Southerners we will here improve the] opportunities to pay tribute to faithful slaves, and it bespeaks the cooperation of our people in sending concise contributions to the honor of those who have ever been faithful. Two illustrations are here given.

William Johnson (colored) lives by Nolensville, Tenn., near his birthplace. He was a slave, and the property of Mr. Ben Johnson, as was also his mother. In 1862 a part of the army commanded by Gen. Forrest was stationed at Nolensville, and young William Johnson (fifteen years old) drove one of the wagons with provisions for the army. Capt. B. F. White, who had been assistant adjutant general on the staff of Gen. Forrest, had been detached, and was in command of a battery of artillery captured at Murfreesboro. Seeing the boy William, he liked him, and proposed to buy him. Mr. Johnson sold him to Capt. White for $1,200, and *he went with Capt. White in the regular field service*.

William Johnson.

Soon after his purchase of William, the great battle of Murfreesboro was fought; and while on the battlefield, during the battle, Capt. White was attacked suddenly with inflammatory rheumatism. His servant William was with the wagon train, and did not reach him until the next day. The day following, the Confederates retreated, and the Federals, who also had been falling back, retraced their movements and occupied the area in which Capt. White was left in that painful and awful predicament, attended only by his servant William. For three months Capt. White was guarded by the Federals in a house on Thomas Butler's plantation, near the village of Salem. One bitter cold night the guard went to his camp some distance away, when the Captain asked William if he couldn't get him away from there. It was soon arranged for him to take a spring wagon and a broken-down army horse on the

Butler farm. He put his charge in the wagon, and by a circuitous route got away without apprehension. Late in the night the horse so nearly gave out that William walked in water and ice over his boots, and would lift the wheels of the vehicle out of the mire, and moved on until they were safe in the Confederate lines. A better horse was procured, and the afflicted officer was taken to Shelbyville, and from there he was permitted to visit Mobile, where he recuperated, William of course going with him. *This faithful servant remained with Capt. White, who went back into field service*, but his health failed, and when his constitution gave down he was put on post duty, and at the end of the war he was paroled at Albany, Ga. He brought William back to Nashville, leaving him with an uncle when he left to reside in Memphis. He afterwards moved to California. They never met again.

Reunion of black Confederates, circa early 1900s.

When the notice of Capt. White's death appeared in the December Veteran for 1899, William saw it, and asked to pay tribute to his memory. . . . He resumed his original name after the war.

William has lived all these years in the neighborhood of his birthplace, and has maintained a reputation as an honest, upright man—such as *will ever have the devoted friendship of the white people, and who will prove it if later in life misfortunes should render him unable to support himself*.

During the time of Capt. White's confinement in the Federal lines he allowed William to carry three young ladies through the lines to

Shelbyville. They were Misses Sallie J. McLean and Lizzie and Julia Lillard. After his return from that trip, Capt. White gave him permission to visit his mother, at Nolensville, before they escaped to the South.

[Now let us pay tribute to another one of the millions of blacks who remained loyal to their white families, the South, and the Confederacy.]³⁰³ Living on the banks of the Rappahannock, in the county of Culpeper, is a venerable old colored man, known by all near him as "Uncle" Ned Hawkins. His fidelity to his old mistress, his loyalty to the Confederacy, and *his devotion to our soldiers were truly remarkable. He risked his liberty and his life more than once for the safety of our citizens and soldiers.* On one occasion some of our scouts called at the house of his mistress—knowing they were always welcome there—and while she and her sister, assisted, of course, by "Uncle Ned," were busily engaged in preparing for them a much needed breakfast, the dreaded cry was heard: "The Yankees are coming!" They were guided by the ever faithful "Uncle Ned" to the pines near by, and he returned to the house. After the Yankees left, he took the breakfast in an old haversack, with a few ears of corn on top, and told our scouts if all was right when approaching them he would raise his hat and scratch his head, and if not, his hat would remain on his head; and should he meet the Yanks, with those ears of corn, his excuse would be that he was hunting his sheep. *Many, many such acts he did for the safety of our soldiers*, and now he and his aged companion are struggling hard for a living; and—O that some brave Confederate could assist them in their good old age! He is certainly worthy of notice.³⁰⁴ — SUMNER A. CUNNINGHAM

"Uncle" Ned Hawkins.

☛ MEMORY OF THE BATTLE OF BRICE'S CROSS ROADS

The place is known as Brice's Cross Roads, but the post office is Bethany. I am unable to explain why so little mention has been made of this engagement even by Southern writers. It was a signal Confederate victory. The slight mention made of it by Northern writers is easily explained, for it was a humiliating defeat. Gen. Grant in his official report of the operations of the war dismissed it with a few sentences.

To guard against any injury to his communications, he states:

> Gen. Sherman left what he supposed to be a sufficient force to guard against Forrest in West Tennessee. He directed Gen. Washburn, who commanded there, to send Brig. Gen. Samuel Davis Sturgis in command of his force to attack Forrest. On the morning of the 10th of June Gen. Sturgis met the enemy near Guntown, Miss., was badly beaten and driven back in utter rout and confusion to Memphis, a distance of about one hundred miles, hotly pursued by the enemy.

The battle occurred about six miles from Guntown, at the crossing of the Ripley and Fulton road with that from Pontotoc to Jacinto.

At this Cross Roads in 1864 was the residence of Mr. William Brice, a large two-story building; also the dwelling of Dr. A. G. Smythe, then unoccupied. Across the road from Brice's house was an unoccupied storehouse, and near by was the Associate Reformed Church of Bethany. The place was about half a mile east of Tishomingo Creek [thus the conflict is also known as the Battle of Tishomingo Creek]. My home was then with my father, Dr. E. Agnew, nearly three miles from the Cross Roads toward Ripley, where I still reside. The Cross Roads were sometimes called "Brice's Cross Roads," because his dwelling was the principal building there. It is so styled in Sturgis's official report in 1864. We had no mails. Our [troop's] intelligence of current events was generally derived from rumors, and these were, as a rule, unreliable.

On June 5 three Federal regiments of cavalry passed through Ripley, taking the Rienzi road, camping three miles from there. They fed off of Yancey, who was said to be ruined. This force was estimated at from fifteen hundred to three thousand men. A large infantry force, said to number ten thousand, was reported to be at Salem, coming on. What this move meant we could not imagine. Russell's Tennessee Regiment was following this cavalry, watching their movements.

Forrest, with his main forces, passed up by the Cross Roads, Tuesday evening, the 7th. The trains on the Mobile and Ohio Railroad that night and the next morning brought up his artillery; and it was evident that he was moving toward Corinth.

That evening (the 7th) [Edmund Winchester] Rucker's Brigade, consisting of [W. L.] Duckworth's Tennessee and Duff's and [James Ronald] Chalmers' Mississippi Regiments, had a fight four miles south of Ripley, fell back and camped at Kelly's Mill on the Tallahatchie, and on Wednesday they went to Baldwyn.

On Thursday, the 9th, we learned that Rucker's Brigade had gone from Baldwyn toward Rienzi. Forrest's command was then all above us.

Friday, the eventful 10th of June, a negro man came in and reported that the Yankees had camped the night before at Stubbs's farm, seven miles from us, in the direction of Ripley. Some scouts had called at Mr. J. O. Nelson's during the night, and warned them of the impending danger. It was not known whether they would go by the Baldwyn or the Guntown road.

Nathan B. Forrest, C.S.A.

I took charge of my father's mules and horses, and with some negroes to help care for them and a little brother thirteen years old, went into a dense thicket a mile and a half southwest of our home, where we hoped to hide our stock and save them from seizure by the Federal troops if they came our way. My father hid in the woods north of his dwelling, where he remained safely till the day after the battle. The anxiety with which we watched and listened can be imagined. From our hiding place we heard a mysterious roaring noise made by the advancing Federal army. *Not long after, one of our own negroes, who came skulking through the woods, told us that the Yankees were then at my father's home; that the yard was "black with Yankees;"* that they had taken everything we had to eat, and that about fifty wagons were in the road in front of the dwelling; also that there were thousands of negroes with the Yankees. We listened intently, and anxiously awaited developments. Soon a volley of small arms was heard—the first shots of the day. The advance guard of Sturgis's force had encountered a squad of Confederate cavalry. This occurred in Dry Creek bottom.

Hon. Newnan Cayce, of Columbus, Miss., has told me that he was with that reconnoitering detachment of cavalry. They fell back and reported the advance of the Federal force. Ere long cannon began to roar in a southeastern direction, near the Cross Roads. The battle, beginning about 10 a.m., raged long and doubtfully, and it was after five o'clock before the Federals retreated.

    Sturgis established his headquarters in Mr. Brice's house. His cavalry was under the command of [Union] Gen. Benjamin H. Grierson, and consisted of two brigades (Waring's and Winslow's) numbering 3,300 men, with six pieces of artillery and four mountain howitzers. His infantry was under McMillan, and consisted of three brigades—Wilkins', Hoge's, and Bouton's. The last was of negro troops. The infantry numbered 4,400 men, with twelve pieces of artillery. Sturgis estimated his force at 8,000, in round numbers, and the estimate is regarded as a low one. He had twenty-three regiments in all.

    Forrest's force consisted of 3,500 men, comprised in four brigades, commanded by Lyon, Rucker, Johnson, and Bell—all cavalry. With the main part of his force he was in Booneville the night of the 9th. I have understood that Forrest was not sure of Sturgis's movements until during that night, when scouts reported him camped at Stubbs's farm. Sturgis was ten miles from the Cross Roads, and Forrest was eighteen miles away. Forrest moved very rapidly, coming, according to Gen. Chalmers, eight miles in a gallop. His wagon train was hurried south on roads east of the railroad. Notwithstanding Forrest's haste, Sturgis succeeded in getting his force south of him, and blockaded his advance at the Cross Roads. Forrest himself moved with a part of his command to the left of the Baldwyn road, and advanced, flanking the enemy's right. The Federal force was placed in the form of a fan. The movement of Forrest was very difficult, owing to thick undergrowth of black-jack which covered the surface all around the Cross Roads. But his men were dismounted, and fought as infantry. The Federal cavalry held their front until their infantry came up. Back of the Porter field the conflict was very sanguinary. At the opening of the battle Forrest ordered Gen. Buford to send a regiment C. R. Barteau's) from Old Carrollville across the country into the rear of the enemy. This command entered the Ripley road in the rear of Sturgis, on the top of the hill west of Camp Creek, five and a half miles from the Cross Roads; and moving down the road a mile and a half, they deployed into the woods and fired on the enemy, who were beginning to fall back.

In my place of concealment I heard the firing of this attack of Barteau's. About six o'clock, when this long, hot, and anxious day was drawing to a close, to my surprise shells began to fall in the woods where we were hidden. We were evidently in an unsafe place, and we retreated, going south, while the shells were flying over us. We had not gone far when I met my uncle, Joseph Agnew, who told me that our fields were filled with Yankees. The battle was evidently now raging at my father's house, and I was anxious about the dear ones at home. The enemy fought desperately, but were finally driven back. Forrest was in the front, pursuing them with vigor, and the last reports were that a desperate stand had been made at our house.

The next morning, as soon as I could see, I started to find out what had happened, and I found that the Federals had been driven away. Our once pleasant home was a wreck. Thanks to a merciful Providence, the lives of the family had been preserved, although they had been exposed to great danger. I found the females of the family all in the back piazza. They were laughing and talking, notwithstanding recent distresses. The fence around the garden and yard had been torn down. Many horses were hitched under every tree in the yard. Soldiers

Edmund W. Rucker, C.S.A.

[Union] were stalking through the yard and house without ceremony. The public road in both directions was lined with wagons as far as could be seen. For more than half a mile, as I came home, I saw on the roadside hundreds of shoes and articles of every description, which had been thrown away by the Federals in their retreat. Several dead negroes in blue uniform were lying by the roadside not far from our dwelling. The public road was filled with soldiers passing to and fro. When I saw these things I knew that Forrest had gained a great victory, but my heart sank at the prospect of our own losses. *The Yankees had taken every grain of corn and every ounce of meat, leaving us nothing to eat. The family had not eaten anything since the previous morning, and the house had been plundered. Everything was turned upside down, and much was missing.* Dead and wounded men were lying in the house, upstairs and downstairs. Bullets had penetrated the walls in various places. Negroes and white men had both plundered our dwelling. Nothing could move their pity, but with vandal hands they rifled trunks and bureaus, entering every room. Destruction seemed to be their aim. *They even entered the negro cabins, and robbed them of their clothing. They cut the rope, and let the bucket into the well.* As they went back, panting with heat and suffering with thirst, they were glad to drink such dirty slop as they could find. [Note: all of this was illegal as it was in violation of the Geneva Conventions, as well as international law, Christian ethics, and common decency. L.S.]

The [Union] negro troops were specially insolent. As they passed down they would shake their fists at the ladies and say that they were going to show Forrest that they were his rulers. *As they returned, their tune was changed. With tears in their eyes, some of them came to my mother and asked her what they must do; would Mr. Forrest kill them?* On the retreat Sturgis was in the front, going at a trot.

The final stand was made at my father's house. When it began, my mother, wife, and sisters closed the window shutters, and all went into an inner room, and, lying flat on the floor, they awaited the issue of the conflict. Two Federal soldiers came into the back piazza, and surrendered to my mother just as the fight began. The yard was a battle ground. They made a breastwork of a picket fence. A Federal battery was in front of our gate. Rice's battery was just below the bend in the public road, and the fight here was nearly as stubborn as at the Cross Roads, and lasted fifty or sixty minutes. Capt. Rice told me that the artillery saved the day here. When he came up our cavalry was being repulsed. It was indeed a signal victory, for the Federal force was fully three times as great as that of Forrest. Forrest completely defeated the enemy, capturing all their artillery and their entire wagon train. To quote Sturgis's own words: "Order soon gave way to confusion, and confusion to panic." The losses incurred in such a rout were necessarily very great. According to the *Official Medical History of the War*, the losses on the Federal side were 617 killed and wounded, and 1,623 missing. The Confederate loss, according to the same authority, was 606 killed and wounded.

The pursuit was continued beyond Salem. On Monday, the 13th, many soldiers returned from the pursuit. Eight hundred prisoners were marched down the road that day. Some officers were among them, and they were nice-looking men. It is certain that a great many negroes were killed. They wore the badge, "Remember Fort Pillow," and it was said that they carried a black flag. This incensed the Southern soldiers [for the white and black Union troops at Fort Pillow had been abusing, robbing, and harassing the locals], and they relentlessly shot them down.[305]

Mr. Brice's house was temporarily made a hospital for wounded Confederates. Some Southern boys died there. I remember a lad who lay there dying, and whose earnest gaze and yearning for a mother's soothing presence aroused my tenderest sympathies. How gratefully did that dying boy receive the kind ministrations of Mrs. Brice, who was watching by his side!

Dead Union soldiers.

Bethany Church was occupied as a hospital, and many a Federal soldier lay wounded on benches on which worshipers had been wont to sit in days when peace reigned. A bullet [had] passed through the pulpit. The monuments and tombstones in Bethany burial ground to this day show the imprint of Minie balls. Thirty or more graves containing the bodies of brave Tennesseans and Kentuckians, who fell in battle that day, are in Bethany burial ground. The graves are unmarked, and the heroes are unknown. A man named King, of Rice's Battery, is buried a few hundred yards below my residence. The little mound which marks his grave can be seen on the roadside. King was from the vicinity of Artesia, Miss. The grave of a Tennessean, A. J. Smith, is not far away. A nice young man, who was brought wounded into my house on the day of the battle, and died there that night, was buried under a large post oak in front of my gate. His name was Rice. His friends removed his remains to the family burial ground in Lauderdale County, Tenn., in 1865.

Forrest, with his subcommanders, Buford, Lyon, Bell, Rucker, and Johnson, won laurels that day which will not soon wither. The day will not soon be forgotten by those who were present. Gen. Chalmers said *it was the most brilliant victory of the war on either side.* And considering the great disparity of the contending forces, the result was certainly most wonderful.[306] — REV. SAMUEL A. AGNEW

☛ SKETCH OF GEN. MAXCY GREGG

Maxcy Gregg, C.S.A.

Gen. Maxcy Gregg, before the war, was a lawyer of note, as was also his father, James Gregg, Esq. He was born and reared in Columbia [South Carolina], living in a house built by his father, in what was then a forest, where deer ran wild, now Senate Street, near the State House and old Trinity Church. Mr. Gregg gave the lot on which Trinity is built, and on condition that the graveyard should not be continued on this side of the church, as it was just in front of his house. Here his quiet childhood was passed and his early youth matured into manhood, and here his mind was imbued with those high principles of honor and right which afterwards made him the noble man he was. It may be said that he was an original secessionist—almost a nullifier, as in his youth he heartily indorsed the nullification proceedings of 1832. He was in 1852 the head and front of the opposition to cooperation in that memorable campaign. On one occasion, at a proposed meeting on the South Carolina College campus, where a dozen prominent speakers had been promised and announced, Col. Maxcy Gregg was the only one on the platform; the others had "flunked." Undismayed, he arose, and in impassioned language stirred the assembly to fever heat, speaking for nearly two hours.

Although an earnest lawyer, Col. Gregg was also thoroughly posted in military matters. Responding [in 1861] to the call from the State, he immediately enlisted and served his country [the C.S.A.] gallantly and efficiently until his death, in 1862, at Fredericksburg, Va. He was then only forty-seven years old, although he looked much older. He was mortally wounded while gallantly repelling [Union Gen. George Gordon] Meade's charge. He was a brave and fearless soldier, and a noble gentleman. After he was mortally wounded he lingered for many hours in terrible pain, which he bore with uncomplaining patience and Spartan bravery. *I heard his old body servant, "Uncle" William Rose, who was his faithful friend until the end, tell with streaming eyes of his sufferings and untold Christian fortitude. This old servant has never forgotten his former master and general, and it is a touching sight every year on memorial day to see him with tottering steps and shaking hands lay a wreath of flowers on Gen. Gregg's monument in Elmwood cemetery.* The old man is truly a veteran, having served in three wars—the Mexican, Florida, and Confederate. *Nearly ever since the war, no matter who is Governor, "Uncle" William has been porter to the Governor's office, and sits at the door day after day in his comfortable chair, and happy in the possession of Gen. Gregg's watch, which he gave him on his deathbed, and a gold-headed cane presented to him a few years ago by the Legislature.*

Gen. Gregg was never married. He was one of the tidiest of men, and was always well dressed in, generally, a full suit of black, with the uncomfortable standing collar of immaculate white. As a lawyer his character was unsullied, and his reputation was never smirched by undertaking a case in the least disreputable. As in his person he was straight as an arrow, with a firm step, so in his character he was an upright man—an honor to his profession—*a true representative of the olden-time gentleman.*

Home of Maxcy Gregg, Columbia, SC.

The following anecdote of Gen. Gregg was told me by an old fellow-soldier: "Near Vienna, Va., in the latter part of 1861, [Confederate] Capt. Del Remper a former resident of Alexandria, was in command of a masked battery of artillery near the railroad. A train loaded with Federal soldiers approached, and Remper's guns gave them such a warm reception that the train was hurriedly backed out of reach. There were several rounds fired with telling effect, and at each discharge Remper would throw himself upon the ground and give vent to his joy by repeated shouts. Gen. Gregg rode up, and with a faint attempt at a smile exclaimed: 'Quite undignified, Capt. Remper, quite undignified.' 'Can't help it, General,' was the reply, as another discharge from his guns played havoc with the fast retreating train."[307] — MRS. A. G. ROBERTSON

☛ STONEWALL JACKSON & MAXCY GREGG

Gen. Gregg's monument, Columbia, SC.

When Gen. Gregg, of South Carolina, was wounded at Fredericksburg, an interesting incident occurred. Gen. Jackson had had a misunderstanding with Gregg, the nature of which I do not now recall. The night after this gallant gentleman and splendid soldier was mortally wounded I told Gen. Jackson, as I generally did of friends or prominent men killed or wounded.

Gen. Gregg was one of the most courteous gentlemen that I had ever known. He exposed himself that day in a way that seemed unnecessary, so much so that Col. [Alexander Swift] Pendleton, of Jackson's staff, rode up to him, and, knowing he was quite deaf, shouted to him that the Yankees were shooting at him.

"Yes, sir; thank you," he replied; "they have been doing so all day."

When I told Gen. Jackson that Gregg was badly injured, he said: "I wish you would go back and see him. I want you to see him."

I demurred a little, saying it had not been very long since I had seen him, and that there was nothing more to be done for him.

He replied: "I wish you to go back to see him, and tell him I sent you."

So I rode back to the Zesby house, saw Gen. Gregg, and gave him the message. When I left his bedside and had gotten back into the hall of the house I met Gen. Jackson, who must have ridden close behind me to have arrived there so soon. He stopped me and asked about Gen. Gregg, and went into the room to see him. No one else was in the room, and what passed between the two officers will never be known. I waited and rode back to camp with him. Not a word was spoken on that ride by either of us. *After we reached camp, as we stood waiting for some one to take our horses, Jackson looked up to the sky for a moment, and said: "How horrible is war!"*

I replied: "Yes, horrible ; but what can we do? These people at the North, without any warrant of law, have invaded our country, stolen our property, insulted our defenseless women, and hung and imprisoned our helpless old men. What can we do?"

"'Do?" he answered, and his voice was ringing. "Do? Why, shoot them!"[308]
— DR. HUNTER MCGUIRE

Stonewall Jackson, C.S.A.

CHAPTER 20

1901

☛ TRIBUTES TO BLACK CONFEDERATES

[Accompanying this article] . . . is a good picture of Fed Ardis, who was the property of Mr. Isaac Ardis. Fed is now living in Texas, and is about seventy-five years old. He was given to Mr. Ardis's wife when he married her in Russell County. Ala., 1841. Fed was a good boy, and won the confidence of his master and mistress, and as the family increased and grew he was a great favorite with the children because of his kindness to them.

When the war came on Mr. Ardis made Fed his foreman, and intrusted all his farm business to him, which he managed very faithfully and successfully. Toward the close of the war the deserters became very troublesome in Southeast Alabama, and to protect themselves the old men of Dale County organized a small company of themselves and elected Mr. Ardis captain. He was a resolute, vigorous man, and made it so warm for the deserters that he incurred their bitter enmity. When away from home he trusted his business, his property, and his family to Fed and other faithful negroes on the place. His mistress would intrust her money and other valuables to Fed to keep them from falling into the hands of the enemy. Occasionally Mr. Ardis would come home for a day or so to see how everything was getting on. On one occasion he came home to stay all night, but by some means the deserters found it out and planned to kill him. After supper Fed went to the lot to see about the mules, as was his custom, and in passing the front of the house he saw two men standing by the yard gate with guns. He went by whistling as though he had not seen them, and passed around to the back of the house and called his master to the window and told him not to go out, as there

Fed Ardis.

were men around to assassinate him. They closed the front door, blew out the lights, and Mr. Ardis passed out the back way. Fed went back to the negro quarters and got several other negro men with their axes and went back to the house, and placed them as guards around the house, and said to his Mistress: "Now. Miss Lizabeth, you go to sleep. If anybody gets in this house to-night, they have got to kill us first."

Fed was always very religious, and he was very able in prayer. During slavery he and other old faithful negroes would attend church and take their places in a cut-off portion of the church, just back of the pulpit, which was provided for them in erecting churches. Strange as it may sound to some people at the North, Fed was frequently called on to pray, especially during prayer meeting services.

He was a very sensible man, and his prayers were very effectual. After the war he obtained some education, and got license to preach, and soon became a "big preacher" among the negroes in Southern Alabama. He became a presiding elder in the Methodist Church.

A few years ago he came to Texas, and Dr. Ardis, of Greenville (who had been his young master), sent him money to come on. He has just lately returned from a visit back to his old Conference in Alabama, the negroes then having written him if he would visit their Conference they would pay his expenses.

Soon after he went to preaching my wife, who was his young mistress, sent him a fine Oxford Bible, which he appreciates highly.

Fed is doing well, and will have a good home on Dr. Ardis's place as long as he lives, and I very much believe will have a far better one when he crosses over "the Jordan."

Hannibal Alexander was a slave belonging to Parker Alexander. He went with his young master, Sidney Alexander, to the war, and did his duty faithfully. "Ham" died recently in Monroe County, Miss. He and his wife Delia by industry made a good living and accumulated a competence, *ever having the confidence and friendship of the white people about their lifetime home.* Writes W. A. Campbell, of Columbus: "In the army he was [the] cook. He was in the siege of Fort Donelson. *He was captured there, and went to Camp Douglass as a Confederate prisoner.* He answered roll call all the time as a white soldier. Being a bright mulatto, he was brought to Vicksburg and exchanged with the others, and again went with his young master into service.

"The Federal sergeant that called the roll was somewhat suspicious as to 'Ham' (as he was called by the boys) being a slave, but he was told that living in Mississippi he was sunburned and that made him dark.

"Hannibal was a very intelligent negro, *and knew if he left his master he could go free, but he elected to stay with him among the white men he had been raised with, and preferred to suffer with them.*

"I knew Hannibal for more than forty years as slave and freeman, and he was ever polite and friendly to all his former owners. In the old days I went on many a hunting and fishing expedition with Sidney, with "Ham" to wait on us.

His old master with whom he went in the army is yet alive, but in poor health.[309]
— A. N. EDWARDS

William McKinley.

☞ PRESIDENT MCKINLEY ON THE SOUTHERN PEOPLE
. . . in a long public life, [President William McKinley] *has never spoken unkindly of the Southern people, or done them a wrong.* On the contrary *he has had the rare courage to proclaim that it is now the duty of the United States to take care of the graves of the Confederate dead.*[310] — F. S. FERGUSON

☞ OUR BRAVE PRIVATE SOLDIERS
Many instances of individual bravery and daring by private soldiers in our Southern army deserve the tribute of public mention, and those who were witnesses of such deeds are not doing justice to their companions, living or dead, in keeping silent concerning them. Let all who were witnesses of individual acts of heroism and sacrifice for our cause hasten to place them on record for the benefit of posterity, and as a just tribute to merit and worth. One such I furnish . . . [here].

For three weeks those two masters in the art of war, Lee and McClellan, had been facing each other like two skilled players in a game of chess. The Confederate army under Joe Johnston had been pressed back until it was at the very gates of Richmond, and with eager eyes McClellan's soldiers from the north side of the Chickahominy gazed at the church steeples in the Confederacy's capital city, only six miles away.

But Lee was in command of the army that stood between them and the coveted prize, and the impression had gone out that not another foot of ground would be yielded without a battle.

The seacoast and gulf cities had been stripped of every regiment that could possibly be spared, and the newspapers were appealing to all who were absent from their commands on furlough to return and save our beloved capital from the invader.

Francis S. Bartow, C.S.A.

Among such absentees was John Krenson, of Company B, Eighth Georgia Regiment, one of [Confederate Col. Francis Stebbins] Bartow's "beardless boys" from Savannah. He had been severely wounded in the memorable "pine sapling" thicket at Manassas, and had never completely recovered from his wound. It was said, in fact, that his surgeon had pronounced him permanently disabled and unfit for further service in the field. But when the news came that McClellan's army was in sight of Richmond, he could stay away no longer, and set out to rejoin his company. He came to us, I think, about the time we took up our position at Price's farm, five miles from Richmond, and a short distance north of Nine Mile road. The enemy's pickets were then less than three hundred yards in our front, and each succeeding morning they appeared in a new position and still nearer to us. As each day drew to its close, those of us on the picket line felt that the battle must certainly begin on the morrow. After a brief trial of his strength, Krenson had found that the surgeons were right. He could not stand active service, and a final discharge had been given to him. But he lingered in camp, and to each surprised inquirer as to why he did not go home he would reply with the question, "Do you think the battle will begin soon?" and to the invariable answer, "Yes," he would add, "Then I cannot leave now."

And so during two weeks he waited, thinking each day that the battle would occur ere the setting of another sun.

Finally, on the 26th of June, upon our extreme left at Mechanicsville, the battle was on. Friday, the 27th, it raged furiously farther down on McClellan's right flank, and in the afternoon at Ellison's and Gaines's Mills and Cold Harbor. McClellan's right wing was doubled back at right angles to his original main line, and what that cautious leader's next move would be not even the astute Lee was able to guess.

Saturday came, and with it an order to Gen. Magruder, holding our center across the Nine Mile road, to make a demonstration against the enemy's lines in his front. [George Thomas] "Tige" Anderson's and [Henry Lewis] Benning's Georgia Brigades were ordered forward. Companies A and B, of the Eighth Georgia, were ordered out as skirmishers to cover the front of the advancing column and drive in the enemy's pickets and sharpshooters. Krenson was in his place in the skirmish line. The running fight was at short range,

George T. Anderson, C.S.A.

and almost at every step some one went down; and among the first to fall, a sacrifice to that attempt to "feel the enemy," was brave, proud John Krenson. An honorable discharge in his pocket, a sharpshooter's bullet in his heart, that brave, young soldier boy was "off duty forever."[311] — B. M. ZETTLER

☛ EIGHTEEN CONFEDERATES FOR RETALIATION

Early in November, 1862, I was, with some other prisoners, en route to Vicksburg to be exchanged. We were stopped at Cairo, Ill., and a few days after we reached there all the [Confederate] prisoners in the pen with me, about two hundred or three hundred, were drawn up in a double line, and some [Union] officers and a guard came in. It was then announced that in retaliation for eighteen men who had been shot by

Gen. Forrest's orders, the same number were to be selected from our ranks for a like fate. The order was then given for us to open ranks, which placed us in two single lines, one in rear of the other. A number of white beans and eighteen black ones were then put in a hat and carried  up and down the lines, and each man was forced to put in his hand and draw out a bean. Before his hand could get out of the hat his wrist would be seized by the guard, who would open it, and if a white bean was disclosed the hat was passed to the next; but if the bean was black, the poor fellow was marched off, and we saw him no more. This was kept up until the eighteen men were drawn. About a week later we were loaded on a boat—960 in number by that time—and started for Vicksburg. We were sixteen days making the trip, with prisoners dying every day like sheep with the rot. At last, while lashed alongside the Confederate boat, the exchange going on, and at least a third of our men had passed over on to our boat, the Federals got a dispatch that one of the eighteen men drawn at Cairo had died, and demanding another victim. So another of our comrades was then and there seized, and, like those at Cairo, we saw him no more.[312] — H. B. RICHARDS

☛ CONFEDERATE SURGEONS

Our ranks are rapidly thinning under the corrosive tooth of time, and whatever remains to approximate, as far as we may, our historic part in *the brilliant, incisive, self-sacrificing, principle-honoring, and glorious chapter, which shall mark the rise and fall of the Southern Confederacy, with all her illustrious Christian men and women, her heroic, all-enduring sons and daughters*, must be done without much further delay.

Exceeding four years of almost uninterrupted campaigns, conducted through all seasons and in all weather, covering an unprecedently vast territory scarred by more than 2,000 battlefields—600,000 Confederate soldiers against 2,865,028 Federal soldiers—engaged in the only decisive method for the settlement of a great national question, must compass materials of signal and crucial historic importance for a reunited people, organized under a [confederate] republican form of government.

Our part had to deal with the stern actualities of a vast array of diseases, ghastly wounds, and with problems of sanitation, on an immense scale, in the execution of our most responsible duties. Medicines, instruments, medical works, provisions, and delicacies for the sick and wounded were [cruelly and unlawfully] made contraband of war [by the Lincoln administration], both as regarded our own sick and wounded as well as the sick and wounded prisoners [of] their government [that is, Union soldiers], by refusing to exchange, compelled us to retain and care for in prison life, in spite of our well-known limited resources of every kind for such a colossal undertaking.

Field hospital and wounded soldiers.

Thus, with a prison list, from first to last, reaching the immense total of 270,000, against 220,000 of our own soldiers held in Federal prisons—with a balance, as the records show, in our favor of 50,000 prisoners, the Confederate surgeons, with proudest Christian consolation, point to their monument of monuments, in that terrible, bloody and contracted contention between brothers of the same land and blood and hopes, to *the 4,000 more lives saved in prison life than were saved by our quondam enemies of the other side with an excess of prisoners in our keeping, and with all the stated disadvantages against us, while all the advantages in resources, with a fewer number of prisoners, were in their favor.* . . .[313] — DR. C. H. TEBAULT (an address to the survivors of the medical corps of the army and navy of the Confederate States)

☛ UNION VETS HONOR CONFEDERATE GRAVES IN ILLINOIS
[What follows is] an account of the decoration of our graves in the North Alton Confederate cemetery on May 31, 1901, in which "the boys in blue participated." The [Yankee] article refers to the graves of "the brave Southerners":

Members of the G.A.R. [Grand Army of the Republic; that is, soldiers of the Union army] assisted in decorating the graves. With tender hands they arranged the flowers upon the little mounds, that from lack of proper care have almost disappeared in the old cemetery. The old soldiers attended to the decoration of the Confederate graves with the same instinct of duty as they did to the decoration of the graves of their comrades. A special street car took the little company of people to North Alton, who from there made their way to the old Confederate cemetery. They had with them a wagonload of flowers, including those that had been sent by the old soldiers of Texas. When the company reached the cemetery the service was opened with a prayer by Rev. M. W. Twing. The song "America" was sung by the audience. Joshua Dixon, President of the Village Board of Upper Alton, delivered the address, and he was followed by Rev. H. K. Sanborne in a short and appropriate address. After the hymn, "Nearer, My God, to Thee," Rev. A. H. Kelso made a short address. Another hymn, "Shall We Meet Beyond the River," was sung, and Mr. Twing pronounced the benediction. *The graves of the Confederate soldiers were then decorated with the beautiful flowers, and each grave was marked by a little mound of flowers, made up of the Illinois rose and the favorite flower of Texas, the magnolia blossom. It was a pretty and impressive occasion.*[314] — The *Republican* of Alton, Illinois

☛ COMPLAINT AGAINST YANKEE SCHOOL TEXT-BOOKS
Extract from the minutes of Confederate Reunion, Belton, Tex., July 2, 3, 4, 1901.

The committee on school histories from Camp No. 122, Bell County Confederate Association, made its report: Your committee, referring especially to *Montgomery's History for Beginners*, recommend the adoption of the following resolutions and urge that we use every effort in our power to discourage the use of the book in our schools:

"Resolved: 1. That the *Montgomery History for Beginners* is partisan in its composition, in that it lauds [Liberal] Lincoln and throws on the [Conservative] South unjustly the burden of the origin of the war. That to remedy this we recommend that the lawmaking powers *expunge this book from the series and substitute a nonpartisan book of its kind in its stead.*

"2. That in case this is not done, and the Lincoln laudation is retained, *a like number of pages be devoted to the history of [Conservative] Jefferson Davis, in which be written the truths of history to the effect that in the early 1830s Jefferson Davis, as an officer in the Black Hawk war, administered to Lincoln, as a volunteer, the oath to support the Constitution of the United States—his first oath—and that Lincoln was the first to aver that he would not be bound by that oath, but by a higher law [in today's terms, "social justice"], and that he first openly declared he and his party would repudiate that constitution as constructed by*  *the Supreme Court in the Dred Scott case in 1857, and that this case decided that slaves could be taken in the territories as any other property, and that by Lincoln's repudiation of the law is constructed by the tribunal of last resorts war resulted, and he and his party were fact the real revolutionists and are morally responsible for all the loss of life and destruction of Southern homes and property that ensued.*

"3. If this course, or one similar in effect is not followed, and a partisan history is to be adopted, we recommend that Mrs. [Susan] Pendleton Lee's series of the history of the civil war as now in use in Virginia be used, in which the truth, the whole truth, and nothing but the truth is narrated in plain, simple language for beginners."[315] — W. I. WILSON (Committee Chairman)

☛ A GOOD CAPTURE BY SEVEN CONFEDERATES

At the age of nineteen years I became a scout for Gen. J. E. B. Stuart, and at the end of one year was promoted to army headquarters, where I served Gen. Lee in the same capacity until the surrender.

On the 28th of June, 1863, Gen. Stuart, seeing a force of the enemy

Jeb Stuart, C.S.A.

at a distance from our advance between Rockville and Georgetown, Md., requested a demonstration, at which I called for volunteers, and William Campbell and five others, whom I newer knew, came forward. We, the seven of us, captured [Union] Gen. Meade's wagon train, consisting of 900 mules, 175 wagons, a number of ambulances and private conveyances under a guard of 50 or 75 men. On account of this demonstration I was promoted and publicly complimented by Gen. Lee.[316] — J. S. CURTIS

☛ LINCOLN'S WAR THROUGH THE EYES OF A CHILD

[This Southern boy's composition caused his expulsion from school, for his teacher was from New Jersey]. . . . When quite a small schoolboy he was very fond of writing compositions; . . . he never got a prize for any, but certainly deserved one. One day his teacher told him to write a composition on the civil war, so he set to work and wrote the following: "The civil war was declared in the year of 1861, and ended in the year of 1865. Abraham Lincoln started the row by sending men down South to steal niggers. These nigger thieves were called abolitionists, and they became such a nuisance that the Southern people seceded. That made the Yanks mad, and they declared war against the South. A [Union] Maj. [Robert] Anderson had charge of Fort Sumter, in Charleston Harbor. Well, on the night of April 12 five Confederate batteries began barking at the fort, and Anderson, fearing that he would get hurt if he stayed there any longer, gave the fort to the Rebs, and went North for his health. That made Lincoln as mad as a hornet. He called for 75,000 volunteers, and started the cry, 'Off to Richmond!' but they never got any farther than Bull Run, because Beauregard and Johnston were there, and objected in such a way that the Yanks cleared out, and did not leave any address. Lincoln was mad at the first defeat,

Pierre G. T. Beauregard, C.S.A.

and he was a 'hot box' after the battle of Bull Run. He cussed out Congress, and then called for more volunteers. After this event came the battle of the Wilderness. Gen. Grant was now commander in chief of the Union army, and was a pretty slick chap, but there were others. Grant marched his army to the Wilderness with the object of making a flank march on Richmond, but got his own flank spanked in the attempt. He tried again at Cold Harbor, but there was nothing done, for whenever his men stuck their heads above their trenches they had part of them taken off. Well, by and by hunger began to visit the camp of the Southern soldiers, and many died from it. So seeing it useless to fight against such a combination as hunger and Yanks, especially hunger, Gen. Lee surrendered to Grant at Appomattox in the year of 1865, and now we are all one, a grand and glorious republic."[317] — Z. F. BARNUM

☛ WHAT NERVE DID IN AN EMERGENCY

On the morning of June 26, 1862, Stonewall Jackson sent me as a scout with strict injunctions to see what was in front of his army. After going a short distance straight forward [near the Chickahominy Swamp], I took

a road to the left, and traveled that a short distance, then turned abruptly to the right and rode on, being on the alert all the while. Suddenly I discovered two mounted men, and still farther could see the top of a tent, so concluded that I was near the Federal army. After taking in the situation, I started back to Gen. Jackson's headquarters. When I had gone a few yards I discovered in front of me twelve men, well armed, seemingly holding a consultation. Taking in the situation at once, I of course realized my peril, and that some strategy must be used if I would save my life, so in a loud, commanding voice I shouted: "Here they are, men, charge them!" They immediately threw their arms up, and I then gave the command: "Arms down! Right about, wheel! double-quick, march!" By that time I was close to them, and "double-quicked" them a quarter of a mile, then allowed them to move at a more leisurely pace until I was in sight of Gen. Jackson's headquarters. I delivered them up in Gen. Jackson's presence, who seemed astonished, and said to me: "Scout, had those men any arms?" I replied that they were armed, and had thrown them down at my bidding. The prisoners remarked that they thought I had a battalion at my command and, not looking around, hearing the command to surrender, they immediately obeyed. So the result of that morning's ride alone was the bringing into Gen. Jackson's headquarters of one dozen Federal prisoners.[318] — WILLIAM B. MEGGINSON (member of Company H, Second Virginia Cavalry, C.S.A.)

Confederate cemetery, Madison, WI.

☛ A UNION GENERAL'S TRIBUTE TO CONFEDERATES

The Salt Sulphur Springs, Monroe County, W. Va., was a Confederate post for most of the great war, the passes in the Alleghenies in its neighborhood being a series of back doors to Lynchburg, Va., and covering that important place. [Confederate] Gen. John Stuart "Cerro Gordo" Williams, Gen. [William Wing] Loring, and Gen. [Henry] "Harry" Heth successively commanded the post at Salt Sulphur. Gen. Heth moved his forces over to Lewisburg, some twenty-five miles away, in 1862, and attacked [Union] Gen. George R. Crook there, but was defeated and obliged to return to the "Salt." After [Gen. Heth's] return some of his badly wounded men died, and they were buried on one of the benches of the Peach Orchard hill. [Union] Gen. [John W. M.] Appleton, the present proprietor of the springs, finding that these graves were uninclosed in a pasture, in 1882 placed a fence about them and put up a tablet inscribed: *"To the Memory of the Unknown Confederate Dead Whose*

Mortal Part Sleeps Here."

Thus it was given to a whilom [that is, "former"] enemy to mark the resting place of these brave men who gave all they had to the cause they believed in. Gen. Appleton was first a private soldier during the war of the sixties, and later an officer in the Union army, serving with Massachusetts troops. He rose from second lieutenant to major of the Fifty-Fourth Massachusetts Infantry in about four months, and later, after recovery from severe wounds, commanded  six batteries of artillery. In the service of his State, West Virginia, he has held various positions, from captain of a company of infantry to brigadier general, adjutant general, and is still connected with the national guard.[319] — SUMNER A. CUNNINGHAM

☛ EXPERIENCES IN & ABOUT VICKSBURG

Circumstances were such that I did not go to the war until December, 1862. I went to Vicksburg, joined the Thirty-First Louisiana, Morrison's Regiment, Baldwin's Brigade, Smith's Division. We were there through the siege, and surrendered July 4, 1863.

We were engaged in building breastworks and mounting guns until the Chickasaw Bayou fight. We fought the Federals there one week during the last days of December and first of January, and defeated them. Gen. Grant tried to cut a canal across the bend of the river to get his army below Vicksburg, as the fortifications were too formidable for him to pass. He tried to pass down two or three gunboats, but they were torn to pieces by our guns. Our winter quarters were five miles east of Vicksburg, and we went on picket duty every third night. Every third week we were on guard at the Backbone Ridge. About the last days of March the Federals sent a flag of truce down, and continued it daily every evening for two weeks or over, until one evening the Federal fleet disappeared from Young's point. The army went west for fifteen miles, then turned southeast to Rodney, where it crossed the Mississippi River.

We were on guard at Backbone Ridge the night the boats ran by to put that army across. I was among the first to reach the top of the hill in the breastworks, before the first vessels rounded the point. There were three or four houses fired on the opposite side of the river from us, and it was light as day on the water by the time the first boat passed. The boats were about half a mile apart, and they passed that way until all nine steamed through. I could see every shot that struck the water from "Whistling Dick" [an 18 pound Confederate gun] down to the depot, and there was but one boat struck out of the nine, and it was not disabled. The papers the next morning stated that the bad shooting was caused by the main gunners being absent at a "big ball," and that the guns were manned by "raw conscripts," and it has always seemed reasonable to me that the place was "sold." No gunboat had ever gotten by the batteries before. The boats put the Federal army across at Rodney, and they went on out to Port Gibson. We met them there with 7,000 men and fought them one whole day, and they drove us back. We crossed Big Black River near Grand Gulf, going up on one side while they were on the other to the railroad bridge on Big Black. They went up to Edward's Depot, where they met Loring's Division and other commands. There the Baker's Creek battle was fought. Our brigade, commanded by Col. Richardson, was held in reserve until Sunday morning, when we met our men who were driven out of the breastworks. It was on Sunday. We covered their retreat inside the breastworks. Monday they surrounded us completely, and we fought them forty-eight days on very scant rations of mule meat and pea bread. We were surrendered on the fourth day of July, 1863. In the fight on Chickasaw [Confederate] Maj. T. C. Humble and private Sidney Robertson were killed. I am an old, worn-out wreck nearly seventy-seven years old . . .[320] — R. F. WILLIAMS

"Whistling Dick," Vicksburg, MS, circa 1862.

☛ TRIBUTE TO GEN. WILLIAM BARKSDALE AT GETTYSBURG
Emerging from the peach orchard into the open plateau beyond, [I, Major John J. Hood] . . . discovered that the brigades to Barksdale's right had been held in check by the enemy. Off to the right some three hundred yards another battery was thrown into position to enfilade his column. In a flash "Right wheel, charge!" rang above the roar of battle, and with the rattle of muskets, the clang of bayonets, and the shouts of victory [George B.] Winslow's Massachusetts [New York?] Battery fell a prize to the sons of Mississippi. Still the battle raged. The Federal general, [Charles Kinnaird] Graham, retreated across Plum Run, and rallied his line behind a battery one thousand feet away beyond the ravine. If that battery can be silenced and Graham routed again, the enemy's line will be completely severed. If severed, victory is ours. . . . in this charge hangs the history of the Confederacy. What a moment! The command is given and the regiment moves forward to the ravine, and under its shelter

William Barksdale, C.S.A.

reforms in line of battle. Up the other side, and out upon the plateau at the base of the ridge, they advance for the last and most desperate charge. [Union General Daniel Edgar] Sickles rode to the front to encourage his men. Up the slope the Mississippians advanced, undaunted by bursting shells or screaming Minies. Thinned by the storm which swept down with such terrific fury from the ridge, the advance line staggered and began to waver. The awful crisis of that awful day had come. As on a thread hung the hopes of a struggling nation. Amid the shifting scenes of this doubtful battle the very course of history swung to and fro in the trembling balance. With its ebb and flow rushed the tide of our country's hopes.

Suddenly, far to the left, a wild shout of victory rings above the din of battle. Looking back toward the turnpike, the majestic form of the heroic Barksdale, like the fabled god of battle, towering in the front of the advancing column, was seen leading the charge on the last line of the enemy at the ravine. The inspiration spread like contagion through the regiment, and with a yell that sounded to the very dome of heaven they rushed upon the enemy's line. As the autumn leaves are scattered by the blasts of winter, so was the Federal line swept away by the charge of that hurricane. On, right on, until the fiery breath of the cannon was hot in their faces they pressed. The brave gunners who manned that battery never deserted their posts, and died with their guns beside them. Sickles fell desperately wounded, but escaped into his line. Graham, who had stood by his men till the last had fallen, fell into the hands of the Mississippians, a prisoner of war. The last line was carried, the last battery was captured, the enemy's line was cut in twain.

Thus it was that the Twenty-First Mississippi Regiment bore the stars and bars to the very farthest point reached in the enemy's line on the bloody field of Gettysburg. [Confederate Colonel William Dunbar] Holder and [Confederate Colonel Thomas M.] Griffin had swept across the turnpike in the pursuit of the Red Zouaves, and were now making the last desperate assault upon the enemy's line. Barksdale stood on the turnpike watching the movements of his heroes as they drove the enemy before them. His bright eyes flashed as though lit by a spark from the fires eternal. His face beamed with the glow of glorious victory. His thin lip curled with that haughty smile which meant defiance. He stood the perfect picture of a true hero. Far to the right he had watched the gallant dash of the Twenty-First Regiment, and saw the enemy's line broken and scattered. He saw its lines re-forming in his front across the ravine, and, drawing his sword, he sprang to the front, the flush of victory on his face, shouting: "They are whipped. We will drive them beyond the Susquehanna." Then it was the cheer went up which had lent the inspiration to [Colonel Benjamin Grubb] Humphreys's wavering column. They charged the ravine as Mississippians were wont to charge; but the

Children of the Confederacy, 1901.

Federal lines, reenforced, had rallied beneath its shelter, and poured volley after volley into his lines. His column, halting beneath the deadly fire, reeled to and fro like a forest beneath a tempest. The gallant Holder fell desperately wounded. Griffin fell. [Colonel John C.] Fizer fell. Once more they dashed against the enemy. Then, waving his sword in the very thickest of the fray, in the last charge upon the enemy's last line . . . this soldier, patriot, hero fell. Amid the wild roar of the cannon, the fierce scream of the shrapnel, and clang and glitter of sabers; midst all the pomp and glorious circumstances of war—the great soul, the unconquered spirit of the immortal Barksdale winged its flight. *No shaft marks the spot where he fell. The Federal authorities refused to allow the point they reached to be designated by appropriate stones, but that gallant charge is written upon the hearts of his countrymen, and will be told in song and story as long as gallant deeds and heroism are virtues.*[321] — MAJ. GEN. JOHN J. HOOD

☛ SKETCH OF GEN. JAMES ALEXANDER WALKER

Gen. James A. Walker died at his home in Wytheville, Va., October 20, 1901. His illness lasted a month, before which time he was in good health and a splendid specimen of physical manhood.

Gen. Walker was born in Augusta County, Va., in September, 1833. He graduated at the Virginia Military Institute, and afterwards studied law at the University of Virginia. He married Miss Sarah A. Poage, of Augusta County, and in 1854 he removed to Newbern, Pulaski County. A

James A. Walker, C.S.A.

notable incident of his early life was that while a cadet at the Virginia Military Institute he challenged Maj. Thomas J. ("Stonewall") Jackson, a professor, to fight a duel.

At the beginning of the great war he was captain of a fine volunteer company, the Pulaski Guards (afterwards Company C, Fourth Virginia Infantry), and was successively promoted until he reached the rank of brigadier general, and was assigned to the command of the "Stonewall" Brigade.

At the "Bloody Angle," in May, 1864, Gen. Walker was severely wounded. In July following, his arm yet in a sling, he was put in command of the reserve troops guarding the line of the Richmond and Southside railroads, feeders of Gen. Lee's army. In January, 1865, he was assigned to the command of [Jubal A.] Early's Division, which he surrendered at Appomattox.

Gen. Walker was with Gen. Jackson in the famous Valley campaign, and participated in all the battles of the army of Northern Virginia. At the close of the war he returned to Pulaski and resumed the practice of the law. He was elected to the Virginia House of Delegates from Pulaski County, serving two terms in that body. In 1877 he was elected Lieutenant Governor, with the late Fred W. M. Holliday as Governor. He afterwards served in Congress.

Gen. Walker was the father of six children. Three of them, Messrs. James A., Frank and Allen P., are dead; and three are living, Mrs. M. M. Caldwell and Mrs. James R. Jordan, of Wytheville, and Mr. A. E. Walker, of Florence, Ala. In 1890 Gen. Walker removed to Wytheville, where he resided thereafter.[322] — SUMNER A. CUNNINGHAM

☛ A UNION TRIBUTE TO GEN. FORREST

Forrest out front.

Col. S. W. Fordyce who "was in the Federal army during the great war, and in the Confederate since," learned through Col. Josiah Patterson, of Memphis, of the Forrest Monument movement, and wrote him:

"Dear Sir: In this please find inclosed my check on the Bank of Commerce, this city, for $250, in aid of the Forrest Monumental Association. I thank you very much for giving me an opportunity to join my old ex-Confederate friends in aid of a monument commemorative of one of the greatest soldiers of ancient or modern times. . . . *You and I and all ex-soldiers of both armies living to-day know well the truth of every word spoken of him by . . . [objective historians]. Much more could be said in praise of this wonderful soldier.* In war as terrible and masterful as a lion; in peace gentle, mindful, and considerate of the feelings and prerogatives of others. It was my good fortune and pleasure to have known him well from 1865 to the  time of his death, October, 1877. *I esteemed him as much for his worth as a citizen in peace as I feared him as a soldier in war.*

As the passions and prejudices growing out of the war subside, the more will this man's military career be appreciated by his countrymen, North as well as South. Never did a general recognize the inevitable and lay down his sword with a sadder heart; and never did a fallen hero rise to the sublimity of a loyal and patriotic citizen more earnestly and honestly.

Had he been living at the outbreak of the Spanish war, he would have been among the first to have offered his services, and if need be die on the altar of his country, in defense of its institutions and its flag. When living *he talked frequently with me of his desire to live long enough to see his country reunited in bonds of brotherly and soldierly love, to the end that each by the other would be forgiven (but not forgotten) for all that happened in that terrible conflict. The present historian has recorded and the future will record the fact that Gen. Forrest accomplished more with less resources at his command than any other soldier or officer on either side in our civil war.*

I have long since been on record as favoring the erection of monuments all over the South in memory of her dead heroes, and I want to say of him, as I said of them, that while the monument itself can but feebly emphasize the veneration felt by the living for the dead, yet the memory of his brave deeds and wonderful achievements will be cherished in the hearts of his countrymen, and will live in other lands and speak in other tongues and to other times than ours.[323] — UNION COL. S. W. FORDYCE (Col. Fordyce was in that department of service which enabled him to know of Forrest's ability and heroism, and they were intimate friends afterwards)

☛ JOHN G. BALLENTINE'S PARTISAN RANGERS

. . . My youngest child, aged fifteen, is ten pounds heavier than I was when I entered the army. Six men in blue had surrounded my aged mother, and with the muzzle of their cocked guns pressing her body, forced her to give them my father's money. This so aroused my Scotch and Irish blood that, young as I was, I felt it to be my duty to take up arms for my home and people. About the time I reached the army, between Jackson and Edwards, Miss., in the summer of 1863, the Federals advanced on the Confederates; and I, with others—McDowell's Company, which I had gone to join—was rushed to the front. I had neither been "mustered in" nor given rations or gun. However, in the hurry and bustle to get ready, one man in the company was found to be violently sick, who tendered me his gun, which I took and used to the best of my ability.

Vendor's sign, Memphis UCV Reunion, 1901.

After returning from the battlefield, Orderly W. H. McKinney said to me: "Mack, I will go with you to the ordnance department, and draw you a gun." On going there we found plenty of "Mississippi rifles," the kind that Company E was armed with; though I selected a "Belgium rifle," because it shot four balls in each charge, which I thought made it a more destructive weapon. Although it was much the heavier and I was the lightest (weight one hundred and five pounds) kid in the company, I kept it until I wore it out, and I left it in a hickory log in Georgia. My

White and black Confederate soldiers with Confederate General William Nelson Pendleton during the War.

name was put on the roll, and I drew rations as the other soldiers who had been "sworn in," when there was any to issue. At the reorganization of the army Capt. [W. W.] McDowell and all the other Tennessee members, except W. H. Lewis, who remained with it, were transferred to Tennessee commands. This left First Lieut. Jeff J. Davis in command. Lieut. [Andrew B.] Knox was absent—sick or wounded. The writer, on the reorganization, was made first orderly sergeant, and in the absence of Lieut. Knox was second in command. . . . I was captured at Selma, Ala., April 12, 1865, by the Fourth Michigan Cavalry, who treated me with kindness.

Many other boys were prompted to go to the front and stay because of the [terrible] treatment their families received by the Federals. Of this class were the McKinney boys of our company, whose father was *insulted, robbed of everything, imprisoned, waylaid, and shot by [Union officer Fielding] Hurst's band of Tories,*[324] *from which wounds he died in the summer of 1867. Mr. McKinney was sent to the "Irwin Block" prison in Memphis, Tenn., because he did not see proper to swear falsely in taking the oath of allegiance [to the U.S.].* However, the officers of the prison released him for $500 in cash sent by Dr. Stovall, of Camden, Tenn.

Doubtless all of the surviving members of Company especially McDowell's messmates, will be pleased to know that Anderson McAllister, my [black] war servant, is still living. He is getting on quite well; has a comfortable home, and plenty around him, and is respected by all the good people who know him.[325] — A. H. MCALISTER

☛ JEFFERSON DAVIS ON THE CONFEDERATE SOLDIER

. . . They who now sleep in the grave cannot be benefitted, it is true, by anything we do; their cause has gone before a higher tribunal than any earthly judgment seat, but their children and their children's children are to be benefitted by preserving the record of what they did, and, more than all, the morale with which they did it. As for me—I speak only for myself—*our cause was so just, so sacred, that, had I known all that has come to pass, had I known what was to be inflicted upon me, all that my country was to suffer, all that our posterity was to endure, I would do it all over again.*

Jefferson Davis and his wife Varina.

It is to me most desirable that *the conduct of our men in defense of that cause should be so presented to the world as to leave no stain upon it.* They went through trials which might have corrupted weaker men, and yet throughout the war I never went into an army without finding their camp engaged in prayer. After the war was over, see how many of these men who bore muskets in the ranks became ministers of the gospel. It is your good fortune to have one presiding over your diocese now, and who is the successor of one who drew his last breath on the field of battle, the glorious, holy Bishop Polk!

It is not necessary that we should have recorded what is conceded by all the world, that our men were brave, that they had a power of endurance and self-denial which was remarkable, but *if you would have your children rise to the high plane you desire them to occupy, you must add the evidence of their father's chivalry and forbearance* from that staining crime of the soldier, plunder, under all the circumstances of the war. . . .[326] — JEFFERSON DAVIS (from a speech to the Southern Historical Society, New Orleans, Louisiana)

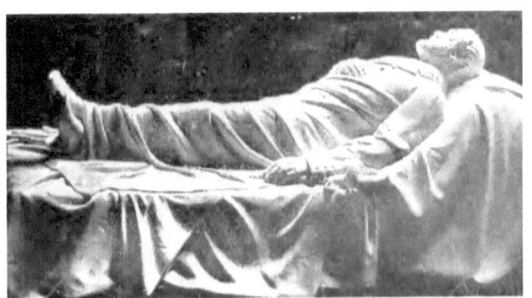

Recumbent statue of Robert E. Lee, Lexington, VA.

APPENDIX A

LIST OF CONFEDERATE DEAD IN THE ARLINGTON NATIONAL CEMETERY IN 1900

J. A. Bennett, Sergeant Seventh Georgia; Unknown Captain, Unknown; Thomas McMeekin; James W. Purse; John Anderson, Sergeant Forty-fourth Georgia; E. F. Howell, Thirty-first Georgia; H. W. Crone, Page's Battery; Harve Barnett (or Bartnett), Nineteenth Mississippi; Michael Quinn, Thirteenth Mississippi; Unknown, Unknown; James Lynn, Twelfth Mississippi; J. C. Cannon, Sixty-first Alabama; P. (or William) Crawford, Forty-fourth Georgia; W. N. Jenkins, Nineteenth Mississippi; George J. Holmes, Twenty-sixth Georgia; James McCord, Sergeant Thirteenth Georgia; J. F. Lloyd, Forty-fifth Georgia; T. H. Hudson, Page's Battery; Willis Kenneman, Twelfth Alabama; Jerry Cronan, Tenth Louisiana; Henry Lahone, Page's Battery; Jesse M. Perry, Twelfth Georgia; Miller C. Pool, Thirteenth Georgia; Thomas King, Sergeant Ninth Louisiana; James Cunningham, Thirteenth Georgia; William C. Cheseltine (Cavalry), First Maryland; Aaron Morris, Third Georgia; Andrew Waldrip, Fourteenth Georgia; William S. Renfral, Lieutenant Company H, Twelfth Alabama; Henry Shann, Company C, Eleventh Florida; Francis M. Thielkeld (or Thialheld), Company F, Twenty-seventh Georgia; Nathaniel S. Bates, Nineteenth Georgia; Patrick Boyle, Company B, Nineteenth Georgia; Fritz Kimple, Company A, Twelfth Mississippi; Elias McElveen, Company E, Twentieth Georgia; B. F. Parsons, Lieutenant Company G, Fourth Georgia; Unknown, Unknown; E. (P.) Stanley, Sergeant Company D, Fourth Georgia; Unknown, Unknown; J. A. Jackson, Company B, Twelfth Georgia; W. L. Brown, Company I, Twenty-first Georgia; William R. Deering, Company A, Nineteenth Mississippi; W. J. Perkins, Seventh Cavalry; James Russell, Forty-third Georgia; Unknown, Unknown; T. W. Farell (or Farrell), Captain Company K. Twelfth Mississippi; Winston Meredith, Corporal Company ?, Jones Battery, Virginia Horse Artillery; W. L. Nicks, Company B, Sixty-first Alabama; Francis M. Autay, Company D, Twelfth Georgia; Reuben Harris, Company B, Sixth Alabama; W. P. Bernhard, Company A, Forty-fourth Georgia; Hannan (or Harman) Howard, Company A, Sixty-first Alabama; William A.

Phillip, Company B, Fourth Georgia; Flemming Jordan, Company G, Fourth Georgia; Thomas A. (or H.) Hickman, Company B, Twelfth Georgia; John A. Curry, Company E, Twelfth Georgia; Leonidas Brewer, Company I, Sixty-first Alabama; John M. Page, Company B, Thirty-seventh Georgia; J. Y. Bendingfield (or Bedingfield), Company G, Sixtieth Georgia; Unknown, Unknown; James Foreman, Company E, Fifty-ninth Alabama; John Abney (or Abbey), Company D, Forty-fifth Georgia; James McClendon, Company G, Sixty-fourth Georgia; John J. Ashley, citizen; Marida Brown, Phillips' Legion (Georgia); James L. Epps, A. Cobb's Legion; A. J. Bayless, Sergeant Sixty-third Tennessee; J. A. Smith, Company H, Sixteenth Georgia; Thomas C. Truner, Corporal Company C, Twelfth Georgia; W. Reynolds, Company F, First Louisiana; Allen H. Early, Company I, Fourth Georgia; Timothy F. Morgan, Company F, Fifty-ninth Alabama; S. Jessup, Company C, Fourth Georgia; William Herod, Company B, Sixth Alabama; James F. Hardy, Sergeant Company B, Sixtieth Georgia; John Roberts, Company D, Fifteenth Alabama; Elijah N. Field, Company N, Twenty-fourth Georgia; George W. Rayner, Company G. Twelfth Alabama; Isaac Neill, Company D, Sixteenth Mississippi; J. F. Graves, Forty-fifth Georgia; Wilson Taylor, Company C, Sixty-first Alabama; John W. Barkley, Captain Company C, Fifty-ninth Alabama; David L. Taylor, Company G, Twelfth Georgia; Theldred S. Lay, Thirty-fifth Georgia; William Worley, Danville Battery; F. G. Pagans (or Hagans), Company H, Forty-fourth Georgia; Unknown, Unknown; William C. West, Fourth Alabama; James Scales, Company I, Seventeenth Alabama; Jesse S. Russell, Company I, Sixty-first Alabama; Thomas Rogers, Company J, Twenty-first Georgia; John H. Rogers, Company B, Cutt's (or Curtis') Battery, Georgia; Thomas McGee, refugee, First Alabama; William Inkfield, prisoner; William Lovelace, prisoner; W. D. Amos, Company D, Fifth Georgia; J. D. Ballowe;

Sons of Confederate veterans, Richmond, VA, 1896.

Robert Beachman, citizen prisoner; Warren H. Brand, Thirty-fifth Georgia; Homer Broxton, Third Georgia; B. B. Burdock, Company D, Twelfth Georgia; John F. Butler, Company B, Eighteenth Georgia; Calvin M. Cannyn, Ninth Georgia; E. R. Coleman, Company A, Seventeenth Mississippi; George Daymend (or Daymud), citizen prisoner; James Emory, citizen prisoner; Joseph Genrard, Eighteenth Georgia; J. C. Green, Company B, Fourth Georgia; W. J. Gray, prisoner of war; Lewis Glease, citizen prisoner; W. A. Heavener, citizen prisoner; G. W. Hall, Company E, Sixtieth Georgia; Samuel Hughes, Company F, Twenty-sixth Georgia; William B. Jones, Company B, Ninth Georgia; Joseph Kirkland, Forty-eighth Georgia; John Leacock, citizen State prisoner; J. McDonald, Company I, Third Alabama; J. R. Mullen, Forty-second Mississippi; U. P. Nichols, First Tennessee; Joseph L. Riley, Company I, Twenty-first Mississippi; W. H. Roberts, Company H, Thirty-seventh Mississippi; C. B. Royston, Company D, Fourteenth Alabama; James Sandlin, Company I, Ninth Alabama; Henry M. Shaw, Company N, Forty-first Alabama; George H. Smith, Fourteenth Alabama; William Snyder, Company D, Sixty-second Georgia; T. B. Thompson, Fifth Alabama; William C. Tipp, Company B, Forty-fourth Tennessee; J. H. Wallace, Company P, Twenty-first Georgia; George Whaley, citizen; James West, prisoner; William Wilkison (or Winkeson), Company F, Forty-third Alabama; J. W. Norwood, Company I, Third Alabama.[327]

Jefferson Davis, the most important American Conservative of the 19th Century.

Confederate reunion, 1895.

NOTES

1. J. Phin Wilson, Confederate Veteran, June 1894, Vol. 2, No. 6, p. 168.
2. Woods, p. 47.
3. On Lincoln's socialistic, Marxist, and communist thoughts, ideas, and tendencies, see e.g., McCarty, passim; Browder, passim; Benson and Kennedy, passim.
4. See J. W. Jones, TDMV, pp. 144, 200-201, 273.
5. See Seabrook, TAHSR, passim. See also, Pollard, LC, p. 178; J. H. Franklin, pp. 101, 111, 130, 149; Nicolay and Hay, ALCW, Vol. 1, p. 627.
6. See e.g., Seabrook, TQJD, pp. 30, 38, 76.
7. See e.g., J. Davis, RFCG, Vol. 1, pp. 55, 422; Vol. 2, pp. 4, 161, 454, 610. Besides using the term "Civil War" himself, President Davis cites numerous other individuals who use it as well.
8. See e.g., Confederate Veteran, March 1912, Vol. 20, No. 3, p. 122.
9. Minutes of the Eighth Annual Meeting, July 1898, p. 87.
10. See e.g., Seabrook, AWAITBLA, pp. 58-59.
11. Seabrook, AWAITBLA, pp. 35, 61.
12. Seabrook, AWAITBLA, p. 329.
13. Seabrook, AWAITBLA, p. 23.
14. Seabrook, AWAITBLA, p. 24.
15. Seabrook, ALWALJDWAC, p. 32.
16. In other words, in 1860 the Republicans were Liberals and the Democrats were Conservatives. For a full discussion of this topic, see Seabrook, ALWALJDWAC, passim.
17. See Seabrook, LW, passim.
18. The previous Conservative president was James Buchanan (also a Democrat), who occupied the White House from 1858 to 1861. Liberal Lincoln (elected November 1860) took office in March 1861.
19. See Seabrook, AWAITBLA, passim.
20. Confederate Veteran, December 1896, Vol. 4, No. 12, p. 422.
21. See Seabrook, C101, passim.
22. Seabrook, AWAITBLA, p. 256.
23. See Seabrook, LW, passim; Seabrook, EYWTATCWIW, passim; Seabrook, AL, passim; Seabrook, C101, passim; Seabrook, ALWALJDWAC, passim.
24. F. Moore, TRR, Vol. 1, pp. 166-167, 174-175. My emphasis.
25. ORA, Ser. 1, Vol. 1, p. 28.
26. ORA, Ser. 1, Vol. 1, pp. 634-635.
27. Confederate Veteran, February 1893, Vol. 1, No. 2, p. 50.
28. Seabrook, ARB, p. 280; ORA, Ser. 1, Vol. 7, p. 64.
29. ORA, Ser. 1, Vol. 14, pp. 100-101.
30. ORA, Ser. 1, Vol. 29, Pt. 1, pp. 58-59.
31. ORA, Ser. 1, Vol. 29, Pt. 1, p. 439. My emphasis.
32. Confederate Veteran, February 1893, Vol. 1, No. 2, p. 62.
33. Confederate Veteran, April 1893, Vol. 1, No. 4, p. 117.
34. F. Moore, APAIOTW, pp. 14-15.
35. Confederate Veteran, May 1897, Vol. 5, No. 5, p. 200.
36. Confederate Veteran, May 1900, Vol. 8, No. 5, p. 204.
37. Confederate Veteran, January 1896, Vol. 4, No. 1, p. 41.
38. Roosevelt, pp. 33-34. My emphasis.
39. Confederate Veteran, October 1897, Vol. 5, No. 10, p. 527. My emphasis.
40. Though his full name was Arnold Elzey Jones, he went by "Arnold Elzey."
41. Confederate Veteran, January 1893, Vol. 1, No. 1, pp. 18-20.
42. Confederate Veteran, August 1893, Vol. 1, No. 8, pp. 233, 234, 236.
43. Confederate Veteran, February 1893, Vol. 1, No. 2, p. 34.

44. Confederate Veteran, February 1893, Vol. 1, No. 2, p. 40.
45. Confederate Veteran, February 1893, Vol. 1, No. 2, pp. 52-53.
46. I Corinthians 13:13 (KJV).
47. Confederate Veteran, April 1893, Vol. 1, No. 4, p. 100. This last scripture is from 1 Corinthians 13:8 (KJV).
48. Confederate Veteran, April 1893, Vol. 1, No. 4, p. 114.
49. Confederate Veteran, April 1893, Vol. 1, No. 4, p. 118.
50. Confederate Veteran, April 1893, Vol. 1, No. 4, p. 118.
51. Confederate Veteran, April 1893, Vol. 1, No. 4, p. 118.
52. Confederate Veteran, April 1893, Vol. 1, No. 4, p. 119.
53. Confederate Veteran, April 1893, Vol. 1, No. 4, p. 120.
54. Confederate Veteran, May 1893, Vol. 1, No. 5, p. 149.
55. Confederate Veteran, May 1893, Vol. 1, No. 5, p. 152.
56. Confederate Veteran, May 1893, Vol. 1, No. 5, p. 154.
57. Confederate Veteran, June 1893, Vol. 1, No. 6, p. 174.
58. Confederate Veteran, June 1893, Vol. 1, No. 6, p. 181.
59. Confederate Veteran, July 1893, Vol. 1, No. 7, p. 195. My emphasis.
60. Confederate Veteran, July 1893, Vol. 1, No. 7, p. 196. My emphasis.
61. Confederate Veteran, July 1893, Vol. 1, No. 7, p. 200.
62. For more on these topics, see Seabrook, EYWTAASIW, passim.
63. See Seabrook, C101, passim.
64. Philippians 4:8 (KJV).
65. This statement is wholly erroneous. For more on the topic of abolition, see Seabrook, EYWTAASIW, passim.
66. For more on this topic, see Seabrook, AL, passim.
67. Confederate Veteran, July 1893, Vol. 1, No. 7, pp. 200-205. My emphasis.
68. Confederate Veteran, July 1893, Vol. 1, No. 7, pp. 206-207.
69. Confederate Veteran, July 1893, Vol. 1, No. 7, p. 207. My emphasis.
70. Confederate Veteran, July 1893, Vol. 1, No. 7, p. 209.
71. Confederate Veteran, July 1893, Vol. 1, No. 7, pp. 210-211.
72. Confederate Veteran, July 1893, Vol. 1, No. 7, p. 214. My emphasis.
73. Confederate Veteran, August 1893, Vol. 1, No. 8, p. 230.
74. Confederate Veteran, August 1893, Vol. 1, No. 8, p. 231.
75. Confederate Veteran, August 1893, Vol. 1, No. 8, p. 236.
76. Confederate Veteran, August 1893, Vol. 1, No. 8, p. 238. My emphasis.
77. Confederate Veteran, August 1893, Vol. 1, No. 8, p. 239.
78. Confederate Veteran, August 1893, Vol. 1, No. 8, p. 246.
79. Confederate Veteran, September 1893, Vol. 1, No. 9, p. 265. My emphasis.
80. Confederate Veteran, September 1893, Vol. 1, No. 9, pp. 265-266.
81. Confederate Veteran, September 1893, Vol. 1, No. 9, p. 266.
82. Confederate Veteran, September 1893, Vol. 1, No. 9, p. 267.
83. Confederate Veteran, September 1893, Vol. 1, No. 9, pp. 268-269.
84. Confederate Veteran, September 1893, Vol. 1, No. 9, p. 269.
85. Confederate Veteran, September 1893, Vol. 1, No. 9, p. 269.
86. Confederate Veteran, September 1893, Vol. 1, No. 9, p. 273.
87. Confederate Veteran, September 1893, Vol. 1, No. 9, p. 274.
88. Confederate Veteran, September 1893, Vol. 1, No. 9, p. 274.
89. Confederate Veteran, September 1893, Vol. 1, No. 9, pp. 274-275.
90. Confederate Veteran, September 1893, Vol. 1, No. 9, p. 276.
91. Confederate Veteran, October 1893, Vol. 1, No. 10, p. 295.
92. See Seabrook, LW, passim.
93. Confederate Veteran, October 1893, Vol. 1, No. 10, pp. 297-298.
94. Confederate Veteran, October 1893, Vol. 1, No. 10, p. 300.
95. Confederate Veteran, October 1893, Vol. 1, No. 10, p. 300.

96. Confederate Veteran, October 1893, Vol. 1, No. 10, p. 306.
97. Confederate Veteran, November 1893, Vol. 1, No. 11, p. 323. My emphasis.
98. Confederate Veteran, November 1893, Vol. 1, No. 11, p. 326. My emphasis.
99. Confederate Veteran, November 1893, Vol. 1, No. 11, pp. 334-335.
100. Confederate Veteran, November 1893, Vol. 1, No. 11, p. 338.
101. Confederate Veteran, November 1893, Vol. 1, No. 11, p. 339.
102. Confederate Veteran, November 1893, Vol. 1, No. 11, p. 340.
103. Confederate Veteran, November 1893, Vol. 1, No. 11, p. 344.
104. Confederate Veteran, December 1893, Vol. 1, No. 12, pp. 356-357. My emphasis.
105. Confederate Veteran, December 1893, Vol. 1, No. 12, p. 357.
106. Confederate Veteran, December 1893, Vol. 1, No. 12, p. 361.
107. Confederate Veteran, December 1893, Vol. 1, No. 12, p. 367. My emphasis.
108. Confederate Veteran, December 1893, Vol. 1, No. 12, p. 371.
109. Confederate Veteran, December 1893, Vol. 1, No. 12, p. 371. My emphasis.
110. Confederate Veteran, December 1893, Vol. 1, No. 12, p. 374.
111. Confederate Veteran, December 1893, Vol. 1, No. 12, p. 371.
112. Confederate Veteran, December 1893, Vol. 1, No. 12, p. 375.
113. Confederate Veteran, December 1893, Vol. 1, No. 12, p. 376.
114. Thomas "Blind Tom" Wiggins was an African-American virtuoso pianist from Georgia who performed for audiences across America during the Victorian Era.
115. Confederate Veteran, January 1894, Vol. 2, No. 1, p. 5.
116. Confederate Veteran, January 1894, Vol. 2, No. 1, p. 5.
117. Confederate Veteran, January 1894, Vol. 2, No. 1, pp. 12-13.
118. Confederate Veteran, January 1894, Vol. 2, No. 1, p. 13.
119. Confederate Veteran, January 1894, Vol. 2, No. 1, p. 14.
120. For more on this topic, see Seabrook, EYWTATCWIW, pp. 188-190.
121. Confederate Veteran, January 1894, Vol. 2, No. 1, pp. 16-17.
122. Confederate Veteran, January 1894, Vol. 2, No. 1, p. 19.
123. Confederate Veteran, January 1894, Vol. 2, No. 1, p. 20.
124. Confederate Veteran, February 1894, Vol. 2, No. 2, p. 33.
125. M. A. Jackson, pp. 534-535.
126. Confederate Veteran, February 1894, Vol. 2, No. 2, p. 33.
127. Confederate Veteran, February 1894, Vol. 2, No. 2, p. 48.
128. Confederate Veteran, February 1894, Vol. 2, No. 2, pp. 48-49.
129. Confederate Veteran, February 1894, Vol. 2, No. 2, p. 33. My emphasis.
130. Confederate Veteran, February 1894, Vol. 2, No. 2, p. 52.
131. Confederate Veteran, March 1894, Vol. 2, No. 3, pp. 67-68.
132. Confederate Veteran, March 1894, Vol. 2, No. 3, p. 70.
133. Confederate Veteran, March 1894, Vol. 2, No. 3, p. 74.
134. Confederate Veteran, March 1894, Vol. 2, No. 3, p. 80.
135. Confederate Veteran, March 1894, Vol. 2, No. 3, p. 86.
136. Confederate Veteran, April 1894, Vol. 2, No. 4, pp. 98-99.
137. Seabrook, WIG, pp. 219-225.
138. Confederate Veteran, April 1894, Vol. 2, No. 4, p. 113.
139. Confederate Veteran, April 1894, Vol. 2, No. 4, p. 115.
140. Confederate Veteran, April 1894, Vol. 2, No. 4, p. 117.
141. The full title of Wilson's unhistorical, anti-South book is *History of the Rise and Fall of the Slave Power in America*. It was published in Boston, Massachusetts, in 1874.
142. Confederate Veteran, April 1894, Vol. 2, No. 4, pp. 126-127. My emphasis.
143. Confederate Veteran, May 1894, Vol. 2, No. 5, p. 143.
144. For more on the topic of Yankee slavery and so-called "Northern abolition," see Seabrook, EYWTAASIW, passim.
145. For a complete discussion of this important moment in America's political history, see Seabrook, ALWAL, passim.

146. The Democratic Party, then Conservative, would not become the Liberal party (as it remains to this day) until the election of 1896. That same year the Republican Party, which since 1854 had been the Liberal party, switched to a Conservative platform (as it remains to this day). Seabrook, ALWAL, passim.
147. Confederate Veteran, March 1896, Vol. 4, No. 3, pp. 75-79. My emphasis. Note: This address was originally given in 1894. This is an 1896 reprint.
148. Confederate Veteran, May 1894, Vol. 2, No. 5, p. 152.
149. Confederate Veteran, June 1894, Vol. 2, No. 6, pp. 162-164.
150. Confederate Veteran, June 1894, Vol. 2, No. 6, pp. 176-177. My emphasis.
151. Confederate Veteran, June 1894, Vol. 2, No. 6, p. 179.
152. Confederate Veteran, June 1894, Vol. 2, No. 6, p. 180.
153. Confederate Veteran, June 1894, Vol. 2, No. 6, p. 182.
154. Confederate Veteran, June 1894, Vol. 2, No. 6, p. 185.
155. Confederate Veteran, July 1894, Vol. 2, No. 7, pp. 194-195. My emphasis.
156. Confederate Veteran, July 1894, Vol. 2, No. 7, pp. 194-195. My emphasis.
157. Confederate Veteran, July 1894, Vol. 2, No. 7, p. 201.
158. Confederate Veteran, July 1894, Vol. 2, No. 7, pp. 204-205.
159. Confederate Veteran, July 1894, Vol. 2, No. 7, p. 206. My emphasis.
160. See Seabrook, EYWTAAAATCWIW, passim.
161. Confederate Veteran, July 1894, Vol. 2, No. 7, pp. 210-211. My emphasis.
162. Confederate Veteran, August 1894, Vol. 2, No. 8, p. 231.
163. Confederate Veteran, August 1894, Vol. 2, No. 8, p. 233. My emphasis.
164. Confederate Veteran, August 1894, Vol. 2, No. 8, pp. 234-235.
165. Confederate Veteran, August 1894, Vol. 2, No. 8, p. 236.
166. Confederate Veteran, August 1894, Vol. 2, No. 8, p. 245.
167. Confederate Veteran, August 1894, Vol. 2, No. 8, p. 247.
168. Confederate Veteran, August 1894, Vol. 2, No. 8, p. 249. My emphasis.
169. For more on this topic, see Seabrook, EYWTAASIW, passim.
170. Confederate Veteran, September 1894, Vol. 2, No. 9, pp. 260-261. My emphasis.
171. Though Rev. McNeilly does not seem to have been aware of it in 1894, secession sentiment has never entirely disappeared in the U.S. If anything it has grown stronger since Lincoln's War. Indeed, there are currently secession movements in nearly half the states, one of the better known being California. According to the White House, this trend was especially evident in 2012 after the reelection of anti-American Liberal Barack Obama, at which time 23 states submitted petitions seeking secession from the Union.
172. Confederate Veteran, September 1894, Vol. 2, No. 9, pp. 265-266.
173. Confederate Veteran, September 1894, Vol. 2, No. 9, p. 270.
174. Confederate Veteran, September 1894, Vol. 2, No. 9, p. 280.
175. Confederate Veteran, October 1894, Vol. 2, No. 10, p. 308.
176. Confederate Veteran, October 1894, Vol. 2, No. 10, p. 311.
177. Confederate Veteran, November 1894, Vol. 2, No. 11, p. 326.
178. Confederate Veteran, November 1894, Vol. 2, No. 11, p. 328. My emphasis.
179. Confederate Veteran, November 1894, Vol. 2, No. 11, p. 330. My emphasis.
180. Confederate Veteran, November 1894, Vol. 2, No. 11, p. 339. My emphasis.
181. Confederate Veteran, November 1894, Vol. 2, No. 11, p. 343.
182. Confederate Veteran, December 1894, Vol. 2, No. 12, p. 354. My emphasis.
183. Confederate Veteran, December 1894, Vol. 2, No. 12, p. 356.
184. Confederate Veteran, December 1894, Vol. 2, No. 12, p. 357.
185. Confederate Veteran, December 1894, Vol. 2, No. 12, p. 373.
186. Confederate Veteran, January 1895, Vol. 3, No. 1, pp. 2-3.
187. Confederate Veteran, January 1895, Vol. 3, No. 1, p. 16. My emphasis.
188. Confederate Veteran, March 1895, Vol. 3, No. 3, pp. 72-73.
189. Confederate Veteran, March 1895, Vol. 3, No. 3, p. 78.
190. Confederate Veteran, March 1895, Vol. 3, No. 3, p. 79. My emphasis.
191. Confederate Veteran, March 1895, Vol. 3, No. 3, pp. 89-90.
192. Confederate Veteran, April 1895, Vol. 3, No. 4, p. 98.

193. Confederate Veteran, April 1895, Vol. 3, No. 4, p. 102.
194. Confederate Veteran, April 1895, Vol. 3, No. 4, pp. 106-107. Note: Anderson did not use the full names of Hurst and Smith in his original article; only their initials. I have added their full names for the convenience of the modern reader.
195. Confederate Veteran, May 1895, Vol. 3, No. 5, p. 132. My emphasis.
196. Confederate Veteran, May 1895, Vol. 3, No. 5, p. 133.
197. Confederate Veteran, May 1895, Vol. 3, No. 5, p. 142.
198. Confederate Veteran, May 1895, Vol. 3, No. 5, p. 132. My emphasis.
199. Confederate Veteran, June 1895, Vol. 3, No. 6, p. 189.
200. Confederate Veteran, July 1895, Vol. 3, No. 7, p. 212.
201. Confederate Veteran, August 1895, Vol. 3, No. 8, p. 226.
202. Confederate Veteran, August 1895, Vol. 3, No. 8, p. 242. My emphasis.
203. Confederate Veteran, September 1895, Vol. 3, No. 9, p. 259. My emphasis.
204. Confederate Veteran, September 1895, Vol. 3, No. 9, p. 261. My emphasis.
205. Confederate Veteran, September 1895, Vol. 3, No. 9, p. 271.
206. Confederate Veteran, October 1895, Vol. 3, No. 10, p. 309. My emphasis.
207. For more on this topic, see Seabrook, C101, passim.
208. Confederate Veteran, November 1895, Vol. 3, No. 11, pp. 343-344. My emphasis.
209. Confederate Veteran, November 1895, Vol. 3, No. 11, pp. 351-352.
210. Confederate Veteran, December 1895, Vol. 3, No. 12, pp. 353-354.
211. Confederate Veteran, December 1895, Vol. 3, No. 12, p. 380.
212. Confederate Veteran, December 1895, Vol. 3, No. 12, p. 385.
213. For more on the topic of the cause of the War, see Seabrook, LW, passim.
214. Confederate Veteran, December 1895, Vol. 3, No. 12, p. 387. My emphasis.
215. Confederate Veteran, January 1896, Vol. 4, No. 1, p. 23.
216. Confederate Veteran, February 1896, Vol. 4, No. 2, pp. 41-43.
217. This was not true of *all* Southerners, but rather only a certain percentage.
218. Again, this is incorrect. South-hating in the North has existed since nearly the beginning of European settlements in North America, but was particularly evident later, during the formation of the U.S.A. and the presidency of George Washington. It was at this time that Liberal Northerners and Conservative Southerners, out of mutual hatred, officially split apart, forming two opposition parties. It was this same friction that caused the South to secede in 1860, culminating in Lincoln's War. In my opinion, as well as that of many others, the differences between North and South have formed a natural division at the Mason-Dixon Line; a deep sociopolitical chasm that is metaphorically light years across; one that cannot and will not ever be bridged. For more on this topic, see Seabrook, AWAITBLA, passim.
219. Confederate Veteran, February 1896, Vol. 4, No. 2, pp. 52, 54. My emphasis.
220. Confederate Veteran, March 1896, Vol. 4, No. 3, pp. 85-87.
221. Confederate Veteran, May 1896, Vol. 4, No. 5, p. 161.
222. Confederate Veteran, June 1896, Vol. 4, No. 6, p. 182.
223. Confederate Veteran, July 1896, Vol. 4, No. 7, pp. 216-217. My emphasis.
224. Confederate Veteran, August 1896, Vol. 4, No. 8, p. 257.
225. Confederate Veteran, August 1896, Vol. 4, No. 8, p. 280.
226. Confederate Veteran, September 1896, Vol. 4, No. 9, p. 288.
227. Confederate Veteran, September 1896, Vol. 4, No. 9, pp. 299-300.
228. Confederate Veteran, October 1896, Vol. 4, No. 10, p. 330.
229. Confederate Veteran, October 1896, Vol. 4, No. 10, p. 354.
230. Confederate Veteran, October 1896, Vol. 4, No. 10, p. 330.
231. Confederate Veteran, November 1896, Vol. 4, No. 11, pp. 361-362.
232. Confederate Veteran, November 1896, Vol. 4, No. 11, p. 388.
233. Confederate Veteran, December 1896, Vol. 4, No. 12, p. 429.
234. Confederate Veteran, December 1896, Vol. 4, No. 12, p. 431. My emphasis.
235. Confederate Veteran, December 1896, Vol. 4, No. 12, p. 440. My emphasis.
236. Confederate Veteran, February 1897, Vol. 5, No. 2, p. 73.
237. Confederate Veteran, February 1897, Vol. 5, No. 2, p. 83.

238. Confederate Veteran, March 1897, Vol. 5, No. 3, p. 113. My emphasis.
239. Confederate Veteran, April 1897, Vol. 5, No. 4, p. 175.
240. Confederate Veteran, May 1897, Vol. 5, No. 5, pp. 201-202.
241. Confederate Veteran, May 1897, Vol. 5, No. 5, pp. 212-213.
242. Confederate Veteran, June 1897, Vol. 5, No. 6, pp. 268-269.
243. Confederate Veteran, June 1897, Vol. 5, No. 6, pp. 277-281. My emphasis.
244. Confederate Veteran, July 1897, Vol. 5, No. 7, pp. 411-412. My emphasis.
245. Confederate Veteran, July 1897, Vol. 5, No. 7, p. 423.
246. Confederate Veteran, September 1897, Vol. 5, No. 9, pp. 475-476.
247. Confederate Veteran, September 1897, Vol. 5, No. 9, pp. 478-480.
248. Confederate Veteran, October 1897, Vol. 5, No. 10, p. 521.
249. Confederate Veteran, October 1897, Vol. 5, No. 10, p. 521.
250. Confederate Veteran, October 1897, Vol. 5, No. 10, p. 528.
251. Confederate Veteran, December 1897, Vol. 5, No. 12, p. 600.
252. Confederate Veteran, December 1897, Vol. 5, No. 12, pp. 627-628.
253. Confederate Veteran, January 1898, Vol. 6, No. 1, pp. 24-25. My emphasis.
254. Confederate Veteran, January 1898, Vol. 6, No. 1, p. 29. My emphasis.
255. Confederate Veteran, January 1898, Vol. 6, No. 1, p. 29. My emphasis.
256. For more on Jackson's "negro church," which he founded with his own money, see Seabrook, TQSJ, passim.
257. Confederate Veteran, February 1898, Vol. 6, No. 2, pp. 53-55.
258. Confederate Veteran, February 1898, Vol. 6, No. 2, p. 55.
259. Confederate Veteran, March 1898, Vol. 6, No. 3, p. 135.
260. Confederate Veteran, April 1898, Vol. 6, No. 4, p. 154.
261. Confederate Veteran, May 1898, Vol. 6, No. 5, p. 216.
262. For more on this topic, see Seabrook, NBFATKKK, passim.
263. Confederate Veteran, November 1898, Vol. 6, No. 11, p. 520.
264. Confederate Veteran, November 1898, Vol. 6, No. 11, p. 529.
265. For more on this topic, see Seabrook, ALWALJDWAC, passim.
266. Confederate Veteran, September 1900, Vol. 8, No. 9, pp. 395-396. My emphasis.
267. Confederate Veteran, January 1899, Vol. 7, No. 1, pp. 26-27.
268. Confederate Veteran, February 1899, Vol. 7, No. 2, p. 59.
269. Confederate Veteran, February 1899, Vol. 7, No. 2, p. 70. My emphasis.
270. Confederate Veteran, February 1899, Vol. 7, No. 2, p. 72.
271. Confederate Veteran, March 1899, Vol. 7, No. 3, p. 119.
272. For more on this topic, see Seabrook, LW, passim.
273. Confederate Veteran, March 1899, Vol. 7, No. 3, pp. 121-125. My emphasis.
274. Confederate Veteran, June 1899, Vol. 7, No. 6, p. 266.
275. Confederate Veteran, July 1899, Vol. 7, No. 7, p. 324. My emphasis.
276. Confederate Veteran, August 1899, Vol. 7, No. 8, pp. 358-359.
277. Confederate Veteran, August 1899, Vol. 7, No. 8, pp. 364-365. My emphasis.
278. Confederate Veteran, September 1899, Vol. 7, No. 9, p. 408. My emphasis.
279. Confederate Veteran, October 1899, Vol. 7, No. 10, p. 446.
280. Confederate Veteran, October 1899, Vol. 7, No. 10, p. 460.
281. Confederate Veteran, November 1899, Vol. 7, No. 11, pp. 492-493.
282. For more on the topic of American slavery, see Seabrook, EYWTAASIW, passim.
283. For more on this topic, see Seabrook, ALWALJDWAC, passim.
284. Confederate Veteran, November 1899, Vol. 7, No. 11, pp. 500-502. My emphasis.
285. Confederate Veteran, December 1899, Vol. 7, No. 12, pp. 536-537.
286. Confederate Veteran, December 1899, Vol. 7, No. 12, p. 557.
287. Confederate Veteran, January 1900, Vol. 8, No. 1, p. 26.
288. Confederate Veteran, February 1900, Vol. 8, No. 2, p. 75.
289. Confederate Veteran, April 1900, Vol. 8, No. 4, p. 171.
290. Confederate Veteran, April 1900, Vol. 8, No. 4, pp. 172-173. My emphasis.

291. Confederate Veteran, May 1900, Vol. 8, No. 5, p. 233.
292. Confederate Veteran, May 1900, Vol. 8, No. 5, p. 237.
293. Confederate Veteran, June 1900, Vol. 8, No. 6, p. 249. My emphasis.
294. Confederate Veteran, July 1900, Vol. 8, No. 7, p. 297. My emphasis.
295. Confederate Veteran, July 1900, Vol. 8, No. 7, p. 302.
296. For more on this topic, see Seabrook, EYWTAASIW, passim.
297. For more on this topic, see Seabrook, ALWALJDWAC, passim.
298. For more on this topic, see Seabrook, AWAITBLA, passim.
299. For more on this topic, see Seabrook, AWAITBLA, passim.
300. A majority of Southerners today would disagree with this statement.
301. Confederate Veteran, July 1900, Vol. 8, No. 7, pp. 313-319. My emphasis.
302. Confederate Veteran, September 1900, Vol. 8, No. 9, p. 392. My emphasis.
303. For more on this topic, see Seabrook, EYWTAAAATCWIW, passim.
304. Confederate Veteran, September 1900, Vol. 8, No. 9, pp. 399-400. My emphasis.
305. For more on the topic of Fort Pillow, see Seabrook, NBFATBOFP, passim.
306. Confederate Veteran, September 1900, Vol. 8, No. 9, pp. 401-403.
307. Confederate Veteran, October 1900, Vol. 8, No. 10, pp. 428-429.
308. Confederate Veteran, December 1900, Vol. 8, No. 12, p. 538. My emphasis.
309. Confederate Veteran, January 1901, Vol. 9, No. 1, p. 36. My emphasis.
310. Confederate Veteran, March 1901, Vol. 9, No. 3, p. 112. My emphasis. President McKinley's exact words were: "I feel that the time has come when we [Northerners] should share with you in caring for the graves of the Confederate dead." Confederate Veteran, September 1901, Vol. 9, No. 9, p. 395.
311. Confederate Veteran, March 1901, Vol. 9, No. 3, pp. 114-115.
312. Confederate Veteran, March 1901, Vol. 9, No. 3, p. 125.
313. Confederate Veteran, April 1901, Vol. 9, No. 4, p. 155. My emphasis.
314. Confederate Veteran, June 1901, Vol. 9, No. 6, p. 259. My emphasis.
315. Confederate Veteran, July 1901, Vol. 9, No. 7, p. 331. My emphasis.
316. Confederate Veteran, August 1901, Vol. 9, No. 8, p. 370.
317. Confederate Veteran, August 1901, Vol. 9, No. 8, p. 370.
318. Confederate Veteran, September 1901, Vol. 9, No. 9, p. 398.
319. Confederate Veteran, September 1901, Vol. 9, No. 9, p. 453.
320. Confederate Veteran, November 1901, Vol. 9, No. 11, p. 498.
321. Confederate Veteran, November 1901, Vol. 9, No. 11, p. 503. My emphasis.
322. Confederate Veteran, November 1901, Vol. 9, No. 11, p. 510.
323. Confederate Veteran, November 1901, Vol. 9, No. 11, p. 514.
324. During the War Union Colonel Fielding Hurst was considered a war criminal of the worst kind by the Confederacy. He was known for, among other things, torturing, murdering, and mutilating Rebel soldiers and even Southern civilians and their children. Forrest swore that if he ever came across Hurst, he would kill him on sight as a "common criminal." Seabrook, ARB, pp. 360-364.
325. Confederate Veteran, December 1901, Vol. 9, No. 12, p. 553. My emphasis.
326. Confederate Veteran, March 1901, Vol. 9, No. 3, p. 119. My emphasis.
327. Confederate Veteran, August 1900, Vol. 8, No. 8, p. 372.

BIBLIOGRAPHY

Note: My pro-South readers are to be advised that many of the books listed here are anti-South in nature (some extremely so), and were written primarily by liberal elitist, socialist, communist, and Marxist authors who loathe the South, and typically the United States and the U.S. Constitution as well. Despite this, as a scholar I find these titles indispensable, for *an honest evaluation of Lincoln's War is not possible without studying both the Southern and the Northern versions*—an attitude, unfortunately, completely lacking among pro-North historians (who read and study only their own ahistorical version). Still, it must be said that the material contained in these often mean-spirited works is largely the result of a century and a half of Yankee myth, falsehoods, cherry-picking, slander, sophistry, editorializing, anti-South propaganda, outright lies, and junk research, as modern pro-North writers merely copy one another's errors without ever looking at the original 19th-Century sources. This type of literature, filled as it is with both misinformation and disinformation, is called "scholarly" and "objective" by pro-North advocates. In the process, the mistakes and lies in these fact-free, fault-ridden, South-shaming, historically inaccurate works have been magnified over the years, and the North's version of the "Civil War" has come to be accepted as the only legitimate one. Indeed, it is now the only one known by most people. That over 95 percent of the titles in my bibliography fall into the anti-South category is simply a reflection of the enormous power and influence that the pro-North movement—our nation's cultural ruling class—has long held over America's education system, libraries, publishing houses, and media (paper and electronic). My books serve as a small rampart against the overwhelming tide of anti-South Fascists, Liberals, cultural Marxists, and political elites, all who are working hard to obliterate Southern culture and guarantee that you will never learn the Truth about Lincoln and his War on the Constitution and the American people.

Abel, Annie Heloise. *The Slaveholding Indians.* 3 vols. Arthur H. Clark, Co., 1919.

Bell, John T. *Civil War Stories: Compiled From Official Records—Union and Confederate.* San Francisco, CA: Whitaker and Ray Co., 1903.

Benson, Al, Jr., and Walter Donald Kennedy. *Lincoln's Marxists.* Gretna, LA: Pelican, 2011.

Boyd, James P. *Parties, Problems, and Leaders of 1896: An Impartial Presentation of Living National Questions.* Chicago, IL: Publishers' Union, 1896.

Brock, Robert Alonzo (ed.). *Southern Historical Society Papers.* 52 vols. Richmond, VA: Southern Historical Society, 1876-1943.

Browder, Earl. *Lincoln and the Communists.* New York, NY: Workers Library Publishers, Inc., 1936.

Bryan, William Jennings. *The First Battle: A Story of the Campaign of 1896.* Chicago, IL: W. B. Conkey Co., 1896.

Burns, James MacGregor. *The Vineyard of Liberty.* New York, NY: Alfred A. Knopf, 1982.

Christian, George Llewellyn. *Abraham Lincoln: An Address Delivered Before R. E. Lee Camp, No. 1 Confederate Veterans at Richmond, VA, October 29, 1909.* Richmond, VA: L. H. Jenkins, 1909.

——. *A Capitol Disaster: A Chapter of Reconstruction in Virginia.* Richmond, VA: self-published, 1915.

——. *Confederate Memories and Experiences.* Richmond, VA: self-published, 1915.

Confederate Veteran (Sumner A. Cunningham, ed.). 40 vols. Nashville, TN: Confederate

Veteran, 1893-1932.
Cruikshank, George M. *A History of Birmingham and its Environs.* 2 vols. Chicago, IL: Lewis Publishing Co., 1920.
Davis, Jefferson. *The Rise and Fall of the Confederate Government.* 2 vols. New York, NY: D. Appleton and Co., 1881.
——. *Andersonville and Other War-Prisons.* New York, NY: Belford Co., 1890.
DeWitt, David Miller. *The Judicial Murder of Mary E. Surratt.* Baltimore, MD: John Murphy and Co., 1895.
Duke, Basil Wilson. *History of Morgan's Cavalry.* Cincinnati, OH: Miami Printing and Publishing, 1867.
Evans, Clement Anselm (ed.). *Confederate Military History.* 12 vols. Atlanta, GA: Confederate Publishing Co., 1899.
Franklin, John Hope. *Reconstruction After the Civil War.* Chicago, IL: University of Chicago Press, 1961.
Fremantle, Thomas Francis. *The Book of the Rifle.* London, UK: Longmans, Green, and Co., 1901.
French, Samuel Gibbs. *Two Wars: An Autobiography of Gen. Samuel G. French.* Nashville, TN: Confederate Veteran, 1901.
Goodloe, Albert Theodore. *Some Relics From the Seat of War.* Nashville, TN: Publishing House of the Methodist Episcopal Church, South, 1893.
Index to the Miscellaneous Documents of the House of Representatives for the First Session of the Forty-ninth Congress, 1885-1886. Washington, D.C.: Government Printing Office, 1886.
Jackson, Mary Anna. *Memoirs of Stonewall Jackson.* Louisville, KY: The Prentice Press, 1895.
Johnson, Charles Beneulyn. *Muskets and Medicine or Army Life in the Sixties.* Philadelphia, PA: F. A. Davis, 1917.
Johnson, Robert Underwood, and Clarence Clough Buel (eds.). *Battles and Leaders of the Civil War.* 4 vols. New York, NY: The Century Co., 1884-1888.
Johnstone, Huger William. *Truth of War Conspiracy, 1861.* Idylwild, GA: H. W. Johnstone, 1921.
Jones, John William. *The Davis Memorial Volume; Or Our Dead President, Jefferson Davis and the World's Tribute to His Memory.* Richmond, VA: B. F. Johnson, 1889.
La Bree, Ben (ed.). *The Confederate Soldier in the Civil War, 1861-1865.* Louisville, KY: The Prentice Press, 1897.
Lee, Susan Pendleton, and Louise Manly. *A School History of the United States.* Richmond, VA: B. F. Johnson Publishing Co., 1895.
Livermore, Thomas L. *Numbers and Losses in the Civil War in America, 1861-65.* 1900. Carlisle, PA: John Kallmann, 1996 ed.
Magliocca, Gerard N. *The Tragedy of William Jennings Bryan: Constitutional Law and the Politics of Backlash.* New Haven, CT: Yale University Press, 2011.
Manly, Louise. *Southern Literature, From 1579-1895: A Comprehensive Review, With Copious Extracts and Criticisms.* Richmond, VA: B. F. Johnson Publishing Co., 1895.
McCarty, Burke (ed.). *Little Sermons in Socialism by Abraham Lincoln.* Chicago, IL: The Chicago Daily Socialist, 1910.

McPherson, James M. *Abraham Lincoln and the Second American Revolution.* New York, NY: Oxford University Press, 1991.

Meriwether, Elizabeth Avery (pseudonym, "George Edmonds"). *Facts and Falsehoods Concerning the War on the South, 1861-1865.* Memphis, TN: A. R. Taylor and Co., 1904.

Miller, Francis Trevelyan, and Robert S. Lanier (eds.). *The Photographic History of the Civil War.* 10 vols. New York, NY: The Review of Reviews Co., 1911.

Minutes of the Eighth Annual Meeting and Reunion of the United Confederate Veterans, Atlanta, GA, July 20-23, 1898. New Orleans, LA: United Confederate Veterans, 1907.

Minutes of the Ninth Annual Meeting and Reunion of the United Confederate Veterans, Charleston, SC, May 10-13, 1899. New Orleans, LA: United Confederate Veterans, 1907.

Minutes of the Twelfth Annual Meeting and Reunion of the United Confederate Veterans, Dallas, TX, April 22-25, 1902. New Orleans, LA: United Confederate Veterans, 1907.

Moore, Frank (ed.). *The Rebellion Record: A Diary of American Events.* 12 vols. New York, NY: G. P. Putnam, 1861.

——. *Anecdotes, Poetry and Incidents of the War: North and South, 1860-1865.* New York, NY: self-published, 1866.

Murlin, E. L. *The United States Red Book: Containing the Portraits and Biographies of the President and His Cabinet, Senators and Members of the House of Representatives.* Albany, NY: James B. Lyon, 1896.

Muzzey, David Saville. *The United States of America: Vol. 1, To the Civil War.* Boston, MA: Ginn and Co., 1922.

——. *The American Adventure: Vol. 2, From the Civil War.* 1924. New York, NY: Harper and Brothers, 1927 ed.

Nicolay, John G., and John Hay (eds.). *Abraham Lincoln: A History.* 10 vols. New York, NY: The Century Co., 1890.

——. *Complete Works of Abraham Lincoln.* 12 vols. 1894. New York, NY: Francis D. Tandy Co., 1905 ed.

——. *Abraham Lincoln: Complete Works.* 12 vols. 1894. New York, NY: The Century Co., 1907 ed.

ORA (full title: *The War of the Rebellion: A Compilation of the Official Records of the Union and Confederate Armies*). 70 vols. Washington, DC: Government Printing Office, 1880.

ORN (full title: *Official Records of the Union and Confederate Navies in the War of the Rebellion*). 30 vols. Washington, DC: Government Printing Office, 1894.

Page, James Madison, and Michael Joachim Haley. *The True Story of Andersonville Prison: A Defense of Major Henry Wirz.* New York, NY: Neal Publishing Co., 1908.

Pollard, Edward Alfred. *The Lost Cause.* New York, NY: E. B. Treat and Co., 1867.

Richardson, John Anderson. *Richardson's Defense of the South.* Atlanta, GA: A. B. Caldwell, 1914.

Rogers, William P. *The Three Secession Movements in the United States: Samuel J. Tilden, the Democratic Candidate for Presidency; the Advisor, Aider and Abettor of the Great Secession Movement of 1860; and One of the Authors of the Infamous Resolution of 1864; His Claims as a Statesman and Reformer Considered.* Boston, MA: John Wilson and Son, 1876.

Roosevelt, Theodore. *Thomas H. Benton.* 1886. Boston, MA: Houghton, Mifflin and Co., 1899 ed.

Rove, Karl. *The Triumph of William McKinley: Why the Election of 1896 Still Matters.* New York, NY: Simon and Schuster, 2015.

Rowland, Dunbar. *The Official and Statistical Register of the State of Mississippi, 1908.* Nashville, TN: Press of the Brandon Printing Co., 1908.

Rutherford, Mildred Lewis. *Truths of History: A Fair, Unbiased, Impartial, Unprejudiced and Conscientious Study of History.* Athens, GA: n.p., 1920.

Seabrook, Lochlainn. *Carnton Plantation Ghost Stories: True Tales of the Unexplained from Tennessee's Most Haunted Civil War House!* 2005. Franklin, TN, 2016 ed.

——. *Nathan Bedford Forrest: Southern Hero, American Patriot.* 2007. Franklin, TN, 2010 ed.

——. *Abraham Lincoln: The Southern View.* 2007. Franklin, TN: Sea Raven Press, 2013 ed.

——. *The McGavocks of Carnton Plantation: A Southern History - Celebrating One of Dixie's Most Noble Confederate Families and Their Tennessee Home.* 2008. Franklin, TN, 2011ed.

——. *A Rebel Born: A Defense of Nathan Bedford Forrest.* 2010. Franklin, TN: Sea Raven Press, 2011 ed.

——. *A Rebel Born: The Screenplay* (for the film). 2011. Franklin, TN: Sea Raven Press.

——. *Everything You Were Taught About the Civil War is Wrong, Ask a Southerner!* 2010. Franklin, TN: Sea Raven Press, revised 2014 ed.

——. *The Quotable Jefferson Davis: Selections From the Writings and Speeches of the Confederacy's First President.* Franklin, TN: Sea Raven Press, 2011.

——. *The Quotable Robert E. Lee: Selections From the Writings and Speeches of the South's Most Beloved Civil War General.* Franklin, TN: Sea Raven Press, 2011 Sesquicentennial Civil War Edition.

——. *Lincolnology: The Real Abraham Lincoln Revealed In His Own Words.* Franklin, TN: Sea Raven Press, 2011.

——. *The Unquotable Abraham Lincoln: The President's Quotes They Don't Want You To Know!* Franklin, TN: Sea Raven Press, 2011.

——. *Honest Jeff and Dishonest Abe: A Southern Children's Guide to the Civil War.* Franklin, TN: Sea Raven Press, 2012.

——. *Encyclopedia of the Battle of Franklin - A Comprehensive Guide to the Conflict that Changed the Civil War.* Franklin, TN: Sea Raven Press, 2012.

——. *The Quotable Nathan Bedford Forrest: Selections From the Writings and Speeches of the Confederacy's Most Brilliant Cavalryman.* Spring Hill, TN: Sea Raven Press, 2012.

——. *Forrest! 99 Reasons to Love Nathan Bedford Forrest.* Spring Hill, TN: Sea Raven Press, 2012.

——. *Give 'Em Hell Boys! The Complete Military Correspondence of Nathan Bedford Forrest.* Spring Hill, TN: Sea Raven Press, 2012.

——. *The Constitution of the Confederate States of America Explained: A Clause-by-Clause Study of the South's Magna Carta.* Spring Hill, TN: Sea Raven Press, 2012 Sesquicentennial Civil War Edition.

——. *The Great Impersonator: 99 Reasons to Dislike Abraham Lincoln.* Spring Hill, TN: Sea

Raven Press, 2012.

———. *The Old Rebel: Robert E. Lee As He Was Seen By His Contemporaries.* Spring Hill, TN: Sea Raven Press, 2012 Sesquicentennial Civil War Edition.

———. *The Quotable Stonewall Jackson: Selections From the Writings and Speeches of the South's Most Famous General.* Spring Hill, TN: Sea Raven Press, 2012 Sesquicentennial Civil War Edition.

———. *Saddle, Sword, and Gun: A Biography of Nathan Bedford Forrest for Teens.* Spring Hill, TN: Sea Raven Press, 2013.

———. *The Alexander H. Stephens Reader: Excerpts From the Works of a Confederate Founding Father.* Spring Hill, TN: Sea Raven Press, 2013.

———. *The Quotable Alexander H. Stephens: Selections From the Writings and Speeches of the Confederacy's First Vice President.* Spring Hill, TN: Sea Raven Press, 2013 Sesquicentennial Civil War Edition.

———. *Give This Book to a Yankee! A Southern Guide to the Civil War for Northerners.* Spring Hill, TN: Sea Raven Press, 2014.

———. *The Articles of Confederation Explained: A Clause-by-Clause Study of America's First Constitution.* Spring Hill, TN: Sea Raven Press, 2014.

———. *Confederate Blood and Treasure: An Interview With Lochlainn Seabrook.* Spring Hill, TN: Sea Raven Press, 2015.

———. *Nathan Bedford Forrest and the Battle of Fort Pillow: Yankee Myth, Confederate Fact.* Spring Hill, TN: Sea Raven Press, 2015.

———. *Everything You Were Taught About American Slavery War is Wrong, Ask a Southerner!* Spring Hill, TN: Sea Raven Press, 2015.

———. *Confederacy 101: Amazing Facts You Never Knew About America's Oldest Political Tradition.* Spring Hill, TN: Sea Raven Press, 2015.

———. *The Great Yankee Coverup: What the North Doesn't Want You to Know About Lincoln's War!* Spring Hill, TN: Sea Raven Press, 2015.

———. *Slavery 101: Amazing Facts You Never Knew About America's "Peculiar Institution."* Spring Hill, TN: Sea Raven Press, 2015.

———. *Confederate Flag Facts: What Every American Should Know About Dixie's Southern Cross.* Spring Hill, TN: Sea Raven Press, 2016.

———. *Nathan Bedford Forrest and the Ku Klux Klan: Yankee Myth, Confederate Fact.* Spring Hill, TN: Sea Raven Press, 2016.

———. *Seabrook's Bible Dictionary of Traditional and Mystical Christian Doctrines.* Spring Hill, TN: Sea Raven Press, 2016.

———. *Everything You Were Taught About African-Americans and the Civil War is Wrong, Ask a Southerner!* Spring Hill, TN: Sea Raven Press, 2016.

———. *Nathan Bedford Forrest and African-Americans: Yankee Myth, Confederate Fact.* Spring Hill, TN: Sea Raven Press, 2016.

———. *Women in Gray: A Tribute to the Ladies Who Supported the Southern Confederacy.* Spring Hill, TN: Sea Raven Press, 2016.

———. *Lincoln's War: The Real Cause, the Real Winner, the Real Loser.* Spring Hill, TN: Sea Raven Press, 2016.

———. *The Unholy Crusade: Lincoln's Legacy of Destruction in the American South.* Spring Hill, TN: Sea Raven Press, 2017.

———. *Abraham Lincoln Was a Liberal, Jefferson Davis Was a Conservative: The Missing Key to Understanding the American Civil War.* Spring Hill, TN: Sea Raven Press, 2017.

———. *All We Ask is to be Let Alone: The Southern Secession Fact Book.* Spring Hill, TN: Sea Raven Press, 2017.

———. *The Ultimate Civil War Quiz Book: How Much Do You Really Know About America's Most Misunderstood Conflict?* Spring Hill, TN: Sea Raven Press, 2017.

———. *Victorian Confederate Poetry: The Southern Cause in Verse, 1861-1901.* Spring Hill, TN: Sea Raven Press, 2018.

Steel, Samuel Augustus. *The South Was Right.* Columbia, SC: R. L. Bryan Co., 1914.

Stephens, Alexander Hamilton. *Speech of Mr. Stephens, of Georgia, on the War and Taxation.* Washington, D.C.: J & G. Gideon, 1848.

———. *A Constitutional View of the Late War Between the States; Its Causes, Character, Conduct and Results.* 2 vols. Philadelphia, PA: National Publishing, Co., 1870.

———. *Recollections of Alexander H. Stephens: His Diary Kept When a Prisoner at Fort Warren, Boston Harbour, 1865.* New York, NY: Doubleday, Page, and Co., 1910.

Thompson, Holland. *The New South: A Chronicle of Social and Industrial Evolution.* New Haven, CT: Yale University Press, 1920.

United Confederate Veterans of Arkansas. *Confederate Women of Arkansas in the Civil War, 1861-'65: Memorial Reminiscences.* Little Rock, AR: United Confederate Veterans of Arkansas, 1907.

Warner, Ezra J. *Generals in Gray: Lives of the Confederate Commanders.* 1959. Baton Rouge, LA: Louisiana State University Press, 1989 ed.

———. *Generals in Blue: Lives of the Union Commanders.* 1964. Baton Rouge, LA: Louisiana State University Press, 2006 ed.

Watkins, Sam Rush. *"Co. Aytch," Maury Grays, First Tennessee Regiment; or A Side of the Big Show.* 1882. Chattanooga, TN: Times Printing Co., 1900 ed.

White, Henry, Alexander. *The Making of South Carolina.* New York, NY: Silver, Burdett and Co., 1906.

Woods, Thomas E., Jr. *The Politically Incorrect Guide to American History.* Washington, D.C.: Regnery, 2004.

INDEX

Abney, John, 558
Abraham (Bible), 339
Adair, W. P., 356
Adam (Bible), 97
Adams, John, 157, 223, 299, 497
Adams, Shelby L., 592
Agnew, E., 525
Agnew, Joseph, 528
Agnew, Samuel A., 531
Akin, A. N., 497
Alexander, Delia, 536
Alexander, Hannibal, 536
Alexander, Parker, 536
Alexander, Sidney, 536
Alfred, King, 90
Allen, J. W., 440
Amos, W. D., 558
Anderson, Charles W., 311, 374-376, 498
Anderson, George T., 539
Anderson, James P., 394
Anderson, John, 557
Anderson, Loni, 592
Anderson, Paul, 485
Anderson, Robert, 29, 455, 461, 464, 544
Anderson, Thomas F., 359
Andrews, Richard S., 51
Appleton, John W. M., 546, 547
Archer, James J., 294, 305, 327
Archilles, 165
Ardis, Fed, 535, 536
Ardis, Isaac, 535, 536
Armstrong, James, 75
Arthur, King, 591
Ashby, Turner, 95, 100, 276
Ashley, John L., 558
Ashley-Cooper, Anthony, 369
Ashton, Clara, 250
Ashton, Willie, 250
Atkins, Chet, 592
Augustus, Caesar, 164

Aurelius, Marcus, 307
Autay, Francis M., 557
Avent, W. B., 313
Bacon, Captain, 418
Bailey, R. Augustus, 35, 37
Baird, Absalom, 141, 143
Baker, Laurence S., 440
Baldwin, John B., 93, 482
Ballentine, John G., 554
Ballowe, J. D., 558
Banks, Nathaniel P., 334, 357
Barbee, A. R., 35
Barkley, John W., 558
Barksdale, William, 96, 100, 102, 103, 549-551
Barlow, Carrie, 250
Barnett, Harve, 557
Barnum, Z. F., 545
Barteau, C. R., 527, 528
Barth, W. G., 38
Bartow, Francis S., 538
Baskette, G. H., 171
Bassett, Dr., 183
Bate, William B., 142, 143, 297, 334, 373, 374, 419
Bates, Edward, 459
Bates, Nathaniel S., 557
Battle, Frank, 452
Baxter, Elisha, 147
Bayless, A. J., 558
Beachman, Robert, 559
Bearden, W. S., 191
Beatan, Etta, 250
Beauregard, Pierre G. T., 10, 28, 29, 44, 48, 61, 62, 71, 72, 154, 194, 196, 219, 225, 345, 379, 394, 461, 463, 544, 591
Bedell, C. A., 203
Bee, Barnard E., 49, 433
Beecher, Henry W., 351
Bell, Dr., 206
Bell, John, 324

Bell, T. M., 356
Bell, Tyree H., 374, 388, 442, 443, 527, 530
Bendingfield, J. Y., 558
Bennett, J. A., 557
Benning, Henry L., 539
Bernhard, W. P., 557
Bernstein, Leonard, 592
Berry, Dr., 489
Berry, William, 477
Bethel, Col., 207
Biscoe, Cameron N., 219
Blaine, James G., 271
Blair, Francis P., 161
Blair, Montgomery, 459, 462
Blakeslee, G. H., 413
Blanton, J. C., 299
Blount, General, 357
Blunt, James G., 71
Boies, Henry M., 24
Bolling, Edith, 592
Bond, Daniel, 353
Boon, Reuben, 292
Boone, Colonel, 279
Boone, Daniel, 591
Boone, Pat, 592
Bowen, John S., 134
Boyd, J. N., 521
Boyle, Patrick, 557
Bradshaw, Captain, 426
Brady, A. J., 145
Bragg, Braxton, 44, 63, 98, 136, 137, 140, 149, 195, 219, 225, 230, 311-313, 315, 324, 345, 349, 374-376, 393, 394, 408, 427, 428, 452, 453, 497
Bragg, Braxton (servant), 497
Braidy, Dr., 429
Bramlett, Peter, 287
Brand, Warren H., 399, 559
Brannan, John M., 140, 142, 143
Breckenridge, William C., 98
Breckinridge, John C., 96, 122, 123, 143, 219, 225, 408, 425, 591
Brewer, Leonidas, 558

Brewer, Mrs. Sarah E., 81, 82
Brice, Mrs. William, 530
Brice, William, 525, 527, 530
Britt, Mrs. Mary N., 448
Broke Arm, Major, 357
Brooke, Edward W., 592
Brooks, Preston S., 592
Brown, A. G., 101
Brown, Aaron V., 323
Brown, H. A., 497
Brown, John, 161, 221, 351, 393, 433, 511
Brown, John C., 142, 143, 155, 156, 195, 211, 323-325, 373, 374, 425
Brown, Marida, 558
Brown, Neill S., 323
Brown, Tom, 370
Brown, Trim, 451
Brown, W. L., 557
Brownlow, William G., 147, 152
Broxton, Homer, 559
Bruton, Lieutenant, 39
Bryant, Jerry, 289
Bryson, Samuel C., 360
Buchanan, Franklin, 10
Buchanan, James, 455, 459, 513
Buchanan, Patrick J., 592
Buck, Adjutant General, 174
Buckner, Simon B., 63, 129, 374
Buell, Don C., 295, 389, 450
Buford, Abraham, 278, 279, 374, 388, 527, 530, 591
Burdock, B. B., 559
Burleson, A. J., 336
Burney, A. M., 268
Burns, Pat, 151
Burnside, Ambrose E., 109, 146, 149, 162
Burt, Erasmus, 100
Butler, Andrew P., 592
Butler, Benjamin F., 471
Butler, Capt., 205
Butler, Colonel, 259
Butler, Dick, 138

Butler, John F., 559
Butler, Thomas, 522
Button, Charles W., 419
Cabell, Benjamin W. S., 193
Cabell, Henry K., 196
Cabell, Powhattan, 193
Cabell, Sarah E., 193
Cabell, Shingo, 196
Cabell, William L., 72, 193-196, 219
Cabot, George, 505
Cahal, Terry, 374
Caldwell, Mrs. M. M., 552
Calhoun, John C., 221, 509, 510
Cameron, Simon, 458
Campbell, John A., 460-462
Campbell, Joseph, 590
Campbell, W. A., 69, 536
Campbell, William, 544
Campeador, Cid, 166
Cannon, J. C., 557
Cannon, Mrs. Newton, 448
Cannyn, Calvin M., 559
Capers, Ellison, 204, 446, 448
Carson, Andrew C., 290
Carson, Martha, 592
Carter, Colonel, 296, 298
Carter, Fountain B., 111
Carter, John C., 497
Carter, Mrs. Robert, 209
Carter, Theodrick, 298, 591
Cartright, Miss, 286
Cash, Johnny, 592
Catchings, Thomas C., 503, 520
Caudill, Benjamin E., 590
Cave, R. C., 239
Cayce, Newnan, 526
Chalmers, James R., 46, 323, 344, 404, 526, 527, 531
Chambliss, N. R., 316
Chandler, Mr., 386
Chandler, Zachariah, 458
Chase, Salmon P., 248, 458
Cheairs, Nathaniel F., 592
Cheatham, Anna B., 180
Cheatham, Benjamin F., 60, 141, 155, 180, 206, 209, 376, 430
Checoti, Sam, 356
Cheseltine, William C., 557
Chesnut, Mary, 592
Chew, Robert S., 463
Clark, Charles, 33
Clark, W. C., 286
Clark, William, 591
Clay, James B., 124
Claybrooke, Miss Annie, 448
Clayton, Henry D., 142, 143, 373, 374
Cleburne, Patrick R., 70, 136, 138, 155, 156, 174, 182, 183, 209, 210, 219, 251, 497
Cleveland, Grover, 21, 196, 204, 253, 260, 337
Cobb, Howell, 102
Cobbs, Norvell, 303
Coleman, E. R., 559
Coleman, Guedron, 218
Coleman, Lewis M., 408
Colley, Thomas W., 74
Colquitt, Alfred H., 143
Colyar, John B., 121
Combs, Bertram T., 592
Conrad, Joseph, 448
Cooper, D. N., 355, 356
Cooper, Douglas H., 358
Cooper, Samuel, 161
Corday, Charlotte, 79
Cowan, George L., 446
Cowan, John B., 346
Cowan, Mrs. George L., 448
Craige, Kerr, 441
Crawford, Cindy, 592
Crawford, Martin J., 459
Crawford, William, 557
Crier, Hardy, 423
Crittenden, John, 203
Crittenden, Nathaniel, 203
Crittenden, Stanley S., 203, 204, 239
Crockett, Davy, 591
Cromwell, Oliver, 187, 430
Cronan, Jerry, 557

Crone, H. W., 557
Crook, George R., 546
Crossland, Ed, 390
Crow, Major, 69
Crow, Robert, 390
Cruise, Tom, 592
Cumming, Alfred, 210
Cumming, Joseph B., 326
Cunningham, James, 557
Cunningham, Miss Birnie, 386
Cunningham, Sid, 411
Cunningham, Sumner A., 15, 83, 108, 113, 117, 132, 146, 186, 189-191, 193, 196, 198, 201, 204, 213, 241, 244, 250, 268, 276, 279, 295, 307, 313, 314, 319, 337, 339, 363, 364, 368, 370, 376, 411, 443, 448, 473, 476, 487, 492, 502, 503, 524, 547, 552
Curran, John E., 275
Currie, Mrs. J. R., 196
Curry, Jabez L. M., 482, 483
Curry, John A., 558
Curtis, Colonel, 284
Curtis, J. S., 544
Curtis, William E., 470
Custer, George A., 63, 105, 121
Cuthbert, George, 29
Cyrus, Billy R., 592
Cyrus, Miley, 592
Daley, E. R., 450
Dalton, R. H., 80
Dangerfield, F. A., 339
Daniel, John W., 131, 179, 302
Daniel, T. M., 266
Darling, Flora A., 114
Davis, Bill, 370
Davis, Dr., 279
Davis, Jeff J., 555
Davis, Jefferson, 9, 13, 15, 21, 24, 25, 27, 28, 30, 80, 81, 103-105, 116, 146, 160, 167, 194, 213, 225, 228, 233, 246, 248, 255, 256, 273, 285, 311, 312, 315, 321, 340, 349, 351, 352, 380, 382, 388, 459, 461, 471, 543, 556, 590, 591
Davis, Jefferson C., 141
Davis, Sam, 230-232
Davis, Varina A., 81, 556
Daymend, George, 559
De Jarnett, E. C., 334, 335
de Toledo, Fernando Á., 352
Deason, John B., 366
Deering, William R., 557
Derrick, Colonel, 36
Devine, T. J., 30
Dickison, J. J., 39
Dickson, Major, 174
Dixon, Joshua, 542
Domin, Fred, 251
Donald, George, 152
Dorrity, Col., 206
Douglas, C. M., 260
Drake, E. L., 172
Drew, Mrs. Charles M., 502
Duckworth, W. L., 526
Duff, Colonel, 345
Duffield, Colonel, 424
Duke of Alba, 352
Duke, Basil W., 246, 247, 425
Dumont, Ebenezer, 424
Dunlap, Sam B., 468
Dupont, Samuel F., 153
Duvall, Robert, 592
Early, Allen H., 558
Early, Jacob, 212
Early, Jubal A., 51, 62, 71, 97, 121-124, 163, 212, 213, 487, 552
Early, Robert, 302
Echols, John, 122, 123
Ector, Matthew D., 140, 219
Edmundson, Miss Sallie, 286
Edward I, King, 591
Edwards, A. N., 537
Edwards, Crit, 390
Eldridge, J. W., 374
Elliott, C. D., 312

Elliott, Stephen, 369
Ellis, John W., 440
Elmore, Captain, 259
Elzey, Arnold, 53
Emmett, Daniel D., 289, 290
Emory, James, 559
Epaminondas, General, 236
Ephraim (Bible), 99
Epps, James L., 558
Erskine, John, 209
Erwin, Mrs. Andrew, 468
Esopah, Captain, 357
Estell, Dr., 79
Evans, Clement A., 316
Evans, H. G., 497
Evans, Nathan G., 100
Eve, F. E., 218
Everett, Edward, 324
Ewell, Richard S., 51, 58, 213, 394, 410, 487
Farell, T. W., 557
Faulkner, Charles J., 88
Faulkner, E. C., 385
Faulkner, W. W., 388, 389
Featherston, Winfield S., 100, 102, 477
Felton, Dr., 279
Ferguson, F. S., 537
Field, Elijah N., 558
Field, Henry M., 187
Fisher, Charles F., 419
Fiske, John, 192, 480
Fitzgerald, Colonel, 138
Fizer, John C., 150, 152, 551
Floyd, John B., 63, 455
Foard, A. J., 313
Foot, Samuel A., 233
Foote, Andrew H., 132, 135
Foote, Shelby, 590
Forbes, Christopher, 592
Fordyce, S. W., 552, 553
Fore, John F., 429
Foreman, James, 558
Forrest, Jeffrey, 346
Forrest, Jesse, 388
Forrest, Mary A., 179
Forrest, Mary E., 179
Forrest, Nathan B., 15, 22, 23, 32, 42, 43, 46, 96, 125, 140, 169, 179, 183, 186, 197, 198, 215, 219, 240, 258, 266, 276, 279, 299, 308-310, 314, 319, 321, 323, 343, 345-350, 367, 368, 373-376, 384, 385, 388-390, 395-406, 413, 414, 417, 418, 426, 428, 430, 443, 450, 451, 467, 474, 476, 490, 491, 498, 502, 503, 522, 525, 527-530, 540, 552, 553, 590, 591
Forrest, Nathan B., II, 179
Forrest, William M., 179
Forrest, William M., Jr., 179
Forsythe, John, 210, 460
Foster, Oliver, 326, 327
Fowler, Adjutant, 137
Fox, Gustavus V., 462, 463
Frances, John W., 361
Frederick the Great, 164, 347
Freemantle, Colonel, 468
French, Samuel G., 111, 117, 155-157, 186, 258
Fretwell, Dr., 30
Frierson, Robert M., 139
Fry, Burkett, 431
Fry, Mrs. George T., 73
Fulkerson, Abram, 147
Gailor, Frank, 362
Gailor, Thomas F., 66
Gardner, Franklin, 54
Gardner, Washington, 177
Garfield, James, 23
Garner, Lieutenant, 125
Garnett, Richard B., 52, 434
Gary, Martin W., 204
Gaus, Jacob, 346
Gay, Miss M. A. H., 447
Gayheart, Rebecca, 592
Genrard, Joseph, 559
George III, King, 14, 225
George, Newt, 327

Gibson, Randall L., 439, 489
Gilbert, Major, 301
Gillespie, Mrs. W. H., 448
Gillmore, Quincy A., 154
Gist, States R., 143, 156, 497, 591
Glease, Lewis, 559
Goodlett, S. D., 34
Gordon, Augustus, 205
Gordon, Chapman, 205
Gordon, Charles, 205
Gordon, George W., 156, 205, 207, 503, 591
Gordon, James B., 205, 440, 441
Gordon, John B., 64, 67, 68, 96, 122, 144, 205, 219, 302, 378, 500
Gordon, Nat, 205
Gordon, Wyley J., 205
Gordon-Law, Sallie C., 204-207, 209, 212
Govan, Daniel C., 141
Graham, Charles K., 549, 550
Granbury, Hiram B., 219, 497
Grant, Ulysses S., 23, 24, 48, 63, 64, 81, 98, 106, 109, 122, 124, 133, 135, 162, 184, 228, 279, 291, 293, 294, 301, 302, 306, 329, 340, 347, 364, 379, 386, 387, 392, 394, 441, 477, 502, 525, 545, 547
Graves, J. F., 558
Graves, Robert, 590
Gray, W. J., 559
Greeley, Horace, 196, 225, 457, 458
Green, J. C., 559
Green, Thomas, 219
Green, William T., 370
Greer, Mrs. James M., 502
Greg, Percy, 456
Gregg, James, 531
Gregg, John, 219
Gregg, Maxcy, 74, 75, 259, 531-533
Greif, J. V., 391
Grierson, Benjamin H., 263, 310, 527
Griffin, Thomas M., 550
Griffith, Andy, 592

Griffith, Richard, 101
Grimes, Bryan, 486, 487
Guaraldi, Vince, 592
Guerry, Dupont, 318
Guice, B. D., 278
Guild, George B., 328
Guild, Mrs. George B., 328
Hagood, J., 33
Hairston, Miss, 212
Hall, G. W., 559
Hall, Tom, 367, 373
Halleck, Henry W., 394
Hamilton, Alexander, 20, 222, 223, 465, 501, 504
Hamilton, Miss Leonora, 286
Hammond, James H., 514
Hampton, Wade, 155, 204, 440
Hancock, Winfield S., 48, 54, 303
Hanner, Mrs. J. P., 295
Hardee, Anna, 208
Hardee, William J., 96, 155, 161, 208, 209, 225, 314-316, 345
Harding, William G., 240, 591
Hardy, James F., 558
Harmon, Adjutant, 117
Harney, William S., 194
Harris, Colonel, 38
Harris, F. S., 328
Harris, Gamaliel, 414
Harris, Isham G., 350, 403, 413
Harris, Reuben, 557
Harrison, Benjamin, 253
Hatch, Edward, 310
Hatcher, Dave, 442
Hatcher, James, 442
Hatcher, Robert A., 373
Hawkes, Florence, 250
Hawkins, Ned, 524
Hawkins, Willis A., 56
Hawthorne, J. B., 411
Hayes, Rutherford B., 253
Hayne, Shubrick, 75
Hays, Harry T., 96
Heavener, W. A., 559
Helm, Benjamin H., 143

Helper, Hinton R., 458
Henderson, J. H., 497
Hendley, H. L., 497
Henlin, John, 327
Henry, John C., 473
Henry, Patrick, 90, 91, 95, 147, 234, 330
Herod, King, 233
Herod, William, 558
Heth, Henry, 122, 123, 546
Hickman, F. G., 287
Hickman, John P., 83
Hickman, Thomas A., 558
Hicks, Thomas H., 465
Higginson, Thomas W., 376
Hill, Ambrose P., 10, 52, 53, 56-59, 95, 100, 103, 213, 291-294, 305, 394, 431
Hill, Ben, 137
Hill, Benjamin H., 165
Hill, Daniel H., 48
Hill, Kenan, 251
Hindman, Thomas C., Jr., 70, 71, 143, 209, 210, 356
Hindman, Thomas C., Sr., 70
Hodge, J. M., 498
Hogan, Needham B., 193
Hogue, Mrs., 429
Hoke, Robert F., 96
Holder, William D., 550
Holliday, Fred W. M., 552
Holman, Daniel W., 215
Holmes, Gadsden, 75
Holmes, George J., 557
Holmes, Theophilus H., 356
Homer, 339
Hood, John B., 60, 75, 117, 141, 143, 149, 156, 161, 176, 180, 190, 197, 219, 279, 298, 305, 313, 376, 379, 405, 466, 469, 477, 490, 491, 494, 591
Hood, John J., 549, 551
Hood, Mrs., 429
Hooker, Joseph, 106, 109, 162, 212
Hooper, Capt., 214

Hooper, O., 214
Howard, H. P., 30
Howard, Hannan, 557
Howard, John, 72
Howard, R. A., 30
Howard, T. G., 30
Howard, Young, 414
Howe, William, 270
Howell, E. F., 557
Hudson, J. Warren, 124
Hudson, T. H., 557
Huger, Benjamin, 360
Hughes, John, 471, 472
Hughes, Samuel, 559
Humble, T. C., 548
Hume, Marie, 250
Humphreys, Benjamin G., 101, 103, 104, 150, 153, 550
Hunter, David, 163
Hunter, Robert M. T., 9
Hunton, Eppa, 100
Hurlbut, Stephen A., 403, 404
Hurst, Fielding, 308, 310, 311, 555
Hutton, C. M., 286
Inkfield, William, 558
Isabella, Queen, 470
Isaiah (Bible), 91
Jackson, Andrew, 116, 221, 281, 294, 318, 457, 499, 512, 591
Jackson, Colonel, 417
Jackson, E. T., 37
Jackson, Henry R., 591
Jackson, Howell E., 239, 240
Jackson, J. A., 557
Jackson, Mary Anna, 430
Jackson, Ridley, 288
Jackson, Stonewall, 22, 23, 44, 48-54, 56, 58, 95, 97, 100, 104, 106, 113, 116, 149, 162, 168, 179, 181, 187-189, 198, 213, 219, 228, 236, 249, 255, 259, 278, 294, 301, 316, 321, 363, 367, 378, 382, 387, 394, 410, 430, 432-436, 533, 545, 546, 551, 591

Jackson, Thomas R., 305
Jackson, William H., 206, 239, 241
James, Frank, 592
James, Jesse, 592
Janney, John, 93
Jarrett, Lieutenant, 389
Jay, John, 20, 480
Jefferson, Thomas, 20, 85, 91, 95, 147, 149, 192, 223, 267, 330, 331, 465, 501, 505, 506, 512, 592
Jenkins, Micah, 477
Jenkins, W. N., 557
Jent, Elias, Sr., 591
Jessup, S., 558
Jessup, Thomas S., 281
Jesus, 54, 56, 65, 66, 95, 163, 233, 406, 408-410, 476, 591
Joan of Arc, 79
John, Dr., 211
John, Elton, 592
Johnson, Andrew, 147, 331
Johnson, Ben, 522
Johnson, Bradley T., 181, 189, 271
Johnson, Bushrod R., 141, 143, 294, 373, 374
Johnson, Colonel, 130, 208
Johnson, Edward, 155, 303
Johnson, J. W., 187
Johnson, Richard W., 141
Johnson, W. Gart, 104, 118, 153
Johnson, William, 522, 523
Johnston, Albert S., 48, 96, 98, 104, 116, 161, 169, 194, 219, 255, 315, 316, 382, 394, 430
Johnston, Edward, 470
Johnston, Joseph E., 15, 44, 48, 62, 71, 75, 116, 161, 169, 174, 194, 198, 209, 210, 219, 225, 246, 250, 312, 324, 346, 378-380, 382, 394, 436, 468, 469, 487, 544
Johnston, Mrs. Joseph E., 211
Jones, J. William, 56, 59, 164, 212, 249

Jones, Major, 286
Jones, Miss Mary K., 73
Jones, William B., 559
Jordan, Flemming, 558
Jordan, Mrs. James R., 552
Jordan, Thomas, 395, 400
Judah (Bible), 99
Judd, Ashley, 592
Judd, Naomi, 592
Judd, Wynonna, 592
Juniper, John, 356, 359
Kane, Lieutenant Colonel, 189
Kavanaugh, Mrs. Judge, 429
Keene, John R., 473
Keller, Martha C., 79
Kelley, David C., 33, 344, 395, 397, 399, 400, 415, 416, 426, 427, 474
Kelso, A. H., 542
Kenneman, Willis, 557
Keough, Riley, 592
Kershaw, Joseph B., 151, 153, 409, 410
Kilpatrick, Hugh J., 105, 310
Kimple, Fritz, 557
King, Captain, 286
King, J. M., Jr., 232
King, Mallory P., 33
King, Thomas, 557
Kirkland, Joseph, 559
Kirtland, Richard, 409
Knox, Andrew B., 555
Kosciuszko, Tadeusz A. B., 233
Krenson, John, 538, 539
Kyle, R. B., 349
LaGree, Dr., 209
Lahone, Henry, 557
Lamar, T. G., 34
Lamon, Ward H., 462
Lane, James H., 189
Lane, John Q., 448
Langhorne, Fannie, 250
Latham, Mrs. T. J., 502
Law, Evander M., 141, 143
Lawrence, James, 111, 113

Lay, Theldred S., 558
Leacock, John, 559
Ledbetter, M. T., 214
Lee, Baker P., 497
Lee, Fitzhugh, 51, 52, 122, 161, 219, 342, 592
Lee, Henry, III, 91, 160, 364
Lee, Richard H., 91, 100
Lee, Robert E., 10, 22-24, 41, 45, 47, 48, 54, 58, 59, 61, 63, 67, 76, 84, 100, 103, 105, 106, 108, 109, 116, 117, 119-121, 124, 128, 130-132, 149, 160-164, 167, 168, 179, 213, 219, 228, 238, 245, 249, 255, 261, 272, 285, 291-294, 301, 304-307, 327-330, 340, 342, 358, 363, 364, 378, 379, 381, 382, 388, 394, 408, 410, 420, 421, 430, 433, 436-438, 441, 477, 478, 487, 494, 500, 538, 539, 543-545, 552, 591
Lee, Stephen D., 64, 155, 196, 198, 239, 591
Lee, Susan P., 543
Lee, William H. F., 219, 592
Leovy, Henry, 285
Leovy, Mrs., 285
Letcher, John, 93, 227
Lewis, Meriwether, 591
Lewis, W. H., 555
Liddell, St. John R., 141
Lillard, Julia, 524
Lillard, Lizzie, 524
Lilly, John, 414
Lilly, William, 414
Lincoln, Abraham, 13, 17, 21, 23-25, 27, 48, 61, 90, 94, 99, 109, 131, 161, 194, 228, 246, 283, 324, 331, 333, 340, 350, 364, 444, 455-459, 462, 463, 465, 471, 473, 474, 482, 505, 511, 541, 543, 544
Lincoln, Robert T., 23, 283
Lindsay, R. H., 490

Littlepage, H. B., 203
Lloyd, J. F., 557
Lomax, Lunsford L., 122
Long, George, 307
Long, Littleton, 474
Longstreet, James, 15, 58, 103, 117, 142, 143, 149, 162, 198, 215, 219, 239, 301, 373, 374, 378, 477, 591
Loring, William W., 133-135, 155, 388, 546, 548
Love, William P., 336
Lovelace, William, 558
Loveless, Patty, 592
Lowrey, Mark P., 155
Luck, Jack, 485
Luckett, P. N., 30
Lynch, Eliza E., 203
Lynn, James, 557
Macaulay, Thomas B., 227, 483
Maddox, William, 414
Madison, James, 91, 92, 148, 192, 223, 504, 512
Magruder, John B., 150, 433, 539
Mahone, William, 487
Major, J. P., 30
Manigault, Arthur M., 591
Manigault, Joseph, 591
Manson, Hal, 327
Manson, Mahlon D., 138
Marion, Francis, 205
Marlborough, Duke of, 45, 47
Marmaduke, Vincent, 430
Marryatt, James, 70
Marsh, John, 369, 370
Marshall, Arthur, 149
Marshall, John, 192, 514
Marvin, Lee, 592
Mason, George, 90, 95
Mason, James M., 9, 81
Mathes, Mrs. J. Harvey, 502
Maury, Abram P., 592
Maury, Dabney H., 436
Maxey, Samuel B., 357, 358
Maxwell, Coot, 427

May, Captain, 415
Mayes, Joel B., 354
Mayes, Thompson, 354
McAlister, A. H., 555
McAllister, Anderson, 555
McCall, Miss Aline, 286
McClellan, George B., 48, 59, 109, 161, 304, 379, 380, 394, 432, 435, 538, 539
McClellan, Irvin, 162
McClendon, James, 558
McCook, Edward M., 310
McCord, James, 557
McCormick, S. D., 283
McCulloch, Alexander, 318
McCulloch, Ben, 194, 219, 354
McCulloch, Henry E., 318, 319
McCulloch, Robert, 347
McDonald, J., 559
McDowell, Irvin, 162
McDowell, James, 88, 379
McDowell, W. W., 554, 555
McElroy, Kennon, 150, 152
McElveen, Elias, 557
McElvey, Captain, 39
McEnery, J., 33, 34
McEwen, Miss, 286
McFarland, Captain, 246
McGahee, T. J., 69
McGavock, Caroline E., 446, 592
McGavock, David H., 592
McGavock, Emily, 592
McGavock, Francis, 592
McGavock, James R., 592
McGavock, John W., 399, 446, 493, 592
McGavock, Lysander, 592
McGavock, Randal W., 592
McGee, Thomas, 558
McGowan, Samuel, 103
McGraw, Tim, 592
McGuire, Hunter, 484, 534
McIntosh, Chilly, 356
McIntosh, D. N., 356
McIntosh, Mrs. M. P., 413

McKenzie, F. M., 427
McKinley, William, 23, 537
McKinney, W. H., 554
McLaurin, J. L., 419
McLaws, Lafayette, 117, 149, 374
McLean, Miss Sallie J., 524
McMeekin, Thomas, 557
McNeilly, James H., 217, 274, 476
Meade, George G., 48, 76, 78, 162, 531, 544
Meade, Thomas, 394
Meade, William, 84, 96
Meagher, Thomas F., 303
Mechling, W. T., 30
Megginson, William B., 546
Memminger, Christopher G., 9
Meredith, Winston, 557
Meriwether, C. E., 32
Meriwether, Elizabeth A., 592
Meriwether, Minor, 592
Meriwether, Ned, 418
Merrill, C. E., 422
Merrin, F. W., 388
Miller, Henry, 419
Miller, John, 354
Milroy, Robert H., 162
Minter, J. F., 30
Minty, Robert H. G., 310
Minus, R. W., 129
Mitchell, John G., 310
Mitchell, John K., 10
Mitchell, Ormsby M., 468, 469
Moab (Bible), 110
Monroe, James, 223, 331, 512
Monroe, Thomas, 285
Moon, G. B., 454
Moore, J. Quitman, 45
Moore, John, 362
Moreau, Victor, 379
Morgan, Daniel, 84
Morgan, Dick, 246
Morgan, John H., 57, 158, 246, 248, 395, 411, 422-425, 430, 450, 591
Morgan, Timothy F., 558

Morris, Aaron, 557
Morris, Dr., 429
Morris, Mary L., 376
Morrison, James J., 451
Morton, John W., 384, 452, 490, 491, 592
Mosby, John S., 105, 591
Moses (Bible), 99, 110
Moses, Mrs. M., 421
Moss, Ed, 391
Motlow, Felix, 370
Mower, Joseph A., 310
Mullen, J. R., 559
Mumford, William B., 10
Murat, Joachim, 72, 375
Napier, Charles J., 344
Napoleon I, 71, 91, 152, 164, 166, 179, 256, 320, 379, 380, 397, 406, 453, 502
Napoleon III, 470, 471
Nash, Mary, 250
Needlett, Dr., 279
Neely, Green, 298
Neill, Isaac, 558
Nelson, Hugh M., 93
Nelson, J. O., 526
Nelson, Samuel, 460
Nelson, Thomas, Jr., 91
Nelson, W. S., 421
Nelson, William, 138, 186
Nero, Emperor, 233
Netherland, John, 147
Ney, Michel, 232, 406, 452
Nicholls, Francis R. T., 96
Nichols, U. P., 559
Nicks, W. L., 557
Nixon, Colonel, 138, 139
Noel, Theo, 284
Norris, John S., 158, 159
Northen, Martha M., 174
Northen, William J., 174
Northway, Mrs. S. E., 413
Norvell, W. T., 302
Norwood, J. W., 559
Nugent, Ted, 592

Nutt, Nannie, 105
O'Bryan, Fannie, 295
O'Mera, Jim, 339
Oaks, Col., 207
Odin, John M., 471, 472
Opdyke, Emerson, 448, 450
Opothleoholo, Chief, 355
Otey, Mercer, 466
Overton, Frank, 414, 415
Ozanne, John M., 376
O'Brien, Colonel, 152
O'Bryan, Martha, 295
O'Mera, Jim, 339
Pagans, F. G., 558
Page, John M., 558
Page, Thomas N., 148
Palmer, B. M., 500
Parks, William H., 413
Parsons, B. F., 557
Parton, Dolly, 592
Patterson, Josiah, 552
Patterson, Robert, 62, 379
Patton, George S., 35
Paul, St., 233
Paul, the Apostle, 66
Payne, Miss, 286
Pelham, John, 10, 198, 200, 255, 326
Pemberton, John C., 133-135, 379
Pender, William D., 96
Pendleton, Alexander S., 51, 52, 533
Pendleton, William N., 554
Perkins, Eli, 106
Perkins, Mrs. Thomas F., 448
Perkins, W. J., 557
Perry, Edward A., 146
Perry, Jesse M., 557
Peters, Janie, 250
Peters, Mary, 250
Pettus, Edmund W., 591
Phillip, William A., 558
Phillips, Colonel, 357
Phillips, George C., 422
Phillips, J. M., 485
Pickens, Francis W., 204, 456, 462
Pickering, Timothy, 505-507

Pickett, George E., 52, 76-79, 118, 294, 431, 476
Pickett, Lieutenant, 256
Pickett, Mrs. W. S., 208
Pierce, Franklin, 331, 513
Pike, Albert, 353
Pilate, Pontius, 255
Pillow, Gideon J., 63, 207, 396, 591
Pinckney, Alfred, 75
Pinckney, Charles C., 192
Pitcher, Mollie, 79
Pius IX, Pope, 470-473
Plato, 26
Poage, Miss Sarah A., 551
Poindexter, George, 506
Polk, James K., 92, 116, 331, 512, 513, 592
Polk, Leonidas, 96, 116, 186, 206, 219, 225, 275, 382, 497, 556, 591
Polk, Lucius E., 138, 592
Pool, Miller C., 557
Pope, John, 109, 162
Pope, William H., 149
Porter, Fitz J., 162
Porter, Horace, 387
Powers, J. L., 284
Prentiss, Benjamin M., 424
Prentiss, S. S., 338
Presley, Elvis, 592
Presley, Lisa Marie, 592
Preston, William, 141, 143
Preston, William B., 94
Price, Sterling, 186, 194, 195, 219, 279, 280, 357
Pryor, J. P., 395
Pryor, R. A., 28
Purse, James W., 557
Quantrell, William, 354
Quarrier, Sergeant-Major, 37
Quincy, Josiah, III, 506
Quinn, Michael, 557
Quintard, Charles T., 369
Rains, Gabriel J., 260, 261
Rains, John P., 193

Rambaut, Gilbert V., 396, 399
Ramseur, Stephen D., 96, 122, 123, 487
Rand, Noyes, 35
Randolph, Edmund J., 84, 90, 91, 465, 592
Randolph, George W., 94, 592
Ransom, Robert, Jr., 440
Rastall, John E., 474
Rayner, George W., 558
Reagan, John H., 230
Reagan, Ronald, 592
Rector, Elias, 196
Reese, James, 362
Reid, Dick, 187
Remper, Del, 532
Renfral, William S., 557
Renfróe, John D., 200
Revere, Paul, 424
Reynolds, Burt, 592
Reynolds, W., 558
Rhett, A. Barnet, 155
Rhett, Albert M., 154
Rhett, Robert B., 153
Rhodes, Elisha H., 103
Rhodes, Harry W., 321
Rice, Captain, 529, 530
Rice, Dorsey, 70
Rice, John, 70
Richard the Lion-Hearted, King, 348
Richards, H. B., 540
Ridley, B. L., 425
Ridley, Samuel J., 284
Riley, Joseph L., 559
Rives, William C., 93
Rizpah (Bible), 173
Robbins, Hargus, 592
Robert the Bruce, King, 166, 318, 591
Roberts, B. T., 157
Roberts, Don, 279
Roberts, J. C., 280
Roberts, John, 558
Roberts, W. H., 559
Robertson, A. G., 533

Robertson, Sidney, 548
Rodes, Robert E., 487
Rodriguez, Jose I., 471
Rogers, John H., 558
Rogers, Thomas, 558
Roosevelt, Theodore, 23, 47
Rose, William, 259, 260, 532
Rosecrans, William S., 279, 374, 393
Rosencranz, Sergeant, 389
Ross, John, 354
Ross, Lawrence S., 219
Rosser, Thomas L., 278
Rou, Captain, 39
Royston, C. B., 559
Rozell, George F., 380
Rucker, Edmund W., 526, 527, 530, 591
Ruff, Colonel, 120
Rupert, Prince, 168
Russell, James, 557
Russell, Jesse S., 558
Russell, Robert M., 443
Rutledge, Henry M., 360, 361
Rutledge, John, 192
Ryan, Abram J., 187
Saladin, 318
Sanborne, H. K., 542
Sandidge, J. M., 489
Sandlin, James, 559
Sansom, Emma, 314
Savage, John H., 341
Saxe, Marshall, 45
Saxton, Rufus, 129
Scales, Alfred M., 103
Scales, J. A., 356
Scales, James, 558
Scott, Dred, 393, 444, 543
Scott, George C., 592
Scott, Harriet, 393
Scott, Robert E., 93
Scott, Thomas M., 421
Scott, Winfield, 92, 160, 161, 378, 513
Scruggs, Earl, 592
Scurry, William R., 219

Seabrook, John L., 591
Seabrook, Lochlainn, 20-23, 25, 590-592, 594
Seddon, James A., 93
Sedgwick, John, 301, 304, 394
Seger, Bob, 592
Seldon, Lieutenant, 146
Semmes, Raphael, 10
Seward, William H., 444, 460-463, 471, 511, 514
Shackleford, John C., 31, 32
Shann, Henry, 557
Shannon, I. N., 378
Shannon, S. F., 157
Shannon, Sam, 297
Shaw, General, 500
Shaw, Henry M., 559
Shea, P. P., 30
Sheridan, Philip H., 23, 123, 141, 292, 294, 394, 395, 441, 487
Sherman, William T., 23, 62, 98, 105, 106, 150, 176, 177, 186, 197, 315, 379, 380, 394, 403, 405, 469, 491, 502, 525
Shields, James, 434
Shuck, Dr., 429
Shuttlesworth, Joe, 477
Sickles, Daniel E., 549, 550
Sigler, Mrs., 368
Simmons, J. W., 384, 470
Simmons, Miss Mary, 338
Sims, Miss Daisy, 114
Singleton, O. R., 101
Skaggs, Ricky, 592
Slack, A. L., 182
Slater, Fannie, 250
Slidell, John, 9, 81
Sloan, J. B. E., 203
Smart, C. H., 127
Smith, A. J., 530
Smith, A. M., 75
Smith, Andrew J., 197, 404
Smith, Baxter, 450, 451
Smith, Edmund K., 63, 65, 66, 81, 136-138, 161, 186, 219, 408,

443
Smith, Frank, 143
Smith, George H., 559
Smith, Henry H., 437
Smith, J. A., 558
Smith, Martin L., 197
Smith, Pessifer F., 194
Smith, Preston, 136, 209
Smith, Thomas B., 297
Smith, W. A., 498
Smith, William S., 310, 311, 404, 405
Smyth, Newman, 364
Smythe, A. G., 525
Smythe, E. T., 213, 214
Snyder, William, 559
Socrates, 165
Sommers, Captain, 276
Spellman, Dominick, 75
St. Clair, William R., 185
Stafford, Fountain E. P., 112
Stanley, David S., 310, 448
Stanley, E. P., 557
Starke, William E., 181
Starnes, James W., 33
Steedman, James B., 142, 143
Steele, William, 356-358
Stephens, Alexander H., 9, 13, 15, 249, 252, 591
Stephens, W. L., 244
Steuart, George H., 270
Stewart, Alexander P., 64, 142, 143, 156, 186, 198, 373, 591
Stiles, Rev., 210
Stockdale, John, 390
Stoneman, George, 161
Story, A. J., 69
Stout, H. S., 312, 313
Stovall, Dr., 555
Stovall, Marcellus A., 143
Strahl, Otho F., 111-113, 155, 156, 368-370, 497
Streight, Able D., 314, 349, 403
Stuart, Alexander H. H., 93, 94, 482
Stuart, Jeb, 16, 58, 95, 100, 162, 168, 198, 200, 219, 255, 278, 339, 440, 441, 543, 591
Sturgis, Samuel D., 347, 402, 404, 525-527, 529
Summers, George W., 93
Sumner, Charles, 353, 444, 458
Sumpter, Thomas, 205
Surratt, Mary, 351
Sutherlin, J. H., 439
Sykes, George, 409
Sykes, Mrs., 298
Talbot, Captain, 463
Taney, Roger B., 444, 461
Tate, F., 30
Taylor, David L., 558
Taylor, James, 75
Taylor, Richard, 15, 96, 177, 240, 323, 347, 348, 591
Taylor, Sarah K., 591
Taylor, Wilson, 558
Taylor, Zachary, 324, 512, 513, 591
Teague, B. H., 114, 442
Tebault, C. H., 445, 541
Temple, Oliver P., 147
Tessier, D. E., 30
Thayer, John M., 357
Thielkeld, Francis M., 557
Thomas, B. S., 498
Thomas, George, 270
Thomas, George H., 48, 161, 315
Thompson, A. P., 388, 390
Thompson, Hugh S., 61
Thompson, Jacob, 455
Thompson, John K., 37
Thompson, Major, 183, 185
Thompson, T. B., 559
Tilden, Samuel J., 196
Tilghman, Llyod, 132, 134, 135
Tilghman, Llyod, Jr., 135
Tillman, J. D., 191
Tipp, William C., 559
Tom, Blind, 179
Toney, Marcus B., 304
Townsend, Dick, 125, 126
Traylor, Albert W., 144, 145
Trousdale, William H., 497

Truner, Thomas C., 558
Tucker, Beverly, 81
Tucker, Joseph R., 117
Tucker, St. George, 20
Tupper, George, 243
Turner, Miss Rosa, 468
Turpin, Dick, 425
Twichell, Reverend, 364
Twing, M. W., 542
Tyler, John, 25, 92, 93, 95, 331, 512, 513
Tyler, Lyon G., 25
Tynes, Ellen B., 592
Ussery, W. T., 497
Van Buren, Martin, 513
Van Dorn, Earl, 29, 30, 72, 133, 161, 186, 194
Vance, Robert B., 592
Vance, S. W., 478
Vance, Zebulon, 592
Vaulx, Joseph, 378
Venable, Charles S., 591
Vernon, Mrs., 208
Vicars, Hedley, 54
Victoria, Queen, 470
Viley, Mr., 425
von Leiberich, Karl M., 379
Wadsworth, James S., 478
Wadsworth, W. W., 69
Waldrip, Andrew, 557
Walker, A. E., 552
Walker, Allen P., 552
Walker, Frank, 552
Walker, James A., 551, 552
Walker, John G., 338
Walker, Leroy P., 28
Walker, William H. T., 140, 143
Wallace, J. H., 559
Wallace, James, 473
Wallace, Lewis, 122
Walthall, Edward C., 140, 156, 198, 383, 425, 491
Walton, Dr., 287
Walton, Lucy M., 300
Ward, J. T., 30

Warren, Gouverneur K., 301, 310
Washburn, Cadwallader C., 404, 525
Washington, George, 13, 20, 48, 67, 84, 91, 95, 116, 128, 148, 149, 164, 167, 192, 222, 248, 294, 330, 364, 465, 479, 505, 512
Washington, John A., 591
Washington, Thornton A., 591
Watie, Stand, 354, 356, 357, 359
Watkins, Samuel R., 252
Watts, Jennie, 250
Watts, Winnie, 250
Waul, Thomas N., 219, 338
Weakley, Hickman, 423
Weakley, T. P., 419
Webster, Daniel, 509, 510
Webster, Miss Rowe C., 469
Wellington, First Duke of, 47
Wells, Julian L., 363
West, James, 559
West, William C., 558
Whaley, George, 559
Wharton, John A., 122, 123, 427, 428
Wheeler, J. A., 183
Wheeler, Joseph, 40, 219, 246, 394, 452, 453
Whitaker, Walter C., 449
White, B. F., 522, 523
White, Jere S., 275
Whitman, Walt, 19
Whitthorne, W. J., 497
Wiggins, Thomas, 179
Wilcox, Cadmus M., 69, 476-478
Wilcox, J. A., 30
Wilkes, John S., 325
Wilkes, Samuel D., 204
Wilkins, Sallie, 210
Wilkison, William, 559
Williams, Camille, 169
Williams, John S., 546
Williams, Martin, 254
Williams, Mrs. Charles J., 72
Williams, R. F., 548
Williamson, J. T., 497

Willie, James, 30
Wilson, B. F., Jr., 158
Wilson, Claudius C., 140
Wilson, Henry, 217
Wilson, James H., 348, 384
Wilson, W. I., 543
Wilson, Woodrow, 148, 592
Winder, Caroline, 399
Winder, Charles S., 51, 592
Winder, John H., 591
Wingo, Harry, 327
Winslow, George B., 549
Winthrop, John, 407
Wirz, Henry, 351
Wisdom, D. M., 309
Wise, Henry A., 433
Witherspoon, Reese, 592
Wofford, William T., 151, 153
Wolseley, Garnet J., 395
Womack, Elder J. K., 485
Womack, John B., 591
Womack, Lee Ann, 592
Womack, Mr. J. K., 453
Woolford, Frank, 150, 215, 424
Wooten, Dr., 280
Wooten, T. D., 279
Worley, William, 558
Wormeley, Mrs. Ralph, 382
Wright, Ambrose R., 360, 361
Wright, Clark, 263
Wyeth, John A., 323, 350
Yandel, Dr., 206
Young, J. P., 406
Youngblood, George W., 215
Youree, William, 172
Zettler, B. M., 539
Zollicoffer, Felix K., 592

Why the South fought . . .

MEET THE AUTHOR

"ASKING THE PATRIOTIC SOUTH TO STOP HONORING HER CONFEDERATE ANCESTORS IS LIKE ASKING THE SUN NOT TO SHINE." — COLONEL LOCHLAINN SEABROOK

LOCHLAINN SEABROOK, a neo-Victorian and world acclaimed man of letters, is a Kentucky Colonel and the winner of the prestigious Jefferson Davis Historical Gold Medal for his "masterpiece," *A Rebel Born: A Defense of Nathan Bedford Forrest*. A classic littérateur and an unreconstructed Southern historian, he is an award-winning author, Civil War scholar, Confederate culture expert, Bible authority, the leading popularizer of American Civil War history, and a traditional Southern Agrarian of Scottish, English, Irish, Dutch, Welsh, German, and Italian extraction.

A child prodigy, Seabrook is today a true Renaissance Man whose occupational titles also include encyclopedist, lexicographer, musician, artist, graphic designer, genealogist, photographer, and award-winning poet. Also a songwriter and a screenwriter, he has a 40 year background in historical nonfiction writing and is a member of the Sons of Confederate Veterans, the Civil War Trust, and the National Grange.

Above, Colonel Lochlainn Seabrook, "the voice of the traditional South," award-winning Civil War scholar and unreconstructed Southern historian. America's most popular and prolific pro-South author, his many books have introduced hundreds of thousands to the truth about the War for Southern Independence. He coined the phrase "South-shaming" and holds the world record for writing the most books on Nathan Bedford Forrest: nine.

Known to his many fans as the "voice of the traditional South," due to similarities in their writing styles, ideas, and literary works, Seabrook is also often referred to as the "new Shelby Foote," the "Southern Joseph Campbell," and the "American Robert Graves" (his English cousin). Seabrook coined the terms "South-shaming" and "Lincolnian liberalism," and holds the world's record for writing the most books on Nathan Bedford Forrest: nine. In addition, Seabrook is the first Civil War scholar to connect the early American nickname for the U.S., "The Confederate States of America," with the Southern Confederacy that arose eight decades later, and the first to note that in 1860 the party platforms of the two major political parties were the opposite of what they are today (Victorian Democrats were conservatives, Victorian Republicans were liberals).

The grandson of an Appalachian coal-mining family, Seabrook is a seventh-generation Kentuckian whose European ancestors came from Virginia, North Carolina, and Tennessee, settling in the Bluegrass State in the early 1700s, thereafter spreading into West Virginia and the Midwest.

Seabrook is co-chair of the Jent/Gent Family Committee (Kentucky), founder and director of the Blakeney Family Tree Project, and a board member of the Friends of Colonel Benjamin E. Caudill. His literary works have been endorsed by leading authorities, museum curators, award-winning historians, bestselling authors, celebrities, noted scientists, well regarded educators, TV show hosts and producers, renowned military artists, esteemed Southern organizations, and distinguished academicians from around the world.

Seabrook has authored over 50 popular adult books on the American Civil War, American and international slavery, the U.S. Confederacy (1781), the Southern Confederacy (1861), religion, theology, thealogy, Jesus, the Bible, the Apocrypha, the Law of Attraction, alternative health, spirituality, ghost stories, the paranormal, ufology, social issues, and cross-cultural studies of the family and marriage. His Confederate biographies, pro-South studies, genealogical monographs, family histories, military encyclopedias, self-help guides, and etymological dictionaries have received wide acclaim.

Seabrook's eight children's books include a Southern guide to the Civil War, a biography of Nathan Bedford Forrest, a dictionary of religion and myth, a rewriting of the King Arthur legend (which reinstates the original pre-Christian motifs), two bedtime stories for preschoolers, a naturalist's guidebook to owls, a worldwide look at the family, and an examination of the Near-Death Experience.

Of blue-blooded Southern stock through his Kentucky, Tennessee, Virginia, North Carolina and West Virginia ancestors, he is a direct descendant of European royalty via his 6th great-grandfather, the Earl of Oxford, after which London's famous Harley Street is named. Among his celebrated male Celtic ancestors is Robert the Bruce, King of Scotland, Seabrook's 22nd great-grandfather. The 21st great-grandson of Edward I "Longshanks" Plantagenet), King of England, Seabrook is a thirteenth-generation Southerner through his descent from the colonists of Jamestown, Virginia (1607).

(Photo © Lochlainn Seabrook)

The 2nd, 3rd, and 4th great-grandson of dozens of Confederate soldiers, one of his closest connections to Lincoln's War is through his 3rd great-grandfather, Elias Jent, Sr., who fought for the Confederacy in the Thirteenth Cavalry Kentucky under Seabrook's 2nd cousin, Colonel Benjamin E. Caudill. The Thirteenth, also known as "Caudill's Army," fought in numerous conflicts, including the Battles of Saltville, Gladsville, Mill Cliff, Poor Fork, Whitesburg, and Leatherwood.

Seabrook is a direct descendant of the families of Alexander H. Stephens, John Singleton Mosby, William Giles Harding, and Edmund Winchester Rucker, and is related to the following Confederates and other 18th- and 19th-Century luminaries: Robert E. Lee, Stephen Dill Lee, Stonewall Jackson, Nathan Bedford Forrest, James Longstreet, John Hunt Morgan, Jeb Stuart, Pierre G. T. Beauregard (approved the Confederate Battle Flag design), George W. Gordon, John Bell Hood, Alexander Peter Stewart, Arthur M. Manigault, Joseph Manigault, Charles Scott Venable, Thornton A. Washington, John A. Washington, Abraham Buford, Edmund W. Pettus, Theodrick "Tod" Carter, John B. Womack, John H. Winder, Gideon J. Pillow, States Rights Gist, Henry R. Jackson, John Lawton Seabrook, John C. Breckinridge, Leonidas Polk, Zachary Taylor, Sarah Knox Taylor (first wife of Jefferson Davis), Richard Taylor, Davy Crockett, Daniel Boone, Meriwether Lewis (of the Lewis and Clark Expedition) Andrew Jackson,

James K. Polk, Abram Poindexter Maury (founder of Franklin, TN), Zebulon Vance, Thomas Jefferson, Edmund Jennings Randolph, George Wythe Randolph (grandson of Jefferson), Felix K. Zollicoffer, Fitzhugh Lee, Nathaniel F. Cheairs, Jesse James, Frank James, Robert Brank Vance, Charles Sidney Winder, John W. McGavock, Caroline E. (Winder) McGavock, David Harding McGavock, Lysander McGavock, James Randal McGavock, Randal William McGavock, Francis McGavock, Emily McGavock, William Henry F. Lee, Lucius E. Polk, Minor Meriwether (husband of noted pro-South author Elizabeth Avery Meriwether), Ellen Bourne Tynes (wife of Forrest's chief of artillery, Captain John W. Morton), South Carolina Senators Preston Smith Brooks and Andrew Pickens Butler, and famed South Carolina diarist Mary Chesnut.

Seabrook's modern day cousins include: Patrick J. Buchanan (conservative author), Cindy Crawford (model), Shelby Lee Adams (Letcher Co., Kentucky, photographer), Bertram Thomas Combs (Kentucky's 50th governor), Edith Bolling (wife of President Woodrow Wilson), and actors Andy Griffith, Riley Keough, George C. Scott, Robert Duvall, Reese Witherspoon, Lee Marvin, Rebecca Gayheart, and Tom Cruise.

Seabrook's screenplay, *A Rebel Born*, based on his book of the same name, has been signed with acclaimed filmmaker Christopher Forbes (of Forbes Film). It is now in pre-production, and is set for release in 2018 as a full-length feature film. This will be the first movie ever made of Nathan Bedford Forrest's life story, and as a historically accurate project written from the Southern perspective, is destined to be one of the most talked about Civil War films of all time.

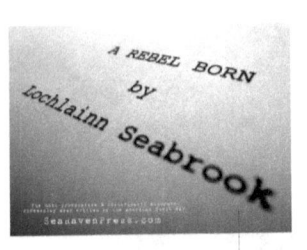

Born with music in his blood, Seabrook is an award-winning, multi-genre, BMI-Nashville songwriter and lyricist who has composed some 3,000 songs (250 albums), and whose original music has been heard in film (*A Rebel Born*, *Cowgirls 'n Angels*, *Confederate Cavalry*, *Billy the Kid: Showdown in Lincoln County*, *Vengeance Without Mercy*, *Last Step*, *County Line*, *The Mark*) and on TV and radio worldwide. A musician, producer, multi-instrumentalist, and renown performer—whose keyboard work has been variously compared to pianists from Hargus Robbins and Vince Guaraldi to Elton John and Leonard Bernstein—Seabrook has opened for groups such as the Earl Scruggs Review, Ted Nugent, and Bob Seger, and has performed privately for such public figures as President Ronald Reagan, Burt Reynolds, Loni Anderson, and Senator Edward W. Brooke. Seabrook's cousins in the music business include: Johnny Cash, Elvis Presley, Lisa Marie Presley, Billy Ray and Miley Cyrus, Patty Loveless, Tim McGraw, Lee Ann Womack, Dolly Parton, Pat Boone, Naomi, Wynonna, and Ashley Judd, Ricky Skaggs, the Sunshine Sisters, Martha Carson, and Chet Atkins.

Seabrook lives with his wife and family in historic Middle Tennessee, the heart of Forrest country and the Confederacy, where his conservative Southern ancestors fought valiantly against Liberal Lincoln and the progressive North in defense of Jeffersonianism, constitutional government, and personal liberty.

LochlainnSeabrook.com

Our immortal Southern heroes and Confederate flags.

594 ∾ RISE UP AND CALL THEM BLESSED

If you enjoyed this book you will be interested in Colonel Seabrook's other popular related titles:

- Everything You Were Taught About the Civil War is Wrong, Ask a Southerner!
- Abraham Lincoln Was a Liberal, Jefferson Davis Was a Conservative
- All We Ask is to be Let Alone: The Southern Secession Fact Book
- Everything You Were Taught About American Slavery is Wrong, Ask a Southerner!
- Confederate Flag Facts: What Every American Should Know About Dixie's Southern Cross
- Lincoln's War: The Real Cause, the Real Winner, the Real Loser

Available from Sea Raven Press and wherever fine books are sold

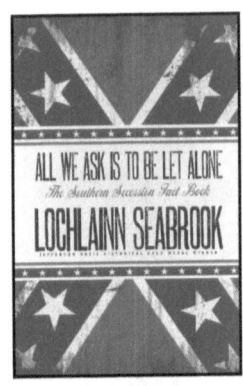

ALL OF OUR BOOK COVERS ARE AVAILABLE AS 11" X 17" POSTERS, SUITABLE FOR FRAMING

SeaRavenPress.com • NathanBedfordForrestBooks.com

www.ingramcontent.com/pod-product-compliance
Lightning Source LLC
Chambersburg PA
CBHW030558230426
43661CB00053B/1761